MW00440896

A FATE WORSE THAN DEATH

INDIAN CAPTIVITIES IN THE WEST, 1830 - 1885

A Fate Worse Than Death

Indian Captivities in the West, 1830 - 1885

Gregory and Susan Michno

Caxton Press
Caldwell, Idaho
2007

Library of Congress Cataloging-in-Publication Data

Michno, Gregory, 1948-
  A Fate worse than death : Indian captivities in the West, 1830-1885 / Gregory Michno and Susan Michno.
     p. cm.
  ISBN-13: 978-0-87004-451-9
  ISBN-10: 0-87004-451-6
  1. Indian captivities--West (U.S.)--History--19th century. 2. Indian captivities--Texas--History--19th century. I. Michno, Susan, 1947- II. Title.

  E85.M53 2007
  978'.020922--dc22

                                        2006025157

COVER

"Scouting the Cabin," by Jim D. Nelson.
www.jdnelsonportraits.com

Lithographed and bound in Canada for

CAXTON PRESS
Caldwell, Idaho
174332

ACKNOWLEDGMENTS

We would like to thank several people who assisted us in locating and collecting information for this book. Thanks to Dr. Jeff Broome in Colorado, for the use of some of his Indian Depredation claims, and to Scott Zesch in Texas, a descendent of Adolph Korn, for sharing his research on Texas captives. We are grateful to Judith Penhiter, a descendent of Lavina Eastlick, who provided genealogical information on several Minnesota captives, and Ronda Jaeger for access to the Roper and Eubank sites along the Little Blue River. We appreciate the help given to us by many folks at the Denver Public Library. We would like to thank all those at the Minnesota, Iowa, Nebraska, and Kansas Historical Societies, and the Butler County, Kansas, Historical Society for their assistance in locating sources and photographs.

TABLE OF CONTENTS

TABLE OF CONTENTS

ILLUSTRATIONS

MAPS

INTRODUCTION

There were several reasons that led us to take up a study of women and children captives of the Indians. The subject is intriguing. The Indian captivity narrative has been part of American literature and history for about 300 years, from when the first colonists of the 1580s disappeared in what was to become North Carolina, leaving only the mysterious word, "Croatoan," carved into a tree, until the Census Bureau declared the frontier was closed in 1890.

From the beginning, European men, women, and children were captured by the Indians, and the threat of capture was a real danger for generations of Americans on the frontier. Many captivity books were written and some of them became bestsellers. They have been discussed, analyzed, and used by scholars for their personal agendas, as symbols of innate violence, to prove the existence of archetypes, to argue Freudian themes, to advance feminist issues, or bash white males. In this study, we choose to use the narratives for what the majority of them were—personal accounts of the horrors of captivity.

The very act of relating the stories is not a politically correct exercise. The stories are replete with details of killing, mutilation, abuse, and rape. There is no particular joy in relating what the captives experienced, but there is a need for it. Over the past several decades there has been a dramatic shift in perception about old heroes and villains. Today, white Americans are depicted as savage and greedy barbarians, while the Indians are said to have lived in peace with ecological wisdom. These role reversals illuminate history less than they simply elevate one group at the expense of another. The old view of the good pioneer and the bad Indian was not correct, but neither is the contrary. In this collection we hope to illustrate the real threat that Indians posed on the frontier—a menace that should not be denied through sugarcoated history. The point here is not to disparage Indians, but rather to let the captives' own words illuminate the true situation, which should then expose as charlatans those writers who would distort or deny the horrors of captivity. The historical scales need to be balanced.

Our choice of geographical area was made because the eastern captivity narratives appear to be more numerous, more documented, and have been studied longer than the western narratives, and, our main interest lies in the trans-Mississippi West. The western captivities have not been studied as thoroughly. Carl Coke Rister, in his 1940 book, *Border Captives*, stated that there were so many captives taken between 1835 and 1875, that "it is quite impossible to follow the fortunes of each captive. . . . This should be done in separate captive sketches."[1] It has been more than six decades and no one, until now, has followed Rister's suggestion.

There were thousands of captives taken on both sides during the years of this study and we cannot hope to record them all. Indians took European and American captives, as well as other Indians—people of all color hues and bloodlines. We limited the examination mainly to white Americans of European ancestry, because of space considerations and the greater availability of historical documents. Certainly a similar book could be written about Spanish and Mexican captives.

In this book we will employ word usages more contemporary to the times we are writing about, therefore "Indian," "white," or "Mexican" will appear instead of the plethora of euphemistic preferences we adopt in our modern, hyphenated society. The language is plain, and the subject is basic. Indian captivity was almost always a horrible experience, and too many women had to judge for themselves whether or not the phrase they had heard so often was true: Indian captivity was a fate worse than death.

Footnote

[1] Rister, *Border Captives*, x.

PORTRAIT OF A CAPTIVE

Nancy Fletcher posed for this portrait at age 15. Nancy Fletcher Morton was 19 when Cheyennes attacked her husband's freight wagons in August 1864 on Plum Creek in Nebraska.

Nancy, wounded by two arrows, watched the attackers kill and mutilate her husband, brother and cousin. The brutal treatment she received from her captors caused her to lose her unborn child. She was held captive for 176 days before being ransomed.

Chapter One

REVOLUTIONARY TEXAS

I felt recreant to mortal existence, and my soul, desperate with the tantalized affections of a wife and mother, would fain have preferred the most cruel death to life such as mine. — Sarah Horn

The scene which here ensued beggars description. A mother meeting with her child released from Indian captivity, rescued, as it were, from the very jaws of death! — John J. Tumlinson

Some of the first emigrants to enter Texas moved to the frontier to establish homes, either not knowing, or not heeding the danger warnings. Then again, possible peril never stopped settlers, and there was little history of hostilities with the wild tribes who inhabited the prairies beyond the forest. As seen in the case of Matthew Martin, the Kiowas, Comanches, and Wichitas had never even met any U.S. soldiers before, and the newly formed Dragoons were on their first mission to Indian Territory to establish contact and make a peace treaty with those tribes. The Martins crossed into the Territory from Texas and put themselves at risk, and Matthew Martin became one of the first post-1830 captives in the trans-Mississippi West.

It was not long before Indians were raiding deep into Texas, stealing, killing, and carrying off hostages. The year the Texans fought their revolution against Mexico was also a year of heavy raiding, and the settlers had not only the Mexican Army to worry about, but also the mounted marauders from beyond the settlements.

In addition to the captivities detailed below, there are a number of other incidents that deserve mention. Two early Texas narratives by Clarissa Plummer and Caroline Harris were not included in this study because there is a question of their legitimacy. The women were said to be from New York, and were captured west of the Sabine River in August 1835. Their husbands and children were killed; they were starved, abused, and raped, until released two years later. Both of their narratives may have been produced

1

to capitalize on the recent experiences of the real Rachel Plummer and Mrs. Harris, whose stories came out in Plummer's book in 1838. There was speculation that Caroline Harris was the Mrs. Harris mentioned in Plummer's narrative, and needing money, she collaborated with the editor to write a semi-fictional story of her ordeal. In the introduction to Rachael Plummer's first edition, editor William S. Reese stated his belief that Clarissa Plummer and Caroline Harris's accounts were fictional. There are similarities in the stories, but the identity of the two women cannot be documented.[1]

On October 5, 1838, the Killough Massacre took place, said to be the largest single Indian depredation in east Texas. About eighteen members of the Killough, Woods, and Williams families were killed and captured in Cherokee County by a force of Caddoes, Coushattas, Kichais, and Mexicans. The names of all the captives, beyond a Miss Killough and Elizabeth Williams, were not recorded, and their ultimate fate is unknown.[2]

Charles and William Bent, who ran a trading post on the upper Arkansas River for many years, were instrumental in freeing some captives. At a July 1840 meeting with Cheyennes and Comanches at Bent's Fort, Jim Hobbs (20) arrived dressed like a Comanche. Charles Bent remembered that four years earlier, Hobbs and John Baptiste left a Bent caravan to chase buffalo and were captured by Indians. Hobbs now belonged to a Comanche named Old Wolf. He was married to an Indian and had one child. Old Wolf had two other white captives, Matilda Brown (18), and her elder sister (21), who had been taken near San Antonio in 1836. They were married to two of Old Wolf's sons. Hobbs asked Bent to help get all of them back. William bought Hobbs back for six yards of red flannel, one pound of tobacco, and an ounce of beads. Baptiste was ransomed for one mule. The sons refused to part with the Brown girls.[3]

* * *

MATTHEW WRIGHT MARTIN
Oklahoma, ca. May 15, 1834

In 1820, Gabriel N. Martin was one of the pioneer settlers of what would become Red River County, Texas. He was appointed county judge in Miller County, but still held the title after the dissolution of those boundaries in 1825. Martin and other settlers, forced south of the Red River by the U.S. Army, congregated in the Pecan Point area and established the village of Jonesborough (present-day Davenport, Texas). Martin ran a farm and established a ferry over the Red River.[4]

Almost every spring, Martin took a buffalo-hunting trip into Indian Territory. In May 1834, he took his son Matthew (8), his Negro slave, Hardy Wright, and Wright's son, Sam. They pitched tents on the prairie near Glasses Creek, near present-day Kingston, Oklahoma, and prepared to spend a month or two killing bison.[5] Their hunt was cut short when a dozen Wichitas attacked their camp.[6] Judge Martin was killed, and Sam, who screamed and fought desperately, was killed because he was too much trouble. Hardy Wright, who was off in the bottoms, saw the attack and hid in a hollow log. Matthew was taken captive. When the Wichitas rode away, Wright crept away and made the 100-mile trip back to Jonesborough.

Wright went to the home of Travis G. Wright, Judge Martin's brother-in-law, who had sold Hardy to Martin the previous year, and Wright quickly organized a pursuit to rescue his nephew. Nearly thirty men volunteered, including Thomas Wright, George W. Wright, John Ragsdale, Zack Bottom, and Richard Styles, who was chosen captain. Hardy Wright guided them back to the scene of the attack where they found and buried the remains of Judge Martin. Continuing on, the party ran into and fought a large band of Indians. They got away, but not before one man was killed and another broke his thigh. Styles's company retreated east of the Washita where they found a company of U.S. soldiers.[7]

The soldiers were from the 1st U.S. Regiment of Dragoons, organized in 1833, and on an expedition into Indian Territory. Their mission was twofold: to find the hostile bands of Comanches, Kiowas and Pawnee Picts (Wichitas) and talk them into attending a peace conference at Fort Gibson, and to locate Private George B. Abbay, who was kidnapped by Wichitas near the Red River the previous year. The dragoons brought along a Kiowa and a Wichita girl, who were recovered from the Osages, and were to be used to trade for Abbay.[8] Colonel Henry Dodge led eight companies of dragoons, about 500 men, plus Indian scouts, out of Fort Gibson on June 15. Accompanying them was the artist George Catlin.

As they moved southwest toward the mouth of the Washita, the weather got hotter, once reaching 105 degrees. Finding fresh water became a problem and men began to sicken and die. Within two weeks, forty-five men and three officers were on the sick list. Colonel Henry Leavenworth, commander of the Western Division, joined them on June 26. Two days later he accidentally fell from his horse while chasing a buffalo. Soon after he caught a "bilious fever." By the time they reached Camp Washita on June 29, Leavenworth appeared to be dying. Typhus and dysentery played havoc with the command. After several days rest, Leavenworth reorganized the command, leaving Lieutenant Colonel Stephen W. Kearny and 109 dragoons to stay behind with the regiment's eighty-six invalids, and ordering Dodge, with seventeen officers, 250 men in six companies, and ten days' rations, to find the Indians.[9]

The civilians in Styles's company explained the object of their excursion, but to their surprise, the dragoons had already heard about it. George Catlin recorded that Judge Martin's fate was already published in the papers, and was known at Fort Gibson before the expedition started. Thus, to their two initial objectives, a third one was added. Catlin wrote, "It belongs to the regiment of dragoons to demand the surrender of the murderers...and it is supposed that his son, a fine boy of nine years of age, had been taken home to their villages by them, where they still retain him, and where it is our hope to recover him."[10]

With the dragoons now on the trail, Styles's company disbanded. Some headed home, while others stayed at Camp Washita. The ailing Colonel Leavenworth died on July 21, and Travis Wright volunteered to take his body to Nachitoches, Louisiana, for shipment to New York.[11] Meanwhile, Dodge's dragoons left the Washita on July 7, passed the site of the Martin attack and continued on. Men continued to get ill and drop behind. The soldiers probably looked more like scarecrows than elite dragoons, but Dodge had to press on or face ridicule by the Indians and have plenty of explaining to do to the American public. On July 14, they met a band of Comanches near an old village near the junction of Chandler and Cache Creek, about ten miles north of present-day Lawton, Oklahoma. Dodge sent out a white flag to parley, and a Comanche warrior rode up to him and shook hands, after which, the remaining warriors rushed in to shake hands with all the soldiers. They agreed to escort Dodge to the Wichita village another two days' march to the west. After leaving behind another thirty-nine sick men with thirty-six fit soldiers to look after them, Dodge's command rode to the Wichita village on the banks of the North Fork Red River, about four miles below the mouth of the Elm.[12]

Dodge's tired command reached the village on July 21. At first, the Kiowas wanted to fight because they saw Osages with the troops, however, a large council was assembled, with about 1,500 Comanches, Kiowas, Wacos, and Wichitas attending. It was well that the tribes took a wait-and-see attitude, for the 183 remaining dragoons would have been no match for them in a battle. Dodge put on a bold front, and declared that they were the first American officers to meet with the tribes, and they came as friends. He said that the American captain, President Jackson, wanted them to visit him in Washington and make a treaty, and then traders would go among the Indians to furnish them with guns and blankets.

Dodge referred to the killing of Judge Martin, the capture of his son, and the capture of Private Abbay, and the meeting became tense, with Comanches blaming Wichitas and vice-versa. Finally, an old chief whose name Catlin rendered as Water-ra-sha-ro, spoke, saying that Indians living around San Antonio had taken Abbay and put him to death, but they knew nothing about the little white boy. Dodge tried a different tact, saying that he heard the Pawnee Picts had the boy, and he was prepared to trade for him. The Indian girl(s) were brought in, and Dodge said he had bought them from their enemy, the Osages, at great expense, to prove that he was their friend. At that, the Indians had a change of heart, with some recalling, "we cried and shook hands with everyone."[13] Finally they told Dodge that they had a white child, whom they were willing to trade.

With that, a little boy was brought in from the middle of a cornfield where he had been hidden. He was naked except for a scanty dress-like covering. His appearance, said Catlin, "caused considerable excitement and commotion in the council room, and as the little fellow gazed around in great surprise, he exclaimed, 'What? are there white men here?'"

Colonel Dodge asked him his name.

"Matthew Wright Martin," he promptly replied. He ran to Dodge's arms, and Dodge signaled to release the Indian girls to their overjoyed friends and relatives. The old chief, said Catlin, embraced Dodge and the officers, "with tears streaming down his cheeks." Twenty-three Indians agreed to accompany Dodge back to Fort Gibson. The colonel hurriedly concluded business and on July 25, marched his ailing command toward home. The return march was nearly as bad as the outward, with forty-three more men doubled over with cramps and fever.

On August 13, on the North Fork Canadian, Dodge's men reached the outlying settlements. There they heard that Mrs. Martin had offered a $2,000 reward for her boy's recovery. Catlin concluded that she would certainly be thrilled that he had been saved without harm or ransom. He was taken to Fort Gibson, Catlin said, "In the arms of the dragoons, who took turns in carrying him; and after the command reached there, he was transmitted to the Red River settlements by an officer, who had the enviable satisfaction of delivering him into the arms of his disconsolate and half-distracted mother."[14]

KIOWA DUTCH
Texas, July 1835

Very little is known about this German boy who became a member of the Kiowa tribe and stayed with them for the rest of his life. He was born in Germany about 1826, and attended school there for a few years. When he was about eight, his parents moved to Texas and settled near the Gulf Coast. He remembered living on a large river with alligators and moss-covered trees, where ships could sail, and which was about a day's ride from the ocean. This may have been Matagorda or Galveston Bay.

Shortly after the Kiowas held their sun dance in the summer of 1835, they raided all the way to the Gulf, plundering and taking captives. The German family had not been there one year and neither of the two sons had learned English. The Kiowas arrived at night, killed the father and captured the mother and two boys. The mother was taken away from her sons and may have been killed. One of the sons committed suicide during the cholera epidemic that hit the Kiowas in 1849. To the last boy, the Kiowas gave the name Boin-edal (Big Blond), or, as he later became known to the whites, Kiowa Dutch.[15]

Boin-edal quickly assimilated into the Kiowa tribe. In the winter of 1837-38, on the Clear Fork of the Brazos, the Kiowas and Comanches had a fight with a band of Arapahos. One Arapaho was killed. The warriors cut his head off, tied a rope to it, and dragged it into the Kiowa camp. Even when he was more than 70 years old, Boin-edal still remembered the barbarous spectacle. Even so, there was a strange thrill to it, and the young German boy grew up to be a Kiowa warrior in all respects.

Boin-edal's adoptive father, Crow Neck, died in the fall of 1842, while the band was on the Double Mountain Fork of the Brazos. By this time Boin-edal was about 16 years old, and could take care of himself. He participated in many raids into Old Mexico, New Mexico Territory, and Texas over the succeeding decades. White settlers and soldiers often recounted Indian raids and mentioned seeing red or blond haired white men riding with the Indians. There were other captives with red or blond hair who rode with the raiders, such as Herman Lehmann and Adolph Korn, or white renegades like Thomas F. M. "Bise" Mclean. Their raiding years, however, would have been much later than Kiowa Dutch's.

One raid in which Kiowa Dutch may have participated took place in Jack County in April 1858, when he would have been about 32 years old. A band of Indians and a few white men pillaged the homes of the Mason and Cambren families, killing all the adults and three of the Cambren children. Mary Cambren (7) and her brother Dewitt (5) were left behind with their dead mother. The marauders put young Thomas Cambren on a horse and rode off, but some mounted travelers chased them and to lighten their load, they threw Thomas from the horse. Later Mary Cambren described one of the leaders as a red-haired man who stole a trunk containing a lot of money, however, she also recalled him speaking English, which probably meant he wasn't Kiowa Dutch. In November 1860, a red-haired Indian participated in another north Texas raid, and was involved in the rape and death of a woman in Palo Pinto County (see Martha Sherman). In July 1867, a red-haired man led a raid on a schoolhouse in Hamilton County, killing the teacher and capturing a student (see John Kuykendall). If Kiowa Dutch participated in these later raids, he would have been in his late thirties or older, and probably on the downside of his warrior days.

In 1898, Kiowa Dutch was more than 70 years of age and the oldest captive member of the Kiowa tribe. He still remembered a few words of German, and picked up a fair knowledge of English and Spanish, but he never remembered his name.[16]

SARAH CREATH HIBBINS & JOHN MCSHERRY, JR.
Texas, January 1836

Of all the unfortunate Indian captives, Sarah Creath-McSherry-Hibbens-Stinnet-Howard may have had the longest stretch of bad luck of all, extending over a period of thirteen years. Sarah Creath was born in Jackson County, Illinois, ca. 1812. About 1828, young Sarah married John McSherry and the couple moved to Dewitt's Colony in Texas. They built a cabin on the west bank of the Guadalupe River, near the southern edge of today's Dewitt County, about ten miles downstream from their nearest neighbor, Andrew Lockhart. Sarah was described as "a beautiful blonde. . . very handsome in person, graceful in manner, and pure at heart." John McSherry was called "an honest, industrious man of nerve and will."[17]

Early in 1829, Sarah gave birth to a son, John Jr. Later that same year Sarah's world began to turn upside down. John McSherry went to a nearby spring to get water when a small party of Indians ambushed and killed him. Sarah saw the attack from near the cabin, grabbed her infant, ran inside, and barred the door. Seizing a rifle, she menaced the approaching Indians by pointing the weapon at them through a window. After circling the cabin a few times, the Indians thought better of attacking the determined white woman and left the area. At sunset, young frontiersman John McCrabb, unaware of the situation, rode up to her door. Sarah explained her predicament; McCrabb helped her and the baby onto his horse and walked through the night the ten miles to Lockhart's house. The Lockhart's took her in and there she stayed.[18]

A few years later, the young widow met John Hibbins (sometimes spelled Hibbons) and they married and settled on the east side of the Guadalupe in the vicinity of the present-day town of Concrete, Texas. In the summer of 1835, Sarah went east to visit her family in Illinois, accompanied by young John McSherry and her second child, the son of John Hibbins. She returned with her children and her brother, George, down the Mississippi, across the Gulf of Mexico, and up the Brazos River to Columbia, arriving in January 1836.[19]

John Hibbins met them and they began the overland journey home. They crossed the Colorado and the Navidad, and then took the old La Bahia Road, where they camped on Rocky Creek, six miles above the later village of Sweet Home, Lavaca County, and only about fifteen miles from their cabin. Without warning, thirteen Comanches swept down on their little camp and in a few minutes, George Creath and John Hibbins were dead. The Indians tied Sarah to one mule, John Jr. and the toddler to another, and they headed northwest along Peach Creek. At night, the Indians forced Sarah to the ground with her boys next to her, threw a buffalo robe over them, and two warriors stretched out on each side of the robe, pinning the three captives between them. The second night out, the youngest boy, tired and hungry, began to cry. An angry warrior killed him.[20]

Another days' travel took them across the Colorado, to a camp in a cedar brake on Walnut Creek where the city of Austin now stands. The Indians, perhaps believing they were far enough from the settlements, let Sarah and John Jr. sleep without a close guard. Sarah had been calculating her chances of escape, and the first night without a guard seemed to be her best chance. Every day would take her farther from the settlements. She hoped to slip away alone, find help, and return to rescue her boy. When the Indians were asleep, she tucked John Jr. under his buffalo robe and slipped away. The night was bitter cold, but, to cover her tracks, Sarah waded down a creek that led to the Colorado River. Her feet were frozen and brambles scratched her arms and legs. She wandered along the twisting gullies for what she thought was two hours when she heard a cry that sounded like, "Mamma!" Was it her son, and after all her walking, was she still so close to the camp, or were the Indians looking for her? Sarah turned away from the sound and hurried off in the direction she hoped was south.[21]

Sarah walked for nearly twenty-four hours, but covered only ten miles before she was ready to drop from exhaustion. In an open pasture by the river she noticed several milk cows. It was late afternoon and she figured she could wait until the cows headed home, hopefully leading her to a cabin. When the cows began to walk, she followed. As the sun was setting she saw two men in the river bottom, and she called as loud as she could, but the men walked on. Sarah continued until she came to Jacob Harrell's cabin. She simply opened the door, saw a chair, and collapsed in it without saying a word. The Harrells were startled by her sudden appearance, but when Sarah was finally able to relate her story, Jacob knew just what to do. He hurried her to the nearby cabin of Reuben Hornsby.

Just arriving at Hornsby's Station was a company of sixty Rangers under Captain John J. Tumlinson. Formed in January 1836, the company was first assigned to an area near Brushy Creek, about thirty miles northwest of the later site of Austin. Reassigned in February, Tumlinson moved his company southeast, to rendezvous at Hornsby's. Just as the Rangers were preparing supper, Sarah Hibbins arrived, described by Ranger Noah Smithwick as, "a young white woman, an entire stranger, her clothes hanging in shreds about her torn and bleeding body."[22]

After drinking and eating, Sarah explained what happened, told the Rangers the direction the Indians were moving, described the mule her son was riding, and implored them to find him. The Rangers finished their supper, saddled up, and Reuben Hornsby guided them up the Colorado in the reverse direction that Sarah had just traveled. At dawn on January 20, they picked up the trail. Smithwick believed the Indians spent a good deal of time searching for their missing captive. "They did not seem to be at all alarmed about the consequence of her escape," he said, because "it was about 10 o'clock in the morning when we came upon them, just preparing to break camp."[23]

The Rangers charged. Smithwick was riding a fleet horse, and the animal carried him among the Indians. One warrior fired at Smithwick from behind a tree, but missed. Noah jumped off and chased him on foot. "I fired on him and had the satisfaction of seeing him fall," Smithwick said. "My blood was up and, leaving him for dead, I ran on." Smithwick chased another Indian through a thicket, lost his hat, and was fired on by another Ranger who mistook him for a Comanche. The Indian Smithwick shot was not dead, for he raised up and fired at Captain Tumlinson, narrowly missing him and killing his horse. Ranger Conrad Rohrer rushed up and brained the warrior with the butt of his rifle. Most of the Indians got away in the thick canebrake. One mule, with a large buffalo robe bundle tied on its back, ran past the Rangers and they gave chase. Someone was wrapped inside the robe. Conrad Rohrer rode up to the frightened mule, placed his rifle against the robe and pulled the trigger, but the gun misfired. He tried again, with the same result. Before he could attempt it a third time, Smithwick reported, "one of the other boys, perceiving with horror the tragedy about to be enacted, knocked the gun up, it firing clear, sending a ball whistling over the head" of the intended target. Inside the bundle, tied to the mule, was John McSherry Jr.[24]

With the battle over, the Rangers gathered up what booty they could salvage, and headed back to Hornsby's. Four Comanches were killed, while the Rangers had only Elijah Ingram and Hugh M. Childress wounded. Late in the afternoon they rode into the station in triumph. Lieutenant Joseph Rogers presented John Jr. to his mother, and Captain Tumlinson explained, "the scene which here ensued beggars description. A mother meeting with her child released from Indian captivity, rescued, as it were, from the very jaws of death! Not an eye was dry. She called us brothers, and every other endearing name, and would have fallen on her knees to worship us. She hugged the child—her only remaining treasure—to her bosom as if fearful that she would again lose him. And—but 'tis useless to say more."[25]

This joyful scene completed, there was little time for anyone to rest. General Santa Anna had led his Mexican Army into Texas and was at that time investing San Antonio and the defenders of the Alamo. For a few weeks, Sarah remained with the Hornsbys and Harrells, until the fall of the Alamo and the advance of Santa Anna's army precipitated the settlers' flight. Sarah and John Jr. hurried northeast with the two families, staying a few steps ahead of Santa Anna. They halted east of the Trinity River, where messengers brought the news of Santa Anna's defeat at the Battle of San Jacinto, on April 21 1836. After that crisis was over, Sarah Hibbins headed west, but only got as far as Washington County, where a sympathetic settler agreed to let her stay. There she met a former neighbor, Claiborne Stinnett, and after 12 months of widowhood, Sarah and Claiborne married. In the spring of 1837, they returned to her former cabin on the Guadalupe.

Sarah's luck had not gotten much better; it was even worse for her several husbands. In the fall of 1837, Claiborne Stinnett went to buy supplies in Linnville. With business done, he headed home, but did not take the usual road through Victoria. Instead, Stinnett took a short cut across the prairie. One night while camped near Arenosa Creek, about twenty miles northeast of Victoria, he saw smoke in a nearby grove. Assuming it was from some hunters, he went to it, but stumbled upon the camp of two runaway slaves who assumed he was hunting them. They killed him, left his body, took his horse, provisions, and money, and fled to Mexico. Sarah did not learn of his fate for five years, until one of the runaway slaves told the story to a white American in Mexico. In the fall of 1842, Stinnett's remains were located and buried. Sarah, not yet 30 years old, was widowed for the third time.[26]

Undaunted, and still young and attractive, Sarah married her fourth husband in 1840, two years before the body of Claiborne Stinnett was found. In June of that year, Sarah and Phillip Howard left her home on the Guadalupe and moved west to Mission San Juan, below San Antonio. The trek took them through 100 miles of country still not secure from raiding Indians, and seven young men from the Guadalupe settlements escorted them. The trip was uneventful, but after arriving at the mission, the party hobbled its horses and rested. John McSherry, now 11 years old, stayed on his pony to watch the small herd. Suddenly, a band of Indians rode in after the horses. One warrior tried to grab John, but he frantically rode back to camp, narrowly escaping a second capture. In a few moments, the Indians were gone, along with most of the horses.

Once more confronted with the harsh realities of living on the frontier, the Howards packed up and moved to the San Antonio River, below the ranch of Don Carlos de la Garza, at the lower edge of Goliad County. Still, Indian forays seemed to follow everywhere Sarah went. In the spring of 1842, Indians swept in, bypassing the Howard home, but striking even further into Refugio County, where they killed members of the Gilleland Family and carried off their children (see Rebecca Gilleland). It was too much for the

Howards. Again they moved, this time to Hallettsville in Lavaca County. Finally, after thirteen years of bad luck, Sarah faced no more Indian raids. Sarah gave birth to a daughter in 1845. Phillip Howard was elected county judge in 1848. Some years later they relocated to Bosque County, where they fade out of history. Sarah died about 1876.[27]

John McLennan
Texas, March 1836

The McLennan clan, including brothers Neil, Laughlin, and John, emigrated from Scotland to North Carolina in 1801. As their families grew they sought new lands, first in Florida, and in 1834, decided to try their luck in Texas. The families, along with some neighbors, bought a schooner and sailed it along the Gulf Coast, reaching the mouth of the Brazos River in January 1835. They snaked the schooner upriver until they hit a snag in what is now Fort Bend County, and the frail craft sank. The McLennans salvaged what they could and continued upriver, leaving the Brazos to head up Pond Creek in Robertson's Colony. The site they chose to build their homes was on a hill known as Sugar Loaf, about 400 feet above the level of a small lake formed by a bend of Pond Creek. The hill later became known as McLennan's Bluff, and is about one mile west of present-day, Rosebud, Texas, in southwest Falls County.[28]

One of the McLennan Brothers, it is uncertain who, was dissatisfied with the location and later in 1835, moved his family southwest to the San Gabriel River. Before they had even built a new home, McLennan and his oldest son went hunting for game. While they were gone, Indians descended upon the camp and took Mrs. McLennan, her second boy, and an infant, captive. The Indians stripped them, tied them, and plundered the camp. Inside a trunk, the Indians discovered a mirror, which they found very amusing. Evening was drawing near, and while the Indians argued over who would "own" the mirror, Mrs. McLennan loosened her bonds, got her children, and crept away into the thickets along the San Gabriel.

When the Indians noticed the prisoners had escaped, they made a quick search, but since night was falling, they gathered up their plunder and left. About this time, Mr. McLennan and his son returned to see the camp destroyed and his family gone. They set out for help in the settlements below. The escaped refugees hid out in the woods for several days, living on grains of corn and

Author's photo

McLennan's Bluff, near Rosebud, Texas. Site of the capture of John McLennan.

wild berries. They did not travel far from their original campsite, and when Mr. McLennan returned with a company of settlers, his wife saw them, thought they were Indians, and fled again into the thickets. She was chased down and caught, emaciated and half-crazed with fear, and only then realized that she and her children had been saved. The reunited family moved back to be near the rest of the clan at McLennan's Bluff.

In the late winter of 1836, Laughlin McLennan and his wife were outside splitting wood when a party of Wacos attacked and killed them. The Indians rushed to the house and found Laughlin's old, crippled mother, who could do little but sit in her chair and watch. One warrior finally buried his hatchet in her head. The three children were captured. The Wacos set the house on fire, leaving old Mrs. McLennan inside to burn.[29]

If it was Laughlin and his wife who were first attacked on the San Gabriel, they were doubly unlucky. In any case, the murders and abductions were enough for brothers Neil and John; they removed their families downriver to the settlement at Nashville-on-the-Brazos. The country was still dangerous, however, for in 1837, Indians attacked Neil, his son John, and a black slave. Neil and his son escaped, but the slave was captured. In 1838, Indians killed Neil's brother, John. In 1839, Neil joined George B. Erath's company of Indian fighters. While scouting farther up the Brazos, Neil found fertile, watered land that looked better than the land

13

at McLennan's Bluff, and he stopped to survey it. His companions thought him crazy, but in 1845, he moved his family there and planted crops. He built a house on the South Bosque River about eight miles from present-day Waco. He was living there in 1845 when he got word about his long-lost nephew, John McLennan.[30]

John, captured when he was about seven years old, was nearly lost to history for almost a decade. His captive sibling and mother either soon died, or were killed, while John was adopted into the tribe. The citizens, not knowing his fate, were nevertheless concerned about the attacks. In October 1837, the Committee on Indian Affairs reported to President Sam Houston, that the Kichais, Tawakonis, and Wacos, who lived on the headwaters of the Trinity and Brazos Rivers, continued to take captives. They "carry off women and children as prisoners," the Committee reported, who "are forced to subserve to pourposes [sic] that any beings other than *fiends* would blush to think of."[31]

The Republic of Texas made several treaties with the Indians. In March 1843, in an Indian council at Tehuacana Creek, Delawares, Shawnees, Caddoes, Ionis, Anadarkos, Tawakonis, Kichais, Wichitas, and Wacos all signed an agreement, including a stipulation that all Indians would give up their captives, "without ransom or price." In a similar agreement in August of that year, the Comanches said that they would give up all white captives. A formal treaty was signed at Bird's Fort on the Trinity in September, that said all sides would "mutually surrender and give up all of the prisoners which they have. . . ." In another council on Tehuacana Creek in May 1844, Texan commissioners told the Kichais that they heard the Indians had a white boy in their possession. The Kichais answered, "The young men got him a long time ago, when he was but a little boy, but if you want to see him we will bring him down to the next council."[32]

Treaties and promises made by the Indians, with tantalizing hints that they were going to return white captives, gave hope to the McLennan family that they would one day see John again. But years passed and promises were not kept. When more meetings were held in 1845, there was probably no reason for the McLennan's to believe the results would be any different. On November 13, 1845, at Torrey's Trading Post No.2, located on a tributary of Tehuacana Creek about eight miles below Waco, Commissioner George W. Terrell spoke harshly to the gathered bands. He affirmed that they had been meeting together for years, and the whites had kept their part of the agreements, but the Indians had not. Terrell pointed at the Kichai chief, Saatzarook, and said, "We know that the Keechi have one prisoner now and that chief there promised some time since to give him up—we expect him now to bring him in."

When Saatzarook spoke, he told a sorrowful tale that he was poor and naked, and he wished the white chief would give him blankets. He said he was glad the white chief loved his red brethren, that he too loved peace, and that he loved "the white women and children, like I do my own." Commissioner Terrell had heard enough.

"Where is the white prisoner?" he demanded.

Saatzarook could delay no longer. His rather lame answer was that, "the reason I did not bring him in is that he had no horse to ride. If you send a horse I can bring him."[33]

The council ended and the treaty was signed November 16, 1845, the last treaty ever made by the Republic of Texas. Commissioner Thomas I. Smith went with Comanche and Kichai agent Paul Richardson and ten rangers to ride to the Indian camp and get the boy. But who was he? Rumor was, a young, white, male captive was held by the Kichais. The authorities assumed it was John Parker, taken by the Indians in the 1836 raid on Parker's Fort. Correspondence among several Texas officials mention Parker as the captive. Superintendent of Indian Affairs, Thomas G. Western, wrote to Agent Benjamin Sloat in July 1845, to get "the young man Parker" from the "Keechi." In November, Western wrote to Agent Richardson to "receive the Parker boy" and bring him to Torrey's Post. The same month, Commissioner Terrell wrote to Secretary of State Ebenezer Allen, that the Kichais had promised to deliver "the white youth named Parker" to the agent. The Texas legislature even appropriated $300 to pay his ransom.[34]

On December 6, 1845, Agent Richardson rode in to Torrey's Post, and delivered "the white boy" to Agent Leonard H. Williams. Williams wrote and asked Isaac Parker to please come and take charge of his nephew. Isaac Parker, 52 years of age, who would serve almost continuously from 1836 to 1856, in the Legislature of Texas as a republic and a state, was the uncle of the famous captives, Cynthia Ann and John Parker. It was still assumed that the returned boy was John Parker. Williams also wrote to Superintendent Western, asking instructions as to what he should do if the boy "is not claimed by Mr. Parker, and turns out to be as is somewhat expected, of another family." From what Williams gathered from the Indians, they killed the boy's parents and took him in the vicinity of Little River, which was about ninety miles from Parker's Fort and much closer to McLennan's Bluff. White men at Torrey's Post suggested to Williams that the boy might be John McLennan.[35]

While Williams was waiting word from Isaac Parker, Neil McLennan heard of a white boy, about 16 years old, who was at Torrey's. His captured nephew would have been about 16. On December 29, Neil McLennan rode to Torrey's, less than a day's journey from his new home. Before McLennan arrived, Agent Williams did not have an easy time with the boy. He was not pleased to be taken from the Indian family he had known for nearly a decade. He was described as, "unable to speak a word of English, dressed in the Indian garb and with all the propensities of that race," and was the "very picture of a wild warrior." Williams described his meeting:

"Mr. Neill McClennan [sic] arrived here last evening and recognizes the boy as being his nephew, and after conversing with the boy through an interpreter he has learnt from him particulars which dispels every doubt-as to the identity of the boy-I have delivered the boy to Mr. McClennan, on his becoming responsible to the government for the boy-and he is willing to pay any legal demands to Govt is disposed to make."

With that, Neil took the teenager, who was sometimes called "Indian John," to other relations near Nashville-on-the-Brazos. A neighbor, Mrs. Robert Davidson, made the first new clothes for John that he would consent to wear, besides his Indian dress: a garment of bright red cloth. She also fashioned him "a straw hat with a red ribbon band streaming down about a yard, of which he was very proud." It took time for John to become reconciled to white society, but, it was said, "with the return of his mother tongue he became more civilized and contented." Nevertheless, John never forgot his Indian "mother," and he often visited her, taking along presents that he knew would please her. Eventually, he accepted the world he was in, got married, and settled down on Hog Creek in Bosque County, where he died in 1866, at only 37 years of age.[36]

Mary Theresa Hennecke Juergens
Texas, ca. April 1, 1836

The Alamo at San Antonio de Bexar, fell on March 6, 1836. Word quickly spread of atrocities committed by Mexican troops on rebellious Texians at San Patricio, Refugio, and following James W. Fannin's defeat on Coleto Creek and the subsequent massacre at Goliad. Many settlers panicked. Families hurried east and north, away from the Mexican Army. The flight was known afterwards as the "Runaway Scrape," and it nearly depopulated some counties. Sam Houston's forces retreated from Gonzales to Burnham's Crossing of the Colorado (La Grange), Beason's Crossing (Columbus), San Felipe on the Brazos, and to Groce's Plantation near Hempstead. Santa Anna and a portion of his army followed in Houston's wake.[37]

The Jeurgens Family did not run. Mary Theresa Hennecke, daughter of Anna Maria Middike and Joseph Hennecke, was born June 18, 1809, in Entrup, Westphalia (Prussia). In July 1833, she married Conrad Juergens and they headed for Texas. In late 1833, they had settled near Cummins Creek west of Post Oak Point, where today's Austin, Fayette, and Colorado counties all meet.

Mary had two sons and was pregnant again at the time of the "Runaway Scrape." The Juergens's imprudent decision to hope the Mexican troops bypassed them was not wholly successful. Santa Anna did pass them by to the south, but with no troops or neighbors around, they were open to Indian attack. One night, Mary awoke to an unusual noise. She roused Conrad and he went outside, only to find the area filled with Indians. He shouted out a warning, was shot and wounded, but ducked into the dark woods and got away. Mary and her two boys ran out into the night, but were seen in their white underclothes and easily captured.[38]

About three months later, Mary Juergens appeared at one of "Coffee's Stations" near the Red River. Holland Coffee, in partnership with Silas Colville, was a trapper and trader who set up several posts along the Red River between the years of 1833 and 1846. Some Texians vilified Coffee, believing that his trading with the Indians encouraged depredations, and members of the Texas House of Representatives recommended that his posts be put under surveillance or suppressed. In spite of Coffee's questionable operations, his posts were sites where Indians occasionally returned captives. One post in operation in the summer of 1836, run by Abel Warren, was located near the mouth of Walnut Bayou, near present-day, Burneyville, Oklahoma. It may have been to this post where Comanches brought a haggard Mary Juergens. A more likely possibility is that she was taken to the post of a Captain Pace, who ran a trading house near the junction of the Blue River and the Red, in present-day Bryan County, Oklahoma. James W. Parker, who was searching for his own captured daughter (see Rachel Parker Plummer), heard that a woman who fit his daughter's description was brought to Pace's.

He hurried there, but learned that the rescued woman was not his daughter, but a "Mrs. Yorkins."[39]

Mary had just given birth to a daughter, Jane (or Ann) Margaret, while being held in Indian Territory. Relatives of the Juergens had been trying to arrange her release. Eventually, the Indians received word that money would be paid for her safe return, and she was released for a ransom of $300. Unfortunately, the deal apparently did not include her two sons. The Indians refused to release them, and they vanished from the historical record. Mary returned to Conrad Juergens for a time, but things were not well with them; stories of his abandoning his family and saving his own skin would have made his life a hell in the frontier community. Sometime before March 1838, Conrad died, and Mary, as administrator of his estate, was given a league and a labor of land in southeast Colorado County. In 1838, Mary Juergens married George Grimes, which evidently ended in divorce or in George's death, for in 1843, she married Samuel J. Redgate. They lived near Frelsburg, Colorado County, a half dozen miles from the site of Mary's capture in 1836. In 1871, the couple moved to Dayton, Ohio, where Mary died on Halloween night, 1891.[40]

SARAH ANN HORN AND MRS. HARRIS
Texas, April 4, 1836

Sarah Ann Horn was born in Huntington, England, in 1809, the youngest of ten children of the Newton family. She was 18 years old in October 1827, when she married John Horn. They had two sons, John, born in 1828, and Joseph, born in 1829.[41] John Horn was a well-established London merchant, but talk of cheap land in America enticed them, and they sailed for New York in July 1833. Having heard of Doctor John Charles Beales and his proposed colony in Coahuila-Texas, the Horn's joined a group of emigrants and set sail on November 11, 1833.[42]

The party, consisting of about fifty-nine emigrants under the direction of Doctor Beales, left Copano Bay, near present-day Bayside, Texas, on January 3, 1834. Their roundabout journey took them to Goliad, San Antonio, southwest to the Rio Grande near present-day Eagle Pass, upriver to the mouth of Las Moras Creek, then up that creek eighteen miles, reaching the selected site on March 16. They named the new town Dolores.

Almost from the first day, the colony was plagued with problems: the soil was not productive without irrigation, the creek was too small, the site was too remote from other settlements, the colonists were not all experienced in forging a new town out of the wilderness, the land company tried to regulate their daily activities, and the land allotted them did not amount to the acreages Texas empresarios had given to other colonists. A clique of Germans argued constantly with Beales or his associates, and some of them abandoned the colony after the first year.[43]

Beales tried to bring in more colonists, but only three families and fifteen men arrived. In fear of Indians and the Mexican Army, the colonists called it quits. The Horns wanted to pull out with four other families and a number of young men, but Sarah and John were sick and unable to travel. The missed opportunity meant disaster.

The colony broke apart in early March 1836. Some members headed east to try and join up with Sam Houston's Army, while others traveled back toward Copano Bay along the same road they had taken west. John Horn and family formed a small party with the Harris family and nine other men. They hoped to head southeast for Matamoros and catch a ship for England, leaving the God-forsaken Texas wilderness far behind. They pulled out March 8, 1836, two days after the fall of the Alamo.[44]

The little band headed out, but fearing Mexican forces along the Rio Grande, they roughly followed the course of the Nueces River. They left the river on April 2, probably near present-day Cotulla, and headed east. On April 4, they stopped at a lake, which was probably southwest of today's Tilden, Texas.

Little is known about Mrs. Harris's antecedents. She was probably not from England, and joined up with Beales's expedition in the States. Sarah Horn was caring for Mrs. Harris's three-month-old baby girl because of her condition, which Sarah called "broken breasts." While dressing the baby, which was probably the only child born in Dolores, Sarah saw Indians riding toward their camp. She ran to her husband, but he said there was no danger. Seconds later, the Indians, probably Peneteka Comanches, attacked, shooting an arrow into the chest of a man standing next to Sarah. Sarah grabbed Joseph's hand while still carrying the baby, but the warriors were upon them. One of them took a rifle and clubbed John Horn to the ground, crushing his skull. They took Sarah and the children to the wagon, where Sarah gave Mrs. Harris back her child. The Indians made short work of the men, then took the women and children to their camp about two miles away. The captives were stripped and given nothing to eat or drink, and that night, Harris and Horn were bound together with a rope, unable to do anything but listen to their children crying.

The next day, the thirsty and hungry baby cried piteously. Sarah, who could speak a little Spanish, asked for some flour to make the baby something to eat. A warrior agreed to get some food, but instead, grabbed the little girl and threw her high into the air. Said Sarah, "This barbarous act having been repeated three times, its sufferings were at an end." An Indian hung the baby's body on a mule's saddlehorn, but the women refused to ride until he removed the corpse.[45]

The next day, to the surprise of the two white women, Mr. Harris and a young German were brought in. They had survived their wounds and were placed nearby so the women could watch them die. Sarah said that Mr. Harris, "cast an agonizing look at his dear wife and myself, but he uttered not a word." The men were shot dead on the spot.

Over the next several days the band moved toward the coast. Horn and Harris were abused, made to alter and sew their own clothing to fit the Indians, and forced to participate in a scalp dance. Nearly naked, the women burned and blistered in the hot sun. They got food only every two or three days. Mrs. Harris's owners were more abusive than Sarah's. One old woman frequently choked her "until the poor unresisting creature would turn black in the face, and fall as if dead at her feet." The woman, Sarah said, was one of the most "depraved beings I have seen."[46]

When the Indians were thirty miles from Matamoros they attacked and killed a small number of Americans, then raided a Mexican's ranch and killed the entire family. Joseph was badly hurt when he fell from a mule, and his cuts and bruises became infected and crawling with maggots. He was taken from Sarah and rode behind another Indian. He lay in the dirt at night, crying in pain and begging for water, but was given no succor. Sarah could not take seeing her children tortured. To end their suffering, she said she "would have rendered it a matter of heart-felt joy could I have seen them share the fate of their murdered father."

The Indians raided another ranch, but two warriors were wounded, a posse chased them, and they abandoned the area. About April 18, they passed the site of the initial attack on the wagon train and Sarah noted the parched and blackened bodies still lying in the sun. They traveled rapidly for three days, when the Indians divided into three groups of about 100 each. Horn and Harris were separated, but Joseph still remained near his mother. They traveled steadily for two months. At one river crossing, Joseph again fell off a mule, but instead of anyone helping him, an angry warrior struck at him with his lance as he attempted to climb up the bank, severely cutting him below the eye and knocking him back into the river. Joseph finally reached shore and Sarah gave the warrior a verbal tongue-lashing in Spanish. The warrior's response was to make Joseph travel on foot the rest of the day, and Sarah was cruelly whipped that night. The punishment, however, "had no terrors for a miserable wretch like me," she said. The strokes of the whip "seemed to me of no more weight than a feather. Indeed, I felt recreant to mortal existence, and my soul, desperate with the tantalized affections of a wife and mother, would fain have preferred the most cruel death to life such as mine."[47] Sarah was suffering her own fate worse than death.

The abuse never stopped, it only waxed and waned. Delighting in Sarah's anguish, the Indians took Joseph and John to a stream and made a game of trying to see how close they could come to drowning them. With the "fun" over, the Indians dropped the boys at Sarah's feet; their emaciated bodies were grotesque with bellies distended and water freely discharging from their noses and mouths. When they next rode off, Joseph could not sit on a mule, so the Indians "choked him until the blood ran out at his mouth and nose."

In June, the Indian bands met up again, and Sarah Horn briefly saw Mrs. Harris, who she described as appearing "barely to exist." After several more days' travel, they split up again, and this time Mrs. Harris and the two boys went off with different groups. Sarah was alone and despondent. She had a new master, and another mistress she described as "an utter stranger to the feelings of humanity." The woman threw things at her and beat her, but this time Sarah took a different tack. Because of what she had "witnessed of savage courage in contact with unresisting and inferior numbers, that they were the most dastardly cowards," Sarah decided she would fight. When her Indian mistress hurled any object at her head, Sarah picked it up and threw it back, "and I found that I fared much better for it."[48]

Sarah Horn and Mrs. Harris met occasionally and Sarah was worried. As bad as her treatment was, she believed it worse for Harris. "[H]er sufferings were greater than mine," she said. "It was with much difficulty that the woman could bring herself to the place of a servant to these wretched beings; and possibly, the rigid discipline under which she was held was proportionably [sic] severe." When they could meet alone, Sarah said, "we mingled our tears as she exhibited to me the marks of savage brutality, which she will bear in her person to the grave."

Sarah had not seen her children for about two months, when a band of Indians moved nearby to camp. She heard there was a little white boy with them and begged permission to go to see him. It was Joseph, but now all painted in black and red, with his hair cut close to his head except for a tuft at the top, and adorned with bracelets and necklaces. He was fast becoming an Indian, but he ran crying to her when he recognized his mother. The meeting was abruptly ended and Joseph taken away again. Four months later she got a glimpse of John, and the meeting was similarly tearful and short-lived.

In late fall of 1836, a few traders visited the Comanche camps. Sarah believed they were employees of Holland Coffee, who owned several posts along the Red River. The men tried to purchase her, but the Indians would not sell. When they left, they said they would contact Coffee to see if he could raise enough money. Coffee visited the camp and parleyed with the Comanches to obtain the release of Horn and Harris, but to no avail. When Coffee left, said Sarah, "He expressed the deepest concern at his disappointment, and wept over me as he gave me clothing, and divided his scanty supply of flour between me and my children, which he took the pains to carry to them himself." Sarah later learned that Coffee was charged "with supineness and indifference" in trying to recover captives, but Sarah had nothing but praise for his efforts.[49]

In June 1837, while the Comanches were at the headwaters of the Canadian, Comancheros visited their camp. American merchant William Donaho had sent them when he learned about the captive women while in Santa Fe (see Rachel Plummer). The Comancheros had ransomed Mrs. Harris, and Rachel Plummer, but they could not obtain Sarah Horn. Sarah tried to talk one last time with Mrs. Harris, but she was not allowed to. She was glad that Mrs. Harris "was released from her sufferings," but now she felt even more alone, and keenly felt "the truth of the saying, that 'misery loves company.' " In her despondency, Sarah pondered that "the God of Heaven only knows why, and how it is, that I am still alive."[50]

Mrs. Harris was conducted to Santa Fe, where she stayed with the Donohos. Three months later, Mr. Donoho packed up his family, Mrs. Harris, and Rachel Plummer, and took them to Missouri. They arrived at Independence in late October, and subsequently moved in with his mother-in-law in Pulaski County, Missouri. Mrs. Harris, with no husband, children, or nearby relatives, had nearly completed her odyssey. She had relatives in Texas, but because of the shame of her captivity, she did not want to go there. She chose to live with some kin near Boonville, Missouri, but soon died of the ravages and abuse she suffered while a prisoner.[51]

Back in New Mexico Territory, Sarah Ann Horn wondered what was to be her fate. In September, while camped near San Miguel, an Indian girl told her she would be sold to the Mexicans, but Sarah did not wish to change one master for another, and be even farther from her sons. The Mexicans, it turns out, were Comancheros working with William Donoho, and after he left for Missouri, for traders William Workman and John A. Rowland of Taos. Sarah, not knowing the Comancheros intended to take her to Taos, heard that Benjamin Hill, a merchant near San Miguel, was interested in buying her. She figured she would rather go with an American than a Mexican, but Hill only teased her; he asked if she would like to be ransomed, then walked away and left her.

The Comancheros finally made the purchase, for a horse, four bridles, two mirrors, two knives, tobacco, powder, and balls, which Sarah estimated to be worth about $80. Hill then changed his mind and demanded that the Mexicans give him Sarah, claiming that he had already given the Indians goods for her release. They demurred, but Hill threatened that if they did not release her, he would take her by force. Sarah was bewildered. She said, "I could not comprehend the meaning of this strange affair." The Mexicans argued with Hill, but he threatened a lawsuit and they gave in. On September 21, Sarah Horn went to her new master, where she worked as his slave for the next six weeks.

Hearing of Sarah's plight, a Mr. Smith, who had made money in the New Mexico mines, sent some of his men with money and weapons to Hill's trading house. They persuaded Hill to let her go, and on November 3, Sarah was at Smith's place near Taos. While at Smith's, Sarah pondered whether to try to leave immediately for the States, or stay in New Mexico to try and rescue her boys. She finally decided to leave, rationalizing that she was no nearer rescuing her sons from Taos than she might be from Missouri, and she did not like the Spanish-Catholic community where she was exiled.

In February 1838, Workman and Rowland sent a gift of two dresses to Sarah, and asked her if she would remain in the territory longer, while they attempted to ransom her sons. Sarah waited, and on March 10, went to Taos to stay with Workman and Rowland. Sarah now had plenty of benefactors. Mr. Smith went out on an expedition to find her children, but apparently a faithless guide led them into waterless country where several died. Workman and Rowland sent out two companies of men to find her sons, but on their return they reported that John was dead. He was ordered to guard the horses one winter night, but was found frozen to death the next morning. The Indians refused to sell Joseph for any price.[52]

With the knowledge that John was dead and that she would probably never see Joseph again, Sarah finally resolved to leave New Mexico Territory. She had a premonition of her fate: "Time shall roll on, and soon my hopes and fears shall be hushed in the silence of death." On August 22, 1838, almost one year after Mrs. Harris left, Sarah Horn bid farewell to those who had befriended her and rode for Missouri, the only female in Workman and Rowland's large wagon train. They arrived at Independence on the last day of September, and Sarah was put up in the house of David Workman, William's brother, in New Franklin, Missouri. William Donoho, after escorting Rachel Plummer to Texas, went back to Santa Fe to finish up his business. He eventually went to Taos to inquire about Sarah Horn, but discovered she had just left for Missouri. With his business completed, Donoho went back to Missouri, where Sarah Horn met him and thanked him profusely for initiating the transactions that eventually led to her rescue. Sarah worked with writer E. House, who recorded her story and published it in 1839. Sarah's premonition of an early death, unfortunately, proved correct. She died in Missouri in 1839.[53]

RACHEL PARKER PLUMMER, JAMES PRATT PLUMMER AND ELIZABETH DUTY KELLOGG
Texas, May 19, 1836

One of the most noteworthy incidents in Texas history occurred on May 19, 1836, when several hundred Comanche, Wichita, Kichai, and perhaps Kiowa and Caddo Indians attacked Parker's Fort. Brothers Silas M. and James W. Parker established the private fort in 1834, on the headwaters of the Navasota River in today's Limestone County, Texas. The wooden stockade protected eight or nine families of the extended Parker clan. Despite Indian warnings, ten men and a boy left the fort with its gate open that Tuesday morning to work in the fields. Left in the fort were six men: the elder John Parker, brothers Benjamin and Silas Parker, G. E. Dwight, Samuel Frost, and his son Robert. The women and children in the fort were Silas's wife Lucy, and their children, Cynthia Ann, John, Silas Jr., and Orleana; elder John's wife, Sallie (Granny) Parker; Patsey Duty Parker, wife of James W. Parker, and a young son; her daughter Rachel Parker Plummer,

Parker's Fort, near Groesbeck, Texas.

and Rachel's son James Pratt; Rachel's sister, Sarah Parker Nixon; Rachel's aunt, Elizabeth Duty Kellogg; Mrs. Frost and her children; and Mrs. Dwight and her children.[54]

When they first saw the warriors about a quarter mile from the fort, the shout, "Indians!" went out, starting a confused rush. Some folks ran outside the walls to try to get to the men working the fields about a mile from the fort. Others saw a white flag and stayed inside, but still neglected to close the gate. Benjamin Parker went out to parley, but quickly returned to warn that he thought the Indians meant to fight. Silas Parker told him not to go back, but Benjamin went out to try and buy time. The Indians closed in.

Rachel Parker Plummer used the extra minutes to try and escape. The red-haired Rachel was born in Illinois on March 22, 1819, and was thus two days short of her seventeenth birthday when the fort was attacked. She moved to Texas with the family and married Luther T. M. Plummer in March 1833, shortly after she turned 15. Her son, James Pratt, was born January 6, 1835, the first baby born in Parker's Fort. By May 1836, she was four months pregnant with a second child. Certain that the Indians would kill her Uncle Benjamin, Rachel grabbed little James and ran. As she headed out the back gate, she saw Uncle Silas. He asked if the Indians killed Ben.

"No," Rachel answered, "but they have surrounded him."

"I know they will kill him," Silas said, "but I will be good for one of them at least."

Rachel turned and saw a warrior lance Benjamin, and then, holding tight to James, she ran out the back gate. The Indians swarmed into and around the open fort and caught them. One warrior picked up a hoe, smashed it on Rachel's head and knocked her down, while another pulled James from her arms. She fainted, only to awaken while being dragged by the hair. Silas and Benjamin were killed, along with Samuel Frost and his son.[55]

Indians caught elder John Parker, shot and scalped him, and stabbed Sallie Parker in the breast. They carried Elizabeth Kellogg away. Sarah Nixon ran screaming to the cornfield to alert the men. James Parker took the refugees to safety, Luther Plummer ran to the neighbors for help, and Lorenzo Nixon went to the fort, but was captured. In a short while, Plummer appeared with several armed neighbors and the nearest Indians ran off, abandoning their captives Nixon, Lucy Parker, Orleana, and Silas Jr. The Indians kept Cynthia and John, plundered the fort, and rode off to the northwest, shooting the settlers' cattle as they went.

The rescuers retreated toward the river, as did Parker with the remaining women and children. In the evening, some of them returned to the fort and found Sallie Parker, still alive. They carried her back to the group hiding by the river and made their way downstream toward Fort Houston. Luther Plummer rode alone into the wilderness, looking for his wife and son, but after only one day's journey, he realized the hopelessness of his task and returned to the settlements.[56]

For Rachel Plummer, the scene was one of confusion and terror. She saw her Uncle Benjamin's body, pin-cushioned with arrows and his face mutilated. She was covered with blood and dizzy. An Indian held her son; he cried for her and she tried to go to him, but two Comanche women beat her with a whip. She saw her Aunt Elizabeth and her two cousins, Cynthia Ann, and John. One Indian carried her grandfather's scalp. When Rachel later wrote about her experience, she was loath to discuss the details. "To undertake to narrate their barbarous treatment would only add to my present distress, for it is with feelings of the deepest mortification that I think of it, much less to speak or write of it; for while I record this painful part of my narrative, I can almost feel the same heart-rending pains of body and mind that I then endured, my very soul becomes sick at the dreadful thoughts."[57]

The Indians didn't stop riding until midnight. Rachel, who had been tied at the wrists and feet so tightly that the ropes cut into her skin and left her permanently scarred, was thrown face down in the dirt and beaten again. "[I]t was with great difficulty I could keep from smothering in my blood," Rachel later wrote. James was brought near enough to her that she could hear him cry when they beat him, but the Indians would not let her go to him. They took pleasure in the captives' agonies. When the other prisoners were near enough to try to talk to one another, the enraged Indians kicked and stomped on them. Rachel "had no idea they could survive" such beatings.

The Indians rode north for five days. Rachel was given a little water, but "never ate one mouthful of food" the entire time. Beyond the Cross Timbers at a place Rachel called the Grand Prairie, the captives were divided up. For a very short time, the Indians gave James Pratt back to his mother. He cried constantly, and Rachel believed he was returned because the Indians were "supposing that I gave suck." When they learned that he had been weaned, they tore him from her grasp and he was taken away by another band. Said Rachel: "This was the last I ever heard of my little Pratt. Where he is, I know not." Comanches, probably of the Kwahadi band, took Cynthia Ann and John Parker. Elizabeth Kellogg was taken by Indians Rachel called "Kitchawas."[58]

Rachel traveled across Red River, north to the Arkansas River in the vicinity of Bent's Fort, and into the Colorado Rockies. She worked dressing buffalo skins, and was constantly hungry, thirsty, and suffered from the vagaries of the weather, having "very little covering for my body." In October 1836, she gave birth to a second son. Rachel hoped the Indians would let her keep it, but caring for an infant interfered with her other labors. When the boy was about six weeks old, warriors took him from her, and while Rachel both fought and pleaded to save him, an Indian strangled him before her eyes. He threw the baby into the air and let him fall to the ground. When the Indians left, Rachel ran to the baby and noticed that he was still breathing. She hoped in vain that they would let him live, but when they discovered he was still alive, they tied a rope around his neck, threw him repeatedly against a cactus, and then tied the rope to a horse and dragged the body across the rocky ground. "I stood horror-struck," Rachel said. The boy was "literally torn to pieces." An Indian then grabbed the body by a leg and threw it on her lap. Strangely enough, Rachel rejoiced that the infant would suffer no more on this earth. She thought about her lost James Pratt and wished that he was dead too, so that he would no longer have to endure the tortures of such an existence. Rachel was ready to die. Her body was already dying.[59]

Elizabeth Kellogg's captivity was not as devastating as her niece's. After being separated from the rest of the prisoners in late

May 1836, she spent only about three months with the Indians. During that time, James W. Parker had begun his obsessive hunt to rescue his kin.[60] In July, Parker called on Sam Houston while Houston was recovering from the wound he received at the Battle of San Jacinto. Parker asked for "a company of men" to help him find the captives. Men had to be paid, however, and the new Republic of Texas was nearly bankrupt. Houston believed that a treaty with the Indians would be the easiest and safest way to get the captives back. Parker's reply was a typical frontier response, but one that was proven true time and again. Parker: "Such a thing as a treaty being formed with hostile Indians until they were whipped and well whipped, had never been known; and the more thorough the chastisement, the more lasting the treaty."[61]

James Parker kept trying to enlist support for his rescue attempt. On August 20, he went to Nacogdoches, where he happily discovered that friendly Delaware Indians had recently purchased Elizabeth Kellogg and taken her to the city. Parker was thrilled to get his sister-in-law back, but the Delawares wanted $150 for their troubles, and Parker had no money. Sam Houston paid the ransom.

Parker and several other men escorted Elizabeth back to Parker's new house near Huntsville, in a location hopefully far removed from potential attack. On the way they met a traveler who said that Indians had just tried to steal their horses, and one of the raiders was shot. Parker's band went to investigate and they saw a wounded Indian on the ground. To Elizabeth Kellogg's great surprise, it was the same warrior who had killed elder John Parker. She was certain it was the same man because, she said, "he had a scar on each arm as if cut with a knife." Parker examined him and, sure enough, there were the scars. "What followed, it is unnecessary to relate—" James said, "suffice it to say that it was the unanimous opinion of the company, that he would never kill and scalp another white man." Elizabeth was reunited with her sister on September 6. She and Patsey were free, but both were scarred from their experiences. James Parker continued his hunt for the rest of his kin.[62]

Rachel Plummer, in the meantime, could no longer continue in her present situation. By the late winter of 1837, she was at the end of her tether. One child was taken from her, her second child was murdered, and her captors constantly mistreated her. "Having lived as long, and indeed longer than life was desirable," she said, "I determined to aggravate them to kill me." When one of Rachel's young female owners attacked her, she fought back with all her strength. They rolled in the dirt, punched, clawed, and bit. A crowd of amused warriors gathered around, but they did nothing to stop the fight. Rachel grabbed a large buffalo bone and beat the woman over the head until she finally cried out for mercy. Rachel let her go.

To her astonishment, no one tried to kill her. Instead, a chief told her that she was brave and kind to take pity on a fallen enemy. When her old mistress, angry at the outcome of the fight, tried to burn her, Rachel fought again, and won again. She had passed a test, and learned that submission was not always the best course to take as a captive. "This answered me a valuable purpose afterwards, in some other instances" Rachel said. "I took my own part, and fared the much better by it."[63]

By June 1837, Rachel had been captive for thirteen months. Her father, James Parker, had made three expeditions to the Red River and Indian Territory, ridden thousands of miles, and spent hundreds of dollars, all for naught. He still did not know where Rachel was. By October, following his fifth attempt, he was ill and exhausted and needed a rest. He asked Lorenzo Nixon to continue the quest. Despite her father's vain search, Rachel was on the verge of freedom. On June 19, Comancheros visited the Comanche camp and bought her. She was joyful, but still did not realize that she was free, for she spoke of her rescuer as "my new master." A seventeen-day trip took them to Santa Fe, where Rachel met her true benefactor, William Donoho. Kentuckian Donoho sought his fortune in the overland trade, and he and his wife moved to Santa Fe in 1833, becoming successful merchants and traders. They had already ransomed several captives from the Indians, including a Mrs. Harris, and were in the process of ransoming Sarah Horn (see Sarah Ann Horn and Mrs. Harris).[64]

The people of Santa Fe raised $150 for Rachel, to help finance her return home, but the money got into the hands of an unscrupulous clergyman and was never used for its intended purpose. Rachel lived in the Donoho home and waited. New taxes and legislation from old Mexico were making it more difficult for foreigners to make money, a drought led to increased food prices, Apaches and Comanches were increasingly hostile, and even the Pueblo Indians were showing signs of insurrection. In September 1837, William Donoho packed up his family, his belongings, Rachel Plummer, and Mrs. Harris in his wagons and headed back to Missouri. The Donoho party arrived at Independence sometime in late October, and subsequently moved in with Mary Donoho's mother, Lucy Dodson. There they waited. Rachel constantly asked about her relatives in Texas, but winter approached, and it appeared she would not get home any time soon. Mary Donoho tried to comfort her, but Rachel's homesickness and anxiety about her family could not be consoled.

On January 20, 1838, a notice appeared in the Houston *Telegraph and Texas Register,* stating that a "Mrs. Plimmer" from Texas was recently purchased from the Comanches and was at Independence, Missouri. She was said to have red hair and was captured with three children and her sister, who were thought to still be with the Indians. The notice contained errors, but the word of Rachel's rescue was out. Even before the newspaper notice, however, a Mr. G. S. Parks had learned of the situation, and in late October, he informed Lorenzo Nixon that Rachel was in Missouri. Nixon tracked her down, and one evening in January 1838, he arrived at Lucy Dodson's house. Rachel was in her room praying. She said, "on stepping to the door, I saw my brother-in-law, Mr. Nixon. I tried to run to him, but was not able. I was so much overjoyed I scarcely knew what to say or how to act." She learned that her father, mother, and husband were still alive, and now, "Every moment seemed an hour." She had to get back home as soon as possible.

William Donoho furnished them with horses and accompanied Rachel and Lorenzo on their journey south. After a long, cold trip, on February 19, 1838, they arrived at James Parker's house in Montgomery County, Texas. "Here," wrote Rachel, "united tears of joy flowed from the eyes of father, mother, brothers and sisters; while many strangers, unknown to me, (neighbors of my father) cordially united in this joyful interview." James Parker was concerned with her condition. "She presented a most pitiable appearance;" he said, "her emaciated body was covered with scars, the evidences of the savage barbarity to which she had been subject during her captivity. She was in very bad health." Rachel was safe, but she never could attain peace of mind. "But oh!" she wrote, "dreadful reflection, where is my little children? One of them is no more—I buried its bloody body in those vast regions of prairies—but I hope its soul is now in Heaven. My body is covered with scars which I am bound to carry to my grave; my constitution broke—but above all and every trouble which haunts my distracted mind is WHERE IS MY POOR LITTLE JAMES PRATT!"[65]

Rachel Plummer was reunited with her husband Luther, and in April 1838, she was pregnant with her third child. Frontier life had not been easy on James Parker either. He had been accused of horse stealing, counterfeiting, and even murder. To prevent vigilantes from harming his family, he sent them from Parker's Mill down to Houston in the late fall of 1838. Once again, Rachel trekked through cold, rain, and mud, further weakening her.

On January 4, 1839, Rachel delivered another son, Wilson P. Plummer, but she knew she was dying. She had been writing a narrative of her capture, and now appended a "closing address." She lamented that her "fast declining physical strength" prevented her from telling her entire story. She realized these were her "last moments, when the 'king of terrors' is staring me in the face and bidding me to prepare to yield up my scarred and emaciated form to its mother earth, and my afflicted and immortal soul to Him who gave it." Once more she asked where her "dear child" was, and hoped that "he too has been taken to his eternal home on high." She had taken all the suffering she could stand. "The fountain of my tears are dried up," she concluded. There was nothing left to do but die. The end came on March 19, 1839, three days short of her twentieth birthday. Her infant son lived only two days longer.[66]

What happened to James Pratt Plummer? James Parker had not forgotten about him. Once a year he took a trip into Indian Territory to look for his niece Cynthia Ann, his nephew John, and his grandson James Pratt. In September 1841, he heard about two children who had been taken to Boggy Depot, Indian Territory. Parker, ill with fever, rode north again, going up the Texas Road which ran from Colbert's Ferry on Red River, northeast to Fort Gibson. When he reached Boggy Depot, in present-day Atoka County, Oklahoma, he learned that the children were not of the Parker clan. He also learned that he was in grave danger, for the Indians at the depot were extremely hostile to Texans. A friendly Delaware Indian named Frank, told Parker that one of the Indians claimed that Parker had killed his brother. When the Indians dispersed, Parker knew he had to leave immediately. He openly took the Fort Towson road, and when about a mile from the depot, cut off easterly into the woods. The Indians were watching and followed him, but Parker lost them in a boggy, wooded patch and made his escape.[67]

Parker's next hope was raised after Colonel Zachary Taylor replaced Colonel Mathew Arbuckle at Fort Gibson in 1842. Taylor arranged a conference with a number of Indian tribes and urged them to give back their white prisoners. Three months later, on 23 August, Kickapoo Indians arrived at Fort Gibson with James Pratt Plummer, now seven years old, whom they had purchased from the Comanches for $400. On September 28, a Delaware brought in a white boy of about 13 years of age, who was assumed to be John Richard Parker.[68] The officers at the post tried to teach James Pratt English. Their lessons were proceeding relatively well until the second boy arrived. The two became quick friends, and preferred to speak Comanche. The officers considered separating them and sending one to Fort Smith, in order to facilitate their schooling, however, they took pity on them and let them remain together.

Once more, James Parker traveled to Indian Territory. Although he had not seen his grandson in six years, he was certain he was the right person because of his resemblance to his daughter, Rachel. When James Pratt learned that a man was coming for him he ran off and hid in the dragoon camp near the fort. He was persuaded to visit with Parker, and after two hours of explanations through an interpreter, the young boy learned that his mother was dead, but his father was still alive, and Grandfather Parker would take him home. The boys agreed to go. On January 16, 1843, Parker placed both of them on his horse and walked back to Texas in the middle of winter. He still could not understand them well, but thought it best that he was "relieved from the pain of listening to their recital of the sufferings they had endured whilst among the Indians." He did note, however, the many scars across their backs, caused by the countless whippings they had received. Parker returned home to another joyous reunion. He gave thanks to God, "on finding myself again with my family, and all in good health. The boys soon became attached to me and my family," Parker said. "They soon learned to speak English, and are now doing well."[69]

How well the boys were really doing is questionable. It was eventually determined that the second rescued boy was not John Parker. He probably left the Parker clan within a few years and went off on his own. James Parker did not give James Plummer back to his father as he had promised. Luther Plummer, he claimed, owed him the ransom money. Plummer had remarried and was doing well financially. He had never made that much of an effort to recover his own son, and Parker figured he should pay him the money. Unable to talk Parker into returning his boy, Plummer wrote to President Sam Houston, and in April 1843, Houston replied that Parker's attempt to "swindle a distressed father on account of his long lost child is in every way deserving of the severest reprehension." Still, they were only words, and Parker would not release the boy. Parker kept him for several more years, but by age 14, James Pratt was living with his uncle by marriage, John Harrold, the third husband of Rachel's older sister, Sarah.[70]

James Pratt Plummer overcame his traumatic experience and gradually fit back into the white world. He married, became a widower, and married a second time. He fathered four children. When the Civil War began he joined the Confederate Army, but his service was cut short. While in camp at Little Rock, Arkansas, James Pratt caught typhoid fever. The illness weakened him so that when the cold weather arrived, he developed pneumonia. He died on November 17, 1862, only 27 years old.[71]

CYNTHIA ANN PARKER AND JOHN RICHARD PARKER
Texas, May 19, 1836

Indians captured Cynthia Ann Parker and John R. Parker, along with three others, in a raid on Parker's Fort on May 19, 1836 (see Rachel Parker Plummer). About five days after the raid, the Indians divided up their prisoners. Cynthia Ann and John were most likely taken by Kwahadi Comanches, who roamed through much of what is today, western Oklahoma and the Texas Panhandle. Brother and sister were eventually separated, and the facts of John's captivity are probably the least known of the five who were taken at Parker's Fort.

John was born either in 1829 or 1830, making him six or seven at the time of his capture. His uncle, James W. Parker searched for him for years, but most of the leads he acted on were concerning female captives. When two boys were returned to Fort Gibson, Indian Territory, in 1842, one of them was James Pratt Plummer and the other was erroneously thought to be John Parker. In 1845, Indians delivered a white boy to Torrey's Trading Post in Texas. Again, it was thought that the lad was John Parker, but once more, the hope proved false (see John McLennan).

Isaac Parker, John's uncle, while serving in the Republic of Texas Legislature, made many attempts to locate his nephew. In June 1845, the Indian Bureau disbursed $300 to Isaac Parker, and in 1845, the Legislature appropriated another $300 for John Parker's rescue, but the money was never used; there was never any bona fide opportunity to ransom him. The vast Texas plains seemed to swallow him up. John eventually forgot the manners and customs of his own people and learned the ways of the nomadic Comanches. In April 1846, Texas Indian Agent Leonard Williams met with Yamparika Comanches on the head of the Washita, and believed he had found Cynthia Ann and John, but the Indians refused to sell or trade for them. Williams wrote to Indian Commissioners Pierce M. Butler and M. G. Lewis, and they wrote to the commissioner of Indian affairs that the Comanches had three white children, one thought to be Warren Lyons, and the other two the Parker children. The white "Parker" boy, however, was described as being ten years old; John Parker would have been about 17.[72]

John's name appears in frontier annals from time to time. In 1852, Captain Randolph B. Marcy, 5th Infantry, led an expedition to locate the headwaters of the Red River. He met with "Middle Comanches" (Nokonis) and saw a woman whom he believed was Cynthia Parker. He reported: "The brother of the woman, who had been ransomed by a trader and brought home to his relatives, was sent back by his mother for the purpose of endeavoring to prevail upon his sister to leave the Indians and return to her family; but he stated to me that on his arrival she refused to listen to the proposition. . . ." Who was the white "brother" who talked to Marcy? It was not John Parker who was ransomed by a trader and taken home to Texas. Was it her cousin, James Pratt Plummer, who talked to Marcy? There is no record of Plummer ever going west to look for his cousin.

The fate of John Parker remains a mystery. Cynthia Ann did not know exactly what happened to him. She later claimed that he "died among the Indians with the smallpox." The most repeated story is that John grew to manhood with the Comanches and often raided with them into Mexico. The Indians took a number of Mexican captives, one of them very pretty, by the name of Dona Juanita. Parker became infatuated with her and she with him. They planned to marry as soon as the Indians returned to their village. On the return trip, smallpox decimated the travelers, and John Parker was one of those stricken. Fearing the disease, the Indians left him behind and fled. Dona Juanita remained to care for John, and the Indians reluctantly agreed. John recovered, and Dona Juanita talked him out of returning to the Indians. They attempted to settle and raise stock on a Mexican ranch. When the Civil War began, John either joined a company of Mexicans serving with the Confederate Army, or became a civilian scout for Lieutenant Colonel John R. Baylor's 2nd Regiment of Texas Mounted Rifles. When his unit was sent to fight in another theater, however, John deserted, for he would not cross east of the Sabine River. To escape repercussions and the strife of war-torn Texas, John Parker and Dona Juanita permanently removed to a small ranch in Mexico, where John was supposed to have passed away in 1915, never once going home to visit his Texas relatives.[73]

Cynthia Ann Parker is arguably the West's most famous Indian captive. She was born in 1826, the first child of Silas M. Parker and Lucinda Duty Parker. The first days after her capture were terrifying. She had seen her relatives butchered, and she was beaten and abused. Not yet ten years old, she may not have been raped, but was stripped of her clothes, and witnessed the rape of her cousin Rachel, and Rachel's Aunt Elizabeth. Captives were chattel property and their captors could do with them as they pleased. They might be tortured and killed, gang-raped, or

Lawrence T. Jones, III Collection
Cynthia Ann Parker

protected by the captor, depending on individual whim.

Once back in the village, captives were almost universally beaten with clubs or lashed with whips by other members of the band. Almost every captive was virtually a slave, having to do much of the backbreaking labor involved in keeping the lodge of his or her master. If a girl captive was young and compliant, the owner might choose to keep her around and eventually marry her.[74]

Cynthia Ann survived and was eventually adopted into the tribe. Sightings of her over the years tantalized the public and kept her relatives' hopes alive that she might one day be rescued. But Cynthia Ann may no longer have wanted to be rescued. She received the name Nautdah or Naduah, which meant, "She carries herself with grace." She married the important warrior Peta Nocona, and gave birth to several children, one of them being Quanah Parker, later to become a Kwahadi chief. Quanah's birth date has been recorded as anywhere between 1845 and 1852. If it was the earlier year, then perhaps it partially explains Cynthia's reluctance to return to her white family when Agent Williams sought her out in 1846. Williams believed that the government's "sword should be made to avenge and liberate" her. He claimed that during his stay with the Indians, which was punctuated by threats on his own life, that Cynthia Ann "continued to weep incessantly." He offered twelve mules and two mule loads of merchandise for her, but claimed that the Indians "say they will die rather than giver her up." Commissioners Butler and Lewis further illuminated the meeting, stating that Cynthia Ann had been claimed by a warrior as his wife, and either "from the influence of her husband, or from her own inclination, she is unwilling to leave the people with whom she associates," and that "she would run off and hide herself to avoid those who went to ransom her."[75]

In 1852, as mentioned, Captain Marcy met with a band of Nokonis, where he saw a "white woman. . .by the name of Parker." He said that she "has adopted all the habits and peculiarities of the Comanches; has an Indian husband and children, and cannot be persuaded to leave them." Cynthia Ann had chosen her new life. She roamed with the Penetekas for a time, and then with her husband's Nokoni band. By then, Cynthia Ann, or Naduah, was very likely contented with her new life and family, however, the very thought that she could happily exist as a Comanche "squaw" could not be tolerated on the Texas frontier. Soldiers who saw her in the hands of the Comanches chafed at not being allowed to attack the Indians and attempt a rescue. The fact that the Indians could take white women and force them into "a fate worse than death," and that some would not care to return to white society, stoked the underlying racial and sexual tensions of the frontier folk.[76]

Peta Nocona's band invaded north Texas in late November 1860. They hit Jack, Palo Pinto, and Parker County, the latter created in 1855, and ironically named for the family whose daughter was a wife of the raid leader. Nocona's marauders stole horses, murdered several people, and captured four (see Martha Sherman). The raid was a catalyst that convinced settlers that the area was too dangerous to live in, and many packed up and headed closer to the coast, or "forted up" with other families. Seventy volunteers under Jack Cureton joined up with Captain Lawrence "Sul" Ross and his company of Texas Rangers. With the help of a twenty-one-man detachment of Company H, 2nd Cavalry, from Camp Cooper, the combined force headed out to search for the Indians. Using Charles Goodnight as a guide, who had first discovered the

Author's photo
Cynthia Ann Parker and Prairie Flower gravesite, Fort Sill, Oklahoma.

raiders' trail, they marched west to the Pease River. On December 19, the Indian hunters got moving in a heavy rain.

At the junction of Mule Creek and the Pease, Ross found the Comanche camp. About twenty-five warriors were packing up and preparing to move. Ross had outmarched Cureton's volunteers, but he decided there was not enough time to wait for them, and attacked with the Rangers and cavalry. Sergeant J. W. Spangler lead the cavalry detachment around some sand hills to cut the Indians off while the Rangers charged. The Indians fled right into Spangler's troops, then scattered. Peta Nocona rode off with someone mounted behind him, and nearby rode another person wrapped in a buffalo robe. Ross and Lieutenant Tom Kelliher chased them down. After a mile, Ross was close enough to pull his pistol and shoot, but before he did, his prey turned, held out a small child, and shouted, "Americano! Americano!"

Ross called to Kelliher to hold the captive while he rode after Nocona. Ross fired, and the Indian and his passenger toppled from their horse. Nocona shot arrows at Ross and Ross shot at him, hitting the chief three times. Nocona crawled away to sing his death song and Ross let him die in peace. The other Indian turned out to be Nocona's wife. She was giving Kelliher all sorts of trouble and he was ready to shoot her when Ross noticed something strange.

"Why, Tom," he said, "this is a white woman! Indians don't have blue eyes." They had found Cynthia Ann Parker.[77]

There are various versions as to how her identity was definitely established. It was either late that night around the campfire, when Jonathan Baker mentioned that she might be one of the Parker children who was carried off years ago, or it might have been after Ross took the command back to Camp Cooper, and Isaac Parker was summoned to identify the woman. In any case, when the name "Cynthia Ann" was mentioned in front of the woman, she finally recognized the sound, stood up, patted herself and said:

"Me Cincee Ann."[78]

The ride back to Camp Cooper was not a triumphal return for Cynthia Ann. Several times she tried to escape. She had left behind two young boys: Quanah (12) and Peanuts (10). She carried her daughter, Prairie Flower (3). The army wives at Camp Cooper tried to help her; they cleaned her, gave her clothes, and fed her, but Cynthia Ann was despondent. She tried to escape again, but was closely guarded. Isaac Parker came to take her "home," and, with an escort, they traveled through Weatherford, Ft. Worth, and to Isaac's home in Birdville. Word spread of her return, and Cynthia Ann became a minor celebrity. Visitors came to see her, but more often than not, they were greeted with tears. One month after her recovery, she was taken to the capital at Austin, but the fuss and ceremony frightened her, and she tried to escape again. The Texas Legislature was generous, and granted her a pension of $100 per year for five years, plus a league of land (about seven square miles).

Cynthia Ann was still unhappy. Her brother, Silas Parker Jr., agreed to take her to his home in the wooded region of Van Zandt County where she would be less likely to run away. When Silas joined the Confederate Army, Cynthia Ann went to live with her younger sister Orleana, who was married to R. J. O'Quinn. Here, Cynthia Ann learned to weave, spin, and sew. She already knew how to tan hides, and neighbors brought in skins for her to work on. She picked plants and herbs for home remedies. She learned to speak English again, and began to read and write. Her main problem was that she missed her two sons. The O'Quinns promised they would take her to visit the tribe when the Civil War ended, and that was probably one of her main hopes. Before the war ended, however, Prairie Flower caught the flu and pneumonia, and died in late 1864.

With her daughter dead and the war over, the O'Quinn's, instead of taking her to the Indians, moved to Anderson County, even farther from the frontier. With little hope that she would ever see her boys again, Cynthia Ann went into a deep depression.

She died in 1870, and was buried at the Fosterville Cemetery. Few Indian captivity and adoption cases captured the public imagination as did Cynthia Ann's. In 1909, the U.S. Congress authorized a monument for her, and the next year, it approved the removal of her and her daughter's remains, to be reburied at the Post Oak Cemetery near Cache, Oklahoma. Her son, Quanah, died in 1911, and was buried next to his mother. Cynthia Ann was finally reunited with her children. Today, they all lie in the cemetery at Fort Sill.[79]

ANN HARVEY
Texas, ca. November 25, 1836

John B. Harvey and his family emigrated from Alabama in 1835, and settled on the east bank of the Brazos, twenty-five miles above Tenoxtitlan, near present-day Calvert, in Robertson County, Texas.[80] Harvey, his wife Elizabeth, and their two children, were sworn in as Robertson's colonists in January 1836. They survived the "Runaway Scrape" in the spring of that year, and returned to their home only to face disaster. In November 1836, the Harveys were gathered for their evening meal when the peace was shattered as Indians burst through the door. Mr. Harvey sprang up from his chair and reached for the rifle hanging on the rack on the wall. A warrior immediately fired, and a bullet struck Harvey in the neck, killing him instantly. They jumped on him and scalped him. Now the attackers could take their time.

In a pathetically futile attempt to save herself, Mrs. Harvey ran into the bedroom and crawled underneath the bed. While she hid, William (10) made the best resistance of all, and the Indians took out their anger on him. Rescuers later found his bloody coat with twenty bullet holes in it. The warriors dragged the screaming Mrs. Harvey out from under the bed, where she fought and kicked for her life. They killed, scalped, and mutilated her, then cut out her heart and left it on her breast.

Six-year-old Ann struggled with the Indians. A healthy young white girl was a worthwhile catch, either to hold for ransom, to trade, or to adopt into the tribe. Nevertheless, during the struggle Ann was roughly handled; a warrior broke her arm before she submitted. The Indians ransacked the house, and took the little girl and a black servant with them. News of the attack appeared on December 30, in the *Telegraph and Texas Register*, spreading more fear in the already harried colony.

Ann Harvey disappeared for almost a year while her relatives searched for her, seeking the assistance of Indian agents and traders. Her captors took her south of the Rio Grande and sold her to some Mexicans. Word of her plight was passed through the Mexican village and eventually a letter was sent to her uncle, James Talbert, who lived in Alabama. After much time and money spent, Talbert went to Mexico and ransomed his niece, who, by this time, had become attached to her Mexican "mother," and was reluctant to leave.

Talbert, nevertheless, talked her into accompanying him back to live with other family members in Alabama. After some time, Talbert and his family moved to Texas, and Ann Harvey settled into a house near where her parents and brother were killed. She overcame the trauma of the experience and the daily reminder of the tragedy, married, and remained in the area. The Reverend Z. N. Morrell visited her as late as 1873, and noted that Ann often used her father's old Bible for worship, a book, he said, "which yet has upon its pages the blood of her parents spilled by the hands of the Indians on that fearful night."[81]

Chapter one footnotes

[1] Hunter, "Southwestern Captivity Narratives," 141-44. The two narratives were: Caroline Harris, *History of the Captivity and Providential Release therefrom of Mrs. Caroline Harris*, NY: Perry and Cooke, 1838, and Clarissa Plummer, *Narrative of the Captivity and Extreme Sufferings of Mrs. Clarissa Plummer*, NY: Perry and Cooke, 1838. Fehrenbach (*Comanches*, 287) incorrectly names Rachel Plummer and Elizabeth Kellogg as the first American females known to be taken by the Comanches. Sarah Hibbins, Mary Juergens, and Sarah Horn were captured earlier.

[2] "Killough Massacre," in www.tsha.utexas.edu/handbook/online/articles/print/KK/btk1; Wilbarger, *Depredations*, 620-21.

[3] Lavender, *Bent's Fort*, 202-03; Brooks, *Captives & Cousins*, 263.

[4] Webb and Carroll, *Handbook of Texas* 1, 928; "Gabriel N. Martin," Handbook of Texas Online.

[5] "Hardy Wright," Handbook of Texas Online; DeShields, *Border Wars*, 93-94. DeShields claims there were more people with the hunting party, including Daniel Davis, James and Robert Gamble, and another Negro slave named Zack Bottom.

[6] The attacking Indians have been described as Comanches, Kiowas, or Pawnee Picts. Pawnee Picts are Wichitas, and it was from them that the captive Wright was recovered.

[7] DeShields, *Border Wars*, 98-99; "Travis George Wright," and "Hardy Wright," Handbook of Texas Online.

[8] Prucha, *Sword*, 366; Mooney, *Calendar History*, 261-62. Mooney says the two children were a Kiowa girl, Medicine-Tied-to-Tipi-Pole (15), and her brother, but the little boy was killed by a blow from an angry ram at Fort Gibson before the expedition started.

[9] Prucha, *Sword*, 244, 365-66; Urwin, *Cavalry,* 61. DeShields, *Border Wars*, 94, incorrectly states that there were two expeditions, one in 1834, and one in 1836, and it was the second that recovered Martin.

[10] DeShields, *Border Wars*, 95.

[11] "Travis George Wright," Handbook of Texas Online; Barry, *Beginning of the West*, 270. Leavenworth was promoted to brigadier general four days after his death, which was then unknown in Washington. His body was taken to Delhi, NY, for burial, but 68 years later his remains were re-interred in the national cemetery at Ft. Leavenworth.

[12] Prucha, *Sword*, 367; Urwin, *Cavalry*, 62; Morris, *Atlas of Oklahoma*, section 17; Mooney, *Calendar History*, 265-66. Sowell, *Rangers and Pioneers*, 60-63, gives a rather confused version of the rescue, and says it was a Kiowa who saw his captured sister with the dragoons, and led them to the Wichita camp.

[13] Urwin, *Cavalry*, 62; Prucha, *Sword*, 368; Nye, *Bad Medicine*, x. The Kiowas only recall one girl being returned.

[14] DeShields, *Border Wars*, 96-97; Wilbarger, *Depredations*, 297; Urwin, *Cavalry*, 62; Prucha, *Sword*, 368. DeShields says that Matthew Wright Martin later grew to manhood and he and his brother William, "made good citizens."

[15] Mooney, *Calendar History*, 269-70.

[16] Mooney, *Calendar History*, 270, 273, 280; Huckabay, *Jack County*, 35-37; Marshall, *A Cry Unheard*, 80-81, 84-87.

[17] DeShields, *Border Wars*, 167.

[18] DeShields, *Border Wars*, 167-68.

[19] Moore, *Savage Frontier*, 77. According to Wilbarger, *Depredations*, 220, Sarah went to visit her mother, who was then living in Tennessee, and returned to Texas with her.

[20] Wilbarger, *Depredations*, 220, says Sarah did not see what the Indian did, while DeShields, *Border Wars*, 168, and Webb, *Texas Rangers*, 35, say the warrior "dashed its brains" against a tree.

[21] Wilbarger, *Depredations*, 220-21; DeShields, *Border Wars*, 169-70; Webb, *Texas Rangers*, 35. The versions of Hibbins's escape vary. Wilbarger mentions her going down Shoal Creek to the Colorado. The nearest present-day Shoal Creek to Austin, flows into the Leon River about 70 miles north of Austin. DeShields said they camped on Walnut Creek, which flows into the Colorado on the east side of Austin.

[22] Wilbarger, *Depredations*, 221; Webb, *Texas Rangers,* 35. Noah Smithwick wrote of his adventures in his 1900 book, *The Evolution of a State*. Much of Hibbins's story comes from Smithwick.

[23] Smithwick cited in Webb, *Texas Rangers*, 36.

[24] Webb, *Texas Rangers*, 37-38.

[25] DeShields, *Border Wars*, 171-72; Moore, *Savage Frontier*, 78-80.

[26] DeShields, *Border Wars*, 172-73; "Sarah Creath Howard," Handbook of Texas Online.

[27] DeShields, *Border Wars*, 173-75; "Sarah Creath Howard," Handbook of Texas Online.

[28] Webb and Carroll, *Handbook of Texas* 2, 120; DeShields, *Border Wars*, 150.

[29] DeShields, *Border Wars*, 151-52; "McLennan's Bluff," Handbook of Texas Online.

[30] "McLennan's Bluff," Handbook of Texas Online; Webb and Carroll, *Handbook of Texas* 2, 120-21.

[31] Winfrey and Day, *Texas Indian Papers* 1, 23-24.

[32] Winfrey and Day, *Texas Indian Papers* 1, 154,229,244; 2,53-54.

[33] Winfrey and Day, *Texas Indian Papers* 2,399-404; Webb and Carroll, *Handbook of Texas* 2,791.

[34] Winfrey and Day, *Texas Indian Papers* 2, 280, 404, 406-07; Webb and Carroll, *Handbook of Texas* 2, 336, 626.

[35] Winfrey and Day, *Texas Indian Papers* 2, 421; Exley, *Frontier Blood*, 166.

[36] Winfrey and Day, *Texas Indian Papers* 2, 429; DeShields, *Border Wars*, 152-53.

[37] Stephens and Holmes, *Atlas of Texas*, 26; Hardin, *Texian Iliad*, 179-86.

[38] Wilbarger, *Depredations*, 237; DeShields, *Border Wars*, 176; "Mary Theresa Hennecke Juergens," "Conrad Juergens," "Abel Warren," and "Coffee's Station," Handbook of Texas Online. Wilbarger and DeShields describe Conrad Juergens as an "old" or "aged" man, who ran for ten miles and died. Conrad was only 40 years old. After his escape he met with other settlers fleeing the Mexicans at Mill Creek Bottom and joined the Revolutionary Army for a short time.

[39] "Mary Theresa Hennecke Juergens," "Conrad Juergens," Handbook of Texas Online; Webb and Carroll, *Handbook of Texas* 1, 619. Mary Juergens could not have been ransomed at the post that has traditionally been called Coffee's Station, for it was the last one built by Holland Coffee in 1837, on the Texas side of the Red River, a year after Mary's return. The likelihood that she was ransomed at Pace's is found in, Exley, *Frontier Blood*, 66-67.

[40] "Mary Theresa Hennecke Juergens," Handbook of Texas Online.

[41] Rister, *Bondage*, 13, 105-06. The two boys were said to be about four and five years old at the time of their capture, but Sarah indicates that one boy was 16 months old at the time of her mother's death in the fall of 1830, and the other boy was 15 months older; thus, they were about seven and eight at the time of their capture.

[42] Rister, *Bondage*, 21, 32, 107, 110. The sailing date is disputed. Horn says they stayed in New York from August 1833 to November 1834, and reached Texas in December, after a five-week ocean journey. Beales says the journey lasted from November 11 to December 12, 1833.

[43] Rister, *Bondage*, 51-61,78-79.

[44] Rister, *Bondage*, 89-92, 123-24.

[45] DeShields, *Border Wars*, 138; Rister, *Border Captives*, 63; Rister, *Bondage*, 124-31.

[46] Rister, *Bondage*, 131-39.

[47] Rister, *Bondage*, 140-52.

[48] Rister, *Bondage*, 153-55.

[49] Rister, *Bondage*, 158-63; DeShields, *Border Wars*, 139-40.

[50] Rister, *Bondage*, 165-66; DeShields, *Border Wars*, 140.

[51] Exley, *Frontier Blood*, 84, 91; DeShields, *Border Wars*, 140; Rister, *Bondage*, 184n. In order to make some money, Mrs. Harris may have cooperated with publishers Perry and Cooke in 1838, to produce a semi-fictional account of her captivity under the name of Caroline Harris. See Hunter, "Southwestern Captivity Narratives," 141-44.

[52] Rister, *Bondage*, 166-80, 183; DeShields, *Border Wars*, 140; Rister, *Border Captives*, 68.

[53] Rister, *Bondage*, 98, 184-87; "Sarah Ann Newton Horn," Handbook of Texas Online. Sarah's story first appeared in *A Narrative of the Captivity of Mrs. Horn, and Her Two Children, with Mrs. Harris, by the Camanche Indians*, written by E. House (St. Louis: C.Keemle, 1839).

[54] Exley, *Frontier Blood*, 53; Webb and Carroll, *Handbook of Texas* 1, 630.

[55] Exley, *Frontier Blood*, 41-42, 44,54; VanDerBeets, *Held Captive*, 334-36.

[56] Exley, *Frontier Blood*, 55-60.

[57] VanDerBeets, *Held Captive*, 337-38.

[58] VanDerBeets, *Held Captive*, 338-40. The "Kitchawas" were either Wichitas or Kichais.

[59] VanDerBeets, *Held Captive*, 341-42. In a bizarre assessment, historian Gary C. Anderson, *Conquest of Texas*, 129, dismisses the captives' horrible ordeal, by simply concluding, "Soon their treatment improved, and the women were ransomed."

[60] Although there were many men who searched for their captured relatives, James Parker devoted the next several years of his life trying to track them down.

[61] Exley, *Frontier Blood*, 63-64.

[62] Exley, *Frontier Blood*, 64-65; Sowell, *Rangers and Pioneers*, 33.

[63] VanDerBeets, *Held Captive*, 353-55.

[64] Exley, *Frontier Blood*, 81,83-84; VanDerBeets, *Held Captive*, 361; "Rachel Parker Plummer," Handbook of Texas Online; Webb and Carroll, *Handbook of Texas* 1, 513.

[65] Exley, *Frontier Blood*, 84, 86-88, 91-93; VanDerBeets, *Held Captive*, 362-63.

[66] Exley, *Frontier Blood*, 101-04, 120; VanDerBeets, *Held Captive*, 364-66; Hunter, "Southwestern Captivity Narratives," 54-55. Rachel Plummer began writing her narrative in Santa Fe, continued it in Missouri, and finished it at Parker's Mill, Texas, in September 1838. It was published as a pamphlet in late 1838. Before Rachel died, she wrote up a second version. James Parker also wrote his story. He attached Rachel's second narrative to it and they were published together in 1844.

[67] Exley , *Frontier Blood*, 110-11.

[68] Exley, *Frontier Blood*, 114. The 13 year-old captive was not John Parker, for he was still being sought in subsequent years. John McLennan, returned in 1845, was also thought to be John Parker. Who the second boy was is not known.

[69] Exley, *Frontier Blood*, 114-15; "James W. Parker," Handbook of Texas Online.

[70] Exley, *Frontier Blood*, 115-17.

[71] Exley, *Frontier Blood*, 177.

[72] Winfrey and Day, *Texas Indian Papers* 2, 375; Wilbarger , *Depredations*, 315, 319; Webb and Carroll, *Handbook of Texas* 2, 336; Exley, *Frontier Blood*, 134-35. Ramsay, *Sunshine on the Prairie*, 28, claims that John Parker was ransomed at this time.

[73] Exley, *Frontier Blood*, 168, 178; Wilbarger, *Depredations*, 315-16; Webb and Carroll, *Handbook of Texas* 2, 336; DeShields, *Border Wars*, 166; Ramsay, *Sunshine on the Prairie*, 50.

[74] Wallace and Hoebel, *Lords of the South Plains*, 241, 261-62; Fehrenbach, *Comanches*, 286-89.

[75] Exley, *Frontier Blood*, 133-35; Webb and Carroll, *Handbook of Texas* 2, 337; Ramsay, *Sunshine on the Prairie*, 52.

[76] Exley, *Frontier Blood*, 138-39; Fehrenbach, *Comanches*, 290, 375. For more on racial and sexual aspects of captivities, see June Namias, *White Captives*.

[77] Sowell, *Rangers and Pioneers*, 38-39; Exley, *Frontier Blood*, 153-58; Ramsay, *Sunshine on the Prairie*, 86-89; Haley, *Charles Goodnight*, 53-57. Goodnight claims that it was not Peta Nocona who Ross killed, but a chief named Nobah. He also says that it was he who first noticed that the "Indian" woman had blue eyes. Ramsay, *Sunshine on the Prairie*, 125-26, states that Nocona got away and died a few years later.

[78] Exley, *Frontier Blood*, 161; Haley, *Charles Goodnight*, 57-59; Wilbarger, *Depredations*, 340; Robinson, *Men Who Wear the Star*, 199-20.

[79] Exley, *Frontier Blood*, 166, 169-79; Webb and Carroll, *Handbook of Texas* 2, 335, 337; DeShields, *Border Wars*, 165-66; Wilbarger, *Depredations*, 341; Ramsay, *Sunshine on the Prairie*, 91-93. The latter three sources say that Cynthia Ann died in 1864, shortly after Prairie Flower.

[80] Moore, *Savage Frontier*, 208. DeShields, *Border Wars*, 175, says Harvey settled near Wheelock, Texas.

[81] Wilbarger, *Depredations*, 230; DeShields, *Border Wars*, 175-76; Moore, *Savage Frontier*, 208; Morrell, *Flowers in the Wilderness*, 68-69. Wilbarger and DeShields say that Ann was nine when captured.

Chapter Two

REPUBLICAN TEXAS

They were loath to return to Austin to inform the grief-stricken mother her loved ones were indeed the prisoners of savages, and would be subject to all the brutal cruelties and outrages of a captivity a thousand times more terrible than the pangs of death. — John S. "R.I.P." Ford.

Texas achieved its independence from Mexico, although its existence would remain tentative for several more years. It existed as a republic from 1836 until annexation by the United States in 1845. The Texas borders would not remain inviolate, for the Mexican Army still made incursions from south of the Rio Grande, while Indian raids originated from almost every corner of the compass. The area around Austin was on the frontier in those days, but Indian raiders occasionally swept to the Gulf of Mexico.

Although Indians captured many people in the early republic years, after the Council House and Plum Creek fights in 1840, Indian raids resulting in stolen captives decreased dramatically. While there were about thirty-seven hostages taken in the six years before the Plum Creek fight, there were only about twenty-one taken in the next twenty years up to 1860. Contrary to the claim that there were more Indian attacks because of the "treachery" of the whites at the Council House fight, apparently the lesson learned was that the Texans meant business and co-existence was safer than constant warfare. Elected president in 1838, Mirabeau B. Lamar stated, "If peace can be obtained only by the sword, let the sword do its work." Modern historians condemn his policy, but it was effective.[1]

Several other captivities occurred that are not detailed below. In January 1841, north of Austin, Texas, Judge James Smith was attacked and killed and his son (9) was captured. The Indians returned him to his mother about one year later because of treaty stipulations. In July 1841, Indians captured Tommy Cox (12) and his brother near Fort Inglish in Fannin County, Texas. The warriors, probably Tonkawas, later killed a one-armed man, cut off his remaining arm, cooked and ate it, and teased the boys that they too would learn to eat human flesh. The boys were ransomed for $600 about six months later. In 1841, Gillis Doyle was captured while out with his father near the Colorado River. In 1847, Jesse Chisholm tried to recover him. Even after six years' captivity, Doyle still wanted to come home, but was afraid to say so in front of the Comanches who held him. Doyle said he would steal a horse and sneak out one night, and asked Chisholm for directions to the Little River settlement in Texas. Doyle got away, but never made it; it was believed that Kickapoos killed him.[2]

* * *

JANE GOACHER CRAWFORD
Texas, February 1837

Among the prominent members of Stephen Austin's Colony was James Goacher, who emigrated from Alabama in 1828. The trail he cut to his home site, from San Felipe, and through present-day Lee and Bastrop counties, and which he later improved, became known as Goacher's Trace. James settled with his son-in-law, Crawford, at Rabb's Creek near the present town of Giddings. By 1835, Goacher and Crawford moved farther west, near Bastrop, where they began working a cotton plantation.[3]

One day in February 1837, Goacher, one of his sons, and Crawford, were cutting wood. Mrs. Nancy Goacher worked outside the house, while her married daughter, Jane Crawford, did her chores inside. Nancy Goacher had just sent two of the children to the creek to fetch some water, when Indians attacked. One party swept in and cut them off. Lest they cry out and warn the others, the boy was immediately lanced and scalped, while the little girl was grabbed and silenced. Despite their efforts to remain hidden, Nancy saw Indians at the edge of the woods, one of them choking the little girl's throat hard enough to make her nose bleed.

"Jane," Mrs. Goacher cried out, "the Indians have got your child!"

She ran to the house, seizing a rifle on the porch. Jane begged her to put the gun down, believing that if she fired it they would kill her. Despite her protests, Nancy fired, and was immediately hit by several arrows. She staggered back to the doorway, but the Indians were upon them before they could bar the entrance. An Indian with a firearm shot Nancy Goacher at close range and put an end to her struggle. They burst in and overpowered Jane. One of Nancy's sons tried to get away, but a warrior caught him by the arm. He caught one of the warrior's thumbs in his mouth and bit so hard that the Indian had to beat him with a ramrod to make him open his mouth.[4]

Mr. Goacher, his son, and Mr. Crawford heard the firing and ran for the house, carelessly leaving their own weapons behind. When they arrived, there was no time to go back for them, so the three ran for the house, hoping to get the other weapons inside and make a fight of it. It was a forlorn hope. The Indians caught them and killed them all. Within minutes, Mr. and Mrs. Goacher, Mr. Crawford, and three children lay dead. Jane Crawford, her young daughter and two brothers, 8 and 12 years of age, were bound and carried off. Their homestead was off the beaten path, and it was some time before a neighbor, Edward Burleson, casually paid them a visit, only to find the decaying corpses in the yard. By the time he could organize a search party it was much too late.

Jane Crawford was forced to carry her daughter as well as a large bag of salt. She became so exhausted that she could not walk any farther, and concluded to set the child down and go on. After taking several steps, the child cried and tried to follow behind her. Jane was overcome with grief, ready to die herself. An Indian then whipped her with his quirt and forced her to pick up the child and keep moving. Once in camp, the hungry and tired little girl would not stop crying. An Indian picked her up and threw her in a stream. Jane, once about to leave the girl behind, now splashed into the water to pull her out. A warrior tore the child from her arms and threw her back in. Jane too, splashed back into the stream to save her. This macabre ritual went on for some time, until one warrior, tiring of the game, grabbed the little girl and drew a knife to her throat. Jane snatched up a tree branch from the ground and knocked him on the head. She thought she would certainly be killed for that action. The remaining warriors, however, laughed at their fallen comrade, knocked almost senseless by this crazy white woman. They gave the girl back to her, reportedly stating, "Squaw too much brave. Damn you, take your papoose and carry it yourself—we not do it."[5]

After nearly two years of captivity, in which Jane and the children were subjected to many indignities and beatings, the Indians brought them to Holland Coffee's trading house on the Red River. After some time of bickering over a ransom price, Coffee traded for them for 400 yards of calico, blankets, and other articles. He sent them back home under the care of a trapper,

47

Charles Spaulding. On the return wagon trip, Spaulding became captivated by Jane, still young and attractive, and without a husband to care for her. By the time they had reached Bastrop County, Spaulding had proposed marriage and Jane accepted. They settled in Bastrop, not far from the scene of her capture. By 1850, Jane had five children by Charles Spaulding, and her two brothers, now 21 and 25 years old, were still residing in the household and helping to work the farm.[6]

Warren Lyons
Texas, Summer 1837

The birthplace of Warren Lyons is in question, as is his place of residence and time of capture. Lyons was either born in Ohio or New York about 1826. His family moved to Texas in 1835 or 1837, settling about sixteen miles southwest of La Grange in what was then Colorado County, and today is south of Schulenburg near the Fayette-Lavaca County line. The family consisted of Mr. Lyons and his wife, their married daughter, Mrs. William B. Bridges, and four sons: Seymour, George, DeWitt, and Warren.[7] In the summer of 1837, about thirty Comanches raided toward Victoria. While in the vicinity of the Little Brushy, about twenty miles southwest of Hallettsville, they battled a dozen settlers, who deflected them from Victoria and altered their course to the northeast. At dawn a day or two later they fell upon the Lyons home.

Mr. Lyons and Warren were up early milking cows, while the rest of the family slept. In a flash, the Comanches killed and scalped Mr. Lyon. They snatched up Warren, stole about ten horses, and were gone. For years Warren Lyons was not heard from, seemingly swallowed up in the vastness of west Texas. One of the only glimpses we have of his activities was brought to light in 1843, with the publication of Dolly Webster's captivity narrative. In her story, Dolly wrote that in the fall of 1839, Comanches held her and a number of other white captives (see Matilda Lockhart, Thomas Pearce, and the Putmans) somewhere to the northwest of San Antonio. As they traveled, Dolly discovered another prisoner in the entourage, "a young man by the name of Lyons," she wrote, "who was taken when young, and raised by the Indians. He was almost a savage."[8]

Because Warren learned to speak Comanche, he helped Dolly communicate with the Indians. Warren was in and out of the camp, apparently taking part in some of the raiding, but being only about 13 or 14, he probably only helped the warriors with

Author's photo

Warren Lyons capture site near Schulenburg, Texas.

their ponies. While in camp, Webster said, "he was frequently with us, but always appeared shy and distant of all the prisoners, and would appear delighted in seeing them punished, and would actually lend his aid in the accomplishment of these cruelties." Webster believed Lyons was jealous of the rest of the captives. "If he saw any of them talking together," she said, "he would invariably inform on them, which caused them a whipping, or some other chastisement."[9]

About ten years passed. In 1846, Indian Agent Leonard H. Williams met with Yamparika Comanches at the head of the Washita and found three white captives. Two were thought to be the Parker children, captured in 1836 (see Cynthia Ann Parker), and one, he wrote, "is a young man by the name of Lyons, who expressed an unwillingness...to withdraw from his association." Williams was unable to procure any of them.[10]

Relatives and friends had given up hope of ever seeing Warren again, all except for his mother. She was said to have had visions of her boy, always knowing that some day he would return to her. In 1847, a party of surveyors, including Wylie Hill, Richard Cheek, George Hancock, and James L. Jobe, were working between the San Saba and Llano, west of present-day Mason. About sixty Comanches confronted them on Honey Creek. The surveyors quickly took cover in a thicket, but the Indians signaled that they wanted to talk. The white men thought it was a ruse, but George Hancock elected to parley. He met a warrior halfway between the two parties and then noticed that Indians had surrounded them.

There was no use for belligerence at that point, and the surveyors tried to play it as cool as possible. The Indians took them to the main camp.

As darkness fell, the men's gloom deepened. Another party of surveyors, under William S. Wallace, was supposed to be in the vicinity. Wylie Hill, perhaps trying to contact the other party of white men, or perhaps in nervous desperation, called out with a shrill, keen, war whoop. The piercing screech startled everyone, and could probably have been heard for a mile. The Indians' reaction was not what Hill expected. They were delighted by the sound. They insisted that Hill yell it out at intervals during the march, and they tried, unsuccessfully, to imitate it. As night fully settled in, Hill spoke what was probably on everyone's mind.

"Boys," he said, "they are going to kill us certain, and we had better take the main bulge on them." Suddenly, a warrior riding nearby turned to them and said, "No these Indians are not going to kill you."

It was Warren Lyons.

The startled Hill turned and asked, "Who are you? Where did you learn our language?" Whereupon, Lyons gave them a brief explanation of all that had happened to him.

Wallace's surveyors heard Hill's whoops. They followed the calls right into the Indian camp, and now all of them were prisoners. One of the chiefs, using Lyons as an interpreter, asked why the white men were making marks on trees. A surveyor answered that they were bee hunting. The chief was no fool, and in a more threatening manner, he told them that they had better stop bee hunting and get out of the Indians' lands.

The surveyors talked with Lyons, learned what had happened to him and tried to convince him to go home. Wylie Hill knew his mother and insisted she had not forgotten him and that he ought to visit her. After ten years the thought of leaving the Indians was a hard decision. Lyons assumed his mother had gone back to her parents in Illinois. He said he could make no promise. The next morning the Comanches let the lucky white men go home, but Lyons rode off with the Indians with no sign of regret.[11]

A few months later, a band of Comanches rode in to San Antonio to trade. Word leaked out that among them was a young warrior who was believed to be a Texan. Two neighbors of Mrs. Lyons who happened to be in San Antonio heard the rumor and went to investigate. One of the men, Waymon Wells, was sure he recognized one of the warriors as Warren Lyons. He struck up a conversation with him and, like the surveyors had done, tried to talk Lyons into going home. The process took several days and much diplomacy. Lyons told Wells he thought his mother was dead. Not so, said Wells. He tried to persuade Lyons by giving him presents. By this time, Lyons had two Indian wives and he did not wish to leave them.

When Wells gave him two fine red blankets, Lyons decided to give one to each wife. He told them that he was leaving only to visit his mother, but he would return. No doubt that was Warren's intention, but when he accompanied Wells to the old homestead and saw his mother sweeping at the front door, he was overcome with emotion. Her hair, once flaxen, was now white, but he exclaimed to Wells, "That is my mother now! I remember her right there, sweeping in that way!" Warren dismounted and ran to her, calling out and dancing in such a manner that it unnerved her. Finally, a neighbor who was standing nearby, put in words what Mrs. Lyons could only have imagined: "It is Warren, your lost boy!" Now it was the mother's turn to smother Warren with hugs and kisses, until it was he who was flabbergasted and embarrassed. It was a Sunday, and when some girls ran to the church to announce, "Warren has come home," the congregation broke up and ran outside before the minister could dismiss them.[12]

In the years since he had been gone the place had grown into a small village called Lyonsville, and things were very strange to him. Warren still felt he should keep his promise to return to the Indians, but his family and neighbors smothered him with presents and kindness enough to make him waver. Finally, his brother DeWitt talked him into staying with the whites and joining the Texas Rangers to fight the Mexicans. Such an occupation was not a bad idea and it would serve two purposes: Warren could fight Mexicans, who were enemies of both the Texans and the Comanches, and it would give him an easier transition period between a wild, roaming lifestyle and that of a settled farmer. Besides, there was one sore point that Lyons wanted to make up for. When he returned to the white world, his hair was shorn on one side of his head—a sign, it was said, of punishment and disgrace because he had fled during a fight between the Indians and Mexicans. Perhaps by riding with the Rangers he could prove that he was no coward.[13]

Warren alternated between his white and Indian homes for a time, but within two years, DeWitt had gotten him to ride on several scouts with the Rangers. He participated in one fight where his Indian skills played a part. Lieutenant Edward Burleson took his company of Rangers to Fort McIntosh in Laredo. On December

23, 1850, near the Nueces River in McMullen County, he spotted a small band of Comanches. Burleson took nine men with him to investigate, but suddenly was confronted by twenty warriors.

Burleson reined up and asked, "Well boys, you see what it is, what do you say?" They told him to make the call. "Well boys, light in," he ordered, and the Rangers readied for battle.

The initial plan was to have the men hand their weapons one by one to James Carr, a noted marksmen, who would do all the firing at long range, and keep beyond the range of the Indians' arrows. In the excitement, however, every man dismounted in a natural move to keep a low profile and defend himself. The Indians, seeing the Texans on the ground, charged at them in a rush. At the same time the Rangers noticed Warren Lyons dismount, throw off his boots, and reach in his saddlebags for his moccasins. Some thought he was going to join the Indians, but Lyons was only preparing to fight, and he could do better in moccasins. Before the Texans could get off many shots, the Comanches were upon them and a tough hand-to-hand struggle ensued. In minutes, all the Rangers were hit; eight were wounded, Baker Barton was dead, and William Lackey was mortally wounded, shot through both lungs. Lyons took a slight wound, while three arrows hit Carr: one in the thigh, one in the side, and one that pinned his hand to the stock of his rifle. The Comanches suffered more, with about thirteen killed and wounded.

The Indians pulled back, but the battered Texans were unsure if it was to retreat or to regroup for another attack. Lyons heard the Comanches calling among themselves and it was certainly with pleasure that he could report to Burleson:

"Lieutenant, they are whipped, they are saying to one another that they will have to retreat." The Comanches put their wounded on horseback and retreated. The rest of the Rangers rode in, packed up their dead and wounded and set out for the fort. They made it, but were in rather poor shape for Christmas festivities. Such activities were more than enough to transition Warren Lyons back into a "civilized" lifestyle, and he soon quit the Rangers to settle into more peaceful pursuits. Little else is known of his adulthood. He married Lucy Boatright and raised a family. Warren Lyons died in Johnson County on August 11, 1870, only about 44 years of age.[14]

THOMAS PEARCE
Texas, May 1838

L ittle is known about the background of the Pearce Family. James Pearce, his wife, two sons, and a daughter, left Nachitoches, Louisiana, about May 1838, and moved to Texas. Perhaps planning to move near relatives who lived in Jackson County. The Pearces' older son, Benjamin, and their daughter Jane (or June), who married James L. Moss, lived fifteen miles above Texana, Texas, in the neighborhood of the "La Baca post office." James Pearce's brother, Jesse, also lived in the vicinity.[15]

The Pearce Family crossed the Sabine River and traveled west toward Nacogdoches. Only a few days later they were attacked by Indians, who might have been Caddoes, Comanches, or Chickasaws.[16] The Indians found an easy target. Warriors swarmed over the Pearces and quickly killed everyone but Thomas. The ten-year-old boy hid under the wagon, but the warriors easily found him. While they dragged him out, Thomas struggled, and a warrior struck him in the head with a weapon, inflicting a slight wound. The Indians destroyed the wagon and rode off.

If the warriors were not Comanches, they soon either sold or traded young Pearce to the Comanches, for he spent nearly two years with them. In October 1839, warriors atop Pilot Knob near the San Gabriel River north of Austin, discovered a wagon train moving upriver toward them. The next day, about 150 warriors attacked the wagons, massacred thirteen men, and took Dolly Webster and her two children prisoner (see Dolly Webster). Assuming that settlers would organize an armed force and come after them, the Indians quickly rode fifteen miles to alert their village. When the captives were brought in, Pearce and a 16-year-old female Mexican captive were ordered to talk to them to see what they could learn. Pearce told Dolly Webster that his father's wagon had been attacked too, that his parents, brother, and sister had been killed, and he had been with the Indians about eighteen months. Unsure of where he was himself, Pearce asked Webster if she knew where Natchitoches was. He told her the Indians had spotted their wagons from Pilot Knob.[17]

The Indians broke camp and headed to the Balcones Escarpment and out onto the high plains. By late October, they were near the headwaters of the Colorado, where several bands met up and consolidated into a large village. Among the occupants were several other captives in various stages of assimilation (see Matilda Lockhart and Warren Lyons). Pearce never had a good chance to escape in the months after he was first caught, and after he learned the Comanche tongue and some of their ways, he was content to wait it out and see what developed. In February, the village broke up, and one group with most of the captives moved south toward San Antonio. Late in the month, several bands again gathered, this time on the headwaters of the San Saba, where Webster experienced what she called a "carnival." About forty-five American, Mexican, and Indian traders gathered together to exchange ponies, blankets, buffalo robes, and captives. Several days later, another group, this time consisting of sixty-five American traders and Caddo Indians, came to do business. The dealing was done about March 5. "After this," said Webster, "I never saw young Pierce [sic] any more among them."[18]

Pearce had been dealt to the Chickasaw Ishteukah-Tubby, who had come down with a trading expedition from Indian Territory. The trip back north was long, and Ishteukah-Tubby did not deliver Thomas Pearce to the Chickasaw Agency near Fort Towson until early June, when Agent A. M. M. Upshaw wrote to Texas President Mirabeau B. Lamar that he had the boy. Ishteukah-Tubby was thanked and treated kindly, for which he was very grateful. He told Upshaw of the several white captives he saw among the Comanches, "all of which he was anxious to get." Unfortunately, the Chickasaw did not have much money, and was only able to buy Pearce. Upshaw told Lamar that the Indian wanted to go back to the Comanches and buy all the Texan prisoners. As Upshaw explained the situation to Lamar, the Chickasaw wanted to know "what would he get for it," and added, "the prisoners are women and boys all of which are in a reached [wretched?] condition."[19]

Upshaw gave Lamar what little details he learned about Pearce's family. Pearce told him he thought he had a brother and sister living in Texas and was very anxious to return to them. In the meantime, until someone came to claim him, Thomas would stay with Upshaw. Word of Thomas's deliverance quickly reached Jackson County, and in late June 1840, Benjamin Pearce journeyed to Indian Territory. On September 16, Texas Secretary of State, Joseph Waples, wrote to James Moss, the husband of Pearce's sister, Jane, that Thomas was waiting at Fort Towson for a family member to take him home. Moss replied that Benjamin Pearce had gone more than two months ago to get him, and he and his wife were becoming worried because there had been no news. It was a long trip to Indian Territory and back, but Benjamin succeeded in bringing his younger brother to Jackson County. It took more than two years, but the last survivor of the James Pearce Family had finally found a new home in Texas.[20]

MATILDA LOCKHART AND JAMES, RHODA, ELIZABETH, AND JUDA PUTMAN
October 1838

The Lockhart Family emigrated from Illinois in 1828, and settled on the Guadalupe River in what is now DeWitt County, Texas. They abandoned their home during the "Runaway Scrape" in 1836, and did not return until the summer of 1837. Joining Andrew Lockhart that summer was the family of Mitchell Putman. Putman had fought in the Battle of San Jacinto, and had just been honorably discharged from the army. For a time the two families shared the same yard.[21]

When the pecans ripened in the fall, the children of both families went along the bottomland to gather the nuts. Matilda Lockhart (13) was the oldest, and the Putman children, James, Rhoda, Elizabeth, and Juda, ranged from about 10 to two-and-a-half.[22] Finished gathering pecans, the children grabbed their buckets and emerged at the edge of the prairie, where they were greeted by a band of painted Comanches. Matilda dropped her bucket, ran for the house, and may have escaped but for the crying of the youngest Putman girl, who pleaded with Matilda not to leave her behind; she turned back and all of them were captured. The Indians tied them to horses with rawhide thongs and rode away. When evening approached, the Lockharts and Putmans began to worry about their children. After dark, they built a signal fire, blew horns, and fired guns. By morning, the parents were disconsolate, with the full realization that their children had been captured.

Captain John Tumlinson and six men were on a surveying expedition and saw about fifty Indians riding past. They headed toward Tumlinson, but the surveyors gave them the slip. When they returned to the Guadalupe, they found the settlers forted up. When Tumlinson learned of the raid he realized that the Indians chasing him were probably the same ones carrying the captives. A company of settlers pursued the raiders upriver to the mouth of the Comal, but they lost the trail when it entered the Hill Country. Andrew Lockhart wanted to continue, but was talked out of it with the promise that they would go back home, reorganize, get more men, and try again.[23]

In January 1839, a band of friendly Lipan Apaches discovered a Comanche camp near the headwaters of the San Gabriel, about fifty miles northwest of Waterloo, Texas, the village that would soon become Austin. The Lipans reported their find, and Ranger companies from Bastrop and LaGrange were organized, with Andrew Lockhart joining the latter. On January 26, sixty-three Rangers and sixteen Lipans, under the leadership of Colonel John H. Moore, rode to the San Gabriel. A norther swept in, pelting them with snow and rain for three days. Horses died of exposure, supplies were low, Ranger Wilson was seriously wounded in the chest by an accidental rifle discharge, and gloom enveloped the expedition.

The Lipans finally spotted the village, probably Penetekas under Chief Muguara, near Spring Creek, in a valley just south of the Colorado and north of the San Saba. On the morning of February 15, Moore arranged his companies to hit the village from three sides, and charged. The quiet was broken by the sound of horses hooves and a few rounds of opening gunfire, but the shouts of Andrew Lockhart were distinctly heard by many.

"Matilda Lockhart! Oh my child! If you are here run to me. I am your father!"[24]

He continued to call out until the sounds of battle drowned him out. Matilda heard him, but Comanche women held her, and then lashed her back into the thickets along Spring Creek. Rangers entered the camp and shot down Indians as they emerged from their lodges, but there were too many Indians, and most of them fled to the cutbanks along the creek and formed up for a counter-attack. Moore realized the bad spot his disorganized men were in and called for a retreat to a line of timber. It was just in time, for the Comanches charged out and nearly broke Moore's line. They repulsed several attacks until about ten a.m., when the Comanches pulled back, surrounded Moore, and opened up a long-range fire. Moore estimated he was facing about 400 Indians.

At noon, a Comanche warrior and a captive Lipan woman with a white flag approached the Texans. Moore went out with a Lipan to talk, while the captive woman translated. The Comanches offered to trade prisoners, knowing that Moore had captured several of their people early in the fight. According to the Lipan woman, the Comanches had a middle-aged white woman, a girl of about 15 years of age, and three children.[25] Moore probably would have made the swap, except that his Lipan allies had already killed the Comanches prisoners without his knowledge.

When Moore indicated there would be no trading, the Comanche said that they had a great number of warriors, with more arriving all the time. Moore put up a bold front.

"Our numbers are small," he said. "Come on."

The parley ended and the Texans awaited the next attack, but none came. The Comanches had probably taken enough casualties themselves—Moore estimated about thirty killed and fifty wounded. The Comanches pulled back, and so did Moore, taking his seven wounded with him. The Lipan Chief Castro, disgusted that the Rangers did not continue to fight, withdrew with his warriors. One of the walking wounded was Mr. Lockhart, disappointed that another effort was not made to rescue his daughter.[26]

Matilda Lockhart's captivity was a horrible ordeal. Whether the abuse began from day one, or was a result of her escape attempt is not certain. The Putman children were not treated with such severity. Matilda was forced to do the bidding of her "owners," always the most unpleasant tasks they could think of. A main job was to herd and guard the ponies. She worked until her fingers bled, and was beaten for all her best efforts. This was not unusual treatment among white prisoners, but the extremes that her particular captors went to was extraordinary. Throughout the year of 1839 she was constantly tortured. Her body was a mass of scars, sores, and bruises. She had been held down while a flaming stick was held against her nose, burning the entire tip off to the bone. When a scab formed, the Indians delighted in surprising her during her sleep while they thrust another flaming torch against her nose. Both her nostrils were charred wide open. She was a ghastly sight to see.[27]

By the fall of 1839, Matilda and the Putmans were prisoners for one year. In late October, more captives joined them in their camp of misery on the headwaters of the Colorado (see Dolly Webster). By this time, Matilda had learned to exist as a tortured slave. She passed on to Mrs. Webster "some instructions in regard to my behaviour [sic] that saved me many a blow." The village held nearly 2,000 Indians, with many white captives (see Thomas Pearce and Warren Lyons), and still included all of the Putman children.[28]

In early January 1840, two war parties went to raid the Mexican settlements along the Rio Grande. The larger band was successful, returning with about thirty prisoners, including twelve adult women. The other raiding party met with disaster; they brought in only one black slave and two scalps, but lost nearly thirty warriors. At the same time, the mother of a Comanche chief died, and there was a great lamentation. To ease their grief, one of the Putman children, probably little Rhoda, was killed and buried with the old woman. Soon after, the village broke up and a large group moved southwest to the head of the Frio River, reaching there in mid-February.[29]

On the Frio the Indians awaited the results of a peace mission. On January 9, 1840, several Comanches, including a Mexican captive, went to San Antonio to see Colonel Henry W. Karnes, who commanded the southern military region. They wanted peace with the Texans and said they turned down offers from Mexicans and other Indians to start a general war. Karnes stated: "These statements may be true; but their known treachery and duplicity, induces me to put little faith in them." He treated them well and sent them away with presents, but warned "that the government would not enter into any Treaty without the release of the American captives, and the restoration of all stolen property." The Comanches agreed to comply and come in within twenty or thirty days. Karnes wrote this up in his report to Secretary of War Albert Sidney Johnston, and added that he thought a few commissioners ought to come to San Antonio, as well as a force of soldiers to ensure delivery of the captives, or to seize the Comanches as hostages should they not deliver the captives as promised.[30]

Johnston ordered Lieutenant Colonel William S. Fisher, First Infantry, to take three companies to San Antonio. President Mirabeau B. Lamar appointed Quartermaster-General Colonel William G. Cooke, and Adjutant-General Colonel Hugh McLeod as commissioners to treat with the Indians. Their instructions included stipulations that any treaty must insist that the Indians return the captives and stay away from the settlements. In addition, the practice of giving presents was to be ended. The Comanches were equally assured that they were in the right. They believed the Texans were eager for peace and they could get a great price for the white prisoners. Muguara argued that they should offer the captives to the Texans one by one, therefore getting the most out of every transaction.[31]

Although Karnes had made it clear that all captives must be returned before any treaty talks, Muguara convinced the Indians to return one at a time. On February 20, the Indian camp on the Frio divided. Lockhart and the two remaining Putman girls remained behind, while one band took James Putman to San Antonio to see if Muguara's plan would work. The Indians hoped to trade the boy for powder and lead. Colonel Fisher, the commissioners, and the First Infantry companies had not yet arrived, and, once again, the white men's response was just what Muguara had believed. James Putman was ransomed for ammunition. The jubilant Comanches returned to the camp. Although they again promised that they would bring in all the captives the next time, the plan was to take in Matilda Lockhart next, and see what she would bring. On March 15, Muguara, twelve other chiefs, warriors, women, and children, totaling about sixty-five Indians, left for San Antonio. The only captives they brought were Lockhart and a Mexican woman named Leno.[32]

The Comanches were arrogant when they rode into town on March 19. They had been to San Antonio many times before, and no one had dared to molest them. The fact that they had brought their women and children along shows that they had no idea this time would be different. They met the commissioners at the old courthouse, a one-story stone building on the corner of Main Plaza and Calabosa Street. The council did not get off to a good start. The Comanches either did not realize the reaction the Texans would have upon seeing the disfigured Matilda Lockhart, or they did not care. At first chance, Matilda told the story of her abuse, said that there were other captives in the village, and that the Indians planned to sell them one at a time. With that news, the troops surrounded the council house.

Still, the Comanches were not alarmed. When the commissioners asked where the other prisoners were, Muguara answered, "We have brought in the only one we had; the others are with other tribes." It was a palpable lie, and the commissioners were stunned into a momentary silence. Perhaps still not realizing the predicament he placed himself in, Muguara curtly asked, "How do you like the answer?"

"I do *not* like your answer," Lieutenant Colonel Fisher replied. "I told you not to come here again without bringing in your prisoners. . . . Your women and children may depart in peace and your braves may go and tell your people to send in the prisoners. When those prisoners are returned, your chiefs here present may likewise go free. Until then we will hold you as hostages."[33]

Fisher signaled for Captain George T. Howard to bring his company into the council house, and soldiers took position at the doors and windows. The Comanche interpreter paled and refused to translate the message, for he knew what the result would be. Commissioner Cooke insisted; the interpreter translated the ultimatum and bolted from the room. The Comanches strung their bows and pulled out their weapons. Fisher ordered, "Fire, if they do not desist!"

A chief dashed for a doorway and plunged his knife into the soldier who barred his way. With this, a confused melee began. Bullets and arrows flew, knives flashed, and rifles were used as clubs. Muguara stabbed Captain Howard in the side, and then was shot to death. A few chiefs fought their way out the door, and the commotion aroused the rest of the Comanches in the plaza. The streets, alleys, and backyards for blocks around became a battleground. It was after midnight when the last two Indians were burned out of a backyard kitchen they had taken refuge in. Casualties were thirty-five Comanches dead, including three women and two children, and twenty-seven women and children captured. Seven whites were dead, and eight were wounded. The captured Indians were locked up, but one woman was given a horse and provisions and told to take word to the tribe that if they wanted their women and children back, they must bring in the rest of the white captives.[34]

After the battle, several townswomen took Matilda Lockhart, washed her, fed her, and clothed her. Yet, one could not cleanse away what the Comanches had done to her. "Ah, it was sickening to behold," said Mary Maverick, "and made one's blood boil for vengeance." "She was in a frightful condition, poor girl. Her head, arms and face were full of sores and bruises, and her nose actually burned off." Matilda was free, but, Maverick reported, "she was very sad and broken hearted. She said she felt utterly degraded, and could never hold her head up again—that she would be glad to get back home, where she would hide away and never permit herself to be seen.[35]

Word of Matilda's liberation spread, and in a short time, her older brother appeared in San Antonio to take her home. Her first ordeal lasted almost two years; her second lasted about two more. Although historian John Henry Brown wrote that Matilda developed into "one of the prettiest" women in the countryside, and was modest, sprightly, and affectionate, one can only wonder if that characterization was meant more for the edification of her surviving family. Matilda, with her nose burned to the bone, and scars covering her body, was more likely to have hidden herself as she told Mary Maverick she would do. In any case, Matilda, broken in body, and likely in spirit, caught a severe cold that developed into pneumonia. She died about two years after her rescue, not even 18 years old.[36]

The Council House fight made it hell for the remaining captives. There were about thirteen of them among the Peneteka bands affected by the fight. Several of them were tortured and killed. With every murder, however, the Comanches reduced their bargaining chips.[37] When they came to their senses, they sent an emissary to San Antonio to reopen negotiations. On April 3,

Chief Piava told the authorities that they had many captives to exchange. On the contrary, scouts reported that there were few white captives in the Indian camp. Nevertheless, a meeting was arranged for the following day, and the Texans brought up nine prisoners to trade. Piava said they would meet on the outskirts of town and exchange two captives at a time. The first two released in trade for two Indians were Elizabeth Putman and a Mexican boy. The Texans, not knowing that some captives had been killed, asked where the other whites were. Piava answered that he only had one more, and if he gave him up, he wished to choose the Indian he wanted.

Tensions were already high, and this news almost brought on another fight. The Texans swallowed their anger, however, and the trading continued. Booker Webster and another Mexican boy were released next, and Piava chose one particular woman whose arm was broken in the Council House fight. When asked why he chose her, he said that she was the wife of a dead chief and owned "muchas mules." He wanted her for his wife. When the woman proved reluctant to go with Piava, the Texans chose another woman instead, and then added a child and another adult. Piava was not pleased, but he accepted the deal. In all, two white Texans and five Mexicans were recovered. There was no use in keeping the remaining captive Indians, and through lax security, most of them escaped. Those who were taken into Texan homes to live and work also ran away at the first opportunity.[38]

Elizabeth Putman, now about five years old, could not remember any English, was very wild, afraid of white people, and tried to run away at every opportunity. Mary Maverick, who took care of her for a time, said she was covered in bruises, and her nose was also partly burned off. Nevertheless, she "cried to go back to the Comanche mother who had adopted her." When word of her rescue got out, Judge James W. Robinson was intrigued. He lived near Gonzales, and a neighbor of his, Arch Gipson, had married Mitchell Putman's elder daughter. He knew her well and was aware that she had lost a sister a few years ago. Robinson went to San Antonio to examine the girl, but he could not see a conclusive resemblance.

Robinson and two companions took the girl back to Gonzales. When they reached the ranch, Robinson went alone to Mrs. Gipson and told her he had a little girl with him, and he wanted her to see if she looked familiar. Mrs. Gipson had been ill, and it was with difficulty that she walked out on the porch. Robinson cautioned her to go easy, but when the child was brought near, she flew to her, "more as a bird than as a person, her eyes indescribably bright." Mrs. Gipson and the girl peered into each other's faces. Said Robinson: "Never before nor since have I watched any living thing as I watched that child at that moment." The instant the girl looked in the woman's face "it seemed startled as if from a slumber, threw up its little head as if to collect its mind, and with a second piercing look, sprang from the horse with outstretched arms, clasping Mrs. Gipson around the neck, piteously exclaiming: 'Sister, sister!'" The three men watching the scene were moved to tears. Elizabeth Putman had come home.[39]

James Putman, released in the swap for ammunition in February, went back to his parents' home, but after two years captivity, in which he claimed to have been carried all across Texas and Arizona, he found it difficult to adjust to "civilized" restrictions. He would not sit in a chair, but sat on the ground with legs crossed; he would not sleep in a bed, but preferred a dirt floor; he would not eat with a knife or fork, but preferred his fingers. And, it was said, "it was impossible to slip up on him." When James grew older he settled down, married a widow named Nash, had a daughter named Sarah, and lived for many years in Guadalupe County. James Putman died in Hays County in the early 1870s.[40]

The last of the Putman children to be accounted for was Juda. She was not exchanged with the others. She may have been adopted, or a warrior held her to marry when she was older, or she was already traded or sold to another band. Juda, about seven years old at the time of her capture, disappeared from white history for about fourteen years. She lived with several Comanche bands and was in Indian Territory when several Missouri traders bought her. She stayed with them for a time, until being sold to Judge John R. Chenault, a former Indian agent then living in southwest Missouri. Chenault cared for her and educated her. In about seven more years, Chenault moved to Texas. Remarkably, they settled in Gonzales County, not far from where Juda was first captured.

After a time, inquisitive neighbors, seeing that she bore a resemblance to some Putman family members, informed old Mitchell Putman and his daughters. Juda remembered next to nothing of her parents or home. One of the Putman sisters figured there was one way to be certain if she was the long-lost Juda. She remembered that Juda had a birthmark in a place that any modest lady would always keep covered. In private, the sister and a few other ladies examined her, and sure enough, the mark was found exactly as described. If the sequence of years is correct, Juda was finally restored to her home and family in the year 1859, twenty-one years after her abduction. The last of the Putman children had come full circle.[41]

THOMAS COLEMAN
Texas, February 18, 1839

In 1830, the Coleman Family settled on the north bank of the Colorado River, near today's Webberville, Texas. Husband and father, Robert M. Coleman, was originally from Kentucky, and had fought against the Mexican Army at Bexar in 1835, and at San Jacinto in 1836. While in Velasco in 1837, Coleman drowned at the mouth of the Brazos River. Elizabeth Coleman was left with three sons and two daughters. The cabin stood at the end of a prairie, flanked on three sides by dense bottom timber, with the only clear approach being from the north. The nearest neighbor was Doctor J. W. Robertson, whose house was about 500 yards away.[42]

The Peneteka Comanches in the area were at war, having fought the Rangers at the Battle of Spring Creek on February 15, 1839, just three days previous. The Rangers were defeated, and nearly 500 Comanches swept down the Colorado River. About ten a.m. on February 18,[43] Elizabeth Coleman and her son, Thomas (5), were outside the house doing chores. Albert (14) was in the house with his two little sisters, ages 11 and 9. James, the eldest, was out working in the fields with a hired man. The Indians appeared so suddenly out of the dense woods, that there was little time to react. James and the hired hand were cut off from the house by a large number of warriors. They immediately ran downstream to try and warn the neighbors.

Mrs. Coleman saw the Indians and ran toward the house, but at the doorstep she turned to look for Tommie when an arrow struck her in the throat. She collapsed inside and Albert barred the door. The Indians snatched up Thomas and turned their attention to the cabin. There were two or three loaded guns inside; Albert grabbed one, shot out the window, and hit a warrior on the doorstep.

"I killed one!" he called out.

Elizabeth, although choking and bleeding profusely, sat down on a chair near a window and tried to aim a rifle. Before firing, she attempted to pull the arrow out of her throat. The barb only tore a gaping wound, and she fell from the chair and bled to death. Albert picked up the rifle and fired, hitting another warrior. When the Indians backed off, Albert reloaded, and then pulled up the puncheons covering a storage space under the floor. He ordered his sisters to get in and told them that no matter what happened, they were not to make a noise until they heard the voices of white men. He then ran back and fired from various windows and apertures, furiously reloading and shooting, so that the besieging Indians must have thought there were several defenders yet inside.[44]

Finally, warriors reached the house and one of them thrust a lance through an opening, stabbing Albert. Others blasted away through chinks in the walls, hitting him again. The fatally wounded boy crawled over to his mother, lay down next to her, and died. Inexplicably, the warriors, either thinking there were still armed defenders inside, or hearing the whooping coming from the house down the road, left the Coleman place and ran off. The two girls were eventually saved. They remembered Albert's final words to them as: "Father is dead, mother is dead, and I am dying, but something tells me God will protect you."[45]

The Indians may have been distracted from the Coleman place by the action occurring at the Robertson house. The doctor was absent, and the Indians had almost a free hand in robbing his place and stealing seven of his black slaves. James Coleman and the hired man, after escaping from the attack on the Coleman place, ran downriver to Robertson's, but when they found Indians attacking there also, they continued on, sneaking through the timber along the river, until they got to a cluster of homes known as Wells' Fort, where resided Mrs. Wells, John Walters, and George W. Davis.

After leaving the Coleman and Robertson places, the Indians rode to Wells' Fort, but evening was approaching, the place may have looked too well defended, and a small force of about fourteen men, under John J. Grumbles, was dogging them. The warriors rode north toward Wilbarger Creek, while the families at Wells' Fort moved southeast to a better position at Wilbarger's Fort. At twilight, John D. Anderson rode to the Coleman cabin and called for the girls. Heeding their brother's advice, the girls answered him. Anderson raised the puncheons, released them, and rode them back to the other families. George Davis took care of them.[46]

The white settlers around Bastrop organized a retaliatory expedition. Captain Jacob Burleson with twenty-five men, joined with Captain James Rogers with twenty-seven men, and the two companies rode off to follow the Indian trail. They rode hard and the next forenoon caught up with the Indians at Post Oak Island, a few miles north of Brushy Creek, near present-day Taylor, Texas, and about twenty-five miles north of Coleman's house. The

Indians saw the whites coming and took position in a tree line. Burleson hurried forward to open the attack before the Indians were ready. He dismounted and ordered his men to open fire; only a few obeyed. The rest, seeing the odds were not good, retreated. Burleson, with only a few men standing with him, had no choice but to join the flight. A bullet caught him in the back of the head as he mounted his horse. He tumbled to the ground and the Indians were upon him.

The Bastrop men fell back three miles and halted, probably pondering their shameful conduct and wondering what to do next. Their response was determined when Jacob's brother, Edward Burleson, rode up with thirty-one more men. The combined force, now totaling about eighty-four men, rode back to fight. Burleson divided the command in half, giving one part to Jesse Billingsley, and tried to hit the Comanches in a two-pronged attack on each flank. The plan was good, but the approaches to the Comanche position led through open areas in plain view of Comanche fire and too dangerous to cross in daylight.

Edward Burleson later wrote: "Thus failing in our attempt to rout and chastise the enemy and recapture the prisoners they held in possession, we were forced to select safe positions...and whenever an Indian showed himself, to draw down on him and send the messenger of death to dispatch him."[47]

The battle turned into a sniping contest. When darkness ended the fight, four white men were dead or mortally wounded: Jacob Burleson, John Walters, Edward Blakey, and James Gilleland. Seven others had lighter wounds. Jacob Burleson's body was found. The Comanches had scalped him, chopped off his hands, and cut out his heart, which they had taken with them.

In the morning, Burleson assaulted the Comanche position, but the Indians were gone, taking Tommie Coleman and most of the slaves. One of Robertson's elderly slaves was found still alive, but with nine arrows in him. He said the Indians lost about thirty killed and wounded, and decided to slip away during the night. They left much of their supplies and equipment behind. Billingsley took thirty men and pursued, but the Indians split up into all directions and Billingsley called it off.[48]

As for Thomas Coleman, little else is known. He was said to have been kept by the Indians until he was "almost grown." His relatives spent much money trying to rescue him. One of his cousins enlisted the aid of several Texas frontiersmen, plus the Delaware guide John Connor, to search throughout Indian Territory. He was found, and with the utmost persuasion agreed to come "home." But, Thomas had lived too long with his Indian family. "He could never," it was written, "adapt himself to civilized life, and soon returned to his wild companions for good."[49]

DOLLY, BOOKER, AND PATSY WEBSTER
Texas, October 1, 1839

John Webster left his Virginia home for Texas in 1837, seeking land, good soil, and a milder climate. The Flesher and Stillwell Families joined the Websters on their long journey down the Ohio and Mississippi River to New Orleans. From there they took a ship across the Gulf of Mexico to Texas, and eventually trekked to Bastrop on the Colorado River. They stayed there for nearly two years. In 1839, Webster purchased military land north near the San Gabriel River, and with typical pioneering spirit, the families moved on.

Accompanying John Webster was his wife, Dolly (32), and their children, Booker (10), and Patsy (3). The Stillwell, Flesher, and Morton families joined, along with the Websters' servant, Nelson, and eight young men seeking new lands on the frontier. The two-wagon ox-train left on September 27, 1839. They passed Austin and in a few days, were between the forks of the San Gabriel. Unknown to them, Comanches were watching their small wagon train from atop Pilot Knob. Near the North Fork, two of the young men of the party rode ahead to hunt, but they heard Indians across the stream and hurried back. They alerted the rest of the train and the men met to discuss options. Some wanted to retreat, but others said, "that they would rather die, than go back and be laughed at as cowards."[50]

Webster volunteered to ride ahead and see if he could determine the Indians' intentions, but they dissuaded him, and after two hours of arguing, agreed to go back home. They traveled all night, hoping to be far away from the Indians before daybreak. Reaching a lower ford of the San Gabriel after the moon had set, and not being able to see their way, they stopped to camp. The next morning, October 1, they got an early start and traveled for two hours before coming to a narrow prairie, with thick timber along both sides. Sixteen Comanches suddenly rode up to their rear and began shouting and shooting. There were thirteen mounted men in the Webster train, and they charged after the Indians, firing and hitting two. It was only a ruse however, for about 150 Comanches attacked the front of the train. Old Indian-fighter Benjamin Reese, encouraged the people with the train. He had them turn the oxen loose and pull the wagons together. The Indians charged by on horseback and the whites fired as they circled, but few were hit. A Mexican in the Webster party tried to escape, but got only fifty yards before being killed.

Mr. Morton was hit next, then Perry Reese. John Webster took a ball in the chest and went down, then Mr. Baylor and Mr. Bezely. Nelson Flesher, Dolly Webster's nephew, fell with a gunshot to the thigh. Warriors ran up to John Webster and were about to scalp him, when one shouted, "blanco, blanco," apparently reluctant to take his full head of white hair. Stillwell was killed, but being bald, the Indians only took his wig. Dolly Webster was wounded. In a short while, only Silsby and Hicks were still fighting, but they too went down. Only Dolly, Booker, and Patsy were still alive. Dolly watched the warriors scalp and mutilate the dead, and then she swooned.[51]

The Comanches plundered the wagons and destroyed what they could not carry off. They seemed most interested in the gold watches and looking glasses, but more than $1,300 in specie was discarded. Dolly revived as warriors were stripping off her clothes; she resisted, and was beaten. The warrior who claimed her dragged her off by the hair. He let her keep the remnants of her clothes, but did nothing to stop the beatings. The Indians traveled fifteen miles west to their village, where the Indian women took turns beating Dolly. Shortly after, a white male captive (see Thomas Pearce) was sent to interrogate her.

Fearing the whites would soon be after them, the Indians packed up camp and headed northwest. Dolly's children were taken from her. Women took the rest of her clothing and made her walk between them, sticking her with spears and rubbing bloody scalps in her face. The women were the worst, Dolly said, "their treatment to me was cruel in the extreme." In late October, they gathered in a large encampment on the headwaters of the Colorado. There, Dolly met more unfortunate captives (see Matilda Lockhart and Warren Lyons). Matilda Lockhart, who had been with the Indians for more than a year, gave Dolly advice as to how she should behave to prevent so many beatings.[52]

In early November, the woman made Dolly go with them to gather pecans. While she filled her sack, she had the fortune to meet Booker and Patsy. They talked about escape. When the Indian women saw them conversing, they "fell upon and beat us most unmercifully, and ran off and left us." Dolly quickly made up her mind. She grabbed the children by the hands and ran off, hoping to find a white settlement. Scratched by mesquite, tired, thirsty, and hungry, with nothing but pecans to eat, the three traveled for eight days until they reached the Colorado River where they got fresh water. The next several days they ate mesquite beans and berries, which made them terribly ill. By the last of November, they had passed the mouth of the San Saba, but Booker was so sick he was unable to travel without a few days of rest. After he regained his strength, they continued on. Dolly's hopes soared when she saw a party of men, dressed in "English costume," but they proved to be a band of Mexicans, Caddoes, and runaway slaves. The Websters were prisoners again.

The band was on its way upriver, and in early January 1840, met up with the same Comanches Webster had escaped from. The Comanches demanded that the Websters be returned, and the meeting grew heated. After some argument, the Comanches agreed to take Booker in trade for one mule. He was loath to leave his mother and sister, but was forced to go with them. A week later, Dolly's old Comanche "master" came after her and traded a horse for her and Patsy. The first night on the journey back to the Comanche camp, the chief and his wife tied Dolly down outside the tipi and placed Patsy inside between them. She worked her way free and picked up the Indian's gun with the intention of killing him and clubbing his wife with the empty rifle. "But," she said, "my heart failed me." On January 10, they were all back in the Comanche camp.[53]

In mid-February the camp moved to the upper Frio, where American, Mexican, and Indian arrived to trade. One white boy (see James Putman) had already been taken to San Antonio to trade for ammunition, and another (see Thomas Pearce) had been sold to a Chickasaw Indian. The women were gathering honey. They located a number of beehives on a rocky ledge, and not wanting to be stung, they tied Mrs. Webster to a long rope and lowered her down the cliff face. As Dolly dangled nearly 100 feet above the canyon floor, she attempted to get the honey, only to be stung profusely. The angry women hauled her back up, and, said Dolly, "they beat me cruelly," and "burned nearly all my hair off my head."

As more punishment, they staked her to the ground for the next two days and nights, then threatened to shoot her. Unable to physically fight back, Dolly thought of a stratagem. "I knew they were very superstitious," she said. "I informed them through young Lyons. . .that if they did kill me, I would rise the next day with the sun, and come back and burn them all up." Strangely enough, her threat was enough to make them desist.[54]

In early March, the Indians moved toward San Antonio. They successfully traded James Putman for ammunition, and decided to take another captive (see Matilda Lockhart) in and find what they could get for her. Dolly was ordered to a chief's tipi to sew a flag of white silk and ribbons for the upcoming trip, and to learn what she knew about the defenses of San Antonio. Warren Lyons interpreted, but he had been in captivity so long that she did not trust him.

Author's photo

Davis Cemetery, Leander, Texas, near the site of the Webster Massacre.

Although the Indians appeared to be returning their captives one by one, Dolly could no longer wait. The day the band left with Lockhart, Dolly talked with Booker and told him of her plan to escape, but he declined the offer, preferring to be traded or escape on his own when he was older. She asked another white captive, whom she called "Mrs. Putman," if she wanted to go with her, but the young lady also refused, saying that the attempt was too hazardous. Dolly explained that the Indians never planned to trade her, but would keep her with the tribe, but the Putman girl, probably Juda, would not take a chance on escaping.[55]

At ten p.m., March 15, Dolly took Patsy by the hand, stepped out into a drizzling rain, and headed for a dense thicket in the direction she hoped to find San Antonio. A short way from the village she walked into an Indian who happened to be a friendly Caddo who knew English and had talked to her at the trading fair. He said her escape would be too dangerous, and if the Comanches caught her again, they would kill her. Dolly told him "I would rather die than to live the way I did," and continued on into the gloom. It rained until late morning the next day. Dolly found the remains of a freshly killed deer, and she and Patsy ate, rested,

69

and continued their journey. She found an abandoned beehive in a tree and took the old comb to eat. It made Patsy sick. On the third day she followed a buffalo trail and traveled all night. The weather turned frigid and Dolly was colder than she had ever been in her life. She thought Patsy would freeze to death. They walked on, passing several bands of Indians, but always avoided being seen. They found the carcass of a dead horse and ate the putrefied marrow from its bones. Likewise, a dead deer sustained them the next day, then prickly pears. After thirteen days the emaciated mother and daughter were about to give up, but Dolly had a vision that if she could just keep going a little farther, she would be saved. On the afternoon of March 28, she saw a house.

Out of nowhere, two Mexicans appeared and called out "Indio! Indio!" In halting Spanish, Dolly made the situation known. They were taken to a house, where a crowd of people gathered. They were given water and food when two men arrived; one asked if she was Mrs. Webster. She replied in the affirmative. It had been nine days since the Council House fight and Matilda Lockhart's rescue, and Matilda had informed the authorities that other captives were in the area.[56]

Dolly and Patsy were taken to John W. Smith's house, where several Texan ladies, Mrs. Maverick, Jacques, Elliott, Higgenbotham, and Smith, attended to them. They fed, bathed, and clothed them and let them sleep. "The stench of the poor woman's clothes was so dreadful," said Mary Maverick, "that Mrs. Jacques fainted away. . . ." Dolly was reunited with Booker on April 4, when the Comanches brought in a few more captives to exchange for Indian prisoners captured in the Council House fight. "Booker Webster's head was shaved," said Maverick, "and he was painted in Indian style." Booker informed them of the murders of many of the other captives. He said the Indians took the American prisoners "and roasted and butchered them to death with horrible cruelties." Only he and one Putman girl were spared because they had previously been adopted into the tribe. If this is true, then it is well that Dolly and Patsy escaped when they did.

Dolly stayed with Mrs. Smith, Mrs. Jacques, and Mrs. Maverick. The townsfolk collected $490 for the Websters, plus, said Dolly, "clothes enough to last us a year." After two months, Dolly Webster was escorted to Austin, where she met President Mirabeau Lamar, who congratulated her on regaining her freedom. With no relatives in Texas, the Websters made their way back to Virginia. Dolly met Doctor Benjamin Dolbeare, a local newspaper publisher, in Clarksburg, and in 1843, they collaborated to print the only known edition of Dolly Webster's story.[57]

LOVICIA HUNTER
Texas, Spring 1840

Doctor Hunter and family moved to Fannin County in 1838. They settled in the valley of the Red River, about eight miles downriver of the little town of Old Warren, named for trader Abel Warren, and located just east of the Grayson/Fannin County line. Old Warren had a trading house with a fifteen-foot stockade and two-story towers at the corners, several cabins, a school, a courthouse, and a tavern. It was also known as Fort Warren and Fort Kitchen, and provided a place of safety for the few area residents.[58] It was still a dangerous area, however, being near major crossings of the Red River leading into Indian Territory.

By the spring of 1840, Hunter had erected a fine cabin and was raising crops in the fertile soil. His 18-year-old daughter had just married William Lankford, of Old Warren, and moved away, thus missing the raid that was about to devastate her family. Days after the wedding, life had about returned to normal. Hunter and his eldest son, John F. Hunter, left home on business, leaving Mrs. Hunter, two daughters, and a female Negro servant behind.[59]

Late in the afternoon, the two girls took buckets and went to the spring for water, only about 100 yards from the house. Suddenly, one dozen Indians appeared, possibly Coushattas, whose lands had been confiscated and who were temporarily living in the area. The youngest girl saw the warrior and made a dash for the house, but warriors shot her with arrows before she could call out. They were on her and scalped her in an instant. Lovicia Hunter was paralyzed with fear, and other warriors easily grabbed and silenced her. They carried her along as they approached the cabin. Neither Mrs. Hunter nor the servant had heard a sound.

The Indians murdered her mother and the Negro woman in front of Lovicia's eyes, but still she could do nothing but stand motionless in terror. They scalped Mrs. Hunter and ransacked the house. They ripped open the beds and poured the feathers over the dead victims to soak up the blood. Warriors broke open Doctor Hunter's medicine chest and amused themselves opening bottles, carefully sampling potions and pills, and throwing the contents about the room. The assafoetida had them coughing, and the aqua fortis (nitric acid) they discarded with disgust. As the sun set over the Cross Timbers they gathered up their plunder and hurried away, dragging Lovicia with them.[60]

Only a minute later, John Hunter rode up to the gate, hallooing toward the strangely dark cabin. Lovicia heard him call out and tried to turn back, but a warrior threw her over his back and they all quickened their pace into the woods. Hunter, seeing and hearing no one at the cabin, walked inside the dark room and immediately knew something was terribly wrong. He smelled the pungent odors of spilled medicines and frantically searched about for a candle. He fell over something in the darkness. His trembling hands finally lit the candle and he beheld his mother's body, mutilated, scalped, and with clotted blood and feathers matted to her skin.

John ran out the door and stumbled to his horse. He mounted, trying not to get sick, and raced toward Old Warren. It was night when he reached town, and his calls for a search party were not answered until dawn. When a party of rescuers reached the Hunter home, they found the place ruined. They found the bodies of Mrs. Hunter and the servant, and a short search around the house and near the spring revealed the body of the scalped little girl. Lovicia was gone. The rescuers located a faint trail, but the tracks soon disappeared. With heavy heart, John Hunter prepared to give the sad news to his father and sister.

With their marauding done, the Indians hurried through a drizzling rain. They put Lovicia down and forced her to walk. At daybreak they stopped to dry their blankets, and then continued on. For the next few nights, Lovicia was given lessons in preparing and dressing scalps, and the first one she was forced to work on was her own mother's. In a few days the band split up and Lovicia arrived at a small village, said to be in the "Keechi Mountains" of Texas.

She was convinced that the Indians would torture and kill her, however, it was her fate to become a slave to several Indian women, who abused her and forced her to labor from dawn until dusk. Thankfully, Lovicia's ordeal was soon over. A red-haired Delaware Indian named Frank, heard of the capture and was familiar with the band of Indians. He and several other Delawares served the Texans well during the Republic years, locating, negotiating, and purchasing captives. Frank found Lovicia after forty-six days of captivity, bought her for $750, and returned her safely to her family.[61]

John Hunter brought his sister back, but readjusting to the drastically altered home situation was difficult for all of them, especially Lovicia, who was haunted by "an everpresent recollection of the ghastly scene she was compelled to witness." From that time on, John Hunter was on a personal vendetta. He donned his leather pants and hunting shirt, shouldered his flintlock rifle, and went on the warpath. He joined a company of Rangers under Edward H. Tarrant, and on May 24, 1841, participated in the Battle of Village Creek. Hunter fought Indians for thirteen years before slaking his thirst for revenge.[62]

NANCY CROSBY AND JULIET WATTS
Texas, August 7-8, 1840

As a result of the Council House fight in March 1840 (see Matilda Lockhart), the Comanches were eager to take revenge on the Texans. More than 500 Indians, mostly Comanches, with some Kiowas and a few Mexicans, descended from the hill country to the north of San Antonio and west of Austin. They headed for the coast, approximately following the courses of the San Marcos and Guadalupe Rivers, intent on death, destruction, and plunder. About four p.m. on August 6, the Indians appeared on the north edge of Victoria. The citizens were caught completely unawares.

At first, they believed the riders were friendly Lipans, who occasionally came to town to trade. They realized their mistake when the Comanches cut loose with their war whoops and galloped in. A small group of citizens counter-charged the Indians, but Doctor Arthur Gray and William M. Nuner were killed, and several men were wounded. Their sacrifice and a hasty defense at other avenues on the outskirts of town prevented the place from being completely overrun. The Indians captured about 1,500 horses and mules, but they were not content.

The next day they continued southeast for the coast. Near Nine Mile Point by Placedo Creek, they swept down on Cyrus Crosby's home. The only ones there were Nancy Crosby and her small child. Nancy was born April 1, 1816, in Missouri, the daughter of Jacob C. and Elizabeth B. Darst, and the granddaughter of Daniel Boone. The family moved to Green Dewitt's Colony in 1831. Jacob Darst was one of the "Immortal Thirty-Two" from Gonzales who went to the aid of the Alamo and died with its defenders on March 6, 1836. Nancy Darst married Cyrus Crosby in Matagorda County, in November 1838.[63]

Alone and frightened, Nancy realized that resistance was useless. The Comanches carried her and her child away. That evening, the Indians camped along Placedo Creek about twelve miles from Linnville. The next morning of August 8, as they rode along, Nancy's hungry and tired child began to cry; the Indians were not tolerant of crying children. The distraught mother did all she could to calm the child, but finally, an angry warrior "snatched the babe from her, cast it upon the ground and speared it before her eyes."[64]

The grief-stricken mother was dragged along as the Indians approached Linnville, at that time in Victoria County, near the head of Lavaca Bay. By the time the surprised townspeople realized what was happening, it was too late to organize a defense. Most of the inhabitants rushed to the bay, where they sought safety in boats, or waded neck-deep into the water. Indians killed Joseph O'Neill and two black slaves of Major Hugh 0. Watts. Major Watts, the customs collector for Linnville, had made it to safety, but apparently returned to shore to recover a gold watch he left behind. He was caught and killed. Watts's wife, a Negro nurse, and a child were captured while knee-deep in the bay, trying to reach a boat.

Juliet Constance Watts, nee Ewing, emigrated from Ireland to Texas in September 1839. She had recently married Major Watts on July 18, 1840, only twenty-one days before he was killed. The women and child were manhandled to shore. The Indians plundered, burned the town, and withdrew to the northwest at dusk. About twenty-three settlers were dead.[65]

As the Indians retraced their route inland, Juliet Watts and Nancy Crosby were mistreated and whipped, with Crosby getting the worst of the beatings. Watts rode a pack mule all day, but around the campfires at night, when it was discovered she could read, Indians made her read to them from the picture books they had stolen. Crosby, who could not read, was frequently whipped and called a "peon" because of her illiteracy.[66]

The Texans were not about to let the Indians get away without a fight. While some mounted citizens trailed the retreating raiders, others concentrated along Plum Creek near present-day Lockhart, Texas, where they believed the Indians would pass. On August 12, 200 volunteers confronted the Comanches and put them to flight. The Comanches lost about eighty warriors killed, while the Texans lost two killed and six wounded. The Indians abandoned most of their stolen horses and attempted to kill their captives. When the fight began, Nancy Crosby slid off her pony and ran toward a thicket, hoping to hide. A warrior saw her and shot two arrows clear through her body. When the Indians retreated, several Texans heard a woman scream and rode to investigate. The

Reverend Z. N. Morrell found Juliet Watts lying in some nearby bushes, crying in pain and clutching at an arrow lodged deep in her breast. He tried to remove the arrow, but Juliet would not release her grip on the shaft because of the intense pain. Doctor David F. Brown was summoned, but, as Morrell explained, "the poor sufferer seized the doctor's hand and screamed so violently that he desisted. A second effort was made with success." The steel ribbed corset she wore deflected the arrow just enough to prevent it from killing her. Morrell laid her down on his blanket and placed his saddle under her head. "She was soon composed and rejoicing at her escape," Morrell said. "Death would have been preferable to crossing the mountains with the savages."[67]

Juliet Watts later married James M. Stanton in November 1842, but the marriage ended in divorce in 1847. Juliet Stanton continued on as the manager of the Stanton Hotel, the first hotel in Port Lavaca, which was established about three miles southeast of the ravaged Linnville. Juliet next married Doctor J. R. Fretwell in May 1852. She kept up correspondence with Reverend Morrell for a number of years, but he never saw her again. She died on August 3, 1878. Nancy Crosby was buried under a large oak tree near the battlefield, about one and a half miles west of present-day Lockhart. Ten years later, her body was reinterred, but the site of the second burial has been lost to history.[68]

REBECCA JANE AND WILLIAM GILLELAND
Texas, April 1842

Johnstone and Mary Barbour Gilleland lived near Philadelphia, Pennsylvania, when they succumbed to the enthusiastic promotions of land in Texas. In 1837, they announced their plans to their children, packed up their belongings, sold their home, and sailed for Galveston. Rebecca Jane, born in Philadelphia, August 31, 1831, reported that the family was excited about the grand adventure, but said that none of them were "used to the hardships and privations of frontier life," and "were ill prepared for the trials which awaited them."[69]

The family lived for a time in Brazoria, and then moved farther down the coast to northern Refugio County, below the large Don Carlos Ranch. Johnstone joined Captain John J. Tumlinson's company of rangers to protect the frontier. In March 1842, Mexicans under General Rafael Vasquez, captured San Antonio, Refugio, and Goliad. The incursion began a second version of the 1836 "Runaway Scrape," as families in west Texas fled east, and President Sam Houston moved the government from Austin to Houston. Rebecca Gilleland remembered the time her family "frequently had to flee through blinding storms, cold and hungry, to escape Indians and Mexicans. The whole country was in a state of excitement. Families were in constant danger and had to be ready at any moment to flee for their lives."[70]

As usual, the Indians made the best of the confusion, raiding in toward the coast almost as far as they had come during the Linnville Raid of 1840. On a warm spring evening when all four of the Gillelands were outside their home they were surprised by a war party of Comanches.[71] Johnstone ran for his rifle at the house, only a few rods away, but he was cut down before he got there. Mary grabbed Rebecca and William and clutched them to her side. Rebecca heard her mother praying for a moment, before a warrior cut her viciously with his weapon. "As she pressed us to her heart," said Rebecca, "we were baptized in her precious blood."

The children were dragged away and thrown on horses. A female warrior, "savage and vicious looking," took Rebecca. At first she handled her roughly, then, strangely enough, comforted her and smoothed back her golden hair. Regardless, both children were weeping piteously. There was a white renegade riding with the Comanches, and he and several warriors threatened to cut off their hands and feet if they did not stop crying. The Comanche woman scolded them and they stopped their threats.[72]

The raiders left Johnstone and Mary dying on the ground, took what they wanted from the home, and fled north. They might have gotten away except the recent incursion of the Mexican Army had alerted the settlers and caused many local militia companies to organize.[73] Lieutenant A. B. Hannum and Doctor A. T. Axsom of the Matagorda Riflemen, and men of other units, including Alfred S. Thurmond, town marshal of Victoria, and Andrew Neill, were in the vicinity of the lower San Antonio River, waiting to see where the Mexicans might move next. Scouting along the San Antonio River, Lieutenant Hannum spotted an Indian trail. As news of the Gilleland murders had just arrived, Hannum quickly got reinforcements and followed the broad, fresh trail north. Among the party rode Albert Sidney Johnston, later to be a Confederate general.

The Indians never stopped moving. They carefully avoided the other settlements, crossed the river, and rode through the night. It was morning when they halted, figuring they had outdistanced any pursuers. The stop proved fatal, for no sooner had they halted, than the volunteer soldiers caught up with them, not far from the site of the 1836 Fannin Massacre.

The Comanches saw the whites approaching and formed a battle line. One old Indian ran up and down the line, playing on a flute-like instrument, as another ornately dressed warrior pranced on his pony in their front. The Indian, said Hannum, "presented too fair a picture to be resisted," and he promptly shot him off his horse. The rest of the Indians took to the woods. The volunteers dismounted and ran to the timber after them, figuring they would battle them from tree to tree. The Indians never stopped running, however, and left behind weapons, shields, and horses. The fleeing Indians had no time for their captives. Rebecca was knocked on the side of her head and dumped off her horse, while her younger brother William was lanced in the side and left for dead. They were alone in the woods. Rebecca prayed, and then she picked up her badly wounded brother and carried him to the edge of the woods. She saw horsemen approaching, believed they were Indians, and went back into the timber and hid. She heard the clatter of horses' hooves and the voices of men calling their names. Gathering up her strength, she lifted up the nearly unconscious William and carried him out to the prairie where they were finally rescued.

Lieutenant Hannum found the children: "a little boy, lanced in the side, and a pretty little girl with long, golden curls and eyes so soft, so mystic; she was one of the politest little things on earth." The boy was in bad shape; blood flowed from his wound every time he breathed. Doctor Axsom looked pale, and Hannum asked him what was wrong.

"Oh, that child's wound makes me sick," the doctor answered. Nevertheless, Axsom got to work and eventually patched him up, the results of the operation being published in the New Orleans *Medical Journal*.[74]

Doctor Axsom took care of William Gilleland for a time, while Rebecca temporarily went to live with Presbyterian minister Doctor Blain, in Victoria, Texas. William recovered from his wounds and became a prominent citizen in Austin, while his sister gained greater fame. In 1844, she attended Rutersville College, the first Methodist college in Texas. Upon graduation in 1848, she married minister Orceneth Fisher, and eventually bore six children.

In 1855, they moved to the Pacific coast. In 1861, Fisher established Corvallis College in Oregon, and Rebecca headed the female department. They later returned to Texas, where Mr. Fisher died in 1880. Rebecca Gilleland Fisher was a charter member of the Daughters of the Republic of Texas, served as state president of that organization for the last thirty-two years of her life, and was known as the "Mother of Texas" for her work in education, politics, and religion.

A. B. Hannum, who helped rescue Rebecca, saw her in 1886, and said, she was "one of the handsomest of the very handsome women for which Texas is justly distinguished," and was "a veritable queen of society." She assisted in saving the Alamo from destruction, and for years, opened many legislative sessions with a prayer. She was the only woman elected to the Texas Veterans Association, and her portrait hangs in the Senate Chamber of the State Capitol. Rebecca died at the home of her daughter, Rebecca J. Blandford, in Austin, on March 23, 1926.[75]

"JOHN" JAYNES
Texas, July 10, 1842

Judge Jaynes and his family came to Texas in 1840, and settled just north of Austin. For nearly two years the family prospered in peace, although Indians frequently raided near the city. In the summer of 1842, one bold band was seen on the slopes of College Hill, where the university was later built. A Mr. Davis had stopped in the valley to graze his horse, when he saw the Indians coming down the slope toward him. He jumped in the saddle and rode south to town. Judge Joseph Lee saw the Indians pursuing Davis and also rode to town, sounding the alarm.

The Indians gave up their pursuit and turned northwest. They next discovered a Mr. Larrabee and chased him into a thicket where he eluded them. Tiring of this sport, the Indians continued on to Judge Jaynes's house. Seeing Jaynes and his family standing near the fence in their yard, they slowed to a leisurely pace, saluted, and came up to the fence. They were friendly Tonkawas, they said. Jaynes, carrying his small child in his arms, stepped out to the gate to greet them. His 14 year-old son stepped out also, as did a hired man. The Indians smiled disarmingly, talking and gesturing. When Jaynes moved closer, a warrior reached out and grabbed the little boy's arm. Jaynes held the boy tightly, and wrenched him free from the warrior's grasp. When the other warriors took out their weapons, all the whites ran for the house.

They were not fast enough. The hired man was killed. The judge made it to his front door when a bullet brought him down. Arrows missed Mrs. Jaynes, but one struck the arm of the little boy. The judge and the child fell at the doorstep. Other warriors caught the 14 year-old, forced him on a pony, and fled as fast as they could.

Joseph Lee, a neighbor, rode up just as the Indians left. He arrived to witness the dying gasps of Judge Jaynes, and tried to help Mrs. Jaynes extract the arrow from her child's arm.[76] The Indians took the boy, whose name was not recorded, away with them. At age 14, he was already "old" for a child who could be successfully assimilated into the tribe. His fate is unknown. If he fought back, he may have been killed early on. If he was pliable and strong enough to survive the physical abuse he would be subjected to, he may have been adopted and possibly become a warrior in his own right. Young "John" Jaynes probably became one of the anonymous whites that were seen from time to time, riding with the Indians of the Plains.

JANE AND WILLIAM SIMPSON
Texas, November 3, 1844

The city of Austin was incorporated as the Texas capitol in December of 1839, but even so, it never was a large metropolis during the Republic years. In January 1840, its population was only 856, and even less after its partial abandonment in 1842 because of the Mexican invasion. The town was only a skeleton for the next few years, and Indian incursions were frequent. One of the remaining stalwarts was the widow Nancy Simpson, who lived on West Pecan Street with two of her three children. The eldest boy had gone to Fayette County to work for his uncle, trying to earn money for his mother. On Sunday afternoon, November 3, 1844, the remaining children, Jane (14) and William (12), went to the valley about 400 yards from the house to bring in the cows.[77]

Minutes later, Mrs. Simpson heard their screams. A small band of Indians, thought to be Wacos, jumped out of the bushes and grabbed them. Jane fought long and hard before she was dragged away. Nancy Simpson knew just what had happened. She ran for the town and stopped everyone she could, pleading with them to organize a force to go after the Indians. Not many men were available, and only a small group formed up, including Columbus Browning, Thomas Wooldridge, and Joseph Lee, who had assisted Mrs. Jaynes (see John Jaynes) in an Indian attack two years earlier. The men reached the scene, saw tracks, and determined the Indians were on foot. This should have made them easier to overtake, but only a few of the would-be rescuers had horses. They trailed the Indians upriver into a section of timber and found shreds of a girl's dress. William later said, "his sister fought the Indians all the time. They carried her by force—dragged her frequently, tore her clothing and handled her roughly."[78]

The pursuing settlers caught a glimpse of the Indians from high ground just before the Indians entered a ravine south of Mt. Bonnell. The Indians saw they were being followed, and doubled back toward Austin. Jane Simpson was kicking and fighting all the way, and her brother pleaded with her to stop, saying that they would kill her if she kept resisting. The Indians then divided up, and William did not see Jane for a short time. When they reunited on Shoal Creek about six miles from Austin, Jane was gone; the Indians had murdered her. All William saw was "his sister's scalp dangling from one's belt." The pursuing settlers probably hastened Jane's death, for a loud, resisting prisoner could not be allowed to slow the Indians down. Shortly after this, however, the warriors crossed a stretch of rocky ground and the would-be rescuers lost the trail. They were loath to return to Austin to tell Nancy Simpson that the Indians got away with her children, for the frontier people were certain that all Indian prisoners were subject to, in the words of Texas Ranger John S. Ford, "brutal cruelties and outrages of a captivity a thousand times more terrible than the pangs of death." Their hesitation was justified, for when they told Mrs. Simpson the bad news, a "wail of agony and despair rent the air."[79]

Word of the raid quickly spread. On November 7, Texas Superintendent of Indian Affairs, Thomas G. Western, wrote to agents Benjamin Sloat and Stephen T. Slater: "On Sunday last at noon two young persons—a Girl of 14 and a boy of 12 years of age Children of Mrs. Simpson were stolen and carried off by Indians supposed to be *Waco*—You will forthwith promulgate this information to the Citizens on your frontier and to the friendly Tribes of Indians throughout your Agency, and use every possible exertion to recover those unfortunate innocents, and chastise the aggressors. . . ."[80]

The agents went to the Caddo, Ioni, and Anadarko camps looking for the children, not knowing that Jane was already dead. In mid-December, Sloat went to Torrey's Trading House to buy the articles necessary to bargain for the children. Obviously they could not produce Jane, and no news was given about William. On the last day of December 1844, the Texas Legislature passed a resolution to appropriate $300 for the redemption of Jane and William Simpson. In January 1845, Superintendent Western got word from Delaware Indians who had been hunting on Brushy Creek, that they saw the Simpson children with a band of Wacos.

This was probably a false report, for if the Wacos ever had William Simpson, they soon sold or traded him to the Comanches.[81]

At the urging of Agent Sloat, Peneteka Comanche Chiefs Pah-hah-yuco and Bear-with-a-Short-Tail came to Torrey's Trading House on January 10.[82] The Indians returned some stolen horses, a runaway Negro slave, and William Simpson. Pah-hah-yuco stated, "The reason I came here was to bring the white prisoner and deliver him up to you as soon as possible, as I know his people are anxious about him. . . ." Pah-hah-yuco acknowledged previous agreements that stated that all parties would give up their captives, and he wanted to comply. Many of his people, including Buffalo Hump, were on a raid into Mexico, but when they returned, the chief would try to convince them to return all their captives. In exchange, Pah-hah-yuco wanted two Comanches, called Molly and Sam, who were held by the whites.

On January 25, Texas President Anson Jones responded, through Agent Sloat, that he was pleased with Pah-hah-yuco's "words of peace." He acknowledged that the Texans held some Comanches, and said "we do not kill them nor harm them but treat them the same as our own Children." Jones continued: "You have sent me the little white boy, that he may go home to his mother and make her heart glad. She was in much trouble. You will receive in return the Comanche boy Sam. Captain Sloat will deliver him to you." Jones said that if the Comanches have any more white prisoners, to deliver them to the agents, "and I will give you more of your people, but your young men must steal no more of my peoples children."[83]

Traders received compensation for their roles in securing William Simpson. The Torrey brothers got $41 and F. Dieterich got $96 for items given to the Indians, including tobacco, salt, clothing, blankets, coffee, sugar, powder, and lead. On February 4, Superintendent Western wrote to Nancy Simpson, "I have the pleasure to restore to the bosom of his Mother, your son. . . ." Western mentioned that they had to thank the "beneficial effects of the Peace Policy of this Government" for the prompt, safe return of the boy. Unfortunately, Western had some bad news: "It is with unfeigned pain I notice the fate of your little Daughter. She died on the day she left you. . .in this bereavement you have the Consolation that She Suffered but little, and is now an Angel in Heaven." He hoped that "Divine Providence" would protect her in the future, and may "He endow you with fortitude to bear with the ills which we as mortals are subject to in this vale of tears and assuage your Sorrows."[84]

Jane Simpson's murderers received their payback in July 1845. Apparently a significant number of Comanches were trying to remain at peace with the Texans. They knew who had led the raid on the Simpsons. Chief Cut Arm and his followers wanted to kill the young man and his accomplices who had caused the trouble, but could not do it right away because of the strength of the young warrior's party. By the summer, Cut Arm had the numbers and the approval. In Chief Mopechucope's village on the San Saba, the young warrior was gathering another war party to raid the Texan settlements. Cut Arm confronted him and said he must not go. A fight erupted in which Cut Arm was killed and some of his followers were wounded, but the belligerent young warrior and his father were also killed, effectively stopping the raid.[85] Fewer captives were taken during the next few years, but the practice had by no means ended.

Chapter two footnotes

[1] Fehrenbach, *Lone Star*, 255; Cashion, *A Texas Frontier*, 21.

[2] Wilbarger, *Depredations*, 140-41; DeShields, *Border Wars*, 318; Corwin, *Kiowa & Comanche Captives*, 126-27; Hoig, *Jesse Chisholm*, 95-96.

[3] Goacher has been spelled several ways, including Gotier, Gotcher, Gocher, and Goucher. John Holmes Jenkins III, *Recollections*, 249, indicates it was spelled Goacher and pronounced "Gotcher" by the early settlers. Wilbarger, *Depredations*, 15, and DeShields, *Border Wars*, 191, say Goacher first came to Texas in 1835.

[4] Wilbarger, *Depredations*, 16; DeShields, *Border Wars*, 192; Jenkins, *Recollections*, 52. The first two sources claim Mrs. Goacher closed the door and fired many times before being overpowered and killed. Story variations also claim that it was the son out chopping wood who either bit the warrior's thumb, or bit him on the neck.

[5] Jenkins, *Recollections*, 52, 249.

[6] Jenkins, *Recollections*, 249; Wilbarger, *Depredations*, 18.

[7] Jenkins, *Recollections*, 226, 256; Wilbarger, *Depredations*, 215; DeShields, *Border Wars*, 206. These sources give Warren's age as anywhere between seven and 13. He was probably 11 at the time of capture.

[8] DeShields, *Border Wars*, 207; Dolbeare, *Dolly Webster*, 12.

[9] Dolbeare, *Dolly Webster*, 23-25.

[10] Exley, *Frontier Blood*, 134-35.

[11] Jenkins, *Recollections*, 227-29; Roberts, "Restoration of Warren Lyons," 24.

[12] Jenkins, *Recollections*, 230; De Shields, *Border Wars*, 208-09; Roberts, "Restoration of Warren Lyons, 24. Wilbarger, *Depredations*, 215, says that when Lyons first rode past the cow pen, he said, "Dar me fadder kill—dar me take off." When he saw his mother, he cried out, "Dar me mudder!"

[13] Jenkins, *Recollections*, 256; DeShields, *Border Wars*, 209.

[14] Jenkins, *Recollections*, 225-26, 256; Michno, *Encyclopedia of Indian Wars*, 8-9; Wilbarger, *Depredations*, 617-19.

[15] Dolbeare, *Dolly Webster*, 9; Winfrey and Day, *Texas Indian Papers* 1, 116.

[16] Thomas Pearce later said that the attacking Indians were Caddoes, however, a Chickasaw purchased him from the Comanches. The Comanches raided east Texas during these years, and the Chickasaws still lived along the Attoyac and Patroon Bayous east of Nacogdoches in the late 1830s.

[17] Winfrey and Day, *Texas Indian Papers* 1, 114; Dolbeare, *Dolly Webster*, 8-9.

18 Dolbeare, *Dolly Webster*, 21-24.

19 Winfrey and Day, *Texas Indian Papers* 1, 114.

20 Winfrey and Day, *Texas Indian Papers* 1, 116-17; Webb and Carroll, *Handbook of Texas* 1, 225-26. John Henry Brown lived in Austin in 1840, where he heard the news of Pearce's rescue. He contacted President Lamar and supplied him with the names and residences of Pearce's relatives. Brown later edited several papers, served in the Texas House, was a justice of the peace, and mayor of Dallas. He wrote several books, one of them, *Indian Wars and Pioneers of Texas*, is cited in this volume.

21 Brown, *Indian Wars*, 51; DeShields, *Border Wars*, 239. Brown says the families lived west of the Guadalupe, opposite the present town of Cuero, in Dewitt County, while DeShields says they lived two miles below Gonzales, in Gonzales County.

22 Brown, *Indian Wars*, 51; DeShields, *Border Wars*, 240; Wilbarger, *Depredations*, 2. The names, ages, and number of Putman children are disputed. Wilbarger says there were four, DeShields says there were three, with James being the youngest, while Brown says there were three, with James four years old, and another daughter two-and-a-half.

23 Brown, *Indian Wars*, 51; Wilbarger, *Depredations*, 2; Sowell, *Rangers and Pioneers*, 226; DeShields, *Border Wars*, 241.

24 Brown, *Indian Wars*, 51; Crosby, "Brushy Creek."

25 Winfrey and Day, *Texas Indian Papers* 1, 58; Brown, *Indian Wars*, 51; Crosby, "Brushy Creek." It is not known who the white woman was, but a possibility is Jane Crawford, who was in Comanche hands at this time. The girl was Matilda Lockhart, and the three children were Mitchell Putman's, which again brings up the question as to whether three or four of his children were captured.

26 Winfrey and Day, *Texas Indian Papers* 1, 58-59; Crosby, "Brushy Creek"; Wilbarger, *Depredations*, 3; DeShields, *Border Wars*, 241. Anderson, *Conquest of Texas*, 175-76, calls the fight an unprovoked massacre of Comanches, by plunder-hunting Texans, and the white captives were "(children, supposedly) taken in earlier raids."

27 Green, *Maverick*, 38.

28 Dolbeare, *Dolly Webster*, 12. Webster reported four Putman children, not three.

29 Dolbeare, *Dolly Webster*, 19-21; Wilbarger, *Depredations*, 4. The death of Rhoda at this time is speculative. Webster claims the Indians killed a little Putman girl. The others can later be accounted for, except Rhoda. Wilbarger says Rhoda never returned home and became the wife of a Comanche chief. Sowell, *Rangers and Pioneers*, 226, says "the oldest girl" became the wife of a chief.

30 Dolbeare, *Dolly Webster*, 21; Winfrey and Day, *Texas Indian Papers* 1, 101-02.

31 Richardson, *Comanche Barrier*, 48-49; Fehrenbach, *Comanches*, 324-25.

32 Dolbeare, *Dolly Webster*, 21, 25; Fehrenbach, *Comanches*, 325. Anderson, *Conquest of Texas*, 181, incorrectly states that James Horn was the boy the Comanches traded for ammunition. James Horn died in the winter of 1838.

33 Richardson, *Comanche Barrier*, 49-50; Fehrenbach, *Comanches*, 325-26; Brice, *Great Raid*, 22-23.

34 Brown, *Indian Wars*, 77-78; Brice, *Great Raid*, 24-25; Green, *Maverick*, 26-29.

35 Green, *Maverick*, 38; Hunter, ed., "Memoirs of Mrs. Maverick," 6. Matilda's reaction was typical of many returned captives. Rape and abuse caused many of them to quickly deteriorate physically and mentally. Maverick also recorded that a sister of Matilda's was still with the Indians, but this may have been a misunderstanding concerning the parentage of the remaining Putman girls.

36 Green, *Maverick*, 38; Brown, *Indian Wars*, 52. Anderson, *Conquest of Texas*, 419, states, "Maverick may have exaggerated Lockhart's condition...."

37 Green, *Maverick*, 30. Fehrenbach, *Comanches*, 330, says that one of the captives killed was a six-year-old sister of Matilda Lockhart, but cites no source. Mary Maverick, in Green, *Maverick*, 31, shocked by the deaths of the white prisoners, later commented: "Our people did not, however, retaliate upon the captives in our hands."

38 Brice, *Great Raid*, 26; Fehrenbach, *Comanches*, 332; Green, *Maverick*, 40-41.

39 Green, *Maverick*, 41-42; Brown, *Indian Wars*, 52-53.

40 Sowell, *Rangers and Pioneers*, 226; DeShields, *Border Wars*, 241.

41 Brown, *Indian Wars*, 51-52; Wilbarger, *Depredations*, 4-5. Brown says that Juda was restored to her family in 1864.

[42] Brown, *Indian Wars*, 61; Sowell, *Rangers and Pioneers*, 55.

[43] Brown, *Indian Wars*, 61, Wilbarger, *Depredations*, 146, and "Battle of Brushy Creek," <u>Handbook of Texas Online</u>, say the attack was on February 18. DeShields, *Border Wars*, 268, Groneman, *Battlefields*, 84, and Crosby, "Battle of Brushy Creek," say the attack was on February 24. Other sources simply say spring of 1839. Brown antedates the others and is the source for many subsequent histories.

[44] Brown, *Indian Wars*, 61; Sowell, *Rangers and Pioneers*, 54-55; Jenkins, *Recollections*, 56-57. Sowell says that there was another child, an infant son, also placed beneath the floorboards.

[45] Sowell, *Rangers and Pioneers*, 55. A year after the fight, Brown, *Indian Wars*, 61, listened to a speech in the Texas Congress that ended with what he termed "an eloquent apostrophe" to "Mrs. Coleman and her heroic boy."

[46] Brown, *Indian Wars*, 61; Sowell, *Rangers and Pioneers*, 56; Jenkins, *Recollections*, 57; Crosby, "Brushy Creek."

[47] Wilbarger, *Depredations*, 149-50; Crosby, Brushy Creek."

[48] Sowell, *Rangers and Pioneers*, 56-57; Crosby, "Brushy Creek."

[49] Jenkins, *Recollections*, 60, 231.

[50] Dolbeare, *Dolly Webster*, 2-3.

[51] Dolbeare, *Dolly Webster*, 3-7.

[52] Dolbeare, *Dolly Webster*, 8-12.

[53] Dolbeare, *Dolly Webster*, 13-19.

[54] Dolbeare, *Dolly Webster*, 20-23.

[55] Dolbeare, *Dolly Webster*, 24-26. Who "Mrs. Putman" was is not certain. The Putman captives were all children.

[56] Dolbeare, *Dolly Webster*, 27-33; Hunter, ed., "Memoirs of Mrs. Maverick," 6. Mary Maverick in Green, *Maverick*, 38, says that Webster walked into the town on March 26.

[57] Green, *Maverick*, 30-31, 38-42; Dolbeare, *Dolly Webster*, ix, 33-34. In 1840, a Texas newspaper assessed Webster's ordeal as "too painful and too horrid to bear description." In response, Anderson, *Conquest of Texas*, 183, incredibly asserted: "This, of course, was not true; Mrs Webster attested to the fact that she had been kindly treated." Anderson's reasoning is incomprehensible.

[58] Sowell, *Rangers and Pioneers*, 18; Webb and Carroll, *Handbook of Texas* 2, 310-11.

[59] Sowell, *Rangers and Pioneers*, 19; Brown, *Indian Wars*, 100; Wilbarger, *Depredations*, 398-99. The latter two sources say the two girls were daughters, about 10 and 12 years old. Sowell says one child was a daughter and the other a seven-year-old cousin.

[60] Wilbarger, *Depredations*, 399; Brown, *Indian Wars*, 101.

[61] Wilbarger, *Depredations*, 400-01; Brown, *Indian Wars*, 101; DeShields, *Border Wars*, 316; Sowell, *Rangers and Pioneers*, 19; Winfrey and Day, *Texas Indian Papers* 1, 192. Brown believes Lovicia was kept for nearly a year, was purchased by Choctaws, and retrieved by John Hunter. Wilbarger thought she was captive for six months, and DeShields guessed six months or a year.

[62] Brown, *Indian Wars*, 101; Sowell, *Rangers and Pioneers*, 19.

[63] Brice, *Comanche Raid*, 28-30, 95-96.

[64] Brice, *Comanche Raid*, 31.

[65] Brice, *Comanche Raid*, 32, 99; Wilbarger, *Depredations*, 27; "Linnville Raid of 1840," <u>Handbook of Texas Online</u>.

[66] Brice, *Comanche Raid*, 45.

[67] Wilbarger, *Depredations*, 32-33; DeShields, *Border Wars*, 301; Brice, *Comanche Raid*, 44-45. The fate of Juliet's black nurse is in question. Morrell said her body was found near Mrs. Crosby's, while another volunteer, Robert Hall, said he found a Negro woman and her child hiding in the grass, and she cried out, "Bless God, here is a white man once more."

[68] Wilbarger, *Depredations*, 33; Brice, *Comanche Raid*, 47, 99; "Linnville Raid of 1840," <u>Handbook of Texas Online</u>.

[69] Webb and Carroll, *Handbook of Texas* 1, 602, 689; DeShields, *Border Wars*, 361-62.

[70] Fehrenbach, *Lone Star*, 261; DeShields, *Border Wars*, 362.

[71] Hunter, ed., "Rebecca J. Fisher," 16, says another son, Thomas, died prior to the attack.

[72] DeShields, *Border Wars*, 362.

84

[73] The year of the Gilleland capture is disputed. Webb and Carroll, *Handbook of Texas* 1, 602, and the <u>Handbook of Texas Online</u>, indicate it was in the spring of 1840. The military situation, the reports of the volunteer soldiers, and the timing with Sarah Hibbins's experience, however, indicate the raid occurred in the spring of 1842.

[74] DeShields, *Border Wars*, 174, 360-63; Hunter, ed., "Rebecca J. Fisher," 16.

[75] DeShields, *Border Wars*, 174, 361; Webb and Carroll, *Handbook of Texas* 1, 602-03.

[76] Wilbarger, *Depredations*, 141-42; Jenkins, *Recollections*, 163-64.

[77] Webb and Carroll, *Handbook of Texas* 1, 85; Brown, *Indian Wars*, 101; Wilbarger, *Depredations*, 139. William is sometimes referred to as Thomas, and Jane is sometimes called Emma. The date of this raid has been recorded as occurring in the summer of 1842, although correspondence between Indian agents and superintendents clearly indicate the raid was in November 1844.

[78] Brown, *Indian Wars*, 101-02.

[79] Brown, *Indian Wars*, 102; Wilbarger, *Depredations*, 140; Jenkins, *Recollections*, 164-65. Emma's skeleton was later found near the home of George W. Davis.

[80] Winfrey and Day, *Texas Indian Papers* 2, 131.

[81] Winfrey and Day, *Texas Indian Papers* 2, 131, 144, 152, 158, 161.

[82] Winfrey and Day, *Texas Indian Papers* 2, 172-73; Richardson, *Comanche Barrier*, 61, 216n23. The date of the conference is listed as either the 10th or 19th. Superintendent Western later wrote that the Simpson boy was in captivity for two months and seven days, *Texas Indian Papers* 2, 192, which would make January 10 his recovery date.

[83] Winfrey and Day, *Texas Indian Papers* 2, 173-74, 179-80; Richardson, *Comanche Barrier*, 61.

[84] Winfrey and Day, *Texas Indian Papers* 2, 176-77, 191-93. Several accounts—Brown, *Indian Wars*, 102; DeShields, *Border Wars*, 365; Wilbarger, *Depredations*, 140; Jenkins, *Recollections*, 164n7—all state that the boy was ransomed in New Mexico a year to 18 months after his capture. Correspondence among those involved in his recovery clearly shows the captivity to be less than three months. Brown's history was the first to give an incorrect time frame, and the error was repeated when subsequent chroniclers uncritically accepted the word of their predecessors.

[85] Winfrey and Day, *Texas Indian Papers* 2, 298-99; Richardson, *Comanche Barrier*, 62, 216n33.

Chapter Three

WAGON TRAINS, EMIGRANTS AND TRAVELERS

I will fight as long as I can, and if I see I am about to be taken, I will kill myself. I do not care to die, but it would be worse than death to me to be taken a captive among them. — Olive Oatman

Every indignity was offered to my person which the imagination can conceive. Nothing could soften them into pity, and I ardently desired death that my torments might come to an end. — Jane Wilson

I was subject to their passions and lusts, and the most brutal treatment that mortal being could be subjected to. — Nancy Morton

Although the isolated pioneer cabin in the wilderness was sometimes a romantic and idyllic setting for many a novel, it was often a dangerous place to be. Emigrants and travelers were somewhat safer, given that they were on the move, traveled often in groups, were comparatively well armed, and usually more alert to trail dangers. The much more numerous, isolated cabins were easier targets than prepared wagon trains. Even so, traveling the roads to California, Oregon, or a hundred destinations in between could be quite perilous, especially when the numbers of travelers were few or they let their guard down.

In 1848 in Manco Burro Pass, on an alternate route of the Mountain Branch of the Santa Fe Trail, Jicarillas attacked a small wagon train. They killed four, wounded eight, scattered the remaining survivors, and captured Mary Tharp (6) and James Tharp (4). About three months later, Taos merchants ransomed them back for $160, but Mary died shortly afterwards. Along the Oregon Trail in 1856, Cheyennes attacked a small four-wagon train on the Platte, thirty-three miles northeast of Fort Kearny. Among the passengers was Almon Babbitt, Secretary of Utah Territory. The Indians killed two men and one child, and carried off a Mrs. Wilson, the mother of the slain child. She too was killed when she could not ride fast enough to keep up with them. Four days later, on August 30, Cheyennes attacked an emigrant party at Cottonwood Springs, eighty miles west of Fort Kearny. They killed Mrs. William Schevekendeck and carried off her 4-year-old boy. On September 6, Cheyennes attacked a Mormon train returning east and killed two men, one woman, one child, and captured another woman. On October 21, 1867, Paiutes attacked a wagon carrying Sergeants Nichols and Denoille, and Mrs. Denoille, from Camp Lyon to Boise, Idaho Territory. They killed Sergeant Denoille and captured his pregnant wife. A search went on for six months before Mrs. Denoille's fate was learned. The Indians had kept her only a short time before crushing her head with a giant rock.[1]

Of the families detailed below, the Sagers almost completed their crossing of the Oregon Trail when a family disaster deposited them at the Whitman Mission. Ann White and Nancy Morton made the mistake of accompanying their husbands on business trips, while Larcena Page erred in going to her husband's lumber mill. Mrs. Snyder tried to visit her husband at a fort. Nelson Lee was riding herd on cattle, while Dorothy Field was just out riding. The Oatmans, Van Ornums, Kellys, Fletchers, and Germans were moving west, while the Wilsons and Blinns were heading back east. They all had close encounters with Indians.

* * *

CATHERINE, ELIZABETH, MATILDA, HANNAH, AND HENRIETTA (ROSANNA) SAGER, ESTHER BEWLEY, AND MARY MARSH CASON
Washington, November 29, 1847

Heinrich (Henry) Sager was born in 1805 in Loudon County, Virginia. Naomi Carny was born in Virginia in 1807, the daughter of a Baptist minister. They married in May 1830, lived in Ohio for a time, and moved to Missouri in 1838. Henry had a farm in Platte County and was a jack-of-all-trades. Naomi did fine needlework and gave Sunday school lessons to the children.

In 1843 the talk of the town was Marcus Whitman, a missionary, who had led a group of emigrants over the Rocky Mountains to Oregon. Henry was restless and Naomi had heard of Oregon's healthy climate, so they made plans to raise their family in the idyllic Willamette Valley. In April 1844, the Sagers packed up their belongings and their children, John Carny (13), Francisco "Frank" (12), Catherine (9), Elizabeth Marie (7), Matilda Jane

(5), and Hannah Louise (3), and joined a wagon train. The large group consisted of more than 700 pioneers in three trains under Cornelius Gilliam, John Thorp, and Nathaniel Ford. The Sagers joined the company of William Shaw (Gilliam's brother-in-law). They left on May 19, 1844.[2]

On the night of May 21, Sac Indians raided the encampment and stole more than 800 cattle, nearly the entire herd. The next day, however, a posse under Gilliam recovered all but six of the animals. On May 31, on the South Fork of the Nemaha River near present-day Seneca, Kansas, Naomi gave birth to Rosanna. Naomi was ill for two days following the birth and the train remained camped while she regained her strength.

On June 7, they camped in a driving rainstorm by the North Fork Black Vermillion River. With little luck keeping warm and dry, Naomi and Henry became ill. On June 15, with the river still flooding, the company had to retreat almost a days' travel to escape the river's wrath.[3]

In early July, the train reached the Platte River, and the emigrants spent a few days hunting bison. The afternoon of 1 August, Catherine jumped down from the wagon, but she fell beneath the wagon wheels and shattered her left leg. Henry Sager set her leg and she was restricted to the wagon for the remainder of the journey. The train reached Fort Laramie that night.

Traveling beyond Laramie, John, Frank, and Henry became ill with "camp fever" (probably typhoid fever). The two boys recovered butHenry Sager died on August 28, after pleading with Captain Shaw to see that his family reached Oregon. He was buried along the west bank of the Green River. Doctor Theophilus Degen told Naomi he would see they got to the Willamette Valley.[4]

Tragically, Naomi began to manifest symptoms of typhoid, with fever and delirium. During one of her sane moments she said her farewells to her children and asked Doctor Degen and Captain Shaw to see them to the Whitman Mission. Naomi Sager died September 25, and was buried at Pilgrim Springs along the Snake River.

Degen and William Shaw and his wife, Sally, cared for the children. The baby was passed among the women of the train who acted as wet nurses for the infant. In mid-October they arrived at Grande Ronde, where one of the Sager girls walked too close to the campfire and her dress caught fire. Doctor Degen extinguished the flames, saving her life, but badly burning his hands. Soon afterwards Captain Shaw heard crying one night and discovered little Hannah had climbed from the wagon, was unable to get back in, and was nearly frozen. He placed her in bed between Doctor Degen and her brother John, where the body warmth revived her.[5]

After crossing the Blue Mountains Captain Shaw rode to the Whitman Mission at Waiilatpu, to see if the Whitmans would take the Sager children. About November 3, Doctor Degen took the six oldest children to their new home. Baby Rosanna remained in the train with a wet nurse and was brought to the mission a week later. Marcus and Narcissa Whitman decided to adopt them all.[6]

The Whitmans were assembling quite an extended family. In March 1837, Narcissa had a daughter, Alice Clarissa, but she drowned in the millpond when she was two years old and Narcissa never bore any other children. Instead, the Whitmans cared for Perrin B. Whitman, Marcus's nephew, Helen Mar Meek, trapper Joe Meek's daughter, David M. Cortez, Mary Ann Bridger, daughter of the famous frontiersman Jim Bridger, and the Sagers, building their "family" to eleven children.[7]

The children were well cared for by the Whitmans. They received an education and religious instruction, and seemed to adjust to their new home. They asked Narcissa to change Rosanna's name to a name that would honor their parents, and Rosanna became Henrietta Naomi Sager.

The Whitman Mission became a haven for travelers. A situation similar to the Sagers brought the Marshes to Waiilatpu in October 1847. Mary E. Marsh was born October 8, 1836, in Springfield, Illinois. Her father, Walter Marsh, ran a farm on the Sangamon River, but by April 1847, they had caught "Oregon fever" and joined a wagon train. Mrs. Marsh became ill near Bear River and died at Soda Springs, where she was buried along the trail. Walter Marsh decided to winter at the Whitman's, and Marcus hired him as a gristmill operator. Mary's older brother continued on to the Willamette Valley. Mary and Walter lived in an adobe structure called the emigrant house, where they shared space with six other families.[8]

Marcus and Narcissa Whitman were at the mission to spread the Protestant gospel to the Cayuse Indians, who were not totally receptive to the idea. Marcus recruited some of the Indians to help construct the mission buildings, which was contrary to their custom, where women built the lodges. The Cayuse considered gift giving an important part of life, while the Whitmans saw it as extortion. Religion and domestic life were inseparable to the Cayuse, yet Narcissa did not allow the Indians into her home for religious services or to eat. In a letter dated February 2, 1842,

Author's photo
Whitman Mission site near Walla Walla, Washington.

Narcissa said the Indians were heathens who "had been serving the devil faithfully." In another letter she explained that the Indians were "so filthy they make a great deal of cleaning wherever they go, and this wears out a woman very fast. We must clean after them, for we have come to elevate them and not to suffer ourselves to sink down to their standards."[9]

It was a strange attitude for a missionary. The Cayuse believed the Whitmans cared more for emigrants than for them. In the fall of 1847, a measles epidemic struck, and Marcus treated both Indians and whites. Most of the white children survived, but half of the adult Cayuse and nearly all their children died.

Jesuits at Forts Walla Walla and Colville told the Indians that there were great differences between Protestants and Catholics, with Protestants falling away from God and into Hell. When the Protestant missionaries Henry and Eliza Spalding, who had a mission with the Nez Perce at Lapwai, heard about the Jesuits interference, they told a contrary tale that Catholics were on a direct road to Hell. Naturally, the Indians were confused. About this time, Joe Lewis, a mixed-blood, began spreading rumors that Marcus was poisoning the Indians in order to acquire their land. Nicolas Finley, another mixed-blood who lived near the mission, supported Lewis's accusations, and his house became a popular meeting place for the malcontents. Making matters worse was a Cayuse custom that made it acceptable for a family of a sick person to kill the medicine man if the shaman's patient died. The practice was to have a tragic impact.[10]

On November 28, 1847, Marcus Whitman responded to a plea from Five Crows and Tauwitwai for medical aid at the Indian encampment at Umatilla, about thirty miles away. Henry Spalding was at Waiilatpu delivering his daughter to the Whitmans for winter schooling, and he accompanied Marcus. When their work was over, Chief Stickus warned Marcus that the Cayuse were planning to attack, and Joe Lewis was plotting his death. Spalding had fallen from his horse on the way to Umatilla and he rested an extra night at the Catholic mission, but Marcus decided to hurry back. He arrived at the mission after dark, tended to Helen Meek, who was very ill, and then discussed what he had heard with Narcissa. They decided to remain and try to keep peace with the Cayuse.[11]

The next morning, November 29, Marcus officiated at a funeral for another Indian child killed by the measles. He was apprehensive, for only a few Indians attended, and he believed something sinister was afoot. After lunch, Narcissa was bathing the Sager girls in the parlor when the two Cayuse chiefs, Teloukite and Tomahas, entered the mission kitchen and asked for some medicine. Marcus complied, but Teloukite began to argue with him. Suddenly, Tomahas attacked him from behind, driving a tomahawk into his skull. One of the Indians then shot him in the neck. Mary Ann Bridger was in the kitchen. She fled out the north door and ran around the building screaming, "They have killed father!" John Sager was also in the kitchen. He tried to fire a pistol at an Indian about to club Whitman, but was restrained and shot a moment after Marcus was struck down.[12]

The slaughter outside of the mission house began at the sound of the first shot. Indians milling around the mission yard watching the butchers cutting up two cows, dropped their blankets and revealed their tomahawks and guns.

Catherine Sager watched from the window as Judge L. W. Saunders struggled with some warriors. "I looked till my heart sickened at the sight," she said. "Mr. Saunders wrestled for life with those ruthless murderers, and they with their butcher knives trying to cut his throat. . . he was overpowered. His body was pierced with several balls when he fell. They beat his head until it was mashed to pieces."

Jacob Hoffman, one of the butchers, struck one of the Indians in the foot with his ax before he fell. They disemboweled him.

From the upper floor of the emigrant house, Mary Marsh (11) saw Hoffman slaughtered, but she was spared the sight of her father being murdered. Walter Marsh was shot at the gristmill where he worked. Isaac Gilliland (Gillmore, Gillian) was sewing in his room when Indians shot him, but he escaped to the emigrant house, and hid under a bed, but died about midnight. Nathan S. Kimball, another butcher, was wounded, suffered a broken arm, and escaped to the mission house. Andrew Rodgers was shot in the stomach and tomahawked in the head while near the river, but escaped to the mission house where Narcissa let him in.

When the Indians ran out of the kitchen to hunt other victims, Narcissa pulled Marcus into the living room, and a group of women and children flooded in, including Mrs. Hays, Mrs. Hall, and Mrs. Saunders. Narcissa saw Joe Lewis in the yard and accused him of starting the uprising. While she called out, a Cayuse, Frank Iskalome, shot her through the breast. Elizabeth Sager was standing next to Narcissa and heard her say, "I am wounded; hold me tight." The women helped her into a chair, while she prayed that, "God would save her children that soon were to be orphaned and that her mother would be given the strength to bear the news of her death."[13]

Narcissa, Kimball, Rodgers, and the children went to an upstairs bedroom. Esther Lorinda Bewley (22) was upstairs, having felt ill that morning. Captain John William Bewley had stopped at the mission that fall with his sick daughter and son. Marcus agreed to treat them, and she agreed to stay if her brother, Crockett, stayed with her. Mr. and Mrs. Bewley went on to the Willamette Valley, where their grown children were to join them in the spring. Until then, Lorinda helped Narcissa with the housework.[14]

The old Cayuse, Tamsucky, convinced them that the Indians would burn down the house, so Rodgers, Narcissa, and a few others attempted to flee. Mr. Kimball, Mary Ann Bridger, the Sager girls, and a few sick children, including Helen Mar Meek and Hannah Louise Sager, stayed inside. Joe Lewis came over to help them out. They placed Narcissa on a settee and carried her outside, but once in the yard, Lewis dropped the settee and nearby Indians shot Rodgers and Narcissa. She rolled into the mud and one Indian lifted her head and whipped her face with a riding crop. She died quickly, while Rodgers succumbed that night. Marcus Whitman lived until nine that evening.

The other children who were not suffering from the measles were in the schoolhouse, where Frank Sager (15) told them to hide in the loft. Joe Lewis and some other Indians entered the school and called to Frank, but he did not answer. Lewis called to mixed-bloods John Manson (16) and Stephen Manson (17) and they responded. He told everyone to come down. They took the children to the mission house kitchen, and while the Indians ate, they taunted the children as to what they might do to them. Undecided, they hauled them to the mission's Indian room and shut them in. Frank Sager finally decided to come out of hiding and Joe Lewis shot him dead. In the Indian room and unknown to them, Josiah and Marguerite Osborn and their three children, Nancy, John, and Alexander, were hiding beneath the floorboards.[15]

Upstairs in the mission house they were all expecting to be incinerated, but after dark, the Indians left. Elizabeth Sager had run back upstairs during the chaos and joined the frightened group. The hungry and thirsty children spent most of the night crying. In the morning, Catherine Sager bound Kimball's broken arm and he went down to the river for water, where the Indians killed him. Inside, Joe Stanfield, a French-Canadian employed by Whitman, ordered the children to stop crying or they would anger the Indians. Stanfield and Catherine Sager (13) talked the children into going to the emigrant house. Helen Mar Meek (10), who was too ill to walk, screamed at the Indians who surrounded her bed.[16]

The Cayuse set the mixed-blood Manson boys and David M. Cortez free, leaving about forty-nine captives at the mission (see Appendix 1). On Tuesday, November 30, Stanfield dug a three-foot deep grave, wide enough for the victims to be buried side by side, and on Wednesday, Father Brouillet arrived and helped bury them.

Then measles began to take a toll on the white children, which should have convinced the Indians that Whitman was not poisoning them. On Sunday, December 5, Hannah Louise Sager (6) died in her sleep of complications of hypothermia and measles. Helen Mar Meek died three days later. Two young men, Crockett Bewley and Amos Sales, had been sick before the massacre but were still alive. On December 13, the Indians congregated around their beds. Catherine Sager saw them pull out the wooden bed slats and beat their heads in. Bewley jumped up, but was pushed to the floor and pummeled. They dragged Sales outdoors and buried their tomahawks into his skull. The Indians stripped off the dead men's clothing and walked away.[17]

Each morning the captives had to prepare breakfast for the Indians, but they feared poisoning and would not eat until the captives tasted each dish. The captives were constantly in fear for their lives. Old Tamsucky came a few days after the killings and searched the house for Lorinda Bewley. She was ill and in bed when he found her, but he began to fondle her. She sprang up and sat beside the cook stove, but the old man cornered her and told her she must become his wife. She refused, so he forcefully dragged her toward the door. Mrs. Canfield intervened, and Tamsucky struck her in the breast with such force that it knocked her breath out. Tamsucky pulled Lorinda outside and tried to force her onto his horse. Lorinda screamed and resisted until he violently threw her to the ground and told her to return to the house. Inside, Mrs. Saunders sent Eliza Spalding and Catherine Sager for medicine for Lorinda.[18]

A few days later an Indian appeared and told Lorinda she must come with him. He successfully got her out of the house, weeping and resisting, and took her to his master, Five Crows. The next day they reached at the Catholic priests' house on the Umatilla, where Five Crows arrived to take her. Despite pleading with Vicars Blanchet and Brouillet to protect her, they took no action. Five Crows took Lorinda Bewley every night, and sent her to the priests in the daytime. Even in her weak and sickly state, the chief continually raped her. Brouillet had the audacity to ask the suffering girl how she liked her new husband. The priests' conduct was inexcusable and they never offered any explanation for their actions.[19]

After Lorinda was taken away, Indians told all the captive females that it would be better to voluntarily become the wives of young chiefs than to be carried off by some disreputable vagabonds. A Cayuse named Clark, a son of Chief Teloukite, chose Mary Smith (15), and a Cayuse named Frank, who had killed Nathan Kimble, took his daughter, Susan (16). Joseph Smith was threatened with death if he did not "persuade" Mary to become Clark's wife, and his daughter complied to save her father's life. Susan wept openly and Mary simply blushed. Edward, another son of Teloukite, asked Catherine Sager to be his wife, but she said she was too young and refused. Clark soon gave up Mary, but his brother Edward took his place.[20]

The captives' days were spent working for the Indians, and they were in constant dread. Mary Marsh said that they were "expecting anytime to share the same fate of the others, but we were spared—only to endure the fear, suspense, and cruel treatment that an Indian is capable of inflicting."

One night a band of renegade Cayuse led by Istulest, entered the emigrant house and harassed the captives. Istulest dragged

Catherine Sager into a room that held only sleeping children, where another Indian said she must become his wife. When she refused, he forced her into the children's bed. Catherine kicked him, ran off, and Mary Smith hid her. The Indians searched for her unsuccessfully and left. A short time later they returned. Catherine hid under the stairs but they found her. Again, the persistent young Indian sat by her and tried to convince her to marry him. Finally becoming frustrated, he said he would whip her if she did not do as he ordered. When he grabbed her, she fought with all her might, kicking and biting. The angry Indian stopped fighting and tried to reason with her again, but Catherine said she hated him. With that answer, the young man tried to carry her outside. Finally, the commotion awoke Joe Stanfield, and he told Mr. Smith, and Mr. Young, and they chased the amorous Indian out.[21]

Mrs. Saunders baked some peach pies and a Cayuse called Old Beardy ate voluminous amounts, went home and began to vomit. He said he was poisoned, told his comrades, and they decided the captives should be killed. Luckily, an Indian woman interceded and convinced Old Beardy it was his own gluttony that had caused the adverse reaction. When the Indians held a council to decide the captives' fate, the vote was evenly split. Tamsucky argued that they must be killed, while a Nez Perce named Old Jimmie, argued convincingly that they should be allowed to live. In the end, the decision was to send the captives to the Willamette Valley in the spring.

On December 19, 1847, Peter Skene Ogden of the Hudson Bay Company brought trading goods to Fort Walla Walla and requested a meeting with the Cayuse chiefs. In council three days later, Ogden made his pitch for surrendering the captives in exchange for money and supplies. The Indians agreed to deliver them in six days, but for a price of twelve guns, 600 rounds of ammunition, twelve flints, sixty-two blankets, sixty-three cotton shirts, and thirty-seven pounds of tobacco. While Ogden bargained for the hostages, a different band of Indians went to Waiilatpu, seized the children, and threatened to kill them. One of them grabbed Matilda Sager. The warrior, she said, "started to thrust a tomahawk into my brains. Just then the Indians outside began laughing and the brutes, on murder bent, concluded the noise was all a joke and did not hurt any of us."[22]

On Christmas Day the captives learned that Ogden had bought their freedom. Early that evening an old Indian named Puke delivered Lorinda Bewley to the emigrant house. Tamsucky tried to lure her away, but she emphatically told him she was not interested in his proposal. Edward tried to persuade Mary Smith to stay with him, and perhaps seeing a way to get revenge, she told him that if he loved her he must come with her. He replied, "White man shoot me if I go with you," which shows he did have a very good understanding of the consequences.

The captives were delivered to Ogden at Walla Walla, and the next morning the Indians came for their payment. Mary Smith, Catherine Sager, and some of the others were locked in a room to prevent the Indians from trying to recapture them. Edward tried three times to see Mary Smith, but she refused. She acted as his "wife" only to save her father and herself; sometimes at night she "wept over her disgrace."[23]

Catherine Sager later wrote: "In giving a history I have had to touch upon a delicate subject—one that I have always avoided in conversation, namely, the treatment of the young women by the Indians. I have endeavored to present them in such a manner as to spare the feelings of those concerned. For this reason I have not related many things that would be interesting. I think it never before appeared upon the annals of American history where female captives were treated with like brutality. We were subject to continual insult while we stayed with them, harassed by fear and exposed to their ill treatment."[24]

On January 1, 1848, Henry Spalding's family arrived at the fort under a guard of forty Nez Perces, for it had been feared that the Cayuse would murder them. Mrs. Spalding was reunited with her daughter, Eliza, who appeared a wasted skeleton of her former self. The ex-captives began their trek to Fort Vancouver, led by Peter Ogden and accompanied by Vicar Blanchet, three priests, and the Manson boys. Priests kept David Cortez at Walla Walla. Henry Spalding and John M. Stanley, an artist and traveler, looked after the Sager girls on the journey to Fort Vancouver. An Indian attack was still feared and Ogden watched over them like a hawk. On the trip, Lorinda Bewley learned that her father had died on the Willamette.[25]

At The Dalles, Mary Marsh's brother came to meet her and took her to his home on the Willamette. The main party reached Vancouver on January 6, where several of the army wives wanted to adopt the Sager girls, but Ogden said it was his duty to deliver them to Oregon provisional Governor George Abernethy. John Stanley bought calico for the Sager girls to make dresses. In Portland, volunteers fired a salute to them and caused Matilda Sager to believe that Indians were attacking. Cornelius Gilliam, who had captained one of the wagon trains back in 1844, met the Sager girls. Some of the captives had friends to meet them and the rest were kept until the governor found places for them.

Lorinda Bewley left the Sagers at Portland, in the company of William Chapman, who would later marry her. They moved to Yamhill County, Oregon, where she lived with her family until her death. The Spaldings and the Sagers went with Abernethy to Oregon City where neighbors took them in. Henrietta and Catherine Sager stayed with Reverend William Roberts. The Morgan Kees Family took Henrietta to live with them for three years. Catherine married Clark S. Pringle in Salem, in 1851, and Henrietta lived with them for a time. She joined a troupe of traveling entertainers led by her Uncle Solomon Sager, and was on the road and away from her sisters for a number of years. Henrietta was married twice, to a Mr. Cooper and a Mr. Sterling, and was shot and killed at Red Bluff, California, in 1870, when an assailant, aiming at her husband, hit her instead.[26]

Mary Marsh lived with her brother until 1849, when he headed for the California gold fields. He left Mary with Mrs. Asa L. Lovejoy, who cared for her as a daughter. Mary married James Pulliam Cason in Oregon City in 1853, and they had ten children. James died in 1887, and Mary died at Spray, Oregon, on April 6, 1907, at age 70. Catherine Sager Pringle lived with her husband, who became a Methodist minister and practiced in the Willamette Valley. They had eight children. In 1888, they moved to Colfax, Washington, and when Clark Pringle retired in 1891, they moved to Spokane to live with their youngest daughter, Lucia Pringle Collins. Catherine died on August 10, 1910, at age 75.[27]

Elizabeth Sager lived with six families in seven years after her release. She went from the home of William Johnson to Mrs. Howland, then to Jacob Robb's. When he decided to take his family to California, she stayed with William Willson. They were cruel to her so she went to live with the Parrish Family. Matilda and Mrs. Parrish apparently had many arguments, and the woman finally demanded that Matilda leave. She then joined her sister, Henrietta, at Catherine and Clark Pringle's home. Elizabeth Sager married William Fletcher Helm in 1855. She died at Portland, on July 19, 1925, at age 88.[28]

Matilda Sager lived with the Spaldings for four months. When they moved to Forest Grove, Oregon, the Geiger Family took her in. In 1855, she married her first husband, Lewis Mackey Hazlett. They had five children. Hazlett died of cancer in 1862. Five years later, Matilda married his partner, Mat Fultz, and they had six daughters. They finally moved to Farmington, Washington, and ran a hotel, a livery, a furniture store, and a funeral home. Mr. Fultz died a year after the move. Six years after his death, Matilda married David Delaney. She began to suffer from crippling rheumatism. On the 50th anniversary of the Whitman Massacre she attended the dedication of the monument in memory of Doctor Whitman and his fellow martyrs. Many bones were discovered while leveling the monument site and Matilda assisted in identifying them. Doctor and Mrs. Whitman's skulls were identified from large eye sockets (attributed to Narcissa), and from the gold fillings in Marcus's back teeth. Additional physical peculiarities helped identify the skeletons of Walter Marsh, Jacob Hoffman, Isaac Gilliland, and Frank Sager. In 1916, Matilda attended a reunion of the Oregon Pioneer Society and the Indian Volunteers of Portland, returning once more to the massacre site. Matilda died in 1928, at age 90, the last of the Sager children.[29]

ANN DUNN WHITE AND VIRGINIA WHITE
New Mexico, October 24, 1849

One of the most famous merchants on the Santa Fe Trail in the 1840s was Francis X. Aubry. His fast mule trains and quick turn-around times were legendary. Joining up with one of Aubrey's expresses heading for Santa Fe in September 1849, was merchant James M. White, who had opened up trading houses in El Paso and Santa Fe the year before. In spite of the danger, White brought along his wife Ann, and his daughter Virginia (10). His employees, servants, and traveling partners manned thirteen goods-laden wagons. The train left Kansas City, Missouri, about September 15, and made good time across the dry prairie. On the Cimarron Cutoff in New Mexico Territory, snow and cold weather slowed them down, and on October 23, the impatient James White left his wagons behind with Aubrey and pulled ahead in two carriages with his family and five other men.[30]

They rode right into a burning powder keg. Jicarilla Apaches and soldiers from Fort Marcy had been fighting for most of the year. Troops attacked a Jicarilla village in April; Indians raided settlers along the Rayado in May and June; and Lieutenant Ambrose E. Burnside, 3rd Artillery, later to be a Union general in the Civil War, led a detachment of soldiers against a Jicarilla camp near Las Vegas in August, killing fourteen and capturing six. Among the prisoners was Jicarilla Chief Lobo Blanco's daughter. The Indians raided Chaparito in September, and the soldiers chased them down again, killing five, including Chief Petrillo, and capturing his widow. By October, raids were occurring almost daily.[31]

In late September, Lieutenant Burnside unsuccessfully chased a band of Jicarillas east to the Canadian River, but figured they had gone back into the Sangre de Cristos. If some Jicarillas were hiding in the mountains, others were still biding their time on the eastern New Mexican plains. Late on October 24, Lobo Blanco and his warriors spied two carriages approaching, and probably could not believe that the whites could be so foolish as to ride the trail in such small numbers. The whites stopped to make camp for the evening. On the Santa Fe Trail near the Point of Rocks, their journey came to an end.[32]

The Indians swept down on the little camp. Ben Bushman, a mulatto servant, and a Mexican were killed first, and the Mexican fell dead into the campfire. The rest tried to run, but didn't get far. James White was killed, as was Aubrey employee William Callaway, and two Germans, including a Mr. Lawberger. Lobo Blanco took Ann White, her daughter Virginia, and a female Negro servant prisoner. He had his revenge for the capture of his daughter. Not content with this coup, Lobo Blanco laid out the bodies in line on the roadside next to the carriages, using them as bait, while his men concealed themselves behind a nearby hill. Shortly after, a small party of New Mexican buffalo hunters came by and investigated. As they examined the bodies and peered into the carriages, the Apaches struck again, killing some and wounding a Mexican boy while the others sped away. Lobo Blanco's warriors then plundered and destroyed the carriages, took their prisoners, and left the area.

The next night, another small party, including Charles Spencer, Alexander Barclay, George Simpson, and Isaac Adamson, passed by the massacre site. In the pale moonlight they noticed carriage parts broken in pieces and saw the bodies scattered on the ground. White's body was lanced several times and wolves had eaten the lower half. A little rocking chair, probably Virginia's, was the only remaining undamaged object. The eerie scene spooked them, and they imagined "the hot breath of the Indians might be near enough to be scented," so they vacated the area as fast as they could, hardly stopping to rest in a seventy-eight-hour ride to Las Vegas. On the way they talked to a small party of Pueblo Indians, who claimed they had just been in camp with a band of Apaches where they saw a white woman and child. Francis Aubry passed the site next, and he hurried on. Word spread from Las Vegas to Santa Fe, where Indian Agent James S. Calhoun was deeply concerned

Author's photo
Point of Rocks, New Mexico. Capture site of Virginia and Ann White.

and wrote to Washington, that if the "two captives could not be liberated, it is to be hoped they are dead."[33]

In November, Captain William N. Grier, 1st Dragoons, organized a rescue expedition. With Antoine Leroux and Robert Fisher as guides, forty volunteers under Captain Valdez, and Company I of the 1st Dragoons, Grier left Taos for the eastern plains, stopping in Rayado to pick up Dick Wootton and Christopher "Kit" Carson for added measure. They went east on the Santa Fe Trail to Point of Rocks, and on November 9, Carson found the bodies and wreckage, with trunks broken open, harnesses cut up, and everything destroyed that could not be carried away.

"We tracked them for ten or twelve days over the most difficult trail that I have ever followed," Carson said. The Indians broke up into groups of two or three and then met again at appointed places. At almost every camp Carson "found some of Mrs. White's clothing." The trail led south to the breaks of the Canadian River, then fifteen miles south of Tucumcari Butte. Carson saw the camp early in the morning of November 17, and he motioned for Captain Grier to follow him with the dragoons. Carson rode ahead, but no one followed. Antoine Leroux, Carson's rival, thought the Indians would want to parley, and he convinced Captain Grier to halt until they could make contact. The Jicarillas, however, seeing the soldiers hesitate, began packing up and leaving as fast as they could. When Grier realized his mistake, he moved his men forward. The retreating Indians sent a few long-range rifle shots in his direction, and one struck Grier in the chest, but the nearly spent ball hit his heavy coat and folded up gauntlets, merely knocking the wind out of him. When he recovered his senses, Grier ordered a charge, but it was too late.[34]

The Indians made their escape, except for one warrior who was shot down as he ran across a creek, and two or three bewildered Indian children left behind. One of the dragoons, James A. Bennett, said he saw Mrs. White "trying to disengage herself from an old squaw," who was trying to get her up on a mule. Ann White broke away, but before she could go very far, the Indian woman "drew her bow and arrow, aimed, and Mrs. White with a shriek fell, pierced to the heart when we were within 15 paces of her." The Indian woman was promptly shot dead.[35]

Carson came upon White's body about 200 yards beyond the campsite. She was found, he said, "still perfectly warm. She had been shot through the heart with an arrow not five minutes before." He thought she had seen them coming and tried to escape. "I am certain that if the Indians had been charged immediately on our arrival," Carson said, "she would have been saved." When he looked at her face, he saw the effects even a short Indian captivity could produce. She was "wasted, emaciated, the victim of a foul disease, and bore the sorrows of a life-long agony on her face," Carson said. Her treatment "was so brutal and horrible that she could not possibly have lived very long." Bennett recorded that White's body "was literally covered with marks of blows and scratches. Her feet were all torn and cut from traveling. . . . Over her corpse we swore vengeance upon her persecutors."

In the deserted camp, soldiers found a book and showed it to Carson. It was a dime novel thriller of the later Ned Buntline-type, and the hero was none other than Kit Carson. The famous scout was illiterate, and a soldier read him some passages. It was, he said, "the first of the kind I had ever seen," and represented him as "slaying Indians by the hundred." Sadly, Carson later thought that Mrs. White must have read it, and imagined that someday soon he would come to rescue her, just as in the novel. Instead, he had failed her, and the knowledge of that forever weighed on his mind. He wanted to attack sooner, and he lamented, "They would not listen to me and they failed. I will say no more regarding this matter, nor attach any blame to any particular person, for I presume the consciences of those who were the cause of this tragedy have severely punished them ere this."[36]

Grier camped on the battleground. That night, dragoons heard a noise in the brush nearby and investigated. They found an Indian child, about eight months old, strapped to a board used for carrying infants. Bennett picked him up, but an old soldier stepped up and said, "Let me see that brat." He took a heavy stone, tied it to the board, and threw the entire rig into the river. His comment was, "You're a little feller now but will make a big Injun bye and bye." Bennett may have been stunned, but he made no protest. The next morning the dragoons burned the camp and marched for home, encountering what Carson called, "the severest snow storm I ever experienced." One man froze to death before they reached Las Vegas.[37]

The bodies of Virginia White and the servant were not found. In Santa Fe, Agent Calhoun contracted with Encarnacion Garcia and Auguste Lacome to find the Apaches and rescue the captives. Garcia was gone for two months, traveling as far south as the Guadalupe Mountains. He found an Apache camp, probably Mescaleros, who heard that the child had been killed with the mother. Lacome went north to talk to the Utes. They heard a similar story: the child was killed during the attack and her body thrown in the river. The Negro servant was unable to keep up with the fast traveling Jicarillas and was killed shortly after leaving Point of Rocks.[38]

There were reward offers. Mrs. White's brother, Isaac B. Dunn, offered $1,000 for the safe return of Virginia White. In 1850, the U.S. Congress authorized Agent Calhoun to offer the Indians $1,500 for the safe delivery of the girl, promising chastisement by the soldiers if they would not release her. As late as 1858, Brigadier General John Garland declared that he had been trying to locate and recover the child for five years, but all the information he received was that the child was dead. As agent to the Jicarillas and Utes, Carson could never learn what happened to her. Lobo Blanco once attended a peace conference with Carson, in which the agent was certain that the Jicarilla chief wore a necklace made out of the teeth of the late James White. Since it was a peace council, Carson could do nothing. Lobo Blanco got his reward in March 1854, however, when he was killed in battle with Lieutenant David Bell and a company of 2nd Dragoons. Bell and his men put several bullets into the chief, but he would not die until a dragoon "got a great rock and mashed his head." Two years after her capture, a girl matching Virginia's description was seen living with the Comanches, but her ultimate fate remains unknown.[39]

OLIVE ANN AND MARY ANN OATMAN
Arizona, March 19, 1851

Royse Oatman had been involved in several unsuccessful farming and business operations in Pennsylvania and Illinois. After injuring himself on his farm near Fulton, Illinois,

Royse answered the call of Mormon Reverend James Brewster, to establish a new Zion near the junction of the Gila and Colorado Rivers in New Mexico Territory (now Arizona). Royse and Mary Ann Sperry Oatman, with their seven children, Lucy (17), Lorenzo (16), Olive Ann (14), Royse Jr. (10), Mary Ann (7), Charity Ann (4), and Roland (1), left Illinois in the spring of 1850, to rendezvous with the gathering colony in Independence, Missouri. There were fifty-two emigrants, including the Oatman, Thompson, Lane, Kelly, Wilder, and Brinshall Families. On August 10, 1850, they set out on the Santa Fe Trail.[40]

Disagreements over religious practices and resting on the Sabbath wasted time and threatened to tear them apart. By the time they reached Mora, New Mexico Territory, they were nearly out of provisions. Near Santa Fe, the group split up, with thirty-two emigrants under Brewster taking the northern route, and the Oatman contingent of about twenty people and eight wagons, taking the southern route. Beyond Socorro, Mr. Lane died of "mountain fever." The road dipped into Mexico, then northwest to Tubac. The year was ending as the slow-moving caravan pulled into Tucson, where they bought supplies and rested for one month.[41]

The Mexican inhabitants convinced most of the party that the road ahead was too dangerous because of Apaches, and they should stay in Tucson, but the Oatman, Kelly, and Wilder families moved on. By mid-February, they had crossed a ninety-mile desert and got as far as the Maricopa and Pima villages. Again, the cattle were weak and provisions were low. They waited until March 11, but the Pimas were poor and the cattle were not recuperating. Kelly and Wilder elected to stay, but Oatman was determined to go on alone. Royse dragged his family across the desert following the nearly dry Gila River. Only one yoke of oxen and two of cows were left, and they were too poor to pull the two wagons uphill. Seven days out of the Pima village, a Doctor Le Conte and his guide rode past. The doctor pitied them, and promised that he would send help once he got to Yuma. About ninety miles east of Yuma, Royse and his family struggled across the uncommonly rain-swollen Gila, made their way to a sandy island where the team became mired, and camped for the night.[42]

That night, in a windstorm, the family huddled around a small fire and talked about Indians. Some said they would run if Indians appeared, and others said they would stand and fight. Olive said, "I will not be taken by these miserable brutes. I will fight as long as I can, and if I see I am about to be taken, I will kill myself. I do

Author's photo
Oatman capture site near Gila Bend, Arizona.

not care to die, but it would be worse than death to me to be taken a captive among them."[43]

The next day, March 19, the Oatmans continued across the Gila, then ascended a mesa about 200 feet above the river. The pull through the muddy sand and up the hill was hard, and the wagons were unloaded to make it easier for the oxen. The crossing and climb took all day, and Royse was overcome with gloom. He sank down near the wagon and groaned, "Mother, mother, in the name of God, I know that something dreadful is about to happen!"[44]

They rested, ate, and when the sun was setting, began to move on, hoping to make a few miles in the cooler evening. They barely started when Lorenzo looked back and saw Indians approaching them from behind. They were nineteen Yavapais, armed with bows, arrows, and clubs. Royse tried to put up a bold front, spoke to them in Spanish, and asked them to sit down. The Indians wanted tobacco and food. Royse said he had little, and by giving it to them, he would condemn his own children to starvation. They demanded food nevertheless. Royse took some bread from the wagon and gave it to them, but it was not enough.

The warriors quickly consulted in their own tongue, and in moments, sprang upon the defenseless family with war clubs. Warriors crushed Royse's skull with repeated blows. Mrs. Oatman jumped from the wagon and grabbed little Roland. Warriors knocked her down and beat both of them to death. A warrior grabbed Olive and yanked her away from the wagon. She saw another Indian club Lorenzo in the head, knocking him to the ground. As Indians beat her mother and father to death,

105

she fainted. A warrior grabbed Lucy by the hair, pulled her to the ground, and several of them beat her head in until she was unrecognizable. Charity was killed with one blow. Royse Jr. stood motionless, in shock, while an Indian came up to him. Then he shrieked and struggled, but they were on him and beat him to death. Mary Ann was standing alone, holding a rope attached to the lead oxen. She dropped the rope and covered her face with her hands. A huge Indian picked her up and carried her away.[45]

Indians took Lorenzo's hat and shoes, dragged him to the edge of an embankment, and threw him twenty feet to the bottom. Incredibly, the next day he regained consciousness. His face was beaten and bruised, part of his scalp was gone, and he could not open his eyes because of the dried, clotted blood. He crawled to the Gila River, drank, and bathed his wounds. After resting, Lorenzo stumbled upriver for two days, driving off coyotes that came around looking for an easy meal. On the third day he saw wagons approaching, walked out into the road, and collapsed. It was the Kelly and Wilder families. When he came to, he told them what had happened, and they turned around and hurried back to the Pima village. Kelly, Wilder, and a number of Pimas went to the massacre site to bury the bodies. Two weeks later they joined another party of white men heading west, took Lorenzo along, and finally made it to Yuma.[46]

The Yavapais took Olive and Mary north across the desert, amusing themselves by threatening Mary with death to the extent that she would run screaming into Olive's arms. Their bare feet were cut and torn from the rocks and cactus. When they camped that night, Olive said, "Food was offered me, but how could I eat to prolong a life I now loathed. I felt neither sensations of hunger nor a desire to live." She wanted to kill herself, but that would leave Mary alone. A few days later they met more Indians, and one of them shot an arrow at Olive, piercing her dress, but missing her. The would-be assassin had lost a brother in a recent battle with the whites, and sought revenge. The two groups nearly came to blows, but the Yavapais took the two girls and moved on.

When they reached a village about 100 miles away, they tied the girls in the center of a clearing, while the Indians danced around them, struck them, threw dirt on them, spit in their faces, and gave them a display "of their barbarity, cruelty, and obscenity." When the ordeal was over, Olive and Mary settled into their new lives as slaves. The Indian women were the cruelest mistresses, giving them the hardest tasks and beating them at the least provocation. Many a day Mary would entreat her sister:

"How long, O how long, dear Olive, must we stay here; can we never get away? Do you not think they intend to kill us?" Olive had little hope, but she encouraged Mary, and they both prayed daily that they would somehow be delivered.[47]

Olive and Mary suffered until early 1852, when a band of Mojaves bought the girls for two horses, three blankets, some vegetables and beads. They traveled north for eleven days to the Mojave village on the Colorado River. Here, the girls worked in the fields, planting and raising wheat, corn, melons, and vegetables, but they were beaten less and given more to eat. Even so, the Indians were concerned that the girls might escape. To facilitate their identification if they ever got away, and to make them ashamed to go back to the whites, the Indians tattooed the girl's faces. Olive pleaded for them to desist, but to no avail. The painful process left the girls' chins decorated with blue-black lines.

The summer of 1853 was especially dry, and the crops failed. The girls spent much of the time gathering mesquite beans, but they were beaten if unable to fill their baskets. Mary could not work as quickly, and as a result, got more beatings and less food. She rapidly lost strength and became ill. With the approach of winter, the entire tribe was starving, and the families hoarded and ate what little food they could obtain. Olive and Mary got little or nothing, and in early 1854, Mary wasted away and died. The Mojaves wanted to burn her body, but Olive would not hear of it, and was finally allowed to bury her.[48]

The next year was better for the Mojaves, with more rainfall and better crops, and the warriors decided to raid the Cocopah tribe. Olive learned that if anyone was killed, she would be sacrificed for the dead warrior in the afterlife. She spent the next five months in dread, but to her great relief, the raiders eventually returned in triumph, bringing five prisoners. One of them, a Cocopah woman, escaped downriver but was captured by a Yuma warrior who brought her back to the Mojaves. They crucified her. With that, Olive gave up all hope of escape and resigned herself to her fate.

She was shocked, when in February 1856, a Yuma Indian arrived in the village with a message from the soldiers at Fort Yuma, demanding her release. The long-delayed rescue attempt came as a result of Lorenzo's efforts, plus the help of a Mr. Grinnell. Lorenzo had gone to California where he repeated his story to the citizens, the newspapers, the governor, and the Indian Department. He even joined a prospecting party that searched the area south of the Mojave territory in 1855, but he could learn nothing about the captive white girls. At Fort Yuma, Grinnell, a carpenter, heard the story and questioned Indians and emigrants about the girls. When the Yuma, Francisco, talked to Grinnell about the captives, Grinnell said that the whites knew they were being held, and would make war upon the Indians if they were not released. Francisco had seen the power of the white men, whereas the Mojaves had not. Grinnell took him to the fort where he explained that if the soldiers would give him four blankets and some beads, he would bring them in.

Francisco arrived at the Mojave village and made his proposal, but the Mojaves insisted she was an Indian taken from a distant tribe. Olive was forbidden to speak to him. The council continued into the next day, when Olive finally blurted out who she was and pleaded to be rescued. The Mojaves wanted to kill them both, but Francisco talked fast, threatened, and finally succeeded in gaining her release. Olive burst into tears of happiness. The surly Mojaves would not let her take any of her personal items, but she and her rescuer decided they should keep quiet and leave quickly, before the Indians changed their mind. In February 1856, Francisco turned Olive over to Grinnell at Fort Yuma, twenty days after he left, just as he had promised.[49]

The community rejoiced. Olive received clothing, food, and care, but she was an emotional and physical wreck, and it took some time for her recovery. Lorenzo learned of her rescue and rode from Los Angeles to Yuma, meeting her in a tearful reunion. Brother and sister went to Los Angeles, and then attended school in Santa Clara. Olive told her story to a reporter from the Los Angeles *Star* in April 1856. They met and collaborated with Royal B. Stratton to publish their story. Two editions were printed in California in 1857. The Oatmans went to Oregon to live with a cousin for a time, and then returned to California, where Stratton arranged for them to accompany him back east. They took a steamship by way of Panama, and arrived in New York in March 1858. That year, Stratton published a third edition of their story. Olive lived with her father's relatives near Rochester, and attended school in Albany. She told her story in a series of lectures between 1860 and 1865. In Rochester in 1865, when Olive was 28, she married John B. Fairchild. They moved to Michigan for seven years and Olive had two or three children. They next relocated to Sherman, Texas. Olive stayed in close contact with Lorenzo for the remainder of their lives. Lorenzo died in Red Cloud, Nebraska, on October 8, 1901. Olive died in Texas on March 20, 1903.[50]

Jane, George, and Meredith Wilson
Texas, ca. September 25, 1853

Jane Smith was born on June 12, 1837, in Alton Illinois, one of five sisters and five brothers. In the mid-1840s, William Smith and Jane Cox Smith, packed up the family and moved to Missouri, where Mr. Smith ran a ferry on the North Grand River near Jamesport. In a short time, wanderlust and news of the greener pastures in Texas prompted him to move again. They settled in Lamar County, near Paris, Texas, where the green pastures proved harsh. In the ensuing years, three of the Smith boys died, and in 1852, Mr. and Mrs. Smith died within a day of each other. The eldest Smith brother was with the Texas Rangers, and came home to care for his orphaned siblings. After securing homes for them with different neighbors, he was taking 4-year-old Ellen to live with an aunt when he caught a fever and died. By early 1853, Jane had lived with several neighbors, and believed the way to get out of her unfortunate circumstances was to wed. In February 1853, Jane (15) married James Wilson, a 19 year-old just starting his own farm.[51]

The farming idea didn't last long. Hearing stories of people striking it rich in California, the Wilsons joined a party of emigrants, which included James's father, and James's three younger brothers. In Hunt County they formed up in a twenty-two-wagon company, all under command of Henry Hickman. The fifty-two men, twelve women, and several children left on April 6, 1853, heading for El Paso. The passage through Texas was slow and uneventful. They probably trailed west to Forts Belknap, Phantom Hill, and Chadbourne, southwest to the Pecos, then upriver to near the New Mexico border, where they left the river and turned west.

On June 1, near the Guadalupe Mountains, Mescalero Apaches attacked the train and stole nineteen cattle. Six men rode out after the raiders, but were repulsed. Chastened, the men of the wagon train proceeded more cautiously and safely reached El Paso. A number of men did not get along with wagon boss Hickman and decided to detach from the company and hook up with another train. James Wilson and family and five other men waited for a month, but Mexicans stole most of their property, and there was little left for them to do but return home.

In late July, the little caravan retraced its tracks. On August 1, they were near the Guadalupe Mountains, when Mescaleros attacked them again. James Wilson and his father had gone only a short distance from the wagons when, Jane said, "they fell into the hands of the Indians. I saw them no more after this. I was told that they had been murdered. . . .I found myself thus bereaved and destitute, in a land of strangers." Jane and her three brothers-in-law turned around again and hurried back to El Paso. On September 8, a small party under a Mr. Hart, four other Americans, one of them a discharged soldier, and one Mexican, was heading east and Jane and the Wilson boys joined them. Moving rapidly, they crossed most of west Texas without molestation, however, about three day's journey west of Fort Phantom Hill, a few men ran off with some of the stock. Hart took the eldest Wilson boy (14) and rode off after the thieves. Jane, the two youngest Wilson boys, and the Mexican, tried to keep up. The discharged soldier fell behind and disappeared.

Hart never returned. Jane kept going, and about noon the next day, southwest of present-day Abilene, about fifteen Comanches appeared in front of them. The Mexican left the wagon and went ahead, trying to show he was friendly, while the mules, hearing the war cries, began to run. One of them fell and dragged the wagon to a halt. The Indians were upon them in an instant. Jane saw them bring the Mexican in, strip him, tie him up, and shoot him in the back. Another warrior stabbed and scalped him, dropped the scalp into the Mexican's hat, and put the bloody mess on his own head. "I was stupefied with horror as I gazed on this spectacle," Jane said, "and supposed that my turn would come next."[52]

The Comanches and their captives headed northeast. The first night the Indians rummaged through all their plunder, keeping some items and burning others. Jane's clothes were taken, "except barely enough to cover my person," she said. One Indian who Jane claimed was the chief, took George Wilson (12). A Mexican, once taken captive himself and now riding as a Comanche warrior, claimed Meredith (7). Another warrior claimed Jane. That night she watched them stretch and dry the scalp of the Mexican who had been her traveling companion. The captives were tied up while the Indians slept.

Starting out the next day, George and Meredith were painted up to look like young Comanches, and given their own bows and arrows and horses to ride. They appeared to enjoy the adventure. Jane was treated cruelly; warriors cut off her long hair and decorated their own hair with hers. The hot sun beat down on her nearly bald head and burned it severely. Every day was rife with what Jane termed, "repeated acts of inhumanity towards me."

After twelve days they met two warriors and a woman. Up to that point, Jane said "my sufferings had been so severe as to take from me all desire to live." She thought she might now receive some compassion from another female, but the woman treated her worse than the men. She took away her horse and made her ride an unbroken mule, which bucked her off constantly, much to the amusement of the Indians. If she did not remount quickly, they beat her with riding whips or sticks, and the chief often rubbed the Mexican's scalp in her face. The Comanche woman stabbed her with a spear when she did not get off the ground fast enough. Jane believed her treatment was motivated because the Indians were well aware that she was about eight months pregnant, and hoped the physical abuse would make her lose the baby.

In camp, Jane "was obliged to work like a slave," carrying large loads of wood on her bare back, which was cut so badly that the blood trickled down her legs. She was forced to chase stock through the briars until her feet were torn to ribbons. Jane could never work as fast as the Indians ordered, and for punishment, she was whipped, stoned, or "knocked down and stamped upon by the ferocious chief." Sometimes they starved her for two or more days at a time, and she was never allowed to drink except while in camp. The sun burned her and she pointed to her parched tongue, begging for water, all to no avail. When her mule was finally tamed, they took it away from her and made her walk. Unable to keep up on her bloody, torn feet, she was beaten "nearly senseless." Jane hated her captors. She often contemplated killing her "inhuman masters," particularly the chief, and "thought if I could only cut him to pieces I could die contented." If murder was not on her mind, it was death. "Every indignity was offered to my person which the imagination can conceive," she said. "Nothing could soften them into pity, and I ardently desired death that my torments might come to an end."[53]

Since Jane could only walk slowly, the Indians pointed her in the right direction and sent her out ahead every morning, catching up to her very soon. About twenty-five days after her capture, they sent Jane out early, as per the routine, but this time she was determined to escape. Instead of plodding along, once she got out of sight she ran off in a different direction as fast as her weary body would go. She didn't care if she died, but only hoped the Indians wouldn't have the pleasure of seeing her expire. When she could go no further, she hid in some bushes. No one came by. The next day she saw the tracks where the Indians had searched for her. Jane had escaped, but she was alone in the wilderness, probably somewhere either in present-day western Oklahoma or the eastern Texas Panhandle, and had no idea which way to go.

Jane collapsed in despair, and only after three days did hunger and thirst force her to move on. She found a little grove and built a shelter of bushes and grass. She ate hackberries and drank at a nearby spring. It was now late October, and the weather grew cold and rainy. Wolves came within five feet of her at night, but she frightened them away. On the twelfth day after her escape, New Mexican Comancheros discovered her. Immediately discerning her predicament, they took her along and gave her clothing, a blanket, and a burro to ride. In a few days, however, they saw a band of Indians, and the Comancheros thought it best if she stayed behind and out of sight while they parleyed. They said they would return that night, but when they did not, Jane went out to look for them. In the darkness she nearly stumbled upon an Indian, but fell to the ground and hid.

In the morning, Jane discovered one of the Mexican traders, Juan Jose, herding the horses and mules. She went up to him. But he hurriedly took her away and hid her again, saying that they were negotiating with the Comanches, and it would be impossible to rescue her if they found she was with them. Jane hid in a grass-covered ravine all day, until Juan brought her some bread and told her she would have to stay hidden longer. Jane waited, and heard Comanches calling out in the distance. Juan returned to her again that night with more food and water. This time he told her she must stay hidden for another week, as they must move on for a time, and could not take her or the Indians would know. Jane watched them all disappear, and with them went all her hopes of rescue.[54]

The next day she went to the abandoned campsite and found a log that was still burning. Using it and adding fuel to the flames, she was able to keep warm. She took shelter at night in a hollow cottonwood stump. With her hackberries and bread almost gone, Jane was once more ready to give up, but eight days after the Comancheros left she heard voices. The traders, on their way back to New Mexico, had returned for her. They could not find her in the place Juan Jose told her to hide, and they were calling for her. "I was so overjoyed," she said, "that I rushed toward them unmindful of briars and sore feet." Juan gave her a horse to ride and they all treated her with kindness. They headed west, reaching the village of Pecos in late November 1853. There she met Captain James H. Carleton of the 1st Dragoons, and received women's clothing from some of the army wives. Raymond Meriwether, son of New Mexico Territorial Governor David Meriwether, escorted Jane Wilson to Santa Fe, where they arrived on December 3. Governor

Meriwether said, "On her arrival she presented the most pitiful spectacle I had ever seen. She was in rags, emaciated, and her mind somewhat disordered." Jane gave birth to a stillborn child, and was taken care of by several American and Mexican ladies.[55]

Jane was concerned about her two brothers-in-law, wanting "the strong arm of Government" to get involved with their rescue. She believed no one had known about the attack on their party, but she was mistaken. There was a survivor from their wagon train, either another Mexican teamster or the discharged soldier. Friendly Comanches found the wounded man, shot in the shoulder, and brought him in to Fort Phantom Hill. His story was slightly different from what Jane remembered. He said one teamster grabbed a rifle and tried to fire when the Indians first appeared, but Mrs. Wilson grabbed his rifle and spoiled his aim. The Indians grabbed the man, tied him to the wagon, scalped him, and rode off with Jane and the two boys.

The rescued teamster told the story to Captain Henry H. Sibley, 2nd Dragoons, in command at Phantom Hill, and the captain sent out two patrols to pursue the Indians. They hunted to the north and west, but neither could pick up a trail. On October 8, Sibley wrote to Texas Indian Agent Robert S. Neighbors, telling him what happened and asking for ransom money to buy back the captives.[56]

Neighbors did all he could. Friendly Delawares and Caddoes went out to various Comanche bands, trying to purchase the captives, but they learned that the Indians had already sold the two boys, one to another band in the north, and the other to a Chickasaw trader named Brown. On December 13, 1853, Governor Meriwether wrote to Texas Governor Elisha M. Pease, saying that Jane Wilson was in Santa Fe, that he had already sent out traders to locate and purchase the two Wilson boys, and asked if Pease would also initiate recovery efforts. Pease passed the news along to Robert Neighbors, and the agent answered that he was already aware of the situation and had friendly Indians out looking for them.

It was not until March 1854, however, that the boys were returned. Either Indians or the Chickasaw trader Brown, brought George to Fort Arbuckle, Indian Territory, where he was placed in care of Major Humphreys. A Kickapoo named Johnson recovered Meredith, the younger brother, and brought him to the fort, where Capain. Seneca G. Simmons, 7th Infantry, took him in.[57]

Governor Meriwether paid $50 to Jane Wilson's rescuers and spent $300 for her care. With the help of Governor Pease of Texas,

Jane was finally sent home in the spring of 1854. Jane Wilson told her story to a correspondent from the Santa Fe *Weekly Gazette*, and the narrative was reprinted in other newspapers, such as the New York *Commercial Advertizer*. Rochester, New York, bookseller, Dellon M. Dewey, printed Jane's story in 1854, and two years later, it appeared in John Frost's anthology, *Indian Battles, Captivities and Adventures*. Jane gave her story in the hope of spreading the news to facilitate the release of her brothers-in-law. She probably never even knew the story was reprinted, that Dewey printed a booklet, or that Frost included it in his collection. She made no money from publicizing her sufferings, and faded out of history like so many of her fellow captives.[58]

NELSON LEE
Texas, April 3, 1855

Nelson Lee was born in Brownsville, New York, in 1807. His athletic constitution and roving spirit did not suit a sedentary life, and he soon left his father's farm to see the world. He was a boatman on the St. Lawrence River, and in 1831, traveled west to fight in the Black Hawk War. Arriving too late for that conflict, Lee went east and enlisted in the navy, staying seven years until reports of fighting in Texas lured him there. He was shipwrecked in the Gulf of Mexico, made his way to Galveston, joined the Texas Navy and fought Mexicans off Yucatan. Eventually, Lee gave up the sea and settled down in south Texas. He joined the Texas Rangers and fought at Plum Creek in 1840, at Mier in 1842, and in the Mexican War with Jack Hays's Rangers. After the war, Lee rounded up wild horses, broke and sold them, and traded in livestock. The money was fair, but Lee looked for a way to increase his profit.[59]

In 1855, William Aikens persuaded Lee to join him in a business venture, driving horses and mules to sell in California. They pooled resources with six other partners, went to New Orleans and bought supplies for themselves and nineteen hired men. Lee bought a silver pocket watch that would play a role in the upcoming adventure. They left San Patricio for Matamoros, and in March 1855, began moving slowly up the Rio Grande, driving all the wild horses and mules they could find. By the time they reached Eagle Pass, they had nearly 400 head. The outfit pushed on toward El Paso, and by the last of March, Lee figured they were in Mexico, 350 miles beyond Eagle Pass, in the vicinity of Presidio, Texas.[60]

In the pre-dawn darkness of April 3, a Comanche war party attacked the sleeping cowboys, quickly killing or capturing them all. A warrior lassoed Lee and a half a dozen more jumped him and tied him up. Only Bill Aikens was able to fire a few rounds before he was captured. The two of them, plus Thomas Martin and John Stewart, were the only ones who survived the initial attack. While stripping the cowboys, an Indian found Lee's silver watch and was examining it, when the alarm went off at half past three, their traditional time of rising. The alarm rang on for two minutes, to the amazement of the gathering warriors. They gesticulated to Lee and the watch, as if they thought he had some power over it, and wanted it to ring again. Lee set the alarm for a few minutes ahead. They listened to it tick, and were startled again when the alarm sounded. One Indian put the treasure in his pouch and they talked among themselves, pointing to Lee and to the sky. Nelson figured they "regarded it as something supernatural which connected me with the Great Spirit."[61]

At first light, the Indians showed the captives the mangled and scalped bodies of their dead comrades, blindfolded them, tied them to mules, and rode off. At the first night's camp, the Indians roasted horsemeat and dripped the sizzling fat onto the captives' bare legs, leaving scars that Lee carried to his grave. Lee, with nothing to eat and little to drink, wondered how God could permit such wrongs to be perpetrated. The next day they crossed the Rio Grande near Presidio and traveled north for four days, finally coming to the village. A warrior gave Lee's watch to Chief Big Wolf, and he and his wives entreated Lee to make it work, but Lee played up the supernatural aspects and indicated that the heavens said it was not an auspicious time.

Lee, Aikens, Stewart, and Martin were stripped and bound to a post, while warriors danced around, taunting them. They stabbed and scalped Martin and Stewart; Stewart only groaned, while Martin implored God to have mercy on him, provoking the warriors' laughter. After about two hours of torture, warriors crashed their hatchets into Martin and Stewart's skulls, finally ending their misery. Aikens and Lee were separated and spared for the time being.

Lee thought about suicide, escape, or killing his captors. Indians ordered him to make the watch ring, but he obstinately refused. He was forced to perform menial tasks, but he was no longer tortured. Aikens told Lee the Indians were going to take him to another camp, and Bill was certain that he would be murdered, but he thought Lee would be spared because of his connection with the supernatural watch. Aikens was led away. Said Lee, "I have never seen or heard of him since."[62]

Lee conformed to the Indian customs, but he was not totally trusted, although some of Big Wolf's wives seemed to like him. He occasionally worked the "magic" of his watch, and his fame spread. In November 1855, Lee and his watch were traded to Spotted Leopard, chief of another Comanche band. His new master was crueler than Big Wolf. Lee labored hard, but was allowed to carry a knife and given more liberty. When Lee wandered from the camp, testing how far he could get without arousing suspicion, several warriors caught him and brought him back. Spotted Leopard tied him down and cut the tendon below his right knee, intending to cripple him and prevent him from escaping, but the wound healed without permanent damage.

Lee accompanied a war party in a fight against the Apaches. Lee hoped the Apaches won, for he believed he had a better chance with them, but the Apaches were defeated, and Spotted Leopard's band joined up with more Comanches. Lee passed through their camp and saw the body of a U. S. soldier by the look of his clothing. He was suspended upside down from a tree limb like a carcass in a butcher shop. Lee wondered why the government would sit back in their line of forts while the Indians killed and captured people by the hundreds. He thought the army should take the offensive and march into Indian lands to teach them "a lesson too impressive to be forgotten."

Lee was with Spotted Leopard for several months when three white women were brought in. They were Marietta Haskins (60), and her daughters, Margaret (21), and Harriet (18). They had been in a wagon train traveling west from Indianola, Texas, when Indians attacked them somewhere beyond Eagle Pass. There were fourteen women and several infants in the party. Now, about three years after their capture, only these three were left. "I turn with disgust," said Nelson Lee, "from the contemplation of the cruelty to which these captive women were subjected by the lustful hellhounds as they bore them off in triumph to their camps." The cruelty was not over. Marietta Haskins, rheumatic and unable to work as fast as her captors demanded, was staked out, stabbed, and scalped, while her daughters were forced to watch the torture. When they were removed from the camp, Lee never saw them again. Once more, he lamented for the many women "dragging out their weary lives in misery and captivity." He hoped to God that the United States would take measures "to reach them in those lonely wilds, and bring them out of bondage."[63]

In his second year of captivity, Lee was sold again, this time to the Comanche Rolling Thunder, but he still kept the secret of his enchanted watch. Lee "married" and got his own tipi, but was still not allowed to roam far away. He was determined to get weapons, a horse, and supplies sufficient to make a successful escape. In May 1858, Rolling Thunder left the camp to attend a council and ordered Lee to prepare his mule to ride with him. The first night they came to another Indian camp, where liquor was available and the chief overindulged. The next morning, Rolling Thunder was able to ride, but by mid-morning, he was parched with thirst on the desert. They rode until they discovered a hollow with muddy water trickling through the grass. Rolling Thunder directed Lee to fetch him a horn full, but what he scooped up was more mud than water. The impatient chief dismounted, told Lee to hold his horse, stretched out on the ground, and tried to drink directly from the rivulet. Lee saw his chance. He grabbed the hatchet hanging from the saddle, and "leaped towards the chief and buried the dull edge a broad hand's breadth in his brain." Lee took the chief's knife, rifle, horse, and mule, and "dashed wildly away over an unknown path towards the land of freedom."[64]

Lee tried to get his bearings. He traveled through mountains and canyons. When unable to shoot game, he killed the mule, cut it up, cooked, and preserved it. He thought he would head to Chihuahua, Mexico, and then go southeast on the route he had taken three years ago, but he became lost in the mountains. His horse failed and he let it go. He killed several deer and fashioned clothes and moccasins from their skins. Lee was so disoriented that he believed he was near Santa Fe. It was nearly two months after his escape that he came to a wide prairie and heard the crack of a rifle. Lee nearly panicked, thinking the Indians had trailed him. Instead, he saw a Mexican riding up with a dead deer slung across his horse.

"How do you do?" the Mexican asked.

"Sick and dying," Lee replied to him in Spanish. "Will you help me, my friend?"

Lee learned the Mexican was with a party on a trading expedition to the Apaches, and were on their way home to San Fernando. The man let Lee ride his horse back to the camp, and three traders, Halleno, Silva, and Lezzez, cared for him and escorted him to San Fernando. Lee recuperated for six weeks until Silva accompanied him down to Matamoros. From there, Lee went to Brazos Santiago, and shipped out to Havana, Cuba. There, he composed a letter to Bill Aikens's friends in Corpus Christi, notifying them of his fate. Lee sailed on the schooner *Elizabeth Jones,* and reached New York on November 10, 1858.[65]

Lee was impoverished and needed to publish his story. His account was first printed in New York in January 1859, buttressed by testimonials from several prominent citizens, including the mayor of Albany. Lee needed the money, plus he sought to broadcast the sufferings of many others, mostly females, "who are still in bonds," and subject to many cruelties. Although he advocated military campaigns to chastise the raiding tribes, he believed that attacks would result in the deaths of the captives. The best solution, he thought, would be for the government to furnish traders with money and supplies to buy their freedom. Lee hoped, although he was now "prematurely old," to devote the rest of his life "to the accomplishment of their ransom."[66]

LARCENA PENNINGTON PAGE AND MERCEDES SAIS QUIROZ
Arizona, March 16, 1860

Larcena Ann Pennington was born in Tennessee on June 10, 1837, the third of twelve children of Elias Green Pennington and Julia Ann Hood. In 1839, when Tennessee became "too populated" for Elias, he moved the family just south of Red River in Fannin County, Texas. Julia died in 1855, and Elias moved the family to Jack County. Two years later, they were on the move again, hoping to make it to California, which was said to be a land of gold and riches.

The Penningtons packed up and trekked across Texas, beyond El Paso, and through the dangerous passes of Cooke's Canyon, Doubtful Canyon, and Apache Pass, where Apaches later killed scores of soldiers and pioneers. At Fort Buchanan, in what would later become Arizona Territory, Larcena took sick with "mountain fever." While Elias waited for her to recover, he went down Sonoita Creek near its junction with the Santa Cruz River at the southern end of the Santa Rita Mountains. There, in the summer of 1857, Elias decided to build a home in the valley at Canoa.[67]

The Penningtons formed bonds with other families in the area, such as the Wadsworths, Akes, Thompsons, Kirklands, and Pages. On Christmas Eve in 1859, the blond Larcena (22) married John H. Page in Tucson. In March 1860, he brought her from the ranch at Canoa, into Madera Canyon in the Santa Ritas, where Page and his friend, William Randall, ran a logging operation. Accompanying Larcena was Mercedes Sais Quiroz (10), the

Author's photo
Madera Canyon, Arizona, site of Page and Quiroz capture.

daughter of a Mexican widow and ward of William H. Kirkland, a rancher who did business with Page. Larcena and Mercedes had stayed in Tucson while the men worked in the mountains, but Page naturally wanted his wife to be closer to him. He asked Kirkland to let Mercedes come down with Larcena. Shortly after arriving, Larcena caught another fever, probably malaria, and he thought it would be healthier for her if she stayed in the mountains. Page talked Kirkland into letting Mercedes accompany Larcena to a cabin he was building in Madera Canyon.

After breakfast on March 16, Randall had gone out to hunt deer and Page went up to the pinery. Larcena and Mercedes had just fetched water from the brook and returned to the tent when the dog began barking. Larcena scolded him when she heard Mercedes scream. An Apache warrior burst through the tent flap. Larcena reached for a revolver, but the Indian grabbed it from her. She ran outside but he caught her. Another warrior grabbed Mercedes. They were the prisoners of five Tonto Apaches from the Arivaipa Canyon country, led by Toodlekiay. One of the participating warriors was Eskiminzin, who would become infamous years later for leading his band in many raids against Arizona settlers, as well as being a victim of the Camp Grant Massacre of 1871.[68]

The Apaches looted the camp and took the captives away. Larcena tried to talk to Mercedes, but the Indians separated them. She tore off small pieces of her clothing to leave a trail. They

119

climbed over a ridge and into another canyon, skirting the western edge of the Santa Ritas heading north. Larcena was exhausted, but an Apache threatened to shoot her and she stumbled on. The Indians spoke in broken Spanish, and Mercedes understood that they planned to kill Larcena if she could not keep up. She got near enough to Larcena to warn her. When they halted, a warrior gave the women a cup of melted snow to drink, and they were on their way again. Near sunset, Larcena could no longer walk. They had gone about fifteen miles from Madera Canyon and a warrior trailing in the rear ran up and said they were being pursued. The Tontos demanded that they travel faster. One of them picked Larcena up and threw her over his shoulder. He walked some distance with her before others took turns. The pursuers were still gaining on them. They stopped, stripped Larcena down to her chemise and told her to turn around. When she did, a warrior lanced her in the back. She fell down a steep slope while others followed behind her, repeatedly stabbing her and throwing boulders at her head. She crashed into a pine tree and the Indians left her for dead. They went back uphill, picked up Mercedes, and hurried on into the twilight.[69]

When Bill Randall returned to the camp after hunting, he found the place wrecked and Larcena and Mercedes gone. He hurried to tell John Page, who immediately took Randall's horse and raced to Canoa, where the horse dropped dead of exhaustion. Kirkland dispatched a rider to carry the news of the attack to Fort Buchanan, and then rode forty miles north to Tucson to organize a search party. Page collected a small number of companions and returned to the lumber camp to set out on the Apaches' trail.

Although the Apaches moved fast, the pursuing whites on horseback were catching up. It was nearly dark when Larcena regained consciousness. She heard the sound of dogs barking on the ridge above her, and then heard her husband's voice call out, "Here it is, boys!" They had found the tracks, but apparently couldn't figure out the riddle of what happened next. Page saw the tracks of her shoes, now worn by an Apache. Larcena tried to call out, but only a gasping murmur escaped her lips. In the shadows, the men did not see evidence of her tumble off the cliff. They continued on and Larcena fainted again. When night was fully upon them they gave up the search and headed back to Madera Canyon, unknowingly passing by Larcena once more.

The next day, Captain Richard S. Ewell, in command at Fort Buchanan, sent out a detachment of Company G, 1st Dragoons, to search for the Indians. They failed to connect up with Page and did not know which way the Indians were traveling. Ewell decided to use a couple of Pinal Apaches he held as prisoner, and sent them back to their people to negotiate an exchange. Kirkland had reached Tucson and organized a search party, while Juan Elias gathered another. On Sunday, March 18, a tearful Elias Pennington went to Tubac to plead with Edward F. Radcliff of the Sonora Exploring and Mining Company for help. Radcliff and twenty men volunteered.[70]

Larcena did not regain consciousness again until the third day after her capture. She was wedged against a pine tree in a snow-filled ravine. The snow may have saved her life, slowing the flow of blood from her eleven stab wounds. She swallowed a handful of snow and began to crawl away. She could not stand, nor make it uphill, so she crawled along the base of the ridge out to more open ground. It took all day to get a short distance down the mountainside when she collapsed again and slept until morning. At sunrise, Larcena could see an isolated cone-shaped hill that she recognized as Huerfano (orphan) Butte. She knew it was miles (ten) northeast of the lumber camp, so she adjusted her direction, finally stood up, and staggered on. She gnawed grass and found a few wild onions to eat. The sun beat down on her, crusted her bloody wounds and blistered her face. Cactus and rocks tore her feet and after one day, she was reduced to crawling again. She couldn't go down into the valley because there was no water, so she had to keep near the craggy slopes and hope to find pockets of snow. At night she dug holes in the sand and covered herself so she would not freeze.

Twelve days after her capture, Larcena saw some men in the valley with an ox team. She tried to call to them and waved her petticoat, but they did not see her and rode away. Two days later she was almost at the site of her capture. She found a still glowing campfire, and small heaps of flour and coffee on the ground. She tore off a piece of her chemise, piled some flour on it, crawled to the creek to wet it down, and rolled it into a ball. Then she stuck a stick into it and cooked it over the glowing fire. She devoured the dough and collapsed again into a deep sleep. By the path she took, Larcena had gone about sixteen miles.

The next morning was March 30, two full weeks after her capture. Larcena awoke to hear the sounds of men working at the lumber camp and crawled on. The sight of her scared the Negro cook, named Brown, who ran to camp to get his gun. In a minute, several men went up the path and saw something crawling out of the woods. A man lifted his rifle to fire, when Larcena gasped out her name. A workman ran to her and picked her up, while Brown continued to insist she was a ghost. A rider went to Tucson and John Page, Bill Radcliff, and Doctor C. B. Hughes rushed back to the lumber camp. Radcliff described Larcena as "emaciated beyond description, her hands and knees and legs and arms a mass of raw flesh almost exposing the bones." Hughes thought she would die, but her husband put her in a wagon and drove her to Tucson, where she was constantly under a doctor's care. It took until mid-summer before she was well enough to go home.[71]

When the Apaches threw Larcena off the cliff they continued on with Mercedes undetected, through the Santa Catalina Mountains within sight of Tucson. When she grew tired, the Indians took turns carrying her. They took her to a Pinal Apache camp at the junction of Arivaipa Creek and the San Pedro River. When word reached there that Captain Ewell would trade his Pinal prisoners for Mercedes, the Pinals said they would buy her from the Tontos who had taken her. Ewell and his dragoons went to Arivaipa Creek with his prisoners in boarded-up wagons, and Kirkland met him there. Ewell let the prisoners be seen and told the Pinals that he would free them when Mercedes was in his hands. They let the girl run to Kirkland, and Ewell opened the wagons to release the Pinals. The first thing Mercedes said to Bill Kirkland was that she was hungry. Two days later, Mercedes was reunited with her mother in Tucson.[72]

Mercedes later went back to stay with Bill Kirkland and his wife at Punta del Agua. In 1868, she married Charles A. Shibell and they lived in Tucson. She had one daughter, but was not destined to enjoy her family for long. Mercedes Shibell died in 1876, at only 26 years of age. John Page was killed in an Indian ambush in February 1861, about thirty miles north of Tucson. Larcena, pregnant at the time, went to live with her sisters, and gave birth to a daughter in September of that year. With the start of the Civil War, many of the original settlers decided to leave the area and go back to Texas. The Ake, Wadsworth, and Thompson families packed up to go, and with them went one of Larcena's brothers, Jack Pennington. Apaches attacked them in Cooke's Canyon and killed several of them. Elias and his eight daughters and three sons remained in Arizona. In 1868, they moved to the Sonoita Valley near Camp Crittenden. In 1869, Elias and his son, Green Pennington, were ambushed and killed by the Apaches. When Jack Pennington returned in the summer of 1870, he talked most of the family into returning to Texas with him. Five of them were already dead beneath Arizona soil. All except Larcena went back to Texas, for that summer she married William Fisher Scott and stayed in Tucson. They had a son, William Pennington, in 1871, and a daughter, Georgia Hazel, in 1872. Larcena and her husband lived to see Arizona Territory become a state in 1912, but they were among only a handful remaining who had been there since the beginning. Larcena died on March 31, 1913, at the age of 76. She was buried in Tucson's Evergreen Cemetery.[73]

ELIZA, MINERVA, LUCINDA, AND REUBEN VAN ORNUM
Oregon, ca. October 9, 1860

Elijah P. Utter had guided the Utter-Van Ornum wagon train all the way from Geneva, Wisconsin, along the Oregon Trail and to Fort Hall in present-day Idaho. There they met men of the 2nd Dragoons under Lieutenant Colonel Marshall S. Howe, who had spent much of the summer escorting emigrants and were looking forward to returning to Camp Douglas in Utah Territory. Howe assigned twenty-two soldiers to escort the wagons to Raft River, and then they would be on their own. Six more soldiers who had recently mustered out of the service decided to join the wagon train. There had been Indian trouble in the area previously, but so far this year, no attacks were reported on trains along the Oregon Branch.[74]

With the addition of the six soldiers, the Utter party now numbered forty-four souls. There were eight wagons, about 100 cattle, and several horses. The Utter family consisted of Elijah, his wife Abagel, and ten children, including three from her previous marriage, Emeline, Christopher, and Elizabeth Trimble. The Van Ornum family consisted of Alexis and his wife Abigail, and their five children, Marcus, Eliza, Reuben, Lucinda, and Minerva. The Myers family included Joseph and Mary and their children, Isabella, Margaret, Harriet, Carolyn, and Eugene, plus Joseph's brother John. Daniel and Elizabeth Chase rode with their three children, Daniel Jr., Albert, and Mary. A number of single men were along: Jacob and Joseph Reith, brothers in their twenties, Judson Cressy, Samuel Gleason, Lewis Lawson, and Goodsel Munson, and the ex-soldiers, Charles Chaffee, Charles Kishnell, Theodore Murdoch, Charles Schaumberg, Henry Snyder, and William Utley.[75]

Beyond Raft River when the army escort turned back, the discharged soldiers took over as guards. After a few days of uneventful travel the train arrived at Salmon Falls, a popular fishing site. The Indians there were surly. At Three Island

Crossing, Utter and Van Ornum decided they would stay on the south bank of the river to save time, and by September 8, they had reached Castle Creek. The next morning they were moving by 7 a.m.

If anyone, after months of hard travel, had any remaining romantic allusions about the western trek, their idyll was shattered that morning. When Indians approached from the west, Utter ordered the wagons to form a tight circle and placed the stock inside. A band of Bannocks rode up, whooping and firing their guns, but they did not charge. The two parties faced each other, and after an hour, the Bannocks signaled that they wanted to parley. They indicated they were hungry and the wary emigrants decided that if they fed them, they would let them move on in peace. After eating, the Indians indicated the emigrants were free to travel on, but they were not convinced. When the Bannocks left, Utter moved the wagons out; he did not head to the river for water, but cautiously kept on the main road.

The Bannocks charged in, this time firing arrows into the cattle and wagons. Utter called for them to circle once more, but while doing so, the lead driver, Lewis Lawson, caught a bullet and tumbled off dead. Ex-soldier William Utley was mortally wounded and died soon after. The emigrants tried to close-up the wagons when another ex-soldier, Charles Kishnell, was killed. For the rest of the day they returned fire from within the dubious protection of their corral. It was said that Charles Utter (13) shot five Indians. Joseph Myers said "it was certain death to an Indian if he showed his head, for we were all pretty good marksmen. . . ." He claimed that they killed twenty-five to thirty warriors.[76]

The claim was likely an exaggeration, for the Bannocks showed no sign of being hurt, or of going away. They besieged the train all Sunday night and kept it up on Monday morning. Soon the sun rose and the soaring temperatures and lack of water made the youngest children wail with thirst. They all needed water, but the river was about 400 yards away, and by late afternoon they could take it no longer. They abandoned four wagons, hoping the Indians would be satisfied with them, then hitched up the remaining four wagons and made a dash for the river. It didn't work. As soon as they broke their protective corral the Bannocks attacked. John Meyers was shot dead, and a few others were hit. The four remaining ex-soldiers, Chaffee, Murdoch, Schaumberg, and Snyder, galloped away at full speed. The two Reith Brothers, although afoot, threw their empty weapons away and ran after them. The remaining emigrants ran headlong for the river.

Wayne Cornell photo
Flat above the Snake River in southwest Idaho where the Utter-Van Ornum train was initially attacked.

Judson Cressy was killed in the melee. Elijah Utter, holding Susan (1), was shot down as he ran. Abagel rushed back to him, and her children followed close behind. Emeline Trimble pleaded to her mother not to go back, but she would not listen. Emeline snatched up little Susan and left them. Abagel was murdered next to Elijah, as were four of her children, Mary, Emma, Wesley, and Abby. As the sun set that evening, twenty-seven people out of the original forty-four were left hiding in the brush near the Snake River.

They spent a horrible night watching the fires from the burning wagons and hearing the yells from the triumphant Bannocks. The warriors were temporarily satiated however, for after celebrating for a few hours, they gathered all the property they could carry, rounded up the cattle and horses, and moved off into the night. The white survivors had only a few weapons and bullets left. Worse, they only had one loaf of bread and a few corncakes for food. They traveled west along the river, moving at night and hiding by day. A few Indians harassed them, but they were kept at bay. After about ten days they arrived at the Owyhee River's junction with the Snake. They were so tired and hungry that they decided to make shelters of willow branches and wait in the hope that someone would rescue them. Surely, they hoped, other wagon trains would be coming along the trail. But there were no other wagons. They were the last of the season.[77]

125

Their only hope for succor would be in the four ex-soldiers and two Reith Brothers who fled during the attack. The six men headed for Fort Walla Walla, 250 miles away. But would they help? They must have realized that in abandoning their comrades they would be seen as dastardly cowards. In addition, Charles Chaffee had not mustered out of service, he deserted, and he was not about to walk into an army post. The six men argued, and split up. Murdoch, Schaumberg, and Snyder made it as far as the John Day River in northeastern Oregon, where Indians caught and killed two of them. Only Snyder escaped, later to be found by a settler, half-starved and on the edge of madness.

Meanwhile, Goodsel Munson and Christopher Trimble (9), the two strongest survivors at the camp on the Owyhee, began to walk for help. By great luck, they came upon the camp of Chaffee and the Reiths, about twenty-five miles further down the Snake River. Chaffee killed his horse. They divided up the meat and sent young Trimble back alone with a large share for the starving survivors. The four men continued on, but Chaffee and Munson dropped out forty miles farther near the mouth of Burnt River. Chaffee was later caught, convicted of desertion, and hanged. On October 2, the Reiths made it to the Umatilla Reservation. The agent sent out rescue parties, but they found no one.

Trimble returned to the survivors with the meat, but it was soon devoured. He left camp, found a band of Shoshones and managed to explain their predicament. The Indians returned several times with food, but each time demanded more for payment. When one of the survivors mentioned the word "soldiers" the Indians became suspicious and angry. They rode off with Trimble and killed him. At that point, some of the survivors decided they would have to get away or they would all be killed.

Van Ornum and his wife, three daughters and two sons, Sam Gleason, and Charles and Henry Utter began walking west. Ten others stayed behind. The Van Ornum group traveled another fifty miles to Farewell Bend, a few miles from the mouth of Burnt River. There they stopped, whether from exhaustion or Indian attack is unknown.[78]

On October 9, word reached Fort Dalles, and Captain Frederick T. Dent, 9th Infantry, took 100 mounted infantry and dragoons, and with Jacob Reith as guide, headed back down the trail. Dent sent an advance detachment of forty dragoons under Lieutenant Marcus A. Reno. On the 19th, Reno found Munson and Chaffee, naked and starving, on Burnt River. Reno left most of his men in camp on Burnt River where the town of Huntington now

Author's photo
Hillside near Huntington, Oregon when the Van Ornum children were captured and their parents killed.

stands, and continued to the Malheur River. Finding nothing, he returned to within two miles of camp when he spotted fresh tracks. Hurrying on, he discovered a ghastly scene: "Gleaming in the moonlight, dead, stripped and mutilated, lay the bodies of six persons." Reno had found the remains of six of the ten who had split off from the rest back on the Owyhee. They appeared to have been dead about five days. Three had their throats slashed, and others were pierced with arrows. Abigail Van Ornum had been whipped, scalped, and "otherwise abused." Reno followed childrens' footprints to the banks of the Snake River. The four of them, Reuben, Eliza, Minerva, and Lucinda Van Ornum, ranging in age from eight to 14, were gone.[79]

Dent pushed another detachment of thirty-five men, under Lieutenant Robert H. Anderson, ahead to the Owyhee River. On October 24, they finally found the first survivors' camp. Dent later reported: "Those still alive were keeping life in them by eating those who had died. I will not attempt to describe the scene of horror this camp presented...those who were still alive were skeletons with life in them; their frantic cries for food rang in our ears incessantly. . . ."[80]

"We became almost frantic," Emeline Trimble wrote years later. "Food we must have, but how should we get it? Then an idea took possession of our minds which we could not mention to

127

each other, so horrid, so revolting to even think of, but the awful madness of hunger was upon us, and we cooked and ate the bodies of each of the poor children, first sister Libbie, then Mr. Chase's little boys, and next my darling little baby sister. . . ." Years later, when Emeline had time to reflect upon her ordeal, she wrote: "Let those who have not suffered as I have pity the fate of the noble red man of the forest. My pity all goes out for their poor unfortunate victims. . . ."[81]

Only fifteen members of the Utter-Van Ornum Train ever reached the Willamette: all seven members of the Myers family, Elizabeth Chase and her daughter, Mary, the Reiths, Munson, Chaffee, Snyder, and Emeline Trimble.[82]

Little is known about the captured children. On November 22, Colonel George Wright, 9th Infantry, penned, "The most energetic measures for the rescue of the Van Ornum children, if they prove to be in the hands of the Indians, as well as for the punishment of the savages concerned in this outrage, will be carried into effect at as early a moment as possible."

Three expeditions, some accompanied by survivors of the massacre, went out to find the Van Ornum children during the next two years, but none were successful. In December 1860, Eagle-From-The-Light, a Nez Perce, with four companions, went to Fort Walla Walla and said he heard that four children were still alive. The authorities made arrangements for the Nez Perce to find and rescue the children. They believed they were taken to the Flathead Agency, but mountain snow prevented their trip that winter, and they lost track of them the next spring. Emeline Trimble heard that the oldest girl killed two Bannock women while trying to escape, and the warriors killed her. The two other girls either wandered off and were lost, or died of starvation; travelers claimed to have seen them at various times, being led around by the Indians with collars on their necks. It was even reported that Indians sold two of the children to the Mormons.

In August 1862, Zachias Van Ornum appeared at Fort Walla Walla. He was the brother of murdered Alexis Van Ornum, and had been searching for his four nephews and nieces, having already spent $5,000 in the process. He accompanied Lieutenant Colonel Reuben F. Maury on an expedition along the Oregon Trail when he learned that one or more of the missing children were seen in Cache Valley, Utah; no rescue was made because the Indians demanded too much money. Zachias went to Camp Douglas near Salt Lake City, and enlisted the aid of Colonel Patrick E. Connor. They learned that Shoshoni Chief Bear Hunter had held the children, but only Reuben remained; the three sisters had died in captivity. On November 20, 1862, Connor sent Major Edward McGarry with sixty men of the 2nd California Cavalry, to rescue Reuben. If McGarry could not get the boy, he was to take three Indians as hostages.

Zachias met McGarry in Cache Valley on the 23rd, and pointed the direction to the Indian camp. When they arrived, the place was deserted. Later in the morning, more than thirty Indians attacked and McGarry chased them up a canyon, but hesitated to advance, fearing an ambush. After two hours of skirmishing, Bear Hunter signaled that he wished to parley. When he told McGarry that Reuben was sent away a few days earlier, McGarry seized the chief and four other warriors as hostages until the boy was brought in. The tactic worked, for the next day, the boy was traded for the Indian hostages.

Reuben Van Ornum, now ten years old, had completely "gone Indian." Only his blue eyes and blond hair suggested his ancestry. He was in good physical shape, but did not appreciate being taken from the Indians. He was said to have acted "like a regular little savage" when reunited with his remaining family, often fighting and kicking when something was disagreeable to him. Zachias and his nephew stayed in Utah for several months, where Zachias was employed by the quartermaster at Camp Douglas and as a scout for Connor.

In the fall of 1864, Reuben and Zachias both guided and interpreted for an army expedition up the Snake River to Salmon Falls. Years later, Zachias went to Chico, California, and in 1896, he was in Douglas County, Oregon, applying for a pension. In 1871, Zachias's granddaughter reported that the old man refused to keep Reuben "because he was so mean to the little kids," and it was likely that "he ran away back to the Indians and Grandpa let him go." Nothing else was heard about Reuben Van Ornum.[83]

FANNY KELLY AND SARAH LARIMER
Wyoming, July 12, 1864

Fannie Wiggins was born in Canada in 1845. James Wiggins, her father, died of cholera while moving the family to Geneva, Kansas, in 1856. They lived there for several years in what Fanny called a "pleasant prairie home." Fanny married Josiah S. Kelly and all seemed well until Josiah's health failed. Hoping that a change of climate would help, Josiah packed up his family to move to Montana, at that time called Idaho Territory. They left in May 1864, for what Fanny called "the golden hills of Idaho." In the wagons were Fanny and Mary Hurley (5), Fanny's niece and adopted daughter, Josiah, two Negro servants, and Gardner Wakefield. During the next couple of weeks Mr. Sharp and William J. Larimer, his wife Sarah, and their son, Frank (8) joined them. The ten emigrants made it safely to Fort Laramie, where they were assured that the road was safe and the Indians were friendly.[84]

Although a few other wagons joined up, they preferred to travel in a small group since they could make better progress. Fanny Kelly tried to ease Mary's fear of Indians, telling her they were civil and harmless. Unfortunately, their idyll was shattered as they crossed the Little Box Elder Creek, about four miles beyond LaPrele Station, where more than 200 Lakotas swept down on the train. Josiah thought they should defend themselves, but, considering the odds, Fanny and Sarah insisted on appeasement. The Indians swarmed around them, professing friendship. One Indian who spoke broken English, introduced himself as "Ottawa," said he was a good Indian, and told them they only wanted food and supplies. They expressed an interest in Josiah's best horse, and he gave it to them.

The emigrants fed the Indians, but with supper over, so was the charade, and the warriors turned on them and began the slaughter. Mr. Kelly, Mr. Larimer, and servant Andy, were wounded, but escaped. Wakefield was shot down and mortally wounded. Franklin, another servant, was pierced with many arrows. Sharp went down a few feet from Fanny, and a Mr. Taylor was shot in the forehead with a rifle ball. The Indians tore through the wagons, looting and destroying. They captured Fanny Kelly, Sarah Larimer, and the two children.[85]

Josiah and Andy ran along the trail and came upon a larger emigrant train about eight miles east. He spread the alarm, but was disappointed when the train leader chose to corral the wagons and wait instead of going out to help rescue the captives. At the attack scene, Sarah Larimer was distraught, saying, "The men have all escaped, and left us to the mercy of the savages." Fanny thought it was better then being killed, because they might still be able to rescue them. She put on a brave front, but admitted, "Those hours of misery can never be forgotten."[86]

That evening, the Indians directed the women to gather up some extra clothing and they headed north. In the darkness, Fanny let Mary slip off the horse they were riding, with instructions to hide, then make her way back along the creek to the main trail. The scheme seemed to work, and soon Fanny tried the same trick.

Author's photo
Little Box Elder Creek, Wyoming, near the Kelly, Larimer capture site.

She slid off her horse and crouched on the ground, but Indians following behind discovered, recaptured, and beat her. She told them Mary had fallen off and she was trying to find her. They placed Fanny back on the horse and said they would find the girl in the morning. Indians did find Mary, but whether warriors of the same party or another, is unknown. Mary was killed, scalped, and left in the trail.

When Josiah Kelly finally got the other emigrant train to move forward the next day, they buried the bodies and rescued Mr. Larimer, who had hidden in the bushes all night. Sullenly, they moved on to Deer Creek Station at present-day Glenrock, Wyoming, and reported the attack. A telegraph message was sent to Fort Laramie, and Colonel William O. Collins, 11th Ohio Cavalry, ordered a pursuit.

Company H, thirty men of Company G, and detachments of companies E, I, and K, 11th Ohio—about 160 men and two howitzers—assembled at Deer Creek Station. Captains Jacob S. Shuman and Levi G. Marshall left at 1 a.m. on July 19, and crossed the North Platte River with the dual purpose of looking for the Indians and rescuing Fanny Kelly. Lieutenant John R. Brown, Company E, accompanied by Mr. Kelly and about one dozen troopers, scouted ahead and ran into a band of about forty warriors. Several of the skittish troopers broke for the rear, while Brown, seeing the hopelessness of running, tried to parley. The

Indians shot an arrow into Brown's back. Kelly sped away with the rest of the troopers. They alerted the main camp and a pursuit was mounted, but the Indians escaped in the darkness. Brown died the next morning. The command searched to Powder River before turning back. Fanny Kelly was gone.[87]

Surprisingly, on the second night after the wagon train attack, while the Indians made their first camp, the Larimers escaped. Fanny had been tied up for the night because of her previous escape attempt, and before they were separated, Sarah made Fanny promise not to leave her. Instead, Sarah and Frank Larimer crept away in the darkness, leaving Fanny behind. After four days of wandering, tired and hungry, they stumbled onto Deer Creek Station and were reunited with William Larimer, who was there recovering from his wound. When he could travel again, they gave up the idea of going to Montana, and returned to Kansas.[88]

One Lakota band claimed Fanny Kelly and took her north to the Tongue River. Along the way she tore up bits of paper, hoping to leave a trail for any would-be rescuers. Fanny was given little food or water, and had no blanket or shelter at night. Incredibly, one of Fanny's notes was found twelve years later by Lieutenant James H. Bradley, 7th Infantry. Bradley was on a scout for Colonel John Gibbon in the preliminary stages of the campaign that resulted in the Battle of the Little Bighorn, when, on May 21, 1876, he was searching through an Indian burial scaffold near the junction of the Rosebud and Yellowstone Rivers. Among the items buried with the warrior was a paper signed by Fanny Kelly, that concluded, "I am compelled to do their bidding." Bradley was angry. "'To do their bidding!'" he wrote in his journal. "Alas, how many poor captive women have suffered this to them worse fate than death! May the end of such atrocities be near at hand! May the military operations. . .result in so complete an overthrow of the hell-hounds called Sioux that never again shall poor women be made the victims of such barbarity at their hands!"[89]

The Indians, with Kelly in tow, moved from the Rosebud and Tongue and passed north of the Black Hills. In late July 1864, they reached a large village near the badlands east of the Little Missouri. Fanny was subjected to numerous cruelties. She narrowly escaped death when she carelessly discarded a chief's pipe. She had few good things to say about the Indians she traveled with. They were wasteful of the buffalo they killed for food, with each Indian taking only a little part that he liked best, and leaving the rest to decay. She saw many mixed-blood children treated cruelly by the full blood boys and girls. On the other hand, she was given a little girl named Yellow Bird, to replace her own dead daughter. Some Indian women threatened to kill her, but another took her in. Fanny realized that the "dusky maidens of romance" she had read about were only fictional, "in strange contrast with the flesh and blood realities into whose hands I had fallen." How different, she lamented, were "the stately Logan, the fearless Philip, the bold Black Hawk, the gentle Pocahontas," from "the greedy, cunning and cruel savages who had so ruthlessly torn me from my friends!" The novels were all fantasy. "The true red man, as I saw him" Fanny said, "does not exist between the pages of many volumes."[90]

Kansas State Historical Society
Fanny Kelly

Whoever the "true red man" was, Fanny had many opportunities to observe the examples. Ottawa, or Silver Horn, traded her to a Hunkpapa named Brings Plenty. The village moved near Killdeer Mountain, where, on July 28, it was attacked by an expedition under Brigadier General Alfred Sully. Sully's 2,200 soldiers faced about 3,000 warriors in what was one of the largest battles of all the Indian wars. By the day's end, Sully's tenacious tactics and punishing artillery fire forced the Indians to abandon the village and flee to the west. Sully pursued them, and on August 7-9, fought them several more times in the badlands along the Little Missouri. Fanny Kelly was caught up in the chaos, and witnessed a wild scalp dance, which she likened to "a picture of fiends in a carnival of battle." The Indians were pushed west toward the Yellowstone, and they lost many of their supplies and equipment. They almost starved during the next few weeks, and some Indians wanted to take revenge on Fanny, but Brings Plenty kept her from harm.[91]

About this time, Fanny met another captive girl, Mary Boyeau. She was at her home near Spirit Lake, Iowa, during the Minnesota Sioux Uprising in August 1862. Her family was murdered and

133

Mary, then 14 years old, was captured. She was treated as a child for one year, until a warrior traded a horse for her and, said Mary, "carried me to his tipi as his wife." She hated him and his other wife, who starved her and beat her, and despised everything about "this fearful bondage." She hoped her younger sister was dead, because, she said, "From a life like mine death is an escape." Mary expressed interest in a book and a pencil that Fanny managed to salvage from the wagon train she had been captured from. Fanny gave her the book and half the pencil, happy for the one small act of kindness she could offer to Mary before she was taken away.[92]

The Indians traveled into what is now southwestern North Dakota, near present day Marmarth, where they attacked an eighty-eight-wagon train of about 200 emigrants under Captain James L. Fisk. They fought on September 2, and the siege that followed lasted more than two weeks. The Lakotas forced Fanny to negotiate for them, making her write a note that demanded supplies in exchange for Fanny and freedom to pass through the territory. Kelly carefully phrased the note, warning of the Indians' treachery. Fisk responded, offering three horses, flour, sugar, and coffee for her, but the Lakotas wanted forty head of cattle and four wagons. The Indians would not release her, and rode away after a few more days. General Sully dispatched 900 men to rescue Fisk and escort the wagon train back to Fort Rice.[93]

By October, the Lakotas had not driven the army out of their territory and it would be a cold, dangerous, winter with so many soldiers nearby. The Indians suddenly became more conciliatory. On October 23, about 200 Hunkpapas and Blackfeet Sioux, led by Bear's Rib, negotiated for peace with Captain John H. Pell at Fort Sully. Pell pressed his advantage and said that the soldiers would not stop fighting until the white woman was released. Brings Plenty would not negotiate until Sitting Bull intervened. Sitting Bull's honor was at stake more than his desire to help the white men, and the chief's implicit menace finally persuaded him. On December 9, a delegation of Blackfeet Sioux brought Fanny Kelly to Fort Sully. The gate opened, and once she crossed the threshold, the gate slammed behind her. "Am I free, indeed free?" she asked.

Fanny had a different recollection in her own narrative. She said her captor sold her to the Blackfeet, who planned to use her as a decoy to get into the fort. She sent a note to the commander and warned him, and a number of soldiers of the 6th Iowa Cavalry stationed there confirmed her version. When the Blackfeet brought her in, she was rushed through the gate and the trailing Indians, decked out in paint and singing war songs, were shut out. She was poorly clad, her limbs were nearly frozen, and she had to be confined to the fort hospital for two months.[94]

For the five months Fanny was captive, her husband had sent many messengers with horses and money to try to ransom her. When she was at Fort Sully, Josiah was at Fort Leavenworth recruiting a company of men to invade Lakota territory to rescue her, but Fanny didn't believe he had made a serious enough effort to rescue her. When word arrived, Josiah rushed to Fort Sully.

Husband and wife started down the Missouri and were engulfed by crowds of people in Yankton, Sioux City, and Council Bluffs, who wanted to see the rescued white woman. The Kellys returned to Geneva, and then moved to Ellsworth, where they opened a rooming house. Josiah died of cholera in 1867. Fanny was invited to Cheyenne, Wyoming, to share the home of Mr. and Mrs. Larimer. After one year, Fanny went to Washington D.C. where she made a claim against the government for restitution of her losses, for her service in saving the Fisk Train, and for warning the soldiers at Fort Sully. President Grant extended his sympathies to her and, in April 1870, Congress awarded her $5,000.

All was not well, however, for in October 1870, Fanny Kelly commenced a lawsuit against Sarah Larimer. Apparently she and Sarah made an agreement in 1865, that they would prepare a joint memoir of their experiences with both names appearing as co-authors. In May 1869, Sarah took the manuscript to Philadelphia where it was published in her name only and as her own work. Clearly, almost all of the Indian captivity experiences were Fanny's. At the first trial, Kelly recovered a judgment of $5,000. Two more appeals followed, and the last one finally declared that the payment should only be one-half of the value of the manuscript when Sarah Larimer took it. Kelly was only awarded $285.50. The case was bitterly contested, with the last hearings dragging on until 1876, and the women becoming enemies.

Fanny Kelly published her own version of the story in 1871. She married a second time in 1880. She still owned the old homestead in Geneva, Kansas, obtained a government job in Washington, and invested her money wisely. She was moderately wealthy when she died in Washington in December 1904. Sarah Larimer later moved to Oklahoma and was still alive after Fanny had passed away.[95]

NANCY FLETCHER MORTON AND DANIEL MARBLE
Nebraska, August 8. 1864

Nancy Fletcher was born in 1845 to Samuel and Charlotte Fletcher of Clarke County, Indiana. The Fletchers moved to Sidney, Iowa, when Nancy was 4 years old. She married Thomas Frank Morton in 1860, when she was only 15. In the span of four years they had two children, Charlotte Ann and Samuel Thomas. Mother and children contracted measles in the spring of 1863; Nancy survived, but both children died. In August 1864, after a long grieving period, Nancy decided to join her husband, her brother William, and her cousin, John Fletcher, on their last freighting trip of the season.

Unbeknownst to them, the old road they were about to take was to become the focal point of shocking Indian raids, soon to be described in the *New York Times* as a route where "devastation, terror, and murder has held a perfect carnival. From Denver to Fort Larimee [*sic*] to the Little Blue in Kansas. . .the Rebel Indians have swept like a hurricane. . . . They have murdered 200 white persons, among them many women and children. The stark bodies lie stripped and mutilated in the glaring sunlight, festering and rotting for the want of burial; or half charred are seen smoldering amid the ruins of ranches, cabins, and stage stations."[96]

The unsuspecting travelers rode into the thick of it. The wagon train consisted of Morton's three wagons, Michael Kelly's six wagons and his six teamsters, and William Marble's three wagons, including James Smith and his wife, Charles Iliff, Mr. St. Clair, and Marble's son, Danny. They spent the night of August 7 camped near Plum Creek, on the south side of the Platte about thirty miles west of Fort Kearny.

The next morning, Nancy Morton climbed into the wagon and took the reins so her husband could rest. Lieutenant Joseph Bone, 7th Iowa Cavalry, was nearby at the Thomas Ranch, when he spied Indians descending the bluffs to the south. A crescent shaped formation of about 100 Indians thundered down upon the wagon train. The wagons scattered, some toward the bluffs and others toward the river. The defenders, armed only with pistols, were little threat to the Indians. From Plum Creek Station, Bone sent a plea for help to Colonel Samuel Summers at Fort Kearny: "Send [a] company of men here as quick as God can send them. One hundred Indians in sight firing on ox train."[97]

There would be no last-second rescue. The Morton wagon pulled off toward the bluffs and Nancy swung over the side, but hit the

Author's photo
Plum Creek massacre site, Nebraska, where Nancy Morton and Danny Marble
were captured by Cheyennes.

wagon wheel and broke several ribs. The last words she heard
from her husband were, "O my dear, where are you going?" Her
brother and cousin stood in the grass firing at the warriors as they
circled. Within minutes almost everyone was slain; Mrs. Smith
escaped into the reeds by the river while Nancy Morton, wounded
by two arrows, and Danny Marble, were captured. "Those killed
were all scalped in my presence," recalled Nancy.[98]

An aged warrior beat Nancy with a whip when she refused
to ride with him. Two warriors threatened to kill her, but she
told them, "I would rather die than to be led into captivity."
Nevertheless, they put her on a pony. An Indian, who Nancy later
remembered as Red Cloud, forced her to ride behind him, while
Big Bear took Danny Marble. Many of the Cheyennes were Dog
Soldiers under Bull Bear. They frequently threatened the captives
with death.[99]

Colonel Summers arrived at ten p.m., much too late to catch
the Indians. He discovered Mrs. Smith hiding in a field and in
a state of shock. The next morning, the soldiers buried eleven
men in a mass grave, and two others where they had been killed
farther down the road. The bodies were stripped, scalped, and full
of arrows. Some had their eyes gouged out, and others had their
tongues cut out. Some had their genitals cut off and stuffed into
their mouths.

The Indians stopped at noon to rest and eat. Danny Marble ran to Nancy for comfort, and with good sense he concluded, "Let's do what they want and then they won't kill us." Then they sat down and cried. A man who Nancy described as a "swarthy Frenchman," helped remove the two arrows still protruding from her side. Later, Big Crow, who would be one of Nancy's main tormentors, rubbed her brother's bloody scalp in her face. Danny became so sick that he thought he would die. Morton tried to sooth him and said, "surely God would rescue us from their demon hands."[100]

The second night, the warriors performed a war dance around a pole decorated with scalps. Nancy thought she would be tortured and killed, but she survived; her unborn baby did not. "I suffered terribly," she said, "I had a miscarriage on account of my severe and ill treatment, and my eyes went blind." Indian women swarmed on Nancy and beat and kicked her. The Frenchman, who Nancy called "John Brown," visited her again.[101] He questioned her and taunted her, and when she demanded that he leave, he told her that she was not the only captive in the village. Thus, Nancy learned that she had partners in misery (see Lucinda Eubank and Laura Roper). Next, George Bent, the mixed-blood son of trader William Bent and the Cheyenne, Owl Woman, came to see her and said he would try to get the medicine man to give her some herbs to cure her wounds. The treatment seemed to work. The other captives, Lucinda Eubank and Laura Roper, were brought to see her for a short visit, but the Indians never left them alone for long, for fear they would plot to escape.

Danny Marble did not fare well. He knew his father was dead and he cried often. Needing security and affection, he converted Nancy Morton into his surrogate mother. She provided what comfort she could, but overwhelmed with their situation and in a moment of despair she proclaimed she wanted to die. The alarmed boy protested, "Then I will be left all alone!" A group of drunken braves began to hurl spears and arrows toward the boy and Nancy told them to stop and leave him alone for, "He is my papoose."

The chief's son wanted to marry Nancy but she refused. Warriors threatened to kill her, and Bent said that she must marry if she wanted to live, but Nancy was adamant. Finally an old chief interceded and declared the marriage did not have to take place. He sheltered Nancy in his tipi and promised to release her when peace was achieved.

As summer drew to a close, the Cheyennes realized that winter was not a good time for war with the white man. Previously they had ignored Colorado Territorial Governor John Evans's peace proclamation. Now, urged on by William Bent, some of the chiefs, led by Black Kettle, had letters written to Agent Samuel Colley at Fort Lyon. The letters said they wanted peace and would trade their seven white captives for peace and for Indian captives they believed were being held in Denver.[102]

Contrary to military orders, Major Edward Wynkoop marched out to the headwaters of the Smoky Hill and met in council with Black Kettle and other chiefs. Wynkoop agreed to take some of the Indians to Denver to see Governor Evans. The next day, Arapahoes Left Hand and Neva took one captive to the soldiers (see Laura Roper). The following day, September 12, Danny Marble and two other captives (see Isabelle Eubank and Ambrose Asher) were released. Wynkoop had four captives, but what about the other three?

During the council, Lucinda Eubank, Willie Eubank, and Nancy Morton were hurried away to a distant tipi and forced to lie under buffalo robes and remain silent. To further demoralize them, after the council ended, the Indians let the women watch, unable to cry out, as Wynkoop and the soldiers marched away. Black Kettle had deceived Wynkoop into believing that the Sioux held the other three prisoners. Wynkoop swallowed the story and marched back to Fort Lyon, taking along Chiefs White Antelope, Bull Bear, Black Kettle, Neva, No-Ta-Nee, Bosse, and Heap of Buffalo. They arrived in Denver on September 25, and four of the ex-hostages began their re-assimilation. It would not be an easy process.[103]

Danny Marble was characterized as perceptive, creative, and talkative. At Fort Lyon, Private William F. Smith of Company D, 1st Colorado Cavalry, took Danny Marble under his wing and the boy was an immediate hit with all the troopers. The company collected $76.50 for clothing and other necessities. Mentally, Danny seemed to have withstood his captivity with little damage, but he was not well physically. In Denver he caught typhoid fever. Doctor W. F. McClelland offered to care for him free of charge, but he was sent to Camp Weld military hospital under Doctor A. A. Smith, Assistant Surgeon of the 1st Colorado. He treated Danny as well as he could, but the boy died on November 9. The army neglected to notify his mother, and it was not until December 1, 1864, that Doctor McClelland wrote a letter to Ann Marble informing her of her son's death. Laura Roper corresponded with Ann Marble, and on January 7, 1865, she wrote, "Hope your wish will come true that every one of the Indians will be extinguished. . .Poor little

Dan wish he was alive. . .Keep up good spirits you will meet him in heaven. . . ."[104]

The three remaining captives were still with the Cheyennes. On September 25, on the same day that Black Kettle and the "peace chiefs" arrived in Denver, their warriors were in Kansas fighting with Major General James G. Blunt's forces on the Pawnee River. Blunt reported nine Indians killed, and when the defeated warriors returned to their camps, the captives felt the brunt of their anger. The Indians rubbed bloody scalps in their faces and threatened them with death. Warriors heaped firewood around a stake and the women feared they would be burned. Instead, a buffalo roast and ceremonial dance took place. One twirling warrior snatched Willie from Lucinda's arms and feigned throwing him in the flames, but another returned him to his mother.[105]

The Indians gave Nancy a test of strength and skill, and by performing well beyond what the Indians thought her capable of, she was allowed to live to see another day. Lucinda Eubank and Nancy Morton plotted an escape. On the pretense of gathering fresh fruit they left camp. About two miles away they felt they had successfully given their captors the slip, but several Indian women discovered them and forced them back to the village.

Lucinda suffered a severe emotional episode when, prior to the departure of a group of raiding warriors, she flung herself to the ground and screamed, "They are going to kill more whites!" She took a bite of the sod, bit her own arm, and went into hysterics. The Indians had to restrain Lucinda, and the chief was fed up with all the disruptions and wanted to kill her. Nancy pleaded for another chance, and the next day Lucinda seemed saner. The bands headed north, and eventually split up near the headwaters of the Republican River. Morton went north and Eubank went west. They would never see each other again.[106]

The Indians holding Morton continued to raid and kill. A few weeks later six traders and Indians from Fort Laramie appeared, bringing news that the soldiers wanted to trade for captives. The traders secretly told Nancy of a plot to have her persuade the Indians to take her to the fort to trade for provisions, and then they would kill the Indians and free her. Her captor suspected treachery, and asked Morton what the trader had said. She told him that they wanted to trade her for provisions, but the suspicious Indian did not believe her. Instead, he said, Nancy would be burned at the stake! She was horrified, but determined that she could take no more of this torment. The post and the firewood were prepared, but Nancy was defiant.

"I was very glad of it," she said, "that all my troubles would cease and I would go to the happy hunting ground and would never see them again." Her defiance of death despite their dancing and chanting in preparation of her barbeque resulted in her release. They called her a "brave white squaw" and held a war dance instead of a roast.[107]

Food was scarce as winter set in. Nancy became ill, fell from her horse, and lapsed into unconsciousness. The Indians later brought her a white man's medicine case and asked her to sample various potions. She spied one, labeled, "strychnine," which she pretended to taste and then passed to a chief who swallowed it down and died within minutes. The Indians declared the bottle an evil spirit and buried it deep in the earth.

For six months Nancy witnessed the Indians going out to steal and kill. It seemed that no matter how she behaved, she was "subject to their passions and lusts, and the most brutal treatment that mortal being could be subjected to."[108] The Indians placed Morton on a wild horse, and she was thrown to the ground and broke her ankle. Once, a trader named Mr. Smith got Nancy to come to his camp to help his Indian wife with some work. Both Smiths spoke English and it was a welcome break for Nancy. Mrs. Smith fixed coffee, bread, and buffalo meat for dinner and gave Nancy a dress. Believing she was trying to escape, the old chief dragged Nancy back to his tipi, whipped her, and starved her. She became so despondent she tried to hang herself from a tipi pole, but her captor caught her and hauled her down.[109]

With starvation threatening the entire village, the Indians decided to trade Nancy for food and supplies. Post commander, Major John Wood, was ecstatic. He sent Spotted Horse and Little Horse with ponies laden with food and gifts to the chief, but the mission was a failure. The Indians felt that the goods offered were insufficient.

In December, Jules Ecoffey and Joe Bissonette Jr. tried to strike a bargain, offering $398 worth of coffee, flour, sugar, and tobacco, but the deal fell through. Nancy's hopes were dashed as the tribe moved into the Big Horn Mountains. Trader John Rousseau told Major Wood the pot wasn't sweet enough for the Indians, who believed that Morton must be the wife of a wealthy man. Ecoffey and Bissonette tried again, taking the major's two prize steeds and a pack train of supplies to the Indian camp. In mid-January, 1865, they trekked 200 miles through the snow to reach their destination. After bargaining until late in the night, the old chief gave in and agreed to release his captive for $2,154 worth of goods.[110]

The next morning, the traders took Morton and hurried away before the Indians changed their minds. They plodded on for seven days to Platte Bridge Station. From there the trip was easier, and Nancy rode in an army ambulance to Fort Laramie, reaching the post January 30. At one of the way stations, Nancy recognized Big Crow, one of the Cheyennes at the Plum Creek Massacre who had tormented her so much. She relayed this information to Major Thomas MacKay at Fort Laramie. Big Crow was caught, thrown in the guardhouse, and in late April, he was hanged. Nancy Jane Morton's 176 days of physical and mental torment came to an end.[111]

On February 26, Nancy left in a wagon train for Fort Kearny. They stopped at Plum Creek to allow her time for reflection. She took a coach from Kearny to Nebraska City, and then made a precarious crossing of the Missouri River on a skiff. At last, on March 19, 1865, Nancy arrived at her parents' home in Sidney, Iowa. "Oh, the joy that reigned supreme in the family is almost indescribable," she said. "It seemed to me like I had arose from the dead, and had awakened and found myself in Paradise."

Nancy married George Stevens on November 19, 1865. She filed a depredation claim in conjunction with Matthew Pratt, who was partner in the freighting business with her late husband. Secretary of the Interior Orville Browning sent a request to the superintendent of Indian affairs to settle the claim in favor of Pratt and Morton. It was settled on December 9, 1868. Pratt was to have received $20,104, and Nancy Stevens $6,041. Her payment was to have included a $5,000 indemnity for her suffering in captivity, which was highly irregular and not usually allowed. The government may have realized it made a mistake and reneged. In January 1871, Nancy filed another deposition, saying that she had previously sold her interest in the claim to Matthew Pratt for $1,500, and likely re-filed because of the small amount of money she actually received.

Years later, Nancy and George Stevens moved to a farm in Jefferson, Iowa. They had four children and remained happily married. Complications from the injuries Nancy received as a captive plagued her in later life. The development of a goiter compounded her other problems, causing difficulty in swallowing and breathing. Nancy Jane Fletcher Morton Stevens choked to death on August 24, 1912, at 67 years of age.[112]

MRS. ANNA SNYDER
Colorado, August 14, 1864

Fort Lyon in Colorado Territory was a focal point for heated Indian/army confrontations during the summer of 1864. Newly arrived in Denver, was a Mrs. Anna Snyder, who had come west at the bidding of her husband, who worked as a blacksmith at Fort Lyon. John Snyder, Company E, 1st Colorado Cavalry, talked the quartermaster into letting him have an ambulance for the 200-mile trip to pick up his wife. A teamster named Bennett and possibly a soldier, Joel H. Dyer of Company F, accompanied them. They picked Anna up in Denver, drove south to Pueblo, and east along the Arkansas. They stopped in Booneville, at the home of Colonel Albert G. Boone, grandson of Daniel Boone and ex-Indian agent at Fort Lyon. There, Eliza, an old woman who had lived with Boone's family for years, told Mrs. Snyder, "You all got a mighty fine head of hair for the Injuns to git, honey."

The frightened woman answered, "Oh, don't say that, for I have heard such terrible stories of how they abuse the prisoners."

The next day the little group headed for Bent's Old Fort, but they never arrived. On August 14 they were attacked by a band of more than forty Arapahoes led by Little Raven's son, who the day before had led a raid at Point of Rocks Agency and stole twenty-eight head of stock. The Indians overwhelmed them. The westbound stage came upon the attack site shortly after the Indians left, and Thomas Pollock reported finding the bodies of three men. John Snyder was scalped and his testicles were cut off and stuffed into his mouth. One of his legs was cut off, while he was hung on the ambulance by the other leg. The two other men were also killed and mutilated. The woman was missing.

Captain Isaac Gray, Company E, 1st Colorado Cavalry, was in command at the new Camp Fillmore, which was built just above Booneville early in the summer because old Camp Fillmore had poor grass for grazing stock. Gray rode eight miles downriver to the murder site very near the grounds of the old abandoned camp. He sent scouts out in all directions but they could not pick up a trail. All Gray found were the bodies, an ambulance, and a wagon containing the remnants of the Snyder's household furniture. He reported that "The inhabitants in this settlement are much excited, and a great many think of abandoning their farms." He only had thirty-eight men and didn't know how he could protect them.[113]

After stealing horses from Charles Autobee's Ranch, the Arapahoes rode away with their plunder. The longhaired Anna Snyder was raped repeatedly and taken to the growing camps on the upper Solomon. Two other white captives being held in the Cheyenne camp (see Nancy Morton and Laura Roper) heard that another white woman was in the nearby sixty-lodge Arapaho village. Neither woman got to see Mrs. Snyder alive, however. Only a short time after she arrived, she tried to escape, getting several miles from camp before being recaptured. The distraught woman, seeing her husband slaughtered and despairing of ever being released, gave up hope. One night she tore her calico dress into strips, twisted them into a rope and hanged herself from the crossed tipi poles in a lodge. Laura Roper was shown the body before she was cut down. Nancy Morton thought that the Arapahoes had killed her.[114]

AMANDA M. AND ELIZABETH FLETCHER
Wyoming, July 31, 1865

Jasper Fletcher was born in Derbyshire, England, came to America in 1861, and moved to Henry County, Illinois. He made good money as a mining engineer in England, received more money from his father, and brought with him about 21,000 English pounds when he emigrated. Fletcher lived five years in Illinois before deciding to move to California. The family consisted of Jasper, wife Mary Ann, and children, Amanda (13), William (11), Jasper Jr. (6), Oscar (5), and Elizabeth (3). All of the children except Lizzie were born in England.

Mr. Fletcher bought two wagons, three horses, and four sets of harnesses for the trip. The large wagon was loaded with tea, tobacco, bacon, sugar, and two feather beds. Jasper had six new suits of clothes, two overcoats, and two sets of carpenter's tools. Mary Ann had a $75 velvet dress, five silk dresses, and a shawl that cost 100 pounds, all purchased in England. They bought an additional $500 of provisions in Rock Island. They left Illinois on May 10, 1865, and went across Iowa and Nebraska to what Amanda Fletcher called "Jewel Station" (Julesburg). From there they went to Denver and rested for two weeks. Amanda was not sure about the route after this point, but she believed they next went to Fort Laramie. At the fort they got orders that they had to have at least seventy-five armed men to proceed, so they hooked up with large train of seventy-five wagons and 300 people and continued west.[115]

144

Author's photo
Rock Creek, Wyoming, near the capture site of Amanda and Elizabeth Fletcher.

The Fletchers never became well acquainted with any other families and kept slightly ahead of the main group. On Monday, the last day of July, they stopped for dinner just east of Rock Creek Station, about twenty-five miles east of Fort Halleck. There was a bridge over the creek and the toll was seventy-five cents per wagon. Joe Bush built the station in 1860, and lived there with his Indian wife.[116] Jasper Fletcher never saw an Indian in his life before this day, when nearly 300 Cheyenne and Arapaho rode out of the mountains and attacked. Mary Ann, Amanda, and Lizzie had strolled closer to the creek and about 300 yards from the wagons. Warriors cut them off, killed Mary Ann, threw Amanda and Lizzie on their ponies, and took them across the bridge and part way up the hillside. An arrow hit Jasper in the right wrist, but he and his boys escaped to the east where they met up with the main wagon train. Amanda watched the Indians plunder their wagons and set them aflame.

Warriors stole all of the clothes, ripped open the feather beds, threw the feathers to the wind, and kept only the ticking. Packed among the wagon's contents was a green sheet iron moneybox, 12 by 18 inches in size. Amanda knew it well. She was in charge of its safety and had counted the money many times. Inside were 17,000 English-pound notes and 3,000 in gold sovereigns. The family had discussed taking so much money with them, but American money fluctuated in value, and they figured the English pound was good

145

and the gold better. "Their money was good anyplace," Amanda said.[117]

The Indians broke open the moneybox and took some of the money to Joe Bush; Amanda saw him take it. The Indians stayed in the area. Three days later, Amanda saw "one family swept out of existence, with the exception of the white woman. She was captured, and killed shortly afterwards." This may have been part of the same sequence of events noted by W. L. Kuykendall, who went through the area in a wagon train about the same time. He saw Indians on a hill north of Rock Creek, "having a white woman with them, whom they treated in a fiendish manner in plain view of all of us." The men of the train were enraged, and they wanted to rescue the woman, but the wagon boss figured she was being used as a decoy to bring them out and ambush them. He corralled up and threatened to shoot the first man who tried to leave. When they didn't take the bait, the Indians rode off and left the woman, possibly a Mrs. Carrick, "because she had gone crazy." She reached the train, but was "in a pitiful condition" and "unable to give any account of herself."[118]

The warriors, many from Sand Hill's band of Cheyennes, took Lizzie from Amanda on the first day. Minimic was Amanda's captor, and his band separated from the main party after two or three weeks. About this time, George Bent, the mixed-blood son of trader William Bent, who was raiding with the Indians, met Amanda. She told him that the Civil War was over. George passed on this important information to the chiefs, believing it was a bad omen because it would probably free up more soldiers to come west and fight the Indians.[119]

The Cheyenne band that held Amanda made its way from present-day Wyoming to Kansas, keeping her well hidden. Amanda turned 14 on August 19, a birthday she dejectedly kept to herself. Indians showed her the stolen money and asked her to count it for them. Minimic alone had about 2,400 English pounds. Amanda suffered through the fall and winter, often times being hungry and cold. Her situation quickly changed in late winter of 1866.

The Indians first used their stolen money when they bought sugar, coffee, flour, and blankets from William Bent, in the sand hills about four days travel south of the Arkansas River. The Indians gave the money to Amanda to count to make sure it was correct, and she passed it to Bent. Amanda was somewhat amused at the Indian woman who made earrings out of the gold sovereigns. After doing business with Bent, the Indians moved on.

Several days later, Charles Hanger, a partner in the firm of Hanger & Morris, and working under the auspices of Agent I. C. Taylor, rode into a nearby Arapaho camp on Bluff Creek about forty miles southeast of Fort Dodge. He traded with the Arapahoes for a few days, then packed up and moved to the Cheyenne camps. The Indians were in the Bluff Creek area for a meeting with U.S. government representatives who wanted to get signatures from the remaining chiefs who had not signed the Little Arkansas Treaty in October 1865. Special Agent Edward W. Wynkoop was charged with getting their approval. He left Fort Dodge with a sixty-man escort of 2nd Cavalry troopers under Captain George A. Gordon. The Indians included bands under Black Kettle, Poor Bear, Heap of Bears, Stone Forehead, Big Head, Little Raven, and Big Mouth. The council began February 28, 1866. After a tense time with the Dog Soldiers, Bull Bear and Porcupine Bear, who had threatened to kill Wynkoop, the recalcitrant Dog Soldiers finally touched the pen. Wynkoop distributed presents and left the camps on March 3 with his hide intact. Nearly 4,000 Indians were still in the area when Hanger rode in with his trade goods.

"I visited a camp of Cheyenne dog soldiers in February," Hanger said, "and found among them a captive white girl, aged about fourteen years." He had done about $14,000 worth of business, and was quite satisfied with the outcome, when he noticed the girl. Minimic had just paid Hanger for his supplies with the money stolen from the Fletcher wagons, and he noticed Amanda handling and counting the money. He immediately knew that he must try to buy her, but Minimic wanted a high price. Since Hanger had just made plenty of money, he met Minimic's demand: $1,665!

"I did the trade that bought Mrs. [Fletcher] Cook at the time," Hanger later deposed, and it occurred either the last day of February or the first of March. Jasper Fletcher's money had served some good purpose. The next morning, Hanger sent Amanda with one of the mixed-blood Poisal Brothers back to the Arapaho camp, where his interpreter was finishing up business. From there, Captain Gordon escorted her to Fort Dodge and then Fort Larned, where she was "given in charge of Major Wynkoop the Indian agent at the post."[120]

Amanda was sent to Davenport, Iowa, where her father had acquaintances who agreed to take her in. Hanger kept in touch with her, and learned that the Fletchers were people of "very good circumstances" until the attack. Amanda learned that her father and brothers survived and were living in Salt Lake City, but her father was nearly destitute, and could not afford to send for her. At first, Jasper and Amanda assumed little Elizabeth had been killed, but they kept seeking information. They heard rumors that she might still be held captive, wrote to Lieutenant Colonel George A. Custer, at Fort Riley, Kansas, and asked him for help in locating her. Custer wrote to Amanda on January 27, 1867, saying that he had news that a little white girl was being held by the Cheyenne Cut Nose. Lieutenant Owen Hale and guide Will Comstock had seen her on the Smoky Hill River, 250 miles west of Fort Riley and near Fort Wallace. Custer told Amanda that Comstock believed the child could be ransomed for a couple of horses. Jasper, unfortunately, did not have enough money to buy horses and send out traders to recover the girl.[121]

When, in the late winter of 1867, Custer heard that the military had in their possession a boy belonging to the Cheyennes, he wrote to General Winfield S. Hancock that it would be a good strategy to trade the boy for Elizabeth Fletcher. Custer explained that the mother was dead, the father was in Salt Lake City, and the elder daughter, Amanda, was in Iowa. He received several letters from them imploring him to get the little girl back, and he wanted to help. The government, however, in a fit of penitence after Sand Creek, thought it best not to further antagonize the Indians. Custer's trade proposition failed and Lizzie was never recovered.

The last he heard of the girl was before the campaign of 1867 began. She belonged to Cut Nose, who was camped along the Smoky Hill near Monument Station. The Indian frequently came in to the stage stations to trade, and was often accompanied by the captive. Custer never saw her, but reports reached him that she was a beautiful girl from four to seven years old, with fair complexion, blue eyes, and silver-gold hair. Cut Nose was said to have given her the name "Little Silver Hair," and did not seem inclined to sell her. When the fighting began in the spring of 1867, Custer heard no more about her.[122]

Amanda married Judge William E. Cook, of Davenport, Iowa, on December 31, 1867. They had six children. On January 2, 1866, Jasper compiled an itemized list of his losses in the Indian attack, which totaled $6,295. Two years later, when no action was taken on his claim and he heard that no cash losses could be declared, he amended his damages to $2,032, and then re-amended them to $2,356. Nothing came of it. In Salt Lake City in 1871, Amanda saw her father for the first time since the 1865 attack. In the 1870s, Jasper, Jasper Jr., and Amanda renewed their compensation efforts. Jasper Fletcher died in October 1875, and finally on December 10, 1875, Agent John D. Miles submitted Jasper's claim to the Cheyennes in council, and they admitted "committing the outrage."

When government representatives asked Amanda if the Indians who attacked her were hostile, she somewhat sarcastically answered: "Well I should think so from appearances that day."

On January 24, 1876, Amanda complicated the affair by submitting her own list of damages, for $7,915. Jasper Jr. submitted a similar list in February. When these conflicting claims wound their way through the bureaucracy, the Commissioner of Indian Affairs made his recommendation to the Secretary of Interior that the case be disallowed because the amount of loss was not satisfactorily shown. The claim was transferred to the House of Representatives in February 1876, which sent it back to the commissioner for reconsideration.

Not until November 1885, due to new legislation about Indian claims, did the department look at it again. The commissioner believed the case was proven, but differences in amounts caused doubts. Still, Assistant Commissioner A. B. Upshaw recommended payment of $2,356. Again, the recommendation was not concurred, and in December 1885, it was sent back to a field representative. In September 1887, Special Agent Leonard H. Poole decided that Jasper's amended amount was the most accurate, although he wanted Amanda to produce more evidence. He stated that money had been deducted from the Indian annuities to cover the expenses of Amanda's recovery,[123] which was *ipso facto* proof that the capture occurred, but he threw a new wrench in the gearbox: Jasper was not a naturalized citizen and was not entitled to compensation from the attack.

By this time, Amanda hired Attorney Giles O. Pearce to help her. They protested Poole's decision, stating that Jasper Fletcher was a law-abiding citizen, and had taken out citizenship papers. They sent him a copy of Jasper's Declaration of Intention to become a citizen, filed in Illinois, on April 24, 1863, and said he would have followed up but for the attack that caused his financial ruin. He was worried sick about the murder of his wife and his missing girls and became a mental wreck. He used what money he made to look for his captive children. It was the depredation itself that prevented his follow-up. He was going to come east to complete the naturalization papers before his sudden death in 1875. Amanda argued that Commissioner Upshaw allowed the claim and the Indians admitted the attack. In March 1890, she was still wondering what the delay could be.

In April, Pearce sent in a copy of section 2168, U.S. Revised Statues, that said children of aliens who have declared intention to become citizens and die before completing naturalization, may become citizens with all rights. If that wasn't good enough, on April 17, 1890, Amanda filed for citizenship, just in case she was not yet "naturalized." If Lizzie, who had been born in Illinois, had been around to file the claim, perhaps it could have been favorably resolved for the Fletcher family years before. Amanda was sick of the whole affair. She stated, "no amount the government would allow could ever repay me for my sufferings while a prisoner with the Indians."[124]

All of Pearce's and Amanda's efforts notwithstanding, when the case went back to Poole for reconsideration, he still ruled against them. He concluded that Jasper's filing for citizenship was made in 1863, and the depredation occurred in 1865, therefore, the required five years for naturalization had not elapsed. The Act of March 1885, was meant for investigation of citizen's claims, and Jasper was not a citizen. Pearce countered by showing that section 2156 said that if Indians in amity take the property of "any citizen or inhabitant of the United States" indemnity may also be demanded, and the right of indemnity descended to the heirs. That the depredation did happen is shown by the fact that Congress directed the Secretary of Interior to deduct $2,000 from the Cheyenne-Arapaho annuities and to pay the same amount to Amanda Fletcher.

The case was finally decided in the Court of Claims. The defendants, the U.S. government, argued that Jasper "corruptly practiced or attempted to practice a fraud against the United States" because he first claimed $6,295 in 1866, and changed the amount to $2,356 in 1867. Both times he was under oath, so the defendants "pray" that under section 1086, the entire claim should be forfeited. They also argued that Amanda Fletcher-Cook also attempted fraud by submitting three different amounts. In addition to that, in December 1892, she claimed that there were an additional 17,000 English pounds and 3,000 in gold sovereigns that they had never mentioned before. This was the equivalent of $96,800 in U.S. money. The government said the demand was outlandish and fraudulent. The court denied the claim.[125]

CLARA AND WILLIE BLINN
Colorado, October 9, 1868

Clara Isabel Harrington was born in Elmore, Ohio, on October 21, 1847, to William T. and Harriet Bosley Harrington. She married Civil War veteran Richard F. Blinn in 1865. One year later they had a son, William Blinn. Clara's parents moved from their Perrysburg, Ohio, home in 1868, to take up a new life in Ottawa, Kansas. The Blinns also pulled up stakes, but Richard thought they would go beyond Kansas. They left Ohio on March 15, 1868, bound for, as Richard wrote in his diary, "Sand Creek Colorado Territory." They took a train to Kansas City, where they got mules and wagons and traveled west with two couples, Jack and Sarah, and Steve and Charlotte.

In late March, beyond Olathe, Kansas, they were stalled three days trying to fix a broken wagon axle. They traveled through Junction City, Abilene, Fort Harker, and Hays City. Beyond Hays they traveled with a train of Mexicans and saw their first Indians. They went south to Fort Dodge, reaching there on April 11. Continuing up the Arkansas River along the Santa Fe Trail, they reached Sand Creek on April 20. "Here we are at last," Blinn recorded. "Avery thing looks nice. I like the plase first rate."[126]

Richard ran the way station near the mouth of the Big Sandy (Sand Creek) and the Arkansas River. On April 23, he wrote: "Commenced boarding the drivers for the Southern Overland Mail Co. at $84 per week and renting them the stable at 50 dollars per quarter." Below that entry he wrote: "Embrer & Johnson, Family Grocery, Adolph Shader, Fort Gibson, and D. A. Brewster, Delphos, Ottawa Co., Kans."[127]

Richard Blinn's job did not go well. Work was hard and Richard's arm, wounded in the Civil War, never fully healed. Clara was reportedly fearful of roving Indians—Utes and Apaches were raiding along the Purgatory River in the late summer of 1868— and the couple decided they would go to Kansas near her parents. Richard formed a partnership with his brother-in-law, John F. Buttles of Fort Lyons, to furnish supplies to government posts as they headed east. They organized an eight-wagon train with 100 head of cattle and ten men, and left Boggsville on October 5. Clara carried all of the outfit's money: nearly $800 in greenbacks and gold coin.

By October 9, they had traveled about fifty miles along the Santa Fe Trail and stopped "this side of Sand Creek at three mile point" for an early dinner. After eating, they decided to put on a few more miles before nightfall. The largest wagon, with Clara and Willie aboard, pulled out ahead of the others. At that moment, a band of about seventy-five Cheyennes attacked, split the train, and ran the lead wagon across the Arkansas River. The warriors kept most of the men with the rear wagons, circled around, and shot flaming arrows, setting several wagons on fire. Richard Blinn and the rest of the men dug a breastwork around the wagons and were trapped there for five days, with the number of attacking Indians grown to nearly 200. Finally, one or more of the men broke out and got back to Fort Lyon, reaching there at three a.m., October 14. At daybreak, Lieutenant Henry H. Abell, 7th Cavalry, and ten soldiers rode to the rescue, but it was too late. They found the burned remains of the supply wagon, but Clara and Willie, who had been hiding under a feather bed, were long gone.[128]

After being captured, Clara had the presence of mind to scribble a note on a card and drop it on a bush about four miles downstream from the attack site. It read: "Dear Dick, Willie and I are prisoners. They are going to keep us. If you live, save us if you can. We are with them. Clara Blinn." The other side read: "Dick, if you love us, save us." The card was found and given to the distraught Richard Blinn.[129]

The Cheyennes took their captives southeast to Black Kettle's camp on the Washita River, where his people had fled after taking part in the Kansas raids of August (see Jane Bacon and Sarah White). Black Kettle may have been considered a "peace chief," but he was never averse to harboring warring Indians and holding captive white women and children (see Laura Roper and Nancy Morton).

The Indians believed they had good bargaining chips with which to deal for peace, much as they had attempted to do with their captives in the late summer of 1864, and which backfired on them and led to the Battle of Sand Creek. In late October 1868, a trader operating out of Fort Cobb, William Griffenstein, who was married to an Indian woman known as Cheyenne Jennie (see Nathaniel McElroy), sent an Indian boy to Black Kettle's camp to inform Jennie's mother, the wife of Lame Man, that her daughter had died. The boy delivered the message, but returned to Griffenstein with the news that there was a white woman and child in the camp. Griffenstein, known as "Dutch Bill," sent a mixed-blood boy known as Cheyenne Jack, to Black Kettle's camp, with pencil and paper and directions for the woman to identify herself. Clara wrote a letter, dated November 7, in which she pleaded for someone to buy her and her child. She said she would work for her rescuer and "do all that I could for you." She did not want to be sold to Mexicans, for fear that they would sell her into slavery in Mexico. Assuming her husband was dead, she asked to please inform her father of her situation, and said that the Cheyennes claim that "when white men make peace we can go home." She also asked that the governor of Kansas and the peace commissioners be informed that if they made peace, she would be freed. "For our sakes," she penned, "do all you can and god will bless you."[130]

The Cheyennes had raped and abused other white captives in 1864, but Clara Blinn was not treated as badly, although Willie was apparently beaten and was

Kansas State Historical Society
Clara Blinn

starving. The Cheyennes probably realized, that if they were to use Blinn as a hostage for their demands, she must not be returned as "damaged goods." Her letter reached Griffenstein, who showed it to Colonel William B. Hazen. The 38th Infantry colonel had arrived at Fort Cobb, Indian Territory, on the same day that Clara had written her letter, to take over as the military agent for the Kiowas and Comanches when their agency had been moved from Fort Larned. Hazen forwarded the letter to General William T. Sherman on November 25, along with his own letter stating that he had charged Griffenstein with negotiating for the Blinns' release, authorizing him to deal with friendly Indians nearest to the Cheyennes and "to spare no expense in his effort to reclaim these parties." The letter did not reach Sherman in St. Louis until December 18.

Also, on November 20, Black Kettle, Big Mouth, and a number of chiefs representing the Cheyenne and Arapahoes, came to Fort Cobb to discuss peace and talk about the ransoming of white captives. Since these tribes were currently at war with the United States, Hazen knew he could not make a separate peace with them or even offer them shelter. Although Black Kettle was ostensibly at Fort Cobb to discuss peace, he did say, as Hazen recorded it, "that many of his men were then on the war path, and that their people did not want peace with the people above the Arkansas." Hazen directed them to go back to their villages and deal directly with General Sheridan. Clara and Willie Blinn were caught in the middle.[131]

On the same day Hazen forwarded Blinn's letter to Sherman, Lieutenant Colonel George A. Custer and the 7th Cavalry were already in Indian Territory. Custer did not know about the white captives in Black Kettle's village, nor did he know whose village it was that his cavalry struck on the icy cold dawn of November 27. Some Indians fought, but most of them scattered. Black Kettle and Little Rock were killed. Custer captured the camp and burned the tipis. He reported killing 103 Indians and capturing fifty-three. Twenty-one soldiers were killed and sixteen were wounded. Among the casualties were Clara and Willie Blinn.

A number of scenarios are given for their deaths, but eyewitness accounts of the discovery of their bodies point to the conclusion that Indians killed them during the chaotic escape. Custer pulled his troops out that evening, went back to Camp Supply, got provisions and reinforcements, including the 19th Kansas Cavalry, and returned to the scene of the fight on December 10. The Blinns' bodies were discovered just east of the village site, in the direction most of the Indians fled. Doctor Bailey described a small white woman and an undernourished child with a bruised cheek. Doctor Henry Lippincott said Clara had one bullet hole above the left eyebrow, her head scalped, and the skull extensively fractured. Willie's body showed evidence of violence about the head and face. There was a report that one or both of Clara's breasts were hacked off, and that Willie was killed by holding his feet and swinging his head against a tree. On Clara's stomach was a piece of cornbread, leading Bailey to speculate that she was trying to hide some food for an escape attempt. Nearby was a wrapped package of paper money and gold coins. Men of the 19th Kansas filed past the bodies until someone finally recognized them.[132]

Clara and Willie's bodies, along with that of Major Joel Elliott, who was killed in the battle, were wrapped in blankets and taken to Fort Arbuckle, Indian Territory. They were buried with military honors on Christmas Day 1868. General Sheridan snipped off the hem of Clara's dress and a lock of Willie's hair to send to her family in Kansas. Richard Blinn still did not know of their fate. On the day they were buried he was stalled at the Arkansas River by high water. He wrote: "Waiting to get across the river. On my way to Fort Arbuckle looking for Clara and Willie. I would give my last dollar to go on." On December 29, Blinn wrote, "It looks dark and gloomy and I feel the same. I would give my life for my little family but I am afraid I have got to go through this world alone. If I only knew where they are I would feel better but to live and think what they have to go through is worse than death."[133]

Blinn struggled through bad weather and high water on the trek through Indian Territory. His diary echoes his despondency in numerous entries: ". . . .everything goes against me. . .I must know what has become of them if it takes all my life. . .I do not expect to see poor Clara again. . .life looks dark and dreary to me. . .wish I was with my wife dead or alive. . .I hope she is in a better world than this." Near Okmulgee on January 8, 1869, Blinn met a man named Campbell who said he was on the Washita battleground and saw the bodies of Clara and Willie. He told Blinn they had been taken to Arbuckle for burial. "I shall try to take them home," Blinn wrote. Campbell offered him a horse and said he was going to Fort Cobb, so Blinn joined him.

On January 15 they camped near "Dutch Bill" Griffinstein's Ranch. Blinn went to see Colonel Hazen and learned that General Sheridan had left. Blinn was given the piece of Clara's dress and Willie's hair, plus Clara's shoes. Blinn learned that the army had marched to the Wichita Mountains where they were in the process of building a new post that was to become Fort Sill. He headed there and met Agent Albert Boone, who said he would try to help the suffering Blinn and hired him "as watchman." They thought he might be able to recover something more from the Indians. "All I want is enough to get toom stones for my family," wrote Blinn. On January 23, Blinn met "a young man that was looking for his sister." Blinn had again run into Daniel A. Brewster, who had joined the army as a teamster for the special purpose of finding his sister (see Anna Brewster Morgan) who had been captured by Indians in Kansas only five days after Blinn's wife was taken.[134]

Blinn did not get to Fort Arbuckle until late February. He built a fence of blackjack logs around the graves, but due to lack of money and means of transportation, he gave up on the idea of taking the remains back to Kansas. Blinn moved back to Perrysburg, Ohio, where he lived with his father. He filed an Indian depredation claim in 1871, asking for $2,400 in lost stock, wagons, supplies, and money. Apparently the amount of money did not match another claim filed by his brother-in-law, and the discrepancy may have been enough to detour the claim into a pigeonhole where it remained for nearly twenty years. Richard Blinn spent much of his remaining days lamenting the loss of his family. He kept two small stones from the Arbuckle cemetery in his pocket until the day he died of tuberculosis on September 18, 1873.

Almost two decades after Richard's death, the family hired a lawyer to track down and reopen the file. The attorney was partially successful, for in 1892, he received a check for $1,200—half the amount claimed. Now, almost all of the Blinn relatives wanted a portion of the money and the lawyer decided that the best way to resolve the issue was to erect a nice tombstone in the Perrysburg Cemetery with all three names on it. The $917 left over was divided among seven relatives.

Some time after Fort Arbuckle was abandoned in June 1870, the bodies in the cemetery were reinterred at Fort Gibson, Indian Territory. By then, the identification of Clara and Willie Blinn's remains were lost. They rest today at the Fort Gibson cemetery simply as "Unknown Woman" and "Unknown."[135]

Dorothy Field
Texas, February 27, 1870

Dorothy Field, the wife of New York broker Patrick Field, and described as "a beautiful society woman," made the unwise decision to begin the new year of 1870 with a trip to Texas. She stopped at Fort McKavett, located on the San Saba River at the western edge of Menard County, to visit "some friends," but whether they were army officers or local civilians is not recorded. The fort was abandoned by the Army in 1859, and only saw sporadic use by the Confederates during the Civil War. Federal forces reoccupied it in April 1868. In 1870, it was home to the 24th Infantry, a black regiment in command of Colonel Ranald S. Mackenzie. In March 1870, the post returns stated, "Scouting parties have been kept out constantly during the past month, but nothing important has been accomplished against Indians."[136]

The post reported it had nothing significant to report—apparently Dorothy Field's disappearance was not newsworthy. Mrs. Field made another bad decision by riding out alone on February 27. It was a beautiful day and there had been no reported Indian trouble in the area for some time. Field took a pony and rode down the San Saba River. About four miles east of the fort she ran into a small band of Lipan Apaches. The pony and Mrs. Field vanished without a trace.

Patrick Field learned about the abduction and quickly wrote to Texas Secretary of State James P. Newcomb on March 1, 1870:

"Sir: My wife was captured by Indians on the 27th of February about four miles from this post on San Saba River Menard County—I will give five hundred in Gold for information that will lead to her whereabouts and hope the state will assist me in her recovery."

A short time later a poster appeared on the frontier, including at Fort McKavett. The reward had increased to $750 in gold, "for the safe delivery at any point in the United States, of Mrs. Dorothy Field, abducted by Indians from Menard County, on the San Saba River. . .on Sunday, February 27, 1870." Information was to be sent to Field's address at the corner of 26th St. and 10th Avenue in New York City, or to the commandant at Fort McKavett, who at that date was Lieutenant Colonel William R. Shafter.[137]

Dorothy Field disappeared from the scene and efforts to recover her brought little result. Word of her plight was sent to citizens and government employees in Texas and surrounding states and territories. Lawrie Tatum, agent for the Kiowas and Comanches at Fort Sill, Indian Territory, was instrumental in recovering many captives, but he was stymied in the case of Mrs. Field. In the fall of 1870, he employed Pacer, an Apache chief, to travel to the Indian camps to try and learn about captive white children "or of Dorothy Field, a woman captured the previous winter." He visited many camps, but not the Kwahadis, who he said were too angry with the Texans to make any deals. Said Tatum, "we never heard of Dorothy Field after she was carried off."[138]

A possible answer to her fate appeared in a Denver journal, *Field & Farm*, in 1911. The reporter indicated that Mr. Field upped the reward to $3,000. He appealed directly to a scout at Fort Sill named Charles Christy, who enlisted the help of Noconi Comanche "Quinevasa." They traveled all over, eventually visiting the Mescalero Reservation in New Mexico Territory. There they learned of a Lipan chief named "Moroitz" who was in the war party that captured Field. They only held her a short while before killing her, but he agreed to take them to the spot where she was murdered. With about twenty warriors to accompany them, they made the long journey back to the vicinity of Fort McKavett. Under a burr oak tree and near an abandoned shack they discovered all that was left of the beautiful Mrs. Field: "the skull, a part of the vertebrae, a forearm, and a few ribs." Christy put the remains in a saddlebag and rode to Fort Sill. They were expressed to Patrick Field in New York, "but he never acknowledged receipt and forgot entirely to forward the reward. . . ."[139]

CATHERINE, SOPHIA, JULIA, AND NANCY GERMAN
Kansas, September 11, 1874

The German Family left Georgia for Colorado in 1870, but four years later they had not arrived. After spending time in Missouri and southeastern Kansas, they finally continued their journey, leaving Elgin, Kansas, on August 15, 1874. Several railroads were in operation, and there were few emigrants using the old wagon roads, but John and Lydia German, both 44 years old, could not afford the fare. With one wagon and several oxen, they walked west. Their seven children, Rebecca Jane (20), Stephen (19), Catherine (17), Joanna (15), Sophia (12), Julia (7), and Nancy Adelaide "Addie" (5), helped in whatever ways they could. They camped on the night of September 10, on the banks of the Smoky Hill about one dozen miles east of Fort Wallace.

By the next sunrise they were awake and driving the wagon up the bluff out of the river valley. Jane and Lydia were on the driver's seat. John walked ahead carrying his musket, and Stephen and Catherine walked herd on their cattle. Stephen thought he saw an antelope and he pointed toward the bluffs, when he and Catherine were both startled to see Indians riding over the hillcrest. They started running. From the wagon, Sophia counted nineteen Indians.

They were Cheyennes, and included Medicine Water and his wife, Buffalo Calf Woman (Mochis), and his brother, Cometsevah. They had all survived the 1864 battle at Sand Creek. One warrior shot John in the back and Mochis plunged a hatchet into his skull. Lydia jumped off the wagon and ran to him, crying, "Oh let me get to father!" She was murdered next to her husband. Sophia saw another Indian tomahawk her. Lydia was pregnant, and the Cheyennes tore her unborn child from her sliced open belly. Rebecca grabbed an ax and tried to defend herself, but she was knocked senseless and several Indians raped her. When they were done and while Rebecca lay unconscious, they covered her with bedclothes from the wagon, set her on fire, and burned her to death.

Indians killed Stephen, and shot Catherine in the leg with an arrow. Medicine Water pulled out the shaft, kicked her several times, and threw her on his bay horse. The Indian pulled the four youngest sisters out of the wagon and tore their bonnets off their heads to see who had the longest locks. Joanna's long blonde hair made her the choice. She was shot in the head and scalped. Addie began to cry, but Julia was so shocked, she said, "I could not cry. There wasn't enough tears in my eyes."[140]

Author's photo
Site of German family capture, near Russell Springs, Kansas.

The Cheyenne raiders took whatever loot they could carry, rounded up four cows and two calves, hoisted the four surviving sisters on horses, and rode south toward the Texas Panhandle. Nearly three weeks after the massacre, a hunter discovered the charred wagons and the news was reported to Fort Wallace. As a result, Lieutenant Christian C. Hewitt, 19th Infantry, led a patrol to the scene. In the dirt was a family Bible with nine names inscribed. The numbers didn't match the bodies, and the soldiers knew that there were four missing girls. For the next few months their rescue was a primary goal for most of the Army on the southern Plains. Nine miles from the massacre site, the Cheyennes camped and divided up the spoils, including the girls. The warriors raped Catherine and Sophia. Over the next weeks the girls were treated very cruelly, suffering from exposure, beatings, and starvation. Sophia's ankles were tied to a horse so tightly with rawhide straps that they ripped through her skin, leaving her scarred sixty years later. The two elder sisters were forced into concubinage, gang raped, forced into backbreaking labor, and abused by the Cheyenne women. Mochis, said Catherine, "seemed delighted to see us tortured or frightened." In one of her ordeals, Catherine said, "I was stripped naked, and painted by the old squaws, and made the wife of the chief who could catch me when fastened upon the back of a horse and set loose on the prairie. I don't know what

Indian caught me." Later she declared that "nearly all in the tribe" had raped her.[141]

On September 24, near North McClellan Creek, southeast of present-day Pampa, Texas, the Cheyennes spotted a herd of bison. In the warriors' excitement, two of them who usually had charge of the two youngest sisters, set them down and rode away. Catherine tried to rein up and see what was happening, but other warriors lashed them forward. Catherine assumed that the girls were such a burden that the Indians had killed them. She told Sophia what she saw and Sophia sadly replied, "They are better off than we are!"[142]

Julia and Addie wandered around until they saw some wagon tracks, followed them to an abandoned army camp, and found hardtack, horse corn, wild berries, and onions to eat. Wolves threatened them, but they drove them away. Incredibly, the little girls survived for about six weeks. During that time, soldiers had been combing the plains, fighting with the Indians in numerous actions that became known as the Red River War, and searching for the captured girls. Stone Calf and his Cheyenne band, in which Catherine and Sophia were now living, was aware that the army knew of the four captive girls, and he realized that if the time came when he was caught and confronted with that fact, he needed to have four girls, not just two. He sent out scouts to find them. On November 7, three Cheyennes found and returned them to the village. The girls were given raw meat to eat, but being near death, neither could even chew.[143]

On Sunday, November 8, it was still uncertain whether Julia and Addie's luck in being "rescued" was good or bad, for that morning, Lieutenant Frank D. Baldwin, with Company D, 6th Cavalry, and Company D, 5th Infantry, came barreling into Grey Beard's village on North Fork McClellan Creek. Grey Beard's warriors held the soldiers off for a time while the women and children scattered. Among those gathered up and taken away were Catherine and Sophia German. Sophia had learned a few words of Cheyenne and heard the Indians say it would be best to kill her little sisters, and one rode back to do so. Julia crawled under a buffalo robe near a fallen lodge. A warrior was seen to sneak up and take a shot at a pile of buffalo robes, but a soldier immediately shot and killed him. As the soldiers rummaged through the wreckage, George James, 5th Infantry, lifted the robes and saw a starved white child.

"What is your name, dear little girl?" he asked.

"My name is Julia German," she answered, "and Addie and Sophia were here a while ago."[144]

The soldiers continued searching the other lodges, and finally found Addie, trying to place logs on a fire as she had been ordered to. The girl could hardly walk. A Sergeant Mahoney arrived and picked Addie up. He held her close to him and wept. One hardened teamster entered the village and was affected as much as many of the soldiers were, He remarked, "I have driven my mules over these plains for three months, but I will stay forever or until we get them other girls." Said George James, "I give you my word, the condition those girls were in almost set us hard boiled soldiers to blubbering." Fifty years later, Addie remembered, "How good the soldiers were to sister and myself."[145]

From The Moccasin Speaks, *page 132*
Julia (left) and Adelaide German

The soldiers hunted the Indians, trying to force them onto the reservation and get the last two captives. In late December 1874, Cheyennes surrendering at Darlington, Indian Territory, informed the agent that one sister (Catherine) was in Stone Calf's village, the property of Long Back, who made money farming

From The Moccasin Speaks, *page 182*
Sophia (left) and Catherine German

161

her out as a prostitute, and the other (Sophia) belonged to Wolf Robe, who was in Grey Beard's Band. In January 1875, Colonel Nelson A. Miles sent a friendly Indian to take a message to the "Misses Germaine" that their little sisters were safe, and that every effort was being made to rescue them. Constant harassment by the troops, starvation, and despair finally had their effect, and on March 6, 1875, Stone Calf, Grey Beard, and 820 Indians surrendered at Darlington. The road was lined with spectators who waved and cheered. Again, tears were common even among the toughest soldiers and civilians. The girls were taken to Lieutenant Colonel Thomas Neill's tent. He tried to question them, but they were so emotionally overcome that he postponed the meeting. They were taken to the Arapaho Indian school and placed in care of Lina Miles, the sister of Agent John D. Miles. Catherine, nearly 18 years old, weighed 80 pounds, and Sophia, nearly 13, weighed 65 pounds. The soldiers and employees took up a collection for them.

On March 12, Neill paraded the surrendered Indians in front of Catherine and Sophia so they could point out the murderers of their family. Sophia quickly identified Mochis as "the woman who chopped my mother's head open with an axe!" She, Medicine Water, and others went straight to the guardhouse. On April 28, seventy-four of the worst offenders—Cheyennes, Comanches, and Kiowas—were sent by rail to prison in Florida.[146]

Julia and Addie went to Fort Leavenworth in December 1874, and Catherine and Sophia went there in April 1875. With no parents or nearby relatives, Colonel Miles was appointed their guardian. Arrangements were made to have the four stay at the nearby home of Patrick and Louisa Corney. Miles tried to secure an appropriation from Congress of $10,000, taken from the Indians' annuities, to be divided up among them when they reached 21 years of age. They stayed with the Corneys three years. Colonel Miles resigned his guardianship in 1877, and Patrick Corney became guardian of the younger girls. Mochis, Medicine Water, and the other Cheyennes who had murdered the German Family and taken their daughters captive, were released from prison in 1878, and returned to Indian Territory for a happy reunion with their families. Meanwhile, the promised appropriations for Catherine and Sophia were still not approved, and the girls had to fend for themselves.

Catherine married Amos Swerdfeger in 1878, and moved to a farm near Wetmore, Kansas. Her three younger sisters joined them. In 1879, Congress finally approved the money for the

German Sisters. In 1880, they moved to Berwick, Kansas, and in 1893, Amos and Catherine and their five children moved to Los Angeles, California. Amos died in 1921, and Catherine lived at the home of her sister, Julia, in Atascadero, California, where she died on August 6, 1932, at age 75.

Nancy "Addie" German graduated from high school in Sabetha, Kansas, and attended two years of college at Kansas State. In 1890, she married Frank Andrews and moved to a farm near Berwick, close to sister Catherine. They later moved to Bern, Kansas, and had eleven children. She was widowed in the 1920s and her home was destroyed by a tornado in 1928. In 1939, she went to New York to appear on a nationally broadcast radio show called, *We the People*, where she talked about her captivity. She died on December 31, 1942, at age 73.

Sophia married Albert Feldmann, a Swiss immigrant, in 1882. The next year they moved from Sabetha, Kansas, to a farm near Humboldt, Nebraska, where she lived for the next sixty years. Albert died of a stroke in 1905. They had three daughters. Sophia remarried in 1907, but it was a big mistake. In 1910, she filed for divorce and her enraged husband, who wanted her property, tried to kill her with an ax, which must have brought terrible memories of her mother's murder thirty-six years earlier. Sophia caught the ax and wrestled her husband for it while he punched her with his free hand. Sophia's grandson, Alfred, had seen the fight and ran for help. Her husband finally knocked Sophia out, and perhaps thinking her dead, and knowing that the authorities would soon arrive, went into the barn and hanged himself.

In 1915, Sophia went to California to visit her sisters and attend the San Francisco Exposition. Registering at a hotel, she noticed that General Nelson Miles was also staying there. They met, forty years after he had been her guardian, and he gave her a copy of his memoirs. She noticed that Miles had misspelled their last name as "Germaine," and it had been repeatedly misspelled in many publications ever since. Sophia died on March 4, 1949, at age 86.

Julia graduated from high school in Sabetha, and received a teaching certificate from Kansas State Teacher's Institute. She married Howard Rees in 1888, and moved near Chicago, Illinois, where Howard died of pneumonia only three years later. Julia, with two children and expecting a third, moved to California to live near her sister Catherine. Four years later, Julia married Albert Brooks and they had one daughter. Her husband died in 1912, and Julia was widowed a second time. Catherine moved in with her in the 1920s. In 1952, Julia went to Pampa, Texas, to help dedicate a monument to the local pioneers. Seventy-seven years earlier, she and sister Addie had spent six weeks alone on the prairie south of Pampa. In 1957, Julia was a guest of the Fort Wallace Memorial Association when the old prairie graves of the German family were located and a new stone was dedicated at the Fort Wallace Cemetery. Julia died on June 1, 1959, at age 92, probably the last of the white captives.[147]

Chapter 3 notes

[1] Lecompte, "Manco Burro," 309-12; Chalfant, *Cheyennes and Horse Soldiers*, 42; Bancroft, *History of Oregon*, Vol. 2, 547.

[2] Sager, *Whitman Massacre*, 9-11, 152, 177-78n9-10.

[3] Sager, *Whitman Massacre*, 12-13, 156-57, 179n12, 179n14, 180n15, 16. Catherine recorded the birth date as May 22, however, Naomi stated it was the last day of May.

[4] Sager, *Whitman Massacre*, 14-15, 159-61, 181n21, 182n22, 23, 186n30.

[5] Sager, *Whitman Massacre*, 15-17, 162-65, 187n33, 188n36, 188-90n37, 38, 190-91n39, 191n40, 41.

[6] Sager, *Whitman Massacre*, 18, 21, 167, 170-71.

[7] Sager, *Whitman Massacre*, 46, 169; Lavender, *Land of Giants*, 218; "Narcissa Whitman," 2, www.tu-chemnitz.de/phil/amerikanistik/projekte/west/narissa.htm.

[8] Marsh Cason, "Massacre Recalled," 3, http://gesswhoto.com/whitman.html; "Whitman Massacre—Whitman Massacre Roster," 4, http://www.oregonpioneers.com/whitman4.htm; Sager, *Whitman Massacre*, 29.

[9] "Narcissa Whitman," 2, www.tu-chemnitz.de/phil/amerikanistik/projekte/west/nariissa.htm; Sager, *Whitman Massacre*, 29; "Letters and Journals of Narcissa," 28, www.pbs.org/weta/thewest/resources/archives/two/whitman2.htm.

[10] Lavender, David, *Land of Giants*, 258, 261-62; Sager, *Whitman Massacre*, 44-5, 48-52; "Narcissa Whitman," 3, www.tu-chemnitz.de/phil/amerikanistik/projekte/west/narissa.htm.

[11] Sager, *Whitman Massacre*, 52, 57-8; Lavender, David, *Land of Giants*, 262.

[12] "Whitman Massacre," http://www.oregonpioneers.com/whitman2.htm, 1; Sager, *Whitman Massacre*, 58, 62, 116; "NPS Historical Handbook: Whitman Mission-The Massacre," 2, http://www.cr.nps.gov/history/online-books/hh/37p.htm.

[13] Sager, *Whitman Massacre*, 59, 117.

[14] "Whitman Massacre—Preliminary Events," 4, http://www.oregonpioneers.com/whitman1.htm.

[15] Sager, *Whitman Massacre*, 64-65, 122. They escaped that night and after a perilous three-day journey reached Fort Walla Walla.

[16] Sager, *Whitman Massacre*, 46-47, 61, 65, 67, 121. "Whitman Massacre—Whitman Massacre Roster," 5, http://www.oregonpioneers.com/whitman4.htm. Later, during Joseph Stanfield's trial, two of the women captives claimed he had told them he knew there would be a massacre. In his possession was found a watch belonging to one of the women, and money of one of the dead men.

[17] Sager, *Whitman Massacre*, 68-69, 70, 118, 124-26, 171;

[18] Sager, *Whitman Massacre*, 71, 73-74.

[19] Gaston, "Centennial History of Oregon," 3, http://gesswhoto.com/centennial-whitman-massacre.html; Sager, *Whitman Massacre*, 74-75.

[20] "Oregon Pioneer Association, Spalding Letter," 96, in http://www.1st-hand-history.org/opa/21/095.jpg; "Whitman Massacre—Whitman Massacre Roster," 1, http://www.oregonpioneers.com/whitman4.htm; Sager, *Whitman Massacre*, 76-77.

[21] Sager, *Whitman Massacre*, 79-81; Marsh Cason, "Massacre Recalled," 3, http://gesswhoto.com/whitman.html.

[22] "Whitman Massacre—The Aftermath, " 7, http://www.oregonpioneers.com/whitman3.htm; Sager, *Whitman Massacre*, 79-80, 127, 200n2.

[23] Sager, *Whitman Massacre*, 84-85.

[24] Sager, *Whitman Massacre*, 90.

[25] Sager, *Whitman Massacre*, 86.

[26] Sager, *Whitman Massacre*, 87, 128-30, 152, 171, 197; "Whitman Massacre—Whitman Massacre Roster," 1, http://www.oregonpioneers.com/whitman4.htm.

[27] Marsh Cason, "Massacre Recalled," 4, http://gesswhoto.com/whitman.html; "Whitman Massacre—Whitman Massacre Roster," 4, http://www.oregonpioneers.com/whitman4.htm; Sager, *Whitman Massacre*, 172-73.

[28] Sager, *Whitman Massacre*, 172, 189.

[29] Sager, *Whitman Massacre*, 137-38, 145,149-150; "Whitman Massacre—Whitman Massacre Roster," 1, http://www.oregonpioneers.com/whitman4.htm.

[30] Barry, *Beginning of the West*, 884-85; Dary, *Santa Fe Trail*, 218. Some sources say Virginia was an infant.

[31] Oliva, *Ft. Union*. 22-24.

[32] Oliva, *Ft. Union*, 24; Sabin, *Kit Carson Days*, 619-20. The attack is said to have occurred near Point of Rocks, which is in the southeast corner of present-day Colfax County, and about 12 miles northeast of Abbott. It is also said to have happened at Rock Springs, ten miles "beyond" Point of Rocks, and 80 miles from Rayado, but Rayado is only about 50 miles from Point of Rocks.

[33] Barry, *Beginning of the West*, 885; Sabin, *Kit Carson Days*, 618-19; Bennett, *Forts and Forays*, xvi-xvii.

[34] Guild and Carter, *Kit Carson*, 186; Oliva, *Ft. Union*, 24; Bennett, *Forts and Forays*, xvii; Quaife, *Carson's Autobiography*, 133.

[35] Bennett, *Forts and Forays*, 24-25. Bennett recorded the expedition dates incorrectly in his diary, but his participation is convincing.

[36] Bennett, *Forts and Forays*, 25; Guild and Carter, *Kit Carson*, 186-87; Quaife, *Carson's Autobiography*, 133-35; Sabin, *Kit Carson Days*, 620-21.

[37] Bennett, *Forts and Forays*, 25; Quaife, *Carson's Autobiography*, 136.

[38] Bennett, *Forts and Forays*, xviii-xix.

[39] Bennett, *Forts and Forays*, xviii; Sabin, *Kit Carson Days*, 619, 621-22; Dary, *Santa Fe Trail*, 218; Oliva, *Ft. Union*, 24n77; Michno, *Encyclopedia of Indian Wars*, 23-24. Dragoon James A. Bennett happily recorded in his diary, *Forts and Forays*, 48, the death of "Old Lobo," who, he said, "has boasted that he has had intercourse with Mrs. White."

[40] Dunn, *Massacres*, 140-41; Stratton, *Oatman*, 26-38; Heard, *White Into Red*, 85; Thrapp, *Frontier Biography*, 1071.

[41] Stratton, *Oatman*, vii, 48-52; Dunn, *Massacres*, 141.

[42] Stratton, *Oatman*, 63-64, 67-68, 72; Dunn, *Massacres*, 142-44.

[43] Stratton, *Oatman*, 75.

[44] Stratton, *Oatman*, 79.

[45] Dunn, *Massacres*, 148-49; Stratton, *Oatman*, 85-86.

[46] Dunn, *Massacres*, 148-51.

[47] Stratton, *Oatman*, 116, 122, 134, 140; Dunn, *Massacres*, 152-53.

[48] Stratton, *Oatman*, 181-83; Dunn, *Massacres*, 155-57.

[49] Dunn, *Massacres*, 157-64.

[50] Thrapp, *Frontier Biography*, 1071; Stratton, *Oatman*, ix-x; Dunn, *Massacres*, 164; Hunter, "Southwestern Captivity Narratives," 184-85, 206, 220n26.

[51] Wilson, *Sufferings*, 9-10.

[52] Wilson, *Sufferings*, 10-14. The Comanches were probably Tehnahwahs, an offshoot of the Nokoni band. Winfrey and Day, *Texas Indian Papers* 5, 171; Fehrenbach, *Comanches*, 144.

[53] Wilson, *Sufferings*, 15-20.

[54] Wilson, *Sufferings*, 21-25.

[55] Wilson, *Sufferings*, 25-26; Hunter, ed., "Capture of Mrs. Wilson," 23; Hunter, "Southwestern Captivity Narratives," 178. Hunter indicates Wilson was cared for by Mexican women in the town of "Ysleta."

[56] Wilson, *Sufferings*, 26-27; Thompson, *Sibley*, 99-100.

[57] Winfrey and Day, *Texas Indian Papers* 3, 182; 5, 169-70, 171-72. Hunter, "Southwestern Captivity Narratives," 177, cites a source that claims one of the Wilson boys was recovered a few months after Jane's escape, and spent some time at Fort Phantom Hill. Meredith's age has been given as seven, eight, and ten.

[58] Wilson, *Sufferings*, 5-6, 28; Hunter, ed., "Capture of Mrs. Wilson," 23; Hunter, "Southwestern Captivity Narratives," 169-70.

[59] Drimmer, *Captured by Indians*, 278; Hunter, "Southwestern Captivity Narratives," 271-73.

[60] Lee, *Among the Comanches*, 81-86, 99. Either Lee's dates or locations are awry. If they left Matamoros in March, and were 350 miles beyond Eagle Pass by the end of March, they had come about 620 miles in less than a month, a very brisk pace of more than 20 miles per day, and extremely difficult to maintain. Lee also said they moved slowly, averaging 15 miles per day. If they were truly near Presidio, they were only about 260 miles beyond Eagle Pass.

[61] Lee, *Among the Comanches*, 87-91.

[62] Drimmer, *Captured by Indians*, 284-91.

[63] Hunter, "Southwestern Captivity Narratives," 275-76; Drimmer, *Captured by Indians*, 300-01; Lee, *Among the Comanches*, 145-51.

[64] Drimmer, *Captured by Indians*, 302-06; Lee, *Among the Comanches*, 165-68.

[65] Lee, *Among the Comanches*, 177-86; Drimmer, *Captured by Indians*, 306-13.

[66] Hunter, "Southwestern Captivity Narratives," 269-71, 288, 289n1; Lee, *Among the Comanches*, 1-3, 187. The truth of Lee's account has been questioned, some calling the information he provides invaluable, and others believing it mostly fiction.

[67] Roberts, *With Their Own Blood*, 11-21.

[68] Roberts, *With Their Own Blood*, 3-6; Schellie, *Domain of Blood*, 92-93.

[69] Roberts, *With Their Own Blood*, 6-8.

[70] Roberts, *With Their Own Blood*, 7-9, 23-24, 26-28.

[71] Roberts, *With Their Own Blood*, 30, 33, 35-6, 38.

[72] Roberts, *With Their Own Blood*, 32, 35, 37.

[73] Roberts, *With Their Own Blood*, 92-94, 105-06, 124, 145, 151, 155, 162, 164, 167, 176, 185, 214.

[74] Smith, "Utter Tragedy," 43.

[75] Smith, "Utter Tragedy," 44. The family names are sometimes incorrectly written as Otter and Van Orman. Shannon, *Utter Disaster*, 5, 11n.

[76] Smith, "Utter Tragedy," 44-45; Schlicke, "Massacre on the Oregon Trail," 42-43.

[77] Fuller, *Left by the Indians*, 22-23; Schlicke, "Massacre on the Oregon Trail," 44; Smith, "Utter Tragedy," 45-46.

[78] Fuller, *Left by the Indians*, 23-26; Smith, "Utter Tragedy," 46-48.

[79] Schlicke, "Massacre on the Oregon Trail," 45-46; Shannon, *Utter Disaster*, 103, 105.

[80] Dent's report, in Fuller, *Left by the Indians*, 62; Smith, "Utter Tragedy, 48.

[81] Fuller, *Left by the Indians*, 27-29.

[82] Smith, "Utter Tragedy," 80. Emeline Trimble married John Whitman three years after her ordeal. When he died she returned to Wisconsin and married Melvin Fuller. In 1892 she wrote a booklet of her experiences.

[83] Bancroft, *History of Oregon*, Vol. 2, 473; Michno, *Encyclopedia of Indian Wars*, 107-08; Schlicke, "Massacre on the Oregon Trail," 50-54. Fuller, *Left by the Indians*, 29; Lockley, *Pioneer Men*, 198; Shannon, *Utter Disaster*, 174; Dent's Report, in Fuller, *Left by the Indians*, 59.

[84] Kelly, *My Captivity*, 11-13, 20; Doyle, *Land of Gold*, 153; Farley, "An Indian Captivity," 249. Mary is said to be either five or eight years old.

[85] Kelly, *My Captivity*, 21-27; Doyle, *Land of Gold*, 154; Farley, "An Indian Captivity," 249.

[86] Farley, "An Indian Captivity," 249; Kelly, *My Captivity*, 37-40.

[87] Farley, "An Indian Captivity, 250;Unrau, *Talking Wire*, 154-55; Vaughn, *Indian Fights*, 6-9; Doyle, *Land of Gold*, 744.

[88] Kelly, *My Captivity*, 54-55; Farley, "An Indian Captivity," 250. Sarah later wrote a book titled, *The Capture and Escape; or, Life Among the Sioux*. Only a few pages deal with her capture, and the book was mainly a plagiarism of the book Fanny would write of her own experience.

[89] Kelly, *My Captivity*, 64; Bradley, *March of the Montana Column*, 112-13.

[90] Kelly, *My Captivity*, 68, 76-78, 84-87; Farley, "An Indian Captivity," 250.

[91] Kelly, *My Captivity*, 95-96, 99, 102-08; Utley, *Lance and Shield*, 60, 344n12; Farley, "An Indian Captivity," 250-51. Fanny says Ottawa was her protector, but Utley says she had already been traded to Brings Plenty.

[92] Kelly, My Captivity, 113-18.

[93] Clodfelter, *Dakota War*, 195-96; Farley, "An Indian Captivity," 251-52.

[94] Clodfelter, *Dakota War*, 199-200; Kelly, *My Captivity*, 208-10; Utley, *Lance and Shield*, 63; Farley, "An Indian Captivity," 252-53.

[95] Farley, "An Indian Captivity," 253-56; Drimmer, *Captured by the Indians*, 331.

[96] Czaplewski, *Captives of the Cheyenne*, sec. 2, 12; *New York Times*, September 8, 1864.

[97] Czaplewski, *Captive of the Cheyennes*, sec. 2, 14; Becher, *Massacre Along the Medicine Road*, 252, 255-56, 260.

[98] Becher, *Massacre Along the Medicine Road*, 258; Czaplewski, *Captive of the Cheyenne*, sec. 1, 69. Hoig, *Peace Chiefs*, 109, incorrectly claims that Daniel Marble was captured on the Blue River in Kansas.

99 Czaplewski, *Captive of the Cheyennes*, sec. 1, 67, sec. 2, 15-17; Nancy Morton Depredation Claim, RG 75, #332.

100 Becher, *Massacre Along the Medicine Road*, 260, 262, 266; Czaplewski, Captive of the Cheyenne, sec. 2, 17-18.

101 Czaplewski, *Captive of the Cheyenne*, sec. 1, 70. "Brown" was probably Joe Barroldo.

102 Becher, *Massacre Along the Medicine Road*, 314, 316; Michno, *Battle at Sand Creek*, 142-43.

103 Becher, *Massacre Along the Medicine Road*, 320; Wynkoop, *Tall Chief*, 93-96, 99; Czaplewski, *Captive of the Cheyenne*, sec. 2, 22; Michno, *Battle at Sand Creek*, 157-59.

104 Becher, *Massacre Along the Medicine Road*, 326-327, 438.

105 Michno, *Encyclopedia of Indian Wars*, 153-4; Grinnell, *Fighting Cheyennes*, 173; *OR*, 41/1, 818. Becher, *Massacre Along the Medicine Road*, 355.

106 Becher, *Massacre Along the Medicine Road*, 356-58; Czaplewski, *Captive of the Cheyenne*, sec. 2. 24-26. See Lucinda Eubank for the rest of her story.

107 Czaplewski, *Captive of the Cheyenne*, sec. 2, 26-27; Morton Depredation Claim #332.

108 Czaplewski, *Captive of the Cheyenne*, sec. 1, 72, sec. 2, 28; Becher, *Massacre Along the Medicine Road*, 356; In Morton's depredation claim, her attorney elaborates: "Defendant further states she suffered from all the abuse and indignity that could be practiced toward her not only by one Indian, but many. . . ."

109 Becher, *Massacre Along the Medicine Road*, 358; Czaplewski, *Captive of the Cheyenne*, sec. 2, 29.

110 Becher, *Massacre Along the Medicine Road*, 359-62; Jules Ecoffey and Joseph Bissonette Depredation Claim #2208.

111 McDermott, *Circle of Fire*, 57; Becher, *Massacre Along the Medicine Road*, 364.

112 Czaplewski, *Captive of the Cheyenne*, sec. 2, 45; Becher, *Massacre Along the Medicine Road*, 366-67, 429, 433n21.

113 Hoig, *Sand Creek Massacre*, 88-89; White, *Hostiles & Horse Soldiers*, 46n30; *OR*: V.41/2, 766-67.

114 Czaplewski, *Captive of the Cheyenne*, 30; Monahan, *Denver City*, 174; "Massacre of Cheyenne Indians," 28; Becher, *Massacre Along the Medicine Road*, 321. Hoig, *Peace Chiefs*, 109, incorrectly states that Mrs. "Ewbanks" was the one who hanged herself.

115 Fletcher-Cook Depredation Claim #5072. Amanda's travel itinerary is suspect. If they went to Denver, it seems unlikely that they would have then gone 150 miles north to Ft. Laramie to join a wagon train, and then come south another 80 miles to get back on the Overland. It also is unlikely that they would have taken such a large train west from the fort into the Laramie Mountains, which was a hard pull through Halleck Canyon and used mainly by small military supply trains. Perhaps from Denver, they went north, picked up the Overland, and made stops at Big and Little Laramie Stations, which Amanda called "Fort" Laramie. (Robert G. Rosenberg, Historical Consultant, 5-12-04. See also, Erb, Brown, and Hughes, *Overland Trail*, 39-40.)

116 Erb, Brown, and Hughes, *Overland Trail*, 45.

117 Fletcher-Cook Depredation Claim #5072.

118 Fletcher-Cook Depredation Claim #5072; Rosenberg, 5-12-04; Erb, Brown, and Hughes, *Overland Trail*, 46; Ellis, "Robert Foote," 58-59.

119 Fletcher-Cook Depredation Claim #5072; Halaas and Masich, *Halfbreed*, 192. It is notable that Minimic was the Cheyenne who, along with One-Eye, came to Fort Lyon in 1864, with a letter from Black Kettle, stating that the Indians wished to give back their white captives and seek peace.

120 Fletcher-Cook Depredation Claim #5072; Zwink, "Bluff Creek Council," 9-11, in http://www.kancoll.org.khq/1977_2_zwink; Halaas and Masich, *Halfbreed*, 208; Gerboth, *Tall Chief*, 26, 116-18, 134n42. The true story of Amanda Fletcher's captivity from her own, her father's, and her rescuer's testimony differs a great deal from the incorrect standard tale repeated by numerous historians. For example, Berthrong, *Southern Cheyennes*, 258; Hyde, *George Bent*, 251; Halaas and Masich, *Halfbreed*, 192, 208; Hoig, *Peace Chiefs*, 113; Powell, *Sacred Mountain* I, 407; Kraft, "Between the Army and the Cheyennes," 52; Gerboth, *Tall Chief*, 26, 134n42, and McDermott, *Circle of Fire*, 81, contain variations of errors in Amanda's name (calling her Mary), age, place of capture, captor, treatment, and rescuer. Halaas and Masich misleadingly indicate that the Cheyennes gave Fletcher to Wynkoop out of respect. Powell claims that the Cheyenne, Sand Hill, owned her for a time, treated her kindly, and turned her over to interpreter John Smith. In her own correspondence, Amanda belies all of this. Wynkoop,

as befitting his numerous acts of dishonesty, Michno, *Battle at Sand Creek*, 262-63, 266, 268-69, 273, took undeserved credit for rescuing Amanda.

[121] Fletcher-Cook Depredation Claim #5072.

[122] Custer, *Life on the Plains*, 62-63. Trenholm, *Arapahoes*, 262, without citing her source, says that Lizzie's sister Mary (*sic*) saw and identified her in Casper, Wyoming, but that Lizzie denied being white and wanted to remain living with the Arapahoes. In fact, Amanda was consistent in 20 years of depredation claim records, stating that she had never seen Lizzie since she was captured, and assumed she was dead.

[123] Fletcher-Cook Depredation Claim #5072. Halaas and Masich, *Halfbreed*, 334, appear confused over the nature of Indian depredation claims. They indicate that George Bent corresponded with Amanda who wanted to know about abductions so she could file a claim. They said, "The Cheyennes had much to gain by Bent's depositions, for successful claimants received payment deducted from the Cheyennes' annuities." Successful claims meant the Cheyennes had much to lose, not gain. Whenever Bent may have gotten them to admit to an outrage, it may have been true, but it did not help them.

[124] Fletcher-Cook Depredation Claim #5072. Amanda's statement contrasts to the picture others painted of her captivity. Hyde, *George Bent*, 258, and Powell, *Sacred Mountain I*, 407, for instance, wrote that she was well treated by her captors.

[125] Fletcher-Cook Depredation Claim #5072. One cannot read through these claims without sympathizing with the settlers and pioneers who saw the government giving hundreds of thousands of dollars in money and annuities to Indian tribes, while so often being denied their own fair claims.

[126] Justus, "Saga of Clara Blinn," 11; Richard Blinn Diary.

[127] Blinn Diary. Apparently one of Blinn's first customers was D. A. Brewster, a remarkable coincidence, because Brewster's sister (see Anna Brewster Morgan) would be captured by the Indians only five days after Blinn's wife.

[128] Justus, "Saga of Clara Blinn," 12; Blinn Diary.

[129] Justus, "Saga of Clara Blinn," 12-13.

[130] Justus, "Saga of Clara Blinn," 13; Hyde, *George Bent*, 279.

[131] Justus, "Saga of Clara Blinn," 13; Kroeker, *Great Plains Command*, 77-80.

[132] Hoig, *Washita*, 211-13, gives a concise sample of the various accounts of their deaths. Reports that Satanta held them are incorrect. Satanta and the Kiowas talked with Hazen at Ft. Cobb on November 20, and they were camped nearby to receive rations at the time of the attack. In her own letter, Blinn said she was with the Cheyennes. Agent Jesse Leavenworth and Agent Albert Boone, who were not there, claimed that Custer's troops shot the Blinns. In his article, "For our sake do all you can," Joe Haines Jr. claims that Custer's men not only shot down the Blinns, but may have scalped them. For proof of this ludicrous contention, he states that the village was under attack and the Cheyennes were too surprised to have killed them. Tall Bull's Cheyenne village was under similar surprise attack the next summer, and it did not prevent the Indians from attempting to kill both of their captives (see Maria Weichel and Susanna Alderdice.) Many times Indians attempted to kill their captives while in the midst of a fight.

[133] Justus, "Saga of Clara Blinn," 17-18; Blinn Diary.

[134] Justus, "Saga of Clara Blinn," 18; Blinn Diary.

[135] Justus, "Saga of Clara Blinn," 19.

[136] "Field & Farm," 8; Sullivan, *Fort McKavett*, 21, 24, 27-28, 29; Robinson, *Bad Hand*, 54.

[137] Winfrey and Day, *Texas Indian Papers 4*, 303; Ashton, *Indians and Intruders*, 83. The particulars of Mrs. Field's capture have been incorrectly reported since 1937, when W. S. Nye published *Carbine and Lance*. He wrote (p. 35) that Satanta captured Field at Menard in 1864, and that Kiowas at Fort Larned in August of that year, held a scalp dance in celebration of the successful Texas raid. Several authors repeated the error. In 1962, Mildred Mayhall, *Kiowas*, 224, cited Nye and told the same story. In 1998, Robinson *Satanta*, 32, 205n4, made the same claim, but compounded the mistake by saying that Agent Lawrie Tatum, who tried to recover Mrs. Field in the fall of 1870, incorrectly believed she was "a recent captive." She was captured in 1870, just as Tatum had described in his book, *Our Red Brothers*, 51. This author made the same error by citing the above authors in his 2004 book, *Battle at Sand Creek*, 124. It illustrates a dilemma for historians: build on what other researchers have done before, hoping they were correct, or expend much time and ink studying the primary sources.

[138] Tatum, *Our Red Brothers*, 50-51.

[139] "Field & Farm," 8.

[140] Jauken, *Moccasin Speaks*, 58-66, 231-32; Lee and Raynesford, *Trails of the Smoky Hill*, 214-16. Powell, *Sacred Mountain* 2, 868-69, typically tones down the Cheyenne outrages, blaming what they did on Chivington's attack at Sand Creek ten years earlier. Among other omissions he does not mention slicing open the pregnant Mrs. German, says Rebecca hit a warrior with the ax, which she did not do, and omits the warriors' act of burning her alive.

[141] Jauken, *Moccasin Speaks*, 71, 73, 78-80; Haley, *Buffalo War*, 145; Powell, *Sacred Mountain* 2, 869. Incredibly, Powell states that the Cheyennes were careful to cook meat and give it to their captives, and claims, that "mistreating of a captive woman was not usual among the People (Cheyennes)."

[142] Jauken, *Moccasin Speaks*, 87-88. As befitting his bias, Powell, *Sacred Mountain* 2, 870, 1352n34, calls leaving the girls alone on the prairie an act of "genuine kindness," because they assumed that soldiers would find them. After all, Powell says, the Cheyennes were "thoughtful of the little girls' well-being."

[143] Jauken, *Moccasin Speaks*, 88-90, 110; Lee and Raynesford, *Trails of the Smoky Hill*, 216-17; Powell, *Sacred Mountain*, 883-84. Powell would have his readers believe that the Cheyennes "were thoughtful of the two white children" so they sent out scouts to find them (after six weeks), but when the girls were brought in they "refused" to eat.

[144] Jauken, *Moccasin Speaks*, 112-15; Lee and Raynesford, *Trails of the Smoky Hill*, 217; Michno, *Encyclopedia of Indian Wars*, 287-88; Powell, *Sacred Mountain*, 884; Hyde, *George Bent*, 363. Powell cites Bent and claims that the Cheyennes left the two sisters behind eating hackberries while a rear guard of warriors stayed behind to watch and make sure that they were safely picked up by the soldiers. Powell says that the Indians "had done all they could to make sure the girls were cared for and quickly returned to their own people." He faults the whites, saying that they "failed to recognize real acts of kindness" by the Cheyennes. The girls could not have lived many more days as the recipients of such Cheyenne "kindness."

[145] Jauken, *Moccasin Speaks*, 115-17; Miles, *Personal Recollections 1*, 175.

[146] Jauken, *Moccasin Speaks*, 165-66, 171, 174; Haley, *Buffalo War*, 200-03; Miles, *Personal Recollections 1*, 179; Nye, *Carbine & Lance*, 231.

[147] Miles, *Personal Recollections 1*, 181; Jauken, *Moccasin Speaks*, 181, 191, 194, 201-09. In 1998, Arlene Feldmann Jauken, the great-granddaughter of Sophia German, wrote *The Moccasin Speaks*, an excellent book about the German Family experience.

Chapter Four

PRE-CIVIL WAR TEXAS

We have every reason to believe that the whole family has been murdered save the little girls, who have been carried into a captivity a thousand fold worse than death itself. — William Windham and Jasper Willis

After Texas had become a state in 1845, there was a remarkable stretch of nearly a dozen years of relative quiet along the edge of settlement. The "quiet" stretch was broken when Captain John S. "RIP" Ford led a force of Texans and Indian scouts into Indian Territory to defeat the Comanches at Antelope Hills on May 11, 1858. On October 1 of the same year, Captain Earl Van Dorn led companies of the 2nd U.S. Cavalry and Indian auxiliaries to Rush Creek in Indian Territory, to once again defeat the Comanches. During the fight, Lawrence S. "Sul" Ross rescued an 8-year-old white girl. Ross took the little girl back to Texas, but she could not remember her name or who her parents were. After strenuous, but fruitless efforts to find out who she was, Ross adopted her, calling her Lizzie Ross, from the name of Lizzie Tinsley, the woman he was soon to marry. Lizzie Ross later accompanied Ross's mother to California, and in 1889, married a wealthy merchant in Los Angeles.

The battles at Antelope Hills and Rush Creek proved the Indians would no longer be safe in their home country, but angry survivors, such as Comanche Chief Buffalo Hump, vowed revenge on the Texas settlements.

In March 1850, the oldest son (12) of Timothy Hart of Mission de Refugio, was captured about two miles from town. Hart offered $200 for rescue of the boy, but he was never returned. In late 1851, Comanches captured the son of Johanes K. Schneider. A captive Mexican later said that the Comanches kept the boy for a while, but killed him. In November 1854, Texas Governor Pease wrote a letter to General Persifor Smith mentioning the recent murder of a Mr. Williams on the Medina River, and the carrying off of one of his children "into a captivity worse than death." In September 1859, Indians attacked the Worman cabin near Eagle Pass, Texas, killed Mr. Worman, Mrs. Worman's mother, and Mrs. Worman's two sisters. They carried off Mrs. Worman and her daughter (3). The little girl's body was found a few miles from the house, but Mrs. Worman was never seen again.[1]

* * *

Peter Johnson Jr.
Texas, December 31, 1857

In December 1857, a band of Comanches came down from the north to raid in Erath, Comanche, Hamilton, and Bosque Counties. They split into three parties. One band stole horses near Stephenville on December 30, and on the same day, another party raided Turnbolt Barbee's home on Resley Creek in Comanche County, twenty miles south of Stephenville. Barbee's Negro slave was herding horses a half mile from the house when the Comanches lanced him and shot six arrows into him. They left him for dead and stole the horses. When the Indians left, the resilient slave crawled back to the house to report that the horses were gone, and allegedly said to Barbee: "The Injuns kill me for awhile, and they think I was dead for good, but I wasn't."[2]

The raiders continued down Resley Creek into Hamilton County, where they attacked Isaac Bean and his Negro slave, who were riding in a wagon to Waco. Both men were killed.[3] One of these bands, or another, consisting of six to eight Comanches, headed northeast into Bosque County. On the last day of December, the raiders spied Peter Cartwright Johnson and his son, Peter Jr. They were returning home from Meridian where they had purchased supplies. Near the base of Meridian Peak—which has since been called Johnson's Peak—located three miles south of Iredell, Texas, the Indians struck. They shot Mr. Johnson with five arrows, cut loose the oxen, plundered the wagon, and captured Peter Jr. (10). Within minutes they were gone, headed up the Bosque.[4]

Shortly after the first raids near Stephenville, civilian scouts took up the Indian trail, went to Barbee's, found the bodies of Bean and the slave, and discovered the murdered Peter Johnson. They tracked the Indians north, who appeared to be driving about 150 stolen horses. People sent letters to State Senator George B. Erath and Texas Governor Hardin Runnels, complaining of a lack of protection. Many believed that the raiders came from the

Texas reservations on the Brazos. On January 8, 1858, Ranger Lieutenant Thomas C. Frost wrote a letter to Governor Runnels, complaining that Indian Agent Robert S. Neighbors was petitioned time and again to control the Indians, but only issued insults and threats in reply. The letter prompted a response from Neighbors, who told Runnels that the Indians were not from the reservations, and were seen passing by them on January 3, heading north with up to forty head of horses. He admonished Frost, stating he ought to spend more time chasing guilty Indians and less time making false accusations.[5]

None of the letter writing did anything to help Peter Johnson Jr. The Indians let him go on their own accord. Perhaps tiring of carrying him along, or worried about retribution, the warriors took Peter's coat, hat, and socks, and turned him loose on the prairie somewhere near the Clear Fork of the Brazos. In freezing temperatures, with nothing to eat, and not knowing which way to go, Peter was in deep trouble. His mother had told him that if he became lost he should follow the cows, which would inevitably lead him to a house. Up to that time the Indians were also driving a number of cattle. The last night he was with them they had butchered and eaten one. The next day when they abandoned him, they also left behind a number of cows. Sure enough, among them was a belled-cow that abruptly turned about and began walking in a southeasterly direction. Peter walked along with them. He had nothing solid to eat besides grass roots, but had enough wits about him to milk one of the cows for a meager nourishment.

For nine days they wandered, and eventually the cows mingled with a herd belonging to Bill Keith. The cattleman had just sent out some of his boys to round up his stock. Dave Roberts and a few other cowboys were riding about six miles west of Dublin, Texas, when they spied cattle in the woods. To their surprise, they also saw the prone form of a boy, nearly frozen in the drizzling norther that was blowing at the time. They picked up Peter, wrapped him in blankets, and gave him food and drink. The little boy was taken to Cora, which no longer exists, but was then a village located about ten miles southeast of present-day Comanche, Texas. Frank M. Collier described him as "the poorest looking object imaginable—a mere skeleton." Collier carried him around Cora and got a donation of one dollar from every man in town. Peter recovered and eventually settled in the area, and was described as "a stout, robust man, and a worthy, good citizen of Comanche County."[6]

REBECCA AND TOBE JACKSON
Texas, October 21, 1858

Joshua (Mose) Jackson was a native of North Carolina. He and his family emigrated to Texas, settled in Harrison County for a time, and then moved to what was then Brown County, on the west side of Pecan Bayou and a few miles up from the junction of that river with the Colorado.[7] Neighbors were few, and the area's scattered families scratched out a meager living, living in dread of Indian attack.

Neither the Rangers nor the U.S. Army had successfully halted the raids. In 1858, Department of Texas commander, General David E. Twiggs, concluded that reacting to raids and staying on the defensive would not solve the problem. He authorized Captain Earl Van Dorn to lead the 2nd Cavalry into Indian Territory to take the war home to the enemy. The resultant battle at Rush Springs on October 1, 1858, was a defeat for the Comanches, but Buffalo Hump, one of the most belligerent chiefs, escaped, vowing to take revenge on the Texas settlements. Whether the subsequent events in Brown County were the direct result of Van Dorn's attack is uncertain, but Buffalo Hump's threat was real. The New York *Weekly Times* warned: "War has now begun in earnest, and there is no saying where it will terminate."[8]

Joshua Jackson lived several miles downstream from the Kirkpatrick and King families. In October 1858, the heads of the three households selected a few large pecan trees to cut down and use for building purposes. Since the trees were lush with pecans, the men agreed to return with their families and collect the sweet nuts before cutting the trunks into board timber. On October 21, the Kings and Kirkpatricks waited, but the Jacksons failed to arrive.[9]

Jackson had a large family. An adult son, John, lived in Lampasas and had protested about his father moving far out into Brown County. On the day of the proposed gathering, another son, Jesse, was sick, so Jason, an older son, agreed to stay home with him. Joshua Jackson hitched up a wagon and loaded in his wife, his daughter (17), his son Tobe (12), his daughter Rebecca (9), and another son (7). They traveled up a buffalo trace, heading for the rendezvous about six miles north. Less than two miles from home, twenty-six Indians dashed up from the timber along Pecan Bayou and shot Mr. Jackson dead. The team bolted and started to run. Tobe struggled unsuccessfully with the reins, while the horses circled wildly into the woods and tangled themselves in the brush.

174

An arrow hit the oldest daughter, pinning her arm against her side. The Indians reached the wagon and pulled her out. Mrs. Jackson got down and fell to her knees, crying, and praying, while Rebecca sat beside her. Tobe stood nearby, not knowing what to do, while the youngest boy peered out from the wagon bed. They watched in horror as the Indians dragged the eldest daughter about forty paces away, stripped off her clothes, and raped her. When they finished, they cut off one of her breasts, scalped her alive, cut her throat, and carried the long auburn hair to Mrs. Jackson and threw it in her face. Another Indian noticed the youngest son peering out from the wagon. He shot an arrow into his eye, pulled his head over the edge of the end gate and cut his throat. Mrs. Jackson, Rebecca, and Tobe were nearly frozen in shock.[10]

The Indians plundered the wagon and divided in two groups; eight of them took the two children, and eighteen of them carried off Mrs. Jackson, but she did not live long. Shortly after they split up, the warriors probably decided the white woman would be too much trouble, particularly if they were to continue raiding. They cut her throat and left her dead on the trail not far from the bodies of her husband and children. The other band took Rebecca and Tobe about twenty miles southwest to Lookout Mountain, in northwestern San Saba County. On the wooded slopes, which rose about 150 feet over the surrounding plain, three Indians guarded the children while the other five went to steal horses. They waited for nine days. Tobe seemed to adapt to the situation, but Rebecca was a nervous wreck, unable to eat or drink, and she appeared to be wasting away. The tenth night the other Indians returned with a herd of stolen horses and they all packed up and headed north.[11]

When the Jacksons failed to appear at the scheduled gathering, the other families were concerned. Mr. Kirkpatrick thought he heard gunfire to the south, but supposed it was a party of hunters. They continued cutting boards, gathering pecans, and after a long day, went home. The next day, King and Kirkpatrick returned to collect the last of the boards they had sawn. Kirkpatrick asked one of his brothers and one of King's sons to ride downstream and round up some stray cattle he had seen. As they rode they spotted an abandoned wagon, and then saw the Jacksons' bodies. When they spread the alarm, the few families in the area fled south into Lampasas and San Saba Counties. Two other settlers, William Windham and Jasper Willis, also discovered the massacre site. In Lampasas they recorded what they saw with the county notary, which included the murdered settlers and a girl's bloody stocking.

They believed the entire family was killed, except for two children, "who have been carried into a captivity a thousand fold worse than death itself."[12]

Although the Indians had won the first round, they had not yet escaped. On October 16, a detachment of ten Rangers under Captain John Williams, left old Camp Colorado near the Bowser Bend of the Colorado. They scouted north in the vicinity of new Camp Colorado on Jim Ned Creek, then east along the divide between the Colorado River and Pecan Bayou. On the 21st they struck an Indian trail near Clear Creek and followed it south for about ten miles, discovering the remains of two butchered cows, and then continued south another ten miles until they reached Jackson's deserted house. The trail ran north, and within two miles they discovered the bodies. None of the fleeing settlers had stopped to bury them, and Williams had them interred.

In San Saba on October 25, Williams met many settlers who had fled their homes, and learned from Jesse and Jason Jackson that two of their siblings were still missing. About fifty men joined them, and the next day, Williams headed out again in pursuit. Also on the 25th, forty-five citizens of Lampasas County petitioned Governor Runnels, asking for military protection to prevent all the people from fleeing the frontier. While some petitioned, others were looking for the Indians. Carter Mays and sixteen men discovered the trail of the eighteen Indians who had split up after murdering the Jacksons. The track led south. Since the Indians had several-days' lead, the settlers and Rangers agreed to form a scouting line from the Colorado across to the Leon River, hoping to pick up the Indians as they returned north after raiding the settlements. While the men organized in San Saba, the Indians holding the Jackson children were still on Lookout Mountain, about twenty miles to the northwest.[13]

One company located an Indian trail about twelve miles north of Lampasas and followed it north to the divide between Cowhouse Creek and Pecan Bayou. They caught up with four Indians driving horses and attacked, killing one and wounding two. They recaptured thirty-five horses and found the Jacksons' clothing. Lieutenant Gideon P. Cowan and twelve men, including Rhome Vaughn, Gabe Choate, Rid Hoy, and Frank Gholson, had gone back to the Jackson house, and on October 29, once again picked up the old trail from there. With so many Indians splitting up and rejoining, and so many whites in pursuit, the tracking was confused. Nevertheless, Cowan luckily hit on the trail of the eight Indians with the children, after they had left Lookout Mountain on the 30th.[14] On November 7, Cowan found the site where the Indians had camped the night before.[15] Nearby was a strip of girl's clothing hanging from a bush and a small footprint in the mud. Cowan sent out two Rangers to scout what appeared to be two diverging tracks, while six more men from Lampasas and Burnet Counties joined them.

That evening, Cowan said, "Boys, we have got to do all possible to rescue those children. The Indians are going toward a certain star, so we will follow that by night and follow the trail by day."[16]

They moved slowly by night, and picked up their pace with the morning sun. The next day they were right behind them. Riding in the lead, Frank Gholson spotted warriors on a hill ahead. He told Cowan and the lieutenant split up his company to try to encircle them, but then he saw two children on the prairie. The Indians had abandoned them and sped off on their fastest horses, hoping that recovering the children would satisfy their pursuers. Eight Rangers rode off after the Indians, but they were outdistanced and gave up the chase.[17]

As the rescuers approached, Tobe rose up from his crouching position in the grass and said to Rebecca, "They are white men; they are white men; they are white men. I see their hats and stirrups."

The first man up to him slid off his horse, grasped Tobe by the hand and asked, "Are you the Jackson children?"

"Yes," Tobe answered, and then asked, "Did the Indians kill mother?"

"Yes," the Ranger sadly replied.

Rhome Vaughn went to Rebecca, who was still hunched over with her elbows on her knees. "Sissy, stand up if you are able; you are safe now," he said. "You are in the hands of your friends."[18]

The Rangers and citizens all said a prayer of thanks for getting the children back unharmed. They rounded up seventy-eight stolen horses and camped until the following afternoon, giving Rebecca a chance to recuperate. At first she could eat nothing and they only made four miles before she was near collapse. They made her a bed of blankets, and finally got her to eat some roasted bacon. At this slow pace it took six days to reach Camp Colorado. There, the officers' wives took care of the children while their oldest brother was contacted. He came to pick them up and a guard was furnished to escort them back to John Jackson's home in Lampasas.[19]

Citizens of Brown, San Saba, Burnet, McCulloch, Mason, Lampasas, and surrounding counties were dissatisfied with the lack of military protection. In late November, Hugh Allen wrote a complaint to Governor Runnels, stating that he had been on the Texas frontier for twenty years and this was the first time he felt compelled to write about Indian depredations. He concluded that "ever since Van Dorn routed them and dismounted so maney they have bin down to get more horses and I think he will drive them down on us."[20] The Texas frontier was no better off after the army took the offensive.

Little is known of what became of Rebecca and Tobe. It was said that Rebecca, who had initially been the most traumatized, coped with her ordeal, married Jack Stroud, and lived in Lampasas County for a time before moving to New Mexico. Tobe, who appeared comparatively unaffected by his captivity, is said to have later revisited the scene of the massacre, only to be taken away in terrible mental anguish. He never recovered, and roamed the countryside, clothed and fed by those who knew what happened to him. Tobe eventually died in an insane asylum.[21]

RHODA AND MARGARET RIGGS
Texas, March 16, 1859

In 1859, Bell County was on the edge of the frontier, and there were few homes west of the town of Belton. One of those, owned by William C. Riggs, was about a dozen miles northwest of town in a cedar brake between North Nolan Creek and Cowhouse Creek, on the present-day Fort Hood Military Reservation. On the bright, clear morning of March 16, from fifteen to forty Indians, probably Comanches, began their raid into Bell County.

About one mile from Riggs's house, warriors found and killed a Mr. Pierce. About that time, Mr. Riggs and a boy named Thomas Elms were leaving the house in a wagon. The Indians jumped them and tried to take them alive. They stripped Elms and beat him with quirts. Riggs broke free and ran toward his house. The Indians left Elms and ran after Riggs, which allowed Elms to hide. Riggs made it home and barred the door. A short while later, thinking the Indians gone, Riggs, his wife, carrying the baby William Jr., and two daughters, Margaret (8) and Rhoda (12), burst from the door and ran.

The warriors easily caught up to them and murdered and scalped the husband and wife. They left baby William lying in his parents' blood, and took the two girls up on their horses and rode back to the house. They plundered its contents, ripped apart the feather beds, wrapped themselves in bright cloth and danced about, teasing and taunting the horrified girls. Done with their sport, the Indians put the girls on horses and rode away.

In mid-afternoon along North Nolan Creek they set up an ambush. Charles Cruger was driving a herd of horses home when he almost rode into the trap. Noticing people moving in a thicket about 100 yards ahead, Cruger halted and tried to turn the horses around. Three Indians chased him almost two miles. He got away, but they captured seven horses. When only about one mile west of Belton, they came upon a man named O'Neil. He tried to escape but the Indians shot him in the back. Margaret Riggs said, "I can remember seeing him bathed in blood and hearing his piteous groans but they did not tarry long with him. . . ."[22] The warriors rode west about seventeen miles from Belton, attacked the Franklin Ranch and stole forty-five horses.

The Indians then came in sight of what Margaret called "cow hunters," who she said, "surprised and excited them and caused them to ride very fast." Margaret fell off her horse and was hurt. Rhoda saw her fall. She struggled to get off the horse, but the warrior hung onto her with one hand. When the galloping horse passed near a tree, Rhoda grabbed hold of a branch and wrenched herself free. The Indians kept on going. Rhoda went back to Margaret and helped her younger sister, who could barely walk. By nightfall they reached a deserted cabin and went inside. The night was cold and Rhoda pulled off her dress to wrap Margaret up. The next morning they were off, limping in the direction of where they thought Belton must be. They found another abandoned house and took shelter, when a rider came up. The girls hid in silence, but when the man began calling out in English they ran to him. The man, named Lee, took the girls to the home of Captain Damern, where they stayed until relatives came to claim them. Citizens of Belton quickly raised a posse to chase the Indians, but the raiders were long gone.

Relatives took care of the Riggs children, and all three overcame the trauma and grew to adulthood. In the 1880s, all three were married and living productive lives. William Riggs Jr. moved to Colorado and became a stock raiser. Rhoda moved to New Mexico, and Margaret moved with her husband to Bandera County, Texas.[23]

William Hoerster
Texas, July 19, 1859

Heinrich (Henry) Hoerster and wife Maria Christina Gelhausen lived for a time in the German community of Fredericksburg, Texas. Wilhelm (William) Hoerster, their fifth son, was born there on April 16, 1850. The family moved to Mason County in 1856, where they settled on upper Willow Creek, at present-day Art, Texas, about six miles east of Mason. It was a dangerous location and life was hard. Mrs. Hoerster died in May 1859, but the family dealt with their grief and persevered. One of 9-year-old William's jobs was to pasture, water, and guard the few horses they owned. His daily routine was shattered on July 19, 1859, when a small band of raiding Kiowas struck the Hoerster farm and other ranches in the area. They shot Bill in the neck and rode off with the wounded lad and his father's four horses. A posse of settlers followed the Indian trail north for 150 miles until rain obliterated the trail. A neighbor, George W. Todd, reported the incident in the San Antonio *Herald*, stating that Mr. Hoerster was "almost insane" about his son's capture.[24]

Bill's neck wound did not prove fatal. He remembered crossing the San Saba River and traveling six days to reach a village containing 1,000 Indians. His life was not easy, for Indians "had beaten him daily," and he had to fight for his life at times just to survive. The Kiowas who held young Hoerster either found him to be too much trouble or were in dire straits themselves, for about three months later they reportedly sold him for a loaf of bread to New Mexican Comancheros at the edge of the west Texas caprock in the Valley of Tears.[25]

Comancheros took Bill north. Christopher "Kit" Carson, Ute Indian agent in Taos, New Mexico Territory, was in Mora on November 19, 1859, when a Mexican approached him with a white boy. He told Carson that he had bought him from the Kiowas for a mule and other goods worth $100. Carson listened to the story and wrote to James L. Collins, Superintendent of Indian Affairs in Santa Fe. He stated that the boy was "in destitute and miserable condition" and he gave him clothing and sent him to school. He supposed he was about ten years old, with light complexion, light hair, and blue eyes. He could speak only a little English, but understood what was being said. Carson learned from him that his name was William "Houston." He named his father as Henry, his mother as Christy, and several of his siblings as Fritz, Daniel, Catherine, Sophie, and Minnie. He couldn't remember where he lived. Carson asked Collins if he could authorize payment to ransom the boy. He also wrote to Texas Governor Sam Houston if he could advertise the information to help locate his parents.[26]

Houston had newspaper ads placed and Henry Hoerster eventually saw the letter in a San Antonio *Herald*. He wrote several letters to Carson, one, on December 28, stated that the description given sounded like his boy, William, and the names of his siblings were correct. Only his name was spelled "Hoerster," not "Houston." Mr. Hoerster added that he was "very much indebted to you for your kindness and humanity, and may our Lord bless you for this." He asked if Carson would keep the boy until arrangements were made for his transportation home. Then he wrote to Houston about having him returned at government expense.

Meanwhile, the Texas Legislature passed a resolution appropriating $500 for Hoerster's restoration. Secretary of State Eber W. Cave wrote to Carson on January 11, 1860, that the money was available, and asked him to send the boy by regular mail stage line to San Antonio in care of Vance and Brother, who would then send him to Frank Stricklin of Fredericksburg. Cave said Carson's expenses would be paid and his ransom payment reimbursed. Cave thanked Carson for his "promptitude in behalf of humanity" and said his kindnesses would be remembered.[27]

Bill Hoerster reached home in May 1860. His return was joyously celebrated, but his ordeal stamped him forever as a man out of the ordinary. The fighting he had to do to survive only three months of captivity was not easily unlearned. He got the nicknames of "Tough Boy" and "Wild Bill," and at age 11 he enlisted in Mason County's "Minute Men." Bill married Anna Alberson in January 1873. They had three children, but only Sophie survived. Bill and his brother Daniel were caught up in the Mason County feud of 1875, where stockmen, farmers, and rustlers battled each other for nearly two years, and fifteen men were killed, including Dan Hoerster. Bill's wife Anna died in 1878. He married Mervia Fripp in 1880, but she died three years later. He married a third time, to Anna Theresa Scholl. In 1898, they sold their land and moved to Hinsdale, Montana. Marital problems drove them apart and Bill returned to Texas, where he lived with the Dietrich Kothmann family for the rest of his years. William Hoerster was visiting relatives in Denver, Colorado, where he died on August 4, 1910. His body was sent back to Mason County and laid to rest next to his father in the cemetery in Art, Texas.[28]

HULDA AND NANCY LEMLEY
Texas, February 7, 1860

For years, citizens had been angry because of the continued presence of two Indian Reservations along the Brazos and Clear Fork in Texas. They were convinced that many of the marauders came from the reserves, while others from north of the Red River used them as refuges. Constant agitation, from men such as John R. Baylor, finally resulted in their removal in July and August 1859. About 1,420 Indians were escorted north to their new home in Indian Territory. Returning to Fort Belknap after having facilitated the exodus, Agent Robert S. Neighbors was gunned down and killed by an embittered assailant. If the settlers thought that Indian removal would solve their problem, they were mistaken, for worse was still to come.[29]

The raids began the following year. In early February 1860, bands of Comanches and Kiowas rode down from the north. They first appeared on the Paluxy River in Erath County, and then near the present-day town of Lingleville. They struck on the full moon night of February 7.

John Lemley and family had lived in Jack County as early as 1854, but for safety reasons, decided to move farther south, entering Erath County in January 1860. William Wood had also recently arrived, building his house about a mile from Lemley. The two men were still constructing their homes, and had gone to the Leon River for timber. Wood's wife, Lucinda (16), was staying with the Lemleys. Mrs. Lemley had taken her baby, John Jr., to the Tucker house to spend the evening, and later in the afternoon, her daughter, Dallie Lemley, joined them. Left behind at the Lemley house were Lucinda Wood, and sisters Liddie, Nancy, and 19-year-old Hulda Lemley.[30]

The Indians attacked without warning, and before the women could take any defensive measures, the warriors captured all four of them. The Indians carried them away from the house and took them southeast a few miles near where Lingleville would later be built. There, with reasonable assurance that they would not be interrupted, the warriors beat and raped the women. At dusk, with their lusts satisfied, the warriors released Lucinda Wood and Liddie Lemley, and motioned to them to go home. The Indians had just begun their raid and apparently there was disagreement among them as to the advantages of either taking the women along, releasing them, or killing them. A few warriors quickly made up their minds. They rode back down the trail, found Lucinda and Liddie, shot them in the back with arrows and lanced them with spears. Lucinda, with a full head of light golden hair, was scalped, but Liddie's thin head of hair was left behind.[31]

Nancy and Hulda Lemley made little protest about their treatment and sought the protection of an older warrior who seemed more kindly disposed. At least they were still alive. They rode away under the light of a full moon. The next morning they stopped about three miles southwest of Stephenville. Nancy and Hulda's clothing was stripped off, and they both probably assumed they were going to be raped again. Instead, the warriors motioned for them to head home—just what they had done to Lucinda and Liddie. The terrified women headed down the trail in the freezing February morning, certain that they would soon be killed, but when out of sight of the Indians, they veered off the trail and headed toward Stephenville. The Indians did not go after them, but continued on their raid, with two less white women to be concerned about. Nancy and Hulda staggered to the home of Will Roberts one mile from town. Townswomen brought them clothing and they told what had happened.

On February 8, the Indians killed the two Monroe brothers six miles northwest of Meridian in Bosque County. The next day they killed Baptist preachers Griffin and White, ten miles north of Gatesville. On the 11th, they murdered M. S. Skaggs and Benjamin Vanhook on the San Gabriel in Burnet County, and a few days later they robbed Newton Jackson of his horses and wagon in San Saba County. Citizens chased them for weeks, but never could catch them. Several months later, some Indians' horses were captured during a raid in Palo Pinto County. Found on one of the bridles was a scalp of light golden hair that was identified as belonging to Lucinda Wood.

Lucinda and Liddie were buried in the West End Cemetery near Stephenville. Nancy and Hulda had been abused so badly that Doctor J. P. Valentine (I.P. Vollintine) of Weatherford, had to treat them for several weeks before they recovered. John Lemley moved the remaining members of his family to Palo Pinto County after the attack. The girls both lived many years after the incident, Hulda marrying Mr. Reasoner and remaining in the area. She related the story in 1926.[32]

KATHERINE MASTERSON, MATILDA GAGE, HIRAM FOWLER, AND MARTHA SHERMAN
Texas, November 26-27, 1860

One of the largest raids to hit the Texas frontier since the Comanches were officially removed in 1859, occurred in the late fall of 1860. It was memorable for its scope and savagery, and because it led to the recapture of Cynthia Ann Parker, kidnapped twenty-four years earlier. Her husband, Peta Nocona, was a leader of the raiders. The Comanches first struck in Jack County, about five miles northeast of Jacksboro, at the home of James Landman. On November 26, Landman and his son were cutting wood away from the cabin, when the Indians murdered Mrs. Landman, plundered the house, and carried off Jane (12) and Katherine Masterson (15), who were visiting the Landmans. Katherine's captor threw her on a horse, but Jane was roped and dragged as they rode away.

The raiders traveled less than a mile west to Calvin Gage's home on the banks of Lost Creek. Before attacking, they cut loose Jane's battered and bleeding body, and shot her dead. At Gage's that day were Anna Gage, Katy Sanders, her aged mother, and Matilda, Jonathan, and Polly Gage. Three children of Anna's previous marriage also lived with them: Joseph (16), Mary Ann, and Hiram Fowler. Joseph and Calvin Gage, were searching for stray oxen about a mile from the house. The Indians slaughtered old Katy Sanders, and shot Anna several times, leaving her for dead. She recovered, but died of complications from her wounds a few years later. They took Polly, not yet two years old, and laughingly threw her high into the air several times, letting her smash onto the ground. They shot and wounded Mary Ann Fowler and Jonathan Gage. Tiring of this sport, the Indians took what property they could carry and rode south, taking Matilda Gage (14), Katherine Masterson, and Hiram Fowler with them. Only a short distance away, the warriors stopped, stripped Matilda and Katherine, and "savagely abused" them. When satiated, the warriors let them go. The two girls heard bells and walked toward the sound, finding Joseph Fowler coming in with the oxen. The piteous, naked, and embarrassed girls told Fowler what had happened and the three of them cautiously returned home to discover the terrible scene. Fowler rode to neighboring houses and spread the news.[33]

Just before daylight on November 27, a messenger reached the home of John Brown in northwest Parker County, about twenty-four miles southeast of Jacksboro. Brown saddled up and went to warn his neighbors. Two hours later, fifty Indians appeared at his house. Mary Brown gathered her children in the cabin's half-story loft. A black female slave hid in the orchard, but her son, Anthony (14), grabbed an ax and took a stand near the front door of the house. The Indians only stole their horses. When it seemed that the Indians left, Mary Brown opened the trap door of the loft. Just then, an Indian, still waiting below, loosed an arrow at her that glanced off her head, taking off some of her hair. She slammed the door and the Indian ran off. The Comanches encountered John Brown on his return, only a half-mile from the house. They lanced and scalped him, then cut off his nose. Mary Brown later buried him in the corner of her yard.[34]

The raiders next went into Palo Pinto County. On Staggs Prairie, a few miles northeast of present-day Mineral Wells, they came to the home of Ezra and Martha Sherman. Martha's maiden name was Johnson. She had lived earlier in Parker County and was previously married to a Mr. Cheairs. When she wed Ezra Sherman they moved to Palo Pinto County. The Shermans had just sat down for dinner when Indians burst in the door. They were taken by surprise, but Martha cautioned everyone to be calm, and not to show any fright. The Indians appeared to be friendly, indicated that they were hungry. William H. Cheairs (7) slipped out the back and hid in an oak thicket.

Martha noticed that one of the Indians had red hair, and realizing that he was a white renegade made her more fearful, although she tried her best not to show it.

"Vamoose—no hurt—vamoose," one of the warriors said in broken Spanish and English.

There was little else they could do. Ezra and Martha took the two remaining children, Mary Cheairs and Joe Sherman (1), and began hurriedly walking east toward the home of their nearest neighbor on Rock Creek. They only got a half-mile away when Indians rode up to them. This time they ordered Ezra to continue walking, and grabbed Martha by the hair and dragged her back to a spot about 200 yards from the cabin. There she was stripped, tortured, and raped by at least seventeen warriors, including one she called "that big old red-headed Indian." One of them pushed an arrow under her shoulder blade. They scalped her, rode their horses over her and left her, no doubt believing she was dead. The warriors returned to the house and ransacked it, drank the molasses, tore up the feather beads and, for whatever reason, stole the family Bible. Then they rode off.

Ezra, meanwhile, went to a neighbor, borrowed a gun, and hurried home. Martha had dragged herself to the cabin, trying to get out of the freezing weather. Ezra found her there, but there was little he could do. She related all the horrible things the Indians did to her, and how hard it was for them to remove her scalp. Neighbors came to see her, and one, rancher Henry Belding, could not get the "fearful" sight of her erased from his memory even fifty years later. Martha lingered four days, delivering a stillborn child before she finally died. Her body was taken to Weatherford, where it was shrouded in a casket and laid out in a cabin for all to view. Naturally, the people of the county were outraged. Martha Sherman was buried in Willow Spring Cemetery, eight miles east of Weatherford.[35]

The raiding Comanches were not finished. With about 300 stolen horses in tow, they rode west to William Eubanks's ranch near the Brazos. Mr. Eubanks was not home, but his daughters smartly donned men's clothing and hats, and took position behind a fortified picket. The ruse was successful and the Indians rode away. They next headed north, crossed Keechi Creek, and turned west. In Dark Valley they stole 300 horses from Jowell McKee, and, on November 28, headed out of the settlements.

According to Ida Lasater Huckabay, the Landman, Gage, Masterson, Brown, and Sherman murders "so enraged the settlers that the cavalrymen and rangers became determined to pursue the Indians to their own doors. . . ." They formed a strike force under Texas Ranger Captain Lawrence "Sul" Ross, a twenty-one-man detachment of Company H, 2nd Cavalry, under Sergeant J. W. Spangler, and seventy volunteers under Jack Cureton. Ross followed the pony tracks to the junction of Mule Creek and the Pease and found the raiders' camp. The night before, on November 18, the Indians had just killed their last captive. Rebellious young Hiram Fowler was proving to be too much trouble. They murdered him and left his body behind. His bones were found about one year later. Ross attacked on the morning of the 19th. Just before he moved out, guide Charles Goodnight found a pillowslip on the trail and picked it up. Inside was a little girl's dress and a Bible with Martha Sherman's name on the inside cover. They had caught the guilty Indians. In the subsequent Battle of Pease River (see Cynthia Ann Parker), Peta Nocona may have been killed and his wife, Cynthia Ann Parker, kidnapped twenty-four years earlier, was finally recovered. The most recent captures, rapes, and murders, were partially avenged.[36]

Chapter four footnotes

[1] Winfrey and Day, *Texas Indian Papers 3*, 155; Winfrey and Day, *Texas Indian Papers 5*, 90, 190; Michno, *Encyclopedia of Indian Wars*, 62, 66-67; Corwin, *Comanche & Kiowa Captives*, 119-21; Abney, *L. D. Lafferty*, 198-99, 203, 206, 209-12. There is question as to the accuracy of the latter narrative.

[2] Winfrey and Day, *Texas Indian Papers 5*, 213-14; Wilbarger, *Depredations*, 498-99.

[3] Isaac Bean is called John Bune in Wilbarger, *Depredations*, 499.

[4] Winfrey and Day, *Texas Indian Papers 5*, 207; Webb and Carroll, *Handbook of Texas 1*, 919; McConnell, *West Texas Frontier*, in forttours.com/pages/tocjohnsn; Wilbarger, *Depredations*, 499.

[5] Winfrey and Day, *Texas Indian Papers 5*, 207-11, 213-16.

[6] McConnell, *West Texas Frontier*, in forttours.com/pages/tocjohnsn; Webb and Carroll, *Handbook of Texas 1*, 412; Wilbarger, *Depredations*, 500.

[7] Wilbarger, *Depredations*, 489; McConnell, *West Texas*, 303. The site of the Jackson home is in present-day Mills County, about 12 miles west of Goldthwaite.

[8] Arnold, *Jeff Davis's Own*, 182-83, 212; Michno, *Encyclopedia of Indian Wars*, 66-67.

[9] McConnell, *West Texas*, 303-04; Winfrey and Day, *Texas Indian Papers 3*, 298. McConnell says the date was October 28, but Lieutenant D. C. Cowan later reported the incident occurred on Thursday, October 21.

[10] McConnell, *West Texas*, 304-05; Winfrey and Day, *Texas Indian Papers 3*, 301; Wilbarger, *Depredations*, 490. Wilbarger says that Mrs. Jackson's throat was also cut at this time.

[11] McConnell, *West Texas*, 305.

[12] Wilbarger, *Depredations*, 491; Winfrey and Day, *Texas Indian Papers 3*, 299-300.

[13] Webb and Carroll, *Handbook of Texas 1*, 279; Winfrey and Day, *Texas Indian Papers 3*, 297-98; 5, 289; McConnell, *West Texas*, 305.

[14] Winfrey and Day, *Texas Indian Papers 3*, 301; McConnell, *West Texas*, 305-06, 308.

[15] McConnell, *West Texas*, 305-06, says the trail was found on November 7, while in Winfrey and Day, *Texas Indian Papers 3*, 306, a letter from Gideon Cowan's brother, Lieutenant D. C. Cowan, dated November 7, indicates that the children were recovered on or before that date.

[16] McConnell, *West Texas*, 306.

[17] McConnell, *West Texas*, 306; Winfrey and Day, *Texas Indian Papers 3*, 306. McConnell says the rescue took place in Nolan County in the vicinity of Sweetwater, but Cowan's report indicates the rescue occurred on the divide between the headwaters of the Leon and Pecan, in southeast Callahan County.

[18] McConnell, *West Texas*, 306-07.

[19] McConnell, *West Texas*, 307-08.

[20] Winfrey and Day, *Texas Indian Papers*, 3, 309-10.

[21] McConnell, *West Texas*, 308; Wilbarger, *Depredations*, 491.

[22] Wilbarger *Depredations*, 593-95; Winfrey and Day, *Texas Indian Papers 5*, 330, 335.

[23] Winfrey and Day, *Texas Indian Papers 5*, 330-31, 335; Wilbarger, *Indian Depredations*, 595-96.

[24] Johnson, "'Wild Bill' Hoerster," 49, 53n8. George Todd's own daughter (see Alice Todd) would also be captured by Indians in the same vicinity six years later.

[25] Johnson, "'Wild Bill' Hoerster," 49-50; "Valley of Tears," in Handbook of Texas Online. The Valley of Tears (Valle de las Lagrimas) was along Los Lingos Creek south of present-day Quitaque in Briscoe County, Texas. It was so named because of the wailing that occurred when captured mothers and children were brought there to be separated from their families and sold.

[26] Johnson, "'Wild Bill' Hoerster," 50-51.

[27] Johnson, "'Wild Bill' Hoerster," 51-52; Winfrey and Day, *Texas Indian Papers 4*, 1.

[28] Johnson, "'Wild Bill' Hoerster," 52-53; Gard, *Frontier Justice*, 52-57.

[29] Marshall, *A Cry Unheard*, 66.

[30] McConnell, *West Texas Frontier*, in forttours.com/pages/toclemley

[31] McConnell, *West Texas Frontier*, in forttours.com/pages/toclemley; Winfrey and Day, *Texas Indian Papers 4*, 8, 24; Wilbarger, *Depredations*, 507. Wilbarger says that two women were killed while trying to escape when the house was first attacked.

[32] McConnell, *West Texas Frontier*, and Gibson, *Painted Pole*, in forttours.com/pages/toclemley; Winfrey and Day, *Texas Indian Papers 4*, 7-16, 19, 24; Wilbarger, *Depredations*, 508.

[33] Marshall, *A Cry Unheard*, 29-30, 135; McConnell, *West Texas Frontier*, in forttours.com/pages/
tocnocona.

[34] Marshall, *A Cry Unheard*, 30-31.

[35] Marshall, *A Cry Unheard*, 32-34, 79; McConnell, *West Texas Frontier*, in forttours.com/pages/
tocnocona; Wilbarger, *Depredations*, 516-17.

[36] Marshall, *A Cry Unheard*, 30, 34-35; Huckabay, *Jack County*, 60; Haley, *Goodnight*, 52-58.
Apologist Jack Ramsay, *Sunshine on the Prairie*, 84, whitewashes Nocona's Raid, citing none
of the Masterson, Gage, and Fowler killings and rapes, and states only that a family named
Sherman was attacked, and the mother was wounded and reportedly died the next day. In a
similar whitewashing, Anderson, *Conquest of Texas*, 330-32, says that the Pease River fight
was "a brutal massacre" of a "camp full of women and children," and fails to mention the vicious
raid by Nocona that precipitated the incident.

Chapter Five

THE MINNESOTA UPRISING

She would either be killed, or share with me what I felt to be a worse fate—that of a captive. — Abigail Gardner

The platform was thronged with relatives and friends to greet us, as restored to them from a fate worse than death. — Urania White

Being threatened with death so often, sometimes I almost prayed that some of their attempts to kill me might prove successful. I thought that death might be a relief to me. — George Spencer

Minnesota experienced one great paroxysm in 1862, but that conflagration was perhaps the greatest single episode of settler killings and captures in American history. Death estimates ran as high as 2,000 according to the St. Peter *Tribune*, and six weeks after the uprising, burial parties were interring as many as forty-seven bodies a day. There were many bodies lying in far off thickets and prairies that were found, and thousands of other settlers fled the state, never to return. Commissioner of Indian Affairs William Dole estimated Indians killed from 800 to 1,000 "inoffensive and unarmed settlers." Twenty-three counties were virtually depopulated. The official count was established at 644 dead. About 300 captives were taken; only four of them were white men.[1]

Although not a temporal part of the Sioux uprising of 1862, the 1857 Dakota attack at Spirit Lake, Iowa, was a precursor to the uprising. The attack, the hostages taken, and the punishments meted out to the Dakota Indians, including withholding annuities as punishment, were links in the chain of events that would lead to the horrors of 1862.

* * *

ABIGAIL GARDNER, LYDIA NOBLE, ELIZABETH THATCHER, AND MARGARET ANN MARBLE
Iowa, March 8-13, 1857

Abigail Gardner was born in 1843, in Seneca, New York, to Roland Gardner and Frances M. Smith-Gardner. The Gardners moved from New York, to Ohio, and finally built a cabin on the south side of West Okoboji Lake in Dickinson County, Iowa. The family was comprised of Roland and his wife Frances, and their children, Eliza Matilda (16), Abigail (13), and Roland (6). Living with them was their eldest daughter, Mary, and her husband, Harvey Luce, and their children, Albert (4) and Amanda (1). Six other families and several single men lived in what was known as "Spirit Lake" settlement. Among the families were Lydia Noble (21), Elizabeth Thatcher, and Margaret Marble (20), all soon to share a common fate. Alvin and Lydia Noble with their child (2), and Joseph and Elizabeth Thatcher with their seven-month-old child, lived in one cabin on the east side of East Okoboji Lake. William and Margaret Marble lived on the west shore of Spirit Lake.[2]

The idyll was shattered in the spring of 1857, when the outlaw Dakota Chief Inkpaduta and his band of warriors swept into the Spirit Lake settlements and committed murder and mayhem. The precise cause of the massacre is still debated. One cause was said to be the murder of an Indian by a white man; another reason was that a white man's dog bit an Indian who then shot the dog, and the enraged owner beat the Indian senseless. This same Indian then claimed to converse with the "Great Spirit," who apparently approved of the destruction of the bad white people who were responsible for all the Indians' suffering. The Dakotas considered the lakes as sacred dwelling places for the spirits. The Indians were not permitted to fish from these lakes or even place a canoe in the waters. The sight of the log cabins and fences incensed the Indians to "bloodlust and butchery," for this was viewed as an invasion of their sacred shores.[3]

On Sunday morning, March 8, 1857, Inkpaduta and his warriors barged into the Gardner cabin and demanded breakfast. Mrs. Gardner fed them while a warrior took Roland's gun and removed the firing mechanism. Roaring Cloud, one of Inkpaduta's twin sons, demanded more food, but none remained. He pointed his gun at Harvey Luce, who grabbed the barrel and prevented the Indian from firing. After a few tense moments, the Indians vacated the cabin. About 9 a.m., Doctor Issac H. Harriott and

190

Author's photo

Abbie Gardner cabin. Spirit Lake, Iowa

Bertell A. Snyder came by, for they knew Roland was about to leave for Fort Dodge for provisions and they wanted him to mail their letters. Roland refused to leave because he felt the Indians were on the warpath. Harriott and Snyder disagreed and soon left. About midday the Indians took Gardner's cattle, killed them, and headed for the Mattock cabin.

After the Indians left the settlers discussed their options. At two in the afternoon, Harvey Luce and a visitor, Robert Clark, went to warn their neighbors of possible Indian trouble. About four p.m., Roland stepped out of the cabin and saw nine Indians fast approaching. He called out, "We are all doomed to die!"[4]

Roland did not want give up without a fight, but Frances Gardner said, "If we have to die, let us die innocent of shedding blood." Honoring his wife's wish, Roland did not resist as the Indians entered his home and demanded flour. As he went to the barrel they shot him in the heart. The Indians then grabbed Frances Gardner and Mary Luce and held their arms tight, while others took rifles, bashed in their heads, and dragged the bodies outside. Abigail sat in a chair in a state of shock. The Indians tore her sister's baby from her arms, dragged Roland Jr., and Mary's toddler outside, beat them with stove wood, and left them for dead. Seeing her family dead or dying around her, begged the Indians

191

to kill her too. They grabbed her by the arm and indicated she would not be killed, but would be taken prisoner. "All the terrible tortures and indignities," she said, "I had ever read or heard of being inflicted upon their captives now arose in horrid vividness before me."[5]

The Dakotas scalped the dead, plundered the house, and took Abigail to their camp about a mile away near Mattock's house. She saw the burning cabin and heard the screams of two victims as they burned to death. Around the house were the dead bodies of five men, two women, and four children. Warriors found Carl Granger at his nearby cabin. They shot him and chopped the top half of his head off with a broad-ax. Isaac Harriott, Bertell Synder, and Joseph Harshman, all bachelors from Red Wing, were also murdered. Robert Clark and Harvey Luce were shot on the southern shore of East Okoboji, bringing the day's death total to twenty whites.[6]

Abigail Gardner spent her first night of captivity at the Indian camp near the ruins of the Mattock house, while the Indians celebrated by singing, dancing, and drumming until early morning. Having whetted their appetites for murder, Inkpaduta's cohorts searched for more prey. They found Joel Howe on the trail, shot him down and hacked off his head. A Mr. Ring discovered the skull two years later on the south beach of East Okoboji. Warriors entered Howe's home, killed his wife, Rheumilla Ashley Howe, sons Jonathan (25), Alphred (16), Jacob M. (14), William P., (12), Levi (9), daughter Sardis (18), a young woman, and old Mrs. Noble.

Next stop was the Noble and Thatcher cabin. Lydia Howe Noble (20) was the daughter of Joel and Rheumilla Howe. She was born in Ohio, in 1836. When she married Alvin Noble, they moved to East Okoboji Lake. The Indians burst into the cabin and shot Alvin Noble and visitor Enoch Ryan. They took Lydia's child and Elizabeth's infant and bashed their brains out on a nearby oak tree.[7] They killed all the livestock, plundered the house, and took Lydia Noble and Elizabeth Thatcher prisoner. Retracing their path to Howe's cabin they stopped to gather more treasures. Lydia Noble discovered her mother, Rheumilla, under the bed with her skull crushed by a flat iron and her red eyes peering out of their sockets "like balls of fire." The Indians found Jacob Howe sitting in the yard, still alive; they quickly killed him, and then continued on to their camp. They ordered the captives to braid their hair and grease their faces so they took on an Indian appearance.[8]

On March 9, Morris Markham, who was living with the Noble-Thatcher family for the winter, returned home after having been gone two days rounding up livestock. Seeing the destruction, he hurried to alert the settlement of Springfield (now Jackson, Minnesota) about eighteen miles north. There he found Eliza Gardner, who had been visiting in Springfield with Doctor and Mrs. Strong, and reported that her entire family had been murdered except possibly for Abigail, whose body he did not find.

The next day the Indians moved their encampment three miles west. Abigail was enlisted to drive one of the

State Historical Society of Iowa
Abbie Gardner Sharp

sleds pulled by a team of stolen horses. On March 11, they moved to Marble's Grove on the west side of Spirit Lake. On March 13, the Indians stumbled upon the Marble homestead. Mr. Marble was unaware that marauding Indians had been in the area for several days. The Marbles welcomed the braves into their home and fed them. Then they traded for Mr. Marble's rifle and challenged him to a target shoot. After several shots the target fell over. As Mr. Marble turned to replace it, warriors shot him in the back and stole his money belt containing $1,000 in gold. Margaret Ann Marble viewed the contest from the cabin. She saw her husband murdered and attempted to escape, but the Indians nabbed her and took her to the tipi containing Lydia Noble, Elizabeth Thatcher, and Abigail Gardner. The warriors concluded another bloody day with a festive war dance.[9]

On March 26, 1857, Inkpaduta's band was headed for Springfield, and Abbie Gardner was in agony over what might happen to her sister. She figured Eliza "would either be killed, or share with me what I felt to be a worse fate—that of a captive." Had it not been for Morris Markham's warning, the entire town might have been destroyed. As it was, the warriors still stole twelve horses, dry goods, food, powder, lead, clothing, and quilts, and killed Willie Thomas (8), William Woods, George Wood, Mr. Stewart, his wife, and two small children.[10]

The Indians headed northwest. Abigail and Lydia Noble carried packs that weighed about seventy pounds. Margaret Marble carried a pack and a pudgy Indian toddler. The Indians had snowshoes to make their trek easier and the captives had none. Elizabeth Thatcher was in great physical distress, suffering from phlebitis, what Abbie called a "broken breast," and a combination of other maladies. She had to trudge through deep snow, cross frigid rivers, chop and carry firewood, cut poles for tents, and perform other drudgery, yet she displayed great perseverance throughout her suffering, but a medicine man did relieve her pain for a short time.

The stolen provisions lasted about a month. "The Indians have no equal as gormandizers;" Abbie Gardner said, "they are perfectly devoid of anything like delicacy of appetite, or taste, or decency in that matter." The captives got the leftovers.[11]

Two days after the Springfield encounter, there was a great commotion when soldiers were seen approaching. The Indian women were sent away while the warriors placed a guard over the captives and readied for battle. The soldiers, a twenty-four-man detachment under Lieutenant Murray sent from Fort Ridgely, searched the area for more than an hour and turned back. Their retreat saved the captives' lives, for they were going to be killed had the soldiers attacked. Inkpaduta cleared out of the area. After a two-day march, Abigail Gardner could no longer walk and refused to move. A female Indian swung a hoe over her head, but Abbie just bowed her head and was ready to die. Instead, the woman dropped her pack, grabbed Abigail's arm, hauled her up and pushed her forward. Finally they stopped to camp for the night.[12]

The Indians continued to push west with minimal rest. Icy river crossings drenched the captives and they froze at night. Two or three days passed between meals and the captives were glad to eat the camp offal. They camped at Red Pipestone Quarry in Minnesota, and then moved into Dakota Territory. They had been on the go for six weeks. On the Big Sioux River in the vicinity of present-day Flandreau, South Dakota, an Indian teenager removed Elizabeth Thatcher's pack from her back as she approached a fallen tree bridge. Elizabeth had a premonition of death.

"If you are so fortunate as to escape," she called to Abigail, "tell my dear husband and parents that I desired to live and escape for their sakes."

When Thatcher reached mid-stream, the boy shoved her into the water. Elizabeth swam to the shore and grabbed a tree root. More Indians took clubs and poles and beat her back into the river. Desperately she swam to the other shore, and once again the warriors clubbed her back in. As she floated downstream the Indians followed along as if it was a grand game, clubbing and stoning her whenever she neared shore. When tired of the sport, they shot and killed her. Abigail called her death "an act of wanton barbarity." Lydia Noble, Elizabeth's cousin, was so devastated by the murder that she gave up hope of rescue or escape, and implored Abigail to go to the river with her "and drown ourselves." Abigail drew deep within her Christian upbringing, found the will to survive, and declined the suggestion.[13]

On May 6, thirty miles west of the Big Sioux River near Skunk Lake, two Sioux brothers, Ma-kpe-ya-ha-ho-ton and Se-ha-ho-ta, from Minnesota's Yellow Medicine Reservation, visited Inkpaduta and offered to trade for Abigail Gardner, but she was not for sale. Instead, they traded for Margaret Marble. Before they took her, Margaret spoke to Abigail and said she thought the Indians might trade her, and as soon as she could she would send someone to rescue her and Lydia. They left in a hurry, before Inkpaduta changed his mind. Two of his warriors accompanied them to collect the rest of the ransom. They traveled east to the Big Sioux River where they came to an Indian camp. A Frenchman approached them and greeted the brothers. They went to his tent where his Indian wife prepared potatoes, pumpkin, and hot tea.

"Surely, I thought this is a feast fit for the gods!" Margaret said. "A great contrast from my former experience with Inkpaduta, where we subsisted mostly on digging roots, and roasting bones and feathers, to keep soul and body together." Inkpaduta's men were paid. Margaret was taken to Yellow Medicine Reservation, where the parents of the brothers who rescued her became her caregivers. In a few weeks, Stephen R. Riggs and Doctor Williamson, missionaries from Hazelwood, came to claim her. The State of Minnesota paid $500 to each of the brothers who rescued her. Indian agent, Major Charles E. Flandrau, took Margaret to St. Paul.[14]

About one month after Marble's rescue, Inkpaduta joined forces with a Yankton band. One of the Yanktons, named End-of-the-Snake, hoped to get a reward by returning the remaining captives so he purchased them from Inkpaduta. In the meantime, he continued to work the women as before. A few nights later, Roaring Cloud burst into End-of-the-Snake's tipi and demanded

Lydia Noble go with him, but she refused. The enraged warrior forced her out of the tipi, picked up a piece of firewood that Lydia had just cut, beat her mercilessly with it, and then left to wash his bloodstained hands. Abigail was not allowed to go to her. She heard Lydia moaning for a half hour before she died.

The next morning the Indians forced Abigail to watch as they abused Lydia's corpse by using her as a target. They scalped her and tied her hair to the end of a stick. When they left, a young Indian walked next to Abbie, repeatedly whipping her in the face with the bloody scalp. "Such was the sympathy a lonely, broken-hearted girl got at the hands of the 'noble red man,'" she said.[15]

While Abigail wondered if she would ever be rescued, Margaret Marble was in St. Paul, where she met William Granger. His brother Carl was killed on the first day of the massacre. He offered her a home with his family in Michigan. Three months after Marble moved to Michigan she filed for damages with the Commissioner of Indian Affairs. According to the Sioux City *Eagle*, August 22, 1857, she claimed the Indians destroyed or stole property worth $2,229, plus $200 for her husband's preemption rights under Section 17 of the 1834 law that provided for such claims to be deducted from Indian annuities. She was finally granted the amount of $1,994, but it did her little good—she granted power of attorney to Granger and he got the claim. When he was asked if he was going to pay her he said that he learned from the investigation that Margaret's husband had another wife still living and therefore she was due no payment.

Margaret may never have learned of Granger's duplicity, for she made no mention of it in a letter she later wrote to Abbie Gardner. She continued to stay with his family. Granger later moved them all to Sioux City, Iowa. There, Margaret met and married a Mr. Oldham, who was working for Granger. Oldham was suspicious of Granger's story and inquired to the Department of Indian Affairs about any payoffs made to him. He discovered that Granger had totally misrepresented the amount the government allowed her. Granger was confronted with demands for restitution, but he disappeared into Dakota Territory.

Little is known about the rest of Margaret's life. Oldham disappeared from the scene sometime after 1857. In 1868, Margaret was living in Napa County, California. At some time she married a man named Silbaugh, for in 1885, she corresponded with Abigail Gardner Sharp and signed the letter M. A. Silbaugh. She lived in California for forty-three years, and died October 20, 1911, at 74 years of age. She is buried in the St. Helena Cemetery.[16]

Abbie Gardner finally was rescued. Inkpaduta moved to a large village on the James River in present-day Spink County, South Dakota. On May 30, 1857, three Wahpetons appeared and began a three-day bargaining session for Abigail. An expensive deal was struck, and for two horses, twelve blankets, two powder kegs, twenty pounds of tobacco, thirty-two yards of blue cloth, and thirty-seven yards of calico, Abigail had new owners. Mazakutemani (Man-Who-Shoots-Metal-As-He-Walks), Hotonhowashta (Beautiful Voice), and Chetanmaza (Iron Hawk), were from Yellow Medicine Reservation and acting under orders of Major Flandrau, who aided in Margaret Marble's rescue, and who supplied the goods for Abbie's purchase. About ten days' travel brought them to Yellow Medicine Agency and to the mission of Doctor Thomas S. Williamson.[17]

Abigail next went to Fort Ridgely, where Captain and Mrs. Bee prepared dinner for them. Mrs. Bee gave Abbie several gold dollars and Lieutenant Murray bought her a shawl and material for a dress. At the head of navigation at Traverse, they boarded a steamboat for the trip to St. Paul, where they docked on June 22, 1857. The following morning the Indians officially delivered her to Governor Samuel Medary with much pomp and circumstance. The people of St. Paul presented her with $500, which she deposited it in a St. Paul bank.[18]

From St. Paul, Abigail, Governor Medary, and entourage, took a steamboat for Dubuque, Iowa, where she debarked and traveled overland to Fort Dodge and waited for her sister Eliza's new husband, William Wilson, of Hampton, Iowa. She reached her sister's home on July 5. In Hampton, Abigail delivered to Elizabeth Thatcher's parents her final message she had entrusted to Abigail just moments before her death. Things happened quickly for Abbie, mature beyond her actual thirteen years. On August 16, 1857, she married Casville Sharp (19), a cousin of Elizabeth Thatcher.[19]

About a year and a half later Abigail returned to the house where her family was massacred and discovered that J. S. Prescott occupied the cabin. He reimbursed her only a small percentage of what the property was worth. In 1859, Abigail and Casville had a baby boy, Albert, and in 1862, a second son, Allen. In 1871, daughter Minnie was born, but she died at age 19 months. The Sharps moved to several locations in Iowa, Missouri, and Kansas. Twice, house fires destroyed the family's possessions, and one of them consumed an early version of her Spirit Lake manuscript. In the late 1870s, the marriage failed. In 1883, Abbie returned to Lake Okoboji and made money by soliciting speaking engagements telling about her captivity. She finished her narrative of the Spirit Lake Massacre in 1885, and, in 1891, used the profits to purchase her family's cabin. She restored it as a historical site where it remains today. Abigail Gardner Sharp stated, "Never have I recovered from the injuries inflicted upon me while captive among the Indians. Instead of outgrowing them, as I hoped to, they have grown upon me as the years went by, and utterly undermined my health." She died at Colfax, Iowa, on January 26, 1921.[20]

MARY SCHWANDT
Minnesota, August 18, 1862

Minnesota in 1862 was ripe for an Indian uprising. Contributing conditions included treaties that had confined the Santee Sioux to a narrow strip of land along the upper Minnesota River in close proximity to the homesteaders, the interference of the missionaries who attempted to convert the Indians to Christianity, and tardy annuity payments. The Indians were also aware that the Civil War had drawn many soldiers to southern battlefields. To make matters worse, the winter of 1861-62 was severe. Crops failed, starvation loomed, and traders denied credit. One shopkeeper, Andrew J. Myrick, replied, "Let them eat grass or their own dung." This inflammatory statement was considered one of the primary causes of the uprising.[21]

When four Indians made an unprovoked attack and killed six whites, it was nearly too late to stop the conflagration. Chief Red Middle Voice listened to his warriors' story and rationalized that punishment would be coming anyway, so they might as well go to war and drive the whites away forever. To be successful, they needed the other Sioux bands to agree to the plan. Red Middle Voice went to Shakopee's camp, and Shakopee's warriors all seemed anxious for war. Mankato, Wabasha, Traveling Hail, and Big Eagle were summoned to meet Little Crow, an influential Mdewakanton Dakota.[22]

Little Crow said that war with the white man would result in certain defeat. "You are full of the white man's devil water," he said. "You are like dogs in the hot moon when they run mad and snap at their own shadows. We are only a little herd of buffalo left scattered. . . . The white men are like the locust. . . . Kill one, two, ten, and ten times ten will come to kill you." Red Middle Voice called Little Crow a coward. Little Crow jumped to his feet and knocked his accuser's headdress onto the floor. He said, "You are little children. . . . You are fools. You cannot see the face of your chief; your eyes are full of smoke. You cannot hear his voice; your ears are full of roaring waters. You will die like the rabbits when the hungry wolves hunt them in the Hard Moon. Taoyateduta [Little Crow] is not a coward; he will die with you!"[23]

Little Crow would lead the Dakotas to war. He ordered an attack on the Lower Agency for the next morning, August 18, 1862. The stage was set for one of the bloodiest episodes in American history.

Among the settlers along the Minnesota River were the Schwandts. Mary Schwandt was born in Berlin, Germany, in March 1848, to John and Christina Schwandt. Ten

Minnesota Historical Society
Mary Schwandt, ca. 1865.

years later they immigrated to Ripon, Wisconsin. In 1862, they moved to Minnesota, north of the town of Beaver Falls and above the mouth of Beaver Creek. Other family members were a married daughter, Karolina (19), John Waltz, their son-in-law, and their sons, August, Frederick, and Christian. A hired man, John Fross, lived with them. Across the river and a few miles south was Chief Shakopee's village.

White neighbors were few and Mary was often lonely. A few weeks earlier they arranged for Mary to help Mr. and Mrs. Joseph B. Reynolds with their housework. This provided Mary with two companions, Mattie Williams, and Mary Anderson; the former was the Reynolds' niece and the latter was a hired girl. The Reynolds also had two children, plus, William Landmeir and a Mr. Davis lived with them. The Reynolds's were teachers at the government school nearby. Their home was south of the Minnesota River above the mouth of the Redwood River on the main road between the Lower and Yellow Medicine Agencies.[24]

As dawn broke on August 18, 1862, Shakopee, Red Middle Voice, and their warriors approached John Schwandt's cabin. Without any warning, they shot him dead as he repaired his roof. The Indians tomahawked and slashed Christina to death.

Her body was later discovered in a nearby field, but her head was never found. John Waltz, Karolina, Christian, Frederick, and John Fross, were similarly dispatched. August, a third brother, was tomahawked and believed dead, but survived. August saw the Indians slice open his sister, remove the fetus of her unborn child, and nail it to a tree. Mary Schwandt might have suffered a similar fate, but she was staying with Reynolds.

At the Reynolds's homestead that morning the two Marys were doing the laundry. Mr. Patouile and a Frenchman had stopped there for breakfast. While eating, Antoine La Blaugh, a mixed-blood, arrived with the disturbing news that the Indians were on the warpath and intended to kill all the whites. The Lower Agency and the Beaver Creek settlement had already been attacked. Everyone prepared to flee.[25]

Mr. and Mrs. Reynolds, their two children, and William Landmier struck out for Fort Ridgley across the prairie and arrived safely. Patouile, Mr. Davis, Mattie Williams, Mary Anderson, and Mary Schwandt took Patouile's wagon, while the Frenchman rode his horse. Patouile took the road and headed for refuge at New Ulm. As they came within two miles of the lower agency they saw smoke in the sky from the burning buildings. Indians spotted them and showered them with arrows, but they were not hit. Near Fort Ridgley, Patouile was doubtful they could cross the Minnesota River without the ferry, which was nowhere in sight. They rolled on. About eight miles from New Ulm, fifty painted warriors surrounded Patouile's wagon and killed Patouile, Davis, and the Frenchman. Mary Anderson was shot in the back and all three girls were captured. Mary Schwandt later recalled: "I was running as fast as I could towards the slough when two Indians caught me, one by each of my arms, and stopped me." The warriors put Mary Anderson and Mattie Williams in one wagon and Schwandt in another wagon driven by a quadroon, Joseph Godfrey. Anderson and Williams's wagon headed for the lower agency while Schwandt and Godfrey, under the guard of some Indian women, went to Chief Wacouta's house in the village half a mile below the agency.[26]

Mary Schwandt met Jannette De Camp and her three children at Wacouta's house. The De Camps had been captured near the lower agency. Several Indians came to the house and pestered Mary with unwelcome attentions. One Indian forcibly touched her. When she screamed in protest he hit her in the mouth, causing it to bleed profusely. Mary said, "They then took me out by force, to an unoccupied teepee, near the house, and perpetrated the most horrible and nameless outrages upon my person. These outrages were repeated at different times during my captivity."[27]

At 11 p.m. the three girls were reunited in Wacouta's house, where he attempted to remove the bullet from Mary Anderson, but was unsuccessful. Mary supposedly took the knife and extracted the wadding and ball, and Wacouta dressed the wound. It was to no avail. Mary Anderson died early the next morning.

Days later Little Crow approached Mary Schwandt as she sat dejectedly by a tipi. He jerked his tomahawk from his belt and sprang at her, seemingly about to cleave her head in half. Mary only stared up at him, expressionless, showing no fear. After a few more threatening swings of his tomahawk, he replaced it in his belt and strutted away laughing.

Mary was beyond concern over her fate. She later recorded: "Now it pleased providence to consider that my measure of suffering was nearly full." An elderly Indian woman, Wamnukawin, purchased Mary for one pony and gave her to her daughter, Snana. Snana, who the whites called Maggie, was the wife of Wakinyan Weste, or Good Thunder. Maggie and her mother treated Mary kindly, and helped save her life. When the hostile Indians threatened to kill all the prisoners, Maggie hid Mary beneath buffalo robes and told the Indians she had gone away. Maggie gave her clothing and beaded her a pair of moccasins, which replaced what she'd worn since her capture.

Schwandt stayed at Little Crow's village a week, and then was hastily moved to Yellow Medicine Agency where she spent two weeks before the Indians fled west. Mary was unaware of the Battle of Wood Lake, September 22-23, 1862, which effectively ended the first phase of the uprising. An Indian attempt to ambush Colonel Henry H. Sibley's command was a failure, the Indians were defeated, and Little Crow fled Minnesota. All the captives were gathered at Camp Release. There, 269 captive whites and 167 mixed bloods were handed over to Sibley's liberators.[28]

Mary was sent from Camp Release to St. Peter, Minnesota, and then to Wisconsin, to stay with friends and relatives. There she met her brother August, the only other survivor of her immediate family. She stayed with the Reynolds's through part of 1863, until she left for Fairwater, Wisconsin, to stay two years with an uncle. In 1866, William Schmidt, of St. Paul, became her husband. In 1889, they moved to Portland, Oregon, but were back again in St. Paul, in 1894. Mary had seven children, three of whom were still alive in 1894.[29]

WILHELMINA, AUGUST AND AMELIA BUSSE
Minnesota, August 18, 1862

Gottfried and Wilhelmina Busse emigrated from Germany to America, in 1858, and settled at Fox Lake, Wisconsin. During the spring of 1860, they moved to Middle Creek, Minnesota, in Renville County. In 1862, the family was comprised of Gottfried (33), Wilhelmina (30), a son, August (14), and daughters Wilhelmina (7), Augusta (5), Amelia (4), Caroline (3), and Bertha (3 months).

On August 18, 1862, Gottfried was working in his hay field about one mile from his home, while August climbed the roof to look for stray cattle. From his perch he heard gunshots and screams from the nearby Roesslers' house. He reported this to his mother, who dismissed it as the Indians simply having target practice. She sent August to the Roesslers' to borrow some sewing needles. The boy returned and described the scene as if "they were all asleep."

August had seen Mrs. Roessler and one son lying dead on the floor. The other boy was outside partially buried in a clay pit. Mrs. Busse correctly guessed they had been killed by the Indians and set off to warn her husband. They gathered their children and headed for the cornfield. Gottfried Busse seemed irrational, took baby Bertha, and ran across the open prairie. Indians saw them. Mr. Busse pled with the Indians to take their possessions but let them live. His appeal was answered with a double-barreled shotgun blast that killed both Gottfried and Bertha. Mrs. Busse and daughter Caroline were murdered next. Another warrior tried twice to shoot August but missed. An Indian superstition was that if after two shots a warrior fails to kill his enemy, he should be given another chance to live, for it was the will of the Great Spirit. The Indians also killed Augusta and captured Wilhelmina, August, and Amelia.[30]

The marauding warriors then returned to plunder Gottleib Boelter's homestead, where they had earlier murdered Mrs. Boelter, her mother, and three of the Boelter children. Four Indian women took the captives to a village two miles south. Wilhelmina and Amelia were placed in a bark shelter and were given buffalo robe beds. The Indians offered them supper, but they could not eat. In the morning the children awoke, and the brutal events of the previous day brought a flood of tears to their eyes. An ax-wielding warrior threatened to split their skulls if they did not cease sobbing. Despite the threat, they cried until an old Indian widow and her daughter comforted them, and cooked them breakfast, but the Indian fare was unpalatable. They were on the move again, and warriors put blankets over the children and threw them into a wagon. Later, they were separated for a week.[31]

The Indians took Wilhelmina to a new camp and gave her to an Indian family. Wilhelmina recognized the man as the one who murdered her parents. She also found her family's clothing and her father's hymnal. An old Indian woman and her son were mean to Wilhelmina most of the time, while a younger woman acted as her protector. One morning the old Indian woman woke Wilhelmina and indicated she should fetch a bucket of water. Wilhelmina was tired and did not want to go. When she refused, the old woman came at her with a big stick. The young Indian woman picked up a corn stalk, beat the old crone, and made her fetch her own water.

Wilhelmina befriended a German girl, Henrietta (4), who could not remember her last name. They moved to a big camp near the Redwood River. During this time Wilhelmina spotted a former neighbor, Mrs. Minnie Inefeldt, and her baby. In the course of their brief conversation, Wilhelmina told her that her entire family had been murdered. She had been told that Amelia and August had their throats cut for crying. That night they all camped in what Wilhelmina described as "a large city on the prairie," and was reunited with Amelia and August. The false tale of their deaths was a psychological torture the Indians forced the young girl to endure. In a similar vein, August had been told that Wilhelmina was killed trying to escape. Three days later they moved again, and Henrietta and Wilhelmina were permitted to ride in the same wagon. During the day Wilhelmina saw an acquaintance, Ludwig Kitzmann (14), and he recognized his cousin, Henrietta Krieger (5). Ludwig visited with them and urged Wilhelmina to stay with the Indians until the soldiers rescued them.[32]

Wilhelmina sickened and lost track of time. While the Indian warrior was gone from the tipi for several days, his son continually tormented Wilhelmina. Later, when Wilhelmina visited August, Ludwig, and August Gluth[33] as they picked hazel nuts, the Indian boy appeared with a big stick to drive the girl home. August and Ludwig gave the boy a taste of his own medicine when they grabbed bigger sticks and drove him home. The old Indian woman was there when they arrived and she scolded them, to which they responded in German, calling her "old crooked mouth." When the German youths left, the Indian boy returned, kicked Wilhelmina in the face and gave her a bloody nose.[34]

On September 23, 1862, Wilhelmina heard cannon fire. Unbeknown to her, the shots represented the beginning of the Battle of Wood Lake, a decisive turning point in the uprising.

There was nothing to eat during the day and bonfires flamed all night. The next day they were again on the move and she went to live with the Indian who was caring for Amelia.

The Dakotas were divided in opinion as to what should be done after the Wood Lake battle. Most of the Sissetons and Wahpetons had taken a neutral course; their chiefs were against the war, even though some of their warriors fought in the battles. They wanted to surrender and release the captives, hoping to lessen the punishment they knew would follow. The militant faction thought the captives should be killed to eliminate witnesses who might testify against them later. Little Crow chose to release most of the captives to the peace chiefs Wacouta and Wabasha, and fled to Devil's Lake in Dakota Territory with 200 followers, seeking other Indians to help him keep the war going.[35]

After the Battle of Wood Lake, Wilhelmina and Amelia were taken to a large circle of Indians, and Wilhelmina again met her brother August, August Gluth, and Ludwig Kitzmann. They explained that the soldiers defeated the Indians, and they were to be released. They were all assigned tents to stay in until Colonel Sibley and his soldiers arrived. The site was known as Camp Release.

On September 25, 1862, Sibley arrived at the camp and met no resistance. The Indians released 269 captives to the soldiers—167 of whom were mixed bloods. Within two weeks Sibley rounded up about 2,000 Dakotas who would be held accountable for the past five weeks of atrocities. The captives went to Fort Ridgely. In Wilhelmina's wagon were Ludwig Kitzmann, Mrs. Urban and Mrs. Kraus and their children, an American lady with two children, and a boy about 8 years old. Along the road they met Mr. Gluth, and Ludwig told him the happy news that his son August was still alive. At the fort the soldiers provided food and beds. When they reached St. Paul an empty store was used to accommodate all the people looking for friends and family.

Reverend Friedrich Emde took Wilhelmina and Amelia to New Ulm. John Muhs (Mrs. Emde's brother) and his wife were Wilhelmina's caretakers for the next two years. Amelia remained with Reverend Emde and his wife. August was sent to a family in Hutchinson. The man of the family was appointed guardian of all three children, for he claimed to be wealthy and wanted to adopt them all. He received $1,200 of Mr. Busse's money for this service. It was later revealed his wealth was a sham and his interest was solely in the money he received.[36]

Author's photo
Beaver Creek, Minnesota, site of the Carrothers, Carrigan captures.

Wilhelmina left her guardian when she turned 15. She worked summers and attended school during the winter. In 1879, she married Owen Carrigan and they had five children. Owen died in 1898. Amelia left her guardian at age 14, and returned to live with Reverend and Mrs. Emde. She later married a Mr. Reynolds from Minneapolis. August departed for Montana at age 19. He corresponded with Wilhelmina for two years. He was thought to be in the army and to have died at the Battle of the Little Big Horn, but his name did not appear on the 7th Cavalry rosters.[37]

Forty years after her experiences in the Sioux uprising of 1862, Wilhelmina Busse Carrigan wrote of her reminiscences of these five weeks, which irrevocably altered the course of her life.

Helen Mar Paddock Carrothers, Urania S. Frazer White, and Amanda M. Macomber Earle
Minnesota, August 18, 1862

Helen Mar Paddock, born in 1843, was only 14 years of age when she married James Carrothers, a carpenter at the Lower Sioux Agency in Minnesota. Since 1858, they lived six miles from the agency in a secluded cabin on Beaver Creek, with their daughter (4), and an infant son, Tommy. The nearby Indians appeared very friendly, visiting Helen daily. She learned the Dakota language and many Indian traditions.[38]

Urania S. Frazer was born February 10, 1825, in Alexander, New York. She married Nathan Dexter White in New York in

1845, and two years later they moved to Pardeeville, Wisconsin, where they lived fifteen years. There they met the Jonathan Earle family, and in May 1862, joined the Earles in moving to Renville County, Minnesota. Nathan built a cabin in the valley of Beaver Creek, about one mile up from its junction with the Minnesota River and about six miles from Little Crow's Indian village.[39]

Vermont native Jonathan W. Earle, graduated from the University of Vermont in 1841 and taught school for nine years. In 1842 he married Amanda M. Macomber of Westford, Vermont. In 1850 they moved to Pardeeville, Wisconsin, where Jonathan practiced law. They had six children: Chalon (19), Ezmon (17), Radner (15), Julia (13), Herman (9), and Elmira (7). The family joined the Earles to move Beaver Creek, arriving in late June 1862. Like Carrothers and White, Earle lived only about six miles from the Lower Sioux Agency. On August 15, Chief Little Crow had given Earle his favorite shotgun in security for the purchase of two cows. Only three days later the peaceful scene drastically changed, when about 400 Dakotas went on the rampage. The Great Sioux Uprising had commenced.[40]

Before breakfast on August 18, four painted Indians came to Earle's house, as Jonathan said, "pretending to be in pursuit of Chippewas." They asked if they could look at his rifle, but the suspicious Earle told them they must leave. He sent his sons out to round up his horses, but the boys reported many Indians wandering the area and they all began to worry that something was up. That same morning Helen Carrothers was at S. R. Henderson's house helping care for Mrs. Henderson, seriously ill with appendicitis. Early in the morning Helen and the Hendersons saw four Indians peek in the window, but they soon left in the direction of Jonathan Earle's house. Earle had gone to warn his neighbors and hurried to return home. A Mr. Veightman (Weichman) came by from the Lower Agency and reported the Indians were killing all the whites.

Nathan White was on his way to Blue Earth County to fetch Mrs. Henderson's parents. Urania, on this day of her 20th wedding anniversary, was doing the laundry when her daughter Julia (14), and her daughter's friend, Julia Earle, excitedly entered the house and warned her that the Indians were on the warpath. Urania grabbed a large purse containing money and important papers, a gun, and her five-month-old son, and they ran to the centrally located Earle's home where about twenty-eight settlers had gathered. They decided to flee to Fort Ridgely. The group included the Hendersons, Carrothers, and Urania White with her sons,

Millard (12) and Eugene (16). Only four were adult males, four were teenage boys, and there were twenty women and children. Only three wagons were available for their exodus, and they only had two weapons, one loaded with nothing but pebbles.[41]

Indians surrounded them before they went a mile. S. R. Henderson and David Carrothers went out to see what the Indians intended to do, and learned that all the whites were to be killed. The men haggled for a time and a compromise was reached— their lives in exchange for two wagons and all three teams. The wagon carrying Mrs. Henderson was kept, and the men began the arduous task of pulling the wagon by hand. Regardless of the deal they made, three gunshots rang out and the Indians attacked.

Helen Carrothers had been shading Mrs. Henderson with an umbrella and at first shot she jumped from the wagon. Mrs. Henderson gave David Carrothers and her husband a white pillowcase to use as a sign of truce. The Indians response was to shoot off Mr. Henderson's fingers, after which, Henderson and David Carrothers ran away. Mr. Wedge was shot dead next. Helen Carrothers was about five yards in front of the wagon and she and her children dove in a ditch. The Indians killed nine people, including two of David Carrothers's children and Eugene White. Jonathan Earle felt he could not save his wife, so he ran away to save himself. He shot once at the Indians and then threw away his rifle. As he ran past his son Radner (15), whose gun was loaded with pebbles, he shouted for him to shoot the Indians. Radner lay in wait in the tall prairie grass and fired. "Noble boy" Earle later wrote, "He saved my life by the sacrifice of his own." Earle overtook his other two sons and Millard White and eventually arrived safely in Cedar City.[42]

As this transpired, another Indian grabbed a violin case and beat Mrs. Henderson's daughter in the head until her face was mangled and unrecognizable, and then he battered her against a wagon wheel. Another warrior held Mrs. Henderson's baby upside down, hacked it to bits with his tomahawk, and threw the pieces in its mother's face. The warriors then set the feather bed afire, with Mrs. Henderson and her mangled children sprawled helplessly on it.

While Helen Carrothers waited to die, a warrior approached, shook her hand, and told her the medicine man said she should not be killed. The Indians rounded up the remaining captives to take to Little Crow's village, where the women would become wives of the Indian warriors. There were eleven captives: Elizabeth Carrothers and her baby; Amanda Earle and her daughters,

Julia and Elmira; Urania White, her infant son, Frank, and her
daughter, Julia; and Helen Carrothers and her two children. All
were placed aboard one of the wagons. They Indians plundered
the Earle, Hunter, Robinson, and Hayden homes as they went.
Carrothers was riding with a man called Indian John,[43] who
claimed he beheaded Mrs. Hayden—a false boast, for she and her
child had escaped to Fort Ridgley. As they passed by the Eune
(Juni) and Isenridge (Eisenreich) homes, Indian John also claimed
to have murdered Mrs. Isenridge, but this was another lie, told
just to strike fear in the minds of the captives.

Across the Minnesota River a warrior told Helen she would be
taken to John Moore's house. She asked if Elizabeth Carrothers,
her sister-in-law, could stay with her, but her request was denied.
Amanda Earle and Julia White's wagon headed toward Redwood.
Whenever the Indians stopped to eat, they made the captives
sample the food first; Helen thought it was their way to insure the
food was not poisoned.[44]

As they stopped for water near Little Crow's house, the chief
appeared, and Helen asked if he would take her in. He knew the
Carrothers and agreed. He had a two-story frame house loaded
with plunder, sugar, coffee, tea, bolts of calico and clothing. Helen
asked Little Crow for something to eat and he pointed to a flour
sack and told her to make some bread if she was hungry. Little
Crow's brother came in and sat beside a German girl he declared
was his "squaw."[45] Amanda Earle, Urania White, and their children
were collected and taken to Indian John's tipi, and then Amanda
Earle and her daughter, Julia, were moved elsewhere. Little Crow
told them all to braid their hair and to sew Indian dresses to wear.
Too-kon-we-chasta (Stone Man) and his wife selected Urania to be
their "big papoose." She was treated well, and said, "Their owning
me in this manner saved me probably from a worse fate than
death."

Helen Carrothers heard Little Crow arguing with four of his
warriors, and an Indian woman told Carrothers that all four
wanted her as a wife; because she was causing dissension, Little
Crow said Helen must die. All day Helen waited to learn her
fate. During an evening drizzle, an Indian woman came to Helen
and her children and told them they were to be executed in the
cornfield. She gave Carrothers a ragged old dress to replace her
Indian dress, for it was considered too good for an execution. The
Indian woman left them standing in the midst of a cornfield, and
Helen reasoned, that since she was to be murdered she might as
well try to escape. Just then, an Indian approached her and said

she would not be killed. Helen could no longer take this emotional roller coaster. When the Indian left, she grabbed her children, crouched down, and ran for the cornfield, helped by a rain and hailstorm.[46]

The escapees reached the Minnesota River the next day; Helen's home was across the river, but she balked because of the high water. Trudging along near the lower agency by the steep riverbank, she discovered a path down the hill and hid until nightfall. Braving the odds, Helen went up to a house and found it empty. She discovered a trap door leading to the cellar and took a feather bed and threw it inside. After securing her children underground, she gathered some tiny potatoes from the garden. The captives spent three nights in the cellar and at times heard Indians in the house, but they were not discovered. When the food was gone Helen knew they must reach the ferry, cross the river, and get to Fort Ridgley.

At the Redwood Crossing all they found were the mutilated bodies of some soldiers.[47] Helen discovered a large wooden box half afloat in the river, and covered by a decaying corpse. She shoved the body into the river and bailed the water out of the box. She and her children climbed aboard their leaky craft and floated about seven miles downriver to the fort. They disembarked on the north bank just before their "boat" sank. Clawing their way through thorny weeds and grapevines, they climbed a hill and found a road they knew led to the fort. They looked for shelter as the sun set. At a deserted house, they found some cucumbers in the garden, and pressed on until the darkness hid the trail and exhaustion overcame them. They spent the night in a grassy field swarming with mosquitoes. The next morning they plodded to Mr. Busche's house about three miles from the fort. Helen found some sugar in a bowl and she shared it with her children, and then went to explore the cellar. While rummaging below, a man peered down into the cellar and asked for food. He was a German, and after his wife and three children were slain, he had spent the last three nights hiding in the haystack. They decided that Fort Ridgley was their best chance if the Indians were not in control of it. The man helped Helen carry her daughter. As they approached the fort, Lieutenant Culver and Warren De Camp met them. De Camp had been using the fort's telescope to search for his own wife when he spotted Carrothers. After an eight-day journey of nearly thirty miles, on a diet of potatoes and cucumbers, Helen and the children were ravenous, and they hungrily ate the meal that was prepared for them at the fort. Helen's relief at finally reaching safety was short-lived. Her daughter became ill from eating more than her emaciated body could digest. Doctor Muller, the fort's physician, said there was no hope for her survival, but Helen, with her knowledge of tribal medicine, collected roots, herbs, and plants and concocted a potion. After one day her daughter improved, and three days later Doctor Muller pronounced her miraculously cured.[48]

Meanwhile, the third day of Urania White's captivity began when Too-kon-we-chasta's wife led her and her baby to a cornfield and told her she must remain hidden there until she returned. Later another Indian woman approached and told her, "Me Winnebago; Sioux nepo papoose." Urania figured that she was hidden there so the Sioux could not kill her child.

Mrs. White used a single scanty cotton sheet for her bed, shawl, and sunbonnet while captive in Little Crow's village. While fording the Redwood River she gave her cover to an Indian to carry, and he kept it. Her Indian mother replaced it with a dirty, odorous blanket. One of Urania's chores was to fetch water from the river. After about a week of captivity a call was issued: "Puckachee! Puckachee!" and the Indians proceeded to pack and move their camp. More than 100 white prisoners and an equal amount of mixed-bloods combined with 800 warriors and their families to string out along three miles of trail. Warriors all decked out in their war paint and feathers were traveling along either side and were ordered to kill anyone who broke ranks.

Recent rains had made the Redwood River treacherous to cross. Julia Earle and Urania White saved Mrs. Earle from drowning by interlocking their arms as they crossed. Urania had been carrying Frank all the way, and by midday she was exhausted. She sat beside the road to rest and admonishments to "Puckachee!" did not motivate her. An old Indian man offered his hand to hoist her up but she didn't budge. They placed her baby in a loaded wagon, and told her if she did not move they would kill them both. With that motivation, Urania grasped hold of the back of the wagon and was able to keep pace. An eighteen-mile march brought them to Rice Creek. After camp was set up, Urania went to look for her daughter Julia. She said, "It was like seeing one risen from the dead to meet her. . . . And oh! How pleased we were that so far we had been spared not only from death, but, worse than that, the Indian's lust."[49]

The next day they traveled ten miles, crossing the Yellow Medicine River by the mills. They camped there eight days. Urania noted, "In order to make myself as agreeable as possible to them, I feigned cheerfulness, and took particular notice of their papooses, hoping that by so doing I would receive better treatment from them, which I think had the desired effect."

Several days later they moved to a new camp, when Urania's Indian "mother" warned her the Sissetons were coming to carry her off, so they hid her and her baby under an old blanket. The Sissetons remained three days, but took only horses and showed no interest in captives. About this time Julia White became highly distraught when she heard an Indian brave had chosen her for his wife and was coming that night to claim her. She waited in anguish for days, but the Indian never came and her honor was preserved.

During the Battle of Wood Lake, many of the captives were put to work digging defensive trenches around the village. After their defeat, Little Crow and his followers abandoned the area, while the "friendlies" surrendered to Colonel Sibley three days later and released all the captives. The freed prisoners were put in army tents and fed applesauce and biscuits. Supper was a feast of rice, hard tack, coffee, and meat. The ex-captives remained at Camp Release ten days to testify in front of a military commission.[50]

On October 5, 1862, Urania White and Amanda Earle were ecstatic to find Nathan White and Jonathan Earle in camp. Jonathan Earle had met up with his sons, Herman and Ezmon, and took them to relatives in Wisconsin. He returned to St. Peter where he joined Nathan White and William Mills, and the three of them followed in the wake of Sibley's army to Camp Release. After dinner, the Whites and Earles began a three-day unescorted trek to St. Peter, which they reached without incident. Urania, Nathan, Julia, and little Frank were reunited with their son Millard in St. Peter. Urania was happy to exchange her Indian outfit for new calico dresses and thrilled to be reunited with her family, "except for our oldest son," she said, "whose life was taken to satisfy the revenge of the Sioux warrior." Two weeks later they went to St. Paul, and then to La Crosse, Wisconsin. Old neighbors had heard of their plight and gave them financial aid. From La Crosse, they traveled to their old home in Columbia County, Wisconsin. At the depot at Pardeeville, said Urania, "the platform was thronged with relatives and friends to greet us, as restored to them from a worse fate than death." In March 1863, they moved to Rochester, Minnesota, and in the fall of 1865, Nathan and Urania returned to their Renville home.

The Earles, with financial aid from friends, also went back to Pardeeville, Wisconsin, where Jonathan taught school for six months and, no doubt, tried to obliterate the memory of his abandoning his family. In 1863, the Earles moved to Arcade, New York, southeast of Buffalo, where Jonathan became the principal of the Arcade Academy. Helen Carrothers and her children, as the Whites had done, traveled to St. Peter, and then to La Crosse, Wisconsin, where they spent the winter. In March 1863, they went to St. Paul, and in June 1863, they returned to St. Peter, Minnesota, to make their home.[51]

SARAH F., JAMES O. AND LUCY E. WAKEFIELD
Minnesota, August 18, 1862

Sarah Brown was born September 29, 1829, in Kingstown, Rhode Island, to William and Sarah Brown. John Lumen Wakefield was born in 1823, in Winsted, Connecticut, and graduated from Yale medical school in 1847. In April 1854, he established a medical practice in Shakopee, Minnesota. Two years later, Sarah married John Wakefield in Jordan, Minnesota. In June 1858, Doctor Wakefield treated many Dakotas for wounds they received fighting with the Ojibwas. Sarah's first child, James Orin, was born in 1858 and their second child, Lucy Elizabeth (Nellie), was born in 1860. In June 1861, Doctor Wakefield was appointed physician for the Upper Agency Sioux Indians at Pajutazee or Yellow Medicine, Minnesota.[52]

On August 18, 1862, John Wakefield was alerted to a rumor that the Indians were attacking whites in the area. Concealing this information from his wife, Wakefield suggested that Sarah and their two children take an early leave to visit his mother-in-law back east. George Gleason, the storekeeper for the Lower Agency, had been visiting in the area and agreed to take Sarah, James, and Lucy to Fort Ridgley, where they could get transportation.

As they passed through the Upper Agency, Stewart Garvie, manager of Myrick's store, flagged them down and warned them that Indians were murdering whites on the north side of the river. Sarah asked Gleason to return to her home, but he told Sarah that her husband wanted her and the children at Fort Ridgely. Half way to the Lower Agency they saw smoke rising in the distance. Despite Sarah's frantic nature, Gleason drove on until six p.m. when they neared the Reynolds's home and two Indians approached the wagon. Sarah told Gleason to draw his gun, but he had no firearm. The two Indians were Hapa and Chaska. After a brief conversation, Gleason tried to drive off, but Hapa fired his gun and hit Gleason in the shoulder. He shot again and Gleason

Author's photo
Site of Sara Wakefield's house, Upper Sioux Agency, Minnesota.

fell from the wagon to the road, crying out, "Oh, my God, Mrs. Wakefield!"[53]

Chaska asked if she was the doctor's wife. She answered yes, and he warned her to say nothing for Hapa was a bad man and very inebriated. Despite his warning she begged to be spared, when another shot rang out. Hapa finished off Gleason and waved his gun in Wakefield's face. Chaska knocked the gun away and the two men argued. Doctor Wakefield had treated wounded Dakotas and Chaska felt obligated to save the doctor's wife. Hapa agreed to spare Mrs. Wakefield, but later declared he would kill the children because they would be trouble. "No," Chaska said, "I am going to take care of them, you must kill me before you kill any of them." The difference in the two Indians was like night and day—Hapa was wild and Chaska was a farmer who had been schooled by the missionaries. In the Indian camp Sarah recognized people who her husband had helped and she had fed. "They promised me life," she said, "but I dared not hope, and felt as if death was staring me in the face."

After supper Chaska took Sarah, James, and Nellie to a house the Indians had taken over where there was another white woman captive. Wakefield went to Chaska's mother to get Indian garb to look less conspicuous. Some of the Indians enjoyed tormenting the captives. An old woman named Lightfoot told Wakefield she would soon meet her maker in the spirit world but her children would be

213

kept alive to be ransomed when they got older. Sarah said she "thought of this all night, and I determined I would kill them rather than leave them with those savages." Wakefield begged a knife from an Indian woman. She was about to slit her daughter's throat when another Indian stopped her and told her that was all a lie. The same afternoon Chaska's mother told Sarah a man was coming to kill her. The old woman took Nellie on her back and led Sarah and James to the river to hide in the tall grass.[54]

They sat through the stormy night until the old lady returned and said the coast was clear. Mosquitoes swarmed on them until her children's faces were swollen and bloody from their bites. The Indian led Sarah to a new camp, three miles away, to stay with Chaska. Unfortunately, Chaska and his mother lived with Hapa and Hapa's wife, Winona, who was also Chaska's half-sister. Winona made Sarah's life very unpleasant when Chaska was away. One day, Chaska's mother burst into the tipi and told Sarah her life was again in danger and she must run. Too exhausted from her recent ordeal, she decided to stay and face death. The old woman hid Sarah and James under a stack of buffalo robes and walked in front of the tipi with Nellie fastened on her back Indian fashion. Later, Sarah peeked out of the tent and asked if there was any news. The old woman said, "Chaska dead, and you will die soon; that man is a very bad man."[55] Soon after this, Chaska rode up and reassured Sarah that she was safe for the moment.

On Thursday, August 21, the Indians prepared to attack Fort Ridgely. Chaska feared that Hapa would try to murder Sarah, so he sent her to his grandfather's (Eagle Head) house. Tipis surrounded the perimeter of his brick house, and Sarah recognized an elderly acquaintance called "Mother Friend" by the whites. The old lady recognized Sarah, and took her under her wing. "Mother Friend" made James new moccasins, and cared for baby Nellie.

That morning they heard a cannon and saw smoke rising from the direction of the fort. The fight did not go well for the Indians and they got a warning that a chief would return to the village to kill all the captive white women. Eagle Head led Sarah and her baby to the woods, where they roamed until daylight. James stayed at the camp with "Mother Friend." At sunrise, Eagle Head hid Sarah and Nellie in a haystack so he could return to camp to get an update on the situation. Eighteen hours later, the old man reappeared and led Sarah back to the village. She learned that the men searching for her were not going to murder her but had planned a fate worse than death.[56]

On Saturday, many Indians got drunk, and Chaska heard that one wanted to kill all white women in the camp. Once again the old woman hid Sarah and her children in the woods, and at sunset brought them back to camp. On their way back they spotted the hostiles and ducked into a nearby tipi. Sarah hid under robes, but the children had been seen. The Indian woman convinced the braves that Sarah was dead. When they left, Sarah crept to Chaska's tipi.

Hapa was drunk and wanted to talk to Sarah. He drew his knife and stumbled toward her, saying she would become his wife or die. Chaska admonished Hapa, saying, "You are a bad man; there is your wife, my sister. I have no wife, and I don't talk bad to the white women." He tried to defuse the situation by proposing that, since he had no wife he would take Sarah as his wife. Reassuring her that he would not harm her, Chaska laid between his mother and Sarah until he was sure Hapa was asleep. According to Wakefield, he then returned to his own bed. When the other captives heard this story they assumed that Sarah and Chaska were lovers. She did not deny it at the time for she feared Hapa would take her as his wife.

One day while still at Redwood, a mixed-blood spread a rumor that all white captives would be killed. Wakefield could no longer tolerate the death threats. She asked Little Six, chief of the band she was with, if she was to be killed. "I told him if he would only spare me that I would help kill the other prisoners," she said. "I also promised to never leave his band, and that I would sew, chop wood, and be like a squaw. . .for all I thought of was, if I can only live a little while longer and get away, my husband, if living, will not care what promises are made, if his wife and children were saved."[57]

On August 26, the Indians moved to Yellow Medicine. While crossing the Redwood River, an Indian asked if Sarah was the doctor's wife, but she denied it. The Indian, whose name was Paul Mazakutemani, insisted that she come with him, for he would give her a mule to ride and she would not have to walk. Sarah asked Chaska if she should take him up on his offer. After conferring with Paul, Chaska left the decision up to her, but, he said that Paul wanted her for his wife. Meanwhile, James, who was suffering from diarrhea and having a hard time keeping up, thought a mule ride sounded good. Sarah declined Paul's offer but allowed James to go with him. Sarah stated, "I traveled in great distress barefoot, trotting along in the tall, dry prairie grass. In some places it was 5' high. My feet and legs were cut by the grass switching and twirling around them as we drove through, regardless of the many prairie snakes we tread upon."[58] When they stopped for a noon meal, Chaska noted her feet were a bloody mess and said she could drive a wagon the remainder of the day.

When they arrived at Yellow Medicine, Chaska went to Hazelwood, Minnesota, to reclaim Sarah's son from Paul. Then he hurried back to warn her that another white woman had been slain by a drunken Indian, and she must hide again. Paul also arrived and began to pester Sarah about becoming his wife; the situation was becoming tense. Wakefield traveled with Chaska's camp sixteen miles to Red Iron's village. There, Little Crow, Wabasha, and Taopee, wrote letters to Colonel Henry H. Sibley, and Sibley replied to both factions. He admonished Little Crow for requesting peace and not releasing the prisoners, and told Wabasha and Taopee that he had come with a large army to punish the Indians who had slain the white settlers, but he would not punish innocent Indians. The letter directed them to gather with the captives on the prairie in full view of his soldiers with a white flag of truce, and when Sibley signaled, they could come forward and surrender. Sibley stated, "I shall be glad to receive all true friends of the whites with as many prisoners as they can bring, and I am powerful enough to crush all who attempt to oppose my march, and to punish those who have washed their hands in innocent blood."[59] Sibley informed Wabasha and Taopee that he and his troops would arrive in three days.

Little Crow called for all warriors to attack Sibley, but the friendly bands gathered all the captives they had, plus all they could steal from Little Crow, in order to release them to Sibley. The hostile bands suffered a crushing defeat at the Battle of Wood Lake. Little Crow and his minions fled the next morning toward the West. Chaska remained behind to release Sarah Wakefield and her children to Sibley.

After the surrender, soldiers questioned Sarah about her treatment as a prisoner and asked who had been her captor. She explained that Chaska was her protector, and he, his mother, and Eagle Head had saved her life numerous times. Soldiers escorted her to camp and placed her in a large tent with other ex-captives and supplied them with food. Despite Sarah's testimony, Chaska was arrested as an accomplice in the murder of George Gleason. Sarah was assured that Chaska would not be executed, but he faced five years in prison.[60]

Wakefield, her children, and four other captive women were sent unescorted to Yellow Medicine, despite the hostile Indians still in the area. From there, two soldiers escorted them to Fort Ridgely. Near Little Crow's abandoned village, the soldiers went to a settler's house in order to get feed for their horses when Sarah Wakefield noticed Indians in the woods. She alerted the soldiers and they all sped off to catch up with another group about three miles ahead. Five Indians approached from behind. The advance group assumed Wakefield's entourage were hostiles, and when they sent soldiers back to attack, they actually did scare off the approaching Indians. At five p.m. they arrived safely at Fort Ridgely. The next morning, Sarah, James, and Nellie were reunited with John Wakefield.[61]

Sibley appointed a five-man military commission to try the Dakotas. It first convened at Camp Release, and then moved to the Lower Agency. On November 5, the verdicts were in. Of the initial 392 prisoners, 307 were found guilty and sentenced to death, and sixteen were sentenced to prison terms. Sibley and his superior officer, General John Pope, favored a swift execution of the condemned Indians. Not wanting to exceed their authority, however, Pope sent a $400 telegraph message to President Lincoln with a list of 303 Indians and mixed-bloods who faced the hangman's noose. Lincoln responded by requesting the complete records of their convictions—by mail. Lincoln appointed two men to review these 303 reports, to distinguish which individuals were rapists and murderers and which Indians simply had participated in battles.

The condemned Indians were moved from the Lower Agency to Camp Lincoln at South Bend. As the shackled prisoners passed through New Ulm, the townsfolk pelted them with brickbats. On December 4, the people of Mankato converged on Camp Lincoln to murder the Indians, but were stopped by the troops. The prisoners were secured in a jail in Mankato.[62]

After studying the situation, Lincoln approved death sentences for thirty-nine of the 303 convicted Indians, one of whom was later reprieved. At ten a.m. on December 26, 1862, in Mankato, thirty-eight Indians mounted the gallows singing their last "Hi-yi-yi"—the Sioux death song. Caps were drawn over their faces, the trap was sprung, and thirty-eight men swung to their deaths. The executioner was William Duley, a survivor of the Lake Shetek murders. Three of his children had been killed there and his wife and two other children were still Sioux prisoners (see Laura Duley). The Mankato hanging was the largest mass execution in the United States.[63]

Sarah was at Red Wing when she heard that Chaska was one of the victims—a mistake because of an unfortunate similarity of names. An Indian named Chaskadon had been convicted for killing a pregnant woman and cutting the fetus out of her body. The authorities apologized, but Wakefield couldn't help feeling they had done it intentionally. She had been the only white woman to testify in front of the commission on behalf of an Indian captor. She had been ridiculed, and called an Indian lover. Other captives said she was Chaska's lover or wife. She explained, "I loved not the man, but his kindly acts."[64]

Sarah Wakefield published a narrative of her experiences on November 25, 1863. In 1866 and 1868, she had two more children, Julia E., and John R. Wakefield. On February 17, 1874, John Luman Wakefield was found dead of an overdose of drugs. Whether this was accidental or if foul play was involved was never determined. In 1876, Sarah and her children moved to St. Paul. In 1897, James Orin Wakefield died. Sarah F. Wakefield died May 27, 1899, at age 69,[65]

JANNETTE DE CAMP
Minnesota, August 18, 1862

Jannette E. Sykes was born July 29, 1833, near Lockport, New York. Joseph Warren De Camp was born October 13, 1826 in Licking County, Ohio. They were married in Ohio, in May 1852. In 1855, they moved to Shakopee, Minnesota, and then to the Redwood Agency in 1861, when Agent Thomas Galbraith appointed Joseph De Camp to run the sawmill. Joseph also built a mill for grinding the Indians' corn.

Joseph De Camp left his wife and three sons on August 17, 1862, to go to St. Paul on business, expecting to return in less than a week. The next day, Jannette De Camp was gardening when she saw an Indian harness her horses from the stable, hitch them to the wagon, and drive toward her. She adamantly asked where he thought he was taking her horses, and he replied that all her property was his. He warned her that all whites at the agency had been killed and she should flee for her life. Two girls who helped De Camp with housework, a German girl and a mixed-blood named Lucy Pettijohn, heard the Indian's warning. The German girl ran away. Lucy, Jannette, and her three children climbed the hill and viewed the scene below. The agency and trader stores were ablaze as hundreds of painted warriors shouted and brandished their weapons. Lucy ran away.[66]

An elderly Indian woman picked up De Camp's son (4), Jannette grabbed her infant, and they, along with Willie De Camp (9), went to Chief Wabasha, who had previously espoused peace with the whites. Near the village they encountered Wabasha, who was with his warriors, and did not appear peacefully inclined at the time. Wabasha drew his pistols and Jannette pleaded for the lives of her and her children, reminding him that she had saved his sick child the winter before with one of her remedies. Wabasha restrained his men and declared that neither she nor her children were to be harmed. He told her that he was not part of the uprising; it was the Sissetons who were causing all the trouble. Janette was suspicious, and wanted to escape across the river, but high water foiled her plan. At dusk, Jannette approached an Indian she recognized and asked him for food. He took the De Camps to a village near the Lower Agency. There, Jannette saw only angry Indians who probably would have killed her were they not busily engaged in dividing up the goods they had stolen. The De Camps crept away and hid in the undergrowth.[67]

Jannette next encountered Chief Wacouta and asked for his protection. He led them to a house, gave them a box of figs, and locked them in. As the De Camp children slept, two Indians unlocked the door and brought in two captive girls, whom Jannette recognized as Mattie Williams and Mary Anderson. Mary Schwandt arrived next. When warriors entered and made sexual advances toward Mary Schwandt, Willie De Camp broke down. "Are we going to be killed now, mamma?" he cried out. "Don't let them kill us with knives!"

Suddenly, Jannette's fright and submissiveness vanished and she gave the Indians a verbal lambasting. She had once taught English to some of these very Indians, and now she demanded that they behave, and asked why they were killing the whites. They said that it was fun to kill cowardly white men who fled, leaving their women behind, and boasted that one Indian could easily kill ten white men. Jannette predicted that they would all hang before another moon had passed. White soldiers, she said, would return in large numbers, and, if the Indians killed their captives, "it would not be long till their hideous forms would be dangling from a rope's end."

The Indians were unimpressed and brandished their weapons in the women's faces. They hollered and threatened until Wacouta appeared, threw them out of the house, and tried to patch up Mary Anderson's wound. On August 19, Wacouta told the captives that he was forced to join his band to attack Fort Ridgely. They were to remain in the loft and stay silent and out of sight. He closed the trap door as he left. The women's ministrations notwithstanding, Mary Anderson was dying and Jannette's baby needed nourishment. If it had not been for Wacouta's warning to remain hidden, they would have gone out in search of food. In the evening of the following day, Mary Schwandt and Mattie Williams crept from the loft and returned with some green corn. Mary Anderson could not chew, and in her delirious state she accused the others of trying to starve her. The warriors returned on the 21st, and took Mary Schwandt and Mattie Williams. A short time later another warrior put Mary Anderson, Jannette, and her three children aboard his wagon and took them to Little Crow's village.

A great thunderstorm broke as they traveled, making the situation even more wretched. At Little Crow's, a warrior demanded that Mary Anderson get out of the wagon and go with him. De Camp explained that Mary was dying. The warrior said, "She is better than two dead squaws yet. Get along out!" Mattie Williams and De Camp never saw Mary Anderson again. She lived only one more hour. They buried her in an old tablecloth.[68]

After being moved to Shakopee's village, De Camp learned that a woman captive was shot while attempting to escape. When the warriors returned from fighting at Ridgely and New Ulm, they moved to Rice Creek. Jannette waded the high Redwood River and lost her shoes. At the spring near Joseph Reynolds's house they rested. As Jannette attempted to get a drink, her Indian captor yelled a warning. She looked up to see Cut Nose charging in to kill her. She dodged behind her captor and her life was saved for the moment. Cut Nose had sworn to kill all the whites.

When they arrived at the 1,000-tipi Rice Creek camp, De Camp discovered her friends, Mrs. Marion Robertson Hunter, Mrs. Andrew Robertson, her son Frank Robertson, and Mattie Williams. Hunter and the Robertsons were staying in John Moore's tipi. Mattie Williams and Jannette often visited Mrs. Hunter and prayed together, for she had the only prayer book in camp. Jannette also met Sarah Wakefield. Since Janette was seven months pregnant, she was concerned about having little food and no blankets for the cold nights. She told Wakefield of her situation, but Sarah did not appear concerned. Sarah said she gave Jannette some of her breakfast, but complained that, "She was very filthy, and so were her children." Wakefield thought that Jannette whined too much. Once, when the Indians returned from a battle and said that many warriors had been killed, Jannette responded, "Oh! that is good: I wish every one dead; I would like to cut their throats." Sarah winced, for she knew that some of the Indians could understand English. Sarah believed that the Indians were only looking for an excuse to kill her.[69]

The captives were next taken above Yellow Medicine Agency. Jannette met up with Lucy Pettijohn and the two hatched an escape plan. Lucy offered to take De Camp and her three sons to Lucy's uncle, Lorenzo Lawrence. A few days later, while Indian runners were in the village looking for more ammunition, the women and children crept away on a three-mile trek to Lawrence's.[70] Early one morning, Lorenzo's mother awoke Jannette and said it was time to escape. The De Camps met Lorenzo Lawrence and his family and they made their way to a marshy lake where they waited until Lawrence could scout the area. He learned that some Indians were threatening to shoot him on sight, and he hurried away with his charges to the Minnesota River where he had previously hidden three canoes. In a storm at the mouth of Yellow Medicine River Jannette lost her paddle and her boat was caught in a swift current that spun her canoe around. Lorenzo pulled them to shore and decided to wait for daylight.[71]

The next morning the weather had not improved. Before they began their journey, Lorenzo sent his sons, Moses and Thomas, to climb a tree and look around. They spotted a woman running. Lorenzo paddled his canoe across the river and returned with the woman and her five children. She was a mixed-blood, Mrs. Madaline Robideau, and she and her children had escaped in the night from their captors. Lorenzo retrieved a canoe they had passed the day before and they continued on their way. Near the Lower Agency, the canoe carrying Willie De Camp and Lorenzo's son, Thomas, hit a snag and capsized. Panicked, Jannette called to Lorenzo for help, and luckily the Indians on shore did not hear her cry. Lorenzo's wife pulled Willie out from underwater, and she found Thomas clinging to the capsized craft. Once ashore, they worked on Willie until he coughed up some river water and revived.

Despite the close proximity of the Indians, they remained there that night and left early in the morning. They spotted De Camp's house and the mill still standing, and she insisted on returning to her home to retrieve important papers she would need for business purposes. Lorenzo thought it was foolish, but Jannette had her way and rounded up some account books and the family Bible. Continuing down river they saw the corpse of Captain John Marsh, who had drowned August 18, after an ambush at the Lower Sioux Ferry. Lorenzo told the others to go ahead a little ways and wait for him. He pulled Marsh's body out of the river and buried it.[72]

De Camp often pleaded with Lorenzo to abandon the boats and continue on foot, but he refused and accused her of ingratitude and having no concern for his safety. Being a mixed-blood, he feared the troops might mistake him for one of the hostiles. On Sunday, they heard drums and bugles and knew they were near the fort. De Camp pleaded for Lawrence to move on, but the weather turned stormy once more, and he said they would wait it out. The storm continued the next morning and they beached the boats. Lawrence had his family and the Robideaus take shelter beneath the overturned canoes, while he took Jannette De Camp and her three sons to Ridgely. On September 15, Reverend Joshua Sweet, the post chaplain, and a number of soldiers found them. Said Jannette: "My clothing was in rags, an old piece of gingham enveloped my head; my feet were bare and bleeding, as were my children's; but, oh, joy! We were at last free!" The De Camps, thanks to the untiring bravery of Lorenzo Lawrence, were finally safe.[73]

Jannette learned that her husband had been mortally wounded at the Battle of Birch Coulee, and was buried by Reverend Sweet ten days earlier. Jannette was devastated. "Every hope seemed blotted out from the horizon of my existence," she said, "and life and liberty bought at such a price seemed worthless as I looked at the future of my fatherless children, without a home and many miles from my people."

Lieutenant Timothy J. Sheehan provided her with an escort to St. Peter. From there the De Camps took a stagecoach to Shakopee, where they once lived and had many friends. Her old neighbors welcomed them back "as if raised from the dead" and gave them clothes, food, and shelter. Jannette's 70-year-old father arrived in Shakopee and took her and the children to his home in the south where the Civil war was still raging. There, she learned that her mother had died only two months earlier. She gave birth to a healthy son, her fourth, a few weeks later. In 1866, Jannette De Camp and her four boys returned to Fort Ridgely as the wife of Joshua Sweet, the garrison chaplain. In March 1893, Jannette De Camp Sweet finished writing a narrative of her captivity experience, and in the concluding paragraphs she heartily thanked Lorenzo Lawrence and others for rescuing her. "To such as those," she wrote, "I owed my safety from dishonor and death."[74]

GEORGE H. SPENCER
Minnesota, August 18, 1862

George Spencer was born in Kentucky on December 20, 1831. By 1851, he had become a fur trader in St. Paul, Minnesota. In 1862, he was employed as a clerk at William H. Forbes's trading post on Big Stone Lake. He was en route to visit friends in St. Paul, when he stopped to spend Saturday night at the Lower Agency. Spencer attended church the next day, and made the mistake of spending one more night.

Early on Monday morning, August 18, 1862, Spencer and six other people were at another of Forbes's buildings when the sound of Indian war whoops drew them outside. A short distance away, Nathan Myrick's store was being attacked. The Indians spotted the men at the trading post and were there in a flash, killing Joe Belland, Antoine Young, George Thomas and William Taylor. George Spencer was shot through his right arm, in his right breast, and in the stomach. George and his two uninjured companions ran upstairs, where they met William Bourat and the mixed-blood Paulite Osier. Osier looked through a trap door to the scene below and saw twenty-five or thirty Indians ransacking the store. A brave looked up and called for him to come down, assuring him he would not be hurt. The two uninjured men climbed down and Bourat bolted out of the store and ran for his life. An Indian blasted him with duck-shot about 200 yards away. Bourat played dead while the Indians stripped his clothes and shoes and piled logs on him. Convinced he was dead, the Indians left to plunder the store. Bourat crawled away and escaped.[75]

Paulite Osier joined with the Indians, sealing his fate. He took part in some of their raids and killed a white woman. When he later surrendered to Sibley at Camp Release, he was convicted of murder and hanged. Back in the trading post, the Indians seemed to have forgotten about the badly wounded George Spencer. He heard them discussing burning the building so he tied a cord to a bedpost and tossed the cord out the window intending to slide down if they did set it afire. The Indians were aware Spencer was upstairs, but were afraid to go after him for they knew that several crates of guns were stored above and they were sure he would shoot anyone who came up.[76]

George heard the familiar voice of Wakinyantawa, his friend for the past ten years and at one time one of Little Crow's head warriors, asking where he was. George answered and the Indian ran upstairs. Wakinyantawa asked Spencer if he was mortally wounded and he responded he was badly hurt but did not know if he was going to die. His comrade helped him downstairs, while other Indians in the store yelled, "Kill him!" "Spare no Americans!" "Show mercy to none!" Wakinyantawa brandished a hatchet and threatened anyone who harmed Spencer. He helped Spencer outside into a wagon and directed two Indian women to take him to Wakinyantawa's lodge in Little Crow's camp. Wakinyantawa treated George's bullet wounds with an Indian remedy, and from this time on chose not to fight the whites. Little Crow realized Spencer's presence was keeping one of his head warriors out of the fighting, and the two often had words about what to do with the white man.

George Spencer stayed in Little Crow's village for five days. The Indians were raiding and bringing stolen goods and white captives to their camp. Besides the mixed-bloods, Spencer was the only adult male captive in the village. He said he was treated well, "But the female captives were, with very few exceptions, subjected to the most horrible treatment. In some cases, a woman would be taken out into the woods, and her person violated by six, seven, and as many as ten or twelve of these fiends."[77] After unsuccessful attempts to capture New Ulm and Fort Ridgely, the Indians decided to move. Spencer, still on the mend, was put in a wagon. Beyond Redwood River, George saw a dead white man and got down to try to identity him. He appeared to have been dead about one week, and his features were too swollen to be recognizable, but on the collar of his shirt, he read, "Geo. H. Gleason" (see Sarah Wakefield). The second day they reached the Yellow Medicine Agency where they camped about two weeks.[78]

While they waited, Colonel Sibley was slowly mobilizing his forces. A strong burial party moved up the Minnesota River, commanded by Major Joseph R. Brown and comprised of fresh recruits of Company A, 6th Minnesota Infantry, under Captain Hiram P. Grant, fifty men of the Cullen Frontier Guard under Captain Joseph Anderson, seventeen teamsters and wagons, and a fatigue detail of soldiers and settlers, including Agent Thomas J. Galbraith and Dr. Jared W. Daniels. They left Fort Ridgely on August 31, and buried fifty-four victims of the uprising over the next two days. On September 1, they found Mrs. Justina Krieger. She had been wounded in an attack on August 19, and had spent the next thirteen days wandering in the woods near Beaver Creek. Doctor Daniels treated her and placed her in a wagon. That night they selected a campsite near Birch Coulee.

Before dawn on the morning of September 2, 200 warriors under Gray Bird, Red Legs, Big Eagle, and Mankato attacked the sleeping soldiers. Within an hour, Major Brown, Captain Anderson, and Agent Galbraith all lay wounded and Captain Grant took command. They strengthened their perimeter and dug in, but they were surrounded on a flat plain. The wagon Mrs. Krieger was in was riddled with bullets, but she escaped further injury. Not so lucky were the soldiers and civilians: twenty-four were killed or mortally wounded and sixty-seven others wounded. About ninety horses were killed. The command was trapped for thirty-one hours without food or water. Far down the river, Colonel Sibley heard sounds of the fighting and sent Colonel Samuel McPhail and 240 men to their aid, but three miles from Birch Coulee, McPhail ran into Indians under Big Eagle and halted. On the morning of September 3, Grant's men were down to five rounds of ammunition apiece, when Sibley, now with 1,000 men, finally appeared. The outnumbered Indians pulled away. They only lost two warriors killed and four wounded, and inflicted the heaviest military casualties of any battle during the uprising.[79]

After the Battle of Birch Coulee, Colonel Sibley attached a note to a stake on the battleground that read: "If Little Crow has any proposition to make to me, let him send a half-breed to me, and he shall be protected in and out of my camp." Little Crow took the letter to George Spencer to have him write a reply, but Spencer's right arm was broken and he couldn't write. Mixed-bloods Tom Robertson and Antoine J. Campbell helped Little Crow frame a response that blamed Galbraith, Myrick, Forbes, and other whites for forcing the Indians into a war that they didn't want. He also closed with an implied threat: "I have a great many prisoners women and children. . . ." A series of letters were sent and Spencer was able to tell his friends he was still alive, but his predicament was perilous.[80]

Each day Indians threatened Spencer's life, riding up to the tipi and demanding he be brought out. He wanted to escape, but he was still too weak. Wakinyantawa protected Spencer when warriors aimed their weapons at him. He pointed his double barrel shotgun at the Indians and said, "Shoot if you like; kill him if you will, but two of you will come out of your saddle if you do." No one doubted Wakinyantawa's word and they backed down. Wakinyantawa hid Spencer in a large hole dug in the ground in the center of his lodge because Little Crow had ordered that he should be put to death. George stated, "My bodily sufferings were very great, but nothing when compared with my mental anxiety. Being threatened with death so often, sometimes I almost prayed that some of their attempts to kill me might prove successful. I thought that death might be a relief to me."[81]

On September 26, 1862, the "Long Trader," as Colonel Sibley was called among the Indians, appeared with his troops. "It was to me a glorious sight," said George Spencer, "I had been in captivity 40 days, and during most of that time my life had been in imminent danger almost every hour." The captives were turned over to Sibley.

After the Great Sioux Uprising of 1862, George Spencer went to work as a bookkeeper in St. Paul. In 1881 he became an Indian agent at Crow Creek, Dakota Territory. In 1887, he moved to Montana, where he died on May 31, 1892.[82]

AMANDA, JENNIE, AND GEORGE INGALLS, JOHN SCHMERCH AND JAMES SCOTT
Minnesota, August 19, 21, 24, 1862

On August 19, 1862, news of the Sioux massacre in Minnesota reached the Jedidiah H. Ingalls family who lived at Hawk Creek, three miles below Yellow Medicine, in Renville County. Jed Ingalls, his wife, daughters Amanda (14) and Jennie (12), son George (9) and one younger son, were on their way to Fort Ridgely when Indians attacked them. Mr. and Mrs. Ingalls were slain and their four children were taken captive by Little Crow's band.[83]

An alternative scenario states that the Ingalls were killed early on August 19, and Little Crow captured their two sons, but the two daughters joined the Samuel J. Brown family. The extended Brown family included his wife; his mother, Susan Frenier Brown; his nine children; Charles Blair and his wife, Lydia Brown Blair; Angus Brown and Nellie Brown, Samuel's brother and sister; hired man Lonsman; neighbors Charles Holmes, Leopold and Frances Wohler, and a few others. They fled from Brown's home eight miles east of the Yellow Medicine Agency, but Dakotas, including Cut Nose, Shakopee, and Dowanniye surrounded them. Susan Frenier Brown, a mixed-blood Dakota, made her Indian connections known. One of the warriors recognized her as having saved his life the previous winter and after a great deal of pleading and arguing, the hostiles let Mr. Wohler and Mr. Holmes go.[84]

Cut Nose led Frances Wohler off when her husband ran back, tore open his shirt, and said, "Shoot me, but I shall first kiss my wife." Leopold Wohler's action astonished the Indians and they froze as he showered her with kisses and then ran away. The white women were parceled out among the Indians. Along the way they the passed four mutilated white bodies, one of them a woman with a pitchfork sticking in her, and another a man with a scythe in him. Cut Nose, Brown said, "gleefully told that he had killed this man. . ." by first shaking his hand, and then stabbing him in the chest. They fought, and the white man almost bit Cut Nose's thumb off before he killed him and stuck the scythe in him. The Dakota proudly showed his bloody thumb to the horrified captives. In a short while they reached John Moore's (a mixed-blood Sioux) house. A few Indians kept the Ingalls girls and Frances Wohler, but little is known about their subsequent experiences. All three were freed at Camp Release.

The other captives—Browns, Blairs, and Lonsmans—were sent on to Little Crow's house, where he gave them water, robes, and blankets and said he would treat them as family.

"The wily old fellow!" Sam Brown said, "He was working for the aid and support of the Upper Sioux. He knew of mother's influence over Standing Buffalo, Waanatan, Scarlet Plume, Sweet Corn, Red Iron, A-kee-pah, and other influential Sisseton and Wahpeton chiefs."[85]

In the middle of the night, Little Crow had an argument with some Indians who wanted to kill all the whites. He diffused the situation, but figured it would be best to get Charles Blair out of the camp. He had his men dress Blair as an Indian, escort him into the woods, and direct him to Fort Ridgely, fifteen miles downriver. Blair, a consumptive and in fragile health, took seven days to reach the fort. Exhaustion and exposure took their toll and he died six months later.

On Wednesday, August 20, Hazatonwin, an old Indian woman that Brown knew, took the captives to her daughter's tipi, fed them, and guarded them. On Saturday, Akipa, Susan Brown's step-father, arrived from Yellow Medicine Agency to take the captives home to his family and friends.[86]

On August 21, while the Browns were awaiting their fate, five men were cutting hay and building a stable and blacksmith shop for Agent Thomas J. Galbraith at Big Stone Lake. George Lott, brothers Anton (Anthony) and Henry Manderfeld, Hilliar Manderfeld, their cousin, and John Schmerch (Julien) (16), had been working there since July 1862.[87] More than fifty Dakota warriors hit their camp at daybreak on Thursday. Henry Manderfeld and George Lott were killed. Anthony and Hilliar Manderfeld ran into the reeds along the lake. They heard the Indians searching for them, and while Anthony crouched down in the marsh, Hilliar decided to run along the bank. It was the wrong choice. Ten minutes later

Anthony heard shots; Hilliar was dead. When night fell, Anthony escaped across the Minnesota River, and after a ten-day flight he found a camp of white soldiers near Fort Ridgely.[88]

When the attack began, John Schmerch, the camp cook, fled to the woods and hid until he thought the Indians were gone. When he returned to the camp to see if anyone else was alive, a friendly Dakota, Eu-kosh-nu, spotted him and tried to protect him. He took John across the lake and sent him off alone, following some distance behind to see that he made it out of the area. When Eu-kosh-nu discovered that hostile warriors were close on John's trail, he caught up with the boy and took him to his own tipi. Later in the day, John and Eu-kosh-nu's son went to the lake when another Indian, Hut-te-ste-mi, saw John, pulled out his pistol, shot him, and ran away. The Indian boy got his father, who patched John's wound. When he set out to kill Hut-te-ste-mi, John overruled his plan. Instead, Eu-kosh-nu took his hatchet, found Hut-te-ste-mi, and smashed his pistol. Now Eu-kosh-nu's own life was in danger. He took John to his cousin's tipi, where the pistol ball was removed from his side and he was cared for.[89]

While John Schmerch was recuperating from his wound, other Indians were creeping up on a lone cabin at "Old Crossing," on Otter Tail River, about fifteen miles from Breckinridge, Minnesota. Old Mrs. Scott (65) lived there with her son and her grandson Jimmy (6). On August 24, 1862, the Indians, ranging about 140 miles away from the center of trouble at Redwood Agency, attacked Scott's house. They wounded Mrs. Scott, tore off her dress, and killed her son, and then ran outside to attack a market wagon going by. Mrs. Scott told Jimmy to do as the Indians said and maybe they'd let him live. The Indians returned, snatched Jimmy, loaded the wagon with their treasures and rode off. The old lady remained motionless until she was sure the wagon was gone, retrieved fifty silver dollars the Indians missed, and crawled to the door. She hid the money in a haystack and then crawled and walked along the Otter Tail River toward Breckinridge for help.

Hearing of Indian attacks near Breckinridge, Captain John Van der Horck formed a squad of six civilians and six men of Company D, 5th Minnesota Infantry, from Fort Abercrombie, and marched to investigate. Van der Houck recovered the bodies of three men killed near the town and discovered Mrs. Scott, barely alive, with three wounds in her breast. They took her to the fort and cared for her.[90]

After Little Crow's defeat at the Battle of Wood Lake, he headed for Devil's Lake in Dakota Territory, where he hoped to join forces with other Indian tribes and continue the war. John Schmerch, still very weak from his wound, was part of the group of departing Indians. He walked the first day because Eu-kosh-nu's cousin had no horse. The second day it was evident he could not travel under his own power so his captor returned him to Eu-kosh-nu. He rode in a wagon and remained with him for the rest of his captivity. Included among Little Crow's fugitives were Jimmy Scott and George Ingalls.[91]

The boys were fed buffalo meat, and their hardships were mostly in the form of hard chores and the severely cold winter. At Devil's Lake the Indians divided up, and the group holding the captives continued on to the Missouri River, where they met up with a group of 500 lodges of Yanktons. They rested and feasted on buffalo for five days. Little Crow joined them, increasing the Mdewakanton lodges to sixty. Around Christmas, Little Crow tried to talk the Yanktons into attacking Fort Pierre, but they wanted nothing to do with the plan. Rebuffed, Little Crow moved his band farther upriver.

Little Crow next tried to open negotiations with the Mandan and Arikara tribes located near present-day Bismarck, North Dakota. Uncertain how they would react to his plan, he forced John Schmerch to go in front as a human shield when he sent his delegation forward. The semi-sedentary tribes on the Missouri were wary, but the groups shook hands and smoked pipes. Little else was accomplished before a war faction among the Arikaras began firing to break up the conference. The meeting degenerated into a battle, with the more numerous Mandans and Arikaras quickly gaining the upper hand. Eight Dakotas were killed and Schmerch was wounded in the leg. As Little Crow retreated, Schmerch tried to keep up, but after five miles his leg was too painful to continue. He hid to avoid the pursuing Arikara and at nightfall he walked on until he caught up with Little Crow.[92]

In late winter, Little Crow set out for Devil's Lake. His band was cold and hungry, and the three boy captives suffered along with them. Little Crow wanted to establish friendly relations in Canada, and in the spring of 1863, moved to the border and camped near St. Joseph. Eventually, the displaced Dakotas grew to several hundred people, and the inhabitants of St. Joseph became alarmed, until they realized the Indians were starving and only wanted to trade for food. Father A. Andre, parish priest at St. Joseph, visited their camp regularly and established trade connections with them. Andre changed his outlook when two traders, Gingras and Bottineau, opened up their stores to the Indians, taking much of the plunder they had collected in Minnesota, and almost ran out of supplies needed by the other inhabitants of the village. In the late spring, Father Andre learned that the destitute Dakotas wished to sell three white captives.

Joseph Demerois, son of the post interpreter at Fort Abercrombie, had been at St Joseph's in May, and returned to Abercrombie with news of the captives. They discussed options to rescue the boys, but another priest from St. Joseph beat them to it. About the first of June, Catholic missionary Father Germaine arranged to ransom Ingalls and Scott. They had suffered much. Ingalls seemed better for the wear, but Jimmy Scott could remember little of the days before his capture, not even his grandmother's name. He cried piteously when questioned. Germaine parted with a horse and nearly all of his worldly goods to buy them. Even so, Jimmy cried bitterly on the neck of his Indian "mother" when he kissed her goodbye.

Father Germaine next worked on Eu-kosh-nu. He was reluctant to sell John Schmerch, and told the priest that he wanted to take him to the settlements himself to deliver him up and prove that he was a friend to the whites. He explained that he had asked nothing unreasonable from Schmerch, and even sold a pony so he could get clothing and blankets for him. Other Dakotas, however, would not let Eu-kosh-nu go to the whites, and supposing that General Sibley would not travel that far north, the Indian finally agreed to a deal. He sold Schmerch to Germaine for a horse and two blankets, and the boy reached St. Joseph on June 13, 1863. Germaine sent him to St. Paul, which he reached on September 17, probably the last of the rescued captives.[93]

Mariah C. Koch, Laura Duley, Julia Wright, Lavina Eastlick, Lillie Everett, Rosa and Ellen Ireland
Minnesota, August 20, 1862

A dozen families established a small settlement around Lake Shetek, Smith Lake, Fremont Lake, and Bloody Lake in Murray County, Minnesota, about sixty-five miles west of New Ulm. Andreas (Andrew) Koch (pronounced Cook) and his young wife Mariah Christina Koch built their homestead on the south shore of Bloody Lake in 1859, and he and the other settlers went about their peaceful business on the morning of August 20, 1862.[94]

The Dakota Indians, however, were not in a peaceful mood. A Dakota proclivity was to ease their anger by making innocent

Author's photo

Eastlick cabin site, Lake Shetek, Minnesota.

parties suffer. Because they felt wronged by white agents, traders, and what they perceived as broken promises, they were determined to wreck vengeance on white settlers. With White Lodge's and Lean Bear's villages located only thirty-five miles west of Lake Shetek, the settlers there were in grave danger.[95] Indians approached the Koch cabin, with one group heading for the house and another for the cornfield. Mr. Koch was at the cabin while Mrs. Koch was in the cornfield firing a rifle to scare crows away. The Indians rode up to Mariah Koch and asked to see the rifle. She gave it to them. The warriors refused to return the gun and told her to go away, for they intended to kill all the white men in the country. The Indians at the cabin asked Andrew for water to drink. He took a pail and walked across the yard to a well when the Indians shot him. Mariah Koch pretended to run away as she had been ordered, but she dallied to watch the Indians plunder the house. When they left she returned and stumbled upon her husband's corpse. She went to warn the other settlers and reached John Wright's cabin where about thirty-four settlers had already gathered.[96]

Charles D. Hatch, the brother of Almira Everett, had ridden from Everett's to Hurd's cabin to get a team of oxen to help William Everett build a sawmill. When he came to the outlet of Bloody Lake he tired of riding, tied his horse, and went to Hurd's on foot. Charlie Hatch had seen dense smoke rising from his neighbor's cabin. He investigated and discovered John Voight, who had been overseeing the farm while Phineas Hurd was away, had been shot.

Alomina Hurd and her two children were nowhere to be found. Hatch continued on to the Koch cabin where he saw Indians ransacking the place, so he ran off to warn the others.[97]

Two tipis stood in a clearing next to Wright's house. Pawn and several other Indians approached and told the settlers that 300 bad Indians were in the vicinity, intent on murder. Pawn and his companions then disappeared into the tipis and soon emerged naked and painted for battle. William Duley scowled at Pawn, who quickly explained that he was attired like this so the bad Indians would not kill him; when the time came he and his comrades would fight for the settlers.

The settlers prepared the sturdy two-story log house for defense. Mr. Wright was away at the time, but Mrs. Julia Wright was calm and helped distribute axes, hatches, and butcher knives to the women, stationed them upstairs as sentries, and removed chinking from the cabin walls to provide rifle slots. Unsure of Pawn's sincerity, the men banished the Indians from the house, telling them to set up a defense in the stable. William Duley, Henry Watson Smith, Thomas Ireland, and Mrs. Wright each had a gun, while John Eastlick had two guns.[98]

The Eastlicks had hurried to the Wright house from their cabin about one mile north. Lavina Day was born May 28, 1833, in Broome County, New York, and married John Eastlick in Ohio, in 1850. They moved to Indiana and Illinois before finally settling at Lake Shetek, Minnesota, in October 1861. They had five sons: Merton (11), Frank (9), Giles (8), Frederick (5), and John "Johnny" Eastlick III (1).

Lavina watched a band of Indians in full war regalia come up from the south. They began firing from long range and then stopped. Pawn, still pretending to be an intermediary, returned and gave the whites a choice: leave peacefully, or stay behind and the Indians would burn them out. The majority of settlers decided it would be wiser to leave and make a stand in the woods rather than go up in smoke. Thirty-two people set off east toward New Ulm. The Indians let Charley Hatch and Mr. Rhodes go to William Everett's cabin to bring back a wagon for the women and children; all got aboard except for Julia Wright, Lavina Eastlick, and her sons, Merton and Frank. About a mile from Wright's cabin, the settlers turned to see the Indians fast approaching.[99]

They tried to run, but quickly realized it was hopeless. They jumped from the wagon, thinking the Indians wanted the horses. About one mile farther east was a low-lying slough in the prairie that became marshy in rainy weather. The slough drained northwest into Lake Shetek. Now, it represented a possible sanctuary for the fugitives. Mr. Rhodes and Henry Smith grabbed rifles and sprinted toward the main part of the slough, ignoring the shouts of John Eastlick to halt. The rest had little choice but to head for the slough. The men tried to form a line behind the women and children but the Indians soon forced them all into the head-high prairie grasses and reeds. A barrage of bullets pierced the air as a second band of Indians advanced. Half of them galloped along a ridge to the east of the settlers. A barren stretch

Minnesota Historical Society

Lavina Eastlick and children Merton and Johnny (baby), ca. 1862.

intersected the patch between where the whites hid and the main slough. With some of the attackers on top of the ridge and some patrolling the bare area leading to the main slough, the settlers were surrounded. William Duley and Thomas Ireland shot at an Indian threatening to ride between the settlers and the grass. The Sisseton Chief Lean Bear fell dead. Atop the ridge, White Lodge, Pawn, and dozens of other Indians dismounted, crouched behind the wild plum trees and stalked their prey. Any rustle of the grass brought a series of well-directed shots. Although the grass was high and green, there was no water on the low ground, only parched hummocks packed so close that the settlers could not lie low. They were trapped.[100]

The Indians zeroed in on their targets. Charlie Hatch was shot and gave out a load groan. Sarah Ireland (5) took a bullet in the bowels and screamed. Lavina Eastlick was shot in the heel and in the side, and a large ball lodged between her scalp and her skull. A bullet hit Almira Everett in the neck. John Eastlick and his son Giles were shot dead. Sophia Smith was shot in the hip. Emma

Duley (12) was shot through the arm. A bullet struck William Everett shattering his elbow.

There was a lull in the gunfire. "Come on out," Pawn yelled, "Nobody will hurt the women and children." He said he wanted Mrs. Eastlick and Mrs. Wright for his wives. They could come out now or be burned to a crisp when the Indians set the grass afire. Once again they believed Pawn and the women and children began to come out of the slough. Almira Everett and Julia Wright and their children walked and crawled to the base of the ridge. Almira, badly wounded, had great difficulty climbing even with help. She reached the top and died. Pawn raised one child on his shoulder and told the rest to hurry or they'd be burned when the grass was set aflame.

Mariah Koch, Lavina Eastlick, Sophia Smith, Laura Duley, and Sophia Ireland got up. Lavina looked back in the slough and saw her little son Fred emerge from the grass. An Indian woman clutched a twisted hunk of wood and swung it at the boy's head. He screamed as blood streamed down his face. Another Indian woman smashed Frank Eastlick in the mouth with a club. Warriors held the frantic Lavina back, and forced her to the bluff top with Merton and her baby, Johnny.[101]

A violent thunderstorm let loose it's fury. While the rain pelted them, the warriors began claiming their prizes. White Lodge grabbed Mariah Koch and led her away. Two warriors claimed the two oldest Ireland girls, Rosa (9) and Ellen (7). They later ended up with Chief Redwood. Pawn claimed Julia Wright and her children and put them on a horse. The badly wounded Sophia Smith and Sophia Ireland struggled up the bluff. Two braves chuckled at their desperate condition, and then shot them both dead. Willie Duley (10) was walking in front of Lavina Eastlick when a young Indian sauntered up next to him and shot him dead.

Laura screamed. Twice, Pawn's promises of safety proved false. Lavina challenged his honesty and asked if he intended to kill her too. He replied in the negative, but they had gone only a short distance farther when Pawn shot her in the back. The ball tore out above her hip and pierced her right arm. She fell to the ground and Pawn moved on, believing she was dead. Several minutes later Merton crawled to her side and she told him to take Johnny and care for him as long as he lived.

Farther on, Pawn ordered Julia Wright to return to the slough and retrieve all functioning weapons. She returned shortly with one defective gun and Pawn hurled the gun to the ground near where Lavina laid. Believing she would be trampled, Lavina rolled

Author's photo
Mariah Koch Cabin, Lake Shetek, Minnesota.

out of the muddy path and into the grass. A young warrior noticed her move, picked up the discarded gun, pounded her head with it, and left her for dead. The Indians took the captives and left the men wounded or dead in the slough. They could not burn them out because of the thunderstorm.[102]

The warriors headed back to Thomas Ireland's house. Mariah Koch was walking with Belle Duley (5) when the same old woman who had murdered Fred Eastlick came along, snatched her away, and whipped her face with rawhide. The woman then grabbed the girl by an arm and a leg and repeatedly slammed her against the ground. They then tied her to a bush and used her as a knife-throwing target. She was pierced numerous times and soon died, all to the horror of Mrs. Duley, who was held back and forced to watch the contest.

At the camp, White Lodge told Mariah Koch to remain in the tipi so no Indian would kill her. They held a war dance, boasting of the deaths they had caused and demonstrating how their victims had suffered and died. Because of Lean Bear's death at the slough, the Indians chose Pawn as the new chief.

Lillie Everett (6) was brought to camp in the morning, shivering from cold and fear. Mariah Koch and Laura Duley tried to comfort her. They wrapped her in a shawl and had her sit close to the fire. The Indians disliked the attention the women showed the little girl and shot at them in a fit of anger. One ball penetrated the

235

skirt of Laura Duley and another tore through Mariah's shawl just below her shoulder, but neither shot hit flesh. The Indians broke camp on Friday, August 22, and moved on.[103]

Mariah Koch was sold to an old Indian who treated her good or bad, and fed or starved her, depending on his mood. One day he decided to take Mariah with him on a visit to another Indian band in Dakota Territory. The old man had a tough time traveling and Mariah offered to carry his gun. He gave it to her, probably thinking she was behaving as a dutiful Indian wife. Mariah removed the percussion cap, dropped it, and spit into the barrel hoping to disable it. Then she refused to travel any further. The Indian snatched the gun and threatened to shoot if she did not move. She boldly bared her breast to receive the death shot. He pulled the trigger and nothing happened. He was amazed at her bravery, spooked by the malfunction of his gun, and superstitiously believed she led a charmed life. He then agreed to go in the direction she chose; they headed north and reached the Upper Agency only ten days after the fight at Slaughter Slough.[104]

Mariah formed an alliance with an Indian woman who wished to run away from an abusive husband and they plotted an escape. On the chosen day they met at the Minnesota River, and crossed ten times in order to conceal their trail. The two women traveled about thirty miles when they stumbled upon Wahpeton Chief Red Iron's band and joined him. Red Iron had opposed a war with the whites and he had gathered about ninety captives who he hoped to give to the approaching soldiers under Colonel Sibley. After being in Red Iron's possession for only three days, they were all surrendered at Camp Release on August 26.[105]

Lavina Eastlick was left for dead at Slaughter Slough. Incredibly, she regained consciousness and crawled away, hiding in the grass. It took her three days to reach the main trail. At that time, August Garzene, a mail carrier on his way from Sioux Falls to New Ulm and unaware of the uprising, saw Lavina in the road. He put her in his one-horse sulky and they sped off. They picked up Thomas Ireland, wounded eight times, but able to crawl out of the slough. The next day they found Alomina Hurd and her two sons. The Indians had found and killed her husband, Phineas. Fifty miles from Lake Shetek they spotted two small figures in the road. Garzene stopped the wagon. It was Merton Eastlick still carrying his little brother Johnny. More than two weeks after the attack they all reached Mankato, Minnesota, where a doctor finally treated Lavina's wounds.

Author's photo

Slaughter Slough, near Lake Shetek, Minnesota.

After her recovery, Lavina met Mariah Koch, and the two women threw their arms about each other. Mariah asked her to join her in testifying against the Indians. In Mankato, Lavina visited the recuperating Mr. Ireland at the hospital and went to see the Indians that Sibley had taken prisoner. Lavina thought they were all being treated too well. "It made my blood boil," she said. "I felt as if I should see them butchered, one and all; and no one, who has suffered what we settlers have, from their ferocity, can entertain any milder feelings toward them."[106]

Lavina went to live with her sister in Wisconsin, returned to her parents in Ohio, and in 1866, bought farmland near Mankato with money she made from selling an account she wrote about the Lake Shetek Massacre. In 1870, Lavina married Solomon Pettibone, but he disappeared about three months after the wedding. In August 1871, Lavina gave birth to a daughter, Laura. Lavina's house burned down in 1883. She rebuilt it and lived there with Laura, all the while her old wounds still troubled her.

Johnny married in 1885 and had two children. He lived for a time a mile away from his mother. About 1901, Johnny and his wife moved to Wright County, Minnesota.

Laura Pettibone married Angus McDonald, and they moved to Alberta, Canada. Lavina went with them. She died in Lougheed, Alberta, on October 10, 1923, at age 90.

Merton worked as a carpenter, while Johnny, now ten years old, helped his mother run the household. Merton married in

237

1873, and had one son, but Merton died of a pulmonary ailment in Rochester, Minnesota, in 1875.

The last that is known of Mariah Koch was that she remarried and was living in Mankato. She could not speak English, so a depredation claim for $1,419 in damages was prepared for her by Ernst G. Koch of New Ulm.

Lillie Everett was freed months after her capture. Four Bear, one of the Indians opposed to the revolt, got her by trading horses and provisions for her freedom. She was taken to Fort Dodge, Iowa, where her father met her. William Everett recovered from his wounds. William and Lillie moved to Wisconsin. In 1866, Everett married Amelia Addison. After the birth of a son, they moved to Waseca, Minnesota, and built its first store. Lillie Everett married a Mr. Keeny and died in 1923.[107]

Some of the last captives rescued were Laura Duley, two of her children, Julia Wright, two of her children, and Rosa and Ellen Ireland. The rescue came about through the efforts of Charles E. Galpin and his Two Kettle Lakota wife, Eagle-Woman-That-All-Look-At (Matilda Galpin). Galpin was a partner of La Barge, Harkness and Company and was in charge of Indian trade along the Missouri River. In the autumn of 1862, when miners were pulling out of Dakota Territory's (present-day Montana) placer mines for the winter amid rumors of a Sioux uprising, Galpin, Matilda, and ten miners were heading down the Missouri toward the states. On November 1, as they approached the mouth of Grand River near present-day Mobridge, South Dakota, a Santee war party attacked their mackinaw boat and forced it to land. One of the warriors recognized Galpin's wife and he spoke with her. The warrior told her White Lodge was camped four miles downriver and there were three friendly Yanktonai there. The Galpins talked some of the war party into sending for them. While the Santee impatiently waited with the beached boat, Matilda Galpin played upon their sympathies by revealing she was transporting her young son home for burial, and then told them she had some provisions as a gift for White Lodge. When the three Yanktonai arrived, they convinced the Santee to take the boat to White Lodge and let him decide if they could pass. The Yanktonai jumped aboard and told Charles Galpin they would divert the Santee so they could escape. As they neared the village, Galpin pretended to land while the Yanktonai jumped ashore and began to vehemently argue with the warriors gathering near the shore. Galpin pulled away and sped off in the current.[108]

As the mackinaw pulled away a white woman ran down along the bank pleading for rescue. It was Julia Wright, who, with the other captives, had come a long, hard road to get to this point. After White Lodge led them away from Lake Shetek they headed northwest into Dakota Territory. One of Wright's sons, John (3), was separated from her and was later rescued at Camp Release. Her daughter Dora (5) was with her, but Indians had taken her infant daughter from her and smashed the baby's head. The Indians traveled incessantly, covering more than 500 miles seeking buffalo. The ordeal was excruciating for Julia Wright, Laura Duley, and Laura's daughter Emma, for they were beaten, starved, and "sold" from one master to another. Laura was passed to four owners, for a horse, for a blanket, and for a bag of shot. Both women were pregnant, and both suffered miscarriages from the "tortures and cruelties heaped upon these unfortunate beings. . . ."[109]

Galpin heard Julia Wright's plea, but knew he could not rescue her without endangering everyone aboard the boat. He called out that he would send back a rescue party. On November 3, Galpin docked at Fort La Framboise, near old Fort Pierre, and told trader Frank La Framboise of the eight captives at White Lodge's camp. La Framboise organized a rescue party of ten Fool Soldiers, Indians friendly to the whites who opposed the uprising, paid them $35 each, and supplied them for the trip. They left on November 10, reaching White Lodge's camp four days later.

After a huge feast, the Fool Soldiers met with the chief, but he refused to give up the captives. The rescuers reproached White Lodge for murdering unarmed people, abusing women and children, and running away leaving other bands to fight the soldiers. They threatened to take the captives without ransom if the chief would not sell them. White Lodge still refused. His sons agreed, however, taking eight horses and half of the Fool Soldiers guns in trade. Laura Duley and six children were given up, but they had to sneak Julia Wright from the chief's tipi. The rescuers shared moccasins and blankets with the women and carried the children to speed their journey out of the area. The next morning White Lodge changed his mind and went looking for Julia Wright but the Fool Soldiers were already safely downriver in the Yanktonai Bone Necklace's camp.

The Fool Soldiers gave the last of their guns and horses for provisions, blankets, and an old cart to carry the children to Fort La Framboise, which they finally reached on November 23. La Framboise supplied each captive with a pair of shoes and calico dresses. The former prisoners were thrilled to be able to wash with a bar of soap. On November 26, the women and children boarded wagons for Fort Randall. Thirty miles from the fort they ran into a force in command of Major John Pattee marching to Fort Pierre. They camped with the soldiers for the night and the men collected $250 for the captives' aid. They arrived at Fort Randall November 30. For three weeks Major Pattee's wife, also a Sioux woman, and Mrs. Galpin, extended their hospitality.

Charles Galpin had reached Yankton November 23, and gave a local paper the first public notice of his discovery of the captives. They had not been forgotten, for General John Pope, commander of the Military Department of the Northwest, had ordered all posts on the Missouri to send out scouting parties to look for them. On December 22, the captives rode in an army ambulance to the Yankton Agency and spent Christmas with Agent Dr. Walter Burleigh and his wife. The captives' names had been published in various newspapers and when they reached Yankton on New Year's Eve, Julia Wright learned her husband was on his way to meet her.[110]

Laura Duley also returned to her husband William. William Duley was selected as the hangman of the thirty-eight convicted Sioux Indians (see Sarah Wakefield). When he sprung the gallows on December 26, 1862, he believed his wife and children were either dead or still in captivity. Duley also joined the 1st Minnesota Mounted Rangers, became captain of scouts, and he and Laura lived in Mankato. Thomas Ireland recovered from his wounds and continued to live in Minnesota with his daughters, Rosa and Ellen.

Charles Hatch and Thomas Ireland returned to Slaughter Slough six weeks after the battle and buried the dead on October 16, 1862. On October 31, 1863, a military burial party under Captain Starkey and Scout William Duley, with the aid of Thomas Ireland, Charles Hatch, and Henry Smith, returned to the area to rebury the remains a few miles west of Slaughter Slough between Lake Shetek and Smith Lake. In 1925, the State of Minnesota completed and dedicated a monument to their memory.[111]

Chapter 5 notes

[1] Oehler, *Great Sioux Uprising*, 234-36; *Commissioner of Indian Affairs 1862*, 171; Carley, *Dakota War of 1862*, 65; Michno, *Encyclopedia of Indian Wars*, 96. See Marion Satterlee's list of released captives in Appendix 2.

[2] Gardner Sharp, *Spirit Lake*, 46, 48, 49.

[3] Folwell, *History of Minnesota Vol. 2*, 401, 402n4; Clodfelter, *Dakota War*, 28-29.

[4] Lee, *History of the Spirit Lake Massacre*, 16; Gardner Sharp, *Spirit Lake*, 71; Clodfelter, *Dakota War*, 29.

[5] Gardner Sharp, *Spirit Lake*, 72-4; Clodfelter, *Dakota War*, 29.

[6] Gardner Sharp, *Spirit Lake*, 76-79.

[7] "Selected Families," in www.pehoushek.com/genealogy/pafg283.htn; Gardner Sharp, *Spirit Lake*, 45, 80-81.

[8] Gardner Sharp, *Spirit Lake*, 82-3; Clodfelter, *Dakota War*, 29.

[9] Gardner Sharp, *Spirit Lake*, 86-91; La Foy, "Margaret Marble," in www.iowagreatlakes.com/_his/_memlane/margannmarble. Margaret Ann Carroll was born in Pennsylvania, September 1, 1837, to William Carroll and Ann Zigley Carroll. She was married at 19 years of age to Mr. Marble. They moved from Linn County, Iowa, to Spirit Lake in the fall of 1856.

[10] Gardner Sharp, *Spirit Lake*, 98, 106-07, 120-25, 156; Folwell, *History of Minnesota Vol 2*, 402-4.

[11] Gardner Sharp, *Spirit Lake*, 159-63.

[12] Gardner Sharp, *Spirit Lake*, 164-70.

[13] Gardner Sharp, *Spirit Lake*, 183-85; Clodfelter, *Dakota War*, 31.

[14] Gardner Sharp, *Spirit Lake*, 189-90, 195-97; Clodfelter, *Dakota War*, 31-32.

[15] Gardner Sharp, *Spirit Lake*, 226-32; Clodfelter, *Dakota War*, 32.

[16] Gardner Sharp, *Spirit Lake*, 197; La Foy, "Margaret Marble," in www.iowagreatlakes.com/_his/_memlane/margannmarble

[17] Gardner Sharp, *Spirit Lake*, 251-55, 258-60; Olson, "Tragedy and the Log Cabin, 61.

[18] Gardner Sharp, *Spirit Lake*, 262-64, 266-69, 275-76. The bank failed a few months later in the Crash of 1857, and Abbie lost every dollar.

[19] Gardner Sharp, *Spirit Lake*, 277-79, 284.

[20] Gardner Sharp, *Spirit Lake*, 287-90, 349; Folwell, *History of Minnesota Vol.2*, 408n12; Olson, "Tragedy and the Log Cabin," 62-63, 68-69.

[21] Tolzmann, ed.,*German Pioneer Accounts*, 5; Utley and Washburn, *Indian Wars*, 202.

[22] Carley, *Minnesota's Other Civil War*, 11.

[23] Clodfelter, *Dakota War*, 37.

[24] Tolzmann, ed., *German Pioneer Accounts*, 9; Schultz, *Over the Earth I Come*, 52.

[25] Tolzmann, ed., *German Pioneer Accounts*, 12, 86n11; Bryant and Murch, *Indian Massacre in Minnesota*, 404. La Blaugh's wife and two children were captured. Martha Clausen's home was also on Beaver Creek. On August 19, Indians attacked the cabin, killed her father, husband, and nephew, and captured Martha and her two children. Also at the house was Margaret Cardenelle. Indians killed her father and brother-in-law and captured her and her child. A Dakota named Te-he-hdo-ne-cha raped her. At his trial, he said, "I slept with this woman once—I did bad towards her once—I tell you the truth. Another Indian may have slept with her." Te-he-hdo-ne-cha was one of the thirty-eight Indians hanged at Mankato in December 1862. Heard, "Dakota Conflict Trials," www.law.umkc.edu/faculty/projects/ftrials/dakota/trialrec1.

[26] Schultz, *Over the Earth I Come*, 53; Tolzmann, ed., *German Pioneer Accounts*, 15-16.

[27] Schultz, *Over the Earth I Come*, 72; MHSC, V6, "De Camp Sweet's Narrative," 357; Bryant and Murch, *Indian Massacre in Minnesota*, 340.

[28] Tolzmann, ed., *German Pioneer Accounts*, 17-19, 85; Clodfelter, *Dakota War*, 57. Anderson and Woolworth, *Through Dakota Eyes*, 225, say four white men, 104 white women and children, and 162 mixed-bloods were released. Mattie Williams was also surrendered at Camp Release. She was one of the few women who agreed to testify about being raped. She named Tazoo as one who tied her arms behind her and raped her repeatedly. Tazoo said, "I ravished her." He was later hanged. Heard, "Dakota Conflict Trials" in www.law.umkc.edu/faculty/projects/ftrials/dakota/trialrec3

[29] Tolzmann, ed., *German Pioneer Accounts*, 22.

[30] Tolzmann, ed., *German Pioneer Accounts*, 33, 35, 44.

[31] Tolzmann, ed., *German Pioneer Accounts*, 36-39.

[32] Tolzmann, ed., *German Pioneer Accounts*, 42-43, 90. Ludwig Kitzmann was the son of Paul Kitzmann, and was captured at Sacred Heart Creek. Henrietta was the daughter of Justina and Frederick Krieger of Renville County.

[33] Tolzmann, ed., *German Pioneer Accounts*, 90. August Gluth was either 10 or 14 years old, and a friend of Ludwig's.

[34] Tolzmann, ed., *German Pioneer Accounts*, 45.

[35] Clodfelter, *Dakota War*, 57; Tolzmann, ed., *German Pioneer Accounts*, 47.

[36] Tolzmann, ed., *German Pioneer Accounts*, 48, 57.

[37] Tolzmann, ed., *German Pioneer Accounts*, 58.

[38] Bryant and Murch, *Indian Massacre in Minnesota*, 283; Schultz, *Over the Earth I Come*, 53.

[39] White, "Captivity Among the Sioux," 395, in *MHSC*, IX.

[40] Bryant and Murch, *Indian Massacre in Minnesota*, 275-76; Anderson, *Little Crow*, 128; Clodfelter, *Dakota War*, 41.

[41] White, "Captivity Among the Sioux," 397-98, in *MHSC*, IX; Bryant and Murch, *Indian Massacre in Minnesota*, 276-77; Oehler, *Great Sioux Uprising*, 53-54. Schultz, *Over the Earth I Come*, 54.

[42] Schultz, *Over the Earth I Come*, 55-56; White, "Captivity Among the Sioux," 399-400, in *MHSC*, IX; Bryant and Murch, *Indian Massacre in Minnesota*, 279-81, 285. Henderson got away, only to be killed at the Battle of Birch Coulee. See Oehler, *Great Sioux Uprising*, 180-81.

[43] Schultz, *Over the Earth I Come*, 55-56; Oehler, *Great Sioux Uprising*, 55-56. This Indian was probably White Spider (Unktomiska), aka John C. Wakeman or Big Thunder (Wakantonka). See Anderson and Woolworth, *Through Dakota Eyes*, 60.

[44] Bryant and Murch, *Indian Massacre in Minnesota*, 286-88.

[45] Bryant and Murch, *Indian Massacre in Minnesota*, 290. Little Crow's brother might have been Little Dog or Sunkacistinna. See Anderson and Woolworth, *Through Dakota Eyes*, 95.

[46] Bryant and Murch, *Indian Massacre in Minnesota*, 292; White, "Captivity Among the Sioux," 404, in *MHSC*, IX.

[47] Clodfelter, *Dakota War*, 41. The bodies were those of Captain Marsh, his men, and a post interpreter who were killed by the Indians at the fight at Lower Sioux Ferry on August 18, 1862.

[48] Schultz, *Over the Earth I Come*, 168; Bryant and Murch, *Indian Massacre in Minnesota*, 294-96.

[49] White, "Captivity Among the Sioux," 405-08, 410-11, in *MHSC*, IX.

[50] White, "Captivity Among the Sioux," 413-17, 422, in *MHSC*, IX.

[51] Bryant and Murch, *Indian Massacre in Minnesota*, 283, 297; White, "Captivity Among the Sioux," 424-26, in *MHSC*, IX.

[52] Wakefield, *Six Weeks in the Sioux Tepees*, 25-26, 43-44.

[53] Schultz, *Over the Earth I Come*, 61; Wakefield, *Six Weeks in the Sioux Tepees*, 66, 68.

[54] Wakefield, *Six Weeks in the Sioux Tepees*, 69, 71-72.

[55] Wakefield, *Six Weeks In The Sioux Tepees*, 74-76.

[56] Wakefield, *Six Weeks in the Sioux Tepees*, 78-81.

[57] Wakefield, *Six Weeks in the Sioux Tepees*, 83-84, 87.

[58] Wakefield, *Six Weeks In The Sioux Tepees*, 89-91, 147-48n47. Paul Mazakutemani or Mosmcoota-Moni (He Who Shoots as He Walks) was a Wahpeton and early Christian convert.

[59] Wakefield, *Six Weeks in the Sioux Tepees*, 94, 96, 98-99; Schultz, *Over the Earth I Come*, 220-22.

[60] Wakefield, *Six Weeks in the Sioux Tepees*, 105, 107, 110-12, 116, 118.

[61] Wakefield, *Six Weeks in the Sioux Tepees*, 119-21.

[62] Carley, *The Dakota War of 1862*, 68-70.

[63] Carley, *The Dakota War of 1862*, 72-3; Clodfelter, *Dakota War*, 58-9.

[64] Wakefield, *Six Weeks in the Sioux Tepees*, 121-23.

[65] Wakefield, *Six Weeks in the Sioux Tepees*, 47.

[66] *MHSC*, Vol. 6, "De Camp Sweet's Narrative," 354-58. Anderson, *Little Crow*, 190. Lucy Prescott Pettijohn was the daughter of Philander Prescott and the Dakota Indian Keya's full blood daughter, Mary.

[67] *MHSC*, Vol. 6, "De Camp Sweet's Narrative," 358-60; Anderson and Woolworth, *Through Dakota Eyes*, 27, 97.

[68] *MHSC*, Vol. 6, "De Camp Sweet's Narrative," 361-65; Schultz, *Over the Earth I Come*, 72-73, 131-32; Anderson and Woolworth, *Through Dakota Eyes*, 97N21. Mary Schwandt has a different verson of Anderson's death.

[69] Anderson and Woolworth, *Through Dakota Eyes*, 78, 177, 97n24, 216n10; *MHSC*, Vol. 6, "De Camp Sweet's Narrative," 366-67, 370, 378; Wakefield, *Six Weeks in Sioux Tepees*, 96-97.

[70] Anderson and Woolworth, *Through Dakota Eyes*, 205. Lorenzo Lawrence (Face of the Village or Towanetaton) was born in 1822. His parents were Left Hand and Catherine Totedutawin. Lorenzo married one of Little Crow's half-brother's widows after he had killed the half-brother.

[71] *MHSC*, Vol. 6, "De Camp Sweet's Narrative," 371-74; Anderson and Woolworth, *Through Dakota Eyes*, 207-209.

[72] *MHSC*, Vol. 6, "De Camp Sweet's Narrative," 374-76; Anderson and Woolworth, *Through Dakota Eyes*, 207-13.

[73] MHSC, Vol. 6, "De Camp Sweet's Narrative," 376-77; Anderson and Woolworth, *Through Dakota Eyes*, 214. In Lawrence's version, he says that in the morning they took the canoes to where they found a large military boat and he had the women and children all go under it for protection. Lawrence then spotted a soldier and told him of the situation. The soldier sprinted to the fort and brought back a squad of soldiers and wagons to bring them in.

[74] *MHSC*, Vol. 6, "De Camp Sweet's Narrative," 377-80.

[75] Anderson and Woolworth, *Through Dakota Eyes*, 66n11; Oehler, *Great Sioux Uprising*, 39; McConkey, *Dakota War Whoop*, 36, 38-41.

[76] McConkey, *Dakota War Whoop*, 35, 41-42. Spencer had learned the Dakota language during his business dealings with the Indians and could understand what they were discussing.

[77] Oehler, *Great Sioux Uprising*, 198-99, McConkey, *Dakota War Whoop*, 43-4, 208.

[78] McConkey, *Dakota War Whoop*, 178.

[79] Michno, *Encyclopedia of Indian Wars*, 101-02; Carley, *Sioux Uprising*, 42-44.

[80] McConkey, *Dakota War Whoop*, 180-81; Anderson and Woolworth, *Through Dakota Eyes*, 235.

[81] McConkey, *Dakota War Whoop*, 206-08.

[82] Oehler, *Great Sioux Uprising*, 197-98; McConkey, *Dakota War Whoop*, 209-11; Anderson and Woolworth, *Through Dakota Eyes*, 66n11, 225, 265n3. Spencer was one out of only four white men who were captured and lived. The others were Peter Rousseau, Louis La Belle, and Peter Rouillard, who were French-Canadian and had Dakota wives.

[83] Bryant and Murch, *Indian Massacre In Minnesota*, 131; McConkey, *Dakota War Whoop*, 308. Bryant said Ingalls had two daughters and two sons. McConkey said they had three daughters and one son.

[84] Anderson and Woolworth, *Through Dakota Eyes*, 73-75; Bryant and Murch, *Indian Massacre in Minnesota*, 130-31.

[85] Anderson and Woolworth, *Through Dakota Eyes*, 76-78, 95n5, 131.

[86] Anderson and Woolworth, *Through Dakota Eyes*, 132-33.

[87] *Commissioner of Indian Affairs 1863*, 272; Bryant and Murch, *Indian Massacre in Minnesota*, 149, 379; McConkey, *Dakota War Whoop*, 97, 316n106. McConkey says John's last name was Julien; Anderson, *Little Crow*, 169, says his last name was Euni; his Manderfeld cousin said John's last name was Smerch.

[88] McConkey, *Dakota War Whoop*, 97-8; Bryant and Murch, *Indian Massacre in Minnesota*, 150, 381-88.

[89] McConkey, *Dakota War Whoop*, 316-317.

[90] Bryant and Murch, *Indian Massacre In Minnesota*, 238-39; McConkey, *Dakota War Whoop*, 123-26; Folwell, *History of Minnesota 2*, 164.

[91] McConkey, *Dakota War Whoop*, 316-17; Anderson, *Little Crow*, 161. George Ingalls's little brother disappeared from the record.

[92] McConkey, *Dakota War Whoop*, 309, 318-19; Anderson, *Little Crow*, 169. Anderson says the Dakotas approached the Mandans in the traditional fashion by whooping and firing guns, and the Mandans' response was to attack.

[93] McConkey, *Dakota War Whoop*, 308-09, 308n104, 319-20, 319n107; Anderson, *Little Crow*, 172, 231n28.

[94] Bryant and Murch, *Indian Massacre in Minnesota*, 153; "Koch Cabin Lake Shetek," in http://www.rrcnet.org/~historic/kcabin.html. Bloody Lake was not named because of the 1862 massacre. It was named years before the incident, because certain tree roots and plants on the

water's edge gave the lake a rusty color (per Wayne and Connie Anderson, who live today on the site of the Koch cabin).

[95] Oehler, *Great Sioux Uprising*, 105; Anderson, *Little Crow*, 31, 42.

[96] Eastlick, *Personal Narrative*, 4-6.

[97] Silvernale, *Commemoration of the Sioux Uprising,* 12; Oehler, *Great Sioux Uprising*, 106

[98] Oehler, *Great Sioux Uprising*, 106-07; Eastlick, *Personal Narrative*, 7-8.

[99] Oehler, *Great Sioux Uprising*, 107-08; Eastlick, *Personal Narrative*, 10. Background, names, and ages of the Eastlick family were supplied by Judith Penhiter, a descendent of Lavina through Johnny.

[100] Oehler, *Great Sioux Uprising*, 108-09; Eastlick, *Personal Narrative*, 10-11.

[101] Oehler, C.M., *Great Sioux Uprising*, 109-13; Eastlick, *Personal Narrative*, 10-13.

[102] Eastlick, *Personal Narrative*, 17-18, 46, 50; Oehler, *Great Sioux Uprising*, 113-14. The death of about 14 settlers in and around the slough gave the area a new name: Slaughter Slough.

[103] Eastlick, *Personal Narrative*, 50-51.

[104] Bryant and Murch, *Indian Massacre in Minnesota*, 155; Eastlick, *Personal Narrative*, 51-52.

[105] "Shetek Massacre," http://www.rrcnet.org/~historic/shetekll.htm; Anderson, *Little Crow*, 156;

[106] Eastlick, *Personal Narratrive*, 49, 52-53; Oehler, *Great Sioux Uprising*, 115-16.

[107] Oehler, *Great Sioux Uprising*, 116; Eastlick, *Personal Narrative*, 59, 60, 64; "The Everett Family," http://www.historical.waseca.mn.us/family.htm; "Shetek Massacre," http://www.rrcnet.org/~historic/shetekll.htm; Penhiter correspondence.

[108] Gray, "*Santee and Lake Shetek*," 48-50.

[109] Gray, "*Santee and Lake Shetek*," 46-47; McConkey, *Dakota War Whoop*, 287; *Commissioner of Indian Affairs 1862*, 523.

[110] Gray, "Santee and Lake Shetek," 50-53.

[111] "The Everett Family," http://www.historical.waseca.mn.us/family.htm; "Shetek Massacre," http://www.rrcnet.org/~historic/shetekll.htm; Eastlick, *Personal Narrative*, 59, 60, 64.

MAPS

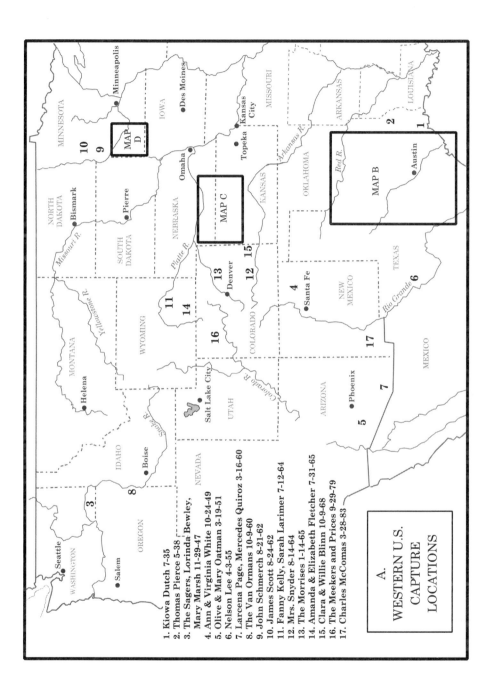

A.
WESTERN U.S.
CAPTURE
LOCATIONS

1. Kiowa Dutch 7-35
2. Thomas Pierce 5-38
3. The Sagers, Lorinda Bewley,
   Mary Marsh 11-29-47
4. Ann & Virginia White 10-24-49
5. Olive & Mary Oatman 3-19-51
6. Nelson Lee 4-3-55
7. Larcena Page, Mercedes Quiroz 3-16-60
8. The Van Ormans 10-9-60
9. John Schmerch 8-21-62
10. James Scott 8-24-62
11. Fanny Kelly, Sarah Larimer 7-12-64
12. Mrs. Snyder 8-14-64
13. The Morrises 1-14-65
14. Amanda & Elizabeth Fletcher 7-31-65
15. Clara & Willie Blinn 10-9-68
16. The Meekers and Prices 9-29-79
17. Charles McComas 3-28-83

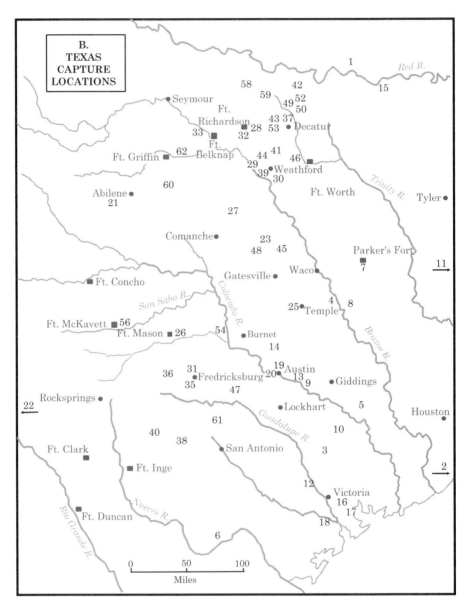

See Appendix 1 for list of names.

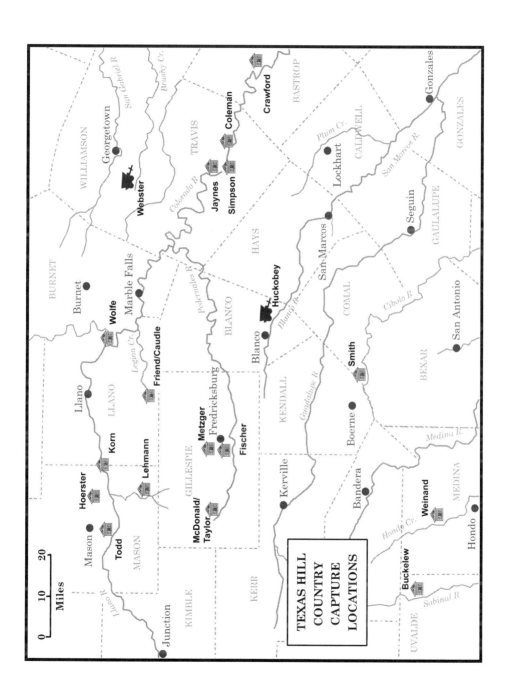

TEXAS HILL
COUNTRY
CAPTURE
LOCATIONS

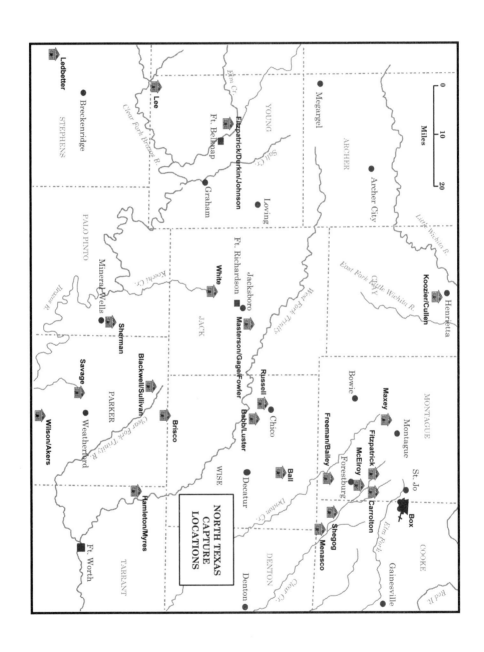

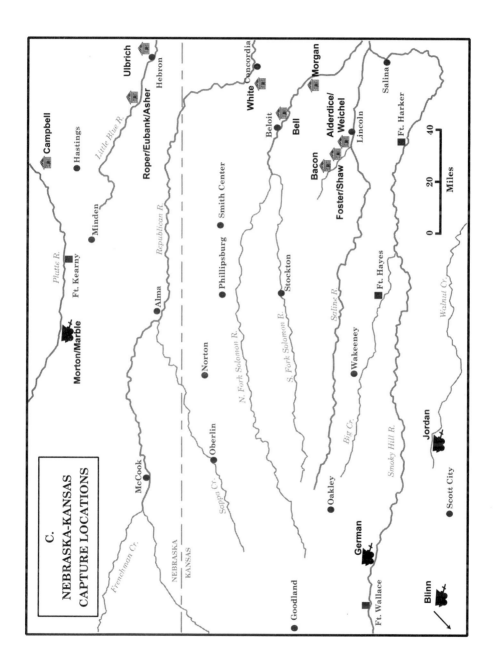

C.
NEBRASKA-KANSAS
CAPTURE LOCATIONS

Campbell

Ulbrich

Roper/Eubank/Asher

White

Concordia

Morgan

Salina

Bell

Alderdice/
Weichel

Bacon

Foster/Shaw

Hebron

Hastings

Beloit

Lincoln

Ft. Harker

Little Blue R.

Minden

Smith Center

Phillipsburg

Stockton

Ft. Kearny

Platte R.

Republican R.

Alma

Morton/Marble

Norton

N. Fork Solomon R.

S. Fork Solomon R.

Saline R.

Ft. Hayes

Wakeeney

Oberlin

McCook

Sappa Cr.

Big Cr.

Smoky Hill R.

Jordan

Oakley

Scott City

German

Goodland

Frenchman Cr.

NEBRASKA

KANSAS

Ft. Wallace

Blinn

Walnut Cr.

0   20   40

Miles

249

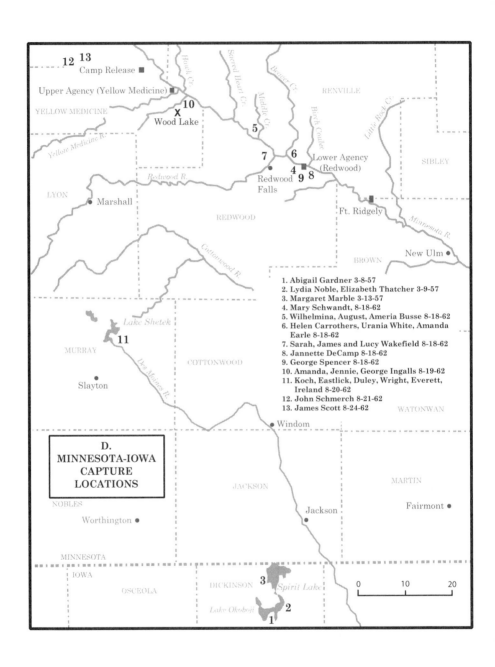

1. Abigail Gardner 3-8-57
2. Lydia Noble, Elizabeth Thatcher 3-9-57
3. Margaret Marble 3-13-57
4. Mary Schwandt, 8-18-62
5. Wilhelmina, August, Ameria Busse 8-18-62
6. Helen Carrothers, Urania White, Amanda Earle 8-18-62
7. Sarah, James and Lucy Wakefield 8-18-62
8. Jannette DeCamp 8-18-62
9. George Spencer 8-18-62
10. Amanda, Jennie, George Ingalls 8-19-62
11. Koch, Eastlick, Duley, Wright, Everett, Ireland 8-20-62
12. John Schmerch 8-21-62
13. James Scott 8-24-62

D.
MINNESOTA-IOWA
CAPTURE
LOCATIONS

250

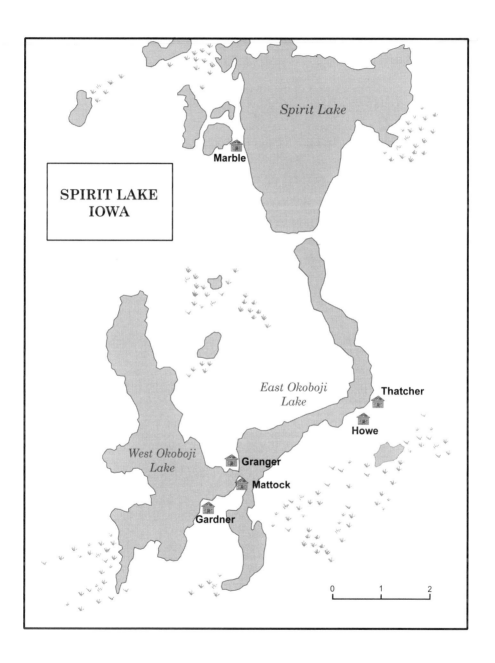

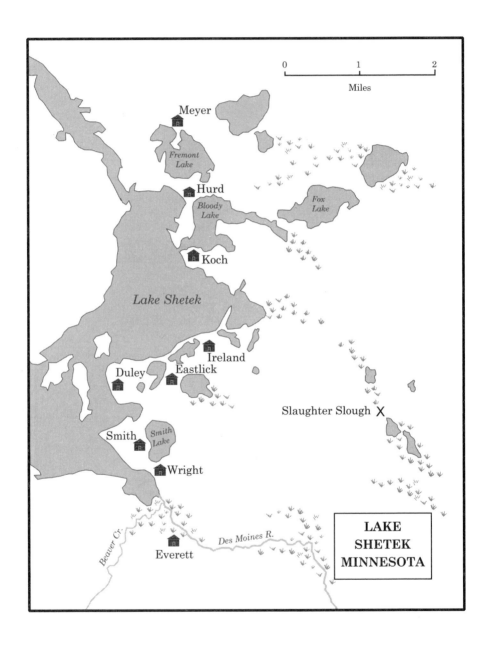

0   1   2
Miles

Meyer

Fremont
Lake

Hurd

Bloody
Lake

Fox
Lake

Koch

Lake Shetek

Ireland

Duley   Eastlick

Slaughter Slough X

Smith   Smith
         Lake

Wright

Beaver Cr.

Des Moines R.

Everett

LAKE
SHETEK
MINNESOTA

Chapter Six

CIVIL WAR YEARS

Don't let them carry me away! — Alice Todd

Merciful God! Have you at last heard me? — Sarah Morris.

The removal of federal troops from the West in 1861 caused an initial decline in fighting between soldiers and Indians, but as state and territorial volunteers were enrolled, the number of fights increased steadily from 1862 to 1865. Likewise, Indian raids on settlers decreased in 1861, with a very noticeable decline in Texas. The respite was short-lived, however, as the Dakotas in Minnesota began a bloody uprising in 1862, and frontier settlers across the Plains had more to fear than they did in antebellum years. Texas was once again plagued with the majority of raids.[1]

In 1861, Henry Scott and a Mexican boy were captured near their homes in Brownsville, Texas, but one night both stole horses from their Indian captors and rode home. In August 1863, Elizabeth J. Brown (12) was captured from her home on Patrick's Creek in Parker County, Texas. The raiders killed Harriet Brown, her mother, and Sarah Brown, her sister, but while the Indians were attacking a nearby cabin, Elizabeth escaped, pulling an arrow out of her flesh as she ran away. James Blair (9) was captured near his home in southeast Callahan County, on February 28, 1864. He shot at one of the warriors but they wrestled him off his horse and tied him up. When they went to steal horses they left him behind, but James untied himself and began walking home across the snowy prairie. His father found him the next day about five miles from home.

In the fall of 1864, five Lipans attacked the George Schwandner home in Real County, on the site of present-day Camp Wood, Texas. They killed Mrs. Schwandner and carried off Albert (8). George Schwandner and a posse pursued the raiders to the Pecos River, where they got in a gun battle with them and Mr. Schwandner was wounded. The Lipans stripped off Albert's clothes and whipped him. Eventually, the Indians evaded the posse and rode west near Paso del Norte, where they traded Albert to a Mexican for a horse and some liquor. He remained with a Mexican family until an American on business in Mexico discovered him one day and learned the particulars of his capture. He went back to Texas, found George Schwandner, and the two men returned to ransom Albert. In 1865, Comanches captured Sarah (10) and Eve Thomas in Nueces County. Eve tried to escape and was stabbed and left by the roadside, but she survived. Sarah was kept until an Indian agent, Church Rollins, discovered her and traded an Indian boy for her.[2]

***

WILLIAM WILSON AND HANNAH AKERS
Texas, ca. July 25, 1863

It had been more than two years since the last large raid into Parker County, and perhaps the settlers had let their guard down. In July 1863, several families living near Mt. Nebo, twelve miles south of Weatherford, Texas, gathered together to make sorghum into molasses at Oliver Fulton's new mill on Spring Creek, about one mile northwest of Mt. Nebo. Living with Fulton were his two orphan nieces, Lou and Hannah Akers. Fulton's brother-in-law, Hiram Wilson, lived one mile southwest of Mt. Nebo. It was customary for the youngsters to have a "candy pull" after the molasses making was done. When Fulton discovered his oxen were too wild to pull the sweep of his ox-powered mill, he asked his nephew, William Wilson (12), to walk the two miles back to his house and ask to borrow his father's oxen. He sent Hannah Akers (12) along with him. Mrs. Richardson, who lived about halfway between the Wilson and Fulton homes, saw the two children go by about ten in the morning.[3]

When the two were only half a mile from the Wilson house, seven painted Comanches rode out of the woods toward them. Bill thought he could have run safely home, but Hannah pleaded with him not to leave her. They both ran, but the Indians were soon upon them. A warrior knocked Bill down with the butt of his lance, and directed him to get on the horse behind him. Hannah cried, and angrily swung her bonnet, but she was soon placed on a horse behind a rider. The Indians rode for Mt. Nebo.

On the way they crossed the trail used by the children to walk to the schoolhouse on Long Creek. Jack and Mary Richardson were

Author's photo
Mt. Nebo, south of Weatherford, Texas, near site of Wilson, Akers captures.

traveling along the path and saw the riders, but mistook them for settlers. Once on top of Mt. Nebo, the Indians spent a long time looking for pursuers and planning their next action. They could see the unsuspecting settlers busy making sorghum, still unaware that two children had been captured. The Comanches were dissatisfied that they had only rustled fifteen head of horses about eight miles southwest of Weatherford, but were soon elated when they saw a wagon train of settlers with plenty of horses, go into camp on the east side of the mountain.

The Indians waited until nightfall. Two stayed behind to guard Bill and Hannah, while the other five crept downhill, rounded up eighteen horses, and brought them back to the foot of the mountain. They were "necked" together for travel and the victorious Comanches with their horses and captives rode off to the west, using the moonlight to illuminate their path.

The "candy pull" at Fulton's place ended about nine p.m. and Jack Richardson (14) walked home. When he reached his yard he heard the rumbling of hooves, and assumed they were runaway cattle. Hiram Wilson and Oliver Fulton were not aware that their children were missing. Each assumed the cousins had spent the night at the other's home. It was not until the next day when Wilson visited Fulton to see how the sorghum making was progressing, that they both learned the children were gone. Just then, a rider approached with the news that Indians were seen crossing the Brazos the day before, heading for Mt. Nebo. They finally realized the children had been taken.[4]

The Indians rode all night and crossed the Brazos before they stopped to rest. They rolled Bill in a blanket so he could not move, and slept on both ends. They let Hannah sleep beside them unguarded. Before daylight, Bill had a nightmare and began talking loudly in his sleep. The voice startled the Indians awake and Bill thought they were going to kill him. Instead, they threw the children on horses and rode off again. At midday they stopped to eat at Sunday Creek near the Erath-Palo Pinto County line. The Indians let Bill and Hannah talk, and they discussed their situation. Bill tried to cooperate, but Hannah fought with them and cried when she realized that she might be forced to live with an Indian family.

The settlers around Mt. Nebo organized a search party, which included Wilson and Fulton, Ike and James Seela, J. W. Richardson, and his son, Jack. They followed the trail two days before losing it, and sadly returned home. Another party had more luck. When the raiders were seen coming through a gap in the Palo Pinto Mountains and heading east to the settlements, about forty-five frontier scouts under Captain Hughes, who were camped around present-day Ranger, moved to the pass, hoping to intercept the Indians when they returned. It was a longshot, but the scouts placed a horse and a mule as bait, in the trail leading up to the pass.

Remarkably, the raiders chose to exit by the same path. Two Indians rode in front, with Bill and Hannah next in line, then the horses, and five Indians bringing up the rear. Part way up the pass, the lead Indians spotted the horse and mule in the moonlight. One had a saddle on it, and tied to it was an old white hat with turkey feathers. The puzzled Indians halted, consulted, and then one howled like a wolf, and others hooted like an owl or gobbled like a turkey at short intervals. There was no answer. The curious warriors rode forward to investigate when the night air was shattered by gunfire.

The lead horses were hit, as was the old roan that Bill and Hannah rode. The children tumbled to the ground and took shelter behind a boulder. Bill was certain that the gunfire came from rescuers at Mt. Nebo and he couldn't understand why they were shooting at him. One of the men was Judge Marvell from Stephenville. He considered himself one of the best shots on the frontier. He fired at Bill six times and couldn't believe he missed him. When most of the horses were killed and the firing slackened, Bill called out for the men to stop. A voice answered, "Just wait till I load my gun and I will be down there."

256

Another voice asked if they were prisoners. Bill answered in the affirmative and told them to come down and see.

"You come up here," the man called out, "and be sure to hold your hands up. If you are a prisoner, don't be afraid."[5]

Hannah was once more in tears and afraid to move, but Bill told her to put her hands up and follow him out. When she saw they were white men, she fainted. The children were safe, but the horses fared badly, almost every one being killed or wounded. The Indians were gone. If any were hit, their comrades had carried them off. After the fight, they rode a few miles to the Clayton Ranch and rested. Captain Hughes sent a rider to Mt. Nebo to tell the families that the children were safe. The next day they rode to Stephenville. Hannah was too weak to ride a horse back to Mt. Nebo, so Judge Marvell put her in his buggy, and with Bill Wilson riding a horse along side, they slowly made their way back home.

The children were captive only about four days, and, compared to how most prisoners were treated, they were in good shape. Just about the only losses were Bill's straw hat and Hannah's bonnet. All things considered, they were extremely lucky. Hiram Wilson and Oliver Fulton, however, were in no mood to tempt fortune. They packed up their families and moved to Dallas County, where hopefully, they would encounter no more Indians.[6]

ANNA METZGER
Texas, February 1864

Peter Metzger emigrated from Nassau, Germany, and settled on the headwaters of Palo Alto Creek in Gillespie County, Texas. About 1861, he moved his family farther south to be closer to his countrymen, on the divide above Palo Alto Creek and about three miles north of Fredericksburg. One of his daughters, Katy, was employed at the Nimitz Hotel in Fredericksburg, while two others, Emma (14) and Anna (11), helped their mother around the farm. One day in February 1864, Mrs. Metzger sent Anna and Emma to Fredericksburg to deliver a message to Katy. It was cold and the ground was covered with snow. The girls bundled up for the little trip that they considered more of pleasure than labor.

In town they delivered the message and lingered, talking to their friends until the sun was getting low. It was nearly six p.m. when they started home. On the way, they passed Charlie Wattenbach, who would become Anna's husband years later. "At that tender age," she said, "I felt inclined to speak a few words to him." She did, but rather shyly, and the two girls hurried on to be home before dark. Two miles from town they saw several riders in the road ahead and thought they were rangers going to Fort Martin Scott. When they closed, the girls saw they were Indians. They tried to run, but were caught immediately. A warrior caught Anna, jerked her by her hair up on his horse, and tied her up. Emma Metzger was stronger, pulled away and ran. They grabbed her and lost her three times. Anna heard her scream that she would never be taken alive by Indians. The last time she broke free she fell to the ground, kneeled down, and began to pray. One warrior, fed up with her resistance, put an arrow through her. "The Indian then scalped her," said Anna, "deprived her of her clothing, mutilated her body in other ways and left her lying upon the cold snow." The Indians rode away with Anna. She remembered Emma's face until the day she died. "I saw my sister's ghastly look as she fell to the ground," she recalled. "It was one of horror mixed with pleading. That look I shall never forget."[7]

That night the Indians camped near Kreuzberg (Cross Mountain), a hill north of Fredericksburg. While the Indians made camp and prepared to eat, they ordered Anna to do things, but when she didn't understand, she said, they "took turns in beating me with their quirts. I cried till my eyes were swollen; but the more I wept the more I was beaten." They also pulled her by the hair "so that I thought none of it would remain." That night she nearly froze, because the Indians had taken most of her clothes and she had only "a blanket of snow" for a bed. While she waited in camp, some warriors went out to steal horses, the brands of which Anna recognized as her neighbors'.

After returning with the stolen horses, the Indians broke camp about midnight and rode west. A posse was formed the next morning, which included young Charlie Wattenbach. They trailed the Indians to Pecan Creek, Town Creek, and to the headwaters of the Pedernales near present-day Harper, after which they lost the tracks. The Indians rode for nine days, with Anna blindfolded the entire time. She had no idea where they went. When they removed the blindfold she found herself in a desert-like prairie like she had never seen before. They crossed a river, which she later learned was the Red, and came to a village. The women jerked her from the horse, Anna said, "and beat me in a most atrocious and unmerciful manner," all the while her captors whooped in hilarity. In the village the children called her "The White Devil," as she understood when she later learned the language. That night they held a scalp dance, and warriors thrust her sister's clothing and bloody scalp in Anna's face. All the while, she said, "the squaws and younger Indians were taking turns in beating me and lacerating my flesh." After the ceremony they painted Anna's face and gave her to a family as a slave.

Some of Anna's tasks were to skin and dress animals and carry wood. They loaded her with such heavy burdens that she often collapsed under the weight. When she fell she "was kicked and beaten unmercifully as if I had been a donkey." She also had to care for several "little naked papooses." When she got to know some of the older children, they asked her her name. She answered, "Anna Metzger," but they could not pronounce it; it came out "Allamot."[8]

Anna later heard it said that some Indians were good; she found that hard to believe, but she did know of one. Her owner had two wives, and while one was a demon, the other was kind to her and saved her from many a beating. Anna was thankful for that. The woman could not help her every time, however. When a mule Anna was tending ran away, it merited another "severe and protracted beating from the warriors." It seemed that Anna was doomed to be pummeled by every person in the tribe.

When spring arrived and the wildflowers bloomed, it reminded Anna of her home in Texas, and she heartily wished she could get away and be with her parents again. She did not know where she was, but guessed it to be either Kansas or Oklahoma. Her remembrances are of little else but "a repetition of savage cruelty on the one hand and suffering on the other."

Things changed in the summer of 1864, when Anna was allowed to accompany the Indians to a trading post run by a man she remembered as Major Floor. He recognized her as a white child and offered to buy her. They haggled over a price and agreed, but when the Indian women heard of the deal, they vehemently protested; apparently Anna was much too valuable to them as a slave. Anna understood the conversation and "kept looking at him (Floor) with imploring eyes," but the deal was not concluded. That night Floor went to the Indian camp and tried again to bargain for Anna's release, but was again unsuccessful. When he left, Anna began crying. Her captor, who Anna called "Snake-In-The-Grass," asked her if she wanted to go home. She said she did. With that, he whipped her with his lariat, and asked her the question again. This time she said no, which ended the whipping for the time being.

That night, Anna resolved to run away. She crawled to the edge of the tipi, pulled up the side, and slid out. She stumbled through the darkness, but was certain she could find her way to Major Floor's store. Then, another thought came to her. Floor "had many Negroes employed" and she was afraid she would run into one of them, so she hid in a field until daylight. She waited until it was broad daylight and no one seemed to be around, then she dashed for the store. To Anna's surprise she ran right into Major Floor talking to a band of Indians. Anna stopped in horror, but Floor took her by the hand and led her past the Indians, "who had looked viciously" at her. He took her upstairs to his wife, and she assured the girl that the Indians would not be allowed to get her. Floor went down and pacified the angry warriors by giving them fine Navajo blankets and $25 in cash. Anna was afraid to leave the store.[9]

Three days later the Indians returned and asked to see the white girl, but Floor told them that she was gone. They eyed the room suspiciously and left. Eight days after that, a white stranger dressed in a soldier's uniform came to Floor's trading post and asked about the white captive he heard was bought from the Indians. He said he had come to take the girl back home to her parents. Anna was standing nearby and Floor suspected treachery.

"Where was the girl captured?" he asked.

"Somewhere near San Antonio," the man answered.

Floor asked Anna where she was taken.

"On Palo Alto Creek near Fredericksburg," she replied.

Floor knew that was not a great distance from San Antonio, but then he asked if the man could show papers to substantiate his claim. He said he could not and Floor told him to leave. When the man hesitated, Floor said if he did not get out immediately he would set his bulldog on him. The stranger stepped outside, ran across the yard, and climbed the fence.

Anna stayed two more months in Floor's home while he advertised in the Texas newspapers about having a freed white captive named Anna Metzger. Finally, a neighbor brought a paper to the Metzger's and they were delighted with the news. Anna's brother, Joe Metzger, William Merta, Jacob Leindecker, and Jim Schmidt prepared to make a journey on horseback to bring her home. At this time, Major Floor went to visit some of his relatives, a family named Spoon, who lived along the Indian Territory side of Red River. Anna accompanied them. They were there about two weeks when a man who Anna remembered as Louis Stoeffens, came to see Floor and explained that he knew the Metzgers in Fredericksburg. After some indecision, Floor agreed to send Anna with Stoeffens. She was at his home another two weeks when her brother Joe and his companions finally tracked her down.

After a happy reunion, they saddled up to return to Fredericksburg. Joe was about to get a wagon for Anna to ride in, but she insisted she would ride a horse and "go back the way I left." They rode south many hours a day. On the way, Anna tried to converse with the men, but she had forgotten much of her German language. She could understand them, but found it hard to express herself. She "talked" around the campfires at night by a combination of German, Kiowa, and sign language, which greatly amused her escorts.

After seven days the country began to look familiar to Anna, and when she saw Kreuzberg she knew she was nearly home. Upon approaching their house, Joe Metzger fired off a couple of shots, a pre-arranged signal to let the family know that they had been successful. Anna remembered it was a Sunday evening in November 1864. Mrs. Metzger ran outside to greet them, but was horrified when she saw her little girl, still with painted face and Indian garb; Anna wanted to show her what she looked like while in captivity. That night, she tried to explain everything that had happened to her, but struggled through her standard combination of languages and gestures to make herself understood. It took months before she could again converse fluently in German. A few days after she returned home, Anna took her family to the exact place she had been captured. There on the ground were her sister's slippers.

Anna married Charlie Wattenbach several years later and lived with him the rest of her life. They lived at Mason, Texas, for many years. About fifty years after her capture, Anna told her story to Leonard Passmore and it was printed in a 1924 issue of *Frontier Times*. Ann Metzger Wattenbach died about 1934.[10]

ELONZO WHITE
Texas, ca. July 25, 1864

The David White and Earl Kemp families were living on the old Jack Bailey place on the Keechi, about nine miles southwest of Jacksboro, Texas. They had recently moved from Palo Pinto County and were just settling in. The women had spent most of the day doing laundry and had hung the clothes to dry on the bushes along the creek. Mr. Kemp was away from the home. In the evening, Mr. White noticed dark clouds gathering and he decided he had better hurry over to see a neighbor that he had to do business with before the storm hit. Mrs. White and Mrs. Kemp were preparing supper and asked the children to gather in the laundry before the rain came. Sarah Kemp (16), her two younger brothers, Elonzo "Lon" White (9) went to gather the clothes, which were about 100 yards from the cabin.

Bursting with energy, Lon went running far in advance of the others, leaving the rest scolding him to come back and help carry the load. Just then, a small band of Comanches sprang out from behind the clothing-draped bushes and surrounded them. When Lon turned around he saw the Indians, but was cut off from home. Sarah put up a fight and broke free, and her struggle made time for her two brothers to run into the brush. Sarah ran, but a warrior shot a bullet into her right side. When she fell, another attacker grabbed her and placed his knife to her head. He tried to get a grip on her hair, but got tangled up in the intricate hair net she wore. While the Indians tried to get the net off, the Kemps' bulldog ran up and bit one of them on the leg. When they turned their attention to the dog, Sarah got up and ran again. She got halfway home where she met Mrs. Kemp and Mrs. White, both armed with rifles. The Comanches were startled by the two armed and determined women advancing toward them, and headed the other way. When they did, they ran right into Lon White.

Everyone made it back to the house, shut the doors and windows, and waited for the probable attack when they realized Lon was not there. In a few minutes it was nearly dark, and the returning David White heard crying before he got to the door. When he learned what happened, he ran to the spot Lon was last seen, but it was too dark to find any tracks. The next morning, White and some neighbors got a search party together. They found Lon's tracks leading toward the Keechi and saw signs of a struggle on a sandbar in the river. Another storm came in and washed away all the remaining tracks. They returned to their homes while Mr. White planned ways to recover his boy. Weatherford physician Doctor Valentine, treated Sarah's wounds, and she eventually recovered.[11]

White moved his family out of Jack County and back to Palo Pinto County, settling near where the town of Santo is now located. He kept up with the news, searching out any information that might help him find his son.

In October 1864, Indians raided along Elm Creek in Young County, and captured members of the Durkin, Fitzpatrick, and Johnson families. A Negro named Britt Johnson was searching for them (see Charlotte Durkin) and David White contacted him. The men went to see Brigadier General James W. Throckmorton, commander of the First Frontier District and one of two

Confederate Commissioners of Indians (the other being Albert Pike). Throckmorton informed them that a meeting would take place in Indian Territory, scheduled for May 15, 1865, at Camp Napoleon, near present-day Verden, Oklahoma. More than 5,000 Indians met with Confederate and Mexican officials in a great peace conference held before news of General Robert E. Lee's surrender in Virginia reached the area. In the end, all agreements fell through with the dissolution of the Confederacy. However, Throckmorton arranged for the release of nine white captives, and White and Johnson were among the beneficiaries, picking up a few other captives in the process.[12]

Many of the captives were being held in Peneteka Chief Tosawi's (Silver Brooch) camp. The Peneteka Asa Havey (Milky Way), who was considered a peacemaker, was instrumental in gaining the captives' release. Asa Havey knew Britt Johnson when the latter worked at Fort Belknap in 1859, while the Comanches were still on their Texas Reservation. With Throckmorton's help, White and Johnson were allowed to accompany Asa Havey up the Washita to bargain for more captives, paying out a number of horses, goods, and a $20 gold piece. White got his son back for a horse, a blanket, and some trinkets.[13]

After nearly a year with the Comanches, Lon White thought he was being tricked when he was told to enter a tipi and go to his father. He hesitated, as if unsure of what awaited him, but once he saw his father, the boy ran to his arms. Lon asked in broken English, "Did the Indians kill Mama and the other children?" David White was shocked at his son's appearance. The Indians had stained his skin with a pecan shell dye, and he was as dark as any Comanche. After bargaining, White and Johnson had no horses to make the journey home so Asa Havey gave them four ponies out of his own herd. In Weatherford, Texas, the citizens came out to show their approval. White returned George Light's boy and two men from Jack County came to pick up the Rowland boy. When they tried to take him, he cried and fought, wanting to remain with "Uncle" White. Thirteen months since Lon White was captured, he was at last reunited with his mother.[14]

ELIZABETH ANN FITZPATRICK, CHARLOTTE AND MILLY JANE DURKIN, AND MARY JOHNSON
October 13, 1864

Nearly 500 Comanche and Kiowa raiders struck Young County in the fall of 1864, along Elm Creek, northwest of Fort

Belknap. As they raided ranches, some settlers hid, while others spread the alarm. A number of them "forted up" at George Bragg's Ranch. The defenders of "Fort Bragg," and another strongpoint, "Fort Murrah," held off the Indians. The Comanche Little Buffalo, who organized the raid, was killed while fighting at Bragg's.

Lieutenant N. Carson, Company D, of Colonel James Bourland's Border Regiment, pursued about 300 raiders who drove off hundreds of stolen horses. Carson's men rode into an ambush and were forced to retreat. As they fell back, the soldiers rescued two women from the McCoy house. During the raid, the Indians lost about twenty warriors, mostly in the fight at Bragg's Ranch and with Carson's soldiers. Carson lost five killed and about five wounded, while seven civilians were killed and two wounded.

The most memorable incident of the raid occurred during the late morning on Thursday, October 13, only a few miles northwest of Fort Belknap, when the Indians swept down on the Fitzpatrick Ranch, a two-story house once called the Carter Trading Post. Milly Susanna Carter Durkin (21) (mulatto) futilely tried to defend the others with a shotgun, but she was tomahawked, dragged outside, tortured, gang-raped, scalped, and killed.

There were no men home that day. Inside the house were Milly's mother, Elizabeth Ann Carter Sprague Fitzpatrick (38); her brother, Elijah Carter (13) (mulatto); Milly's daughter, Charlotte Elizabeth "Lottie" Durkin (5) (quadroon); Milly's daughter, Milly Jane (2) (quadroon); and Milly's newborn, unnamed son (quadroon). A black family also lived there, with Britt Johnson the head of household, but Britt was working at the mill. Britt's pregnant wife, Mary Johnson (24), was home with her daughter (4), and two sons (5 and 7).[15]

While Milly Susanna was being raped, another older boy, Jim Johnson, ran from the house, but Indians killed him before he reached the gate. These violent murders caused the others to decide resistance was useless. Even so, when the Indians found the Durkin baby hidden in a box under the bed, they pulled him out and smashed him against a wall. The rest of residents of the house were tied on ponies, and when the Kiowa Satanta blew a bugle, the raiders took them away.

They rode northwest for almost two days and nights before stopping on Saturday morning near Pease River. Elijah Carter was sick, probably from drinking gypsum water, and he was too ill to travel. The Indians built a fire in a brush heap and threw the boy in it. They forced Elizabeth Fitzpatrick to watch her grandson burn to death. From there the Indians headed into the north

Texas Panhandle. It is uncertain if all the captives were kept together, but at least some of them were in the Indian village on the Canadian River near Bent's old adobe fort when the soldiers attacked on November 25.

Colonel Christopher "Kit" Carson left Fort Bascom on November 12, with about 335 cavalrymen and infantrymen, plus Ute and Jicarilla scouts, searching for Kiowas and Comanches who had been raiding along the Santa Fe Trail. Carson first hit the 150-lodge village of Little Mountain's Kiowas. They fled downstream and Carson followed, coming upon more Indians as he went. When he approached Stumbling Bear's 350 lodges, about 1,000 warriors confronted him. Satanta was present, again blowing his bugle, and now it was Carson's turn to fall back. Kiowas had reoccupied the first village, and Carson's soldiers had to fight their way in again. Only the howitzers kept the charging warriors at bay. Carson wisely vacated the area, but he torched the lodges and supplies before he left—a severe blow to the Indians at the onset of winter. Three soldiers and a scout were killed, and twenty-nine soldiers and scouts were wounded, while the Indians lost about sixty killed and wounded. Some of the captive whites were indirect casualties of the attack.

Milly Jane Durkin had been hidden in the bushes when Carson approached Stumbling Bear's village, and she was whisked away when the Indians counter-attacked. When the soldiers were gone, the angry Indians rode off for help from their kinsmen on the Cimarron River. The months of December 1864, and January 1865, were cold and harsh, and the Indians and their captives suffered greatly. People of all ages perished due to disease, starvation, and exposure. Milly Jane was one of them, dying during what the Kiowas called the "Muddy Traveling Winter." The Indians blamed the "Great Father" for all of their deaths.[16]

The five remaining captives spent the winter and spring in various Comanche and Kiowa camps between the Cimarron and Arkansas Rivers. Few inquiries were made concerning their fate, possibly because they were illiterate, they had few relatives in Texas, and Young County had a very small population and an inefficient government, barely able to manage its own affairs, let alone to organize any rescue attempts. Apparently, the only male relative able and willing to try to rescue the captives was Mary's husband, Britt Johnson. Johnson was strong, honest, respected, and a brave Indian fighter, and he may have made a trip or two into Indian Territory looking for his wife, children, and the Fitzpatricks and Durkins, but he probably did not do all the things he was credited with doing.[17]

Johnson went to Indian Territory with David White (see Elonzo White), who was looking for his own son. In late May 1865, a grand council with many of the Plains tribes was held at Camp Napoleon at Cottonwood Grove, Oklahoma. There, Brigadier General James W. Throckmorton arranged for the release of nine white captives, including members of the Fitzpatrick-Durkin clan, the Johnsons, and White's son, Elonzo.[18]

The Comanche Asa Havey (Milky Way) was instrumental in gaining their release. For a number of horses, blankets, supplies, and a $20 gold piece, he got the captives from Tosawi's Comanches and turned them over to Texas agents at Cottonwood Grove. The first to be released were Mary Johnson, her son and daughter, an infant born to Mrs. Johnson during her captivity, and Lottie Durkin. Britt Johnson gave seven ponies for the return of his family. Lottie was separated from her grandmother and her sister after Carson's attack in November 1864. Lottie reflected her African heritage, and was described as having "dark skin, dark eyes, and dark hair." The Indians tattooed her arms and tattooed a dime-sized blue moon on her forehead, marking her for life. The freed captives were sent to Decatur, Texas. By mid-summer of 1865, they all went to Veal's Station in Parker County, where Britt Johnson had relocated after the Elm Creek attack.[19]

Elizabeth Fitzpatrick was still with the Indians. She had not been sold with her granddaughter or the Johnsons, but was held by different bands, and at one time was with Satanta's Kiowas. The Indians met the whites again for a peace conference, this time on the Little Arkansas in Kansas, in October 1865. Again Britt Johnson was there, trying to recover Texas captives. Before the commissioners would distribute the treaty goods, they demanded that the Indians turn over their prisoners. The Kiowas admitted to having four, and the Comanches had three, but all of them, they claimed, were not with the bands on the Little Arkansas. Five Texas captives were eventually brought in (see Caroline Taylor McDonald), but Elizabeth Fitzpatrick was not among them.[20]

Jesse H. Leavenworth, at times colonel, commissioner, and agent, was busy rounding up any other captives he could locate. With the help of mixed-blood Cherokee Jesse Chisholm and a soldier escort, he rode to Fort Zarah on the Arkansas River. On November 2, 1865, north of the post on Walnut Creek, Leavenworth found a white woman and a small white girl (see Alice Taylor) working like slaves in a Kiowa camp. The woman was Elizabeth Ann Fitzpatrick, and she knew right away what the soldiers were doing there, although she "thought they must be beings from another world," because "their white faces and blue uniforms looked so beautiful."[21]

Elizabeth had been captive just over one year. She had been starved, beaten, and raped, and her obviously pregnant belly was a constant reminder of her treatment. Even now, she and the little Alice Taylor did their chores while nearly naked. Leavenworth took both captives and moved on to a nearby Comanche camp. There he collected another captured Texan, James Benson (9), who was taken from near his home in Backbone Valley in 1865, twelve miles southwest of Burnet, Texas, after the Comanches killed his father. A Mr. W. Dunlap, of Kansas, reclaimed Benson for some cattle. Leavenworth took the three freed captives to Cow Creek Ranch, 115 miles west of Council Grove, arriving there on November 9. After resting, the captives were escorted to the Kaw Agency at Council Grove. On the trip, Elizabeth questioned Leavenworth and learned that her granddaughter, Lottie, had been returned to Texas four months ago. She also learned that Milly Jane died the previous winter, but she refused to believe it.[22]

At Council Grove, Elizabeth Ann Fitzpatrick once more resumed familiar duties: running a household and caring for children. She was born in Alabama on March 29, 1825, and, at 16 years of age, married a free black man, Alexander J. Carter. They lived in Red River and Navarro County, then moved to Milford, Texas, and did business with Fort Graham on the Brazos, engaging in freighting, stock raising, and farming. When the fort closed, the Carters followed the emigration to the frontier at newly established Fort Belknap. Elizabeth Ann raised her children while she ran the rooming-boarding-trading house near the fort. Her husband was murdered in September 1857, her daughter Milly Susanna married Private Owen Durkin in October, and Elizabeth remarried Lieutenant Owen A. Sprague in February 1858. Apparently, the lieutenant did not relish his situation, for by October, he paid off his creditors at Belknap and disappeared. A pregnant Milly lost her husband in February 1859, when soldiers at Belknap murdered Owen Durkin. Milly had another child out of wedlock in 1862, and the same year, Elizabeth Ann married Thomas Fitzpatrick. This marriage lasted eighteen months, until Fitzpatrick was murdered in February 1864. Once again, Elizabeth Ann was a widow. The next disaster occurred in October, when Indians raided Elm Creek.[23]

At the Kaw Agency, Elizabeth Ann met the other Texas women and children who had been held captive and were now at Council Grove: Caroline McDonald, Rebecca McDonald, James Taylor, Dorcas Taylor, and James Ball. Along with Alice Taylor and James Benson, "Grandma" Elizabeth, only 39 years old, took on the duties of supervising and caring for seven women and children. In addition, Agent Hiram W. Farnsworth hired Elizabeth Ann at three dollars per week to cook, clean, sew, and nurse the growing number of people and employees at the agency. In December, Elizabeth was expected to deliver her child, but apparently the baby was stillborn.[24]

With the new year of 1866, the ex-captives were still at the Kaw Agency, with no money, no family, few friends, and no word as to when they might be sent home to Texas. Mrs. McDonald was expected to give birth shortly, and her mid-wife was Elizabeth Fitzpatrick. Amid all her work, Elizabeth still had the spirit to constantly agitate for the ex-captives' return home, plus for the rescue of other captives still on the prairie. "If all the captives still unaccounted for belonged to those whom the business of rescuing them was committed," she complained, "they would have been rescued long ago."

Commissioner D. N. Cooley appointed Leavenworth to accompany the captives back to Texas, but the agent demurred, replying on January 14 that Mrs. McDonald "might be confined any day" and that the trip south would be too hazardous. He figured it would be easier in the spring for the captives to travel to St. Louis, down the Mississippi, and up the Red River to Shreveport, Louisiana. The postponement might also allow him to recover Fitzpatrick's and McDonald's little girls, and Willie Ball, who the Indians still held. Additionally, the women did not want to be sent home 1,000 miles by wagon, as they were in fear of being captured again.

Mrs. McDonald gave birth to a boy in March 1866, and was ready to go home, if only she could yet get her last daughter, Mahala, back from the Indians. Elizabeth too, was sure that Milly Jane was alive and did not want to leave without her. Colonel Leavenworth was still trying to obtain the other captives, but the government was becoming concerned over the cost of maintaining them at the agency. All was in a state of flux, but nothing appeared to be getting resolved. In June, Leavenworth delivered Willie Ball, James's cousin, to Council Grove, and Elizabeth convinced him that she knew where Mahala McDonald (5) was being held. She and Leavenworth rode out, and returned with the girl in two weeks. Finally, it seemed that everyone was together, except for Milly Jane. For Elizabeth, it was more work, for she became the surrogate mother of the two Ball cousins.

By July, the women were frantic to get home. Elizabeth and Caroline tried to make a deal with Thomas H. Green, who had come up to Kansas to take the Ball cousins home. When Elizabeth announced to Farnsworth that they would all go home with Green if the government could not afford it, he notified Superintendent Thomas Murphy of the situation. They had talked about sending the freed captives home by a roundabout water route, but it was too expensive, and Farnsworth did not trust Green to get them home safely. Farnsworth told Elizabeth that he could not pay her yet, and asked if she'd work to September 11. He also suggested that Joseph Dunlap, a government contractor and teamster, could take them home in a government-train. The women jumped at the chance, but an argument continued about the cost for the round trip. Farnsworth eventually discussed the tangled situation with Kansas Senators Samuel C. Pomeroy, Edmund G. Ross, and Congressman Sidney Clarke. They agreed to go to Washington and see that the bill was paid for the captives' return to Texas. Finally, on August 27, 1866, Farnsworth got them all loaded up in five wagons and on the road home.[25]

The trip was long and arduous, and not without dangers. The same month that the freed captives set out, Kiowas under Satanta raided Montague County, in the very area they would pass through, attacking the James Box family, killing the husband and a baby, and carrying off five females (see Mary Box). After the Kiowas cleared the area, the Dunlap train came through and continued south to Decatur, where the passengers were split up into several parties to continue on to their various homes. Elizabeth reached Parker County in October, where she met the Johnsons and her granddaughter, Lottie Durkin.

Elizabeth stayed for a time with the Miers Family, who had been taking care of Lottie. Elizabeth met Isaiah Clifton, and married him in 1869. They moved west to Shackleford County, near the booming area around Fort Griffin. The Miers Family and Lottie moved with them, and Indian troubles seemed to follow them. In Young County, on January 23, 1871, Kiowas killed Britt Johnson and two companions on the Fort Griffin-Fort Richardson Road. In May, General William T. Sherman was at Fort Griffin, and Elizabeth Ann Clifton and Lottie Durkin called on him. They described their ordeal during the 1864 Elm Creek Raid and their subsequent captivity. Elizabeth made it clear that she was not convinced that her granddaughter, Milly Jane, was killed in the winter of 1865. She pleaded with Sherman to re-institute the search, and the general promised that he would.[26]

In November 1880, Isaiah Clifton had a stroke and died; Elizabeth Ann had been abandoned by one husband, and buried three others. Elizabeth Ann appeared more depressed and morose than anyone had seen. Her spirit was gone. Seemingly older than her 57 years, she steadily deteriorated in health, until she died on June 18, 1882. Elizabeth Ann Carter Sprague Fitzpatrick Clifton was buried next to Isaiah, in a mesquite-covered graveyard near the Clear Fork of the Brazos, somewhere below Fort Griffin. The graves were unmarked.[27]

Of the captives of 1864, only Lottie Durkin remained. In 1874, at age 15, she married David H. Barker, the marshal of the town of Fort Griffin. They had two daughters, Ada and Ida. When the buffalo played out, Fort Griffin began a quick decline also, and Barker took his family west to the Panhandle, stopping near the Sweetwater, a few miles from Fort Elliott, at a place that would eventually become Mobeetie. Barker became a deputy, but Mobeetie was doomed also, from drought, prairie fire, cattle fever, and lack of a railroad. In 1886, they moved on to Tascosa, Texas. Lottie's health was never good since her captivity, and she declined more after the birth of a son on July 30, 1887. On August 10, cholera took the life of her little baby, and on the same day, "childbirth fever" claimed Lottie. The lady with the blue moon on her forehead was only 27 years old.

The last of the Elm Creek Raid captives was gone. The story persisted that Milly Jane Durkin was still alive and living with the Kiowas. Britt Johnson was said to have made several trips looking for her. Elizabeth Ann insisted she had seen her with Chief Sun Boy's Kiowas near the Little Arkansas in 1865. Vincent Colyer, Secretary of the Board of Indian Commissioners, met a band of Kiowas near Fort Bascom who claimed to have a girl named "Molly" in captivity, but Colyer's questions assured him that the captive was too old to be Milly Jane. Agents Lawrie Tatum and James Haworth initiated searches for the girl, but could not locate her. The Indians always insisted that Milly Jane died during the first harsh winter after her capture. The woman who married the Kiowa Chief Goombi and died in 1934, at Mountain View, Oklahoma, was not Milly Jane Durkin.[28]

Author's photo
Todd Mountain, south of Mason, Texas, where Alice Todd was captured.

ALICE TODD
Texas, January 7, 1865

The defense of frontier Texas during the Civil War was constantly on the settlers' minds and almost always on the government and military agendas. Although undermanned and underpaid, the official and *ad hoc* organizations did a fair job protecting the western counties from Indian raids. In 1864, the frontier was divided into three districts. Mason County, on the border between the Second and Third District, and with Fort Mason abandoned, was vulnerable. Nevertheless, settlers still struggled to exist in their precarious positions. George Todd, a Virginian, moved to Texas and organized Mason County in 1858. He was the first county clerk, postmaster, and became a lawyer and businessman. George, his wife, Dizenia, and their 13-year-old daughter Alice, lived four miles south of the town. Dizenia's father, Joshua Peters, lived near them on a large plantation and owned several slaves.[29]

Alice had been home from the San Saba Female Seminary for Christmas vacation and was due to return to school. Before leaving, however, she would go into the town of Fort Mason with her parents to see Dizenia's newborn nephew. On January 7, 1865, they rode out, Alice and her father on one horse, and Dizenia and a black female servant on another. Their dogs ran alongside. While crossing a small pass just west of a low mountain, they

271

noticed some men on horseback and assumed they were ranchers out hunting for stray cattle. When the men were right upon them they realized they were Indians. In a flash, the warriors attacked; the black servant was killed first, and Dizenia was hit by an arrow and fell. The Indians even killed the dogs. George's horse reared back and Alice slid off.

"Don't let them carry me away!" Alice shouted to her father, but he sped off, later explaining that he could not stop the frightened animal.[30]

In town, George Todd gathered up some men and rode back to the attack site. Dizenia was still breathing, and would linger for five days before dying. The searchers first followed horse tracks to the east, until they found some travelers who said they saw Indians go by, but insisted that they did not have a white girl with them. The pursuers doubled back, found another trail heading west, and followed it. The weather turned cold and snowy. In Kimble County, a family awoke one morning to find an Indian campsite nearby, with a snowy circle of small footprints around a tree, as if a young person had been tethered to the trunk. The rescue party followed the trail north into Menard County, then west to the Concho River. The trail divided into three branches, and the cold, exhausted pursuers gave up.

George Todd sent word of the abduction to Alice's stepbrother, James H. Smith (19), then serving in the Confederate Army in Arkansas. Smith obtained a furlough to look for his stepsister. His search continued after the war ended in the spring, and Smith's new ally became Colonel and Agent, Jesse. H. Leavenworth. Leavenworth devoted much of his time as an Indian agent hunting captives. Leavenworth arranged for Smith to attend the October 1865, peace council on the Little Arkansas River in Kansas. The Indians admitted to having several captives, but they told Leavenworth that Alice Todd had been killed shortly after her capture. The agent was not convinced and didn't tell James Smith what they had said. Smith returned to Texas with nothing new to report.[31]

The search for Alice Todd ran hot and cold for the next several years. George Todd, perhaps plagued by the thought that he had abandoned her to the Indians, was relentless in his agitation for something to be done, writing to U.S. officials, state officials, the military, and the press. In the spring of 1866, Comanches told Leavenworth that Alice was dead, but he wrote to Todd, telling him that he would continue to search. In August 1866, Todd wrote to Texas Governor James W. Throckmorton, stating that he was poor, and he hoped that the legislature could set aside some money to be used to reclaim Indian prisoners. Jim Smith continued his search, which he partially financed by gathering wild honey in the Texas Hill Country and selling it in town. He fell to his death one day while trying to get honey out of a cave in a bluff above the Llano River.[32]

In 1868, George Todd again heard news of a possible sighting of his daughter. Captain Emil Adam, 39th Infantry, pursued some Kiowa cattle thieves, and when he confronted them in their Kansas camp, he believed he saw Alice. He wrote to Todd, but the questions were, why didn't Adam rescue her if he saw her, or was it perhaps that she didn't want to leave? Her method of rescue, like many others of the time, was snarled in the ongoing argument of whether or not to ransom captives. The military and the agents were handcuffed by the government refusal to encourage the captive trade by paying for prisoners. Todd was angry. He wrote to the Indian commissioner that it was "too cruel to allow her to remain a captive simply on account of a bad precedent." Later, the tormented father pleaded, "For God sake, for my dear child's sake, for humanities sake, aside from my feelings will the Government allow anything to stand between my dear child and liberty?"[33]

Captain Adam continued writing to Todd, stating that he learned that Alice was claimed by a Mexican and had a child. Todd was devastated. If his daughter had a husband and child of her own, how willing would she be to go back to a father who had deserted her? The dickering over how to best recover Alice was given a new twist in July 1868. The Kiowa band moved, and with it disappeared the girl—if it was Alice to begin with.

Todd sent more letters to the commissioner, expressing his dissatisfaction with Agent Leavenworth and everyone else who couldn't, or wouldn't, get his daughter back when they had the chance. Todd rued the day he moved to Texas. He pleaded for the bureau not to give the Indians guns and ammunition, "for they come right down here and use them on us." He wanted to get away, he said, "but I am too poor." He had been on the frontier since 1853, he said, "and I now curse the day when I commenced it."[34]

The next news about Alice was darker. Indians told interpreter Philip McCusker that Comanches killed the girl shortly after they captured her, and the one Captain Adam had seen was a different girl. In the summer of 1868, General Alfred Sully recovered a female captive (see Elizabeth Brisco) and for a time, Todd's hopes were again raised, but the girl did not prove to be Alice. In the summer of 1869, John Friend, the father of a captive boy (see Lee Temple Friend), stopped by to visit George Todd. He had been searching for his son when he heard from an Indian agent that Alice Todd was alive, living with Comanches, and married to a Mexican. Friend told Todd that the agent said the girl's father knew about her, but if he didn't want to come up and retrieve her, she'd stay where she was. Todd was flabbergasted. Again he wrote to Washington, asking why the agents wouldn't reclaim a captive if he had the chance. The commissioner said there must have been a mistake, because they had no news about Alice. As far as they knew, she was dead.

In 1870, a captive Comanche woman at Fort Griffin described a girl that resembled Alice Todd. She said the girl was now 18 and was owned by the Kiowa Prairie Oats. The information led nowhere. Lawrie Tatum, the new Kiowa-Comanche agent at Fort Sill, tried to find Prairie Oats, but hit a dead end, and the federal government also gave up the search. Todd was destined never to learn what became of his daughter. Perhaps it was his destiny to remain tormented and guilt-ridden for the rest of his life, for, after all, it was he who had first fled and abandoned her.[35]

Alice Todd's mother, Dizenia, and the black servant girl were buried near the foot of the mountain where they were attacked, and where Alice was carried away. The eminence, with a height of 1,720 feet, and rising about 160 feet above the surrounding countryside, became known as Todd Mountain. About eighty miles northwest of Todd Mountain, on the Concho River, is a seventy-foot limestone cliff known as Paint Rock. The cliffs and caves are covered with hundreds of paintings and pictographs done by generations of natives from ancient times to the 19th Century. Among the newest pictographs is one of two crossed lances and two longhaired scalps. Nearby is a horizontally drawn figure of a woman, a typical captivity depiction. The pictographs are thought to record the Todd attack and kidnapping. If so, Alice Todd's legacy may last much longer in rock than in human memory.[36]

SARAH, JOSEPH, AND CHARLIE MORRIS
Colorado, January 14, 1865

After the Battle of Sand Creek, November 29, 1864, the Indians who would normally have gone into winter camp during that season, were leaving Colorado Territory. In January 1865, thousands of Cheyennes and Lakotas attacked forts and ranches along the South Platte, including Fort Rankin, Julesburg,

274

Dennison's Ranch, Valley Station, Godfrey's Ranch, Wisconsin Ranch, and American Ranch. The latter was located on the south side of the South Platte, opposite present-day Merino, Colorado. Present were current owners William and Sarah Morris; their son, Charlie (1), their adopted son, Joseph (3); William's brother; hired hands Gus Hall and a man known as Big Steve; and several other employees.[37]

About ten a.m. January 14, Hall and Big Steve took a wagon to cross the frozen South Platte to chop wood when about 100 Indians appeared. A dozen warriors came after them, shooting and wounding both men. A bullet fractured Hall's ankle, and Big Steve may have taken a more serious wound. They took refuge in a sand pit near the river, firing and ducking down. A warrior sprang from concealment and was upon them. He shot an arrow that grazed Hall's chest, and Hall fired back, killing the Indian. After a several-hour siege, the Indians left, and the two men stumbled twelve miles down the frozen river to Wisconsin Ranch, where they crawled into a burned building, hiding in a smoldering pile of grain for warmth.[38]

When the Indians cut off Hall and Big Steve, Morris and the remaining men hurriedly prepared a defense. Bill Morris knew there were dangers living on the frontier, but that did not deter him when an opportunity arose to take over the rebuilt American Ranch. Morris, a fair violinist, and his educated wife, Sarah, took the chance and moved from Delaware County, Indiana, in the summer of 1864. Bill had been entertaining the family and hired hands with his violin when the Indians struck. They barricaded the doors and windows, but there was a haystack close by. The Indians set it ablaze, and the flames soon reached the house. The men kept firing as long as they could, killing at least two Indians, but the fire eventually drove them outside. William picked up Joseph and Sarah grabbed Charlie.

"We ran towards the river," said Sarah, "through the corral, hoping to make our escape."

The Indians were on them in a flash. An arrow hit Sarah in the shoulder and she fell. William rushed up behind her, brushed aside her beautiful long black hair, and jerked the arrow free. He told her not to resist, that the Indians would probably take her prisoner. He dropped off Joseph with her and tried to escape with the other men. They went down in a hail of bullets and arrows. Sarah tried to cover the two boys with her body as blows rained down upon them, and she was stabbed and whipped. A Minneconjou named White White stepped in to try and stop the frenzied Cheyennes. He offered a horse to the first warrior who could get the others to stop beating her. One Cheyenne understood his message and stopped the assault. White White tried to calm the bleeding, bruised woman, and eventually he got her and the two children up on ponies and rode away. The ranch was burned. When soldiers later examined the site, they counted seven white bodies, and three Indians. Finding dead Indians in the ruins amid open whiskey decanters caused Gus Hall to speculate that Morris doctored them with strychnine, as he once said that he intended to do.[39]

Sarah was bleeding from eleven wounds when she was taken away, but White White and an old woman dressed them. An Indian who could speak English told her to make sure the other warriors saw all her wounds, because they were planning to kill her, and her injuries would probably prevent it. They traveled south to a camp, possibly near Summit Springs on White Butte Creek, and stayed several days while the Indians held scalp dances and celebrated.

The confederated Indian bands struck along the South Platte again in early February, then they moved north toward the Powder River. White White was not as harsh to Sarah as many Indians were to their captives. He gave her enough meat to eat, and when her wounds began to heal, he only made her "pack on my back a few kegs of water and saddle my pony."

His kindness did not extend to the children. Joseph was too young to understand discretion, and he fought whenever an Indian came near him. He was becoming troublesome, but eventually he won over a few chiefs with his pluck. When they saw him as a possible asset they took him from Sarah. She only saw him one more time when an Indian woman brought him for a visit. Charlie's condition deteriorated. Not yet two, he seemed to know his world had changed, and he constantly asked, "Where Daddy?" He cried a lot, and Sarah tried to hold him to keep him quiet, but then she could not do her chores. The Indians quickly grew tired of the boy's behavior. About three months into their captivity, White White gave Sarah a command, but Charlie clung to her and cried if she tried to move away. The chief flew into a rage, grabbed the boy, slammed him into the ground, and stomped on him. Sarah screamed and threw herself over his body. Charlie was never the same. He never cried; he never uttered a sound, and he seemed to waste away. One day when it looked like he was dead, the old chief picked him up and tried to bury him. Sarah let out an anguished cry and the chief handed the boy back to her. It was too late, however, for in a few days the boy was dead. The Indians put him in a coffee sack and tossed him in a ravine, barely covering him with dirt. Sarah scratched the ground with her hands, trying to bury him properly, and two Indian women took pity on her and helped her cover the body.[40]

In the spring of 1865, many of the warring Indian tribes concentrated on the upper Powder River. White White, who had been traveling with the Cheyennes, joined back up with Minneconjous of his own tribe. For a brief time in late April, he camped with some Oglalas who had a captive (see Lucinda Eubank) initially taken by Cheyennes along the Little Blue in Nebraska in August 1864. Sarah was allowed to visit Lucinda for an hour. It was a blessing to both women that they could comfort each other. The next day, Sarah asked to see Lucinda again, but was forbidden. Soon after, White White's band moved toward Fort Berthold on the Missouri River in present-day North Dakota. The Indians offered the post commander a captive white woman and some horses in return for peace, but Captain Benjamin Dimon, under orders prohibiting military interference in Indian Bureau affairs, hesitated to make a deal. The Indians went downriver to Fort Rice to negotiate with Captain Dimon's brother, Colonel Charles A. R. Dimon of the 1st U.S. Volunteers, a regiment of "Galvanized Yankees" (ex-Confederate soldiers).

The Minneconjou chiefs Red Horn, Lone Horn, White Shield, and White White, with twenty lodges, came to Fort Rice on June 21. Colonel Dimon, using the Blackfeet Lakota, Grass, as an interpreter, stated that all white prisoners must be given up before any peace could be made. White White agreed to surrender Sarah for two horses, just what he had paid to retain her, and the other Indians got sugar and coffee.

Sarah did not know that the Indians made a deal to trade her, and when they rode within 200 yards of Dimon and a detachment of soldiers, she figured her chance for escape had come at last. Sarah broke from the Minneconjous and ran as fast as she could toward the soldiers. She had nothing on but a buffalo robe tied around her waist, and her long black hair, now tangled and dirty, flew behind her in the wind. She threw herself down by Dimon's horse, grasped the stirrups, and cried:

"Merciful God! Have you at last heard me? Am I dreaming? God bless you! God bless you!"[41]

Sarah Morris had a high fever and was put in the hospital. She recovered in a few days and related her story to Colonel Dimon. The sympathetic soldiers' wives cried when they heard Sarah's story and saw her unhealed wounds. They babied her, washed her, combed her hair, and sewed her some new clothes. On June 28, the steamboat *Montana* stopped at Fort Rice. Sarah Morris was as fit for travel as she was going to be, Captain Joseph Throckmorton welcomed her aboard at his own expense, and Sarah was off for St. Louis.

Rezin Iams,[42] Sarah's father, met her at the dock on July 14, and took her back to his home in Granville, Indiana. He wrote to Holon Godfrey, who successfully defended his ranch the same day that American Ranch was overrun, telling him about Sarah's ordeal and rescue, so that the remaining settlers along the South Platte Trail would know what became of her. Sarah lived in Granville with her parents for a time. Her father died in the late 1860s and Sarah remained there with her mother into the 1870s. Rumor has it that the wounded Gus Hall, who escaped the ranch that January morning, eventually lost his leg, went to Omaha, had it replaced with a cork leg, and traveled to Indiana, where he married Sarah Morris. The story is probably apocryphal. By 1880, Sarah and her mother were no longer in Granville, Indiana, apparently all having died or moved elsewhere.[43]

Rudolph Fischer
Texas, July 29, 1865

In 1851, Gottlieb and Sophie Fischer purchased a 110-acre farm six miles southwest of Fredericksburg, Texas, on the north bank of the Pedernales River. The German-American community in Gillespie County was in a beautiful country, but life was hard, and fourteen years later the Fischers were still struggling to make a living.

On July 29, 1865, Gottlieb sent his oldest son Rudolph (13) out to look for stray cattle.[44] The boy spoke only German. He was healthy, strong, with curly black hair, dark eyes, and a fair complexion. On his stomach was a prominent birthmark in the shape of a catfish. Kwahadi Comanche raiders spotted the barefooted boy, wearing buckskin pants and a striped shirt, all alone herding cattle. The raiding Indians swept him up on a horse. He knew not to resist and maybe they would let him live.[45]

A scouting party tried to follow the Indians but failed. The Indians rode to their homeland in the Texas Panhandle. In December 1865, citizens of Gillespie County wrote to Texas Governor A. J. Hamilton, decrying the Indian raids in their county and asking for help in rescuing the captives. One of the signatories was Gottlieb Fischer. The citizens learned some of the prisoners had been reclaimed, but they did not know who. Gottlieb wrote to President Andrew Johnson, giving him a description of Rudolph and asking him for help in locating him. By the spring of 1866, Gottlieb Fischer came to believe his son was dead.[46]

Rudolph was alive, and given the name Gray Blanket. In 1866, he saw another white captive (see Bianca Babb) and talked to her in German when she was in his village. Later, a white visitor recognized Rudolph among the Indians. In April 1866, a trader, the German Jew, Marcus Goldbaum, visited Indians camped on the western edge of the Staked Plains in New Mexico Territory. The bands may have been Comanches under Paruaquahip and Kiowas under Little Heart.

Goldbaum noted the Indians held about twenty captives of all ages. Goldbaum was able to strike up a conversation with Rudolph in German and learned his age and the circumstances of his capture. Rudolph appeared afraid to speak openly to Goldbaum and he soon learned why. When the Indians saw them talking, said Goldbaum, it "roused the jealousy of the red skin. The Indians held council to kill or not to kill me." The results would have been fatal for Goldbaum had it not been for Puertas, the leader of another Comanche band, who professed friendship for the whites. After Puertas pleaded to spare his life, Goldbaum was treated better and allowed to continue trading.

The band moved east to Quitaque on the eastern edge of the Staked Plains. There, in early May, Goldbaum wrote a letter to the military in New Mexico, stating that he tried to buy the captives but did not have enough money or goods. He asked for help to rescue them, indicating that he promised Paruaquahip that he would return in June to make the deal. Goldbaum said he had done everything he could to get them, "particularly Fischer whom I feel particularly attached." He concluded, "To see that boy a slave of the wild Comanches is heart rending."[47]

Before Goldbaum could return, he received a verbal message from Puertas that there was danger in Paruaquahip's camp and he should not return, but deal directly with Puertas. Instead, Goldbaum and a New Mexican, Diego Morales, accompanied Captain Edward H. Bergmann and a detachment of soldiers from Fort Bascom on an expedition to seek out Paruaquahip and Little Heart and demand a return of the captives. Bergmann met the Indians at Arroyo de Nuez, but after two days of heated discussion, the Indians affirmed that the chiefs had no power to force their people to give up prisoners. Bergmann, who had been accused of profiting from the Comanchero trade, upon the Indians' refusal to give up the prisoners, made the statement, "You have made your bed, you shall sleep in it." Bergmann vented his anger, but it did not help Fischer. The boy disappeared from the record for another year.[48]

Because of pressure from Gottlieb Fischer and other citizens, on May 1, 1867, New Mexico Territory Superintendent A. B. Norton, ordered Agent Lorenzo Labadi to locate and rescue Rudolph. Labadi took six men and searched the Staked Plains, and in August, located the Indians at Quitaque in the Valley of Tears, in present Briscoe County, Texas. Labadi called for a council and about 500 Comanches and Kiowas attended. "I demanded of them the delivery of Rudolph Fischer," he said, "and all white captives of the United States held by them, and without ransom; also to cease their depredations on all citizens." The Indians demurred, telling Labadi that Paruaquahip and Mowway were out raiding and they could not discuss the issue until October. Labadi agreed to meet them then. Before he left, Labadi, said, "I saw the boy Rudolph Fischer, one other boy about 18 years of age, and a Negro boy about 13, but I had very little talk with them, as they seemed afraid of the Indians, and the Indians disliked it when they spoke to me. I believe they were in earnest, and that they will deliver up the captives to me at the time and place specified."[49] It was not to be.

Knowing that Labadi was trying to negotiate for Fischer's release, the U.S. peace commissioners who were assembling at Medicine Lodge in October 1867, instructed the agent to find and tell the Yamparika and Kwahadi Comanches to attend the meeting. When Labadi returned to Quitaque, cholera had broken out, Paruaquahip was dead, and the Indians had scattered. Rudolph Fischer disappeared again.

In February 1871, Texas Congressman E. Degener, representing Gottlieb Fischer, wrote to Commissioner Ely Parker about the boy. Degener said that Goldbaum had again gone to the Indians in the fall of 1870, to bargain for Rudolph's release, but this time, Rudolph refused to leave. "It is not stated," Degener wrote, "whether from fear of being recaptured, or whether the roaming life had gained such a charm for him that he preferred it to rejoining his parents and friends." Regardless, Degener asked, "Is there no possibility of getting news from the boy, and eventually redeem him?" Commissioner Parker wrote to Agent Lawrie Tatum at Fort Sill, that efforts to obtain Fischer's release were unsuccessful, and that Tatum was "instructed to make inquiry concerning the boy, and if possible, ascertain his whereabouts or secure his return." It was nothing new to Tatum, for he had been attempting to recover captives since he became an agent in 1869.[50]

In April 1871, Tatum reported that he learned of a 19-year-old captive fitting Fischer's description, but the Indians told him that he had married a Yamparika Comanche woman and did not want to leave. Tatum wanted to know if Fischer should be taken from the Indians without his consent. Acting Commissioner H. R. Clum wrote that it was not advisable to compel him to leave against his will, especially if he had a family, however, he should still be found, talked to, and persuaded to return to his relatives in Texas. If the only objection to his return was the unwillingness of the Indians to part with him, then Tatum should make a demand that the Indians deliver him and any other captives they held. The Indians would not let Fischer go, and Tatum was not allowed to talk to him.[51]

Fischer participated in the Battle of Adobe Walls on June 27, 1874, where a combined force of Comanches, Kiowas, and Cheyennes attacked a camp of buffalo hunters near the Canadian River in north Texas. The Indian leader was Quanah Parker, the mixed blood son of Peta Nocona and Cynthia Ann Parker. Fischer was said to have been Quanah's right-hand man. The battle ended in an Indian defeat and led to some Comanches going to the reservation. Colonel Ranald Mackenzie sent out Jacob Sturm, who was instrumental in securing Bianca Babb's release from the Indians, to seek a truce with the Comanche holdouts. His quest was successful, and on June 2, 1875, Quanah and 400 followers rode in to Fort Sill. Rudolph Fischer was probably with them.[52]

Although many Comanches surrendered in 1875, through some bureaucratic oversight, no one knew that Fischer was among them. Not until 1877, did agency employees finally question the identity of the big, curly-haired, 25-year-old who didn't quite look like the other Indians. When approached, he admitted his birth name was Fischer. He couldn't remember his parents' names, but remembered the city of Austin. On that slim note, an ad was published in an Austin paper, and the Fischers of Fredericksburg saw it. Sophie was certain this was her son, and she was "almost frantic with joy at the recovery of a son, whom she believed dead already."

Rudolph was found, but arrangements for his return to Texas dragged on all summer. William Nicholson, the superintendent in Kansas, didn't want to furnish transportation. After all, he was a mature man, well versed in survival, and fully able to take care of himself. Kiowa-Comanche Indian Agent James Haworth never made much of an effort to send him home either. Gottlieb Fischer, who still spoke only German, got a friend to write letters to Fort Sill, and contacted U.S. Congressman Gustav Schleicher, to see if he could help. When Schleicher contacted the commissioner of Indian affairs, orders finally went out to approve $100 to pay for his transportation home. Still nothing happened. In September 1877, Gottlieb got a letter from the agency that said Rudolph didn't want to go home, that he was not sure he could make a living in the white world, and might only go for a visit.

That was enough for Gottlieb. He left Fredericksburg and reached Sill on September 12. He recognized Rudolph but, it was reported, "the boy was cold and indifferent." He did not want to return with his father, but Colonel Mackenzie forced him. Supposedly at the bottom of his reluctance was a "dusky maiden" that a chief promised to give to Rudolph as his wife if he stayed with the Indians. Regardless, on September 16, 1877, father and son left Fort Sill for Texas. Rudolph had been captive for about ten years, and lived freely at the agency for two years after that.[53]

Back in Fredericksburg, Gottlieb quickly realized that his son was not happy in white society. He never caused trouble, but he did not want to stay. His father tried to talk him into bringing his Indian wife and family, but Rudolph said, "The white people would always look upon my wife as a squaw, and she would not be happy here." Rudolph took a job with a local man named Crocket Riley to help him drive a herd of horses to Nebraska Territory. They left in May 1878. Rudolph got as far as Fort Concho before his urge to leave got the best of him. He discarded his white man's clothes, took one of the best horses, and rode to the reservation. Rudolph promised his father that if he left it would only be to visit his Indian family. The visit turned out to last for twenty-two years.

Fischer stayed with the Comanches and spent much of his time on a farm near Apache, Oklahoma Territory, raising cattle and cultivating a fruit orchard. He lived well and was considered a good citizen. For a time, Rudolph had two wives, but when he converted to Christianity, he gave one up. As a devout Catholic, Rudolph's farm became a gathering place for priests and nuns. He wanted his children to have a good education and sent them to a Catholic boarding school. Gottlieb Fischer died in 1894, leaving Rudolph an interest in his farm. Rudolph wanted nothing to do with it, but finally, in 1900, he came back to Fredericksburg to settle the estate by selling his share to his brother, Arthur, and a brother-in-law, Otto Rabke, for $150. He remained only a few days to visit his mother, and then returned to the Territory. He did not return again until 1935, at age 83, when his grandson took him to Texas to visit Arthur. He returned again in 1939, to attend Arthur's funeral. Rudolph died at age 89, on Easter Sunday, April 14, 1941. He was buried in Apache, Oklahoma. Rudolph Fischer had spent more time with the Indians than any other captive taken in post-Civil War Texas.[54]

COLA CAROLINE TAYLOR MCDONALD, MAHALA MCDONALD, REBECCA J. MCDONALD, ALICE ALMEDA TAYLOR, JAMES AND DORCAS A. TAYLOR
Texas, August 8, 1865

Pioneer preacher Matthew Taylor and his wife, Hannah Axley, moved from their farm on the Llano River in 1863, to build a new homestead near the head of the Pedernales River. The site is in Gillespie County, in present-day Harper, Texas, on Highway 783 just south of the junction with Highway 290. They had ten children, and three of their adult children and their families moved with them. The extended clan included son James Taylor, married to "Gilly" Taylor; daughter Cola Caroline Taylor (26), married to Elijah McDonald; and their daughters Mahala (4), and Rebecca Jane (1). Son Zedrick Taylor had married Margaret A. Halliburton. They had two children, Alice Almeda and James (7). When Margaret died, Zedrick married Angelina Dorcas Hays and had one daughter, Dorcas Angelina (3). Zedrick died sometime before 1865, and the three children were living with their grandparents. Matthew and James Taylor were away in Kimble County when the Indians struck.[55]

Gilly Taylor had just gone to the spring to get water when about twenty Kiowas sprang out from behind the trees, and one shot her in the breast with an arrow. Despite the wound, she ran to the cabins shouting, "Indians!" Near the porch another arrow hit her in the back. She fell and hit the ground with such force that the arrow was driven through her body. Eli McDonald grabbed his gun, but Cola Caroline and Hannah pleaded for him not to fire, for it would only enrage the Indians. Nevertheless, he fired for a time, driving the Indians back and forcing them to resort to an old trick. They waved a white flag near the front of the cabins, and while engaged in this ruse, Grandmother Hannah Taylor slipped out the back and made her way through the brush, until she found and hid in a small cave along the creek.

With the Indians no longer shooting and apparently wanting a parley, Eli McDonald stepped outside to talk. The move was fatal, for as soon as he showed himself, warriors rushed him from around the cabin, shot him full of arrows, and burst inside. One of them pushed Mahala McDonald into the cooking fire and her hand was burned so badly that the fingers were charred and permanently curled out of shape. When they found there were no more men around, they dropped their guard and began pilfering. Warriors took their clothing, ripped open the feather beds, and tore through the houses like tornadoes. When Cola Caroline realized they were not being closely watched, she tried to usher the children away, but when Mahala went outside and saw her father and Aunt Gilly lying dead, stripped, and scalped, she screamed. Warriors quickly rounded them up and put a close watch on them. When finished plundering, the Indians set the cabins aflame, grabbed Cola Caroline by the hair, threw her and the five children on ponies and rode off.[56] Grandma Hannah watched the cabins go up in flames from her hiding place. That night she started walking to a neighbor's house, but wandered around in the darkness, and it was daybreak before she came to the Doss Ranch about seven miles to the north.

The Indians rode east near Fredericksburg, captured some horses, then headed north, crossed Red River, and dispersed in Indian Territory and southern Kansas. Mrs. McDonald was treated brutally. She was about two months pregnant when captured, and often sick and feverish. She and the children were given so little water that their tongues blackened and swelled. When the children cried for water while near a stream, the warriors amused themselves by throwing them in and seeing if they could swim. In Indian Territory, the Indians took their clothing, and they blistered and burned in the hot sun. One of Mrs. McDonald's worst memories of her captivity was her forced nudity in front of her children, nieces, nephew, and all the warriors and women. Cola Caroline lost track of time, forgetting when she was captured or how long she was with the Indians. Mahala and Alice were separated and given to different bands.[57]

The Gillespie County captives could be considered fortunate in one respect; they were not destined to remain prisoners for long. With the Civil War over, and the United States desperate for peace, the government arranged for a council with Kiowa, Comanche, Cheyenne, Arapaho, and Kiowa-Apache bands. In October 1865, on the Little Arkansas in southern Kansas, Commissioner John B.

Author's photo
Taylor and McDonald capture site near Harper, Texas.

Sanborn made his peace overtures, but cautioned the assembled chiefs that he knew they held white prisoners.[58]

In order to collect the promised presents, the Indians went to gather up the captives—at least some of them. They brought them in on October 24, stating that the others were with distant bands but would be brought in later. The five returned prisoners were Cola Caroline McDonald, Rebecca McDonald, James Taylor, Dorcas Taylor, and James Ball.[59]

The army escorted the freed captives to Council Grove, Kansas, to stay with Agent Hiram W. Farnsworth at the Kaw Agency. Mrs. McDonald was still ill, and was not recovering well from her ordeal. She worried about her daughter Mahala, and her niece Alice, who were still somewhere out on the prairie. Agent Leavenworth was actively working to obtain the rest of the captives (see Elizabeth Fitzpatrick). With the help of mixed-blood Cherokee Jesse Chisholm, he located Alice Taylor and Elizabeth Fitzpatrick, the latter being captured in Texas, in October 1864, at a Kiowa camp near Fort Zarah. Leavenworth found Alice nearly naked, bruised and dirty, carrying wood and water while she slaved for the Kiowas. The Kiowa women were the worst, constantly kicking them and knocking them down. They had been fed only small amounts of raw liver, buffalo, and dog meat. Leavenworth took them, moved on to a Comanche camp where he obtained another captive, James Benson, and took all three to the Cow Creek camp,

285

where they arrived on November 9. An army ambulance conveyed them the rest of the way to Council Grove, where they arrived five days later.

Mrs. McDonald was happy that more captives were freed. Her niece Alice was restored to her, but her daughter Mahala was still being held. While arrangements were being made to take the women and children home, and efforts were being made to find Mahala, the children were enrolled in the Agency Indian school. While Fitzpatrick helped care for Mrs. McDonald, she buoyed up her hopes by insisting that she had seen her daughter in one of the villages where she had been held.

News of captives being rescued filtered down to Texas, and in December, a number of concerned citizens of Gillespie County wrote to Governor Andrew J. Hamilton. They named Mrs. McDonald, Mahala, Rebecca, Alice, James, Dorcas, and Rudolph Fischer, as being captured the previous fall. They read in the papers that a treaty was made with the Indians and that at least six prisoners had been returned. "Could you not find out from the 'authorities' in Washington," they asked the governor, just who these released captives were, and if they could count on his help for their "speedy and safe return."[60]

The new year of 1866 began and the ex-captives were still not in good shape. Cola Caroline's pregnancy was troublesome, the children needed shoes, clothing, and blankets, and their skin was ulcerated. The sutler issued them spirits-of-camphor and castor oil. On March 20, Mrs. McDonald gave birth to a baby boy, and named him Elijah. She said, "If I can get my daughter Mahala from the Indians, I will be ready to go to Texas in two weeks."[61]

In June, Elizabeth Fitzpatrick convinced Leavenworth that she could find Mahala, and the two of them went after her. In two weeks they returned with the five-year-old girl. Mrs. McDonald was thrilled, and now even more anxious to get home. In the summer, Fitzpatrick and McDonald were sick of the delays, and made a deal to pay Thomas Green, the uncle of the Ball cousins, to take them home at their own expense. The threat may have embarrassed the government bureaucrats into expediting matters (see Elizabeth Fitzpatrick), for finally a wagon train was readied and the captives left Council Grove on August 27.

The Taylors and McDonalds made it back to Gillespie County in late October, finding that most of their relatives had moved back to a safer part of the county. Cola Caroline had the daunting task of caring for her three children, her nephew, and two nieces. She married Peter Hazlewood in 1868, and they had two children,

Eddie and Pleasy. In October 1873, Indians raided the area. The settlers fought them, but Hazlewood took a bullet in the head; Cola Caroline was widowed again. She later married L. F. Pope, had one daughter by him, Carrie Eva, who died in infancy. Cola Caroline Taylor McDonald Hazlewood Pope lived in Kerrville until her death in 1898, at age 59. She and Carrie were buried in the Hunt Cemetery between Kerrville and Ingram.[62]

Rebecca Jane McDonald always remembered being thrown into the river by the Kiowas. She later married Monroe Herrin and had several children. The baby Elijah McDonald grew up, married, raised a family, and lived to the age of 64. James Taylor lived into young adulthood and disappeared from the record. Dorcas Taylor married Charles Nabors, and four years later married John West. Alice Taylor married William G. Rayner and they had five children.

Mahala McDonald always bore the scars of her burned hand. She married Allen McDonald and they had seven children, but they all died in one disaster and were buried in the Spring Creek Cemetery in Gillespie County. Mahala and Allen lived until 1931, and 1932, respectively, both dying at age 70. They were buried in Melvin, McCulloch County, Texas.[63]

James "Bud" and William "Willie" Ball
Texas, September 20, 1865

The Ball families moved to Wise County, Texas, about 1852. James S. Ball Jr. was born in Kentucky in 1820. He married Nancy Green (1820 – 1892) and they had seven children: three girls and four boys. His brother, Moses P. Ball (1816 – ca. 1895), married Levina Jane Jones (1818–1902), and they had nine children: six girls and three boys. They lived about ten miles north of Decatur, Texas.[64] To complete some work he was engaged in, Moses Ball sent his son, James "Bud" Ball (7), over to neighbor Preston W. Walker's house, to borrow a hand saw (or an auger). On the way, he stopped at Uncle James's house to ask his cousin, William "Willie" Ball (7), to accompany him. This probably occurred on September 20, 1865.[65]

The boys made it to Walker's place about one mile away, got the tool, and headed for home. They never made it. Kiowa warriors were in the area. They had just stolen two horses from James Ball's place, and swung around to hit the next ranch when they found the two cousins strolling down the road. They swept them both up. Moses Ball wondered what was taking Bud so long and he went to Press Walkers, only to learn that Bud and Willie had picked up the tool and left hours ago. Moses's son, Carlo, joined him, and they followed the boys' tracks back down the road. The dropped hand tool lay in the dirt, and the boys' bare footprints disappeared amidst numerous pony tracks. Moses and Carlo followed the tracks. They found hand and knee prints at a waterhole where they boys were let down to drink. They followed the trail west to the Jack County line, but lost it when night fell.

The Kiowas rode hard for three days, blindfolded and separated the cousins, and then two different bands took them in opposite directions.[66]

In October 1865, the U.S. arranged a peace council on the Little Arkansas in southern Kansas. Commissioner John B. Sanborn told the assembled chiefs that he knew some bands held white prisoners, that there would be no treaty until they were returned, and if returned, "compensation will be given you for them." The Kiowa Little Mountain admitted having four captives and the Comanche Eagle Drinking, said he had three white boys. Although the usual gifts were ready to be distributed, Commissioner Thomas Murphy cautioned the chiefs that, "when the treaty is made and concluded, and all the prisoners in your hands given up, then the presents will be given to you, and not before."[67]

Apparently the Americans were easily fooled and the Indians realized they had a good arrangement going. They could capture white women and children, sell them back to the authorities, and go right out and capture more. Kicking Eagle, Satank, and others went to gather five captives. On October 24, they brought them to the council grounds, stating that the others were not in the immediate vicinity, but would be delivered to Agent Leavenworth as soon as possible. The commissioners thanked the Indians for their cooperation. The five captives were Cola Caroline McDonald, Rebecca J. McDonald, James Taylor, Dorcas Taylor, and James Ball.[68]

The captives were sent to Council Grove, Kansas, under an army escort led by Lieutenant Mark Walker, to stay with Agent Hiram W. Farnsworth at the Kaw Agency. "Bud" Ball was a captive for a little more than one month. Willie Ball's rescue took longer. He was in the camp of the Nokoni Red Feather, who did not want to give him up. In February 1866, Agent Farnsworth wrote to his superiors to remind them that William Ball was still with the Indians, even though the ransom money had been paid. He sarcastically added that neither Leavenworth nor the Indians seemed to be making a good faith effort to bring the boy in. Leavenworth would have begged to differ, since he continually complained about the great efforts he made to secure all the captives and how worn out he had become.[69]

Back in Texas, the Balls had been making efforts to regain the children. They raised $450 to buy the boys back, and Thomas H. Green, their uncle, rode a wagon to Kansas to bring them home. Willie was finally secured in the spring. When Red Feather was gone on a raid in March, Leavenworth arranged for the boy to be brought to the Cow Creek camp, east of Fort Larned, but still 115 miles west of Council Grove. When Red Feather returned he was furious, and vowed he would get his "adopted" boy Willie back.

Leavenworth and Farnsworth wanted the freed captives out of their hair, but red tape and the cost-effective need to get all of them home in one shipment took time. Tom Green had arrived in Council Grove, wanting to take the boys home, but he soon took sick, and Willie was not there yet. Leavenworth finally got Willie to Council Grove on June 6, but there were more hold-ups (see Elizabeth Ann Fitzpatrick). When other captives at the Kaw Agency tried to make a deal with Green to take all of them to Texas, it motivated Farnsworth to cut through the bureaucratic hold-ups. Green was getting impatient waiting for the captive women to make up their minds if they were coming with him or not. Finally, Farnsworth completed arrangements for contractor Joseph Dunlap with a government train to take them home. They climbed aboard on August 27, 1866. Green followed along with "Bud" and Willie Ball in his own wagon. They reached Decatur, Texas, in early October.[70]

It was not to be the last adventure with the Indians for Willie Ball. If Red Feather really wanted his captive back, or if the story is apocryphal, will probably never be known for sure. Nevertheless, the Noconi and a band of raiders revisited the Ball residence in November 1868. According to some accounts, the Indians surrounded and besieged Moses Ball's ranch in an attempt to recapture Willie Ball. Willie, and John Bailey, the husband of James Ball's daughter, Easter Melvina, had gone to the field that morning to gather corn. While they worked, Mr. Shira, a neighbor, dropped over to visit. Just then, Indians appeared all along the fence and wood lines. They peppered the place with gunfire and arrows and made directly for Willie. Bailey was armed with two six-shooters and held them at bay, while Shira and Ball ran for the house. About the same time, two passers-by, John W. Hunter and a man named Holford, chanced to blunder into the fight and rode to the house. Bailey ordered Willie to crawl under the wagon, while he fired until his pistols were empty. When he was gunned down, Easter Bailey fainted in the yard. Indians crawled closer to the wagon, trying to get Willie, while gunfire from the house made it hot for them.

"Shoot all around the boy! Don't hit the boy," Moses Ball told Hunter and Holford as they added their guns to the defense.

Suddenly, Willie broke from under the wagon and ran, but a big Indian darted out and grabbed him. Mrs. Ball screamed for the men to shoot. Two or three bullets plunked into the Indian at once, and as he dropped to the ground, Willie ran to the house. The Indians grabbed the fallen warrior, thought to be Red Feather, and dragged him away. With that, the fight ended. The men buried Bailey's body, and a few days later they discovered another grave in the timber about 150 yards away. They dug it up and discovered the dead Indian, complete with a "scarlet feathered cap," various army accoutrements, and a deed to a settler's ranch in Kansas. Red Feather would take no more captives.[71]

The "battle" at Ball's Ranch was not quite so dramatic when described by James Ball in his depredation claim filed in 1894. He said the incident took place on his ranch, not Moses,' and it would probably have been his son "Bud," not Willie, that the Indians tried to capture. Strangely enough, in the claim, neither James, nor his daughter Easter, nor Preston Walker, made any reference to a battle. James Ball was only concerned about his lost horses and oxen. Easter Bailey (now Easter Helm) said she lived on her father's place when the raid occurred. She mentioned her husband, John Bailey, being killed, but said she did not see it happen. Press Walker only said the raiding Indians stole two of Ball's horses and killed a yoke of oxen. They all said the raid occurred in September 1871, and none of them even mentioned Indians trying to capture either "Bud" or Willie. In another strange twist, Ball's attorney was Cliff D. Cates, who later wrote a history of Wise County, in which he stated the boys were captured in 1866. The discrepancy in dates, as discussed in a footnote above, was remotely possible because they all forgot the actual year, or more likely due to the fact that the tribes in question needed to be in "amity" with the United States, which was the case in 1871.[72]

James S. Ball Jr. did recover $465 for the loss of his horses and oxen in the raids of 1865 and 1868 (which he said occurred in 1870 and 1871). The U.S. government allowed no compensation for injury, death, or capture of human beings. Neither of the two captured cousins were destined for long, happy lives. "Bud" Ball married Betty Fletcher, but later died and was buried in an unmarked grave in Hopewell Cemetery in Wise County. Willie Ball, who federal authorities described as "an intelligent young man" when he was rescued from the Indians, died sometime between 1880 and 1885. All James Ball had to say about their passing in his 1894 depredation claim was that, "they are both dead."[73]

Chapter 6 notes

[1] Michno, *Encyclopedia of Indian Wars*, 353-54; Smith, *Frontier Defense*, 39, 190n6.

[2] Marshall, *A Cry Unheard*, 99-101; McConnell, *West Texas Frontier*, in www.forttours.com/pages/tocblair; Hamilton, "Albert Schwandner," 403-05; Hunter, "Indian Captivity Retold," 194; Hunter, ed., "Once a Prisoner," 7.

[3] Marshall, *A Cry Unheard*, 93.

[4] Marshall, *A Cry Unheard*, 94-95; McConnell, *West Texas Frontier*, in forttours.com/pages/tocwilson. Brown, *Indian Wars*, 122, and Grace and Jones, *History of Parker County*, 72, name the girl Diana Fulton and incorrectly date the capture in August 1866.

[5] McConnell, *West Texas Frontier*, in forttours.com/pages/tocwilson. Grace and Jones, *History of Parker County*, 72, name the white scouts' leader as Captain Marthell.

[6] McConnell, *A Cry Unheard*, 96-98, 196; McConnell, *West Texas Frontier*, in forttours.com/pages/tocwilson.

[7] Passmore, "Captivity of Mrs. Wattenbach," 20; McConnell, *West Texas Frontier*, in www.forttours.com/pages/tocmetzger. McConnell says that Emma was staying in Fredericksburg with her uncle, John Metzger, and Anna was sent to town alone. She accompanied Anna home when the Indians attacked.

[8] Passmore, "Captivity of Mrs. Wattenbach," 21-22.

[9] Passmore, "Captivity of Mrs. Wattenbach," 23-24.

[10] Passmore, "Captivity of Mrs. Wattenbach," 24-25; Hunter, "Indian Captivity Retold," 194.

[11] Cox, "Capture of Lon White," 59; McConnell, *West Texas Frontier*, and Nowak, "Painted Post Crossroads," in forttours.com/pages/ewhite. David White is sometimes called Daniel White. Dr. Valentine, may by I. P. Vollintine, Marshall, *A Cry Unheard*, 257.

[12] Nowak, "Painted Post Crossroads," in forttours.com/pages/ewhite; Ledbetter, *Fort Belknap*, 135, 156n5; Smith, *Frontier Defense in Civil War*, 143; Richardson, *Comanche Barrier*, 233n17; Huckabay, *Jack County*, 511. There are conflicting stories as to whether White and Johnson accompanied Throckmorton to the council, or were notified later that the captives could be ransomed. They also purchased an orphan being raised by George Light of Parker County, and the son of Mrs. Rowland of Jack County.

[13] The time and location of the captives' release remains controversial. Ledbetter, *Fort Belknap*, 135-36, says the captives, with no mention of Elonzo White, were turned over to Throckmorton's agents at Camp Napoleon on August, 15 and then sent to Decatur, Texas, where Britt Johnson claimed them. Nowak, "Painted Post Crossroads," in forttours.com/pages/ewhite, says White and Johnson were both present at Camp Napoleon in May and secured the release of Lon White, the Johnsons, and other captives, after riding another 200 miles to a Kiowa village to get them. Cox, "Capture of Lon White," 60-61, says White and Johnson made two trips to the Indian camps because they didn't have enough money to buy everyone. Nye, *Carbine and Lance*, 35-36, says Johnson rode to the Indian camp on the Washita, and with the help of Asa Havey, traded horses for all the captives. Huckabay, *Jack County*, 511, has a similar story.

[14] Nowak, "Painted Post Crossroads," in forttours.com/pages/ewhite; Huckabay, *Jack County*, 512; Cox, "Capture of Lon White," 61.

[15] Groneman, *Battlefields*, 151-52; *OR*: V.41/1, 886; Gallaway, *Dark Corner*, 228-30; Ledbetter, *Fort Belknap*, 117-18, 121, 135-36; Smith, *Frontier Defense in the Civil War*, 132-33.

[16] Ledbetter, *Fort Belknap*, 6-7, 12n36, 118-19, 145-46; Michno, *Encyclopedia of Indian Wars*, 156-57; Nye, *Carbine & Lance*, 37. The standard story, first begun by historian W. S. Nye, is that Milly Jane married a Kiowa named Goombi, and lived as an Indian until her death in 1934. Nye later admitted that his scenario was in error.

[17] According to Ledbetter, *Fort Belknap*, 135, contrary to what many historians claim, Britt did not rescue Fitzpatrick, Durkin, or his own family.

[18] Nowak, "Painted Post Crossroads," in forttours.com/pages/ewhite; Ledbetter, *Fort Belknap*, 135, 156n5; Smith, *Frontier Defense in Civil War*, 143; Richardson, *Comanche Barrier*, 233n17; Huckabay, *Jack County*, 511.

[19] Ledbetter, *Fort Belknap*, 135-36, 157n11, 12; Nowak, "Painted Post Crossroads," in forttours. com/pages/ewhite; Kingman, "Diary of Samuel Kingman," 6, in http://www.kshs.org/publicat/ khq/1932/32_5_kingman; Phin W. Reynolds, Gallaway, *Dark Corner*, 230, later went to school with Lottie Durkin and remembers she had "a red and blue circle on her forehead."

[20] *Commissioner of Indian Affairs 1865*, 531-32, 535; Ledbetter, *Fort Belknap*, 140, 200; Kingman, "Diary of Samuel Kingman," 6, in http://www.kshs.org/publicat/khq/1932/32_5_kingman. The five captives were Caroline McDonald, Rebecca J. McDonald, James Taylor, Dorcas Taylor, and James Ball. The latter is sometimes recorded as James Burrow. Ledbetter, *Fort Belknap*, 8, 68, discounts much of Britt Johnson's exploits, although it is clear that he made a few excursions to Indian Territory and Kansas to rescue captives. Sam Kingman specifically mentioned him being at the Little Arkansas Treaty on October 15, 1865, where Kingman commented, "I hope no treaty will be made till all the prisoners are delivered up."

[21] Ledbetter, *Fort Belknap*, 141, 143. Hoig, *Kicking Bird*, 93, confuses many of the captives. He believes Mrs. Fitzpatrick and Mrs. Sprague are two different women, when she is only one person—Elizabeth Ann Carter Sprague Fitzpatrick. He incorrectly calls Milly Jane Durkin, Milla Jane Sprague, and calls the McDonalds the McDaniels.

[22] Ledbetter, *Fort Belknap*, 143, 145-46, 151; Winfrey and Day, *Texas Indian Papers 4*, 165; McConnell, *West Texas Frontier*, in www.forttours.com/pages/tocbenson. James Benson was also said to have been from Hamilton County, Texas. Apparently few, if any, relatives initiated any inquiries about him.

[23] Ledbetter, *Fort Belknap*, 33, 34, 42, 55, 64, 73, 75-76, 88, 104, 106.

[24] Ledbetter, *Fort Belknap*, 147-49.

[25] Ledbetter, *Fort Belknap*, 163-176; Foreman, "Jesse Leavenworth," 21.

[26] Ledbetter, Fort Belknap, 177-79, 193-94, 196, 199-200.

[27] Ledbetter, Fort Belknap, 213, 215, 217n18, 218-20.

[28] Ledbetter, *Fort Belknap*, 5-8, 200-01, 209, 223-26, 231-33; *Commissioner of Indian Affairs 1869*, 86-87.

[29] Smith, *Frontier Defense in Civil War*, 30-33, 39, 41-42, 150, 160; Zesch, "Alice Todd," 3-4.

[30] Zesch, "Alice Todd," 4-5, 15.

[31] Zesch, "Alice Todd," 5-7.

[32] Winfrey and Day, *Texas Indian Papers* 4, 106; Ledbetter, *Fort Belknap*, 159n47; Zesch, "Alice Todd," 7-8.

[33] Todd letters of June 18, July 12, 1868, quoted in, Zesch, "Alice Todd," 9-10.

[34] Todd letter of July 22, 1868, quoted in Zesch, "Alice Todd," 11-12.

[35] Zesch, "Alice Todd," 13-15.

[36] "Paint Rock," in Handbook of Texas Online.

[37] Michno, *Encyclopedia of Indian Wars*, 161-64; Propst, *South Platte Trail*, 75-76; Tucker Butts, *Galvanized Yankees*, 133. A depredation claim indicates that the correct surname might be Morrison.

[38] Monahan, *Denver City*, 212; Propst, *South Platte Trail*, 75-76. Propst says that Big Steve died on the riverbank.

[39] Propst, *South Platte Trail*, 76, 90; Monahan, *Denver City*, 212: OR: V.48/1, 41.

[40] Propst, *South Platte Trail*, 92-93; Monahan, *Denver City*, 230.

[41] Propst, *South Platte Trail*, 89-90; Monahan, *Denver City*, 230; Tucker Butts, *Galvanized Yankees*, 133-34.

[42] Tucker Butts, *Galvanized Yankees*, 134, 176; Propst, *South Platte Trail*, 90; Monahan, *Denver City*, 231. The surname is spelled Iams and Iames, but might actually be James.

[43] Monahan, *Denver City*, 231-32.

[44] Zesch, *The Captured*, 39; The name is sometimes rendered as Randolph Fisher.

[45] Ledbetter, *Fort Belknap*, 151-52; Zesch, *The Captured*, 39-40. Another version of Fischer's capture, McConnell, *West Texas Frontier*, in http://www.forttours.com/pages/tocfischer, is that he and a friend, Peter Webber, had been to the home of Ludwig Kneese who lived five miles southwest of Fredericksburg. They were only a mile from home when Indians attacked. Webber, riding a horse, got away, but Fischer, on a slower mule, was captured.

[46] Winfrey and Day, *Texas Indian Papers 4*, 88-89; Zesch, *The Captured*, 40.

[47] Ledbetter, *Fort Belknap*, 152-54; Kavanagh, *Comanches A History*, 406-07.

[48] Kavanagh, *Comanches A History*, 407; Ledbetter, *Fort Belknap*, 153-54; Kenner, *Comanchero Frontier*, 156-57.

[49] *Commissioner of Indian Affairs 1867*, 214-15.

[50] Kavanagh, *Comanches A History*, 411-12; Ashton, *Indians and Intruders*, 86, 87.

[51] Ashton, *Indians and Intruders*, 92-93.

[52] Zesch, *The Captured*, 205-08.

[53] Zesch, *The Captured*, 222-26;

[54] Robinson, *Bad Hand*, 237; Ledbetter, *Fort Belknap*, 160-61n79; Lehmann, *Nine Years*, 105; Zesch, *The Captured*, 233-35, 250-51, 282-83.

[55] McConnell, *West Texas Frontier*, in forttours.com/pages/toc/tayhome; Ledbetter, *Fort Belknap*, 150, 160n74, n75, n76; Texas Historical Commission, roadside marker. Gilly's given name has been recorded as Gillette, Gilead, and Gill.

[56] Ledbetter, *Fort Belknap*, 150; McConnell, *West Texas Frontier*, in forttours.com/pages/toc/tayhome; Wilbarger, *Depredations*, 646-47.

[57] Wilbarger, *Depredations*, 646-47; Ledbetter, *Fort Belknap*, 146, 151, 178.

[58] *Commissioner of Indian Affairs 1865*, 528, 530-32.

[59] Ledbetter, *Fort Belknap*, 137, 139-40, 146; *Commissioner of Indian Affairs 1865*, 534-35. James Ball's name was recorded as James Burrow.

[60] Ledbetter, *Fort Belknap*, 143-44, 146-48; Winfrey and Day, *Texas Indian Papers* 4, 88-89.

[61] Ledbetter, *Fort Belknap*, 163-64.

[62] Wilbarger, *Depredations*, 648-50; Ledbetter, *Fort Belknap*, 168-71, 180, 184.

[63] Ledbetter, *Fort Belknap*, 180, 184, 274.

[64] Ledbetter, *Fort Belknap*, 161n85. The Balls' homes are placed at various distances from Decatur, usually within a few miles. James S. Ball Jr. and Preston Walker, in Ball's depredation claim, RG 123, #10172, say they lived 10 miles north of town.

[65] Various sources list the capture in different years. Cates, *Wise County*, 188, has the year 1866; Winfrey and Day, *Texas Indian Papers* 4, 314, say it was 1865; Hunter, "Battle at Ball's Ranch," 31, says the fight at the ranch occurred in 1868, and the capture was three years earlier; Sowell, *Rangers and Pioneers*, 287, thinks it might have been in 1869; and Ledbetter, *Fort Belknap*, 146, dates it in 1865. The most curious dating comes from James Ball's depredation claim, RG 123, #10712, made in 1894. He indicates his place was raided in September 1870 and again in September 1871, with his son and nephew captured in 1870, and the battle occurring in 1871. Whether his memory was faulty decades after the fact, or he purposely changed the dates to give his claim a better chance of success is unknown. In order to collect damages against a tribe, it had to be in "amity" with the U. S. The Kiowas and Comanches, although they had signed previous treaties with the U.S., were at war after that date. They did not again sign treaties until October 1865, on the Little Arkansas, and in October of 1867, at Medicine Lodge. To have any chance of approval, the depredations Ball claimed would have to have occurred after those treaties.

[66] Cates, *Wise County*, 188-89; Hunter, "Battle at Ball's Ranch," 31; Ball Depredation Claim #10172.

[67] *Commissioner of Indian Affairs 1865*, 528, 530-32.

[68] Ledbetter, *Fort Belknap*, 137, 139-40, 146; *Commissioner of Indian Affairs 1865*, 534-35. James Ball's name was recorded as James Burrow.

[69] Ledbetter, *Fort Belknap*, 146, 155, 164; Hunter, "Battle at Ball's Ranch," 31.

[70] Winfrey and Day, *Texas Indian Papers* 4, 314; Ledbetter, *Fort Belknap*, 167-73, 176-79.

[71] Hunter, "Battle at Ball's Ranch," 22-34; Sowell, *Rangers and Pioneers*, 287-94.

[72] Ball Depredation Claim #10172. Documents in Winfrey and Day, *Texas Indian Papers* 4, 316, also show John Bailey, age 35, was killed 10 miles from Decatur in 1868.

[73] Ledbetter, *Fort Belknap*, 155, 161, 275; Ball Depredation Claim #10172.

Chapter Seven
THE CENTRAL PLAINS

He forced me, by the most terrible threats and menaces, to yield my person to him. — Lucinda Eubank

Two young ladies and two little girls were carried away by the red-handed assassins, to suffer a fate worse than death. — Governor Samuel J. Crawford

Besides indignities and insults far more terrible than death itself, the physical suffering to which the two girls were submitted was too great almost to be believed." "There was much in their story not appropriate for these pages. — George A. Custer

Although the majority of captives were taken in Minnesota and Texas, the central Plains were not immune from Indian attack. In addition to the dangers on the Oregon, California, Overland, and Santa Fe Trails that coursed through the area, living in an isolated frontier cabin was also fraught with peril. The pioneer settlers who lived in Kansas and Nebraska were also the victims of raiding Indian bands, although the hostage-takers in this region were more often Cheyennes and Lakotas instead of Kiowas and Comanches. The late 1860s were the years of the most Indian-military conflicts in American history, and the instances of hostage taking were on the rise.

* * *

LAURA ROPER, AMBROSE ASHER,
AND LUCINDA, ISABELLE, AND WILLIE EUBANK
Nebraska, August 7, 1864

The summer of 1864, in Kirksville, Missouri, Joseph Eubank, his wife Ruth, their children Hannah, Dora, George, William, James, Henry, and grandson Ambrose Asher, were about to lose their farm at public auction. Joe Eubank's son, William, was

Author's photo

Eubank Ranch site near Oak, Nebraska.

married to Lucinda (23), and they had two children, Isabelle (3) and Willie (six months). Hoping to start over and find a better life they headed west, moving to Nebraska Territory to be near another son, Joseph Jr., who had built a log home and worked as a rancher just west of Kiowa Station along the Little Blue River. Living with Joe Jr., was his brother Fred, his wife Hattie, and Hattie's brother, John Palmer. Joseph Sr. built a log house for his extended family about nine miles from his son's ranch, and George Eubank found work as a drover, while Hannah found employment with the stage line.[1]

The Joseph Roper Family was also on the move in 1864, going from Cub Creek near the Big Blue River to a ranch one mile from the Narrows in present-day Nuckolls County on the Little Blue River. Their family group included Joseph, his wife Paulina, daughters Clarisa, Laura, Francis, Kate, and their partner Marshall Kelley. Kelley and Laura (16) had a baby out of wedlock, named Clarence Marshall Kelley, who Laura's parents were raising. Among the oak, ash, and cottonwood, and amid the wild plums and grapevines along the Little Blue, the Ropers and Eubanks settled in to start life anew.[2]

Fighting had begun in Colorado Territory in April 1864, and spread to the surrounding countryside. By August, with winter approaching and war preventing the usual winter preparations, the Indians needed supplies from other sources. Captives too, would be good insurance and would give the Indians bargaining power.

296

Author's photo

Roper and Eubank capture site, near Oak, Nebraska.

Early in the morning of August 7, 1864, Joseph Eubank Sr. rode west of Kiowa Station to help his sons, Joe Jr. and Fred, with their haying. In the wagon with Joe were his son James (13), and his grandson Ambrose Asher (7). One half mile from Oak Grove, a lone Indian approached to ask for tobacco and old Joe cut him a plug. The Indian bit off a hunk, and then drew his bow and arrow and aimed at the oxen. Joe called and signed to the Indian to leave the animals alone. The Indian redirected his aim and shot several arrows into Joe Eubank. James jumped from the wagon and ran, but fifty more warriors appeared and shot him dead. One warrior pulled Ambrose from the wagon and tied him to a pony. The Indians stampeded the oxen toward Eubank's home and followed behind with their boy captive.

The same morning, Laura Roper visited her friend Lucinda Eubank. Marshall Kelley and Jonathan Butler were preparing to get supplies and offered Laura a ride in Butler's wagon as far as Eubank's place. After a day of socializing, Laura asked for someone to walk her home, for recent Indian raids made her feel unsafe. Laura, Lucinda, William, Isabelle, and Willie set out for Roper's home one mile away. Only a few hundred yards from the Eubank cabin, William heard the screams of Dora, his mentally challenged sister, and he ran back home to help her. Near the house he saw Indians surround Dora, throw her to the ground, rape her, and murder her. Brother Henry tried to defend his sister, but he was

297

mortally wounded. His body was later discovered about 100 yards from the cabin in a bushy ravine. Knowing he could do nothing, William fled toward the river, but the warriors caught and killed him. Laura, Lucinda, and the two children watched the massacre from cover in a nearby thicket. One man, Dan Freeman, who later buried the bodies said, "the men were scalped, their limbs unjointed, privates cut off; the women were scalped, their bodies mutilated and the private parts scalped." After ransacking the home, the Indians went down the road, when Isabelle cried out and gave away their position. In seconds, the warriors grabbed them. The Indians took Laura's shoes and tore Marshall Kelley's signet ring from her finger. The Indians returned to the house, plundered it, and set it aflame.[3]

The Indians gathered their captives and headed southwest. Laura's saddle broke while descending into a deep ravine, she fell to the ground, and the horse kicked her in the face, breaking her nose. For days, the pain was agonizing, until a Cheyenne doctored her face with a red poultice. The Indians did not tolerate unruly children, and when Isabelle cried, a warrior threatened her with a knife. Laura pled for mercy. The warrior laughed, but did not carry out his threat. Because Laura defended the child, the Indians believed that Isabelle was Laura's baby. They continued across the high plains to the main village, where Cheyenne women pulled Laura from her mount and severely beat her. Finally, a woman called Yellow Squaw spirited her away to her own tipi. Laura decided that being submissive would lessen her abuse. Soon after, the Cheyenne who captured Laura sold her to an Arapaho. Apparently regretting the sale, he later repurchased her, then changed his mind again and sold her to the Arapaho, Neva. Lucinda was taken by an old chief whose name she did not remember. But she remembered her treatment: "He forced me, by the most terrible threats and menaces, to yield my person to him," she stated.

The captives' adaptability and the type of treatment they received varied greatly with each situation. Laura tried to fit in to her new environment. She was allowed to pick wild fruit with the Indian women and some of them treated her well. Lucinda had a worse trial, for she was often raped, beaten, and abused. When Isabelle cried, she was tortured by being cut with arrowheads.[4]

Toward the end of August, the Cheyenne Black Kettle, and some of the other chiefs realized the current intense raiding could not be sustained all winter and white retribution was inevitable. Fall was coming and, as usual, the time to make peace was at

Author's photo
Oak Grove Ranch on the Little Blue River, Nebraska. Raided in August 1864. Near Ambrose Asher capture site.

hand. Even so, only some of the chiefs thought peace was advisable. Many bands were still fighting and had no desire to stop. Finally, William Bent notified them about Colorado Territorial Governor John Evans's plea for peace, and urged them to accept it.

The chiefs were suspicious of their own agent, Samuel Colley, due to the theft of their annuities, so they had George Bent and another mixed-blood, Edmund Guerrier, write two identical letters, one to Colley and one to Major Edward W. Wynkoop, the commanding officer at Fort Lyon. The letters stated, "We heard that you have some (Indian) prisoners in Denver. We have seven prisoners of which we are willing to give up providing you give up yours." It was dated August 29, 1864, and was signed Black Kettle and other chiefs.

The letters were entrusted to Lone Eagle (One Eye) and Minimic (Eagle Head) to deliver to Major Wynkoop. When the Indians appeared at the fort on September 3, Wynkoop was faced with a dilemma. In May, he had received orders from Colonel John M. Chivington, which said, "the Cheyenne will have to be soundly whipped before they will be quiet. If any of them are caught in your vicinity, kill them, as that is the only way."[5] Instead, the guards escorted the Indians into the fort. The furious major calmed down when he received the letters. Apparently awed by the Indians' bravery in the cause of peace, Wynkoop later affirmed that this marked the point in his life when he changed from exterminator to peacemaker. One Eye said that if Wynkoop would go to the Indian village he could get the captives.[6]

Although he would be violating his orders, Wynkoop was anxious to free the captives, and he feared that any delay waiting for permission might anger the Indians and drive them to kill them. General Curtis, however, had already ordered General Blunt to find and fight the Indians, and Colonel Chivington would soon be ready. If the soldiers struck before peace was made, the white captives would be as good as dead.

After a great deal of discussion and contemplation of the consequences, Wynkoop decided to risk a meeting with the Indians. He left Fort Lyon on September 4, with the Cheyennes and 127 soldiers. Near the Smoky Hill River, Wynkoop faced 800 Cheyennes, but he stood his ground while One Eye explained their mission. When they met in council, Wynkoop explained that he was interested in the Indian peace proposal and for the release of the captives, but he did not have the authority to grant peace. If they would agree to give him the captives, however, he would escort a group of chiefs to Denver to meet with Governor Evans.

The Indians argued among themselves, and Bull Bear accused Wynkoop of treating them like stupid children by asking them to release the captives and giving them no guarantees in return. The warriors' argument became heated, but Black Kettle finally calmed the situation and told Wynkoop to take his soldiers away from the village and wait. Later that day, Neva told Laura Roper about her pending release, and the next day, accompanied by Chief Left Hand, Neva took Laura to the soldiers. Her thirty-seven-day captivity was over. The following day, Isabelle Eubank, Danny Marble, and Ambrose Asher were released.[7]

Black Kettle had promised seven captives in his letter, but only delivered four. No doubt, Bull Bear's argument that it would be foolish to give away all the captives with no guarantees made the other chiefs hedge their bets. They made up the story that the three other captives were with the Sioux. It was a lie. During the council and in another part of the camp, Lucinda and Willie Eubank and Nancy Morton were forced to lie under buffalo robes and remain silent under threat of death. The women obeyed, and when Wynkoop rode away they were released, beaten, and taunted. The white soldiers would not get all the captives back so easily.[8]

Wynkoop, happy to get out with some of the captives and his life, marched to Fort Lyon, taking along Chiefs White Antelope, Bull Bear, Black Kettle, Neva, No-Ta-Nee, Bosse, and Heap of Buffalo.

Nebraska State Historical Society
Captives given up by the Cheyennes in September 1864 before the Camp Weld Council. Left to right: Ambrose Asher, Laura Roper, Isabelle Eubank and Danny Marble.

At the fort, they were joined by a soldier escort and continued on to Denver, where the newly freed prisoners (see Danny Marble and Nancy Morton) began their transition back into the civilized world. The citizens of Denver collected donations to help them, especially the three young children who were ailing and needed clothing. Laura Roper enjoyed the spotlight, stating, "We stopped at the Planters Hotel and created quite a sensation." But when her celebrity dimmed she got most of the donated money and went on a spending spree purchasing a new wardrobe. Of the $247.75 collected for the four of them, all but $8.36 was spent on Laura. She took passage on a wagon train to Fort Kearny, and then a coach to Nebraska City, where Pauline Roper met her and took her home. Early in 1865, the Joseph Roper kin were all reunited and returned to Pennsylvania for a time. In November of that year, Joe Roper wrote to the Commissioner of Indian Affairs: "My daughter has been rescued but her mind is somewhat impared."[9]

Laura Roper turned 17 in February 1865, and she married Elijah Soper. A year later they homesteaded in Gage County, Nebraska. They had six children; one of them died at age 14. Laura never took responsibility for her first child, born out of wedlock before her captivity. Her parents adopted him, raised him, and changed his name to Clarence Roper. Laura had problems adjusting to society

301

where there was always gossip about her cohabitation with the Indians. In October 1884, Laura deserted Elijah and the children and ran off with James Vance. They moved to Oklahoma, and Laura had three more children. Never excelling at motherhood, Laura caroused about the community while her daughter Nellie acted as surrogate mother for the brood.

On January 13, 1929, a gathering was arranged at the Narrows and the site of the family cabin near Oak, Nebraska. The commemorative event offered Laura a degree of closure for the events of her captivity. On April 11, 1930, Laura Roper Soper Vance passed away at her home in Enid, Oklahoma.[10]

Ambrose Asher had a chaotic childhood, and his captivity added to the turmoil. He was two when his father died. His mother remarried and had another child. Ambrose was sent away to live with Daniel Walton's family. Ambrose's mother may have been Mary Eubank, because his name was changed to Connie (Conrad) Eubank. Next, he went to Missouri to live with his grandparents, Joe and Rose Eubank. Early in 1864, Connie/Ambrose moved with his grandparents to the valley of the Little Blue, where he was captured. After his release from captivity he was taciturn. It took weeks to find out his mother's name. Shortly after he was reunited with her, she died, and this time Ruth Eubank moved him to a boarding house in Quincy, Illinois. On February 24, 1881, Ambrose married Belle Harrison (16) and sired five children. Ambrose worked off and on as a teamster for many years, and the family lived in abject poverty. Sometime between 1894 and 1900, Ambrose disappeared, either dying or deserting his wife. Belle lived until 1940.[11]

Isabelle Eubank suffered great emotional and physical trauma as a captive, resulting in bizarre nightly behavior. In Denver, Mollie Sanford, wife of Lieutenant Byron Sanford, was going to adopt Isabelle, but her behavior was too disturbing and uncontrollable. "I could not stand it," Mollie said. "She would wake up from a sound sleep, and sit up in bed with staring eyes, and go in detail over the whole thing. She was scarred all over with the prints of arrow points that the squaws tortured her with." Doctor Caleb Burdsal, a surgeon in the 3rd Colorado became her guardian until military duty called him away. The damaged waif was passed among the Denver townsfolk. One family changed her name to Mary. The frail little girl, with poor health, and emotional problems, died on March 18, 1865.[12]

Three captives still remained in the Indian village. On September 25, while the "peace chiefs" were arriving in Denver,

Nebraska State Historical Society
Laura Vance Roper visits the site of her capture, 1929.

their warriors were fighting the soldiers in Kansas (see Nancy Morton). When the defeated warriors returned to the camp, they rubbed bloody scalps in the captives' faces and threatened them with death. Lucinda once went into hysterics, biting the ground and her own arm. The Indians wanted to kill her, but Nancy Morton dissuaded them. The bands split up at the headwaters of the Republican River; Morton went north, Eubank went west, and they never saw each other again.[13]

Lucinda Eubank suffered more acutely than the other two adult captives, for she resisted and did not cooperate with the Indians. They abused her and passed her among the warriors. Isabelle was gone and murdered for all she knew. Willie was beaten, threatened with death, and she was powerless.

Lucinda Eubank, "married" to her Cheyenne chief, remained with the Indians as winter approached. As they headed west they encountered a band of Oglala Lakota, led by Two Face. He bought Lucinda and his band headed toward Powder River. Two Face, usually friendly with the whites, went to ranches and forts for handouts, and Lucinda and Willie shared the bounty. Two Face did not make any sexual demands on Lucinda, but the whippings and abuse continued. As the nights lengthened, the Indians were cold and hungry, but at least Willie remained healthy, for he had not been weaned.

During the winter, a Lakota-Blackfoot, purchased Lucinda, and she was forced to endure his sexual advances as well as severe treatment from his wife. Lucinda hated Blackfoot more than any of her previous captors. Blackfoot, she said, "treated me as his wife, and because I resisted him his squaws abused and ill-used me. Blackfoot also beat me unmercifully, and the Indians generally treated me as though I was a dog, on account of my showing so much detestation towards Blackfoot."[14]

With spring came an increase in military activity, and Two Face was concerned that the presence of white captives in camp might bring retribution. He tried to repurchase Lucinda so he could release her at Fort Laramie, but Blackfoot refused. Two Face convinced Lucinda to steal away from Blackfoot's tipi at night, while he waited outside the village with horses to take them to the fort. This plan worked, but within ten miles of the fort they ran into a camp of Indian police under Charley Elliston. He arrested Two Face and took Lucinda and Willie to the fort.

The wife of Captain William D. Fouts cared for Lucinda and Willie. After nine months of captivity, enduring rape, beatings, illness, and starvation, Lucinda had persevered, and saved the life of her little boy as well. The physically battered woman, wearing dirty rags for clothing, told her harrowing, disjointed story to the soldiers, who became angrier at each new revelation. Colonel Thomas Moonlight and Lieutenant Colonel William Baumer were incensed. They barked out orders to hang Two Face and Blackfoot. Charley Elliston and his police rode out to arrest Blackfoot. On May 24, 1865, Two Face and Blackfoot were hanged beside Big Crow, punished for his treatment of Nancy Morton, with trace chains from an artillery caisson. At the end of July, the trio still swung from the gallows.[15]

General Grenville M. Dodge ordered the friendly Indians near Laramie to be moved to Fort Kearny. Starting June 11, 1865, the 1,500 Oglala and Brule Lakota trailed behind 140 cavalrymen under command of Captain Fouts, while Captain Elliston and his Indian police rode along to maintain order. James Bordeau and George Beauvais joined their wagons with the military procession for protection. Riding with them was Fouts's wife, Charity, their two young children, Lieutenant Triggs's family, and Lucinda and Willie Eubank.[16]

Near Horse Creek on the morning of June 14, the soldiers moved out, but the Indians hesitated. Fouts rode to the rear to hurry them along. As he approached, a group of warriors attacked and shot Fouts in the head and the heart. The Indians charged to distract the soldiers while their women and children escaped over the North Platte. Four soldiers were killed and four were wounded. Six warriors were wounded in the charge, and the soldiers executed one of their prisoners, the Oglala, Osape. The Lakotas killed four of their own chiefs who opposed the escape.[17]

The wagons and escort reached Camp Rankin near the ruins of Julesburg. Mrs. Noble Wade, camp laundress, extended her home and hospitality to Lucinda and Willie while they awaited an eastbound stage for Fort Kearny. Lucinda told Mrs. Wade she was pregnant with Blackfoot's child and it would never see the light of day. She never had any more children. While at Rankin, Lucinda met a Mr. Davenport, who rode from Denver to see her and give her the torn dirty remains of Isabelle's dress. He had cared for Isabelle until her death. On June 22, Lucinda and Willie took a coach to Fort Kearny, and then rode past the Narrows of the Little Blue where they had been captured. They finally arrived at the Walton's home in Missouri. After more than ten months, they were free.

Lucinda never wanted to talk about her experiences. She later married James Bartholomew and lived in Missouri. As a teenager, Willie lived with his aunt, Hannah Eubank Walton. Bartholomew died about 1888, and Lucinda and Willie moved to McCune, Kansas. There she married a farmer, Doctor F. Atkinson. In 1895, Willie married Jennie Frogue, and they had a large family of three daughters and five sons. Upon the death of Lucinda's third mate, she went to live with Willie's family until her death on April 14, 1913. William Joseph Eubank died in Colorado in 1935.[18]

VERONICA ULBRICH, CHRISTIANA, JESSIE, DANIEL, AND PETER CAMPBELL, JR.
Nebraska, July 24, 1867

Peter Ulbrich (43) and his wife Mary took advantage of the newly passed Homestead Act and moved their family from Nebraska City, Nebraska, in October 1862, and settled near the Little Blue River. His place, about three miles south of Thompson's Stage Station and several miles east of present-day Hebron, Nebraska, was spared in the devastating raids made by the Cheyennes and Lakotas along the river in August 1864. With the help of his wife and two children, he cultivated fifty acres and sold garden products to soldiers, freighters, and emigrants traveling the Overland Road. Ulbrich's brother-in-law, Albert Kalus, with his wife and children, built a farm about three miles west of him. By

1867, things appeared safe, at least until General Winfield Scott Hancock stirred up a hornet's nest with his spring campaign.

Angry Cheyennes, likely led by Chief Turkey Leg, swept into the area on July 23. Albert Kalus and a friend, Joseph Piexa, were riding in Kalus's wagon to check some land that Piexa hoped to buy. The Indians caught the men and butchered them. His wife, Margaretha, and their four small children waited, she said, "from week to week, from morning till night. . .crying and weeping." A scouting party of settlers from Swan Creek finally found their bodies, buried them by the roadside, and placed a marker by the grave: "Two men killed by Indians."[19]

The Indians swept past Kalus's homestead. At 9 a.m. on July 24, about thirty Indians rode into Ulbrich's pasture and took some horses and mules, then jumped his fence and seized his daughter Veronica (13) and his son Peter Jr. (12), who were pulling weeds in the potato field. They whipped the children with rawhide quirts and drove them toward the house, which Mr. and Mrs. Ulbrich quickly barricaded. One Indian called out in English:

"Father, father! Come out. We give you papooses."

Ulbrich was upstairs with his musket and observed Indians at all corners of his house with their weapons ready. He knew it would be death to all to open the door.

"Give us the papooses free," his wife called out. "You got horses and mules, take it, that is enough!"

The Indians walked to the stable where Ulbrich could see them talking. They made Peter Jr. get the harnesses, bridles, and straps and secure them to their horses. At 10 a.m. the children were lifted up on the stolen horses and they all rode away. Only a short time later the Indians arrived on the east bank of the Little Blue. Peter Jr., who was big and strong for his age, was probably considered to be potential trouble. The Indians shot him off his horse and left his body in the brush by the river. They continued on with Veronica.[20]

On the same day, about ninety miles northwest of the Ulbrich's, just east of present-day Doniphan, Nebraska, Cheyennes attacked Peter Campbell's ranch. Campbell moved his family from Glasgow, Scotland, to Nebraska Territory in 1865. When Mrs. Campbell died in January 1866, Peter and his four daughters (Christiana, Jessie, Agnes, and Lizzie) and three sons (John R., Daniel, and Peter) remained. In the spring of 1867, Peter filed a homestead claim and declared his intention to become a citizen. On the day of the raid, Peter, and his son, John, were away from home, helping a neighbor harvest wheat on a ranch six miles east. On the way home they passed a farm, one-quarter mile east of their farm, where they discovered Mrs. Thurston Warren dead on the threshold of the house with her murdered baby in her arms, and her 14 year-old boy lying nearby with a gunshot through the thigh. They hurried to their own farm to find the cabin ransacked. Agnes (9) had escaped by hiding in a field of grain, but four children, the teenage daughters Christiana and Jessie, and the twin four-year-olds, Daniel and Peter, were gone.

A party unsuccessfully hunted for the Indians. A week later, six soldiers from Fort Kearny searched for twenty-five miles to the south of the home, but found no trail. The settlers were convinced that the garrison at the fort was inadequate to protect them and they vacated the area. Campbell was distraught, but he hung on.[21]

Ulbrich did not. Although he only had three months to wait before officially owning his 160 acres under the preemption law, Ulbrich packed up his wife and light possessions, traded his cattle for a wagon and horse, and headed east for Nebraska City. He said he left behind "all my crop, 45 acres of corn, one acre of potatoes, a large patch of onions, a rail fence around the field, five hogs, 80 hens, 40 bushels of shelled corn, two-story house, cellar, well, stable, crib and other outhouses behind."[22]

The captured children went through the usual hell reserved for most Indian prisoners in the West. After the Cheyennes killed Peter Ulbrich, Jr., they halted for the night along the Little Blue. The next morning they took Veronica and rode southwest for three days until they reached a village of about 500 lodges on the Republican River. They moved five times during the next three months, and for Veronica, each day was hell. "I did not get enough to eat, suffered from thirst, had to wash and do other work; sometimes they whipped me, sometimes they wanted or threatened to kill me," she later wrote in her father's depredation claim. "Soon one Indian, soon another belonging to the band forcibly violated my body, causing me immense pain and anguish thereby. This was almost a daily and nightly occurrence, which would have killed me, if I had not been liberated almost exhausted." Veronica was happy when the Campbells joined her. "I was glad to have white company in my misery," she said. "I was afraid I never could get away and had to stay with these brutes and devils all my lifetime." Christiana and Jessie Campbell undoubtedly suffered similar indignities and abuse, although their oldest brother, John, only stated of their experience: "They had suffered greatly from hunger and general ill treatment."[23]

The only thing that may have saved Veronica from the death she believed was imminent, was that the army had captured some Cheyennes, and the Indians wanted to trade prisoners. On August 6, 1867, Cheyennes under Turkey Leg and Spotted Wolf tore up tracks on the Union Pacific Railroad a few miles west of Plum Creek Station (present Lexington, Nebraska). They attacked workers who came out to repair the damage and derailed a train, killing seven civilians. Colonel Richard I. Dodge ordered Major Frank North and his Pawnee Battalion to the scene. On August 17, North and Captain James Murie found the Indians still loitering in the area. The Pawnees attacked, scattered the surprised Cheyennes, and chased them twelve miles south of the Platte River, garnering fifteen scalps and capturing thirty-one horses and mules. They also caught a woman and a boy. The boy was Turkey Leg's nephew.[24]

The Cheyennes might capture and hold white women and children for their pleasure, but could not countenance their own people being held by the whites. In September 1867, a peace council was arranged to take place in North Platte, Nebraska. Among the white representatives were Generals Sherman, Terry, Harney and Augur, John B. Sanborn, Commissioner N. G. Taylor, Senator John B. Henderson and civilian Samuel F. Tappan. Most of the Indians attending were Brule and Oglala Lakotas and Cheyennes. Reporter Henry M. Stanley, later to become famous as the finder of the lost missionary, Doctor Livingstone, left a record of the proceedings that produced almost nothing of note except tedious speeches, unfulfilled promises by both sides, and a plan to meet again at Medicine Lodge in October. About the only noteworthy accomplishment was the return of the white captives. The Brule Spotted Tail was said to have used his influence to bring some of the chiefs to council, and induced Turkey Leg to swap his prisoners. Turkey Leg, however, needed no inducement. He sent a runner to North Platte, saying that the captured Cheyenne boy (later called Pawnee) was his nephew, and that in exchange for him and the captured Cheyenne female (Island Woman), he would bring in six captive whites.[25]

On September 18, reporter Stanley wrote: "The Indians and their white captives arrived here last night. There were two hundred warriors, fresh from bloody exploits, and with their hands dyed with the blood of the unfortunates at Plum Creek." Stanley's jibe at the sincerity of the Indians notwithstanding, Turkey Leg brought in his prisoners and the exchange was made two days later at the Union Pacific eating house near the tracks in North Platte.

Ulbrich and the Campbells were free, and, as Veronica explained, in her case it was not a minute too soon.[26]

The freed captives were sent by rail, courtesy of the Union Pacific, to Grand Island, where Peter Campbell met them and took them to his home. Peter Ulbrich, who had fled to Nebraska City, was notified and he rode out to the Campbell farm to pick up his little Veeney. "She was nothing but skin and bones," Ulbrich said. When Veronica was able to travel, she took him back to the spot along the Little Blue where the Indians killed her brother, so his remains could be collected and receive a proper burial.

From the collection of Dr. Jeff Broome
Veronica Ulbrich

After that experience, Peter Campbell moved his family to Saunders County, closer to Omaha, where he believed they would be safer. He died in 1875. The oldest daughter, Christiana, wed J. P. Dunlap, of Dwight, Nebraska. Jessie died in St. Louis about 1903. Agnes died about 1904. Lizzie, the youngest daughter, died about 1907. As of 1913, one of the twins, Peter, was living in Weston, Nebraska, and the other, Daniel, was living in southern Illinois. The oldest son, John R., was living in Omaha.[27]

In 1889, Peter Ulbrich filed an Indian depredation claim for his losses. The value of his lost or destroyed property he estimated at $2,750. He figured the loss of his son's labor was worth $2,000. "For transporting my daughter Veeney. . ." he wrote, "into savage captivity, for her defloration, for numberless violations of her youthful body I claim damages as her father to the amount of Five thousand Dollars."

Poor Mr. Ulbrich, now 70 years old, did not realize that the U.S. Congress only paid (in a low percentage of cases) for loss of property, but did not offer compensation for suffering, injury, or loss of human life. The petition Veronica added to her father's claim further illustrates the family's dire situation. She bared her innermost secret to the commissioner of Indian affairs, writing of the abuse and humiliation she experienced. Her father also explained to the commissioner that in 1887, Veronica married Alfred Megnin, but such was the onus attached to anyone who had been "deflowered" by an Indian, the husband was not told about her captivity, and they altered the date of her birth if he should ever find out, making Veronica appear to be 28, when she was really 34. Thus, she could hope to explain that she was only seven at the time of her captivity, not 13, and was not likely to have been raped. Ulbrich explained that similar trouble was caused in the Roper family when the husband found out about Laura's sexual abuse, and it was likely to be a problem "if Mr. Megnin should find out, that my daughter was a subject of the Indian's bestiality." Ulbrich pleaded with the commissioner not to let the information become public, "so that her husband cannot hear the testimony."

The pleas were unsuccessful. Ulbrich's claims were denied. Perhaps the commissioner blew the secret or someone else gave it away, but the next year in the Census of 1890, Albert Megnin was listed as living alone as a single man. He remarried in 1892. Peter Ulbrich's poor Veeney, most likely broken-hearted, faded into oblivion.[28]

JANE BACON, MRS. SHAW, MISS FOSTER, ESTHER AND MARGARET BELL
Kansas, August 10, 12, 1868

Compared to Texas, the Kansas frontier was comparatively quiet in 1868—at least until June. Trouble began that month when Cheyennes attacked Kaws living at their agency near Council Grove, Kansas, reportedly because of defeats the Cheyennes had suffered at the hands of the Kaws the previous year. Perhaps because of their losses, the Cheyennes may have taken out their frustrations against settlers living in the area, shooting livestock, ruining crops, robbing people, raping one woman, plundering homesteads, and destroying property.[29]

After the raid, Agent Edward W. Wynkoop questioned the Cheyenne Little Robe about what occurred. Little Robe said that after the raid they were hungry, but they only killed seven settlers' cattle. They also met a band of Texas cowboys driving a herd north, and, according to Little Robe, the Texans "invited them to kill what they wanted to eat," but they only killed four cattle. Beyond that, "they did not interfere with any person or thing."[30] Wynkoop believed the story.

Complaints, however, were enough to prompt Commissioner of Indian Affairs N. G. Taylor to write to Kansas Superintendent Thomas Murphy on June 25, to hold up delivery of arms and ammunition to the guilty Indians until reparations were made. When Wynkoop told the Cheyennes they could not get the weapons they believed had been promised to them at the Medicine Lodge Treaty, they were incensed.[31] Of course it made little difference to the Cheyennes, or to the Kiowas and Comanches, that they had already broken the treaty when they committed depredations. Wynkoop tried to issue the other goods, but the Cheyennes refused to accept anything unless the guns were included. General Philip Sheridan sent Lieutenant Colonel Alfred Sully to Fort Larned to assess and calm the situation. The Indians protested to him that "only a few bad young men were depredating" and "all would be well and the young men held in check if the agent would but issue the arms and ammunition." Sully was inclined to agree that issuing the weapons might solve the problem, but he did not give the order. Approval came from Commissioner Taylor on July 23. Wynkoop was given the go ahead if he was "satisfied that the issue of the arms and ammunition is necessary to preserve the peace and that no evil will result from their delivery." The agent, who had been defending his charges all along, had to put up or shut up. On July 29 he issued arms to the Arapahos and Kiowa-Apaches: 200 pistols, 100 rifles, fifteen kegs of powder, two kegs of lead, and 20,000 percussion caps. The Cheyennes came in a few days later and collected theirs. On August 10, Wynkoop wrote to Superintendent Murphy that the Indians "have now left for their hunting grounds, and I am perfectly satisfied that there will be no trouble with them this season, and consequently with no Indians of my agency." That same day the Indians were already in their "hunting grounds" raiding the settlements.[32]

This was a large raid, with more than 200 Cheyennes, Arapahoes, and Lakotas participating. Among those involved were bands under Red Nose, Tall Wolf, Porcupine Bear, Bear-That-Goes-Alone, Little Rock, Medicine Arrow, Bull Bear, Man-Who-Breaks-the-Marrow-Bones, and Black Kettle.[33] Ostensibly, the war party was on its way to raid the Pawnees, but of more than 200 warriors, only about twenty ever went to Pawnee country. The rest found much easier targets in north-central Kansas. On August 10, a few Indians first hit the home of David G. Bacon on Bacon Creek near present-day Ash Grove in Lincoln County.

Jane Bacon (27) had recently delivered a baby. When they saw the Indians approaching, they ran to the timber along the creek. David got away and hid in a hollow log, but warriors caught Mrs. Bacon. They clubbed her on the head, which cut her badly and knocked her senseless, then they raped her. The Cheyennes who perpetrated the deed, Man-Who-Breaks-the-Marrow-Bones and Red Nose, left her unconscious on the prairie and continued their raid. Later in the day the two returned and found Jane Bacon where they left her. This time they picked her up and carried her to their camp.[34]

Other raiders attacked Simeon Shaw's home on Spillman Creek a few miles north of present-day Denmark, Kansas. With their large numbers—Shaw guessed about 400—they hung around the entire day and leisurely plundered and destroyed all they wanted while Shaw, his wife, his sister-in-law Miss Foster (16), and a neighbor, Ben Smith, watched helplessly. At one time, the angry Smith aimed a rifle at an Indian, but Shaw prevented him from shooting. Perhaps because of this, a chief allowed Shaw to keep three of his own horses. That night, the settlers tried to take the three horses and escape. They didn't get far before about fifty warriors caught up to them. One clubbed Simeon in the head and knocked him off his horse, unconscious and seriously hurt. Others threw Mrs. Shaw and Miss Foster to the ground, tore off their clothing and gang-raped them. They took them back to the camp, where Jane Bacon was added to the mix. The three women were outraged until midnight. In the confusion, Ben Smith crept out of the camp and hid. He heard the women screaming long into the night. Finally, either cooler heads prevailed or the Indians satisfied their lust, and the three women were placed on the horses and ordered to ride home. Shaw and Foster only had a short distance to go and made it home; Bacon, who had been more seriously injured and had to ride several miles farther, fainted, fell from her horse, and lay alone on the prairie all night.[35]

When he escaped from the Indians, barefooted David Bacon hardly stopped running until he got to Martin Hendrickson's home, about twenty-six miles away near the Saline River. Hendrickson said that Bacon's feet were "a gore of blood," and that his story was nearly incoherent. Hendrickson was exasperated because Bacon seemed more concerned about his property "than for the dreadful fate of his wife." Bacon would not return to the scene, and the next day, Hendrickson found another man to accompany him in a search for Mrs. Bacon. Avoiding the Indians who were still raiding in the area, the men approached Bacon's claim and miraculously found Mrs. Bacon stumbling along naked, except for "the yoke of a bodice." The day was cool and Hendrickson had a coat with him. He handed her the coat while averting his eyes and she covered herself. He got her up on his horse and had to hold on to her the entire way back to his place. When Jane Bacon recovered she went back east to live with her parents. David Bacon could never live in the area again, and, said Hendrickson, "became a wanderer on the face of the earth." Simeon Smith and Mrs. Smith recovered, but they separated shortly after the incident. Miss Foster died sometime before 1890.[36]

The Indians moved north into Mitchell County and attacked homes along the Solomon. It has been said that the great majority of warriors did not want to attack the settlers, but Red Nose and Man-Who-Breaks-the-Marrow-Bones forced them.[37] Southeast of present-day Beloit, Kansas, the "reluctant" raiders hit the Bogardus and Bell families, who were among the first settlers in the county. The families were related. Hester Ann Bell married Civil War veteran David Bogardus and had two children, Matt (8) and infant William. They shared a house with Hester's brother's family: Braxton B. Bell, wife Elizabeth (21), and their daughter, Ella. Farther down the Solomon near Asher Creek lived Braxton and Hester's parents, Benjamin and Mary Bell, and other relatives. They shared a house with another daughter, Sarah Bell Farrow and her husband James Farrow. Nearby lived Ben and Mary's son Aaron Bell, and his two daughters, Margaret (6) and Esther (8). The two girls were visiting their Aunt Hester and Uncle David.

On August 12, warriors approached the Bell-Farrow house under the guise of friendship, but the suspicious settlers closed the doors and made a stand. The Indians moved on to easier prey. When they left, the Bells and Farrows climbed aboard a hitched wagon and fled. The Indians next appeared at the Bogardus-Bell place. Margaret and Esther Bell were playing outside and ran to the house to warn their uncle. Once more the Indians pretended to be friendly and asked for food. Although there were more than fifty warriors, Elizabeth Bell made a feeble attempt to cook for them. When one group of them finished eating they threw coffee into Elizabeth's face, and seized David Bogardus and Braxton Bell.[38]

Chaos erupted. The children scattered. Matt Bogardus (8) ran into a field and watched. The Indians made a great sport of forcing David and Braxton to run in circles around their house, all the while whipping them as they ran. When David finally stopped to defend himself from the beatings, an Indian shot him. They ordered Braxton to keep running, but as he turned, they shot him down. The Indians plundered the house, and when they were done, they tried to get Hester Bogardus on a horse, but the family dog defended her. The Indians tried, but failed, to kill it. Hester yelled "Soldiers!" which distracted them long enough for her to escape. The Indians secured Margaret and Esther Bell to ponies and tried to get Elizabeth Bell on one, but the distraught woman refused to go. She struggled so much that the angry Indians shot her. The bullet entered her back and came out through her left breast. As she lay in agony several warriors raped her. They speared baby Ella in the back of the head. Finally, the Indians rode off, taking only Margaret and Esther.[39]

On the night of August 12, the Indians crossed the Solomon and held a council. If the Indians ever had any thought of fighting the Pawnees, they must have shelved the plans, for after the Bogardus-Bell attack, only a small party continued north where they attacked settlers along the Republican River (see Sarah White). The majority swung south thirty-five miles back to the Saline. When word of the August 10 attacks reached Fort Larned, Captain Frederick W. Benteen, with Company H, 7th Cavalry, and Lieutenant Owen Hale, with Company M, were dispatched to the scene. Benteen marched rapidly with the fastest horses, leaving Lieutenant Hale to follow along. At Fort Harker, Benteen collected a few extra men, and with a force of about forty soldiers, rode north about twenty miles to the Saline. As he approached on the late morning of August 13, Benteen topped a rise and saw about fifty Indians threatening the Lon Schermerhorn place, a stoutly built house and stockade on Elkhorn Creek about five miles southeast of present-day Lincoln, that served as a meeting place for the locals.

After dropping off ten men with the pack mules, Benteen and his men "were into that gang of astounded reds before they were aware of it." The surprised warriors fled down the Elkhorn and up the Saline. The chase went for about ten miles, with Benteen unknowingly driving away 150 Indians. His aggressiveness did not allow either side to count numbers, and after a time, Benteen said, they got so close to the warriors they were "almost trampling on their 'gee-strings.'"[40]

The Bell sisters had spent the previous night in a tipi. That day while warriors sought to invest the Schermerhorn place, they were left behind with an Indian woman. When the cavalry attacked, the fleeing warriors rode back, picked up the woman, and left the sisters alone on the prairie. Benteen saw the girls near the mouth of Spillman Creek, but he was in the middle of a chase. He might have detached at least one soldier to take the girls back to the settlements, but he only slowed to cross the river and rode on, leaving the girls behind with the instructions "to keep moving down the river and they would be all right." They were not all right. Said Esther: "We wandered there. We slept out two nights with nothing to eat, until a searching party found us. . . ."[41]

The party of settlers searching for victims of the raid included Mart Hendrickson, who had earlier found Jane Bacon. The girls spent the previous night in a vacant dugout and waited by the river, picking berries to eat. About four the next afternoon Hendrickson found them huddled in the grass. "They were very much afraid, and so starved as to be like some ravenous wolves." It was good that the settlers found the girls, for the Indians later returned to look for them. Henderson took them home and cared for them a few days until they were taken to Fort Harker. Benteen reported killing three Indians and wounding ten more. It was the first undisputed victory of the 7th Cavalry and brought accolades to Benteen, however, the abandonment of the Bell girls left his victory tarnished.[42]

Aaron Bell, the girls' father, came to take them home. Little Ella Bell recovered from her head wound and was taken in and raised by Sarah Farrow. Her mother, Elizabeth, shot through both lungs, died in agony about three weeks later. The death of Braxton Bell was said to have so affected his father that Benjamin Bell "died of grief" within a year. Mary Bell died two years later. David Bogardus, Braxton and Elizabeth Bell, and Benjamin Bell were buried in a cemetery on West Asher Creek, the first burial ground in Mitchell County.[43]

SARAH CATHERINE WHITE
Kansas, August 13, 1868

Benjamin and Mary White's first child, Sarah Catherine, was born December 10, 1850, at North Elk Grove, Wisconsin. The Whites and their seven children settled in Cloud County, Kansas, about eight miles west of present-day Concordia. Their homestead was about five miles southwest of the Republican River on a small stream then known as Granny Creek. Because of the tragedy that would occur there, the stream would later be known as White's Creek. The family was unaware of the massive raiding that was occurring in adjoining counties to the south and west (see Jane Bacon). Smaller parties of Cheyennes separated from the main band and moved north.

On the morning of August 13, while the main war party was raiding in Lincoln County, four to six warriors suddenly appeared at the White home. Ben and his sons John, Martin, and Charles were out near the Republican River cutting hay. The Indians walked right into the cabin and demanded that the startled Mrs. White feed them. The frightened woman cooked for them and tried to remain calm. As was often the case, however, when the Indians finished devouring the food, they turned on their hosts. They began smashing dishes and furniture, and then seized Sarah (17) and took her in the yard. They came back and tried to grab another daughter, but Mary White fought so hard that the Indians temporarily gave up. They ordered them to remain in the yard, and went in to plunder the house. In the confusion, Mary and the younger daughters hid in the heavy brush along the creek east of the cabin. The Indians gathered their booty, but could not find the woman and children. They tied the screaming and resisting Sarah on a horse, rode north about five miles, crossed Buffalo Creek, and met up with about fifteen other warriors. Several warriors threw Sarah to the ground and raped her. The rest went down Buffalo Creek to look for more unwary settlers. On the south side of the Republican they found Ben White. He saw them coming and calmly told his boys to walk slowly toward the horses, while he went to get his gun. If the Indians made any hostile moves they were to jump on the horses and escape. When warriors rode up and promptly shot Mr. White down, the boys fled, with Martin and Charles on one horse and John on the other. An Indian caught up to John and pulled him off the horse. When the horse ran off, the warrior went after it, giving John a chance to hide in the high grass by the river. The boys reached some haymakers who frightened the Indians away. They found Ben White but he died a short time later. They put his body in a wagon and started for his house when they met Mrs. White and the girls running toward them. The next morning about thirty-five volunteers assembled to follow the Indian trail. It led southwest to a very large camp on Asher Creek and the settlers demurred. They waited until nightfall for more help but none came, and they decided to leave, reasoning that they would only be defeated, plus almost guarantee that Sarah White would be killed. Only seven men stuck to the trail until they ran out of food and turned back.[44]

The Indians remained in the area for a few more days, hitting the homes of Alfred Schull in Cloud County, the Shafer, Fowler, and Hay families in Ottawa County, and the Marshall and McConnell families in Mitchell County. They killed two of

Author's photo

Marker at site of Sara White's capture.

the McConnell children near the Asher Creek settlements where the Bogardus and Bell murders occurred just two days earlier. Forty-six families filed for losses in the Indian raids of August 1868. Hearing of the raids, Kansas Governor Samuel J. Crawford took a train to Salina, and then organized a volunteer company to ride to the settlers' relief. They arrived in time only to assist in burying the bodies. On August 17, Crawford wrote to President Johnson about the "terrible Indian massacre," where forty citizens were killed, with many of them scalped and mutilated, and with women "outraged and otherwise inhumanly treated," and with several women and girls carried away "to suffer a fate worse than death."

The Indians had stirred up a hornet's nest. On August 21, General Sheridan responded to Governor Crawford that he would immediately remove all Cheyennes, Arapahoes, and Kiowas "out of your State and into their reservations, and will compel them to go by force." The raiding continued for three more months and resulted in the winter campaign that led to the Battle of the Washita and the death of Black Kettle. Even George Bent, a mixed-blood white-Cheyenne who had raided with the Dog Soldiers, admitted that the affair was a "bad mistake," and believed the Indians were at fault.[45]

317

Most of the Indians didn't wait for Sheridan. When some of the raiders went back to the camps of Black Kettle and Little Rock, the chiefs began to strike the lodges. Little Rock, meanwhile, at Agent Wynkoop's request, had been trying to learn the details of the raids. On August 19, he met Wynkoop at Fort Larned and told him the main troublemakers were Red Nose and Man-Who-Breaks-the-Marrow-Bones (see Jane Bacon). Wynkoop didn't believe that two minor chiefs could sway 200 Indians into committing all the depredations and he asked for more names. Little Rock also named Tall Wolf, Porcupine Bear, and Bear That Goes Alone. Wynkoop asked if Little Rock could persuade the Indians to turn in all the guilty warriors. Little Rock answered that he believed only the two main troublemakers should be delivered. Wynkoop wanted the rest, and he told Little Rock that if he could arrange for all of them to be surrendered, that the whites would consider him their friend and he would be protected. Little Rock considered Wynkoop's proposition and agreed to return to the village and try to round up all the guilty warriors. When Little Rock got back he saw that Black Kettle intended to make a run for it. Little Rock fled with him.[46]

When the Indians, whom Sarah White remembered as Cheyenne Dog Soldiers, finished their raid along the Republican, they joined other bands and they all moved west. Sarah was a devout Christian and whenever possible she would get on her knees and talk with the "Great Spirit." Her seemingly strange behavior apparently kept some warriors away from her, but did not deter others. She was "traded repeatedly" from the hands of one chief to another and kept nearby to "amuse the warriors." When not being outraged, Sarah labored for the Indian women, who made her carry huge burdens on her back. She was fed only enough to keep her alive so that she rapidly lost weight; an inch-square of mule meat being her food allowance for an entire day. The women beat her unmercifully whenever the men were not around to prevent it. It was a no-win situation.[47]

On the upper Republican another band of Indians brought in a second white captive (see Anna Brewster Morgan) and from that time on the two women were companions in misery. From the headwaters of the Republican, the bands moved south with the onset of fall. In October, they captured more prisoners along the Arkansas River (see Clara Blinn) and moved into western Indian Territory for the winter. Sarah and Anna tried to escape, but were recaptured and subjected to more punishment. Sarah nearly lost her feet to frostbite. In November, Custer destroyed

Black Kettle's village, and in the following months he pursued the Indians who still refused to come in to the reservations. Custer led units of the 7th Cavalry and part of the 19th Kansas Volunteer Cavalry on a search through western Indian Territory and into the Texas Panhandle. On March 15, 1869, he found Stone Forehead's Cheyennes on Sweetwater Creek and learned that they held two white captives, although he did not know their names. Custer met Stone Forehead in conference and tried to negotiate a settlement to bring them to the reservation without a battle, realizing that hostilities would certainly cause the Indians to kill the captives as they had done at the Washita. After the meeting, instead of coming in, the villagers began to flee. Custer quickly nabbed four hostages to hopefully force the release of the white prisoners.

He released one hostage with a message to Stone Forehead that the Indians would not be released unless the women were turned over to him. On March 17, with no answer, Custer said that he would hang the three hostages unless the women were immediately released. This did the trick. Before sundown the next day, Cheyennes brought the two women to a hill at a distance from the soldiers' camp. Custer sent his interpreter, Romero, to guide them in. The Indians let them go, both women riding one pony and clinging to each other. Romero told them to dismount and walk slowly toward the army camp. Lieutenant Colonel Horace L. Moore of the 19th Kansas moved forward to meet them. The women were Sarah White and Anna Morgan, the latter being captured in Kansas two months after Sarah. Anna did all the talking. Said Moore: "Miss White asked no questions about her people," for she believed "they were all dead before she was carried away."[48]

Men of both regiments were moved to tears at the women's deliverance. Custer described Miss White as "not beautiful," but she "possessed a most interesting face." Their joy at being freed, however, "could not hide the evidences of privation and suffering to which they had been subjected by their cruel captives." They were dressed in government stamped flour sacks, showing that the Indians who had held them obtained their rations at an agency.

Major Milton Stewart, 19th Kansas, stated: "I was a witness to the recital of the wrongs and brutal indignities which had been heaped upon these poor innocent sufferers." Among other things, they had to work "like beasts of burden, to pack wood and water," and "they were whipped almost daily." Stewart learned from them that they were treated better after Custer destroyed Black Kettle's village. They were also near starvation, but for the past two days "they had feasted on mule meat," perhaps in an attempt by the

Indians to fatten them up before their release. Both women were forced to live with several warriors, and they were reported to be pregnant at the time of their release. "Their joy," wrote Custer, "therefore at regaining their freedom after a captivity of nearly a year [sic] can be better imagined than described."[49]

After obtaining the Cheyennes' promise to go to the reservation, Custer led the troops to Camp Supply in Indian Territory, then to Fort Dodge and Fort Hays in Kansas. Sarah White thought her entire family was dead, but upon rejoining her mother and siblings in Cloud County, she seemed to recover mentally. She lived quietly in the community, and became a schoolteacher in nearby Clyde, Kansas. Within a year of her release, she married H. C. Brooks, a Civil War veteran with a farm near Clyde. Sarah continued to support her mother until her brothers were old enough to take over the farm. Sarah had seven children, five of whom reached maturity.

In 1870, Sarah wrote to her congressman, Sidney Clarke, telling of her experiences, the murder of her father, and her captivity. She asked Clarke to bring the facts before Congress to possibly "appropriate me money for hardships and privations endured." Clarke apparently was unable to help her, for in 1874, Sarah petitioned the U.S. Senate Committee on Claims for compensation due as a result of her captivity. She wrote: "My back is weak from the effects of carrying burdens. I have also been afflicted ever since my recapture with weakness and faintness that is of a nature to last as long as I live."

This time, Sarah White Brooks gave the petition to a congressman named Ingalls, who mishandled the entire matter. As a result, Sarah's claim was denied, the committee declaring, "The statement is unsupported by any proof, not even the affidavit of the petitioner being furnished. The committee report adversely, and ask to be discharged from further consideration of the case." As in so many instances, a claimant's unfamiliarity of procedures or an incompetent attorney botched the case. Sarah got nothing.

Mr. Brooks died in the early 1920s and Sarah had to vacate the home they had shared for so long. Several years of drought had caused the crops to fail, and her income could not meet her expenses and taxes. She moved in with her only son, Walter, who had lost his wife a few years earlier. They still lived near Concordia, Kansas, only about one mile from where she had been captured. Sarah White Brooks died May 11, 1939, at age 88.[50]

ANNA BREWSTER MORGAN
Kansas, October 13, 1868

Anna Brewster was born December 10, 1844, at New Brunswick, New Jersey. Her father, John W. Brewster, died four months before she was born and the family lived in poverty. One of her brothers, Daniel A. Brewster, joined the 1st New Jersey in the Civil War, while another brother died at Chancellorsville in 1863, fighting in the 7th New Jersey. After the war, Dan Brewster moved his mother and sister to Pennsylvania where their mother, Prudence Nau Brewster, died in an insane asylum. Daniel and Anna next moved to Illinois. In 1867, Dan moved to Kansas, on a 160-acre claim on the Solomon River in Ottawa County, near present-day Delphos. When the cabin was built, Dan sent for Anna to come out and help keep house for him.[51]

Anna Brewster (23), said to be "a beautiful young woman with blue eyes and thick lustrous hair of yellow hue" married James S. Morgan (29) in September 1868.[52] James Morgan was also a Civil War veteran, having fought in the 2nd Colorado Cavalry. Anna moved to his cabin, where he had lived since 1866, two miles southwest of present Delphos, and just a few miles from her brother's place. They had only been married a few weeks, when on October 13, James went out to work in the field of his neighbor, David Mortimer. It was a damp, foggy morning, and Morgan figured it would be too wet for Indians to effectively use their bows, so he left his gun at home. He did not realize the Indians had been armed for years, and had gotten a new supply of weapons from Agent Wynkoop just two months ago. About eight a.m. Morgan spied three or four Lakotas coming at him through the cornfield.[53] Morgan motioned for them to go away, but they kept coming. He hurriedly untied his horses from the wagon and as he did, one warrior fired a bullet into his hip. At the rifle's report the horses bolted and ran. James limped off into the high corn, reached the Solomon River, and swam across where he hid in the willows. The Indians left him alone and went after the horses. Morgan later crawled to Daniel Yockey's home. Several settlers joined up and took him to a doctor in Minneapolis, Kansas. The wound took several months to heal.

The Indians did not catch the horses, for they quickly ran right back to the Morgan cabin. Anna heard the clatter outside and saw the horses snorting heavily. She assumed James was hurt, so she strapped on a revolver, mounted one horse, led the other one, and headed to where he was working. She could not see him, so she rode to the tall grass near the river. The warriors were concealed all around her and sprang up; she turned to ride away, but one grabbed the bridle while another hit her in the head with a war club and knocked her unconscious. When she came to, she was "in a strange country among the hills, bound tight to my horse."[54]

The Indians headed west for several hours before stopping for the night, where several other small bands joined them. That night Anna Morgan was gang raped. The days blended together, and a week or more of travel brought them to the headwaters of the Republican. The area was a common hunting ground of both the Cheyennes and Oglala and Brule Lakotas, and there the bands met, celebrating and trading. About one month after her capture, Anna Morgan was traded to the Cheyennes and joined a camp with another white captive (see Sarah White).

The women were put to work, said Anna, doing "menial service such as carrying wood from the creek for the more favored squaws." When the weather turned colder, the bands moved south, reaching the Arkansas and moving downstream. Sarah and Anna tried to cooperate and obeyed all orders in order to gain the Indians' confidence. All the while, said Anna, "we were laying by a supply of dried buffalo meat so we could escape for civilization the first opportunity presented." One day, when the warriors were occupied in a council, they crawled past the guards, struck a trail and "traveled for dear life." They walked at night, badly lacerating and bruising their feet, and hid in the day. They could see the Indians looking for them in the distance. The next night they saw a light in the distance and hoped they might be near Fort Dodge. Hoping that soldiers would see them they made an ill-advised move in the daylight and the Indians caught them. "I fought hard and said I would not go back," said Anna. "But they took me by main force and whipped me and bound me onto the pony."[55]

The women were taken back to the village where they were beaten and placed under more restrictions. The village moved to the upper Washita in Indian Territory, just downstream from the camp of Black Kettle, which was attacked on November 27, 1868. When the soldiers attacked, the Indians killed two white captives (see Clara Blinn). Fortunately for White and Morgan, the village they were in escaped, and they were not murdered.

Strangely enough, after Custer's destruction of Black Kettle's village, the women's treatment improved. Perhaps the Indians realized that the soldiers might strike them someday, or that they would eventually have to return the captives and it might be easier on them if they were treated better. Soon after, an Indian "proposed" to Anna Morgan, and, she said, "I married him, thereby choosing the least of two evils and never expecting to see a white person again." The warrior brought her small gifts and the Indian women treated her more kindly.

Troops searched for the Indians through the winter of 1869. Lieutenant Colonel Horace Moore, 19th Kansas, said the men were weary of the long marches, short rations, and cold storms, but when they thought "of Mrs. Blinn and her little boy, [and] of the hundred murders in Kansas," they tightened their belts and marched on. The Indians evaded the soldiers until March 1869, when detachments of Custer's 7th Cavalry and the 19th Kansas Cavalry caught up to Stone Forehead's Cheyenne village on Sweetwater Creek (see Sarah White). Marching with the 19th Kansas was Dan Brewster. He had been searching for his sister since her capture, and he caught up with Custer at Camp Supply, Indian Territory. He explained his situation to Custer, stating that he required no horse, weapon, or pay, but only wished to search for his sister. Custer put him on the payroll as a substitute teamster. Later, he would write that Brewster "displayed more genuine courage, perseverance, and physical endurance, and a greater degree of true brotherly love and devotion, than I have ever seen combined in one person."[56]

Custer took Cheyenne hostages from Stone Forehead's camp to force them to return the two white women. Late in the afternoon on March 19, the white captives were put on one pony and sent toward Custer's camp. Custer and other officers watched through field glasses as they approached. Dan Brewster stood by his side. Custer described one of the women as being short and heavy and the other as tall and slender.

"The last one must be my sister," Brewster interjected, "she is quite tall. Let me go and meet them, this anxiety is more than I can endure." But Custer would not allow it, fearing that if one of them was his sister, the sight of her might provoke him into taking revenge on the nearest Indian. When the women got a bit closer, they dismounted and were met by a few officers Custer had sent out ahead. Brewster then bounded away, running full speed for them. Custer watched him run up to the taller of the two and throw his arms around her. Lieutenant Colonel Moore was one of the first on the scene. Before Brewster could reach them he took the elder woman by the hand and asked if she was Mrs. Morgan. She said she was, and then introduced the other as Miss White.

"Are we free now?" Anna asked. Moore said yes, and she then asked, "Where is my husband?" Moore said he was wounded and recovering. Her next question was, "Where is my brother?" Moore told her he was in camp, but the situation was soon revealed when Brewster came running up to her.[57]

When the women reached the soldiers' camp a cheer went up, and Custer said there were many a tear shed at the happy reunion. The women wore government flour sacks, Indian leggings, and moccasins, and one of the first things Custer heard Dan Brewster say was, "Sister, do take those hateful things off." Fortunately, Custer had a female cook in camp, and she was able to spare some extra clothing for the women.

Most of the soldiers were completely satisfied to have rescued them without a fight, yet there were those in the 19th Kansas who were disappointed, because they had enlisted especially to fight the Indians who had been devastating their state. Sarah White and Anna Brewster Morgan had been rescued without an attack that would have cost many lives. The military so outnumbered the Cheyennes on this occasion, that had they attacked, they would certainly have had a greater victory than at the Washita. Custer, however, weighed his options and chose to negotiate for the release of the women rather than seek battle. He successfully rescued them without loss of life, and without paying a ransom, showing that he could learn from experience and that he was also a diplomat and negotiator as well as a proven fighter.[58]

The women were very much worse for the wear. David L. Spotts, a private in Company L, 19th Kansas, said one of them (Morgan) "appeared to be 50 years old, although she was less than 25. She was stooped, pale, and haggard, looking as if she had been compelled to do more than she was able." She was tall, with formerly blond hair now "dirty brown from exposure." She wore several "kinds of material, pieces of tents and blankets, all worn out and sewed together with strings." Of Miss White, Spotts said she was dressed about the same and was pale, but was "younger looking and did not show the hard usage."[59]

Several officers and enlisted men heard a "recital of the wrongs and indignities" heaped upon them, including Custer, Major Milton Stewart, and Lieutenant Colonel Horace Moore. They were things that could not be printed in Victorian literature of the times. Custer reported that the story of their treatment was a litany of such "cruelties, and enormous indignities that it is surprising that civilized beings could endure it and still survive." In his book, he wrote, "There was much in their story not appropriate for these pages," but he did say that they suffered "indignities and insults far more terrible than death itself." His wife, Elizabeth, later penned: "The young faces of the two, who not a year before were bright, happy women, were now worn with privation and exposure, and haggard with the terrible insults of their captors, too dreadful to be chronicled here." Spotts too, writing of Mrs. Morgan, said, "It is impossible to imagine the mental agony and physical torture endured. . ." and "Only those who know what Indians are capable of doing, have any idea of how she spent the night."[60]

Years later, Anna Morgan related the events of her captivity to a neighbor, Emily Harrison. Harrison printed the story in a 1907 article. Here, we get a slightly different take on the devastating experience of her captivity. As Mrs. Harrison told it, when Anna was rescued, she heard that "there were two white men in the camp, [and] I did not care to see them. I was surprised to see my own brother walk into the tent." Harrison also wrote, that Anna said, "After I came back, the road seemed rough, and I often wished they had never found me."[61]

After rescuing the women, Custer headed back to Fort Dodge. There, James Morgan, still not fully recovered from his wound, met them and took Anna back to their claim. Life for her would never be the same again. James Morgan resented the fact that Anna had become an Indian's "wife." The situation deteriorated several months later when Anna gave birth to a half-Indian son. She named him Ira Arthur and declared "that the babe's blood was as pure as any of the rest of my children." James, however, did not think so, and their marriage became more strained.

About a year later, some officers of the 7th Cavalry were riding in Ottawa County when they saw a boy with Indian features playing in front of a house. They were inquisitive, knocked on the door, and much to their surprise, recognized Anna Morgan, one of the women they helped rescue. They talked for a few minutes and learned that all was not well. Her husband, instead of trying to help her "forget the misery through which she had passed," often upbraided her as if she was responsible for her misfortunes. Perhaps James's anger was calmed somewhat after the child died, at the age of 17 months.[62]

Anna lived with James Morgan until 1880, when she finally left him. He sued, and obtained a divorce by her consent. Journalists and writers came to her door, asking for her to tell of her experiences, but she would not do it. She considered it a disgrace, and telling the story would only add to the infamy. Her brother agreed with her. In 1893, Anna wrote to a friend that, "rather than the world should know what I have been forced to endure, I would rather live the remaining days of my life in poverty than have these dreadful facts known."

In another letter, Anna wrote: "My life received a blight at that time [her capture] which will go with me to the grave. Life has been worth nothing to me since then. Do not mention my husband to me. He reproached me times without number for my misfortune, for having been a helpless victim to the atrocities of the wild savages." She also wrote, "They say, each cloud has a silver lining, but that has not turned to me yet."

Anna never found the silver lining. Her situation deteriorated and about 1900 she was placed in the Kansas Insane Asylum in Topeka. Perhaps the condition was hereditary, but certainly the anguish, physical, and mental stress she was under for decades must have contributed to her condition. Anna Brewster Morgan died in the asylum on July 11, 1902.[63]

SUSANNA ALDERDICE AND MARIA WEICHEL
Kansas, May 30, 1869

Susanna Zeigler was born in 1840 in northeastern Ohio, the first of seven children of Michael and Mary Zeigler. By the early 1850s they had moved near Independence, Missouri. While living there, Susanna met James A. Daily, and the 20-year-olds married in 1860. A few years later they moved to Salina, Kansas, where they staked a claim to take advantage of the new Homestead Act of 1862. Soon after, Susanna's family joined them. These were years of turmoil as the Civil War raged, and James Daily answered the call by joining the 17th Kansas Infantry in July 1864. They had one child, John, born in 1863, and Susanna was pregnant again when James marched away. He died of typhoid fever in November 1864, one month after his second child, Willis, was born.

In June 1866, Susanna married Tom Alderdice. Formerly a Confederate soldier in the 44th Mississippi, Alderdice was captured at Chickamauga in 1863, was a prisoner at Rock Island, Illinois, took the Oath of Allegiance, and joined the 2nd U. S. Volunteers. The volunteers were regiments of former Rebel soldiers who could get out of prison if they swore to fight for the Union. They were called "Galvanized Yankees" and were used in the west to fight Indians. The couple moved near Spillman Creek, in Lincoln County, Kansas, west of present-day Lincoln. Again, much of the Zeigler family moved nearby, as did John Alverson, who married Susanna's sister Mary. Susanna had two more children, Frank, in 1867, and Alice, in 1868.[64]

Less is known about Maria Weichel. Many of the settlers along Spillman Creek were Germans or Scandinavians. Families such as the Weichels, Meigerhoffs, and Lauritzens were recent immigrants and tended to stay in close-knit communities. Many stayed at a Danish settlement several miles up Spillman Creek from its junction with the Saline. George and Maria Weichel probably emigrated from Hanover, Germany. Unsure as to where to stake a claim, they were warned by Ferdinand Erhardt to stay south of the Saline, because it was safer from Indian attack. Erskild Lauritzen, however, had a place north of the Saline near the Danish settlement and they convinced the Weichels to stay with them and look for land in that locale. They agreed. Maria, described as a shapely and beautiful woman, was three months pregnant in May 1869. They were said to have been educated and well off financially. Maria supposedly owned twenty-four silk dresses. They were only in the area a few months when the Indians struck.[65]

The Indians were mostly Cheyennes under the Dog Soldier Tall Bull. In May, Tall Bull fought with Major Eugene Carr's 5th Cavalry in several actions, including Elephant Rock and Spring Creek. When Carr left to re-fit at Fort McPherson, Nebraska, Tall Bull was free to turn his vengeance on the settlements. In the week prior to May 30, the Cheyennes killed fourteen civilians in north central Kansas. On Sunday, the 30th, they turned their attention to Spillman Creek.

About two in the afternoon, Tall Bull and sixty warriors began their murder spree. The first people attacked were Eli Zeigler and John Alverson, heading up creek to attend to an abandoned farm. Zeigler's sister, Susanna Alderdice, warned him that morning to be careful because of recent reports of Indian depredations. The two men were near the junction of Trail Creek and Spillman Creek when Indians charged them. Zeigler and Alverson abandoned their wagon and made for the thickets along Trail Creek. The Indians fired at them a short while, and then plundered the wagon.

The Cheyennes next went to a small settlement near the present-day town of Denmark. Out tending their garden, Erskild Lauritzen and his wife Stine were killed, stripped, and scalped. Their son was visiting the neighboring Christensen home and lived. A houseguest of the Lauritzens, Otto Peterson, escaped the initial attack, but he could not run far or fast enough and he too was killed. When the Indians came upon the Christensen home, they found the occupants armed and ready and a few shots kept them away.

Continuing downstream, the Cheyennes next came upon Fred Meigherhoff and George and Maria Weichel. The three were inspecting a possible farmstead when attacked. Fred and George fired at the Indians and fled south along Spillman Creek. They went more than three miles before they ran out of ammunition. The Indians quickly killed the men and took Maria captive. One warrior cut off her husband's finger. A small party broke off from the main raid, put Maria on a horse and rode away, then stopped and threw her on the ground. Four warriors held her arms and legs while they took turns raping her.[66]

One mile southeast, Susanna Alderdice, her four children, a Mr. and Mrs. Noon, a Mr. Whalen, and Bridget Kine and her daughter, had been staying at the Michael Healy homestead. When the shooting was heard to the northwest, about six p.m., the Noons and Whalen quickly made their escape on horseback, leaving the rest of the women and children behind. They left the house and tried to make it to the thick brush along the Saline River. Herding along her four children, Susanna could not keep up. Bridget clutched her baby daughter and waded across the river, hiding in the brush on the opposite side. Susanna was caught about fifty yards from the river. She sat down, holding her two youngest children. The Indians were brutal. They shot John (5) with four bullets, put five arrows into Frank (2), then bashed him against the ground, and shot Willis (4) with five arrows, two bullets, plus speared him in the back. For some reason they let Susanna keep eight-month-old Alice.

Another mile down the Saline, the Cheyennes met two 14-year-old boys, Arthur Schmutz and John Strange. The Indians said they were good Pawnees and the boys relaxed enough for one teenage warrior to approach close enough to crash his war club into Strange's head. The boy only yelled, "Oh Lord," before he fell dead. Schmutz took off running, but caught an arrow in his side that pierced his lung. Somehow he kept running, pulled the shaft out, and was rescued by two of his brothers who heard the commotion and hurried to him with rifles. The Indians retreated. Schmutz was taken to Fort Harker but he died about ten weeks later, the eleventh fatality of the deadly raid.[67]

The Indians, finished with their killing for the day, crossed the Saline and camped on the south side near Bullfoot Creek. They were only about two miles from Lieutenant Edward Law and his Company G, 7th Cavalry, who were camped unaware of the raid on the opposite side of the Saline. The soldiers pursued the next day, but the Indians got away. The suffering was not over for Susanna Alderdice. Three days later, perhaps tired of little Alice's crying, the Indians took the baby from her mother, strangled her, and hung the limp body in a tree. Susanna and Maria, subject to constant abuse and rape, remained captives.

On July 11, Major Carr, with seven companies of the 5th Cavalry and three companies of Pawnee scouts under Luther North, finally caught up to Tall Bull and Black Shin's eighty-four-lodge village at Summit Springs, Colorado Territory. Just moments before rescue, a warrior may have grabbed Susanna and tomahawked her in the head, shattering her skull and probably killing her instantly. He also shot her through the head above the eye. Tall Bull himself shot Maria through the chest. Sun Dance Woman, one of Tall Bull's wives, who was taken captive after the battle, said that it was Tall Bull who smashed Susanna in the head with his rifle and then shot Maria. She said, "Both had been used as wives of Tall Bull and one was with child." Sun Dance Woman was jealous and shot Maria again with a pistol, then ran out of the tipi and jumped on a horse with Tall Bull. She said she knew Susanna would die "by the sound of the rifle blow when it hit her head. It cracked like a split from a ripe pumpkin."[68]

While Carr chased the Indians out of the village, the badly wounded Maria Weichel crawled out of the lodge about the time Luther North and Captain Cushing were about to enter it. She fell at their feet and grasped Cushing by the leg, sobbing and speaking in German. Surgeon Louis Tesson made her as comfortable as he could, and later that evening, removed the bullet from her breast. Trumpeter Henry Voss, who could speak German, interpreted for her as she told the story of the abuse that the women were subjected to. Later, Tesson prepared Susanna's body for burial.

The command loaded six wagons with captured goods, yet still burned a staggering amount of Indian property, about ten tons of it, including many articles stolen during the May raids. They also found a gruesome necklace containing the fingers from many white people. Incredibly, the ring taken from George Weichel's cut-off finger was found and returned to Maria. About eight the next morning, Susanna was wrapped in a buffalo robe and buried in a deep grave in the middle of where the village stood. Doctor Tesson read an Episcopal service for the dead, a bugler played the funeral dirge, and the command headed out.[69]

Before they reached Fort Sedgwick on the South Platte, the concerned soldiers took up a collection for Maria, giving her much of the recovered property and about $838. She was placed in the post hospital from July 15 to August 4. Maria remarried soon, but the stories say it was to a 5th Cavalry soldier, a hospital steward at Sedgwick, an army surgeon, or the first white person who helped her at Summit Springs. Her new married name did not survive for posterity. She did not return to Lincoln County for nearly a year, and white thieves had taken much of her property. A neighbor named George Green saved some of her belongings and returned them to her.

The fate of Maria's unborn child carried during her captivity is unknown, but it is likely that she lost the baby. She gave birth to a healthy daughter, Minnie, by her second husband, in Omaha, Nebraska, in December 1870. Maria lived at various locations in Kansas, and possibly Lincoln, Nebraska. She visited Lincoln County, Kansas, in 1909, to talk with the old settlers about the Indian raid of 1869, possibly to obtain evidence to file a depredation claim, although nothing is known of the outcome. Maria then fades out of history. Her daughter, Minnie, married a Mr. Wurthmann, lived in California, and had three children.[70]

Tom Alderdice trailed the Indians after the raid and found his dead daughter, Alice, at a campsite the Indians recently vacated. The information he forwarded to Major Carr helped him catch Tall Bull at Summit Springs. Tom was with a 7th Cavalry detachment on the Saline River on July 23, when word came in of the fight at Summit Springs and the death of his wife. Tom Alderdice was devastated. All his family was dead. He moved to western Kansas and then to Iowa, where he remarried in 1873, and had eight more children. They moved to Milan, Kansas, in 1891. Tom did not return to Lincoln County until 1911, hoping to find the graves of John Daily and Frank Alderdice and remove them to a cemetery. The land had changed, however, and Tom could not remember exactly where they were buried. They remain undiscovered.

Susanna's last child, Willis Daily, incredibly survived his wounds. Some citizens and 7th Cavalry soldiers found him the day after the attack. Army Surgeon Renick refused to remove the arrowheads, including one lodged five inches into his chest, and civilians Washington Smith and Phil Lantz finally had to do the job. Susanna's parents, Michael and Mary Zeigler, stayed in the area and raised Willis. In 1886 he married Mary Twibell, whose parents lived on land adjoining the Zeiglers. They had three children. In 1893, Willis moved his family near Blue Rapids in Marshall County, Kansas. Willis always had trouble from his wounds. His daughter Anna once said, "Daddy never talked about it but I have seen the five big arrow scars on his back many times." By 1917, his legs were giving out, and further examination showed that they were cancerous. He had several operations, the last one removing his leg at the hip, but it was too late to stop the spread. He died in Blue Rapids on June 16, 1920. He was buried in Lincoln County at the Spillman Cemetery, only two miles from where his grandparents raised him.[71]

MARY SMITH JORDAN
Kansas, August 19, 1872

Widow Martha A. Smith moved to Ellis, Kansas, in August 1870, with her five girls and two boys, where she managed a bunkhouse for the Kansas Pacific railroad workers. Some of the Smith girls got jobs as waitresses in John Edwards's hotel. In a town where women were scarce, all of them, Mary, Angeline, Laura, Josephine, and Jennie, were married within three years. Mary Smith married Richard Jordan, a 25-year-old buffalo hunter, in November 1871. The Jordan family moved to Ellis from Kentucky in 1871. They bought the Western Hotel, but managing the business was more than they could handle, and they moved to a cabin a mile west of town. The Jordans had six sons and three daughters. Richard, the oldest son, moved to Parks' Fort (WaKeeney) and built a headquarters for a buffalo hunting business. He brought his new bride to the tiny settlement.[72]

Mary Jordan was soon pregnant, but lost her baby in the late spring of 1872. To snap out of her depression, she decided to go with her husband on a buffalo hunt. In July, she visited her mother, who tried to talk her out of it. Mary thought the trip would be good for her, besides, she understood the Indians were all on reservations, and she would be safe with her husband and his companions.

They left on August 1, with Richard's brother George, a hired man named Fred Nelson, and their Newfoundland dog, Queen. Mary told her parents not to worry about them for six weeks. The small party went southwest to the Smoky Hill, moved upstream, and then south to the Middle Fork of the Walnut. Near the junction of the North and Middle Fork, about five miles northeast of present-day Dighton, in Lane County, Kansas, they set up camp and went about the hunt. On August 16, another hunter stopped at Jordan's camp, saw their Newfoundland dog, learned that their hunt was successful, and that they soon would be heading for home. Unfortunately, the Jordans were in the path of several Cheyennes who had left their agency in Indian Territory and were heading north.

On August 19, Old Bear, Buffalo Meat, Coon, and Broen-hi-o came upon the camp. Whether incensed at the killing of the buffalo, or if there were some other difficulties involved is not known, but the Indians surprised and killed the men. They shot Richard Jordan in the shoulder and chest and scalped him. Fred Nelson was shot about 300 yards away, the bullet entering his hip and breaking his spine. He was scalped twice. George Jordan may have been able to run for a distance before the Cheyennes caught him near a ford of the Middle Fork Walnut. They shot him with five arrows, one of them entering his mouth, and one going five inches into his heart, then scalped and mutilated him. The Cheyennes took Mary Jordan with them; all that remained was her sunbonnet.[73]

About three weeks after the Jordans and Nelson departed, the dog Queen arrived at the Smith farm one night, whining at the door. Mrs. Smith was concerned, but not alarmed, for they said they would be gone six weeks. Perhaps the dog was troublesome and they sent it home. After six weeks without any news, the family was very concerned. On September 30, a hunter named Kent arrived at Buffalo Station (now Park, Kansas) and reported finding deserted wagons and cut up harnesses about forty miles south. In a wagon was a grain sack with the name "R. Jordan" on it. The news was telegraphed to Ellis, and forwarded to Fort Hays. On October 2, Lieutenant Colonel Thomas H. Neill, 6th Cavalry, sent out Sergeant Daniel Ahern and ten privates to investigate. They took a train to Ellis, picked up Nick Jordan, one of Dick's brothers, and Thomas K. Hamilton, Mary's brother-in-law, and continued to Park. There they got Kent to guide them and started south to the Walnut. On October 3, they found the bodies. Jordan and Hamilton rode the sixty-five miles back to Buffalo Station and sent out a telegram. The news reached the Smith Farm and one of the daughters read it and passed it around. None of them wanted to inform their mother. Finally, Mrs. Smith divined what was going on and screamed out, "Read it!"

Jennie, the youngest daughter, read it: "Have found three boys, Mary missing. Suppose she has been carried off by the Indians." "Mother stood straight up for a moment," Jennie said, "then threw her hands over her head and giving a piercing scream, fell to the floor in a dead faint."[74]

Mary's description was sent out across the frontier: five feet tall, black hair, gray eyes, rather pleasing in manner and looks, dark complexion, and a slight limp. General John Pope, commanding the Department of Missouri, wrote to Kansas Governor James M. Harvey, sending Mary's description, and adding that her friends wished to do everything possible "that may lead to her recovery and the punishment of the fiends guilty of the hellish deeds." Tom Hamilton went to Fort Hays to get help to bring back the bodies, and Neill sent three enlisted men and a wagon to return with him to the scene. There was no undertaker in Ellis in October 1872, but carpenters fashioned three wooden coffins and the funeral was held. About one week later, an eight-person search party of civilians, including John Smith, Mary's 15-year-old brother, rode south to take up the Indians trail and find Mary Jordan. They reached the Arkansas River about six miles west of Fort Dodge, crossed over and rode south to the Cimarron on the border of Indian Territory. There, soldiers from Dodge arrested them, because it was against the law to carry weapons into the Territory. When the soldiers tried to escort them back, John Smith cussed and fought them for not looking for his sister and for preventing anyone else from looking for her. They slapped him in irons and took him to the fort.[75]

First reports indicated that the arrows found in the bodies appeared to be Kiowa, but General John Pope, commander of the Department of the Missouri, believed that the Kiowas hadn't been north of the Arkansas for two years. He thought Osages might have committed the murders. From Camp Supply, Indian Territory, Colonel John W. Davidson said he spoke with Medicine Arrow (Stone Forehead) and Little Raven of the Cheyenne and Arapaho tribes, and both men assured him that none of their people committed the crime.

Word of the abduction went to General Edward O. C. Ord, commander of the Department of the Platte, and he forwarded the news to Forts McPherson, Laramie, and Fetterman, with the suggestion that a reward of five or ten ponies be offered for Mary Jordan's safe return. When he asked General Sheridan for approval, Little Phil replied: "After having her husband and friends murdered, and her own person subjected to the fearful bestiality of perhaps the whole tribe, it is mock humanity to secure what is left of her for the consideration of five ponies."[76]

Sheridan, hardened by the realities of war, was saying that if she wasn't already dead, she might as well be. The Smith Family, however, wanted her back in any condition. By this time, the government had finally realized that they could not stop hostage taking by continually paying ransoms, and General William T. Sherman stood by the policy: "So long as ransoms are paid to Indians, so long will they steal women, to use, and sell." He sent orders "forbidding the practice of ransom in future cases," and Secretary of War, William Belknap, agreed. Thus, was Mary Jordan dismissed.[77]

It was not until September 1873, that superintendent of the Cheyenne and Arapaho Agency in Indian Territory, John D. Miles, learned that four Cheyenne Indians, two of whom belonged to the agency and two northerners, left the agency in Indian Territory and were returning to the north. Miles wrote to Commissioner Edward A. P. Smith, that in the Walnut country, "they run on the Jordans, murdering the men and taking captive the Mrs. Jordan whom I believe they kept a day or two for the purpose of gratifying their fiendish desires and after having exhausted their animal desires in outraging her person, killed her." Miles said Old Bear and Buffalo Meat were up north, Coon was accidentally shot and killed in August 1873, and Broen-hi-o, who belonged to Miles's agency, had disappeared.

Nothing else was done to apprehend Mary Jordan's murderers. For most of the white settlers on the frontier it was just another example that the authorities cared little for their safety. Mrs. Smith did not forget. In 1876, she spoke in Hays, Kansas, and said she wanted the Indian "problem" to be left up to the settlers, and then, "many of the murdered ones would be avenged." She never believed the official story that Mary was dead and faulted the government for not looking for her. "How many more sorrowing mothers could tell the same tale?" she pondered. "Mother" Smith died in 1910.[78]

Chapter seven notes

[1] Joseph Eubank Depredation Claim #1117; Becher, *Massacre Along the Medicine Road*, 138; Ellenbecker, *Tragedy at the Little Blue*, 2.

[2] Becher, *Massacre Along the Medicine Road*, 139-40.

[3] Becher, *Massacre Along the Medicine Road*, 149-50, 155, 157-58; Ellenbecker, *Tragedy at the Little Blue*, 21; Charles Emery Depredation Claim # 1019.

[4] Becher, *Massacre Along the Medicine Road*, 159, 162, 181-82, 186-87, 315, 329n7; Ellenbecker, *Tragedy at the Little Blue*, 22-23; Carroll, *Sand Creek Massacre*, iii.

[5] Michno, *Battle at Sand Creek*, 141-43; Becher, *Massacre Along the Medicine Road*, 314-16; *OR*, 34/3, 531-32.

[6] Wynkoop, *Tall Chief*, 16.

[7] Becher, *Massacre Along the Medicine Road*, 318-20; Wynkoop, *Tall Chief*, 17-18, 90-93, 95-96.

[8] Michno, *Battle at Sand Creek*, 157; Czaplewski, *Captive of the Cheyenne*, sec. 2, 22.

[9] Wynkoop, *Tall Chief*, 96, 99; Ellenbecker, *Tragedy at the Little Blue*, 29; Becher, *Massacre Along the Medicine Road*, 323, 329n6, 424.

[10] Becher, *Massacre Along the Medicine Road*, 424-25, 427-28, 445-46.

[11] Becher, *Massacre Along the Medicine Road*, 314, 423-24.

[12] Sanford, *Mollie*, 189-90; Becher, *Massacre Along the Medicine Road*, 328, 329n7.

[13] Becher, *Massacre Along the Medicine Road*, 355-58; Czaplewski, *Captive of the Cheyenne*, sec. 2, 24-26.

[14] Becher, *Massacre Along the Medicine Road*, 369, Carroll, *Sand Creek Documents*, iii.

[15] Ellenbecker, *Tragedy at the Little Blue*, 9; McDermott, *Circle of Fire*, 57, 60-62; Becher, *Massacre Along the Medicine Road*, 370-73.

[16] Nadeau, *Fort Laramie and the Sioux*, 179; McDermott, *Circle of Fire*, 70.

[17] Bettelyoun and Waggoner, *With My Own Eyes*, 88. Nadeau, *Fort Laramie and the Sioux*, 181; Michno, *Encyclopedia of Indian Wars*, 175

[18] Carroll, *Sand Creek Documents*, iii; Becher, *Massacre along the Medicine Road*, 376, 430-31.

[19] Peter Ulbrich Depredation Claim #6220; Margaretha Kalus Depredation Claim #454. Thanks goes to Dr. Jeff Broome for generously sharing these claims with the author.

[20] Peter Ulbrich Depredation Claim #6220.

[21] Campbell, "Indian Raid of 1867," 259-61; Becher, *Massacre Along the Medicine Road*, 384. In her statement, Veronica said she thought Jessie was about 20, Christiana (who she called Catherine) about 18, and the boys five or six. Grinnell, *Fighting Cheyennes*, 268, says that the girls were 19 and 17, and the twins were six.

[22] Peter Ulbrich Depredation Claim #6220.

[23] Peter Ulbrich Depredation Claim #6220; Campbell, "Indian Raid of 1867," 262. Veronica's story is told in Broome, *Dog Soldier Justice*, 133-40.

[24] Michno, *Encyclopedia of Indian Wars*, 207-09.

[25] Stanley, *My Early Travels*, 197-216; Grinnell, *Fighting Cheyennes*, 268; Grinnell, *Two Great Scouts*, 146-47; Hyde, *Spotted Tail's Folk*, 138. Hyde speaks of six white captives being returned. Grinnell also mentions six captives: three girls, two boys, and a baby. Who this sixth unnamed baby was is not explained. Grinnell said two of the girls were named Martin and were captured south of Grand Island. This is incorrect. There was a Martin family attacked in the vicinity in 1864, but the captured girls were Campbells. He also incorrectly claims another girl and two boys were captured on the Solomon.

[26] Stanley, *My Early Travels*, 198; Grinnell, *Two Great Scouts*, 147.

[27] Peter Ulbrich Depredation Claim #6220; Campbell, "Indian Raid of 1867," 262.

[28] Peter Ulbrich Depredation Claim # 6220; Broome, *Dog Soldier Justice*, 139-40, 261n39.

[29] Broome, *Dog Soldier Justice*, 7-9, 230; Burkey, *Custer, Come at Once*, 39. Broome has the most complete account of these raids. Agent Albert G. Boone confirmed that the Indians plundered several settlers' houses. Some, including John Nance, David Lucas, Aaron Grigsby, Patrick O'Byrne, and Hubert Pappan filed depredation claims. Halaas and Masich, *Halfbreed*, 252, because they relied on George Bent's stories, incorrectly claim that in addition to the cattle, the Indians only took "a few things from houses vacated by settlers."

[30] Broome, *Dog Soldier Justice*, 9; Powell, *Sacred Mountain*, 567.

[31] Sheridan, *Memoirs*, 448; Kappler, *Indian Treaties*, 987. Sheridan, as well as several writers, Berthrong, *Southern Cheyennes*, 304, Brill, *Custer, Black Kettle*, 104, Hoig, *Washita*, 44,

Halaas and Masich, *Halfbreed*, 251, states that the Indians were either promised guns and ammunition at Medicine Lodge or expected them. The treaty provided no promise of guns. It stated that the Secretary of the Interior could purchase such articles as "the condition and necessities of the Indians may indicate to be proper." In addition, the treaty stated that delivery of annuities was not to be made until October 15.

[32] Sheridan, *Memoirs*, 449; Burkey, *Custer, Come at Once*, 39; Berthrong, *Southern Cheyennes*, 304-05; Broome, *Dog Soldier Justice*, 230-31n16; Garfield, "Defense of the Kansas Frontier," 455-56; Unrau, "Role of the Indian Agent," 296-98; Barnitz, *Custer's Cavalry*, 174-75. The date of issuance of arms to the Cheyennes is disputed. It is said to have taken place between August 3 and 9, with Wynkoop reporting the latter date, hoping to show that the arms he issued could not have been used by the Indians the next day. Captain Albert Barnitz, 7th Cavalry, stated in his diary that the distribution began on July 29. The controversy is rather irrelevant, since many Indians were already on their way to commit murder and mayhem whether they had new weapons or not. Powell, *Sacred Mountain*, 569, makes the inane statement that this "was another case of warfare starting because the government had failed to keep its word."

[33] Broome, *Dog Soldier Justice*, 11; Berthrong, *Southern Cheyennes*, 306; Powell, *Sacred Mountain*, 568; Hyde, *George Bent*, 288-89. The fact that warriors from Black Kettle's band participated in the atrocities should be no surprise. They had been raping and killing for years (see Nancy Morton and Lucinda Eubank). Black Kettle never could, or never bothered, to make his village off limits to marauders. Man-Who-Breaks-the-Marrow-Bones, a leader of the raid, was a member of Black Kettle's band. Another raider was the son of the Arapaho Little Raven, who already proved how he would treat captured white women (see Anna Snyder).

[34] Broome, *Dog Soldier Justice*, 12; Roenigk, *Pioneer History*, 94-95; Powell, *Sacred Mountain*, 568. Powell explains the rapes by saying that the Indians were "doubtless remembering" what had been done at Sand Creek. Brill, *Custer, Black Kettle*, 109-10, has a similar explanation, but the Indians were committing similar atrocities before Sand Creek.

[35] Broome, *Dog Soldier Justice*, 13-14. Sheridan added details of the assault, stating that Indians "forced sticks up the persons," while another took a saber "and used it on the person of the woman in the same manner." Powell, *Sacred Mountain*, 568, only mentions the rape of one white woman (Bacon) and claims that the other warriors were so upset at the deed that they took her back home. Brill, *Custer, Black Kettle*, 110-11, also mentions only one capture and rape and says the Indians "returned the white woman to her people." Brill whitewashes the entire raid, saying that the Cheyennes were going to fight the Pawnees when they ran into "soldiers and vigilantes." Brill's book is peppered with falsehoods and distortions, and should be included in a bibliography only to illustrate the extent some writers will go to spread propaganda. Hyde, *George Bent*, 289, only says that Indians found a white woman, took her to the camp, and others returned her to her home. Using Bent's explanation, Halaas and Masich, *Halfbreed*, 254, also say that the Indians "escorted the frightened captive back to her home." Bent's refusal to tell the whole truth makes many of his tales nearly worthless as primary source material.

[36] Roenigk, *Pioneer History*, 90, 95; Broome, *Dog Soldier Justice*, 14-15. Broome cites an alternate ending that has David and Mrs. Bacon, with two daughters, still living on Bacon Creek in 1870.

[37] The tale that two Indians coerced 180 others into killing whites instead of raiding the Pawnees is found in several sources, including Powell, *Sacred Mountain*, 568-69, Halaas and Masich, *Halfbreed*, 253-54, and Hyde, *George Bent*, 289.

[38] Broome, *Dog Soldier Justice*, 15-19; Stratton, *Pioneer Women*, 122. A feeble explanation, Sheridan, *Memoirs*, 449, Halaas and Masich, *Halfbreed*, 254, for the Indians' sudden attack on Elizabeth Bell is that she served them coffee in a tin cup, apparently an insult sufficient to cause the ensuing massacre.

[39] Broome, *Dog Soldier Justice*, 18-19; Stratton, *Pioneer Women*, 122.

[40] Roenigk, *Pioneer History*, 110; *Secretary of War 1868*,Vol 2, 11; Sheridan, *Memoirs*, 450; Mills, *Barren Regrets*, 150-51; Michno, *Encyclopedia of Indian Wars*, 219.

[41] Mills, *Barren Regrets*, 151-52; Broome, *Dog Soldier Justice*, 19-20.

[42] Roenigk, *Pioneer History*, 96-97; Stratton, *Pioneer Women*, 122; Powell, *Sacred Mountain*, 569; Mills, *Barren Regrets*, 152.

[43] Broome, *Dog Soldier Justice*, 19-21, 24; Stratton, *Pioneer Women*, 122-23.

[44] Broome, *Dog Soldier Justice*, 28-29; Stratton, *Pioneer Women*, 123; Spotts, *Campaigning With Custer*, 211-13; White, "White Women Captives," 336.

45 Broome, *Dog Soldier Justice*, 29-32; Crawford, *Kansas in the Sixties*, 291-92; Halaas and Masich, *Halfbreed*, 256.

46 Berthrong, *Southern Cheyennes*, 306; Hoig, *Washita*, 47-51; Halaas and Masich, *Halfbreed*, 255.

47 Spotts, *Campaigning with Custer*, 213; Custer, *My Life on the Plains*, 373-74; Dixon, "Sweetwater Hostages," 83.

48 Dixon, "Sweetwater Hostages," 87-98; Thrapp, *Frontier Biography*, 1553; Custer, *My Life on the Plains*, 353; White, "White Women Captives," 340-41.

49 Custer, *My Life on the Plains*, 372-74; White, "White Women Captives," 341-42. Some historians with political or social agendas continue to reject abundant evidence of Indian cruelty to their captives. Broome, *Dog Soldier Justice*, 141-44, addressed this issue. In particular, Powell, *Sacred Mountain*, 717, distorts the captives' experience to make it look like they were on a pleasant picnic.

50 Broome, *Dog Soldier Justice*, 145; Dixon, "Sweetwater Hostages," 101-02; Spotts, *Campaigning with Custer*, 214-15; Thrapp, *Frontier Biography*, 1553.

51 Spotts, *Campaigning with Custer*, 155-56, Broome, *Dog Soldier Justice*, 52; 207-08; Thrapp, *Frontier Biography*, 1014.

52 Thrapp, *Frontier Biography*, 1014; Stratton, *Pioneer Women*, 123; Spotts, *Campaigning with Custer*, 208. Dates for Sarah's marriage are given as September 13 and 24.

53 James S. Morgan Depredation Claim #3644; White, "White Women Captives," 337; Spotts, *Campaigning with Custer*, 208; Broome, *Dog Soldier Justice*, 53-54. Morgan said they were Sioux, and Anna later told him that Sioux had taken her. Oglala Lakotas Pawnee Killer and Whistler were known to have been in the area at the time.

54 James S. Morgan Depredation Claim #3644; Spotts, *Campaigning with Custer*, 208-09; Stratton, *Pioneer Women*, 123-24; Broome, *Dog Soldier Justice*, 53-54.

55 Spotts, *Campaigning with Custer*, 209-10; Broome, *Dog Soldier Justice*, 55; Stratton, *Pioneer Women*, 124.

56 Stratton, *Pioneer Women*, 124; Broome, *Dog Soldier Justice*, 69; Crawford, *Kansas in the Sixties*, 332; Custer, *My Life on the Plains*, 280-81.

57 Custer, *My Life on the Plains* 371-72; Dixon, "Sweetwater Hostages," 98; Crawford, *Kansas in the Sixties*, 334.

58 Custer, *My Life on the Plains* 371-75; Dixon, "Sweetwater Hostages," 100; White, "White Women Captives," 342. Custer's hope that his course would do away with the practice of paying ransoms was not to be successfully implemented as official policy for a few more years.

59 Spotts, *Campaigning with Custer*, 159.

60 White, "White Women Captives, 341-42, Broome, *Dog Soldier Justice*, 69; Custer, *My Life on the Plains*, 373, 374; Custer, *Following the Guidon*, 60; Spotts, *Campaigning with Custer*, 209.

61 Stratton, *Pioneer Women*, 125. Some of this story, printed 38 years after the fact, is wrong. For instance, Anna's brother did not walk into her tent in the Indian camp. Authors have used this statement to "prove" that Indian captivity was not all bad.

62 Spotts, *Campaigning with Custer*, 210; Broome, *Dog Soldier Justice*, 144; Custer, *Following the Guidon*, 62. Re-adjustment of ex-captives to white society was often very difficult and many did not want it known what the Indians had done to them (see Veronica Ulbrich and Laura Roper.)

63 Stratton, *Pioneer Women*, 125; Broome, *Dog Soldier Justice*, 144-45.

64 Broome, *Dog Soldier Justice*, 1-4. This is the most thorough book written about Alderdice and Weichel.

65 Bernhardt, *Indian Raids in Lincoln County*, 27, 45, 199; Broome, *Dog Soldier Justice*, 93-94, 251n16.

66 Broome, *Dog Soldier Justice*, 94-96.

67 Broome, *Dog Soldier Justice*, 96-101.

68 Bernhardt, *Indian Raids in Lincoln County*, 28-32; Michno, *Encyclopedia of Indian Wars*, 235-36; Broome, *Dog Soldier Justice*, 176-78. Carr had only one soldier wounded, while killing about 52 Cheyennes, including Tall Bull. The fight at Summit Springs broke the power of the Dog Soldiers.

69 Broome, *Dog Soldier Justice*, 179-84; Grinnell, *Two Great Scouts*, 196-97.

70 Broome, *Dog Soldier Justice*, 182, 199-202.

71 Broome, *Dog Soldier Justice*, 191-94, 203-04. Susanna Alderdice's remains still lie hidden in the middle of a pasture at Summit Springs. Dr. Jeff Broome was instrumental in erecting a

monument for her nearby. The dedication ceremony took place on July 11, 2004, on the 135th anniversary of Susanna's death.

[72] Millbrook, "Jordan Massacre," 219.

[73] Millbrook, "Jordan Massacre," 220, 223-24, 229; Barnett, *Touched by Fire*, 178; Lee and Raynesford, *Trails of the Smoky Hill*, 203.

[74] Millbrook, "Jordan Massacre," 220-24; Ashton, *Indians and Intruders*, 102; Barnett, *Touched by Fire*, 178.

[75] Millbrook, "Jordan Massacre," 224-25; Miner, *West of Wichita*, 22.

[76] Millbrook, "Jordan Massacre," 225-26; Barnett, *Touched by Fire*, 179.

[77] Barnett, *Touched by Fire*, 179.

[78] Miner, *West of Wichita*, 24; Millbrook, "Jordan Massacre," 229-30.

Chapter Eight

RECONSTRUCTION TEXAS

I could not find any language to repeat what the poor mother and eldest daughter told me of their horrible sufferings.... The girl, then nineteen years old, in the captivity which was worse than death, had lost all trace of girlhood. — Elizabeth Custer

Texas in the years following the Civil War experienced some of the most sustained raiding and captive taking in its history. With manpower depleted, the economy in shambles, and political upheaval common, Texans couldn't afford to pay a military force to guard her frontiers. Worse yet, the U.S. Army, burdened with post-war cutbacks, fewer troops, and stretched thin with reconstruction duties across the South, seemed little inclined to protect the borders of a state recently in rebellion. Frontier settlers petitioned for help, but little was forthcoming. The federal government deferred frontier defense because believing troops were more needed to protect the freedmen. With the Texans not allowed to form their own companies and the United States unable or unwilling to protect the frontier, Indian raids increased. It took nearly two years before the regular army began to occupy the outlying forts. The frontier was devastated and the settlement line retreated about 100 miles in the Reconstruction years, more than it did during the war.

In addition to the captivities detailed below, in the early summer of 1866, Thomas Ewbanks was taken from his home in Stephens County, Texas. Because he had no money, his father, John A. Ewbanks, wrote to the governor to seek help in ransoming the boy. Some time later, a skeleton was discovered along with personal items that identified the corpse as Thomas Ewbanks. In September 1867, Kickapoos captured Bernave Landin in a raid through Webb County, near Laredo, Texas. About the same time, Frank Gebhard (10) was captured in Medina County. Also in September 1867, Indians raided Montague County, Texas, and carried off Alexander Holt (12) who was recovered the next year by Agent Jesse Leavenworth.[1]

* * *

HERBERT WEINAND
Texas, January 27, 1866

The Lipan Apaches enmity with the Comanches began far back in the Spanish period, and although they did not relish the Tejanos as neighbors, they disliked the Comanches even more. In the 1830s and 1840s, Lipans helped the Texans fight the Comanches (see Matilda Lockhart). While the Lipans had tentatively friendly relations with the Texans, it did not prevent them from raiding into Mexico.

By the late 1850s, treaty obligations saw the United States making efforts to stop the border crossings; more forts and more patrols seemed to have an effect. The reaction of the Indians was simply to raid less in Mexico and more in Texas. When the Lipans felt betrayed by what they saw as the breaking of an informal peace between them and the German settlers in the Texas Hill Country (see Frank Buckelew), they further increased their raids. The Kickapoos also had a feud with the Texans. Although they once helped rescue captives from the Comanches (see James Pratt Plummer and Meredith Wilson), when part of the tribe tried to relocate from Indian Territory to Mexico, Texans attacked them in a bloody battle at Dove Creek, January 8, 1865. Ever since, they had warred with the Texans from their bases in Coahuila, Mexico, making the Rio Grande border one of the most dangerous places in Texas in the late 1860s.[2]

In January 1866, a band of Lipans or Kickapoos crossed the Rio Grande and raided Medina and Bandera County. Three boys, Augustus Rothe, George Jacob Miller (17), and Herbert Weinand (13) were on upper Hondo Creek in northwest Medina County hunting stray cattle.[3] The Indians surprised the boys, but Rothe was well armed, and he made a fighting retreat. The other two were caught, and Miller, it was reported, "was murdered after having suffered nameless tortures." Weinand was probably still young enough to be assimilated and was kept alive. The Indians killed some cattle, stole horses, and circled back across the river.

Herbert Weinand was swallowed up in the vastness of Mexico. His father, of the same name, lived in D'Hanis, Texas. He did what he could, writing letters and searching, and after a year his efforts began to bear fruit. In February 1867, he learned that either Kickapoos or Lipans held a boy of Herbert's description in a camp above Monclova, about thirty miles from Eagle Pass, and he went to Eagle Pass to arrange for his release. Mr. Weinand returned in mid-March, unable to buy back his son. The situation was relatively unchanged for another year, when a wealthy Mexican merchant from Monclova learned about several white captives being held at Santa Rosa. Mr. Weinand tried again to bargain for his son. There was progress; the influential Mexican was able to buy the boy, but apparently wanted to be reimbursed before he would give him up.

In May 1868, Mr. Weinand went to Medina County Judge H. J. Richards for help, and the judge wrote to Governor Pease about the situation. He said that the Mexicans aided the Indians in their incursions into Texas, and harbored them on their return. He asked if something could be done to stop the raids or make Mexico pay for the damages. Richards asked Pease if "there are any funds at the disposal of your Excellency to indemnify that good man who bought off young Hubert Weinand. His parents have not the means, and I am certain that the ransom will amount to about $300."[4]

Apparently there was little or no follow-up, for in May 1870, young Weinand had not yet been recovered. That month, Commissioner Ely S. Parker wrote to James P. Newcomb, Texas Secretary of State, regarding Indian prisoners. Weinand's was one of the names mentioned, and Lawrie Tatum, their agent in Indian Territory, was instructed to "endeavor to obtain the captives," and was to "use every means at his command" to do so. Either Newcomb or Parker had some new information that indicated Kiowas and Comanches held Weinand or they were grasping at straws. During Tatum's tenure as agent, he was instrumental in recovering twenty-six Anglo and Mexican captives, but Weinand was not among them.

Another year passed. In June 1871, Acting Commissioner H. R. Clum addressed a letter to an unnamed agent, indicating that trader William Chisholm and his interpreter Caboone, "had seen a captive taken from near San Antonio, four or five years ago named Albert Winning."[5] Nothing came of this information.

We get one more glance at the effort to find the elusive captive in an undated letter from Judge H. J. Richards to Secretary Newcomb. The secretary served under Governor Edmund J. Davis from 1869 to 1873, so the letter had to be within that time frame. Richards said that Mr. Weinand had visited him again. Apparently there was another deal in the making; the brief details mentioned by Richards indicated that he and Weinand both trusted a man named Ian to carry out the transaction. Weinand told Richards he "expressly desired to write Ian that he will pay Ian Fifety [*sic*] dollars in gold and would give me the note now, if by Ian's intercession he gets his poor boy and he will stick to his word, I warrant."[6]

After this effort, references to the recovery of Herbert Weinand are silent. It may be that this mysterious Ian made good the transaction and young Weinand was finally united with his father. It may be that he lived out the remainder of his life with the Indians.

JAMES AND SAMUEL SAVAGE, AND JENNIE BELLE SAVAGE
Texas, March 2, 1866

It had been thirty years to the day since Texas declared its independence from Mexico, and Indians still raided the settlements and captured white settlers. The fact that March 2 was a special day may, or may not have been on the minds of Civil War veterans and brothers, Bolin (34) and James Savage (40), as they worked their farms, four and five miles southwest of Weatherford, Texas. At ten in the morning, Marion Savage (11), James Savage (6), and Sam Savage (5), left their cabin to help their father, Bolin, as he plowed his field near Sanchez Creek. As the boys approached their father, nine Comanches rode across the field, shot arrows into him—one missile going through his neck—and scalped him in front of their eyes. The boys ran for home, but the Comanches easily swept James and Sam up on their ponies. The fleeter Marion got away in the brush by the creek, but not before an Indian put a bullet into his shoulder. Elizabeth Savage saw the attack from the cabin, grabbed a rifle, and defended her home and younger children. The raiders took two of Bolin's horses and rode west.[7]

The Indians next hit James Savage's farm on Patrick Creek. James was also plowing his field. He did not feel well that morning and did not eat breakfast. His daughter, Arrena (11), fixed him a snack, and with Jennie Belle (5), and Jim (2), walked across the field to take it to him. James's wife, Caroline, and his daughter, Sarah Jane (22), were hanging laundry near the cabin. Sarah saw about fourteen Indians approaching and ran to the cabin, got two guns, and rushed out to defend her father, but she was too late. James also saw the Indians, shooed his children home, and turned to defend himself. He fought like a wild man, severely injuring one of the warriors before they overwhelmed and killed him. Mounted Comanches caught Jennie and Jim and hoisted them up on their ponies. Arrena tried to pull Jim down, but a warrior thrust a lance through her arm and into her side. When he tried to pull the lance free the shaft broke, leaving the point pinning her arm to her ribs. The Indians saw Sarah coming with two weapons. They circled around her, rode to the cabin, stole two horses, and rode away. Nearby settlers quickly formed a posse and pursued them. After a several mile chase they found little Jim by the roadside in a tangle of brush, abandoned, most likely for crying.[8]

The raiders crossed into Palo Pinto County east of Mineral Wells and stopped to rest. There, a warrior decided to ride one of Bolin Savage's horses. He tied a rope to the animal and wrapped the excess length around his waist. When the horse bolted, it threw the rider and dragged him over rocks and cactus. The rope slipped up over the Indian's neck, strangled him to death, and nearly pulled his head off. The horse ran free and found its way back to Savage's farm. Other warriors severed the head of the dead Comanche, most likely to prevent it from being scalped by pursuing Texans. They took the body away for burial and gave the head to a mounted Indian woman who carried both it and little Sam Savage. While the horrified children watched the burial ceremony, warriors pinched them until they cried, joining in the general wailing for their dead comrade.

The Indians only offered the children raw meat to eat. Sam refused it, and became so weak that James had to help him walk. Sam's stubbornness angered his captors, and they treated him roughly. They may have been on the verge of killing him when his hunger finally got the best of him. When they got hungry enough, they all ate the raw meat and were treated better. The Indians went to western Indian Territory where the children were kept for several months. In the way that pigs are marked for identification, the Comanches "took and underbit" one of Jim Savage's ears.[9]

In November 1866, John Fields, a trader from McKinney, Texas, visited the Comanche camp and discovered the Savages, sun-darkened and painted up like Indians. Nevertheless, Fields recognized them as white children and offered to buy them. The deal was made at Fort Arbuckle for $414, a prize pony, a saddle, and a bridle. Fields left them at Arbuckle and went to Texas and advertised in the newspapers to try to locate their families. At the fort, the Savage children were virtual prisoners, kept locked up at night so that the Comanches could not recapture them. Finally, William and John Stephens, half-brothers of Bolin and James Savage, came north to fetch them home.

The boys found it hard to discard their bows, arrows, Indian clothes, and manners. Their uncles insisted they throw everything into the Red River. In an opposite frame of mind, Jennie wanted to throw away her Indian dress, but her mother made her keep it to show her descendents. She secretly slipped the garments outside one by one and burned them. Sam's mother cried as she scrubbed him with soap and water in an effort to clean his discolored skin. It took months before Sam Savage again felt comfortable in the white world. When strangers came to the house, he would run and hide near the creek. The boys had to be watched constantly to prevent their running away, but eventually they readjusted.

James and Sam Savage moved with their mother and stepfather to Palo Pinto County. Sam only received limited schooling; he could read, but never learned to write, and worked trailing cattle. He returned to Palo Pinto County, married a farm girl named Arizona Pierce in 1881, and settled on Kent Mountain a few miles northwest of Mineral Wells. In 1911, forty-five years after his rescue, Sam Savage visited John Fields in Dallas for a tearful reunion of sorts. In the 1920s and 1930s, Sam was acclaimed as a champion fiddler. James died in 1933, and Sam died in 1951.[10]

FRANCIS MARION "FRANK" BUCKELEW
Texas, March 11, 1866

Frank Buckelew was born in Union Parish, Louisiana, on August 10, 1852, the youngest of seven children.[11] In 1854, his parents moved the family to Cherokee County, Texas, to get more "elbow room." Mrs. Buckelew died in 1856, and Frank said he lost his "only true, earthly friend." Mr. Buckelew remarried, but died a short time later. Frank's oldest sister, who never got along with their stepmother, took Frank and his little sisters to live with their uncle, L. B. C. "Berry" Buckelew, on the Sabinal River near present-day Vanderpool in Bandera County. It was a beautiful location, near where the stream issues from a canyon, but it was also on the frontier where several Indian paths crossed.[12]

Settlers in the area took turns going to San Antonio for supplies. When Berry Buckelew's turn came he hitched his oxen to a wagon and went on the several-day journey. Buckelew was nearly home when he stopped to see his friend Crossgrave on Seco Creek. It was late on a Friday evening, January 26, 1866, and Crossgrave told Buckelew to spend the night, but he wanted to hurry home. While taking a short cut on the Little Seco, Indians ambushed and shot him, then crushed his head with a rock. Crossgrave rode to Buckelew's place on Sunday, but the children told him their uncle was not yet home. A search party went out and discovered his remains. His dog, Cuff, was still keeping vigil over his master's body.

Maryanna Buckelew could not run the ranch herself, nor could she take care of her nieces and nephew. She moved to a safer location, and once again the Buckelew children went to another home, this time to James Davenport's ranch farther up the Sabinal. One of Frank's tasks was to watch the cattle, which he did with a companion, a Negro boy named Morris. One day, Morris failed to securely fasten the bell to the lead steer and it fell off. When Mr. Davenport had trouble rounding up his cattle, he learned about Morris's gaffe and told him he had better find the bell or he would "beat him to death." Morris begged Frank to help him find the bell. The next morning, March 11, they started out. Frank took an old shotgun that Davenport had given him, but on the way out of the house, Mrs. Davenport told him to leave it behind, for there were no Indians about, and he was more likely to kill Morris or himself than any Indians. The two boys hunted through the thickets, but Frank tired of the search and began picking flowers for his sister. Several cattle ran out of a thicket and startled him. Frank told Morris he thought there might be Indians about, but Morris dismissed his fears and reminded him to help him find the bell. Frank only took a few steps when he saw an Indian watching him from the thicket. He ran toward Morris, calling out a warning. The boy turned, saw the Indian too, and, Frank said, "with a yell of terror fled from me like the wind." Frank ran too, but the Lipan Apache warrior was behind him in an instant, with bowstring drawn. Frank stopped in his tracks. When the Indian came up, he looked at the back of the fleeing Morris and laughed, then he rapped Frank in the head, pointed in the other direction, and said, "Vamos."[13]

The warrior took Frank to a glade where they met two other Indians. The three stripped off his clothes and one of them whipped him across his naked back with a thorny catclaw branch. They moved at a trot across the rugged terrain, the one warrior in the rear continually whipping Frank to keep him moving. His flesh was torn and blood trickled in rivulets down his body. They climbed out of the Sabinal Valley and over the divide to the Frio. On top they met a fourth Apache. He extended his hand to Frank and said, "Howdy! How old you be? You be Englishman or you be Dutchman? You be Englishman me killie you; you be Dutchman me no killie you?"

Frank had heard that Indians would kill boys more than 10 or 12 years old, so, although he was nearly 14, he said he was ten. To the second question he told the truth, regardless of the consequences. He was an Englishman and not a Dutchman (German). It turned out that the Lipans were killing all Germans for what they considered treachery in breaking an informal peace treaty between them. The truthful answer saved young Buckelew, although the Lipan, a chief named Custaleta, eyed him warily.

"Heap big ten-year-old boy," he said.[14]

Custaleta led them away, but Frank pleaded with the chief to let him go, telling him that he was the sole support of his widowed mother and young sisters. The route led them near Davenport's house, and Custaleta took him to the edge of a bluff near enough to the house so that Frank could shout to his family. His sister heard him and ran outside.

"It is Frank!" he heard her call out, but that was as near as he got. The Indians raised a war whoop and led him away. They crossed over to the Frio and for sport, shot arrows into several cows, which led Frank to remark: "This display of wanton cruelty . . .made a deep impression on my mind, and caused me to forbode much evil for myself. . . ."[15]

Every night, Bezaca, the Indian who captured Frank, slept with him. This "hideous bedfellow," Frank said, hugged him tightly to his breast, wrapped a blanket around them, and fell asleep. Frank was awake with thoughts of slipping out of the blanket, grabbing a knife, and stabbing every one of them before they awoke, but every time he stirred, Bezaca would tighten his bear hug.

They headed up the Sabinal, then west to the Frio, and on to the Nueces, which they reached about one week after Frank's capture. There, the Lipans discovered half a dozen wild horses, which they attempted to capture. Frank was given the task to block their escape route, but failed, and was knocked out by a club wielded by an enraged warrior.

Their journey continued across Devils River by Beaver Lake, and on to the Pecos, finally reaching the Lipan camp. For his welcome, an old woman whipped his naked skin until it bled, then shoved him along to the end of a double row of Indians with whips and clubs, where Frank ran the gauntlet, pummeled with a hundred blows. At the end, he collapsed into the old woman's arms as she laid him down and again tested his courage by slowly drawing a knife across his throat. Frank was certain he would be killed, but the woman signaled him to go into the lodge. He would live there as the captive of the old woman and Bezaca.[16]

The Lipans frequently moved their camp of about 150 people, up and down the Pecos and its tributaries, and Frank tried to adjust to a life of slavery, whippings, and starvation. In October 1866, Lipans raided into Bandera and Uvalde Counties, stealing horses and murdering settlers. When they returned, Frank saw some of the spoils. "I noticed some boys clothing," he said, "which I at once recognized as belonging to the children of Mr. Kinchelo." Among the stolen horses he saw "a gray mare belonging to my aunt." He realized another one of his neighbors had been attacked, but he didn't learn what happened to the family until after his rescue.[17]

The Lipans split their camp in November 1866, and half of them, including Buckelew, moved south of the Rio Grande in the vicinity of San Vincente, Mexico, about fifteen miles from Eagle Pass, Texas. An old Mexican visited the Lipan camp, saw Buckelew, and managed to converse with him. He asked if Frank wanted to get away, and he said he most assuredly did. At this time, a Mr. W. B. Hudson was engaged in building an irrigation canal on the Rio Grande and employed Mexican and Indian workers. One of Hudson's Mexican assistants was in the Indian camp seeking laborers when he talked to the old Mexican who had been with Buckelew. The old man passed on the news of the captive and the assistant passed it to his boss. Hudson reported the news to James Moseley of Eagle Pass. Moseley knew James Davenport, and wrote to him that the boy could probably be purchased. Davenport, in December 1866, wrote to Judge W. B. Knox, telling him that he had been supporting the Buckelew children for two years and that neither he, nor they, had the money to ransom the boy. He heard that the government had appropriated money for this purpose, and hoped Knox could help make arrangements for his release.

In February 1867, Hudson sent his man back to Buckelew. He offered the Lipans $100 for boy, but they would not sell. The next visit, Hudson's Mexican assistant made no offer; he and Frank stole two Indian horses and rode out one night. In several hours they were across the Rio Grande and at Hudson's house. The next morning, Frank was introduced to Hudson's wife and daughters. The girls wanted Frank to take off his blanket and show them how an Indian dressed, but Frank, long-haired, painted, and half-naked, was much too embarrassed to remove the blanket. In case the Lipans were tracking them, Hudson saddled up his horses and he, the young Mexican rescuer, and Frank rode north to Fort Clark. Once at the fort, the soldiers, few of whom had ever seen an Indian, made a great ado over Frank's presence, much to his continued discomfort. Frank wanted to get home, and after the post surgeon concocted a potion to rid him of the lice that had tormented him since he became a captive, the party continued on to Bandera County.[18]

They reached the old homestead on the Sabinal, but learned that Frank's sisters had moved away. On January 24, 1867, they stopped at the home of Uvalde County Judge Numan M. C. Patterson. The kindly man informed them that Davenport and Frank's sisters were now living on the Medina River in Bandera, and then drafted a petition that collected more than fifty steers and a large sum of money to help pay Hudson for his troubles. When they reached Davenport's, the family and the townsfolk could not believe he had returned. "We all thought you had been killed by the Indians," Davenport said. "Morris told us that you were." The fuss made over Frank's return was more than he could stand. He rushed inside and hid under a bed.

Hudson stopped at Fort Clark to learn that the Indians had discovered his involvement in Frank's rescue, and they were planning a retaliatory raid. Soldiers escorted him home and waited until he packed up and moved his family elsewhere. The Lipans did attack. Custaleta led his warriors across the Rio Grande, swept through the area Hudson just vacated, stole many horses, killed their owners, and tried to cross the river into Mexico. A white posse ran them down and killed and wounded a number of them. Among the bodies found was that of Custaleta.[19]

As was the lot of orphans, Frank continued to change homes. When he was 16, he moved in with the Sheppard Family, who lived about eight miles north of Bandera. In August 1870, Frank married Nancy Witter. They had three girls and three boys. Frank joined the Methodist Church and became a preacher when he was 41 years old. In Frank's biography, related to S. E. Banta in 1911, he said he was glad to have been an early settler of Texas, sharing with its people the hardships and dangers. He watched the forests give way to farms, the log cabins change to modern homes, the "Redman" replaced by the cowboy, the ox wagon replaced by the iron horse, and old-fashioned hospitality superseded by modern "commercial madness." Nevertheless, Frank Buckelew was proud to have participated in building a frontier society and watching its transition to the Twentieth Century.[20]

ELIZA AND ISAAC BRISCO
Texas, June 1866

Isaac Brisco[21] lived in Jack County for some time, but the chaos of the Civil War did not bode well for families on the far frontier, and Brisco moved from five miles north of Jacksboro, to Parker County, which he considered to be a safer place. Brisco's daughter, Cynthia, stayed in Jack County and married James McKinney; on April 12, 1858, theirs was the first marriage license issued in the county. In the spring of 1865, the McKinneys, with their three children, took a wagon to Springtown in northeast Parker County to mill their grain and visit relatives. Being short of money, Jim McKinney even traded in his pistol for provisions. Business in Springtown done, they turned around to go home, planning to stop at Cynthia's parents' home on the way.[22]

Isaac Brisco did not move to a safer place. His home was located three-fourths of a mile northwest of present-day Agnes, Texas, and about fifteen miles north of Weatherford. The home was built near a break in a line of hills along the Wise-Parker County border that was a favorite route for Indian raiders to approach the lower settlements.

The McKinneys filled their kegs at a spring known as Jenkins Water, then traveled two miles farther west until they were about two miles east of Brisco's home when Indians attacked them. The warriors quickly slaughtered Jim and Cynthia, scalped and mutilated them, killed the baby, lanced Joe (3), and carried away Mary Alice (6), only to kill her near Bridgeport in Wise County. The next day, two settlers hunting for stray cattle, found the massacre site, and the naked boy hiding in the bushes. "Papa!" he called out to them. When they tried to find out what happened, little Joe could only say, "The booger-man did it." The bodies of the four killed were buried in a single grave in Goshen Cemetery, west of Springtown.[23]

Isaac Brisco and his wife grieved over the loss of their daughter, son-in-law, and grandchildren, but carried on, perhaps not realizing how dangerous the place they lived was, or perhaps realizing it, but being too poor to do much about it. Isaac was a furniture maker by trade. He owned a turning lathe and may have been working in the shade of a grapevine arbor near the house when Kiowas struck his home in late June 1866. The Indians killed and scalped Mr. and Mrs. Brisco, then mutilated their bodies in the presence of the children. The warriors plundered the house and carried away Eliza (10), Isaac (3), and a younger sister.

Jim Mayo, who lived one mile east, discovered the Brisco corpses and hurried to spread the alarm. The Indians moved on to Sam Stack's ranch and were stealing his horses when the Tackett Brothers, members of the Texas Rangers, ran into them. They charged into them, firing their guns, but were outnumbered and fell back. The Indians next went to W. H. Allen's home, but Mrs. Allen and her five children got out and hid in a nearby creek. The Indians destroyed the house then went to the Caldwell place, where Mrs. Caldwell and her children hid in a cornfield. Next, the raiders hit J. T. Gilliland and Jack Wynn's ranch. The men tried to protect their horses, but the Indians' fire drove them into the house. They stole the horses and rode north.

The bodies of the Briscos, like their daughter Cynthia and her family, were buried in a single grave in the Goshen Cemetery.[24]

The Brisco children were swallowed up into the vastness of the high plains and little was heard about them for two years. In October 1867, at the Treaty of Medicine Lodge, Kansas, the Kiowas and Comanches agreed that they will "never capture or carry off from the settlements white women or children." The Cheyennes, who had made the same promise, were raiding in Kansas in the spring and summer of 1868. The Kiowas, perhaps because of their promise, perhaps because of an increased military presence in Kansas, or, most likely, because it was simply an opportune time to sell their captives, finally brought the Brisco children to light. In July 1868, while Generals Grant, Sherman, and Sheridan were taking the Smoky Hill Trail to Denver, Kiowas brought in the Briscos to Fort Larned.[25]

On July 11, 1868, the Kiowa Timber Mountain appeared at the fort and sold to post trader John E. Tappan, who was the cousin of peace commissioner Samuel F. Tappan, a little boy who appeared to be about 4 years old. The reason for giving him up, said Tappan, was "as a proof of their friendship to the whites." Nevertheless, Tappan did pay for the boy with goods and supplies. The boy was Isaac Brisco, who was nearly 6, but his poor treatment and undernourishment made him appear to be 4 four years old. On July 20, Timber Mountain was back, this time selling Eliza Brisco. The Indians kept the youngest Brisco girl, now about four years old. Tappan turned both children over to General Alfred Sully, in command of the District of the Upper Arkansas. Without orders as to what to do with the children, and about to lead elements of the 7th Cavalry and 3rd Infantry in a campaign against the Indians, Sully handed over care of the children to army guide and interpreter Hugh Bradley.[26]

Author's photo
Site of capture of Eliza and Isaac Briscoe, near Agnes, Texas.

Bradley could not get any leads as to the whereabouts of any relatives, and once more the Brisco children seemed to have been swallowed up in government red tape. Eliza told authorities that her father and mother were killed where they lived in Parker County, that she had a brother-in-law named Jack Cummings in Parker County, and a brother named Jack Brisco who lived in Jack County. No one responded. In April 1869, Kiowa and Comanche Agent Albert G. Boone, wrote to the commissioner of Indian affairs from Indian Territory, that Hugh Bradley still had the Brisco children and was caring for them at his own expense with "nothing having been furnished by the government." They were now living with Bradley's family. Boone asked that Bradley be reimbursed for his expenses and that some effort be made to find the children's relatives, or, if that proved impossible, to instruct him what disposition to make of them.

In turn, newly appointed Commissioner Ely S. Parker wrote to Texas Provisional Governor Elisha M. Pease and asked if he could help find relatives of the freed captives. Passing the same request along, Pease wrote to the Parker County judge to try and locate the family and requested that the children be sent down to Fort Richardson where they could at least be closer to any living relatives. Finally, word reached the garrison at Fort Richardson, that some children, possibly from the Brisco family, had been recovered from the Indians. William Brisco, the 25-year-old son of Isaac Brisco and his first wife, got the news and rode north to find the children. Before Billy Brisco could get to Oklahoma, authorities, despairing of ever finding a responsible relative and ever conscious of the cost of keeping the children, sent them to an orphan's home. Eliza and Isaac Brisco disappeared into the maw of a poorly served government benevolence.[27]

MARY MATTHEWS BOX AND MARGARET, JOSEPHINE, IDA AND LAURA BOX
Texas, August 15, 1866

Mary Matthews was born in Gibson County, Tennessee, in 1824. Her family moved to Texas in 1832. At age 18 she married James Box, lived for a short time in Titus County, then moved to Hopkins County, where, she said, they lived "for a long time" and where all but one of her children were born. James Box was a Union man, and when the Civil War began in 1861, he moved his family far out on the frontier in Montague County because he did not want to join the Confederacy. The family lived a precarious existence on the frontier, where Union supporters were scorned and feared, and even hanged for their sympathies.[28]

The Boxes survived the war and hoped to achieve a peaceful, comfortable life, but it was not to be. In June 1866, one of James's brothers was deathly ill, and another had a leg amputated. The Boxes hurried to Hopkins County to help them out. They remained about five weeks, and on August 10, stocked up with household goods and leather hides, started back to Montague County. It rained for much of the five-day journey, and during the melancholy trip, James Box declared to the family that he had a premonition that he would never get home. On the 15th, only about three miles from their cabin at Head of Elm (now Saint Jo), which consisted of a blacksmith shop, a store, a few homes, and a stockade, James spotted someone moving along a hill and assumed it was his neighbor.

"I wish that man would come down to us," James told Mary, "so that I could borrow his horse for our jaded one, and then we could get home faster."

When Mary looked in the direction he pointed, she said, "Why, there are three or four of them."

"They are Indians—" James realized, and said, "we are gone." Turning to his 17-year-old daughter, he said, "Margaret—get my six-shooter, quick!"

Before she could get the pistol out, the Indians, twenty-three Kiowas under Satanta, were upon them. One of them shot an arrow into James's chest and he fell backwards into the wagon. He sat up, yanked the arrow free, took the pistol and fired. Another arrow hit him in the head, this time knocking him out of the wagon. Somehow, James Box rose again and stumbled to the far side of the wagon before he fell dead. The warriors were upon him, scalping him twice and cutting open his jaw. A Kiowa grabbed Mrs. Box by the hair and pulled her out of the wagon. The screaming girls, Josephine (13), Ida (7), and infant Laura, were quickly grabbed and tied to ponies. Margaret broke free and ran to her dead father, holding tight to him until the Indians pulled her away. When the Indians stole everything from the wagon, they tied Mrs. Box and Margaret to horses and rode off at a gallop.[29]

Charlie Grant, Bill Grant, John Loving, and Zeke Huffman, saw the attack from atop Wheeler's Mound about one-quarter mile from the road. The men were unarmed and watched in horror. They rode to Charlie Grant's father for arms and reinforcements. They returned at night and found the leather hides and wagon contents scattered all over the prairie. Feathers and broom weeds stuck to Box's bloody body. The next day a larger posse gathered, including Jim Coursey and Dan Brunson. They followed the trail into Indian Territory and discovered the baby Laura's body, and then gave up and returned home.

The Indians traveled north night and day for two weeks. Margaret ripped off pieces of her dress from time to time, hoping that pursuers would spot them. Instead, the warriors saw what she was doing, and tore the remaining clothing from her body. Whenever they stopped to rest, Mary and Margaret were repeatedly raped. On the eleventh day, Mary Box dropped little Laura as they rode horseback. She was badly injured and the crying irritated the warriors. Laura was either on the threshold of death or had just expired, when an Indian grabbed her from Mary's arms, threw her against a tree in a ravine, and left her behind. They mounted up and rode on. Warriors would not allow Mrs. Box to drink, and her tongue swelled. One of her daughters took off her slipper as they crossed a stream, and filled it with water to give to her mother. She managed to drink most of it down before a warrior saw her and knocked it from her hands. Then they almost beat the girl to death. After reaching the main village near the Arkansas River, the Boxes were together for four days. A scalp dance was held and the spoils and prisoners were divided up. Mary was separated from her children and taken to another camp about six miles away. She was beaten, abused, and slaved from dawn to dusk.

"I had to pack wood and water," Mary said. "When I delayed they would hit and beat me and even the squaws would knock me down. I was very sick while with the Indians, notwithstanding they would beat me. It was a terrible life. . . ."

Margaret, described as "a beautiful girl just ripening into womanhood," fell into the hands of a chief who forced her "to become the victim of his brutal lust," and then bartered her to another Indian for two horses. This Indian used her until he tired of her, and traded her to a third Indian, who used her and passed her on. Ida, too young to be sexually abused, nevertheless spent much of the time alone and crying uncontrollably. Occasionally she would see her mother when the bands camped near each other, and she tried to run to her. Her behavior so enraged her captors that they stuck her bare feet into a campfire "until every portion of the cuticle was burned therefrom." Now, with charred feet, she could not run. Months later her feet were not fully healed.[30]

It is unlikely that any of them would have survived a long captivity with such treatment. Comparatively speaking, they were fortunate that the Indians realized that they had more to gain by selling their prisoners than by keeping them as slaves and concubines. They had been taking captives for decades, and the white men always gave money or supplies to get them back. The Indians had returned a dozen captives at the Little Arkansas Treaty the year before, and they were rewarded with many presents. The captive "trade" was a lucrative business for these unsophisticated, budding capitalists.

Eager to turn a profit, Satanta rode from his camp twelve miles south of Fort Larned on September 9, to talk to Major Cuvier Grover, 3rd U. S. Infantry. Satanta told Grover that they had gone to Texas "to make peace with the whites there, but had been received in a hostile manner, and, in consequence, had taken the captives." Now, however, Satanta was ready to give them up. Grover told him he must wait until he could contact Agent I. C. Taylor to learn what disposition he wanted of the captives. Taylor left Fort Zarah and rode to Larned, meeting Satanta there on the 12th. Satanta proposed to give up the captives, "providing I would pay him liberally for them." Instead, Taylor angrily asked if Satanta had forgotten the Little Arkansas Treaty where the Indians promised not to take any more prisoners. He told the Kiowa "that he knew perfectly well that it was in violation of the treaty." Taylor said he "would not pay him one dollar for them" but that he must bring them all to the fort, deliver them to Grover, and wait until Agent Leavenworth arrived to settle the matter. Satanta asked Taylor for ten days to talk over the proposition in council, and he would return with an answer. Taylor agreed.[31]

Satanta was not about to be rebuffed. He rode to Fort Dodge, met Captain Andrew Sheridan, 3rd U.S. Infantry, and made a similar offer. Sheridan sent Lieutenant Gustave A. Hesselberger, an interpreter, and two soldiers, Lee Herron and John Mclaurie, to the Indian camp to negotiate for the prisoners. In the village, Satanta refused to give up the prisoners without a suitable ransom. They negotiated and finally agreed on a combination of money and supplies of about $2,800 in value. The Kiowas demanded powder and lead, but Hesselberger insisted he would be unable to get that for them. Hesselberger's party quickly returned to Fort Dodge, procured the ransom, and rode back to the village. That evening, the lieutenant paid cash to the two Indians who owned the two eldest girls to prevent "a repetition of indignities to which. . .they had been continually subjected." The next morning, Hesselberger took Margaret and Josephine back to Fort Dodge. A few days later, Indians brought Mary and Ida in, and they were given additional blankets and provisions. General William T. Sherman, on an inspection tour, arrived at Fort Dodge shortly after the affair, and instructed Captain Sheridan not to purchase any other captives from the Indians. The Boxes had been rescued just in time.[32]

When Agent Taylor learned of Satanta's duplicity, and that the military was contradicting his instructions, he wrote to Commissioner of Indian Affairs D. N. Cooley on September 30. Taylor wanted to know under whose authority Sheridan was allowed to pay the Indians. He "urgently" called the attention of the department "to the fact that every prisoner purchased from the Indians amounts to the same as granting them a license to go and commit the same overt act. They boastfully say that stealing white women is more of a lucrative business than stealing horses." Taylor added that he believed it was time that "the strong arm of the government" brought the Indians to their senses.[33]

In November 1866, Lieutenant Hesselberger escorted the four Box women to Fort Leavenworth. The soldiers at Dodge took full responsibility for the move, not even letting Agent Leavenworth see them, nor letting his representatives talk to them as they passed through Fort Zarah. Leavenworth was furious at the military action, and complained in a letter to Special Agent Charles Bogy. It was simply an incident of the ongoing feud between the military and the Department of Indian Affairs.[34]

As the Boxes traveled through Kansas, they stopped at Fort Riley, where they met Lieutenant Colonel George A. Custer and his wife, Elizabeth. Both of them commented on their horrible condition. George and Libbie both understood Mary to say that the Indians dashed Laura's brains out against a tree, that many Indians raped and abused the mother and the oldest girls, and that Ida's feet were severely burned. Said Libbie: "I could not find any language to repeat what the poor mother and eldest daughter told me of their horrible sufferings during...their captivity." From what Libbie learned from Margaret, she came to believe that Indian captivity truly "was worse than death." The story of the Boxes ordeal made a lasting impression on the Custers, and it was one of the reasons that the general later ordered his trusted officers that if it ever became inevitable that Libbie would fall into the hands of the Indians, they were to shoot her dead before she could be taken. The Box killings and captures were significant incidents that led to General Winfield S. Hancock's expedition to the Kansas plains in 1867, and later to the Washita Expedition in 1868.[35]

With few relatives in Texas having any money to arrange for their trip home, the Boxes stayed at Leavenworth for some time before arrangements were made to send them to Texas, by way of St. Louis. Little is known about their subsequent lives. Ida, perhaps because of her burned and infected feet, died shortly thereafter. Josephine reportedly married a man named Crowe, while Margaret, apparently surviving her traumatic experience, married Dan Brunson, a childhood sweetheart and one of her would-be rescuers.[36]

THEODORE ADOLPUS "DOT" BABB, BIANCA LOUELLA BABB, AND SARAH JANE LUSTER
Texas, September 14, 1866

Theodore Babb was born near Reedsburg, Wisconsin, on May 17, 1852. In 1854, his parents, John S. and Isabel Babb, began a journey to Texas that would last years. Bianca was born in a covered wagon on August 26, 1856, near Lecompton, Kansas. They first stopped in Grayson County, Texas, but in 1860, the Babbs settled on a farm near Dry Creek in Wise County, south of present-day Chico, Texas. Staying with the Babb's in 1866, was Sarah Luster (25), a pretty young widow. Sarah Renfrow was born in Gasconade County, Missouri. She married Mr. Luster in 1860, and they moved to Wise County, Texas. Mr. Luster was killed fighting for the Confederacy, and Sarah secured a home with the Babbs.[37]

Author's photo

Site of Babb, Luster capture, near Chico, Texas.

In mid-September 1866, about forty Noconi Comanches led by Persummy, raided through Jack and Wise County. John Babb and H. C. Babb, his oldest son, were gone to buy or trade for cattle and horses in Arkansas when the Indians struck. Dot (14) and Bianca (10) were at play about three in the afternoon when they saw riders approaching their cabin. Isabel Babb called to Dot and asked him to see if they were cowboys.

"No," Dot answered, "they are Indians!" They ran inside and Isabel and Sarah slammed the door, then Sarah went upstairs to hide in the loft. Dot tried to take an old gun down from the rack, but the Indians burst inside, grabbed the gun from him and beat him. Isabel tried to ease the situation by shaking hands with them, but to no avail. The warriors plundered the cabin, pulled Sarah down from the loft, tied her up tightly, and threw her on a horse. Others tried to take Isabel but she resisted. Walking Face drew out a big knife and stabbed her four times. Dot ran to his mother and pulled her to the bed, trying to patch her wounds.

Warriors dragged Bianca, who described herself as "a typical platinum blond," outside, but she grabbed hold of a fencepost and would not let go. A warrior threatened her with a knife several times, but she resolved to die before letting go. Finally, the Indian laughed, put his knife away and, Bianca said, "jerked me so hard that the rough bark on the post tore the flesh from the inside of my hands until the blood ran freely from the wounds." But, she said, "I did not cry." When the warriors finished securing Bianca,

357

they came back inside to find Mrs. Babb still alive, clinging to her infant daughter. Walking Face shot her with an arrow that entered her left lung. Dot, nevertheless, pulled the arrow out and tried to console her. The Indian nocked another arrow and pointed it at Dot, motioning for him to leave. The dying Isabel Babb told him, "Go with him and be a good boy." Another warrior jerked him by the arm and took him outside. Soon, all three prisoners were bound and thrown on horses. The baby, Margie, was left crying beside its dead mother.[38]

The Indians rode half a mile where they found a remuda of John Babb's horses, stole some, and continued on, heading rapidly northwest to get away from any pursuing settlers. Ironically, John Babb and about 220 settlers in Wise and surrounding counties had recently signed a petition to Governor Throckmorton, complaining of murders and horse theft and asking for protection.[39] The people of frontier Texas were rightfully concerned, for during the several years after the Civil War they never did get the protection from federal forces that pro-union states such as Kansas received.

The Indians moved rapidly for three days and nights, stopping for only minutes to rest, until they believed they were beyond pursuit range. On the afternoon of the third day the captives were finally given something to eat. Bianca was so hungry she reached for another piece of meat and an Indian hacked at her hand with a knife. Sarah Luster, described by Dot as "a shapely vivacious brunette at the very climax of a vigorous young womanhood," unfortunately was "made to suffer an excruciating penalty for her captivating personal charm and beauty." Had she known the future, Dot speculated, and could have seen her brother and husband killed in the Civil War, and "her captivity and maltreatment that followed, she doubtless would have preferred the forfeit of her life to the terrible ordeal." Sarah suffered the abuse and planned her escape. Near the Red River, while most of the warriors were out hunting buffalo, the captives heard shouting and a commotion in camp. They thought that whites were trying to rescue them and they ran to the bluffs for a look. It turned out to be Indians chasing game, and the three returned downhearted. Bianca later learned that "the Indians would have killed us rather than have us recaptured by white men."[40]

They crossed the Red River near the mouth of the Pease and moved into Indian Territory, joining a large village on the Canadian River. While riding north, Dot and Sarah talked about escaping as soon as they had a chance. The first night in the village, Sarah nudged Dot awake about one in the morning. They crept from the dying campfire toward the horses. Sarah located a bridle and fastened it to a fast horse that had been stolen from a neighbor of Babb's. She was ready to go but Dot was struggling with a bridle when the Indians awoke. He told her to go, and tried to nonchalantly walk back to the fire as if nothing had happened. The ruse worked for a time, for it took about one hour before the Indians discovered Sarah was gone. In the morning, Dot was beaten and knocked down, but, said Bianca, "he would walk up and toe the mark again." When they saw he would take a beating without flinching or crying out, they tied him to a tree, placed dead grass and branches around him and commenced to build a fire. Bianca threw a blanket over her head and began wailing, but Dot stoically awaited his fate. The Indians were impressed with his courage and finally cut him free, believing that he would make a fine warrior.[41]

That same day the Indians separated and Dot and Bianca went off with different bands.

Sarah Luster, meanwhile, had ridden hard back toward Red River. Reaching there, she found the water high, but made a perilous nighttime crossing. Exhausted, and feeling safer on the Texas bank, Sarah paused to sleep. By morning, somewhat refreshed, she continued her journey, only to run into another band of Indians, this time Kiowas. Instead of trying to run, she boldly rode up to them and put on a brave front. The Kiowas didn't kill her, but she was again "subjected to all the inhumanities of the tribe."

She stayed with the Kiowas about one month, forever watching for another opportunity to escape. One night during a rainstorm somewhere out in the north Texas Panhandle, she again slipped away from the camp and secured a horse, but this time rode off to the northeast. The rain obliterated the tracks. Sarah rode night and day, only stopping to rest for short moments when she was about to fall from her horse from exhaustion. When she rested she kept the horse's lariat tied around her body. In late November 1866, after four days and nights she reached the Running Turkey Ranch east of Fort Dodge. Luster had unknowingly ridden through an area occupied by Satanta and his Kiowas, who had just been at Fort Dodge to sell the Box captives. The ranch owner took Sarah in, let her rest, fed, and clothed her. He contacted Jesse Leavenworth and the agent made arrangements for Luster to be taken to Council Grove. Sarah stayed for a time at J. Hammond's, who was the postmaster in Council Grove. On December 10, Hammond contacted Texas Governor Throckmorton to ask if he should send her to Texas, and would the state reimburse him for his expenses.

Perhaps the governor didn't respond favorably or Sarah Luster did not want to return to Texas, for in June of 1867, when the Junction City *Weekly Union* newspaper recorded her story, she was still living in Council Grove. Shortly thereafter, Sarah married a Mr. Van Noy, and they established a home in Galena, Kansas. Sarah died in 1904. Dot Babb wrote a fitting tribute to her. She spent the rest of her life, he said, not with bitter, brooding memories, but "in a spirit of serene repose, reciprocal happiness and affection." Pioneer women were special, Dot wrote. Even though his mother faced a "cruel inhuman massacre" and Luster suffered "inexpressible abuses and sorrows," they were typical "illustrations of the sacrifices and perils of the pioneer women. . . ." That they simply met the dangers with unwavering fortitude, he said, is more of a sufficient theme for any tribute that could be expressed by the most eloquent pen.[42]

While Luster was riding to freedom, Dot and Bianca Babb were learning to adjust to Comanche society. Persummy had captured and claimed Dot. After seeing Dot's bravery, Persummy took him under his tutelage and began to show him the ways of a warrior. He got to accompany the Indians on raids into Mexico, and on the last one they killed seven Mexicans and captured two girls and one boy. Dot quickly learned what the fate of a female captive would be. He said, "Occasionally a warrior would capture a white woman for the purpose of adding her to his harem. . . ."

The Indian who captured Bianca turned her over to his sister, who had no children of her own and whose husband was killed during the same raid in which Bianca was taken. The woman was always good to her. From Bianca's limited viewpoint, and not knowing the hell of abuse and slavery that other captive children often faced, she came to believe "that my life was to be a regular Indian life, every day seemed to be a holiday, children came to play with me and tried to make me welcome into their kind of life." Her recollection, written about sixty years later, was obviously focused on a few idyllic memories of her youth. Not so pleasant was the incident with an old woman who sometimes chased Bianca with her dogs. When Bianca "sneaked a pice of wood" from the "old squaw," the woman came at her with an ax. As she swung the blade at Bianca, a young Indian girl ran in between and was killed by the blow. The old woman was herself killed in revenge for taking the life of another member of the tribe.[43] Quite a "holiday."

While the Babbs were being initiated into Comanche life, efforts were being made for their rescue. When Sarah Luster reported their capture to Leavenworth in December 1866, he called in the chiefs of the bands and said that they would get no annuities until they handed over the captives, and he would pay no ransom. The Indians left, but they did not return with the children. In January 1867, John Babb joined the search, asking for $800 from his relatives in Wisconsin to help pay for their ransoms, and traveling to Indian Territory to look for them. At Fort Arbuckle, post interpreter Horace Jones agreed to help.

In April 1867, Jacob J. Sturm and his Caddo wife located Bianca with a Comanche band on the Washita River, near present-day Verden, Oklahoma. The two emissaries made their quest known, but Bianca's new "mother" did not want her to go. Bianca, even though she acculturated well, told her she wanted to go back to her father. The woman tried to take Bianca out of the village to hide her until her rescuers left. They walked for a day and a half, but Sturm trailed and caught them. He put Bianca up on his horse and made her "mother" walk back to camp. He paid the Nokonis $333 and took her back to Fort Arbuckle. She stayed overnight with Horace Jones and the next morning he took her to her father. "Of course," she said, "I was tickled to death to get back to him."[44]

Dot was located on the Canadian River in Chief Horseback's band through the efforts of Chief Asa Havey, who had been instrumental in gaining the release of several other captives (see Elonzo White and Charlotte Durkin). Horseback, the uncle of Walking Face, who had killed Dot's mother, was sure that the white boy "would elect to stay with them. However," Dot said, "in this they were in great error, as my decision was instant and unalterable to return as quickly as possible to my father and kindred."[45]

Asa Havey still had to bargain and cajole for two weeks before Horseback agreed to sell the boy for several horses, saddles, bridles, blankets, and other gifts. Asa Havey and his small entourage took Dot and quickly rode to Fort Arbuckle. When Dot approached a group of white men, his father kept his back to him, hoping to surprise him. John Babb, still facing away, asked Dot several questions, including when was the last time he saw his father.

"I am looking at him now," Dot answered. Finally John Babb spun around and embraced him. "This is my long lost darling boy," he exclaimed.[46]

The ransoms were paid against the wishes of General William T. Sherman, who saw the payments as incentives for the Indians to keep taking captives. Regardless, the men at Fort Arbuckle knew there was no other way to get the children back alive. Bianca later proudly recalled, "They demanded more for my return than they did for the return of my brother Dot," however, that does not appear to be the case. John Babb had to repay Asa Havey out of his own pocket, $210 in cash, about $23 worth of clothing, as well as replace the horses he had given away. Dot was bitter about the transaction, saying "All this was done solely and independently by my father, who was not assisted to the extent of one cent by the United States government." When Dot met his sister, they embraced and cried, happy to be rescued, but overcome with "anguish and consuming grief" when they learned their mother was dead. Dot quickly recovered: "Finally when I realized the curtain was about to descend and shut out the hideous life of savagery, my feelings and spirits began to rise. . . ."[47]

Dot and Bianca assimilated rather easily into Indian life, but they also easily reentered white society. It was said that they retained some Indian habits, such as Dot's reticence to be among strangers, or Bianca's habit of frequently moving, but these are no more Indian characteristics than they are white.

John Babb built another cabin not far from the place where his children were captured. In 1868, Dot worked with his older brother driving cattle to markets in Kansas and by the early 1870s, worked on a cattle ranch in north Texas. In 1870, John Babb took Bianca and little Margie and moved back to Wisconsin. She moved back to Texas in 1881, and the next year married Jefferson D. Bell. They lived in Henrietta, Denton, and Greenville, Texas, and also in New Mexico and California.

When the Comanche Reservation was being divided up into farms, Bianca, strangely enough, tried to obtain an allotment as an adopted Comanche. The government was taking claims for property losses, but former captives could get no reparations for their captivity or suffering. Bianca, who had lost no tangible property, sought to get something from the government by another means. For three years she tried to get the government and a Kiowa-Comanche council to acknowledge she was an adopted Comanche and thus eligible for land. She wrote: "I honestly believe that my self and my children are entitled to a right in that Country. The Indians did me a great wrong, murdered my mother, took me captive and destroyed or stole every thing that my Father possessed. They can partially recompense me for loss of property by adopting me, and I believe if they now had an opportunity that they would do so." Both the Indians and the government, however, rejected her request.[48]

Dot Babb married Pattie Graham in 1875. They lived in Wichita Falls from 1879 until 1898, with the exception of one year when they moved near Fort Sill. Like Bianca, Dot learned that he might have a chance to get some Indian land if he could show he was an adopted Comanche. A special agent investigated Babb's claim but denied it, and Indian police were sent to tell him to move out of Indian Territory. Dot wanted to fight the decision, but his wife talked him into moving back to Texas. They moved to Clarendon, Texas in 1898, and to Amarillo in 1906. Dot moved to Dallas, and in 1931, suffered a stroke that left him partially paralyzed. He died in 1936.

Bianca wrote a narrative of her captivity in the mid-1920s, probably when she lived in Greenville, or Denton, Texas. She helped take care of her brother in Dallas for a time before he died. When she was asked why she had never published an account of her captivity, she replied, "I suppose I've just taken those early experiences as a matter of course and haven't thought that others were much interested." Bianca Babb Bell died in Denton, on April 13, 1950, the last of Texas's Indian captives.[49]

FREMONT BLACKWELL AND THOMAS JEFFERSON SULLIVAN
Texas, October 1866

Four months after the murder of Isaac Brisco and his wife and the capture of their children, the Indians were back raiding in northern Parker County. In October, they appeared at the Blackwell-Sullivan farm on the eastern slope of Slipdown Mountain, four miles southwest of present-day Poolville, Texas, and about eight miles from the Brisco place. Margaret Sullivan was leaving to visit a sick friend, and she and her sister, Charlotte Blackwell, cautioned their children to be on guard for Indians.

The four boys were in the garden picking peas, but watchful or not, they were soon surprised by five Comanches who had been spying on them from a favorite lookout spot on Slipdown Mountain. The boys realized the Indians were upon them when they saw one trying to lasso one of the workhorses. Robert Harvey Sullivan (13) grabbed the hand of his brother, Tommys (6), while their cousins, Joe Blackwell (10) and Fremont Sullivan (7), also took off running. As the Indians gained on the boys, the older Robert and Joe realized that none of them would escape if they tried to drag their little brothers along with them. They quickly made a decision that haunted them the rest of their lives. They let little Fremont and Tommy go, and ran for their own lives. An arrow hit Robert in the shoulder and a rifle ball clipped Joe's hip, but they still outran the rest and dove safely into a cane thicket. When they peered out they saw the Comanches sweep Fremont and Tommy up on their horses.[50]

The two cousins stayed in the cane until they heard their fathers, Upton O. Blackwell and Thomas Sullivan, calling for them. Back at the house their wounds were dressed while the fathers organized a rescue party. The pursuing homesteaders found the trail and soon picked up a small cowbell that was Tommy's favorite toy. They knew they were on the right trail, and a twenty-mile ride took them to a point just south of Weatherford, when the horses shied up at the smell of blood. There was little Tommy's body, "bruised and mangled almost beyond recognition." Crows had even pecked out his eyes. He was killed because he would not stop crying. They buried Tommy's body right there and took his clothes home. Most of the searchers were so sickened by the sight that they could not continue the pursuit. The remaining few continued on the trail, which turned north. They followed it to the Red River before losing it.[51]

Once the Indians were in Indian Territory, it was almost hopeless for pursuers to catch them, because the U.S. government protected them from vengeful Texans. The only hope they had now was that an Indian trader or army officer might learn of the captive boy's existence and offer to buy him. The Indians took Fremont to the Big Bend of the Arkansas River in Kansas. After a rough breaking-in period, Fremont learned the Comanche language, how to shoot a bow and arrow, and became thoroughly "Indianized." In the same camp were two other white children, a girl and a boy (see Ole Nystel).

In the spring of 1867, white trader Charles Whitaker noticed three white captives in the Indian camp and notified federal authorities, and word got to Agent Leavenworth, who arranged for their release. On June 9, 1867, Parker County Judge A. J. Hunter learned of Fremont's rescue and wrote, "The Blackwell child has bin bought at Fort Dodge Kansas but not yet got home I have not bin in formed as to what it cost." Fremont could not remember his name, but he did tell Whitaker that his father's name was Upton and he lived near Weatherford, Texas. Whitaker inquired in Parker County, found his father, and Upton was soon on his way to Fort Arbuckle to pick up his son, or so he thought. Upton waited at Arbuckle for ten days, but Fremont did not arrive. He returned home empty-handed and his wife, Charlotte, was heart-broken. It had been another government mix-up, and new arrangements were made to send Fremont to his grandmother's home in Collin County, Texas. This time, Upton rode the 100 miles to her home, found Fremont, and brought him home. The boy was sick with scurvy, but a diet of vegetables soon cured him. Not so easy to remedy was Fremont's preference for the wild life of an Indian. It took some time before he fit back into the white world, and for months he used to shoot his brothers and sisters with blunt-tipped arrows until they were "blue all over."

The Blackwell family troubles with the Indians were not over. About four years later, Upton was killed and scalped, and his body left hanging in a tree on the Perrin-Whitt Road. In 1886, widow Charlotte Blackwell and family, and her sister Margaret Sullivan and family, pulled out of Parker County and moved to Greer County, Oklahoma Territory.[52]

OLE T. NYSTEL
Texas, March 20, 1867

The Nystel family moved to Texas from Norway in 1850. In 1851, Terje Nystel married Signe Knudsen in Henderson County, and they had three children. Ole Tergerson Nystel was born on January 4, 1853, followed by his sisters, Tone and Anna Marie. Signe Nystel died in 1861. Terje married Gunnar Grann in 1865, and the family moved to Bosque County, where many Norwegian immigrants gathered. The Nystels were farmers, just as their ancestors had been. Ole spent most of his youth helping his father run the farm. He described himself as "headstrong, self-willed, mischievous, though, withal, I think, kind at heart."[53]

On March 20, 1867, Ole's peaceful world was shattered. A neighbor, Carl Questad, stopped by to ask Ole's father if Ole could help him cut poles. His father agreed and the two headed to a cedar brake on Bee Creek, about five miles from Ole's house and about eight miles southwest of present-day Meridian, Texas. Unluckily, the place was next to a camp of six Comanches, who were then in the process of cooking a horse carcass. Ole was only about fifty steps from Questad's wagon when two war-painted Indians rushed him. Ole broke for the wagon but did not get far before an arrow pierced his right leg. Another warrior caught Ole, placed a gun in his face, and motioned for him to come with him.

Mr. Questad ran about the same time Ole did, leaping over a twenty-foot bluff above Bee Creek and didn't stop until he was about four miles away. He got back to Nystel's, cut, bleeding, and down to his underwear after his desperate dash through the brambles, no doubt trying to figure out how he would break the news to Mr. Nystel. A search party was quickly organized. One night they got within half a mile of the Comanches, but never could catch the fast-moving Indians. Later, Ole looked back on the incident as a "plain case of God's providence," he rationalized, because if they caught the adult male Questad they would have killed him, while he, being only 14 years old, was likely to be spared.[54]

Just before sundown the Indians came upon James Hasty, a black freedman hauling corn. He begged for his life but they pierced him through the heart with a spear. They left him unscalped, showing by signs their disgust for his hair, and pointing to Ole's fine locks, indicating with a laugh that his was the fine type of scalp they desired. They commanded Ole to laugh too, and he did, while thinking, "what a sickly effort it was." Before abandoning the settlements, the Indians killed Clint McLennan, another black freedman. On the way west the warriors abused Ole badly.

"They would kick and knock me about just for pastime it seemed, whip my bare back until it was perfectly bloody, with frequent repetitions fire their pistols held so close to my head that the caps and powder would fly in my face, producing powder burns and bruises, until I was very much disfigured." Ole said, "my head was a solid sore, and the scab had risen above my hair. Oh! horrible condition. The Lord deliver any of my countrymen . . .from ever being brought into it as I was."[55]

On the fifth day, the Indians camped near Double Mountain in Stonewall County. The weather grew cold and Ole nearly froze. About the eighth day of his captivity, Ole could take it no longer. He was forced to dig roots out of the hard ground with his fingers. Finally, he stood up and refused to work. An Indian knocked him into a pond. Ole got right up and punched the Indian, knocking him to the ground, and then he ran as fast as he could, wounded leg notwithstanding. The warrior chased him but Ole outdistanced him. They had to get on their ponies to catch him. When they caught the boy and brought him back, Ole thought they were in awe of him, seeing that he could outrun them even with a wounded leg. He fell to his knees, prayed, and thought he heard a voice from heaven saying that everything would be all right. Ole believed that there must have been divine intervention at this point, for the Indians began to treat him a little better, and finally, on the ninth day after his capture, they gave him a little boiled beef to eat.

They traveled three weeks until reaching the Comanche village at the edge of the Staked Plains. Ole's duties included herding horses, hauling water, chopping wood, and occasionally hunting buffalo. He was not allowed to wear a shirt, and his skin blistered badly, eventually cracking and peeling off, which, he said, "occasioned the greatest suffering I think I ever endured . . . ." When a violent thunderstorm struck, the Indians appeared to be terrified, but Ole, convinced that he would be spared, walked unperturbed in the wind and rain. Again the Indians appeared astonished at his bravery, and, said Ole, "My life from this onward was as one of them."[56]

Part of the band or not, Ole always schemed of ways to escape. One rainy night he took a horse and rode away, but by daylight the Indians were right behind him. His horse was exhausted, so Ole simply stopped, got off, sat down, and began laughing uproariously when the Indians approached him. He treated it as a huge joke and the Indians were confused—Ole having learned that laughing was the best way to get out of trouble.

Back in camp the Comanches discussed what to do with the strange white boy, finally deciding that he was too much trouble to keep and that they would be better off selling him. The Indians had slowly moved near the Big Bend of the Arkansas River in Kansas. They took Nystel to a trading post operated by Eli Bewell, his family, and two other partners. The Indians offered Ole for sale and Bewell said he would give brown paper, blankets, sugar, flour, and tobacco in the amount of $250 for the boy. Nystel was nearly naked, and Bewell gave him a suit of clothes. The deal was made, and in June 1867, after three months with the Comanches, Ole Nystel was freed—but he was not home.

After a week, the Bewells took Ole to the Indian agent at the Kaw Mission in Council Grove, Kansas. Then they began to see him as a son, had second thoughts about turning him over. Before the agent could take charge, Bewell spirited Ole away and kept moving for two months, hoping that in time, the boy would become attached to his surrogate parents. Bewell moved Ole to a hotel in Emporia, then to a few different residences in eastern Kansas. Eventually, Agent Leavenworth heard of Nystel, and located Bewell to find out the true situation. Bewell told him that Nystel no longer wanted to go back to Texas. When Leavenworth arranged to see Ole, the boy told him he definitely wanted to go home. That was that. Leavenworth arranged for him to start the very next day.

Bewell was saddened, but helped Ole on his way by giving him three dollars, a blanket, a buffalo robe, and a bow with arrows. When he rode off, Mrs. Bewell ran and hid to keep from seeing him leave. Leavenworth reimbursed Bewell the $250 he had paid for the ransom and the two men, riding with a government wagon train, accompanied Nystel as far as the mouth of the Little Arkansas River. There, Ole came across the same Comanches who had captured him and paid them a visit. They wanted him to return with them, but Ole refused, saying he was going back to Texas. The Comanches were astonished. They could not understand why anyone would want to go there. They could see him staying in Kansas, but were certain that the Texans were "bad" and would kill him. Ole understood the situation: "Here were these Indians receiving at the hands of the government in Kansas and other points their supplies—*tame Indians you know*—and still the same miserable creatures going off along the frontier of Texas, committing their acts of atrocity, killing, plundering, stealing, etc."

Ole knew that the Indians knew the people of Kansas would not fight them to the death, as did the Texans. The Comanches also realized that when Ole returned home he would tell of his experience as a captive and make the Texans want to fight them even more. They told Ole that if he tried to go to Texas they would kill him. A warrior grabbed him by the wrist and they struggled. The Indian tried to pull out a knife, but Ole had a hidden pistol that he drew and fired at the warrior's head. The blast made the Indian loosen his grip and Ole ran back to the government wagon camp. He didn't know if the bullet hit its target.[57]

Ole bid farewell to Leavenworth and Bewell, and the old man was so choked up that he fell to the ground and could hardly speak. Ole thanked them, and rode off with the government train that continued on to the abandoned Fort Washita in Indian Territory. From there, Ole joined with some ox wagons heading to Sherman, Texas, walking all the way. From Sherman, he went to Milford, where he was taken very ill. He fainted and when he came to three days later, he found himself in bed in a hotel, never knowing who carried him there. He was there a week when he noticed three acquaintances, Knud Hanson, and Jorgen and Kittel Grimland, who were just passing through and stopped to ask directions. Ole jumped up to meet them and the subsequent relation of Ole's adventures attracted a crowd. The three friends decided their trip could wait, and escorted Ole home. News of his stay in Milford traveled fast, and Ole's father was on the way to Milford, as Ole was traveling south. They met on the road in a joyous reunion. Ole reached home six months after his capture.

Ole never had a problem returning to white society; he never fully accepted or integrated into the Comanche lifestyle. In 1872, at age 19, Ole married Serena Hoel. They had one daughter, Signe Ameli. Serena died in 1877. Ole married Annie Olena Anderson in 1879, and they had eight children. Ole remained a farmer all his adult life, living in Bosque County until 1890, when he took his family and joined several other families who moved to Floydada in the Texas Panhandle. They lived there until 1899, when they returned to central Texas. Ole was a Lutheran until he converted to the Seventh Day Adventist Church in 1881. Ole Nystel died November 18, 1930. He was buried in the Seventh Day Adventist cemetery in Bosque County, on the south bank of Meridian Creek, only a few miles from the place of his capture.[58]

Mary and Gus Hamleton and Sarina Myres
Texas, April 1867

James Myres, his wife, and six children, moved from Missouri to Texas in 1860, and settled on Walnut Creek in the northwestern corner of Tarrant County. Life was hard and Mr. Myres died in 1861, leaving Sally to care for William (16), Mahala Emilene (15), Eliza (13), Sarina (11), Samuel (9), and John (7). A year later Sally married William Hamleton and settled in the same area, a few miles north of present-day Azle, Texas. By the spring of 1867, Sally had two more children: Mary (5), and Gus (18 months).[59]

By 1867, the area was well within the outer frontier line of settlement, but few places in Texas were safe from Indian raids. About sixty Kiowas, led by Satank and Satanta, crossed the Red River by Doan's Store, passed by Fort Belknap, and traveled down the Brazos to the Tarrant County line. As the warriors neared the Hamleton log cabin, they saw a number of adults and children in a cotton field. They attacked, killing two, while the rest scattered, including Mahala, Eliza, Samuel, and John Myres. The warriors wanted to get to the house before whoever was inside could bar the door. William Hamleton was away at the mill having his corn ground, and William Myres was rounding up cattle. Sally Hamleton was in the cabin weaving cloth on a handloom, while Sarina Myres, Mary Hamleton, and little Gus played inside.[60]

Kiowas burst in the door before Sally, who the Indians called, "a great big fat woman," could get a gun. "The woman tried to defend herself," a warrior explained, "so we killed her." They grabbed the three children and quickly rode off. The next morning, as the Kiowas broke camp, they spied a cloud of dust in the distance. "The Texans are chasing us!" one of them exclaimed, and they hurriedly rode off. Sait-aim-pay-toy had wrapped Mary Hamleton in a blanket, but when they rode away, he left her beside an oak tree, thinking she would slow him down. After riding a few minutes they discovered that the dust cloud was coming from stampeding cattle and they slowed down.

"I left a child behind!" Sait-aim-pay-toy said. Others asked him if he killed it, but he said no. Hah-bay-te said he would go back after it. "I want to give it to my daughter," he said. "She has no children of her own." Hay-bay-te took Mary home with him and gave her to his daughter. Sarina Myres recalled that Mary was crying a lot and the Indians were angry with her. When Sarina did not see her on the second day after their capture, she assumed the Indians had killed her, and this is what she later reported.[61]

The Kiowas went north to Indian Territory. Sarina, believing Mary's crying resulted in her death, resolved to "endure without murmur the indignities and hardships incident to her condition . . . ." The Kiowas held Sarina about six months before selling her at Fort Arbuckle in Indian Territory. Word was sent out to try and locate her family, and soon Sarina's brother, William, came north to get her and take her home.[62]

Satank's eldest son, An-pay-kau-te, saw Mary Hamleton when she was brought to the village. He said she had "fair hair and light blue eyes," and "ran around the camp in a lively way." She was given to Tope-kau-da (Oak Tree) and brought up "in a good Kiowa family." In October 1867, the Indians met in Kansas for the Treaty of Medicine Lodge. The government wanted to make a treaty with them, said An-pay-kau-te, but they never would have gone just for that. "The reason that we went there," he claimed, "was that we were told the soldiers were going to give us some free food."

The Kiowas learned that the government wanted to put them on a reservation, and said that all white captives must be given up. Tope-kau-da and her husband, Tan-goodle, hurriedly took Mary Hamleton off into the prairie and hid her. "We all told the army officers that she was dead," said An-pay-kau-te.[63]

Mary was first called "Tay-han," which was what they usually called captives from Texas. Later she was given the name To-goam-gat-ty, which roughly translated to "the woman who holds the medicine." Her name was later shortened to To-goam. She was always hidden whenever whites came around, for the family did not want to give her up. She grew up strong, tall, and rather heavy. Her hair turned light brown. To-goam became an expert in raising, training, and caring for animals. Gotebo, a leading member of Tope-kau-da's family, arranged for To-goam to marry a Mexican captive. Neither she nor her foster mother wanted it, but such was the custom, and besides, the Mexican had many ponies to buy her. After her marriage, at age 17, she would lie at night in her tipi and cry for her foster mother.

In her later years, To-goam used to go to Mountain View, Oklahoma, to buy supplies. She wore a shawl over her head and always cast her eyes down when in the presence of white people, a habit she learned while growing up. She lost all command of English and became a Kiowa in thought and deed. Regardless, she converted back to Christianity when a Baptist missionary came to Mountain View and baptized her. Agency officials realized she was a white woman, but because she had a husband and children, they made no attempt to return her to Texas. To-goam/Mary Hamleton had a heart attack and died on July 22, 1924. She was buried in the Rainy Mountain Baptist Cemetery and was survived by two sons, five daughters, and many grandchildren. Her Texas relatives, if any of them even remembered her, thought she was killed fifty-seven years earlier.[64]

THOMAS HUCKOBEY
Texas, July 3, 1867

William Riley Huckobey was born in Nashville, Tennessee, in March 1816. He moved to Texas and may have first settled near Lockhart, in Caldwell County. Little is known about him. He married and had at least two sons and two daughters. His wife apparently died, for he remarried a widow named Tanner who already had several children of her own, including Isaac, James, and Sam Tanner. The Tanners lived near Blanco in Blanco County. Huckobey apparently maintained two households with both families and this was the situation prior to the beginning of the Civil War.[65]

On the morning of July 2, 1867,[66] a small party set out from Huckobey's place near Lockhart. It consisted of Irvin Shepherd (23), his wife (18), who was William Huckobey's daughter, their child Joel (1), and Huckobey's son, Thomas.[67] Remaining behind was Mary Caroline Huckobey (16), and at least one brother. She watched her brother Tommy ride away with her older sister—she on a sidesaddled mare and he on a mule. It was the last time she ever saw them. The four riders were heading to Blanco City. It was a long day's ride. Irvin Shepherd was employed by William Huckobey and they were all supposed to help round up cattle as they rode to a cow camp that Huckobey had set up near the Tanner place three miles from Blanco.

The four did not make good time, for they had to stop short of their destination. In the morning of July 3, they continued on, but ran into a band of Comanches who were raiding into Comal and Blanco County, the first time they had penetrated that far into the settlements in the past fifteen years.[68] The raiders made quick work of the whites. They shot a bullet and nearly ten arrows into Mr. Shepherd and put at least seven arrows into Mrs. Shepherd's back, one of them coming clear through to her breast. They cut Joel's head off and threw it some distance from the body. All were stripped and scalped. Thomas Huckobey was carried off.

When they did not arrive at Tanner's or the cow camp, William Huckobey became worried and rode back down the trail. Four miles away and seven miles from the Blanco County courthouse he found the bodies. William Huckobey rushed back with the news. Sam Tanner rode all the way to Lockhart to tell the other Huckobey children what happened. Huckobey went back to the massacre scene with his stepson, Isaac Tanner, neighbor, John R. Palmer, and a few others. They recognized the arrows and one moccasin left behind as belonging to the Comanches. Realizing they could do nothing more there, they gathered up other settlers, and followed the Indian trail.

In addition to Huckobey's two horses and mule that they took from Shepherd, the Comanches stole about forty horses from Bill Jonas and several more from Ben Shropshire and the Trainer brothers, who lived only a half mile from the Tanners. They hit the Kneuper, Fisher, Reszezynski, Wagenfuhr, and Harsdorff places and got another fifty horses. Then they quickly vacated the county. The pursuers traveled more than 100 miles, said Palmer, "to see if we could not get back the boy." They finally gave up and rode home. "We never saw or heard of him afterwards," said Isaac Tanner.[69]

About twenty-four years later, in 1891, William Huckobey, then living in Amphion in Atascosa County, Texas, filed a depredation claim for his losses in July 1867. He claimed the loss of two horses, a mule, two saddles, and one sidesaddle, for a total of $224. He also claimed $20,000 for the loss of his killed and captured children. The bureaucracy worked slowly, and Huckobey died in July 1893, before his claim was resolved. His daughter Mary Caroline, now Mrs. M. C. Slaughter, became legal representative for her deceased father. Witness depositions were still being taken as late as 1905. Finally, the court ruled in favor of a $224 payment to Mrs. Slaughter, minus $44 in attorney fees. Since the government did not pay for injury or death to humans, the $20,000 claim was dismissed.[70]

No one knew what happened to Thomas Huckobey. Or did they? If he was 16, and "small for his age" as Isaac Tanner claimed, perhaps the Indians discovered he was not assimilation material and killed him. There is a possibility, however, that Huckobey became "Tehan," one of the otherwise unnamed captives who rode with the Comanches and Kiowas. The word was the Mexican pronunciation of Texan, and was frequently used by the southern plains tribes to describe white Texans. There were two comparatively well-known Kiowa captives called Tehan. One was Mary Hamleton, the other was a strong, tall, red-blond haired young man of about 18 years of age in 1874.[71]

The boy known as Tehan lived with the Kiowas for a number of years and became an accepted member of the tribe. In September 1874, his band was camped near the Canadian River in the Texas Panhandle when Tehan went out to round up some stray ponies. He ran into a detachment of 5th Infantrymen under Lieutenant Frank Baldwin and was captured. Tehan, who could still speak some English, told the soldiers he was a captive and would be happy to be taken back to his family in Texas. The soldiers dropped him off in the care of Captain Wyllys Lyman, who was in charge of a wagon train hauling supplies from Camp Supply to Colonel Nelson Miles as he campaigned against the hostile tribes in the Panhandle. Tehan pretended to be pleased with his situation while looking for an opportunity to escape. It came after September 9, when Kiowas and Comanches attacked Lyman's train near the junction of Gageby Creek and the Washita, and began a five-day siege. On the third night, the soldiers were desperate for water and a number of them volunteered to slip out of the corral and get some. Shots were fired, a soldier was hit, and in the darkness and confusion, Tehan crawled away to the Indians.

The soldiers dogged the Indians so much in the fall of 1874 and the winter of 1875, that most of them conceded defeat and rode in to Fort Sill. There were holdouts, however, and Tehan was said to have joined Big Bow, who was going to link up with the Kwahadi Comanches on the Staked Plains. According to Hoodle-tau-goodle, Tehan's "sister," it was the last anyone saw of Tehan. She heard that Big Bow, who was suspicious of anyone with white blood, killed Tehan. Another version is that Tehan joined up with

Big Bow and raided with him for a while, but when it looked like they would have to give up, Big Bow killed Tehan, in whose "veins courses the white man's blood," because he might tell the soldiers about Big Bow's murderous deeds. Another story comes from a Comanche, later known as George Maddox, who said that he was with Tehan on a few raids after most of the bands had surrendered, and the last he saw of him was when Tehan decided to turn himself in to Fort Sill after many of the warriors had been sent to prison in Florida. No one saw him after that.[72]

In 1895, a man named Joe K. Griffis, visited El Reno, Oklahoma Territory, and claimed to have been an Indian captive, telling a story that had some vague similarities to that of Tehan, although he did not mention that he was called by that name. His tale was printed in the local papers and seemingly forgotten. In 1930, Griffis visited several members of the Oklahoma Historical Society and talked at length with Dan W. Peery, who actually edited the El Reno *Globe* that printed Griffis's 1895 story. Now, Griffis was telling everyone that he was Tehan. Again, some of his story matched what was known of Tehan, and some didn't.

Peery decided to put Griffis in touch with his former "sister," Hoodle-tau-goodle, who was still alive and living near Carnegie, Oklahoma, but Griffis had to return to his home in Vermont. He and Hoodle-tau-goodle corresponded, and, according to Peery, "the old lady was convinced" that Griffis was Tehan. She said that she, and the other old Indians, knew all along that the story of Big Bow killing Tehan was just a lie. Yet, when Hoodle-tau-goodle asked Griffis about a certain scar that Tehan had, Griffis did not answer.

In 1933, Lieutenant Wilbur S. Nye arrived at Fort Sill to attend field artillery school. He began writing a history of the fort, and in the process, talked to many old Indians. Nye talked to Hoodle-tau-goodle. She told him that Griffis did make it back to Oklahoma to visit her. "I did not recognize him as my foster brother," she said, "but he may have been some other Tehan. He did know some Kiowa and something of our customs. But no Kiowa ever learned the final end of our Tehan."[73]

That Griffis was Tehan seems unlikely. That Huckobey was Tehan is possible. In any case, his story is one of the many without a known finale. He became another statistic—part of the price the pioneers paid for trying to scratch out a living on the wild frontier.

JOHN M. KUYKENDALL
Texas, July 11, 1867

The families from a score of farms and ranches scattered along the Leon River, sent their children to a new school on the south bank of the river, six miles northeast of Hamilton, Texas. The one-room schoolhouse was constructed of unfinished logs with a crawl space underneath, wide chinks between the logs to let in the summer breeze, and a door at one side and a window on the other. The first schoolteacher was Miss Ann Whitney. Among her pupils were Olivia Barbee, Jane and John Kuykendall, William Badgett, Mary Jane and Louis V. Manning, Gabriella and Alex Power, John H. Cole, and some children from the Dean, Gann, and Massengill families.

About two p.m. on July 11, Olivia Barbee was looking out the door on the south side of the building. She had been expecting her father, John Barbee, a stockman who had been away rounding up cattle, to come by and get her. Gabriella Power also looked out the door, saw riders approaching, and identified them as Indians. She told Miss Whitney, but the teacher dismissed her concern and told her to take her seat, saying that it was either Mr. Barbee or some other ranchers. Gabriella looked again and cried out, "They are Indians."[74]

Gabriella grabbed her brother and they crawled out the window on the north side and ran to the brush along the river. When Ann Whitney finally went to the door she saw Indians untying Mary, her horse. She loved the horse, and had often said, "If the Indians ever take Mary I want them to take me too." When faced with that very likelihood, however, she slammed the door and ushered the children out the window. Most of them escaped, but Mary Jane Manning clung to her teacher. Olivia and Louis Manning lifted a floorboard and crawled underneath. Jane Kuykendall hid behind a desk in the corner.

While some Indians stole the horses, four of them came to the cabin. One of them, who had reddish hair and appeared to be a white man, looked through the chinks between the logs and in fair English, said to Ann Whitney, "Damn you, we have got you now." Ann answered that they could kill her if that would satisfy them, but pleaded for them to leave the children alone. Her plea was answered by a shower of arrows that flew between the logs. Ann was hit several times, but continued to shield the remaining children. As she tried to push Jane Kuykendall out the window, an arrow hit the little girl in the back, inflicting a severe, but not fatal wound. The Indians then burst through the door and finished off Miss Whitney.

The English-speaking Indian asked John Kuykendall and John Cole if they wanted to go with them. Kuykendall (8), with auburn hair and a freckled face, said "yes." Cole said, "no." Strangely enough, the Indian said, "Damn you, sit there," to Cole, and picked up Kuykendall and took him outside. At the back of the schoolhouse, a warrior saw children emerging from underneath and caught Olivia Barbee. He tried to throw her on his horse while she screamed and kicked. Just then, the Indians saw horsemen coming through the valley. They dropped Olivia, but John Kuykendall was already secured on a pony, and they went after the approaching riders.

The riders were two women, Amanda Howard and her brother's wife, Sarah Howard. The women turned their horses, and rode to the east like the wind. Sarah leapt over a rail fence and made it safely to a neighbor's house. Amanda (17) continued riding, like Paul Revere, spreading the alarm. The Indians turned west, and before they left the area, came upon a family riding in a wagon. They killed Mr. Standley and wounded his wife, a daughter, and their baby. Olivia Barbee, now free, ran away screaming. She was not found until the next day, when Mr. John Massengill found her; even so, he had to chase her down and secure her until she calmed down.[75]

Because of Amanda Howard's efforts, a posse was quickly formed and went after the raiders. They rode west about twenty-five miles to the head of Cowhouse Creek, with hunting dogs doing the trailing. The next day the tracks separated in a dense chaparral. When the dogs' feet were cut and bleeding and they could go no farther, the pursuers called it off. They had ridden about 100 miles.

Kuykendall saw the posse about sundown the first day, but after that the Indians outdistanced them. He was tied to his horse and was not let down for two days and nights; when he finally dismounted, the skin peeled from his legs. He faced countless hardships and was almost starved to death. It was his red-haired captor who finally gave him some food. John Kuykendall was kept a prisoner for about two years, when a Hamilton County woman read that a boy fitting John's description had been purchased from Indians in Kansas. Isaac Kuykendall, John's older brother, traveled to Kansas, repaid the ransom price, and took his brother back to Texas.[76]

RICHARD FREEMAN AND THOMAS BAILEY
Texas, September 1867

William Freeman built a cabin in southeast Montague County, Texas, about six miles south of Forestburg at New Harp. After the Civil War he became a stockraiser. His son, Dick Freeman, became an expert horseman and his father placed him in charge of a herd of cattle when he was only 12 years old. Staying with the Freemans was Thomas Bailey (12), whose parents, John and Easter Ball Bailey, lived with Easter's parents on the James Ball Ranch (see James Ball) about six miles south of the Freemans in northern Wise County.[77]

In late September 1867, the two boys were herding cattle in a clearing just east of the Freeman home, when a band of Comanches surprised and captured them. Tom Bailey was riding a splendid, large red sorrel called "Billy Button." Had Tom had a warning he probably could have easily outraced the Indians. As it was, they captured a fine horse along with the two boys. Since the boys believed the Indians punished any show of emotions, they tried to wear stoic faces. They gave up without a struggle and as the Indians took them north they passed by the Freeman home.

"Let's take a last look at home Tom," Dick said, "for we will never see it again."[78]

The Indians moved north and came to Levi Perryman's place. They tied the two boys to a tree and searched Perryman's fields for his horses and cattle. Neither the Indians nor the Perrymans were aware of each other's presence; Levi and his wife were both asleep in the cabin. Tom Williams, who lived about one mile south of Perryman, saw the Indians and trailed them to his house. He watched them steal his stock, then crept away and came back the next day, telling Levi about his close call.

After stealing more stock, the Indians crossed Red River. At first, Dick Freeman and Tom Bailey were treated very cruelly. Warriors roped and dragged them and made them walk barefoot in the snow. At the Indian village along the Washita they were teased and abused by the Indian boys. Finally, Dick reasoned that he was never going to be able to escape and he would be killed anyway, so he would no longer stand being abused. When the next Indian boy pushed him, Dick sprang upon him. As the two fought, a circle of warriors closed about them and watched the contest. Dick thought his time was up, but he was determined to give the Indian boy a beating. He pounded on him, tore his hair, and scratched his face until the Indian begged for mercy. Dick got up, folded his arms, and looked defiantly into the warriors' faces, even though he expected to be killed. To his astonishment they patted him on the back and called him a "heap big warrior." From that time on, both boys were treated better, and they were taught roping, dancing, and swimming. After nearly a year in captivity they could speak Comanche fluently.[79]

When the boys failed to return home, William Freeman organized a search party, but when they located Dick's discarded saddle, he figured his son had been killed. They returned home, but Mr. Freeman continued to ask authorities in Indian Territory about the two missing boys.[80] Nearly a year passed before traders discovered them in Comanche camps on the upper Canadian and Washita. The boys had been separated and the traders were only able to purchase Tom Bailey. With the help of Agent S. T. Walkley, they arranged his trip back to Texas. When Tom returned he told his story to Mr. Freeman, stating that Dick was alive before they were separated. The news spurred Freeman to make a trip to Indian Territory. He armed himself with goods, money, and weapons, found a brave friend to accompany him, and rode out to the upper Washita. There, to his great joy, he found Dick still alive, but to all appearances he was a young Indian, with long hair, painted face, rings, and bracelets.

In spite of this, Dick recognized his father at once, ran to him, and begged him to take him home. Dick's Indian owner was very fond of the boy, however, and very reluctantly entered into a discussion of selling him. Finally, Mr. Freeman offered the fine iron-gray horse he was riding, valued at $150, two pistols worth about $60, and $250 in gold. The chief agreed, but made it abundantly clear that he never wanted to see Freeman again, and if he did, he would kill and scalp him. Freeman paid up and they hurried out of the Comanche camp.[81]

Back in Texas, the neighbors gathered at Freeman's cabin to hear Dick tell the story of his captivity. The local boys, however, made so much fun of Dick's Comanche speech and habits that he quickly dropped the Indian customs he had learned. Dick Freeman grew to manhood, stayed in the area, and built his own cabin. It became almost impossible to get him to talk about what had happened to him.

Tom Bailey's father did not have long to rejoice over the return of his son. John Bailey, who lived at the James Ball Ranch in Wise County, was killed in an Indian attack in November 1868, while defending his little brother-in-law, Willie Ball, who was also a recently freed captive of the Indians (see James Ball).[82]

ELIZABETH SHEGOG, MRS. FITZPATRICK, SUSAN AND ALICE FITZPATRICK, PAULA CARROLTON, AND LIZZIE AND MAY MENASCO
Texas, January 5-6, 1868

There were numerous families affected by the Indian raid of January 1868. They lived along Willa Walla, Dye, Blocker, Spring, Williams and Clear creeks, and the Elm Fork of the Trinity, in the area where Montague, Cooke, Wise and Denton County meet. Some were new residents and some had lived in the area for a decade. Daniel G. Menasco married Sophia Brown, and in 1859, built a cabin on Clear Creek in Cooke County, just north of the Denton County line. In 1861, Daniel Menasco's father, Joseph, along with his wife and two remaining children arrived from Arkansas and moved in with him. Montague County, which was created out of Cooke County in 1857, reported at least seventy-three raids between 1857 and 1861, when about 230 horses and numerous cattle had been stolen. James and Louisa Shegog, who lived near the Menascos, reported three horses stolen in September 1859. The raids, however, were not severe enough to drive the hardy settlers away. Daniel Menasco, his brother, and some of the Shegog boys served with the Confederacy during the Civil War. Old Joseph Menasco looked after the families while they were away. Raids seemed to let up during the war, but things changed for the worse in 1868.[83]

If any of the settlers had faith in treaties with the Indians, perhaps some of them were encouraged that the new year of 1868 would bring peace and prosperity. The October 1867 council at Medicine Lodge, Kansas, and the resulting treaty, sounded, at least on paper, as if it would curtail much of the strife. The Comanches and Kiowas pledged that they would no longer carry off white women and children and promised to maintain a lasting peace on the frontier. One of the newsmen at the council reported that the Indians specifically promised to maintain peace in Texas, although the final treaty had no such detailed provision.[84]

The Comanches and Kiowas had no intention of honoring the agreement. After they received their presents they split up and continued their various pursuits. Most of them went down to their assigned reservation around Fort Cobb, but within a month, they were complaining about insufficient rations. The Senate had not yet ratified the treaty, and the Indians' agent, Jesse Leavenworth, had not made adequate preparations to feed them during the oncoming winter. Some warriors went west to attack

Navajos, while others went east to attack the more peaceably disposed Wichitas, Caddoes, and Chickasaws. In January 1868, the marauders stole about 4,000 horses from the Chickasaws and killed a number of them. Cyrus Harris, governor of the Chickasaw Nation, wrote for help, and said, "The wolf will respect a treaty as much as Mr. Wild Indian."[85]

If the Comanches and Kiowas were truly hungry, then buffalo, cattle, and horses could have supplied their needs. There was no just reason for their murder spree into north Texas.[86] On Sunday, January 6, about 300 Kiowas and Comanches, many under the leadership of the young Kiowa Big Tree, swept across Red River and into Montague County. They first appeared in the Willa Walla Valley at the homes of A. H. Newberry and W. D. Anderson. They saw the Indians approaching, barred the doors, and pointed their weapons. The Indians, seeking easier prey, moved on. Riding nearby, W. A. "Bud" Morris and D. S. Hagler saw the Indians and spurred their horses downstream to warn the other settlers. They reached the home of W. R. Eaves, and they all galloped on, spreading the alarm.

The Indians were not all in one large band, however, and small war parties were already ranging up and down hill and valley. The white riders rode up to Charles McCracken's home, but too late; it had already been burned to the ground. George Masoner had already warned the McCracken's and they were hiding in the woods. Masoner sped down another valley. Morris, Hagler, and Eaves proceeded to the home of Alfred Williams, but found they were losing the race; the Indians had already hit the place. They rode to Morris's house where his family and mother-in-law, Mrs. Dennis, lived. He learned that they had just returned from church and had gone home with W. H. Perryman and family. The riders, now joined by F. R. McCracken and Sam Dennis, sped to warn the Perrymans.

After passing by the Newberry and Anderson cabins, the Indians surprised John and Dan Leatherwood on Clear Creek; they killed John, but Dan escaped. They next plundered McCracken's place before burning it. Down the road, the warriors ran into Dave McCracken, who out-raced them to Alf Williams's cabin. When he got there he discovered that Masoner had already warned them and the place was vacant. McCracken rode on, with the Indians at his heels. He slowed them down by occasionally turning and bluffing them back with his gun. One band of warriors crossed over a ridge to the Carrolton home on Clear Creek. George Masoner had

Author's photo
Willa Walla Valley, Texas. Near Shegog, Menasco capture sites.

warned them, but they could not get out fast enough. The Indians killed Mrs. Carrolton and captured her daughter, Paula (15).[87]

The Indians next appeared at the Perryman home, but the fast-riding Masoner had already warned them. Mrs. Perryman put on a hat and some of Austin's clothing, and joined her husband at the window, with rifles pointing out. The Indians, again seeing a potential fight on their hands, swerved around the cabin and kept going. Nathan Long was the next one in the warriors' path. He tried to hide in the timber, but they found and killed him. Masoner warned Mrs. Long and her children, who lived at Joe Wilson's place four miles east of Forestburg, and they had time to hide in the woods before the Indians arrived.

Next in line was Savil Wilson's cabin. His wife was dead and he was not home, but George Masoner rounded up his children and took them into the woods. The Indians found the place vacant, robbed it, and burned it down. They just rode away when Morris, Hagler, Eaves, McCracken, and Dennis arrived, followed a minute later by Savil Wilson. He saw his house aflame, did not know Masoner had already gotten his children out, and went crazy with grief, believing they had been captured or burned to death. Shortly after, they came out of the woods, as did Mrs. Long and her children. There were now six men there to protect them. Mrs. Long, however, recognized a saddle that the Indians left behind as belonging to her husband, and knew that he had been killed.[88]

Bands of Kiowas and Comanches continued down the valleys into Cooke County and swept past the Shegog place. James and Louisa Shegog lived there with their five children: Anna (24),

R.E. (21), Louis (19), W.E. (17), and Jennie (15). Edward (called Captain Shegog), either lived as part of an extended family with his parents, or had a cabin nearby. He was married to Elizabeth Menasco Shegog. One mile east of the Shegogs, Joseph Menasco lived with his extended family: a few remaining grown children, his son Daniel G. Menasco, wife Sophia (32), and their four children. That morning a rider appeared to spread the word of an Indian raid. Joseph Menasco, knowing that Edward was away, decided to hurry to the Shegogs and bring back his daughter and two of his grandchildren who there were visiting their Aunt Elizabeth. Joe Menasco placed them in a wagon, but only made it 200 yards from the house when the Indians struck. The old man was shot first and then scalped. The Indians captured Elizabeth Shegog, her infant child (18 months), her nieces, Lizzie Menasco (8) and May Menasco (6), and a Negro boy who stayed with the Shegogs.[89]

About three in the afternoon in her cabin on Clear Creek, Sophia Menasco heard shots and screams that she recognized as coming from her sister-in-law. Daniel was about 200 yards away from the house when the Indians appeared, and he ducked into the woods and watched. Sophia saw about fifteen Indians coming toward the house. They had her sister-in-law and her child, and two of her little girls and a Negro boy. "I gathered my two little girls that were with me and put them in a room and gave them some play-things," Sophia said, then "returned to the hall of my house, took my husband's gun and went back to the room where my children were." The Indians came within twenty yards of the window and she clearly recognized all of the prisoners. Luckily, the warriors may have been suspicious about who was defending the house and did not attack it. They went to a back lot and took four horses, put the prisoners on them and rode off. Only three miles from the Menasco home, Elizabeth Shegog's baby began to cry, and a warrior took it by the heels and bashed its head against a tree. At this time, one of the Menasco girls may have begun to fight or cry, and the Indians may have killed her on the spot.[90]

Daniel Menasco returned to his house when the Indians left, got his wife, two daughters, and went to Julius McCracken's house for help. He left them there and convinced another neighbor, Thomas Berry, to go with him to where his father was killed. Realizing they could do nothing for the dead, but still might be able to save the captives, the men rode back to their home. In a short time about twenty citizens were ready to follow the Indians' trail that abruptly turned north. The sun went down early in January, and a storm was brewing. Nevertheless, the pursuing settlers caught up to one band of Indians on Blocker Creek. In the gathering darkness and approaching snow clouds, a short, sharp fight occurred. In the confusion, Paula Carrolton slipped down from her horse and hid in a thicket. Pressed by the settlers and in the fading light, the Indians had no time to search for her. They rode away, veering northeast toward Gainesville. Paula was lost in the darkness and wandered around for a time before hearing dogs barking. She followed the sound and came upon the home of Doctor Davidson on Williams Creek. Afraid to go to the house because she thought it was either an inviting target for the Indians, or that they may have already captured it, she took shelter in a ravine and covered herself with brush. About one in the morning, January 6, a strong blizzard blew in from the northwest, covering Paula Carrolton in her brush shelter under a carpet of snow and dropping the temperature to only a few degrees above zero. She waited until morning when she saw a number of white men in possession of the dwelling. Davidson took her in and slowly began to give her warm fluids to thaw her out.

The Indians moved to a point about six miles east of Gainesville. The storm was bad and they may have lost their way. They backtracked around the town before stopping to camp about a mile southwest of the unsuspecting residents. One band actually rode into Gainesville before realizing their mistake and quickly exiting. An Indian's horse was found next morning standing near the door of the hotel. That night the captives, who wore only lightweight clothing, began to freeze, but the warriors gave them no robes or blankets. To the contrary, Elizabeth Shegog was stripped nearly naked, and one warrior found the time to take his knife and hack off her long hair. She was not scalped, but her hair was raggedly cut nearly to the skin. She was so cold she could not ride, and either she fell, or a warrior threw her off the horse and left her in the deepening snow. Hours may have gone by when she regained consciousness. She could barely move, but she discerned a lightening sky to the east and she thought she heard a rooster crow. Elizabeth dragged herself toward the sound. Eventually she crawled to the door of Sam Dause, who lived about one mile southwest of Gainesville. He took her in, warmed and fed her. Her limbs were badly frostbitten and she was unable to move for several days, but was said to have "partly recovered from her experience."[91]

The Indians moved west of Gainesville on the Elm Fork, then turned north and crossed Red River into Indian Territory. Behind them they left the Negro boy and the other Menasco girl. They either killed them first and threw their bodies in the snow, or just dumped their frozen forms to the ground, knowing that the storm would soon finish them off. The settlers assumed the raiders were gone, and began to assess the damages and look for the bodies. Big Tree, however, with the storm waning and perhaps angry that he had once had six captives and now had none, circled back and re-crossed the Red. On Monday evening he was back in Willa Walla Valley.

Arthur Parkhill, who lived one mile from "Bud" Morris, one of the horseback criers of the previous day, somehow escaped the Indians' attentions and didn't know anything about the raid until Morris rode over to see how he was. Parkhill hurried to his brother's place and convinced him to come to his cabin because it was better fortified and had a picket palisade. Parkhill next rode one mile to Thomas J. Fitzpatrick's place, which was in Montague County two miles north of Forestburg, and convinced them to come to his cabin until things quieted down. Fitzpatrick got his wife, their two daughters, Susan (6) and Alice (8), and their son (2), and hurried to Parkhill's. Just then Big Tree's Kiowas struck again. They killed Parkhill and Fitzpatrick, scooped up Mrs. Fitzpatrick and the three children, and were gone.

Once more the settlers tried to follow, but it began snowing again and they gave up. The next day, settlers found Mrs. Fitzpatrick's body frozen in the snow. She had been raped, and her skirt was pulled up and tied around her head. A short time later, "Bud" Morris found the body of the Fitzpatrick boy, half eaten by animals. Susan and Alice were gone. It wasn't until February, when the snows melted that the skeleton of the last Menasco girl was found, about five miles west of Gainesville. It was buried on the Elm Fork near Mr. Piper's farm.

Cooke County Judge J. E. Wheeler wrote to Governor Pease on February 15, that nearly all the people in the western part of the county were moving out, and almost hourly their wagons were passing through the streets of Gainesville. The settlers were beaten down, tired, with few resources, and with little money to pay for a rescue effort. Once their initial despair was over, they began to blame the Reconstruction government, which they saw as taking the army from its rightful mission of guarding the frontier, and diverting it to unneeded constabulary missions, protecting the freedmen, and persecuting former Confederates. It seemed as if the state and U.S. government had forsaken the Texas frontier.[92]

Joining the families vacating the frontier was Daniel Menasco and Edward Shegog. They did not go far, but did pull back about twenty-five miles east to Pilot Point, in the northeast corner of Denton County. Although he had no money to pay a ransom, Dan Menasco wrote an appeal to Agent Leavenworth: "Colonel, I would give the world if I had it for my dear children back again. Their broken-hearted mother is grieving herself to death for them. It is a hard trial; it looks like it is more than we can bear, but we have no way to help ourselves." In another letter Menasco said he was willing to sell all his property in order to raise the money to ransom his children.[93]

The tale of this murderous winter raid spread across the countryside. It was horrid enough—seven people were killed outright, and six out of the ten captives killed later—but its proportions grew as it was repeated. Kiowa and Comanche Agent S. T. Walkley claimed twenty-five people killed, nine scalped, and fourteen children captured. By 1869, the Commissioner of Indian Affairs included in his annual report the inflated assessment that, after the Medicine Lodge treaty, the Indians "brought away in the coldest weather a whole school of children, most of them freezing to death. . . ." The tale has been repeated in various forms ever since.[94]

The raid was one of the final straws that convinced Jesse Leavenworth to resign. Before the winter of 1868, he had been a champion of the peace policy, but since then he began to send letters to his superiors indicating that the Indians were uncontrollable and needed chastisement. "They have all," he wrote, "without an exception, as bands, been engaged in acts of violence and outrages in Texas, and should be dealt with severely." He recommended their annuities be stopped and the guilty brought up for punishment. A disgusted and exhausted Leavenworth spent the spring of 1868, again trying to buy captives. It seemed that the more he rescued, the more were taken prisoner. In May 1868, he located Susan and Alice Fitzpatrick and purchased them. Then, on May 26, he walked off his job and left Indian country.

Agent S. T. Walkley charged Leavenworth with deserting his post after hearing that the Kiowas were going to kill everyone in the valley. For whatever reason, since no family members claimed the Fitzpatrick girls, Leavenworth took them along with him and never returned. He placed them in the Protestant Orphan Asylum in Washington, D. C. and the government secured $10,000 for their care and education, the money being deducted from Kiowa treaty appropriations. The girls' names were changed to Helen and Heloise Lincoln and at least one of them grew to womanhood and married.[95]

Daniel Menasco wrote a sworn statement of his losses in 1870, claiming $100 for one stolen horse, $500 for "damages and loss of property on account of having to abandon my home," and $10,000 for "two children captured and found dead on the Indian trail." Apparently it was never filed with the Department of the Interior and nothing came of it. In Denton County in April 1888, Menasco officially filed a new claim. Probably learning that he could get nothing for the deaths of his children, he only claimed $400 for the loss of four horses. While being questioned by the government claim examiner, Menasco tried to relate the stories of the murders and captures, but he was cut short, the government attorney indicating that "all questions and answers relating to other than claimants loss of stock objected to as incompetent, immaterial, and irrelevant. . . ." Lost stock was more germane to the issue than lost life.

James Shegog died in 1884, and his wife died two years later. In 1898, son Louis Shegog filed a claim. He didn't even bother about the deaths and losses in 1868, but filed for four stolen mules and horses in an Indian raid in 1859. It didn't matter; neither the Shegogs nor the Menascos received anything.[96]

LEE TEMPLE FRIEND AND MALINDA ANN CAUDLE
Texas, February 5, 1868

The winter of 1868 was one of the worst seasons for Indian raids and killings that the frontier people of Texas ever experienced, and in February there occurred the bloodiest tragedy ever in Llano County.[97]

Methodist minister Jonas Dancer moved to a picturesque spot called Honey Creek Cove near Sandy Creek in Legion Valley, about fifteen miles south of Llano, Texas, in 1852. In 1859, while helping build a road from Llano to Austin, Jonas Dancer was ambushed and killed by Indians. He left a widow and several children; one of them, Matilda Jane Dancer, was 11 years old at the time of his death.

Arriving in the valley in 1856, was John S. Friend, a stock raiser and farmer. He had two children, daughter Florence, and a younger son, Lee Temple, who was born in 1860. When his wife died, John Friend stayed in the area, married Matilda Jane, and moved to what he called the "Dancer Ranche" in March 1867.[98]

In February 1868, there were comparatively few households in Legion Valley; the Bradfords and Johnsons lived near the Friends, and some members of the families were related. On the morning

Author's photo
Legion Valley, Texas, near Friend, Caudle capture site.

of February 5, John Friend left for the mill at Fredericksburg. Brothers Asa G. "Boy" Johnson and Thomas "Babe" Johnson were both away on business, and several people congregated at Friend's place: the pregnant Samantha Johnson Johnson and her child, Fielty (1); Rebecca Stribling Johnson and her child, Nancy (3); Amanda Townsend (18); Malinda Ann "Minnie" Caudle (8); Lee Temple Friend (8); and the pregnant Matilda Friend (20). Florence Friend was not home. The night before, Becky Johnson had a nightmare and told her Aunt Betsy Johnson about it. She dreamed Indians murdered her and wild animals were eating her remains. It was horrible. Aunt Betsy just laughed at her foolishness.[99]

They were undisturbed until almost sundown, when Lee and Minnie came running in to the house, exclaiming that someone was taking "Button," a pony hobbled about 200 yards away. The women went out and stepped up on the rail fence to see. An Indian was taking the horse. They ran back to the cabin and barred the door. The Indian got "Button" and rode off to the southwest. In a few minutes he returned and about fifteen Comanches surrounded the house. Several held the horses, while the rest went to the house and tried to force their way in. Matilda gave a shotgun to one of the Johnson women and told her to shoot if the door was broken open. The Johnsons counseled submission, believing they would not be harmed if they meekly gave up. The warriors discovered that the walls, made of thin, picket-like boards, would be easier to breach than the door. A few of them pulled away a section of wall and got in. Matilda grabbed a Spencer rifle, but a warrior wrested the weapon from her. He was about to shoot her, when

387

another warrior, probably concerned about the alarm being given by the report of a rifle, pulled his arm back. Matilda grabbed a smoothing iron and struck one of them, while the other shot her in the side with an arrow. The projectile hit a rib, glanced around her breastbone, and came out the other side. Matilda collapsed on the bed, feigning death.

The others quietly gave up. They were led outside and secured, while other Indians came back in to plunder. They took supplies, clothing, food, a double-barreled shotgun, the Spencer, a Navy pistol, a sidesaddle, four more horses, and $287 in currency. Then they decided to take the bedding. They threw Matilda to the floor, took the straw ticks into the yard, cut them open, poured out the contents, and kept the cloth. They came back inside one last time to see what else they could take. Matilda lay where she fell, with face to the floor. A warrior bent down and severely slashed her left hand three times, cutting the nerves. He jerked the arrow in her side up and down several times to make sure she was dead, then cut a two- by four-inch "scalp" from the front right side of her head, and a two- by three-inch patch from the middle back of her head. The pain was intense, but Matilda still played dead. As the Indians tied their captives to the horses, Matilda was able to see out the broken walls and watched them ride off to the east. Somehow, she forced herself up, wrapped a cloth around her head, and half-walked, half-crawled toward the Bradfords, about a mile to the southeast. She stopped at times to slake her thirst with snow, which had fallen lightly that day. It was after eight p.m. when she reached Bradfords. Their dog announced her presence, but Mr. Bradford would not come out until he was convinced who she was. When he got her inside the family was shocked at her appearance and Mrs. Bradford insisted upon fleeing immediately. Mr. Bradford helped pull the arrow from her side, but did not stay to dress her wounds. They built a fire, left her with a bucket of water, and fled.[100]

Matilda Friend sat in a chair all night. At eight the next morning, two women, apparently the bravest of those remaining in the area, came to her rescue. The cloth had dried to her head, and they could remove it only after bathing her with hot water. Her body was so swollen that it was very difficult to remove her clothes. During the day her husband came to her and a doctor finally arrived that night.[101]

The Comanches probably had no intention of letting all of their prisoners live. Only a mile and a half from the Friend cabin a warrior choked Fielty Johnson. Samantha panicked and tried to take the baby away, but the angered Indian smashed its head in.

A posse of about one dozen men from Llano, including men named Luce, Miller, Oatman, Holden, and Amanda's father, Spence Townsend, picked up the Indian trail about thirty-six hours later. One of them, Mr. Luce, said, "we found on a large rock, six or eight feet high, Mrs. Johnson's babe, with its brains knocked out." In another mile, the Indians murdered Nancy Johnson (3). Minnie Caudle watched the warriors cut the girl's throat and hold her in front of Rebecca's eyes, "up by the feet with its head down right before her, as if to see the blood flow. Mrs. Johnson screamed and fainted, at which they laughed as if it

Photo courtesy Dave Johnson
Malinda Caudle

were great sport." They scalped the girl, leaving one small tuft of hair near her neck.

The Comanches camped the first night near the top of Cedar Mountain, several miles east of the attack site. They built a fire, roasted some meat, and gang-raped the women. Minnie Caudle watched the warriors draw their knives, "but just then," she said, "my squaw threw a blanket over my head." Minnie couldn't see, but she knew what was going on. She could hear and imagine. "They cried and prayed all the time and they knew they were going to be murdered," Minnie said. In the morning, Samantha Johnson either refused to move, or could not go any farther. The posse found her in a sitting position, with a lance entering her right shoulder blade and coming out above her left hip. Her throat was slashed and she was scalped. It looked like Rebecca Johnson had run before she was killed, near the J. C. Talley place, where she too was raped again and murdered. The posse found her "stripped of nearly all her clothing, and the body nearly eaten up by the hogs." Her nightmare had come true.

The trail led down Cedar Mountain another four miles to a place described as Hell's Half Acre, or Cut Off Gap. There, the posse found Amanda Townsend's body. Said Mr. Luce: "She had been tied down upon the cold ground, which was covered with snow, and from all appearances, had been outraged in the most brutal manner. She was then killed, and her body mutilated almost beyond recognition." Spence Townsend picked up a piece of flesh with a lock of long yellow hair attached. He screamed, "This is my poor child's hair!" She was "tied in a position that the fiends could satisfy their brutal lusts." He was so distraught that he began to have chest pains. The others made him go back home.[102]

The posse found it nearly impossible to continue trailing, especially after a new layer of snow covered the ground. They split up, and one party followed a trail that appeared to swing south along Coal Creek, then west. They followed it for five days until reaching the headwaters of the Devils River, where they ran out of food and their horses gave out.

Over the following months, John Friend spent $1,000 "doctoring his wife." Both he and his father, Leonard S. Friend, spent much time and money trying to rescue the children. Back in October 1866, the Texas Legislature passed a law that appropriated $2,500 to be used at the governor's discretion to aid in rescuing Texans taken prisoner by the Indians. Leonard Friend gained the confidence of Governor Pease, and on July 18, 1868, he appointed Leonard as an agent of Texas, armed him with a letter of credit enabling him to withdraw up to $1,500 of that fund, and a request for all military or territorial officers to assist him, and sent him off to procure any captives he might be able to obtain.

Rumor was that the children were being held somewhere in the neighborhood of Council Grove, Kansas, and off went Leonard Friend. Before he arrived, however, one of the children was already back in government hands. Agent Edward W. Wynkoop, working out of the Upper Arkansas Agency at Fort Larned, accidentally discovered Malinda Caudle in a Comanche camp. On August 4, he wrote to Superintendent Thomas Murphy that he "compelled them to give her up to me without ransom." He said that she answered to the name "Minnie," and told him of the circumstances of her capture. Wynkoop and his wife took care of her until he received instructions to send her to Fort Leavenworth. From there Malinda was sent to Fort Arbuckle, and thence, returned to her relatives in Texas.[103]

John and Leonard Friend were not so lucky in their search for Lee Temple. They corresponded with Governor Pease and with agents of the Indian Bureau and Department of the Interior in Washington D. C. In September 1868, John Friend and family and Leonard Friend left Texas and moved to Butler County, Kansas, near the present-day town of El Dorado. In the winter of 1869-70, Indian traders reported seeing two white boys, likely Rudolph Fischer and Lee Temple Friend, being held by a band of Yamparika Comanches. During the next few years,

Butler County (Kansas) Historical Society
Lee Temple Friend (seated) and John Valentine Maxey, at Fort Sill, 1872.

Leonard traveled more than 15,000 miles in Texas, New Mexico Territory, Indian Territory, and Kansas in his search. He made three trips to Washington to personally talk to officials who he hoped could tell him the best way to affect a release of his grandson. The years passed. In February 1871, Leonard Friend was at Fort Sill to talk to Agent Lawrie Tatum. All Tatum could say was that he heard that the Kwahadi Comanches might have him, but he could not induce them to come to the reservation. In March 1871, Leonard learned that there was to be a general council with the Indians at the Wichita Agency, and he wrote to Tatum that he would like to attend. In April, Acting Commissioner H. R. Clum learned that one Comanche band held Rudolph Fischer and Lee Temple Friend, and suggested that they be traded for two Indian captives. Nothing came of these efforts.[104]

The catalyst that brought about Lee Temple's return, along with several other white captives, was Colonel Ranald S. Mackenzie's November 29, 1872, attack on the Kotsoteka and Kwahadi Comanches on the North Fork of the Red River in present-day Gray County, Texas. Mackenzie took eight casualties, but killed at least thirty-two Comanches and captured 124. He burned their lodges, destroyed their property, and marched his prisoners to

Fort Concho. If the Comanches wanted their women and children back, said Mackenzie, they must return all their white captives to the authorities at Fort Sill.[105]

As was the case with the Cheyennes the previous year (see Veronica Ulbrich), the Comanches could not tolerate the white soldiers holding their people. Within a month, Parra-o-coom surrendered at Sill and promised to send the Comanche children to school, but before they would do this, he wanted Tatum to restore their women and children. Tatum said if the Indians gave up four white children, he would ask Mackenzie to release four Comanche women. The friendly Noconi, Horseback, was instrumental in arranging the releases. In late October, he brought in two white boys (see Clinton Smith and John Maxey) and on November 14, he brought in Adolph Korn and Lee Temple Friend. Mackenzie sent back five Comanche women, and although one died on the trip north, the others made it safely to Fort Sill.[106]

When Temple Friend was turned over to Agent Tatum he could hardly remember a word of English, having been in captivity about four years and ten months. He could only remember his father's name was John, that he had an older sister, and that he believed his mother and aunt were killed. Tatum thought the boy might have been the grandson that Leonard Friend was looking for, and he wrote to Butler County, Kansas, to inform him. Leonard got his horse and buggy and hurried to Sill. In the meantime, Tatum had Temple's long, dirty hair cut, washed him thoroughly, and gave him to the care of Quaker missionary and teacher, Thomas C. Battey, to try to restore some memory of his forgotten English language.

When Leonard Friend arrived on December 15, 1872, Tatum took him to the schoolhouse. They asked the white boy to speak to the old man, but he said nothing. Leonard gently put his arm around him and said, "Temple Friend." The boy looked up with surprise, and his forgotten name sprang back into his memory.

"Yesh," he replied.

Leonard looked at him and spoke his sister's name, "Florence Friend."

"Yesh," Temple replied again, and his eyes sparkled.

Leonard explained to Temple that his mother was not dead, and that his father and sister were anxiously awaiting his return. He told Tatum all about the circumstances of Temple's capture, said he had traveled thousands of miles searching for him, and was ready to pay a reward of $1,000 for his recovery, but was very thankful to have recovered him free of any more costs. Temple

Friend, now 13, rode in a buggy with his grandfather to his new home in Kansas.[107]

As with almost every captured child held by the Indians for several years, it was difficult for Temple to let go of the Indian lifestyle. He still kept a bow and arrow, and used them to kill ducks around the house. He never re-adapted well. Although he appeared healthy, there was some underlying malady that affected his constitution. Lee Temple Friend died suddenly on June 2, 1876, at only 16 years of age.[108]

The struggle went on for John and Matilda Friend, as they tried to get compensation for their losses and suffering. They presented their case to the Bureau of Indian Affairs. The claim was brought before the Comanche Indians in council with Agent James M. Haworth on December 2, 1874. The Indians admitted having the boy, but said, "they bought him of the Esa-que-ta (Mescalero?) Apaches," and denied committing the depredation. In 1875, John Friend explained the situation to Edward P. Smith, the Commissioner of Indian Affairs. John had spent $1,000 in medical bills for his wife, and nevertheless, she was never able to use her left hand again, plus the wound on the right side of her head never healed properly, causing her constant pain. John claimed $3,000 for her injuries and $2,500 more for money spent searching for his son. Smith submitted the claim for $6,500 to the Secretary of the Interior, believing it deserving of consideration and asking that it be presented to Congress for just and proper action.[109]

Despite Commissioner Smith's recommendation, the usual bureaucratic delays ensued. Three times it was sent to Congress and twice it came up for debate in the 44th and 45th sessions. Still, no final action was taken until 1885, when it was returned with no decision, back to the Indian Office for re-examination. In 1887, John Friend filed a supplementary petition with a long list of property losses totaling $2,517. The Interior Department studied it again, but only allowed the original claim of $897. Friend filed again in July 1891. Finally, in January 1894, Friend's attorneys, Lockwood and Coggeshall, summarized the past forty years of proceedings, claiming that the Indians had been in amity with the United States since an 1853 treaty declared peace to be perpetual, and that the Indians agreed to make restitution "for any injuries done" by them. The attorneys referenced several other passages in various treaties that stated the Indians were responsible for "depredations or injuries to the person or property" of American citizens. Treaties on the Little Arkansas in 1865 and at Medicine Lodge in 1867, reaffirmed that the Comanches and Kiowas were in amity. The attorneys, however, agreed to drop the additional $2,517 property loss claim because it was impossible to collect further evidence so many years after the fact. They asserted that the original $6,500 claim as recommended by the Commissioner, plus the $897 in property loss, although small in comparison with the total loss and suffering the family sustained, was a fair and reasonable claim.[110]

In June 1894, Assistant Attorney-General Charles B. Howry, presented the government's brief. The document illustrates the official mindset in so many depredation cases, and the government's penurious attitude and specious, even ludicrous arguments. Howry complained that the case never should have been allowed because it was filed more than three years after the initial raid, but since the Secretary of the Interior concurred that it had merits and it was reported to Congress, he was required to continue the argument for the defendants (the United States). Howry argued that the Act of March 1891, made no provision for injuries, that the Comanches were not in amity with the United States, and that the Secretary of the Interior had no authority to allow a claim for personal injuries. He said that depredation "means robbery, plunder, laying waste, the destruction of property and has no application to personal injuries or homicides."

Howry then tried to separate the Comanches into northern and southern tribes. He claimed that the northern Comanches might have been in amity, but the southern ones were not, and that the locality of the attack would indicate that the southern Comanches were responsible. Howry went on to describe the details of the injuries, murders, and captures, and rhetorically asked, "Is it possible these were friendly Indians? Is it possible that they belonged to a friendly tribe?" He continued with the ridiculous assertion that friendly Indians are friendly and non-friendly Indians are not friendly, and that the depredation had to be committed by non-friendly Indians, who must have been a band not in amity with the U. S. But even if the Indians who committed the depredations were in amity, these friendly relations were destroyed by constant treaty violations; thus the tribe was no longer in amity! Howry stated that "while the existence of a treaty not actually dissolved, cannot create a presumption of amity in the face of such facts as are herein presented, the entire absence of a treaty is of itself, strangely suggestive of a condition of unfriendliness and enmity." He concluded that while the attack was terrible, "the sympathy it awakens and the sentiments it inspires have no place in this Court." He submitted, "that the petition should be dismissed."

At long last, Court of Claims Judge Charles J. Richardson delivered the decision on October 29, 1894. He cut through all the fallacious circular arguments used by the defendants and ruled the tribes were in amity with the U.S., but he disallowed the claimant's assertion that medical bills, injuries, and suffering were covered under treaty stipulations. Strangely enough, the judge made reference to the Treaty of 1868, which was after the fact, and should not have been part of his argument. That treaty said that if guilty Indians are not given up for punishment, then the person injured shall be reimbursed for his loss from annuity monies. The judge said that "reimburse for his loss" are not words to describe personal injuries, scalping, or for capture of a son. Besides, he argued, no one proved who the guilty parties were, nor did the tribe refuse to give them up. Until that part was performed, there was not even a *prima facie* liability on the part of the Indians. The Indians were never liable and it was incorrect for the Secretary of Interior to include injuries in the claim. The Court dismissed the injuries and only agreed to pay for the loss of property. The Friends received $897.[111]

Throughout their long ordeal, the loss of their son, and the constant pain that Matilda experienced, there were bright spots. Despite her wounds, Matilda did deliver a healthy daughter. When the baby was able to travel, they moved to Kansas. Over the succeeding years Matilda had five more daughters, but John never got another boy to take the place of Lee Temple. Matilda and John both died in El Dorado, Kansas—she on January 24, 1909, and he in 1929. Malinda Ann Caudle outlived them all, and died in Marble Falls, Texas, on March 11, 1933, sixty-five years after being captured.[112]

NATHANIEL, DORA, AND ELLEN MCELROY
Texas, May 1868

In May 1868, the Kiowa Satanta, and Noconi and Kotsoteka Comanches raided again in Texas. Late in the month they swept into Montague County in the same area that Big Tree had devastated in January 1868. John R. McElroy[113] lived a few miles from Forestburg. When the Indians struck, John and his wife, Josie, were at the cabin, while their children, Nathaniel (10), Dora (8), and Ellen (12), and their nephew Bob Lackey, were in the field picking dewberries.[114]

The Indians quickly killed and scalped the oldest boy, Bob Lackey, and swept up the three children on their horses. Nearby, Levi Perryman was in his oat field when his dogs began barking, his wife came out of the house with a pistol, and a Negro boy ran up to him and said the Indians were attacking. Perryman ran back to his cabin and met his wife.

"The Indians are killing Mr. McElroy's folks," she exclaimed. "Can't you hear them screaming?"

Perryman got his horse and rode to the McElroy's. He saw Lackey's body and Mr. and Mrs. McElroy hurrying afoot in the directions the Indians had taken. Josie was crying out, "Oh, the Indians have stolen my children; my little children are gone, and we will never see them again."

Perryman followed the trail and Jim White joined him. Topping a rise they saw the Indians half a mile away. The children saw riders following them and thought they would be rescued, but it was not to be. Badly outnumbered, Jim White went for more help, while Perryman tried to keep on their trail. The delay was costly, however, for the Indians went north, and Perryman took a trail they had made earlier in the morning which headed east toward Clear Creek. He headed east to the cabins of Williams and Newberry. When they got up a search party they realized they were on the wrong trail and darkness ended they day. Perryman went back to the Willa Walla Valley to warn the settlers.

The Indians took the children north to the Arkansas near Fort Larned, arriving about June 10. Thankfully, they were not held captive for long. The McElroys immediately contacted authorities in Indian Territory and Kansas, and the children were located and purchased a few months after their capture, but for a high price. Instrumental in their release was an Indian woman called Cheyenne Jennie. She was the wife of Fort Cobb trader William Griffenstein, and worked as a go-between with Agent S. T. Walkley and the Indians to secure the release of white captives. Jennie was an invalid, and often traveled in an army ambulance that her husband bought for her. Through Jennie's efforts—she had to give up some of her own horses in the deal—the children were ransomed. They were released about August 1868, at the same time that another captive (see Dick Freeman) was reclaimed.[115]

MARTHA "LUCY" RUSSELL
Texas, August 1868

Some of the same Indians who devastated parts of Montague, Cooke, and Wise County in January 1868, returned in August. The Russell family lived too far out on the frontier for safety, building their cabin in northwest Wise County on Martin's Prairie about four miles southwest of the present-day town of Chico, Texas. When Mrs. Polly Russell's husband died, she considered moving out, but decided to hold on to the farm. She lived there with her four children: Dean (22), Martha "Lucy" (18), Harvey (16), and James (11).[116]

During June 1868, one dozen buffalo hunters returning from an expedition on the plains to the west, stopped to camp near the Russell place. One of the hunters, John O. Allen, was chosen to go to the house and see if he could buy some milk. There he met Polly Russell and her children, and was immediately smitten by the sight of Martha. Allen was nearly at a loss of words, but Mrs. Russell knew that he and Martha were attracted to each other, and she invited the young hunter to return to visit them after supper. He returned and they spent a pleasant evening. When it was time for him to leave, Martha requested that he talk to her oldest brother Dean, about how dangerous it was where they lived, and tell him he should move the family back into the settlements. He promised that he would. That night, John Allen thought of nothing but the girl he had just met. "Lucy was a perfect brunette," he said, "and the finest specimen of womanhood that I had ever beheld, and Cupid at once got out his arrows and sent one into the most vital parts of my life. Just think of an eighteen year old boy looking at the first woman he ever loved." The next morning, before the hunters pulled out, John Allen hurried back to the cabin to talk to Dean, but he had not returned from the mill and his promise went unfulfilled.

Before he left, Allen asked Martha, that since she had made a request for him, he had a request for her. They drew close together, and, said Allen: "I told her that the Comanches had not captured me, but that she had, and as I said this, I saw two big tears coming from those black eyes and jumped down and brushed them away. . . . I asked her if she was going to grant my request, and she said she would. I took her face in my hands and sealed our troth with a kiss." He said he had to go, but he would come back next year.[117]

Martha did not have that much time. They knew well of the Indian danger, but the family earned its living from the soil and the work had to go on. In August, a band of Comanches or Kiowas crossed Red River and raided the Texas frontier. A short distance from the Russell cabin was a dense cane patch, and the warriors hid there and consumed a quantity of cane while they planned out their attack. Dean Russell was working at the mill, and the warriors saw only two boys, a girl, and a woman. Figuring they had the numbers and the element of surprise, they finally attacked. Even so, they did not count on Harvey Russell. He opened fire with a Winchester rifle and put up a good fight. His stand, however, was to no avail, for the warriors slaughtered James in the yard and killed Polly in the doorway. Harvey fell back into the house, firing until he ran out of ammunition. He tried to crawl under the bed, but the Indians caught him and killed him in the corner against a wall. They kept the beautiful Martha for themselves.

After breaking the windows, destroying the furniture, and slicing open the feather beds, the warriors rode off, with their prize prisoner tied to a horse. When Dean Russell got home that evening, he was shocked at the scene of horror. He found James dead and mangled in the yard and his mother on the doorstep, lying in a pool of blood, but did not see Harvey or Martha. He ran back to the mill. The next day, Dean returned with a search party. They found Harvey part way under the bed, and gathered the three bodies for interment. Among the burial party was Theodore "Dot" Babb, who had been captured nearby two years earlier.

When the Indians left the Russell cabin they headed east, nearly capturing the boy, Dick Couch. Mounted Indians chased him home, where he dove under a wagon. One was about to grab him when he looked up and saw Mr. "Uncle Dick" Couch aiming at him with his rifle from the porch. The warrior pulled up and galloped away. The Indians next went to J. D. White's on upper Catlett Creek, destroyed much of his corn and melon crop, continued east into Denton County, stole some horses, and headed north across the Red.

It is likely that Martha Russell fought with her captors all the while. Had she meekly submitted she would likely have been raped, but kept alive as excellent ransom material. As it was, the warriors got only three miles away from the Russell cabin when they stopped, threw Martha to the ground, raped, scalped, mutilated, and killed her. The Couches told Dean Russell that they had seen the entire Indian band, and Martha was not with them, which led him to believe that she was killed somewhere between the Russell and Couch place. Dean Russell was a nervous wreck for ten days after the attack, with the premonition that his sister had been killed nearby and left on the prairie for the wolves to devour. He rode with men from Decatur taking several trails that crossed through the area. Finally they came upon the gruesome scene about three miles from the Russell home. All that remained were parts of her nude body, with scattered bones and a disjointed frame from which wild animals had torn the last bits of flesh. Beside the remains lay Martha's sunbonnet.[118]

John Allen only received two letters from Martha Russell and then the letters stopped. He anxiously waited all winter until he could get back to north Texas, when the next party of buffalo hunters went out again in June 1869. The cabin was wrecked and abandoned. He made inquiries from neighbors, but learned of the massacre and that only Dean Russell survived. The heartbroken John Allen continued west to the buffalo range. While hunting they had a sharp skirmish with Indians. One hunter was wounded, but they thought they killed three Indians. John Allen walked over the skirmish area and found a warrior's buffalo hide shield that was decorated with the beaded scalp. Allen examined the scalp closely and his heart skipped; in color, length, and texture it was very familiar.

"The minute I found this scalp on the shield," Allen said, "it flashed through my mind that it was Lucy Russell's scalp. The time that it had been killed, the color of the hair, the length of the hair, and the trail on which it had been captured, all corroborated and convinced me at once, that was my Lucy Russell's scalp." He choked back his feelings, hid the scalp in his saddlebag, and said nothing.[119]

WASHINGTON WOLFE
Texas, June 22, 1869

George Washington Wolfe, a Methodist preacher from Mississippi, lived at Wolfe Crossing between the junction of the Llano and Colorado River, about one mile up from the Llano's mouth, in what is today Kingsland, Texas. He had three sons, Hiram (17), Washington (13), and W. B. (6). On June 22, 1869, the two oldest brothers had tied up their horses and were hunting hogs near the confluence of the two rivers, both armed with Colt pistols. When they saw Indians moving toward them they both ran to the wooded bank of the Llano and took cover. Hiram fired several shots at the attackers and held them back for a short time, when one warrior jumped off a fifteen-foot bank and ducked behind a large pecan tree behind the boys. From there he had a clear shot and Hiram fell dead. The rest charged in and grabbed Washington. George Wolfe later found Hiram's body lying on the riverbank half in the water.[120]

The Indians, probably Comanches or Kiowas, took the boys' horses, headed west, and passed very close to the village of Llano. William Haney, who lived at the edge of town, heard a noise, stepped outside, and was very nearly hit by a bullet fired by the passing Indians. They continued west, generally following the course of the Llano River. About six miles southwest of Mason, and not far from where Alice Todd was captured four years earlier, Jim Bidy saw them coming. He hid in the bush and took a shot at them as they passed, wounding an Indian woman. The warriors did not know where the shot came from and didn't know how many enemies were near. They hurriedly split up, leaving two men with the wounded woman. Bidy also saw what appeared to be a white boy with them.

Bidy hurried to Mason and spread the alarm. A search party quickly gathered, including William Gammer, James Johnson, Boy Johnson, and a half dozen others. The men picked up the Indian trail and followed it about fifteen miles west of Mason, to Leon Flats not far from the Little Saline River in Kimball County. The slow-moving Indians with the wounded woman dropped Washington Wolfe and ran off, probably hoping that the pursuing whites would be satisfied with recovering the boy. And indeed they were. Wolfe had only been captive three days, but his face was painted and he was already learning to eat jerked meat and prickly pears.

George Wolfe lost a paint mare in another attack on his ranch in November 1869. He moved up the Colorado River about fifteen miles near Bluffton, but the move didn't prevent more Indian visits. In October 1871, they ran off two more of his horses. Some years later, Wolfe moved to San Angelo, in Tom Green County, Texas. In 1902, Washington B. Wolfe was living in Ardmore, Indian Territory.[121]

Chapter eight notes

[1] Winfrey and Day, *Texas Indian Papers 4*, 122, 245, 246, 299, 307; Marshall, *A Cry Unheard*, 23-25; Pace and Frazier, *Frontier Texas*, 132-33; Foreman, "Jesse Leavenworth," 28.

[2] Richardson, *Comanche Barrier*, 20, 52, 83, 102; Michno, *Encyclopedia of Indian Wars*, 162-63; Fehrenbach, *Lone Star*, 516, 532.

[3] Winfrey and Day, *Texas Indian Papers 4*, 134, 136, 178, 228, 306. Weinand's first name is spelled Hubert and Herbert.

[4] Winfrey and Day, *Texas Indian Papers 4*, 178-79, 262-63.

[5] Winfrey and Day, *Texas Indian Papers 4*, 262-63, 306; Tatum, *Red Brothers*, 154; Ashton, *Indians and Intruders III*, 96. Albert Winning is an incorrect hearing and transcription of Herbert Weinand.

[6] Winfrey and Day, *Texas Indian Papers 4*, 451.

[7] Marshall, *A Cry Unheard*, 119; Grace and Jones, *History of Parker County*, 72; Winfrey and Day, *Texas Indian Papers 4*, 219, 223.

[8] Marshall, *A Cry Unheard*, 120; Winfrey and Day, *Texas Indian Papers 4*, 219.

[9] Marshall, *A Cry Unheard*, 121-22; McConnell, *West Texas Frontier*, in forttours.com/pages/tocsavage.

[10] Marshall, *A Cry Unheard*, 122-24, 231.

[11] Banta, *Buckelew*, 6. Buckelew's name has been spelled Buckalew, Buckaloe, Buckeloe, and Bucklew.

[12] Banta, *Buckelew*, 7-10.

[13] Banta, *Buckelew*, 16-22; Winfrey and Day, *Texas Indian Papers 4*, 202, 226.

[14] Banta, *Buckelew*, 23-26.

[15] Banta, *Buckelew*, 27, 29-30, 33.

[16] Banta, *Buckelew*, 35, 42, 56, 61, 63-68; Winfrey and Day, *Texas Indian Papers 4*, 259.

[17] Banta, *Buckelew*, 79-81; Winfrey and Day, *Texas Indian Papers 4*, 202, 229. Lipans attacked the home of R. H. Kincheloe in Uvalde County on October 11, 1866. Frank's aunt, Mrs. Bolden, was working for the Kincheloes. The two women tried to fight off the Indians, but both were killed—Kincheloe after sustaining 13 wounds. Little Ella Bolden got away during the struggle. The warriors rounded up the Kincheloe children and ransacked the house, but were frightened away by other settlers. The pursuing whites killed one warrior and wounded another.

[18] Banta, *Buckelew*, 91-102; Winfrey and Day, *Texas Indian Papers 4*, 129-30, 143, 229, 259.

[19] Banta, *Buckelew*, 104-08; Winfrey and Day, *Texas Indian Papers 4*, 143, 260.

[20] Banta, *Buckelew*, 110-12.

[21] The name has also been spelled Briscoe and Bursco.

[22] Marshall, *A Cry Unheard*, 135-36; Huckabay, *Jack County*, 23; McConnell, *West Texas Frontier*, in www.forttours.com/pages/tocmckinn.

[23] Marshall, *A Cry Unheard*, 136-37; Huckabay, *Jack County*, 94-95; McConnell, *West Texas Frontier*, in www.forttours.com/pages/tocmckinn and www.forttours.com/pages/toc/brisco.

[24] Marshall, *A Cry Unheard*, 137-38; McConnell, *West Texas Frontier*, in www.forttours.com/pages/toc/brisco.

[25] Kappler, *Indian Treaties*, 980; Broome, *Dog Soldier Justice*, 7-10; Athearn, *Sherman*, 213-14.

[26] Winfrey and Day, *Texas Indian Papers 4*, 266, 268, 294-95; Michno, *Mystery of E Troop*, 9.

[27] Winfrey and Day, *Texas Indian Papers 4*, 266, 268, 270, 294-96; McConnell, *West Texas Frontier*, in www.forttours.com/pages/tocbrisco; Marshall, *A Cry Unheard*, 138.

[28] White, "White Women Captives," 332; Gallaway, *Dark Corner*, 110-11.

[29] White, "White Women Captives," 333; Winfrey and Day, *Texas Indian Papers 4*, 107; Herron, "Box Rescue." This band of Indians also stole 72 horses and 52 mules from brothers James and John Davenport in Cooke County. James B. Davenport, Depredation Claim #5732.

[30] White, "White Women Captives," 330, 333; Herron, "Box Rescue"; Potter, *Montague County*, 25-27; Custer, *Life on the Plains*, 60, 62; Custer, *Following the Guidon*, 223.

[31] Winfrey and Day, *Texas Indian Papers 4*, 114; *Commissioner of Indian Affairs 1866*, 280-81.

[32] White, "White Women Captives," 330-33; Herron, "Box Rescue." Herron states that for volunteering for the dangerous mission, he and McLaurie received "words of personal congratulation" from General Sherman.

[33] *Commissioner of Indian Affairs 1866*, 281.

[34] White, "White Women Captives," 334-35.

[35] Custer, *Life on the Plains*, 59-60, 62; Custer, *Following the Guidon*, 222-24; Custer, *Tenting on the Plains*, 355; Hancock, "Difficulties With Indian Tribes," 93.

[36] Potter, *Montague County*, 26. Potter says it was Mrs. Box who married Brunson; White, "White Women Captives," 333; Herron, "Box Rescue." Anderson, *Conquest of Texas*, 349, calls Margaret's statement of her abuse, "weak on details and somewhat inconsistent."

[37] Babb, *Bosom of the Comanches*, 19; Gelo and Zesch, "Holiday," 39; White, "White Women Captives," 329. In some reports Sarah Luster is called Sarah or Lizzie Roberts.

[38] Babb, *Bosom of the Comanches*, 20-24; White, "White Women Captives," 328; Gelo and Zesch, "Holiday," 49-50; Bianca Babb, untitled manuscript. Bianca's and Dot's recollections of their capture differ slightly.

[39] Babb, *Bosom of Comanches*, 24; Winfrey and Day, *Texas Indian Papers 4*, 97-99.

[40] Gelo and Zesch, "Holiday," 51.

[41] Gelo and Zesch, "Holiday," 53-54; Babb, *Bosom of Comanches*, 30, 32, 34. Bianca remembered Dot's stand against the tree somewhat differently. She said Dot "laughed or smiled from hysteria and fright."

[42] Cates, *Wise County*, 176-78; White, "White Women Captives," 329; Winfrey and Day, *Texas Indian Papers 4*, 128-29; Babb, *Bosom of the Comanches*, 36-38. In December 1866, while Leavenworth hoped to send Mrs. Luster back to Texas, he also said he had recovered a "small white boy" named John Charles Fremont Houston, who he wished to send to Texas with her. We have been unable to discover details of Houston's capture. "Letters Received Office of Indian Affairs, 1821—1881," Microfilm Roll M234/375.

[43] Babb, *Bosom of the Comanches*, 40-41, 120, 136; Gelo and Zesch, "Holiday," 56, 59. Anderson, *Conquest of Texas*, 348, wrote, "But as in the past, the captive children were treated amazingly well." As in whose past?

[44] White, "White Women Captives," 330; Gelo and Zesch, "Holiday," 44, 65-66.

[45] Babb, *Bosom of the Comanches*, 56-57. Anderson, *Conquest of Texas*, 348, in another of his distortions, says that Dot "debated over leaving" the Indians.

[46] Babb, *Bosom of the Comanches*, 58-60.

[47] White, "White Women Captives," 330; Gelo and Zesch, "Holiday," 44; Babb, *Bosom of the Comanches*, 58, 62-63. Dot's belief that his father paid the entire ransom is disputed. Bvt. Captain Mark Walker, 19th Infantry, claimed "the child Babb was ransomed by me while in command of Fort Arbuckle in the Spring of 1867." "Letters Received Office of Indian Affairs, Kiowa 1864—1868," Microfilm Roll 375.

[48] Babb, *Bosom of the Comanches*, 68, 70, 76, 86; Gelo and Zesch, "Holiday," 46-47.

[49] Babb, *Bosom of the Comanches*, 100-02; Gelo and Zesch, "Holiday," 40, 47-48.

[50] Marshall, *A Cry Unhead*, 141-42; Grace and Jones, *History of Parker County*, 100

[51] Marshall, *A Cry Unheard*, 142-43. A different version appears in McConnell, *West Texas Frontier*, in www.forttours.com/pages/ben, where the Blackwell-Sullivan home is said to have been located on Rock Creek two miles east of Whitt, Texas, and a Ben Blackwell and a Harve Sullivan were captured, but Harve made his escape.

[52] Marshall, *A Cry Unheard*, 143-45, 147; Winfrey and Day, *Texas Indian Papers 4*, 223.

[53] Nystel, *Lost and Found*, vii, 3-4, 24n21.

[54] Nystel, *Lost and Found*, 5-6.

[55] Winfrey and Day, *Texas Indian Papers 4*, 186; Nystel, *Lost and Found*, 7-8.

[56] Nystel, *Lost and Found*, 9-13.

[57] Nystel, *Lost and Found*, 14-16.

[58] Nystel, *Lost and Found*, vii, 16-17, 27.

[59] Brown, *Indian Wars*, 118-19; McConnell, *West Texas Frontier*, in www.forttours.com/pages/tochamil.

[60] Marshall, *A Cry Unheard*, 160-61; Nye, *Bad Medicine*, 136-37.

[61] Nye, *Bad Medicine*, 137-38. Brown, *Indian Wars*, and McConnell, *West Texas Frontier*, both state that Mary Hamleton was murdered.

[62] Brown, *Indian Wars*, 119; Marshall, *A Cry Unheard*, 161; McConnell, *West Texas Frontier*, in www.forttours.com/pages/tochamil. Gus's fate is uncertain. McConnell indicates he was "partly scalped" when captured, which likely mean he did not survive long. Brown indicates that William Myres picked up only Sarina at Fort Arbuckle. Marshall says Gus was recovered with Sarina.

[63] Nye, *Bad Medicine*, 138.

[64] Nye, *Bad Medicine*, 138-42. An-pay-kau-te said that they also owned many Mexican captives. "They preferred to stay with us;" he said, "they all liked the Indian life." Many Mexican ex-Indian captives would beg to differ with that assessment.

[65] William R. Huckobey Depredation Claim # 3474. Huckobey's name has been spelled Huckabee, Hockobee, and Huckoby. Huckobey is used because that is the way his daughter and other claimants and attorneys spelled it in his depredation claim.

[66] Winfrey and Day, *Texas Indian Papers* 4, 265, 326-29. The year of Huckobey's capture may have been 1868. A letter from Blanco County clerk John W. Speer to Gov. Elisha M. Pease, detailing the massacre and capture, was dated July 7,1868. In 1870, Blanco County Clerk J. W. Herrman compiled a list of depredations in the county from 1865 to 1870, which indicated the attack took place on July 3,1868. Yet, Huckobey and several witnesses claimed the attack occurred in 1867.

[67] Mr. Shepherd was called Irvin by his sister-in-law, Nestor by a neighbor, and William by the county clerk. Thomas Huckobey's age was said to have been between 12 and 16, but he was supposed to be small for his age.

[68] Winfrey and Day, *Texas Indian Papers* 4, 265; William R. Huckobey Depredation Claim # 3474.

[69] Winfrey and Day, *Texas Indian Papers* 4, 265, 327; William R. Huckobey Depredation Claim # 3474.

[70] William R. Huckobey Depredation Claim # 3474.

[71] Nye, *Bad Medicine*, 208; Marshall, *A Cry Unheard*, 89. Huckobey appears to be a prime candidate for "Tehan." Of the other possible captives, Rudolph Fischer would have been about 23 and had black hair; Hubert Weinand would have been about 20, but was held by the Lipans or Kickapoos in Mexico; Herman Lehmann would have been 15, was with the Apaches, and made no mention of being captured by soldiers in 1874; John Ledbetter, who disappeared for ten years between 1871 and 1881, would only have been about 12 in 1874.

[72] Nye, *Carbine & Lance*, 214-17; Nye, *Bad Medicine*, 209-15; Methvin, *Andele*, 90-92.

[73] Nye, *Bad Medicine*, 215; Peery, "White Kiowa," 257-58, 261, 267-71.

[74] Wilbarger, *Depredations*, 472-73; McConnell, *West Texas Frontier*, in www.forttours.com/pages/tocwhitne.

[75] Wilbarger, *Depredations*, 473-76; Winfrey and Day, *Texas Indian Papers* 4, 231; McConnell, *West Texas Frontier*, in www.forttours.com/pages/tocwhitne; Marshall, *A Cry Unheard*, 86. Marshall says the boy who said "no," was Louis Manning. Wilbarger says Standley's name was Strangeline.

[76] Wilbarger, *Depredations*, 477-78; Marshall, *A Cry Unheard*, 86.

[77] Potter, *Montague County*, 54; Winfrey and Day, *Texas Indian Papers 4*, 246; McConnell, *West Texas Frontier*, in www.forttours.com/pages/tocfreeman. Potter calls Bailey an orphan boy who was taken in by Freeman. Bailey was not an orphan, but his father, John Bailey, was killed in November 1868, during an Indian attack. Hoig, *Kicking Bird*, 125, incorrectly states that the boys were from Grayson County.

[78] Potter, *Montague County*, 54-55. Potter transposes the names of the Baileys, calling John the son and Tom the father.

[79] McConnell, *West Texas Frontier*, in www.forttours.com/pages/tocfreeman; Potter, *Montague County*, 55-56.

[80] Sowell presents an alternative in *Rangers and Pioneers*, 283-85. He says men named Freeman and Vance, who lived in Wise County, chased Indians who had taken their sons. After a tough fight, a few Indians were killed and several of the pursuing settlers were killed and wounded, including Freeman, while the Indians tantalized the whites by showing them that they still had the boys. Sowell admits he might have the details wrong and places the incident sometime in 1868. Sowell's fight is suspiciously like one that occurred in Clay County in 1871.

[81] McConnell, *West Texas Frontier*, in www.forttours.com/pages/tocfreeman; Potter, *Montague County*, 57-58.

[82] Potter, *Montague County*, 58-59.

[83] McConnell, *West Texas Frontier*, in www.forttours.com/pages/tocbigtre; Wilbarger, *Depredations*, 586-87; Winfrey and Day, *Texas Indian Papers* 4, 56-62; Louis Shegog Depredation Claim #4360. The spelling of Menasco and Shegog's surnames comes from their depredation claims. They have also been rendered as Monasco, Manascos, Shegogg, and Sligog.

[84] Kappler, *Indian Treaties*, 980; Jones, *Medicine Lodge*, 129-30.

[85] Nye, *Plains Indian Raiders*, 111-113.

86 Richardson, *Comanche Barrier*, 158, 238n37. Scout and interpreter for the Kiowas and Comanches for many years, Philip McCusker stated that the Indians "are going to Texas to steal horses continually, and if they get them without any trouble, they do so, but if in order to get them it is necessary to kill a family or two, they do so." McCusker's statement was only half right. This time it appeared that the Indians were in Texas to kill and capture people, and if they got any horses it was a bonus. McCusker also said that the Indians told him they went to Texas for scalps because the Caddoes had killed three Comanches the previous summer. This was a murder raid, pure and simple.

87 McConnell, *West Texas Frontier*, in www.forttours.com/ pages/tocbigtre; Brown, *Indian Wars*, 119. Paula Carrolton's name has been rendered as Paula and Perilee Carlton.

88 McConnell, *West Texas Frontier*, in www.forttours.com/ page/tsocbigtre; Potter, *Montague County*, 32-34. Brown, *Indian Wars*, 119, says that "an old man named Loney" was also killed.

89 Wilbarger, *Depredations*, 587; Louis Shegog Depredation Claim #4360; Daniel Menasco Depredation Claim #4211.

90 Daniel Menasco Depredation Claim #4211. Which girl this was is unknown. Sophia Menasco later said, "One was buried by the side of her grandfather, Menasco, who was killed when they were captured." Sophia saw her captured daughters from her window, so one of them could not have been killed at the same time as her grandfather. Whether she was killed at his death site later, or killed elsewhere and then buried next to her grandfather is unclear.

91 Daniel Menasco Depredation Claim #4211; McConnell, *West Texas Frontier*, in www.forttours. com/ pages/tocbigtre; Wilbarger, *Depredations*, 588; Brown, *Indian Wars*, 119-20; Potter, *Montague County*, 37.

92 McConnell, *West Texas Frontier*, in www.forttours.com/pages/tocbigtre; Winfrey and Day, *Texas Indian Papers* 4, 257-58; Brown, *Indian Wars*, 120; Potter, *Montague County*, 29. Tom Fitzpatrick's father, who escaped the massacre, continued to live alone on the homestead. Months later Indians attacked the cabin and Fitzpatrick fired at them, scaring them away. One warrior rode his horse right into an abandoned well 40 yards from the cabin. The next day, settlers pulled out the dead Indian, but left the horse. Hoig, *Kicking Bird*, 124, 294n5, claims that Heap-of-Bears led the Indians who attacked the Fitzpatricks, and incorrectly places the Fitzpatrick home in Denton County. He also says it is not known whether this Fitzpatrick family was related to the Fitzpatrick family captured in the Elm Creek Raid. It was not.

93 Rister, *Border Captives*, 143. Menasco's letter to Leavenworth, written in April 1868, shows that he was still not certain that his girls were dead. One of the skeletons had been found in February, but apparently the body of the other still had not been located, or, perhaps identification of the remains were not conclusive. Another possibility is that Menasco learned that the Indians had two white girls (the Fitzpatricks) and hoped, somehow, that one, or both of them might be his daughters.

94 *Commissioner of Indian Affairs 1869*, 393; McCusker to Hazen, July 19, 1874, "Some Corrections of Life on the Plains," in Custer, *Life on the Plains*, 405; Unrau, "Role of the Indian Agent," 279, 286; Robinson, *Satanta*, 77. General Sheridan, in *Report of The Secretary of War 1869*, 49, wrote, "fourteen of the poor little captive children were frozen to death." Rister, *Border Captives*, 142, says 14 children froze to death. Brown, *Indian Wars*, 120, says 17 women and children were carried into captivity. Mayhall, *Kiowas*, 244, says 25 people were killed and 14 children captured, all of them freezing to death.

95 Richardson, *Comanche Barrier*, 160; Hoig, *Kicking Bird*, 124; Foreman, "Jesse Leavenworth," 27; McConnell, *West Texas Frontier*, in www.forttours.com/pages/tocbigtre.

96 McConnell, *West Texas Frontier*, in www.forttours.com/pages/tocbigtre; Daniel Menasco Depredation Claim #4211; Louis Shegog Depredation Claim #4360.

97 Richardson, *Comanche Barrier*, 158; Wilbarger, *Depredations*, 633.

98 Wilbarger, *Depredations*, 630-31, 633; John S. Friend Depredation Claim #3379.

99 John S. Friend Depredation Claim #3379; Winfrey and Day, *Texas Indian Papers* 4, 269, 310; Zesch, *The Captured* 69-70; McConnell, *West Texas Frontier*, in www.forttours.com /pages/ toclegion; Wilbarger, *Depredations*, 633; "Legion Valley Massacre," Handbook of Texas Online; Reeves, "Scalping of Matilda Friend," 50. The relationships among the families are confusing. Matilda was stepmother to Florence and Lee. Malinda Caudle was a daughter of Mayne Green Caudle, and niece of Betsy Johnson, and a half-sister of Samantha. Malinda had three brothers named William T., Mark W., and Jerry G. Caudle. Amanda Townsend was a niece of Betsy Johnson and cousin to Rebecca and Samantha. Lee Temple said one of the women was his aunt. Amanda was reported to be either 16 or 18 years old. Malinda Caudle's name is sometimes spelled Cordell, Cordle, and Caudull.

[100] John S. Friend Depredation Claim #3379; McConnell, *West Texas Frontier*, in www.forttours. com /pages/toclegion; Wilbarger, *Depredations*, 634-35.

[101] John S. Friend Depredation Claim #3379. John Friend said that he found her on the floor of his cabin, but this does not appear to be the case.

[102] McConnell, *West Texas Frontier*, in www.forttours.com /pages/toclegion; Wilbarger, *Depredations*, 636; Hunter, "Tragedy in Legion Valley," 22; Reeves, "Scalping of Matilda Friend," 51; Zesch, *The Captured*, 76-78.

[103] John S. Friend Depredation Claim #3379; Winfrey and Day, *Texas Indian Papers* 4, 266-69; Wilbarger, *Depredations*, 636. Hoig, *Washita*, 52, writes of Caudle's rescue, but inexplicably states that following the Medicine Lodge Treaty the Comanches and Kiowas "had ceased their raiding into Texas, where they had previously committed excessive depredations, including the taking numerous children prisoners." Hoig, *Washita*, 52, and *Kicking Bird*, 124, incorrectly spells Caudle as "Candle."

[104] Ashton, *Indians and Intruders III*, 86, 91, 92, 96

[105] Michno, *Encyclopedia of Indian Wars*, 258-59.

[106] Tatum, *Red Brothers*, 135-39, 144; Nye, *Carbine and Lance*, 162-63. The freed Comanche women told Tatum that they had been treated with kindness and respect and had not been mistreated. Tatum asked them how their treatment compared with how the Comanches treated white women, and they replied "that Indians never treated white women with the kindness that they had received, but always abused them."

[107] Tatum, *Red Brothers*, 140-41; Battey, *Quaker Among the Indians*, 88-89.

[108] McConnell, *West Texas Frontier*, in www.forttours.com /pages/toclegion; "Legion Valley Massacre," Handbook of Texas Online.

[109] John S. Friend Depredation Claim #3379.

[110] John S. Friend Depredation Claim #3379.

[111] John S. Friend Depredation Claim #3379.

[112] "Legion Valley Massacre," Handbook of Texas Online.

[113] Mayhall, *Kiowas*, 244; McConnell, *West Texas Frontier*, in www.forttours.com/pages.toclackey; Winfrey and Day, *Texas Indian Papers 4*, 299. McElroy has been spelled McLeroy and Muckleroy.

[114] There are variations of the names of the children: J. N. A. McElroy, Ira McElroy, Hellen McElroy; Natt and Dara McLeroy; Nat and Dora Ellen McLeroy; Nathaniel, Dora, and Ellen Muckleroy; and John Lackey or Bob Lacky or Lackey.

[115] Potter, *Montague County*, 39-41; Mayhall, *Kiowas*, 244; McConnell, *West Texas Frontier*, in www.forttours.com/pages.toclackey; Hoig, *Washita*, 95; Hyde, *George Bent*, 279, 282.

[116] McConnell, *West Texas Frontier*, in www.forttours.com/ pages/tocruss; Cates, *Wise County*, 168; Hunter, "Trail of Blood, 14. Dean is sometimes called Bean.

[117] McConnell, *West Texas Frontier*, in www.forttours.com/ pages/tocruss.[118] McConnell, *West Texas Frontier*, in www.forttours.com/ pages/tocruss; Hunter, "Trail of Blood," 15; Winfrey and Day, *Texas Indian Papers* 4, 316; Cates, *Wise County*, 169-70; Babb, *Bosom of the Comanches*, 121-22.

[119] McConnell, *West Texas Frontier*, in www.forttours.com/ pages/tocruss.

[120] McConnell, *West Texas Frontier*, in http://www.forttours.com/pages/tochiram; Winfrey and Day, *Texas Indian Papers 4*, 310; George W. Wolfe Indian Depredation Claim #10315.

[121] McConnell, *West Texas Frontier*, in http://www.forttours.com/pages/tochiram; Winfrey and Day, *Texas Indian Papers 4*, 310; Wolfe Depredation Claim #10315. W. B. Wolfe thought his brother was recovered on the Big Saline.

Chapter Nine

THE LAST CAPTIVES

Death just then would have been a relief to me. — Herman Lehmann

It was made known to me that if I did not submit I would be killed. — Arvilla Meeker

Eventually, by attrition, the last roaming Indian tribes in the southwest were placed on reservations. The coming of railroads, destruction of the buffalo, and unrelenting military pressure finally ended the traditional life styles of the Indians. Captive taking waned as military restrictions curtailed raiding, but the activity was already on the decline as Indian agents and the military increasingly refused to pay ransom demands. With the payment source dry, there was no return in the captive-for-profit venture, and with the military ringing the reservations there was little opportunity to seize captives for tribal incorporation. The practice continued, but with decreasing regularity in the 1870s and 1880s.

In 1870, Indians stole Bud Davis from his home in Wise County, Texas. They held him near Fort Sill and when the authorities learned of it they demanded his release. The Indians complied, telling the military, "We were in Texas, and this pale faced boy followed us off."

Mr. and Mrs. Whitlock and their baby were killed near their Llano County home in December 1870, while William Whitlock (4) was taken prisoner. Mary Wright was carried off from Presidio County on February 22, 1871, and four days later, Indians captured two sons of Henry M. Schmidt (or Smith) in Comal County. On March 16, 1871, Indians killed Thomas Stringfield and his wife at their home in McMullen County, Texas, and carried off their sons, Adolphus (7) and Thomas (4). In February 1873, the Terry family was living in a tent near Center Point, Kerr County, Texas, when Lipans attacked them, killed Mr. Terry and two of his children, and wounded Mrs. Terry. They rode off with little Martha Terry

407

in their possession. Outside of Center Point they also captured a young Negro boy named Jack Hardy.

On the Rio Frio, near the present-day town of Leakey, the Indians stopped to steal more horses and Jack Hardy escaped. He warned nearby white ranchers who formed up a posse and caught the Indians stealing horses. They pressed the Lipans so closely that one of them, in a hurry to escape, threw Martha Terry from his horse. She had been captive for eight days. The rescuers kept Martha because Jack Hardy told them both of her parents were killed. Mrs. Terry did not get Martha back until April 1873.

On April 16, 1879, Apaches captured Fred Schman (11) on the Llano River in Texas. In September 1885, Geronimo's Apaches captured James (Santiago) McKinn (10) near the Mimbres River, east of Silver City, New Mexico Territory. They killed and stripped his older brother, Martin. After being roughly treated, including being clubbed in the head by Geronimo, the blond-haired McKinn rapidly adjusted to tribal ways. He was returned after Geronimo's surrender in March 1886. McKinn later grew a long red beard, became a blacksmith, and raised a family. He died in Phoenix in the 1950s.[1]

* * *

Adolph Korn
Texas, January 1, 1870

Louis Jacob Korn moved to America from Germany in 1836. He lived in New York and Louisiana before moving to Texas in 1845. After farming at New Braunfels for a time, he went into business as a confectioner. Business was good, and in 1848, Korn married a neighbor, Friedrika Grote. Over the next nine years they had five children. By the mid-1850s, Louis Korn moved his family to San Antonio, which was a bigger market for his candies and cakes. In 1858, Friedrika died of a fever, and Louis, with five children under 10 years old, soon married Johanna Bartruff (21), a recently widowed German immigrant and only half Louis's age. She had twins named Adolph and Charlie, born May 8, 1859, and Louis adopted them. By 1860, the Korns had nine children, and Louis, seeking to make more money in the cattle business, moved the family out of the city and to the Hill Country of Mason County.[2]

Korn invested his life savings—$1,200—in cattle, but with the start of the Civil War and his inexperience he lost his total

Author's photo
Llano River, near Castell, Texas. Site of Adolph Korn capture.

investment. Korn tried to raise sheep for a neighbor, then moved farther west to the Saline Valley, but the country was rougher and Indian attacks were more frequent, five pioneers being killed in 1862. Indians killed Frank Johnson in 1867, and Betsy Johnson moved back to their old home in Legion Valley, only to face a horrible massacre in 1868 (see Lee Temple Friend). One by one, the Saline Valley settlers gave up. In 1869, Korn moved back near Castell.

On January 1, 1870, the 10-year-old twins were out herding sheep for August Leifeste. They were eating lunch in a thicket when three riders approached. Adolph sat watching them, but Charlie dove into the bushes. When Adolph realized the riders were Indians he tried to run, but one of them grabbed him, clubbed him in the head, and threw him on a horse. Charlie ran home, and Louis Korn and Leifest heard his shouts, but Adolph was gone.[3]

Adolph remained silent, afraid that his captor would hit him again or slit his throat. The three Indians were either Kiowa Apaches or Mescaleros. They traveled north for twelve days, hardly stopping for rest or water, and eating only a few times. Out on the Staked Plains of west Texas, the Apaches traded Adolph to the Kwahadis, where he worked as a slave. One of his jobs was to care for a sick child, but when the child died, the Indians wanted to kill him. An old woman intervened and saved his life, but he was severely whipped.

409

Little is known about Adolph's life with the Comanches; he never discussed what happened to him, and much of what was known about him came from the narrative of a fellow captive (see Clinton Smith). He became as wild as the Indians, stealing horses, shooting at settlers, and even burning one of their houses.

Shortly after Adolph was kidnapped, his father had a notice printed in the San Antonio *Daily Herald*. Two months later, Korn wrote to Texas Governor Edmund J. Davis for help, but the governor said he couldn't do anything but publicize the fact. Texas Secretary of State, James P. Newcomb, tried to gain sympathy from the reconstruction government by playing up the fact that Louis Korn was a Union sympathizer during the Civil War, and he got results. Commissioner Ely Parker wrote to his Kansas superintendent, Enoch Hoag, to "make diligent inquiry" concerning the whereabouts of Adolph. Korn's description was given as eleven years old in May 1870, about four feet ten in height, flaxen hair, grey eyes, broad face, high forehead, a scar in the center of his chin, and speaking only German.[4]

In early 1871, Comanches with Adolph Korn met up with a band of Apaches with another captive, Herman Lehmann. The two spoke in German and talked over their situation. According to Lehmann they "had a good time and would have devised some means of escape," but their plans were foiled when the bands split up. Apparently Adolph had not been fully "Indianized" at the time he met Herman, but in another six months or more, when he met another captive, Clinton Smith, who was captured in February 1871, he was quite the daring young warrior. Once, when the Comanches were being pursued by a band of rangers, Adolph and another Comanche were used as "bait" to lure the rangers into a trap. The trick worked, and several white men were killed or wounded.

Adolph fought against Colonel Ranald S. Mackenzie when his 4th Cavalry attacked their village on the North Fork Red River on September 29, 1872, and took many Comanches prisoner.[5] The wild bands learned that they could not get their people back until the white prisoners were given up, but some of the newly "Indianized" white boys no longer wanted to return. Their wishes did not matter. John V. Maxey and Clinton Smith were delivered to Fort Sill on October 24, 1872, and Adolph Korn and Lee Temple Friend were delivered on November 14. Tatum talked to the older one, who knew a little German and English, and understood his name was "Kohn." The next step was to strip, bathe, delouse, groom, clothe them, and enroll them in school. Korn, Tatum later wrote, "was delighted with the idea of being restored to his parents, brothers, and sisters."[6]

Just how happy Korn was is debatable. He didn't like the school and when a photographer came to take his picture for identification, Korn, afraid of the strange black box, gave out a yell and the ex-captives scattered. On November 26, Tatum sent Korn and Clinton Smith to San Antonio, with Captain Joseph Rendlebrock, and his 4th Cavalrymen. On the first night out they tried to escape, but the soldiers caught them. The caravan stopped at Fort Concho, where the post doctor examined the boys. He guessed that Clinton was nine and Adolph was seven. Apparently living on a spare Comanche diet had stunted their growth. They reached San Antonio on January 7, 1873. Louis Korn left his confectionary shop on Market Street and found his son. He examined the scar on Adolph's chin and knew it was his boy. He hugged him and "cried like a baby," but Adolph showed no emotion. Louis took the boys to his shop and gave them all the candy they wanted, but they remained aloof.[7]

Adolph did not appear happy, but he made no attempt to run away. He was wild, and got into trouble with the authorities. Sometime later, Clinton Smith visited Adolph in San Antonio. Smith said that Adolph talked to him about going back to the Indians, but Smith said he was happy with his own people. In 1876, Louis Korn again moved his family from the city to the wilds of Mason County. Adolph broke horses for Jacob Bauer near his childhood home in Castell. He tried cattle-raising, but never was successful in any endeavors, and for the rest of his life he appeared caught between two worlds. He and his brother Charlie worked for the county in 1879, and Adolph opened a charge account at a Mason dry goods store in 1889. About that time, Charlie moved away and Adolph was on his own. He never married and was always a loner.

In 1892, Adolph was asked to testify in an Indian depredation claim for a neighbor, Adolph Reichenau, who had lost fifty horses to raiders in 1868 and 1869. One of the questions the government attorney asked Adolph was if a condition of war existed between the Comanches and Apaches and the Texas and U.S. government between 1865 and 1876.

"Yes, of course there was war!" Adolph said. "They killed one another whenever they got a chance." The attorney asked if Adolph ever went on raids with the Indians. "I was too little," he answered. "They left me at their places of rendezvous of their women and children, which was always being moved. I never stayed over fifteen days at one place."

Was Adolph telling the truth? If so, then all the raids that Clinton Smith said Adolph participated in were lies. Perhaps Korn was not the unholy terror that Smith made him out to be, calling him "about as mean an Indian as there was." Or, maybe Korn was afraid to admit his part in the raiding and killing for fear of prosecution or retribution. Likely his true participation was somewhere between the two extremes.

In his last years, Adolph became a hermit, living in some small caves known as Diamond Holes on Rocky Creek, near Hilda, Texas. He became ill around the turn of the century and moved in with his stepsister, Hannah Hey Wilson. He was listed as a boarder in her Mason home in the census of 1900. It was there he died, on July 3, 1900, at the age of 41. Adolph Korn was buried in the Gooch Cemetery in Mason, beneath a lone mesquite tree. One hundred years later a headstone was finally placed over his grave.[8]

HERMAN LEHMANN
Texas, May 16, 1870

Moritz and Auguste Lehmann emigrated from Germany in 1846, and settled near Fredericksburg, Texas. Their son, Herman, was born June 5, 1859, followed by a daughter, Caroline, in 1861, and another son, Willie, in 1862. Moritz Lehmann died in 1862, and Auguste married Philip Buchmeier in June 1863.[9] They moved to Squaw Creek, near present day Loyal Valley, in southeastern Mason County. There were several other German families scattered along Squaw and Beaver Creeks, but the land was still wild and open. Only four miles to the east in Loyal Valley, lived ex-captive Minnie Caudle, who had been rescued less than two years earlier.

On Monday, May 16, four children went to scare away the birds from the wheat. Willie (8) was sitting with Auguste, his 17-month-old stepsister, while Herman (10) and Caroline (9) played. Just then, half a dozen riders approached. The children heard them speaking, but they assumed it was English, for all they could speak was German. The riders were Lipan Apaches. One Indian knocked little Auguste from Willie's lap and grabbed him. A warrior named Chiwat caught Caroline. Herman, slender, and with sandy hair and light gray-blue eyes like his brother, ran across the field. An Indian named Carnoviste caught him, punched and choked him into submission, and tore off his pants and shirt. Herman fought back with all his might, kicking, biting, and pulling Carnoviste's long hair, while Willie put up no resistance. As the Indians tried to secure Herman, Caroline broke free and ran for the house. An Indian shot at her but missed; she fainted and dropped into the wheatfield. Auguste and Philip Buchmeier heard the commotion and ran outside, but the Indians were gone before Philip could shoot.[10]

Buchmeier tried to round up a posse, but all the men were out looking for cattle. Herman was tied to a horse "stark naked" and his skin was torn by mesquite thorns and catsclaw and blistered by the sun. "Death just then would have been a relief to me," he said. When they stopped to rest, the two boys tried to escape, but Carnoviste caught them again, beat and gagged them, and indicated he would torture them if they made another escape attempt. The next night the Apaches killed a calf. Carnoviste cut open its stomach and ate the milk it had nursed. He told Herman to do the same, but he refused. The warrior shoved Herman's face into the bloody mess and forced some into his mouth. Herman vomited. Carnoviste cut off a piece of raw liver and made Herman eat it. He vomited again. This time the Indian scooped up the vomit and shoved it into his mouth. Once again he threw it up. Lastly he soaked another piece of raw liver in blood and forced it down Herman's throat. Finally he held it down. Carnoviste appeared satisfied. For whatever reason, Willie was not treated as severely and got to keep his clothes. The Apaches and their captives continued to ride northwest.[11]

Unlike the Korns, who moved back to San Antonio, or the Friends, who moved to Kansas, the Buchmeiers stayed. They wrote to Forts Concho and McKavett and asked for help. Sergeant Emanuel Stance took nine troopers of Company F, 9th Cavalry, on a scout from Fort McKavett toward Kickapoo Springs, located about twenty-five miles north of the fort. His orders were to try to intercept the Indians who stole two children from Loyal Valley. Although Stance and his black troopers did not know it, they did have a brush with the very Apaches who had Willie and Herman in their possession. About fifteen miles from the fort in the northwest corner of Menard County, Stance saw Indians driving a herd of horses and charged with Spencers blazing, knocking one Apache from his horse. In their mad dash to get away, they threw Herman on a horse with the lead Indian, while Willie was pulled up behind the last man in line. After a short ride, the warrior pushed Willie off, still holding a piece of the Apache's shirt in his fist. Herman couldn't see his brother and thought the Apaches killed him.

Willie hid in the brush and was not found by the Indians or the cavalry. He wandered for three days when a freighter picked him up and deposited him at Kickapoo Springs Station in care of the agent, Mr. Flannagan. On his return trip from Fort Concho, the freighter placed Willie aboard his wagon and took him back to Loyal Valley, where he reached home on May 28. Willie made an enigmatic summation of his four-day sojourn with the Indians. He was treated well, he said, "besides scares, hard rides, and starvation. . . ."[12]

Herman had no such "easy" time. The Indians wouldn't let him eat or drink. After he wandered away looking for water, they tied him to two posts and suspended him face down, just above the ground, then placed a large rock on his back which pressed his nose and mouth into the sand. They left him hanging all night long. "I suffered all the agonies of death," said Herman, but when he groaned they pulled his hair and ears and beat him.

Out on the Staked Plains a few days later the Apaches killed a buffalo, cut off a piece of raw liver and gave it to Herman. He ate it and vomited. Once again, Carnoviste forced him through another eat and vomit routine. When they reached a village, it was the women and children's turn to beat him. Then, as they held him down, they ran a red-hot iron rod through both of his ears, after which they threaded buckskin "earrings." Not yet finished, they then burned great searing holes in his arms. Herman fought until he grew exhausted and fainted.[13]

Carnoviste, who had adopted Herman, used him as a slave to care for his horses, bring his food, light his pipe, and pick lice off of his body. Herman was overcome with homesickness, so much that "I would sit there on my pony and cry." One day he tried to escape and the Indians chased him. He had gotten a long way before his pony stumbled and threw him to the ground. The Indians caught him, tied and whipped him, and brought him back to camp. From then on another boy was assigned to stay with him all the time. Carnoviste taught him the ways of a warrior, and as Herman learned those skills he became more comfortable with his new life.

Only a few months after Herman's abduction, the same Apaches raided Squaw Creek again. This time they attacked Herman's house, and this time Auguste Buchmeier wounded two of the raiders with shotgun blasts. The wounded men were Genava and Carnoviste. When the wounded men returned to the village, Herman was severely beaten in revenge. They showed him some clothing and a toy they had stolen from a storeroom near his house, and said they had killed his entire family. Herman was devastated; now he had no hope or reason to return home.[14]

Herman participated in many raids, once finding an ox-team with a man, a woman, and three children beyond Fort Terrett. The Indians killed the man, woman, and baby, and took the little boy and girl. Herman said, "The poor little things would not eat," and they cried for four days. Tiring of the children's behavior, warriors rode up on each side of the girl, took her left and right arm, lifted her from the horse and swung her, said Herman, "the third time turning her loose. She cut a somersault in the air, and when she struck the ground she was dead, and every Indian rode over her mangled corpse. The boy was served the same way at the same time by two other warriors." They picked the bodies up and hung them in trees for the vultures.[15]

On May 4, 1871, Auguste Buchmeier left her home to go to the camp of General William T. Sherman, who was making an inspection tour and stopped near Loyal Valley. Auguste got an audience with the general and asked his help in rescuing Herman. Sherman, who believed that the complaints by Texans on the frontier were exaggerations, was moved by Auguste's plea and promised he would do his best to find the boy.

In January 1873, the ex-captive Adolph Korn met with the Buchmeiers and told them he had seen Herman, alive and living with the Apaches. They had always assumed he was with the Comanches. In April 1873, a man passing through Loyal Valley told the Buchmeiers that Herman was at Fort Sill and would soon be home. Herman was there. His band of Kiowa-Apaches spent about six months in proximity to the reservation and the Kiowa Kicking Bird told Tatum that he'd seen a white boy among them. When soldiers went to investigate, Herman hid beneath a blanket until they left.[16]

Herman believed his parents were dead, and besides, he was in love with an Apache girl, Topay. By this time, Herman saw the whites as enemies and viewed soldier attacks on Indians as barbarous murders; not realizing that he too was committing the same acts for which he condemned the soldiers.

In August 1875, Herman was sixty miles west of Fort Concho after stealing about forty horses in Menard and Mason Counties, when the Texas Rangers attacked them. They shot Herman's horse and he was pinned underneath it. Rangers Jim Gillett and Ed Seiker, ran up. Gillett put his pistol to Herman's head. He closed his eyes when the explosion blasted powder into his face and the bullet grazed his temple. Just then, Seiker shouted, "Don't shoot

him! Don't you see he is a white boy?" The confused Rangers ran
off after another Indian and Herman crawled away to hide in the
grass. When the Rangers returned they couldn't find him. Herman
walked for five days, living off insects and roots, before finding the
Apache camp. When he arrived, he learned that they had thought
he was dead and had already destroyed all his possessions. It took
him two months to regain his health.[17]

Carnoviste was killed by an old medicine man during a
drunken brawl in the spring of 1876, and then the old man came
after Herman. Herman shot him full of arrows. Knowing the dead
man's family would seek revenge, Herman ran away. He roamed
on his own for nearly a year, until in late winter of 1877, he came
upon a band of Comanches and approached them in peace, and
through an interpreter he explained he hated the whites and
wanted to join them. They welcomed him into the band.[18]

Although Herman rode with the Comanches now, most of them
had gone to the reservation. In 1877, Colonel Mackenzie sent
out Quanah Parker to talk the last holdouts into surrendering.
He found Herman's band in eastern New Mexico near the Pecos
River. Quanah told them they were treated well on the reservation
and that it was useless to fight any more, for the white men were
more numerous than the stars in the sky. Finally, on August 20,
1877, Herman's band rode in to Fort Sill. Even so, Herman had
a last-second fright and ran off to hide in the nearby Wichita
Mountains.

In early 1878, when word reached the authorities that a white
boy was still in the mountains, Quanah went to tell him that his
parents were still alive and he must go to them. Herman did not
believe it. At the post, interpreter Horace Jones explained the
situation to him, but Herman became so angry and confused that
he threatened to kill Jones. Quanah finally convinced him to visit
his white family. In May 1878, Herman returned to Loyal Valley,
where the Buchmeiers had since built a hotel. His mother ran out
to greet him, threw her arms around him and kissed him, but
Herman, now 18 years old, didn't even recognize her. That night
a crowd celebrated, ate, drank, and sang. People called the boy
"Herman," and it sounded familiar, but the commotion was too
much, and he took a blanket and went to sit quietly in the yard.[19]

The first few months after Herman's return he acted more like
a petulant child than a 19 year-old man. He disliked sitting at the
kitchen table. When he was served ham he flew into a rage and
kicked over the furniture, not wanting to dine "with hog-eaters."
He slept in the yard instead of in his bed. Nothing pleased him; he

was used to being in a society where the Indian women did all the hard work. When he hunted and brought home game, he expected his mother or sisters to clean and cook it, plus to curry and feed his horse.

"I would not work at first," Herman said, but he did want possessions like other folks and realized he had to find a job. He hired out to do manual labor, then tried to raise cattle, but nothing suited him. In 1890, he opened up a saloon at Cherry Spring, near Loyal Valley, but he got into fights, drank up all his profits, and got fat. His relatives began to see him as a ne'er-do-well and came to believe he would have been better off to stay with the Indians.

Herman married a Miss Burks in 1885, but she left him after a short time. In 1896, he married Fannie Light. They had five children and never got along well, but remained married. In 1900, Herman moved his family to Duncan, Oklahoma Territory, and like the Babbs, tried to apply for a land allotment as an adopted Comanche. The trouble was, he couldn't prove he was adopted. In 1901, he talked Quanah Parker and the council of chiefs into enrolling him in the tribe, but the Secretary of the Interior concluded that he needed to be adopted into the tribe when he lived with the Comanches, not in 1901. The secretary said Herman could be enrolled as a Comanche, but it was too late to receive a land allotment. A disgruntled Herman Lehmann was enrolled on the reservation as a Comanche on September 16, 1901.

It took eight more years of legal wrangling before the government, perhaps just to get him out of its hair, granted him the land. Herman selected a tract west of Grandfield, but he wasn't happy there either. He didn't like farming and he missed his brother, Willie, and the Texas Hill Country. Herman's mother died in Castell, Texas, in 1912. In 1926, Herman left his wife and children in Oklahoma, and returned to live out his remaining years on Willie's ranch. He never held a job. In 1927, perhaps knowing that his time was running out, Herman collaborated with J. Marvin Hunter to write his life story. He tried to explain his past transgressions by stating: "When I was a savage I thirsted to kill and to steal, because I had been taught that that was the way to live; but I know now that that is wrong." Late in his life Herman developed a heart condition and became bedridden. He died in Willie's home on February 2, 1932, at age 72, trusting that his brother would pay for his funeral.[20]

ELIZABETH, CHARLES, IDA AND DANIEL KOOZIER, MINA AND GEORGE CULLEN, AND MARTIN B. KILGORE
Texas, July 9-10, 1870

President Grant's "Quaker" Peace Policy was inaugurated in the summer of 1869. So named because a delegation of Quakers convened him that they should manage the Indians because they were honest, just, and non-political. "We will substitute brotherly love for the sword," they claimed, "and in a spirit of toleration will lift these wards of the nation from barbarity to Christian civilization." Grant gave them a go ahead.[21]

The new policy did not work well. The Quakers had good intentions but few of them understood the character of the Plains Indians, the majority of whom would more likely respond to a show of force and see kindness as a weakness. On June 12, 1870, a Kiowa, White Horse, ran off seventy-three mules from the post corral at Fort Sill. A few nights later, Big Tree and his warriors killed a woodcutter near the fort, shot a Mexican herder, and ran off horses.

Such was the situation when the new Quaker Agent Lawrie Tatum took over from Colonel Hazen on July 1. He was an honest farmer from Iowa, but he had little conception of what he was dealing with. He called his charges together and told them to be good. Benjamin Grierson, 10th Cavalry colonel in charge at Sill, was supportive of Tatum and the new policy, but he could do little when he had orders that prevented him from assuming jurisdiction or exercising control over the reservation Indians. The Indians quickly realized there was a new regime, and they responded by making a big raid into Texas.[22]

White Horse led a large band of Kiowas and Comanches across Red River and into Montague County, in early August 1870. White Horse had a reputation as a tough and reckless young warrior. He had already led many raids, and had taken a number of prisoners. White Horse first hit settlements in the Willa Walla Valley, where Big Tree had raided in January 1868 (see Elizabeth Shegog). Perhaps finding slim pickings, the Indians swung west, passed by the Jett Davis Ranch on the head of Denton Creek and attacked a loose settlement of about one dozen families living near Victoria Peak.[23]

On Saturday, July 9, the Indians rounded up hundreds of horses. Hard hit were the McDonald and Kilgore places. Jerrell McDonald lived there with his four boys, Cash, Charles, Clark, and Dean. Word of the raid spread fast, and several of the families forted-up at McDonald's. Others didn't get the word until too late. Martin Boone Kilgore (12) and a man named Johnson were outside that morning herding cattle when the Indians approached. They killed Johnson and then went after the boy. Kilgore was small, but an expert rider. The Indians noticed this, and since they used boys to tend the horses, hoped to capture him alive. Kilgore saw the Indians and gave them a ride for their money. He might have escaped, but there were too many, and a band cut him off before he could reach home. One warrior finally caught up to him and clubbed him off his horse with a blow to the head. They threw the unconscious boy on another horse and took him away, all in plain sight of Mr. Kilgore. He was so consumed with grief and rage that his friends had difficulty holding him back from riding alone after the Indians.[24]

About 150 Indians approached McDonald's, but thirteen men and women defending it made an attack too dangerous a proposition. Instead, two miles from McDonald's, they found a group of cowboys working for W. B. and John B. Slaughter, driving a herd of cattle north to Kansas. The Indians jumped them, killed Sam Lewis, who lived in Parker County, a cowboy named Adams from Palo Pinto County, and a man named Vaughn. The Indians headed into Clay County.[25]

Gottlieb Koozier[26] and Doctor Albert Eldridge were in Montague on Saturday when word of the raid came in. The two men had known each other in Illinois, and moved to Texas to set up a frontier colony. The place they chose was near the site of Henrietta, Clay County, between the Dry Fork and the East Fork Little Wichita. The town was abandoned during the Civil War because of Indians, but, despite warnings, Koozier, Eldridge, and several other families moved in. Eldridge lived on the East Fork, about three miles east of Koozier. When they heard about the raid, Eldridge said to Koozier, "Well, I am going through tonight." He was going to try to get his people out. Koozier tied his horse to Eldridge's wagon and rode to his camp where he had four families working for him and tending his horses. Eldridge stayed in his wagon that night, between Montague and his ranch, and Koozier rode home.

At first light, Eldridge told his field boss, "You take these families and get them to Montague the best you can. I'll go out and watch and see if it's reality." The doctor then rode to Koozier's, reaching there about 7 a.m. He talked to Gottlieb and told him to leave, but the passive Quaker said he had never fought the Indians, never carried arms, and would live on peaceful terms with them. Eldridge saw he could not change his mind, and rode away. He went to the East Fork to a timbered ridgetop about seven miles from his ranch. There he took out his "glass" and spied hundreds of Indians and horses coming directly toward him from the direction of Victoria Peak. His son-in-law, Tom Wade, lived at Old Man McDonald's, and he wondered if his horses were included in the massive herd. "Then," Eldridge said, "I left the country."[27]

Gottlieb Koozier and his wife Elizabeth hoped they made the right decision. Before moving to Texas, they both lived near Washington, Illinois, east of Peoria. They had known Doctor Eldridge since 1852, when he treated Elizabeth (then Mrs. Cullen) for an illness. Gottlieb and Elizabeth married about 1857. Koozier brought 200 fine horses from Illinois, selected purposely for breeding. Koozier was a citizen and spoke English with a German accent. It was mid-morning on July 10, when about 100 warriors rode up to Koozier's place.

"There is the Indians," Elizabeth said. Husband and wife came out to greet them. Staying inside and warily watching the proceedings were Charley (10) and Ida (8), children of Gottlieb and Elizabeth; Dan (12), Gottlieb's son from his previous marriage; Mina Cullen (17) and George Cullen (12), Elizabeth's children from her previous marriage. Mina celebrated her 17th birthday the day before. Edgar, another of Gottlieb's sons from his first wife, was out looking after horses. When he saw the Indians coming he ran to the spring and hid under a rock. They rode right over him but didn't see him.[28]

Several Indians walked up to the Kooziers. "We were pretty badly frightened," said Elizabeth, but "we went out and tried to make friends with them; several of them shook hands with us." White Horse shook Gottlieb's hand and grasped it tightly. Another warrior grabbed his other arm. With his other hand, White Horse pulled out a pistol and shot Koozier down. Another warrior put an arrow into him. While Elizabeth watched in horror, the Kiowas scalped him and stripped off his clothes and shoes. Other Indians swarmed into the house and yard. Some grabbed the children while others went on a rampage, killing the chickens and hogs. They took bed ticks, saddles, clothing, pistols, shotguns, dishes, silverware, watches, and destroyed glasses, stove, clock, pictures, bedding, and "a patent washing machine." What was not destroyed outright was burned when they set the cabin afire. They also ran off about 250 horses, every one the Kooziers owned. The Indians also got hundreds of Eldridge's horses.

They grabbed Elizabeth and the children and headed north. At the Little Wichita, which was running full, they stretched a rope across the river to help in fording, but as Elizabeth rode across, a warrior knocked her into the water. She swam, but Indians kept pushing her under and away from the bank. Finally tiring of their sport, they let her swim to shore, exhausted. Elizabeth was suffering from rheumatism at the time, and one arm was in a sling. The sling was lost and her arm was in terrible pain.

On the way north, warriors rode up to Elizabeth and the children, struck them, and, she said, would "throw my husband's scalp up and show it to us." The prisoners were not fed during four days' travel. When they reached a large village in Indian Territory, Elizabeth and the children were separated. A Mexican named "Oyer" kept Elizabeth, White Horse kept Mina, a mixed-blood named Cooper had Ida, and Satanta had Charley. On the fifth day, Elizabeth was offered some raw liver. Even though she was starving, she could not bring herself to eat it. Mina was given some puppy stew and she hungrily ate. Finally, Elizabeth got a chance to eat some bread and buffalo meat and she ravenously accepted it.

"We were treated very roughly," Elizabeth said. "Several squaws pelted me with rocks." In her owner's tipi one day, a woman came in, bit her on the shoulder, and "shook me like a dog," Elizabeth said. "White Horse tried to shoot my oldest daughter Mina," she reported, but Ida saw him and screamed, which caused him to put his pistol away. After three weeks, an Indian from another tribe came with a letter. Elizabeth read it, but an Indian grabbed it from her, threw it on ground, and shot it a few times with a pistol. Elizabeth took the "dead" letter and threw it in the fire, which seemed to make them happy. She didn't know who sent the letter, only that it said help was coming. She was afraid, however, they would be murdered if soldiers came to rescue them, for she estimated that there were more than 4,000 Indians in the village somewhere near the Wichita Mountains, which she could see in the distance. Elizabeth noticed that the Indians had thousands of horses, and occasionally she saw her own horses, with the half-circle K brand. While held captive, Elizabeth said, "The Indians burned seven holes in Charley's ears and put two rings in them."[29]

Immediate efforts were made to recover the captives. Pursuers gathered near Victoria Peak from as far away as Gainesville, and included Louis S. Fisch, Jett Davis, Kilgore, Perry Cook, Tom Wade, several of the McDonald clan, and Jesse Maxey, whose own son (see John Maxey) would be captured in the same area two months later. The posse reached Victoria Peak on Sunday evening to meet the McDonald's. They saw a destroyed wagon with two oxen still hitched to it. The animals' hamstrings had been cut and their sides sliced open so their entrails were protruding. The posse tied its horses up close to McDonald's stable and stayed up all night watching for an attack.

Sunday morning they saddled up and followed the massive trail. On the way they came across some Slaughter's dead cowboys and searched for more bodies. They did not hit the trail again until Monday. They reached the little settlement of Cambridge, where Doctor Eldridge and a few other families lived. The cabins were destroyed and the people gone. By this time, other neighbors were gathering, including, A. L. Burch, Joe Bryant, and a man named Murphy, who was Koozier's son-in-law. They reached Koozier's burned house and found his body lying in the yard. Said Burch, "He had been scalped and they had driven a beef horn through his throat." Edgar Koozier had stayed under his rock until the Indians left, then ran to Murphy's and was saved.

At Fort Sill, Agent Tatum wondered what he was going to do. The Indians were threatening to kill him and his employees, and Tatum told them they were free to go home if they wished, and a number of them vacated the dangerous post. Tatum consulted with Grierson, and they both agreed that Tatum should withhold rations until the stolen stock was returned. When Kiowas and Comanches came in asking when they would get their beef, Tatum said they must return the stolen animals. Sullenly, they left, and Tatum hoped his threat had worked. A week later, however, he learned that instead of rounding up the stock, the Indians had been in Texas rounding up horses and white captives. In an understatement, Tatum said, "The way the Indians were acting was very discouraging."[30]

Mr. Kilgore wrote a letter to Tatum, giving him the details of the raid, the names of the captives, and asked for his help in recovering them. On July 29, Tatum wrote to Superintendent Enoch Hoag, asking if the department would sustain him in paying a reward for the prisoners. On August 7, 300 Kiowas came to the agency to obtain rations. They returned twenty-seven of the seventy-three stolen mules, believing that the good agent would reward them. Tatum, however, grimly broke the news: unless they delivered up all the captives they had recently taken, they would get nothing. The Indians blamed White Horse, and said he was the one who stole the mules and led the latest raid into Texas.

Tatum was adamant—no rations without the captives. While the Indians loaded their guns and nocked their bows, Tatum stood his ground. Eventually, the sullen Indians departed. One came up to Tatum and placed his hand under his vest and over his heart to see if he could "feel any scare," but the mild Quaker passed the test. He was learning that a hard line got more results.[31]

The Indians brought in the Kooziers and Cullens on August 18. Oyer did not want to give up Mrs. Koozier and one of the children. There was a tense moment when little Ida, who had been separated from her mother for a while, began crying. When a warrior threatened her with a knife, some of the soldiers grabbed their weapons. The Indians backed away with the children and Tatum finished talking.

"The chiefs then went to work on the Mexican, a despicable fellow," said Tatum, "and soon procured them, the last of the family." Martin Kilgore was not among them, however, Tatum and Grierson believed that had better take what they could get. The chiefs said they had been very liberal in turning over the captives and they told Tatum they wanted a liberal amount of presents in return. Elizabeth Koozier remembered Tatum's statement as, "If you will make our hearts glad, we will make yours glad in return." Tatum allowed the chiefs to take their men to the beef pen "and see that they behaved," but while cutting out a number of beeves, Tatum said, they "killed a good many more than they were entitled to." Still, Tatum paid them a reward. According to the long established custom," he wrote to Superintendent Hoag, "I paid for the captives or rather gave them presents after they were given up, by giving orders on the stores for $100 each, making $600."

On September 1, the last recalcitrant chief brought in Martin Kilgore. Acting as a go-between as he had before, Asa Havey told Tatum the owner wanted more than $100. Tatum kept his hard stance, saying that the band would get no rations until the boy was delivered. While they discussed the matter, a company of cavalry serendipitously rode into the post, perhaps influencing the decision. The Indians agreed to turn over Kilgore. Tatum gave them $100 worth of goods, but this time, when issuing their portion of rations, he withheld half of the coffee and sugar, to make up for the extra cattle they had killed two weeks earlier. The Indians were angry, but Tatum drove home the idea that both sides must live up to their agreements. The Kiowa, Lone Wolf, finally accepted half the coffee and sugar and left. "My plan of withholding rations from a tribe or band that had white captives until they were delivered was new and experimental," Tatum later wrote. "But I thought it was right, and therefore the thing to do. In practice it worked grandly. I procured many captives of them afterwards without paying a dollar. That treatment made no inducement for them to obtain captives, while paying for them was an inducement."[32]

About three weeks after the July raid, Jesse Maxey, Perry Cook, T. W. Bogard, Louis Fisch, and a man named Taylor rode up to Fort Sill to see if they could recover any of the stolen horses. Fisch was there for a second reason; he was "courting one of the girls." He had met Mina in May 1870, and fallen in love with her. They had seen each other several times, and Fisch was agonizing over what the Indians might do to her. A day after they got to Sill, they saw Indians riding and herding McDonald's, Eldridge's, and Koozier's horses. Bogard recognized Koozier's half circle K brand. "Texas horses," they said, and the Indians replied, "Yes, heap bueno; heap more back," motioning to the Wichita Mountains. The settlers told Tatum, but he said it would be useless and dangerous to try and get them back.[33]

The Kooziers stayed at Grierson's house for several days. While there, Tatum removed the rings from Charley Koozier's ears. The army escorted them to Montague, Texas. There, Edgar Koozier joined the family. They bought a horse and wagon and went back to their home near Henrietta, only to find everything destroyed. Gottlieb Koozier had bought 160 acres, and he had improved 160 more under the Homestead Act, but Elizabeth had no means to stay there. She abandoned the place and moved back to Illinois, about twelve miles from Peoria.

"My hands is all I have," Elizabeth later said, indicating her destitute condition. She married a Mr. Johnson in 1884. They moved to a new homestead about five miles from Humboldt, Allen County, Kansas, and raised chickens. Of her children and stepchildren, Elizabeth later recalled that Dan was killed "out west;" Edgar died in Arkansas; Mina got married and lived in Humboldt, Kansas; George and Charley also lived in Humboldt; and Ida was dead.

In 1893, Elizabeth Johnson decided to file a depredation claim. John S. Hagler was appointed administrator for the estate of Gottlieb Koozier. In 1894, he filed the initial statement, listing destroyed property and stolen horses amounting to $16,850. Not until 1898, did the Department of the Interior acknowledge the claim, taking a long series of depositions and conducting interviews with witnesses for the claimant and for the defense (the U. S.

Government). Koozier's main witnesses were Louis Fisch, and Albert Eldridge. Both men claimed they knew Koozier well and said that he owned from 250 to 300 horses that were stolen by the Indians. Fisch did not marry his sweetheart, Mina, yet he was still concerned about the Kooziers' welfare. "I only hope, for the girls' sake, that they get their dues," he stated.

Other claimant's witnesses were Elizabeth Johnson, Jett Davis, John B. Loring, J. C. Carter, Elijah Hodges, and T. W. Bogard, who all testified that they knew Koozier and knew he owned 250 or more horses. Both sides agreed that the Koozier home was burned, their property was stolen or destroyed, and that the family was taken prisoner. The only question was how many horses Koozier owned. The defendant's attorneys brought three witnesses to testify: J. P. Earle, S. M. Satterfield, and A. L. Burch. They stated that they didn't believe Koozier owned so many horses. Earle and Satterfield didn't live in the area until a year or more after the raid, and had no direct knowledge of Koozier or his horses, but they testified that they never heard anyone say he had that many. Burch, a farmer who lived near Doctor Eldridge in Cambridge for about two years, testified that he never heard about Koozier having so many horses, and thought he could not have owned them without him knowing about it. Burch said Koozier farmed on "a small scale, being a man of little means." He thought he only owned five horses.

The proceedings took years. In 1898, Silas Hare became the claimant's attorney and in 1901, John P. Slayton took over as administrator for the estate. In 1902, Fisch and Carter made supplemental depositions. They stated that in 1901, they attended a settler reunion and talked to A. L. Burch. They asked him why he had testified that Koozier only owned five horses. Burch did not want to talk, but on Fisch's insistence, he replied "in a desultory way" that he did remember that Koozier had many horses and he remembered that he brought some with him when he moved to Clay County. Carter said that he remembered when Koozier first moved to Texas. He lived south of St. Jo in 1868, and had about 140 horses back then. Carter asked Burch if he remembered, but Burch, Carter said, "did not seem disposed to talk." Fisch, Carter, and Attorney Hare believed Burch's motive was because he did not receive the dues he expected after testifying in Albert Eldridge's depredation claim. Eldridge won his case and Burch wanted money for his testimony.

In the spring of 1902, both sides filed their briefs. Hare summed up the claimant's case by stating there was only one question remaining. How many horses did Koozier own? His eight witnesses testified that Koozier had from 250 to 300 horses. The defendant's had three witnesses, two of whom did not even live there, and only surmised that Koozier did not have many horses because they never heard of them. Burch's testimony was unreliable because of a grudge he held.

The government representative, Assistant Attorney-General John G. Thompson, hoped to "show that he never owned any such number of horses and, therefore, could not have lost them." He said the horses lost actually belonged to Eldridge, and that Koozier did not lose more than six horses, his house, wagon, and household goods. They depicted Fisch as a liar because he "evinces a disposition to testify in behalf of the claimant to an extent almost in utter disregard of what the real facts of the case were." Thompson argued that Eldridge never knew how many horses Koozier had, but Fisch, who knew him only a short time, knew everything about his horses. He pointed out that Mrs. Koozier said she owned many silk dresses, but Fisch did know about them. Thompson thought that his three witnesses were more reliable.

The defendants argued that the claimant's witnesses only heard or guessed about the number of Koozier's horses; they really could have been Eldridge's horses. Wrapping up his brief with hollow sincerity, Thompson said that because of Mrs. Koozier's sufferings, the defendants do not want "a judgment for one cent less than the actual amount of loss from a most liberal standpoint; yet the defendants do insist that the Government and the defendant Indians should be protected from an unconscionable judgment in this case." In 1903, the Court of Claims found that Koozier only lost six horses. It ordered a settlement for lost property worth $5,830, to be recovered against the Kiowa and Comanche. Attorney Silas Hare got $884 of it.[34]

JOHN VALENTINE MAXEY AND RHODA MAXEY
Texas, September 5, 1870

Kiowa and Comanche Agent Lawrie Tatum believed that he was achieving positive results in curbing captive taking. Nevertheless, only eighteen days after the Indians had turned in the Kooziers and only five days after they gave up Martin Kilgore, other raiders were back in Texas. This time, the Maxey Family was the victim. Jesse Maxey had ridden with the posse that trailed White Horse's raiders in July, and he rode with a few other men to Fort Sill late that month in an unsuccessful bid to recover the stolen Koozier, Eldridge, and McDonald horses.

Jesse Maxey lived with his wife, his son John Valentine "Volly" (6), daughter Rhoda (3), a baby daughter, and Jesse's father, John Maxey. They occupied one end of a double log house, the other side being the home of T. W. Beale, his wife, their son, Hezekiah, and daughter, Anna. The families were separated by about half a mile from others cabins known as the "Stroud Settlement," which consisted of the families of Jonathan Stroud, Hiram Leaf, Tom and Bob Savage, Will Davis, and Jett Davis. The settlement was located at the head of Denton Creek about five miles southwest of Montague and a similar distance east of the settlement at Victoria Peak.

In the summer of 1870, a measles epidemic broke out in several Montague County settlements, killing many young children and even a few adults. Jesse Maxey and T. W. Beale feared for their children, and the two families recently moved to the old Rice place, distancing themselves from the other families at Stroud's. They escaped the measles, but met up with a worse fate.[35]

On September 5, a party of Kiowa raiders again swept through Montague County.[36] Jesse Maxey and T. W. Beale were in Montague on business, leaving John Maxey to protect the families. The old man and the children were out at the woodpile, and while John chopped, the children picked up the wood chips. A large stump stood between the woodpile and the creek, and behind it, two Indians hid. Before old Mr. Maxey could react, they shot him dead. Mrs. Beale and Mrs. Maxey spotted the Indians about the same time. They shouted out a warning and the children began running. Several other warriors appeared and chased them down. They shot Hezekiah dead, and chased Anna close to the cabin. A warrior got so close to her when he fired that the flash ignited her clothes.

Mrs. Maxey was running, holding her baby to her breast. An Indian fired and the bullet went through the baby's head and lodged in Mrs. Maxey's arm. She held on to the dead child and ran into the house. Mrs. Beale saw Anna fall just short of the cabin and ran out to slap at the flames that were burning her dress. When she realized she was dead, she rushed to the cabin. The two women slammed the door just when a bullet crashed through it and cut a three-inch long gash across the top of Mrs. Beale's head. The two women escaped out a back door and ran into the woods behind the cabin.

When the Indians first charged out, Volly and Rhoda Maxey ran, but were trapped in an angle of the fence. One warrior shot an arrow into Volly's leg so he could not run, and then they easily grabbed the children as they huddled together. They plundered the cabin, drove off Maxey's two oxen, and rode to the Stroud Settlement. Stroud and the other families saw the raiders coming and forted up in his cabin. A brisk fire kept the Indians at bay, but they stole Stroud's horses, stabbed and sliced up Maxey's oxen, and rode away.[37]

In the evening Mr. Maxey and Mr. Beale returned from Montague to discover John Maxey dead in the yard and the two Beale children dead by the woodpile. Frantically they called out for the others, and in a few minutes, the terrified Mrs. Maxey and Mrs. Beale emerged from the timber by the creek. Mrs. Maxey still held her dead baby tight in her arms. Volly and Rhoda were gone. The men gathered up the dead and the two wounded women and took them to John Stroud's cabin where Doctor John A. Gordon was treating Stroud's son with the measles. Gordon dressed the women's wounds. The next morning the four bodies were buried in the Stroud graveyard.

Rhoda Maxey did not get far. The first night out she cried incessantly and the warriors smashed her head and left her naked body impaled on a broken mesquite branch. Volly Maxey quickly learned he had to bear his pain in silence if he wanted to live. He disappeared among the Indians for two years.

Twenty days after his children's capture, Jesse Maxey was at Fort Sill. He reported the raid and capture to Agent Tatum, who was once again flustered that his preaching apparently did little good. Maxey stayed at the agency until the Indians came in for their rations. Tatum questioned them, but he said, "I could hear nothing of the captured children. Their poor father went home disconsolate." Tatum had a Kiowa-Apache Indian named Pacer, travel to the Indian villages to learn what he could, but no one seemed to have anything to say about the captives.[38]

The Indians made it clear to Tatum what it would take for them to make peace. The Kwahadi Comanches were particularly recalcitrant. They said "they would never go to the agency and shake hands until the soldiers would go there and fight with them. If whipped they would then go to the agency and shake hands."[39]

Their wish was complied with when Colonel Ranald S. Mackenzie and his 4th Cavalry defeated them on the North Fork of the Red on September 29, 1872. Valentine Maxey was in the village at the start of the attack and he mounted his horse to ride up the valley and warn the other Comanches. Mackenzie destroyed the village and took 124 Comanche prisoners. If the Comanches wanted their women and children back, said Mackenzie, they must return all their white captives. The Noconi, Horseback, brought Tatum two white boys on October 24. One identified himself as Clinton Smith. The other, about 9 years old, couldn't speak a word of English, and through the interpreter, Tatum learned his name was "Topish."[40]

The boy remembered being taken a few years earlier and thought his father was killed in the yard. He also believed his mother and baby sister were dead. The sister captured with him was killed the first night. He didn't remember where he lived or his relatives' names. Apparently both Clinton Smith and "Topish" were in the village Mackenzie attacked. "Topish" even mounted a pony and raced to another Indian camp to warn of the soldiers' approach. Tatum asked why they ran from the soldiers. "One of them," said Tatum, "replied it was because they were foolish little boys, and the other assented to it."

Tatum advertised in the Kansas and Texas newspapers. Meanwhile, he had the boys' hair cut, dressed in "citizen clothes," and placed in the agency school. Back in Montague, Bob Savage overheard people talking about a little boy who was up at Fort Sill. The description sounded like Volly Maxey. Savage rode to Maxey's cabin and gave him the news. Maxey immediately wrote to Tatum, saddled his horse, and rode to the agency. Thomas C. Battey, a teacher at the agency, was impressed by the change in "Topish" after his father arrived. Before then, the boy could not recall anything which may have proven his identity, but when he saw his father, Battey said, "it seemed as though a new light had suddenly broken upon him, and not only his name, but several incidents of his early life, were unsealed to his memory, proving his identity beyond a question." Jesse Maxey had gotten his son back.[41]

One year after Valentine Maxey was captured, Jesse Maxey filed a depredation claim. The poor man had no recourse to get compensation for his murdered or captured children. All he could hope for was to obtain payment for his two slaughtered oxen. The report went to Indian Agent George H. Smith, who was required to ask the tribes named in the claim if they took responsibility. He met with the Kiowas and Comanches in council on December 21, 1871, and later reported, "that they know nothing of it and refuse to give satisfaction." All Maxey asked for was $100. In 1873, it was sent to the Department of the Interior with a recommendation for payment of $75. Even this trifling amount would not go uncontested by a penurious government. It still dragged on as late as 1890, when special agent David Moore re-examined it. He obtained testimony from W. A. Morris, the postmaster of Montague, as to the value of oxen, and Hiram Leaf and his wife, who lived at Stroud's and saw Maxey's oxen killed. Leaf's valuation of $65 threw the case into further confusion and it took more time to finally figure out that Leaf evaluated the oxen at 1890 prices, rather than the higher value placed on them on the frontier in 1870. It was not until 1895, that the Court of Claims finally agreed to pay Jesse Maxey $100. By then, Jesse Maxey had been dead about six years.[42]

JOHN C. LEDBETTER
Texas, January 1871

The mysterious disappearance of John C. Ledbetter was the subject of numerous speculations in early Shackleford County, Texas, and has many variations. William H. Ledbetter settled at the salt springs on the Salt Prong of Hubbard Creek in 1862. The salt was bitter, but it could be raked up loose or boiled in kettles to a bright white crystal. A few settlers got salt there until Ledbetter moved in and began evaporating salt to sell during the Civil War. Ledbetter's pre-emption did not go unchallenged by Comanches, who came there either looking for salt or passing through on nearby war trails. In 1862, Ledbetter, his wife, and a hired hand had a gun battle with Comanches, successfully defending their cabin and killing a few warriors. The area remained dangerous.[43]

Ledbetter had two boys, Harve and John. The boys played a game in the winter, which was to become significant years later. They sat near the fireplace, made twists of strong wire, and burned brands on corncobs. With mischief on his mind or by accident, Harve branded John on the small of his back, leaving an identifiable scar.

It was customary for several ranchers in an area to get together and hire someone to conduct a community school, classes which were usually held in the summer. A building on J. C. Lynch's property was used as the schoolhouse, located at the confluence of Hubbard and Deep Creek and about two miles from the Lynch house. In the Ledbetter family version, eight or nine students of the Ledbetter, Lynch, Hazlewood, and Gonzales families had left Wash Hullum's classes for the day and were walking home. As the children walked along and dispersed to their homes, John Ledbetter lagged behind. When Harve got home, he realized that John was nowhere around. A search revealed pony tracks, but no trace of the boy.

Another version has John becoming homesick one day, slipping out of the school, wandering home, and disappearing. Another one has him gathering mesquite wax near his house while supper was cooking. John Gonzales was the last to see him wandering farther from the cabin. When he didn't arrive for supper, searchers went out. They thought he might have gone to his father's salt works, but all they found was his cap. There was no Indian sign. Searchers combed the area for thirty days but could find no clues.[44]

Efforts were made to locate Johnny Ledbetter, but no word of him was heard. He disappeared for eleven years and the family moved near Fort Griffin. In the family version, about 1882, a young man resembling John Ledbetter came to the fort in a wagon with a man named Tiger Jim who was selling buffalo hides. He traded with Comanches for the white captive and brought him in. William Ledbetter learned of his arrival and went to see him, believing he had a strong family resemblance. The young man went home with him and met Harve, who looked on his back and recognized his scar. They all agreed he must be John Ledbetter, and the young man agreed—at least for the time being.

"John" said he was on his way home from school when Comanches kidnapped him. He said he lived with them out on the Staked Plains for ten years. "John" finished school, worked for the railroad in Texas, and then moved to Ohio. He worked for an insurance company and studied law. He wrote home to Texas, at first signing his letters, "Your son," but later signed them "S. W. Wesley," and wrote the greetings as "My Dear Adopted Mother." He explained that his real father was Robert Wesley from Missouri, a man who apparently was wealthy. "John" wrote, "How can you blame me for doubting that I am a Ledbetter?" Later, writing as S. W. Wesley, he said he joined the Comanches on his own accord. Years later he ran into some cowboys near the Pecos River, worked with them a while, and eventually went to Fort Griffin where he met a man named Ledbetter who claimed he was his father. He was convinced of it against his will. As a Wesley, he had wealthy family connections and went on to become inspector general of the Federal Guaranty Company in Washington, D.C.[45]

Another story is that Wesley was hired to play the role of the lost boy to please Mrs. Ledbetter, who was old and blind, and allowed her to die believing that her lost son had returned. Wesley/Ledbetter wrote letters and articles both confirming and denying that he was really John Ledbetter. He lived in San Antonio for a time and was still alive in 1912. After that, Wesley/Ledbetter disappeared again, but certainly, this time for good.[46]

Clinton and Jefferson Smith
Texas, February 26, 1871

Henry M. Smith was born in Pennsylvania, became an orphan at an early age, and moved to Texas. In Austin in 1841, he married Fanny Short, who had moved from Alabama. Henry Smith served as marshal of San Antonio for some years, joined the Rangers and fought on the frontier, and after the Civil War, freighted between Indianola and San Antonio. Later, Henry Smith moved his family out on the Cibolo River, about twenty-three miles northwest of San Antonio, in west Comal County. It was a large family with nine children: five girls and four boys. Clinton Smith was born on August 3, 1860, and Jefferson D. Smith was born on August 31, 1862. Their mother died in 1866, and Henry and his children ran the place, raising cattle and sheep.[47]

The boys had dodged Indians several times while they worked outside. Their luck ran out on February 26, 1871. Henry Smith was a short distance from his house looking for horses, while Clint and Jeff were across the Cibolo herding sheep. Clint (10) was slender, with dark eyes and black lashes, but with light blond hair. Jeff (8) was heavier built, fair complexioned, with a large head, dark eyes, and hair that was nearly white.

Clinton spied something moving in the grass and told Jeff that they should slowly move toward home without arousing suspicion that they had seen anything, however, about two-dozen Indians came galloping up to them. The boys grabbed hands and ran; when Jeff tired, Clint hauled him on his back and kept going, but the Indians easily caught them. Harriet, the boys' stepmother, saw men ride up, but they appeared well dressed, wore hats, and looked like cowboys out for a Sunday ride. She saw them racing around the boys but assumed they were just playing with them. It looked so peaceful that she never realized they were Indians. When her husband came home she told him what she had seen. The boys could not be found. "Then," Harriet said, "the awful truth burst upon our minds."[48]

Henry Smith quickly rounded up some neighbors and followed the trail across the Guadalupe River near Kendalia, then north to the Pedernales. The posse followed the trail until it disappeared. All they found was one of Clinton's shoes. Because captures happened so often, a San Antonio paper rather blandly reported that two Smith brothers were captured, and presumed they would be soon "offered for ransom by the savages, who have learned by experience, that a hundred dollars is the accredited value of stolen children."[49]

That night the boys were freezing and exhausted. The Indians tied them up, but Clinton worked a pocketknife open and Jeff cut his bonds. They tried to sneak out of camp, but were caught. The next day the Indians killed a cow, cut it open, and forced the boys to drink the bloody, milky mixture. Clint refused and they held him down by the ears and forced his head into it. It was three days later before they gave the boys another chance to eat. The Indians threw Jeff and Clint pieces of raw cow liver and they hungrily gulped it down.

Ex-Ranger Henry Smith was not about to give up. He spread word of the abduction and John H. Sansom, a cousin of the Smiths, got word of it. He and his company of Rangers at Kerrville took up the chase. They followed the Indian trail up the Llano River and toward Fort Concho, but a heavy rain obliterated the tracks. Meanwhile, the Smith's saw their first murder, as the Indians killed a man splitting rails. They made Clinton turn the body over for them to see the victim. Later they got into a fight with two cowboys and killed their horses, but the cowboys shot two of the Indian raiders.

Finally, the Indians reached the Kotsoteka Comanche camp of Mowway, high up on the Staked Plains. The warriors made the Smith brothers fight against some Indian boys. Clinton was beat up the first day, but the Comanche Tosacowadi explained how he should fight. In the next match, Clinton was knocked down again, but he grabbed the Indian boy and bit him, holding on by his teeth like a bulldog. Some women tried to separate them, but Tosacowadi forced them back. The Indians were having a grand time, until two male Comanches tried to separate the boys. Clinton would not let loose until they strangled him and he nearly lost consciousness. Tosacowadi was satisfied he had won the bet. Said Clinton, "I was learning the wild savage life pretty fast, but it was in a rather tough way."[50]

Tosacowadi was impressed with Clinton and bought him from his Lipan captor for four horses and some ammunition. Clinton got the name Backecacho (End of a Rope). Soon he took part in the raiding. He said that these were "deeds which I was forced to do, taught to do by savages, whose chief delight was to kill and steal. It must be remembered that I was just a mere boy, and that I had, without choice, absorbed the customs and manners of a savage tribe. I was an Indian."

In one raid on a wagon train, Clint was hit in the face with some buckshot, pieces of which stayed embedded in his skin until he died. The next spring they were back in Texas and raided a ranch, but the woman put up a good fight, shooting a chief in the neck. They stole thirty horses, came upon two men on the way back to camp, killed them, cut off their arms, and strung them up in a tree. Whenever they ran out of ammunition they rode to Fort Sill and got some from the authorities.

In late winter the Comanche band met up with a group of Apaches. Unfortunately for the boys, Jeff's Comanche captor sold him to a Lipan. The last Clinton saw of Jeff was when the Apaches tied him up, "branded him like a cow," and stuck thorns through his ears to make holes for earrings. Then the bands split up. An Apache woman who owned Jeff made clothes and moccasins for him and Jeff felt better, he said, because, "The Apaches gave me plenty to eat, which was more than the Comanches had done." They named him Catchowitch (Horse Tail) and taught him how to ride and shoot, but because he was too young, he never went on raids, but stayed in camp and worked with the women.[51]

In New Mexico, Clint's band captured two Mexican boys and a white girl, about nine years old, who was still with them when he was recovered. His band had about eighteen captives. In Texas, they captured a white boy about 14 years old and in camp the women beat him severely, even torturing him and cutting off one of his toes. Clinton felt sorry for him but could not help. One night, the boy stole a mule and escaped, and the women wanted to beat Clinton for it. He was caught in the middle of two worlds, but had finally passed over the threshold. Sometimes at night, Clinton could see the lamps burning in the windows of places they passed, and he often thought about escaping, but he could never muster the courage. Besides, he said, "I considered myself an Indian, and an Indian I would be."

The Comanches once caught a buffalo hunter and brought him to their camp. They made signs that they were going to torture him but the man remained stoic and calm. Three boys approached him and fired pistols with blank loads at his face, but he didn't flinch. The warriors were so impressed they freed him and let him "escape" on one of their horses without pursuing him. The three boys who fired at the hunter's head were Clint Smith, Adolph Korn, and a Mexican captive. Later, Clinton believed it was in Colorado, his band met up with the Apaches who held Jeff, and the brothers held a happy reunion. They traveled together for a time but the Apaches wanted to remain in the mountains when the Comanches headed back to the plains. Clinton pleaded with Tosacowadi to buy Jeff, but the Apaches wanted ten good guns for him and they did not have them. Back in Texas, the Comanches attacked a homestead and slaughtered a family that Clinton remembered as Honeywell, and after that they went to Brown County, killed another family and captured an eight-year-old boy. Tosacowadi did not keep this one, but took him to Fort Sill for ransom money.[52]

In March 1871, Henry Smith wrote to Texas Governor Edmund J. Davis, giving the particulars of the capture, and listing his address as Boerne, Texas. Davis sent a letter to Agent Lawrie Tatum, presuming the Indians came from his jurisdiction. Smith also wrote to Tatum, asking for his help in getting his boys back "from these merciless, inhuman creatures." Smith even made one trip to see Tatum at the Kiowa-Comanche Agency in Indian Territory, but no one had news of the Smith boys.[53]

As in the case of other white captives, Clinton was restored to his family because Colonel Mackenzie took many Comanche prisoners in a fight in September 1872. During the battle, Tosacowadi was mortally wounded and Clinton lost his protector. Some of the women threatened to kill all the white captives in revenge, and Adolph Korn, John V. Maxey, Temple Friend, and Clinton were all in jeopardy. The Kiowa, Lone Wolf, went to see Agent Tatum and said they had fought the white soldiers and had been whipped. Tatum said, "Now they were ready to be friends, and do as their agent advised them." The Indians also wanted their captives restored, but Tatum would make no deals until the white captives were returned. The Indians, said Clinton: "wanted me to go in too, but I would not consent to do so." His stubbornness was preventing the release of Indian captives and one day Clinton was again "captured" by two Comanches who sought to forcefully deliver him to Fort Sill. He escaped from them, joined up with another band, but was found once more. This time the warriors made a deal with him: they would take him to the fort, exchange him for some of their relatives, and then steal some horses and escape back to the wilds. Clinton figured it would work.

Many white captives were rounded up and sent to the fort. Clinton and John V. Maxey were taken in on October 24, 1872, but were locked in a guardhouse to prevent their escape. They were washed, groomed, fed, and given new clothes. Clinton seemingly forgot his wish to escape. When Henry Smith learned Clinton was at Fort Sill, he wondered how he would get him, as he had no money for the trip. He wrote to Governor Davis, who promised him that he would cover the travel expenses. Smith headed for Sill, however, in a misunderstanding, Tatum sent Clinton and ex-captive, Adolph Korn, back to Texas with an army escort. The boys were hellions on the return trip and had to be guarded the whole way. Henry Smith arrived at Sill on December 5, only to learn his son had left nine days earlier. The strain was too much. Smith broke down and cried. Quaker teacher, Josiah Butler, commented, "He has one more son with the Indians—poor man, how I felt for him as he sat and wept."[54]

In San Antonio, Clinton Smith seemed to enjoy the attention as crowds came out to welcome them. He went to Louis Korn's home, where Adolph didn't appear too pleased, but Clinton sat down at the table and enjoyed a good meal. Then Korn took the boys to his candy shop and gave them all they wanted. Clinton's brother-in-law came for him and took him to his home nine miles away on the Salado, where he was smothered in kisses from his sister Caroline. Clinton said, the "manifestations of great joy soon made me realize that I was really and truly among my own people at last." When Henry Smith made it home from Indian Territory, he took Clinton home and broke down and cried. It was "a happy reunion, which no words of mine can describe."

The only thing lacking was Jeff Smith. After Jeff was separated from Clint, he went with the Apaches and learned their language and ways, much as Clint had learned from the Comanches. In the southwestern desert, water and food were at a premium, and Jeff learned to eat cactus and on occasion had to drink the blood of recently killed horses. He took part in a raid in Arizona Territory, where the warriors attacked a ranch, killed and scalped the family, and captured a 12-year-old boy. They gave Jeff three fresh scalps to carry. Jeff was becoming used to the Indian life, but sometimes at night around the campfires, he would get melancholy and hang his head and cry. "I felt that I was without a friend in all the wide world," he said.[55]

His time as a captive was nearly over, however. In April 1873, William Schuchardt, with the American consulate in Piedras Negras, Mexico, learned from a Mexican trader that Jeff was with a camp of Lipans, Mescaleros, and Kickapoos in San Rodrigo Canyon, about sixty miles from the border. The trader, Alejo Coy, described the boy and his circumstances of capture. Schuchardt got with Albert Turpe, a district clerk in Eagle Pass, Texas, to come up with the ransom money. They got Coy to return to the Indian camp to bargain for the boy, successfully, for $150 in gold. Coy brought Jeff to Eagle Pass. Schuchardt reported that Mr.

Smith was too poor to pay for the ransom, so the U.S. government reimbursed him. On May 1, 1873, Jeff Smith was placed in the custody of Agent Thomas G. Williams. Smith's rescue came just in time, for less than three weeks later, Colonel Ranald Mackenzie and his 4th Cavalry attacked the Indian camp near Remolino, killing nineteen Indians and taking forty-two captives. Had Jeff Smith still been in the village, he might have been accidentally killed by the soldiers, or in revenge by the Indians.

Agent Williams cleaned Jeff up, fed him, cut his hair, and on May 2, placed him on a stagecoach and sent him to San Antonio. Crowds gathered around him, much as they did when Clinton returned, but Jeff didn't know what was happening. He assumed he'd been sold to a new owner. A man named Steeneken came and took him to his father's farm. When they neared his old home he finally began to recognize the place and smiled, pointed, and grunted. His family hugged and kissed him, but Jeff was unresponsive. Henry Smith paced the floor and said that it was God's blessing that he got his boys back. Clinton, who was still shy around people, hung back until the commotion subsided. The brothers finally got together and no doubt talked over their experiences. In front of white strangers, however, they appeared frightened and reticent.[56]

The Smith brothers didn't cause as much trouble as Herman Lehmann or Adolph Korn, but it took them time to readjust. As Jeff said, "Everything seemed mighty tame by comparison after I got home." Clint thought he might run away, but, he said, after a while "I had become reconciled to the ways of the white people, and did not want to return to the Indians." He went to west Texas and worked as a cowpuncher at $25 per month. The next year he went on a cattle drive to Nebraska, and the following year, on a drive to Wyoming. He was home in 1878, herding cattle locally, then joined other outfits and drove cattle to Colorado and New Mexico, and later worked in south Texas on the King Ranch. Jeff Smith joined his brother and they worked on various ranches in the San Antonio area.

Clint Smith married Dixie Alamo Dyche in 1889, but his roaming life did not stop. He was seldom home, and Dixie raised the children by herself. She wasn't happy about it, and didn't have much good to say about her nearly always absent husband. They moved to Rocksprings, Texas, in 1910, but their relations didn't improve. They finally separated in 1924, and Dixie divorced him in 1929.

Jeff Smith married Julia Harriet Reed in 1894, and moved to San Antonio. Their marriage wasn't quite as rocky.

Like Herman Lehmann and the Babbs, Clint Smith wrote to the Claims Commission in Washington to see if he could recover damages for his captivity or get a pension as an adopted Comanche. The commission denied his request. In 1935, Jeff Smith applied to receive federal money, but he was turned down. The law was not set up to allow a person to claim damages for being an Indian captive, and the commissioner explained that Jeff could not prove he was adopted by the Apaches, nor would it entitle him to any benefits if he could.

Both brothers appeared in several western shows and rodeos as late as the 1920s, where they and Herman Lehmann were the centers of attention as former "white Indians." They could still ride, rope, and shoot. Like Lehmann, Clint Smith collaborated with J. Marvin Hunter to produce a story of his life, which was published in 1927. Dixie Smith thought Clint would make a lot of money from it, but Clinton gave away many copies for free. "Just like an Indian," his granddaughter joked. At the Old Trail Drivers Association meeting in San Antonio in 1927, Clint Smith met three Comanches who he hadn't seen since 1872. They shook hands and hugged each other and that evening, Clint, Jeff, and the Comanches spent hours smoking and reminiscing. It was a reunion that could not be repeated many more times, as the old men were rapidly reaching the end of the trail.

Clinton spent his last years as a nomad, spending time with his children. He died in Rocksprings at the home of his daughter, Zona Mae, on September 10, 1932, at the age of 72. Jefferson Smith spent his last years in San Antonio, where he worked in his garden. His wife, Julia, died in 1933, and Jeff stayed with his relatives. He was active up until his last day on earth. He spent the evening of April 20, 1940, at a San Antonio tavern, drinking and fiddling, and then rode home with some friends. The next day he was sitting in a rocking chair when he died of a heart attack at the age of 77.[57]

Susanna, Millie F. and John A. Lee
Texas, June 9, 1872

The raid on the Abel Lee home had it antecedents in a previous raid in south Texas. In April 1872, Big Bow and White Horse led about 100 Kiowas near the Rio Grande, killing Texans and Mexicans, and stealing horses. On April 20, a ten-wagon train under Anastacio Gonzales was trailing up the Devil's River to Fort

Stockton. When they stopped for water at Howard's Well, about twenty miles southwest of Fort Lancaster, the Kiowas struck. The warriors charged through the camp, shooting and destroying. They quickly killed most of the men, and lashed the survivors to wagon wheels where they soaked them with kerosene and burned them to death. Among the train passengers were Marcela Sera, her baby, and her elderly mother. The Indians killed the baby and captured Sera and her mother.

When Colonel Wesley Merritt's 9th Cavalry caught up with the raiders, the Indians killed Sera's mother and dumped Marcela in a thicket. The warriors fought the black cavalrymen to a standstill until dusk. When they pulled out, Sera ran and the soldiers rescued her. White Horse and Tau-ankia, the son of Lone Wolf, were wounded. White Horse left behind his young brother Kom-pai-te, and a small group of young Kiowas, who were not yet ready to go on a major raid. They guarded the horses on the Brazos near Fort Belknap. The impatient youths attacked a group of surveyors seven miles east of Round Timbers, near present-day Megargel, Texas. One surveyor was killed, but Kom-pai-te and another Kiowa boy were killed, and the brother of Comanche Chief Tabananica, was wounded.[58]

When White Horse returned and learned his brother had been killed, he was furious and organized a revenge raid. He vowed that he would not return from Texas until he had killed a white man. Five warriors and a woman accompanied him back to north Texas. In the first week of June, they were hunting along the Clear Fork of the Brazos, looking for an unsuspecting victim. On June 8, Henry G. Comstock left Fort Griffin with a supply wagon, heading for Dallas. Before nightfall he stopped at a house near the junction of Kings Creek and the Clear Fork, on the north edge of Stephens County. Abel John Lee and his family now occupied the picket house abandoned by old Mrs. Dodson, who once ran a tidy ranch there, surrounded by hedges of bois d'arc (Osage orange) along the banks of the Clear Fork. The river was too high to cross, so while Comstock set up camp, Abel Lee came out and wanted to ask him over for supper, but confessed that he didn't have the money to buy flour at Fort Griffin. Comstock supplied the flour, and the Lees provided the bacon fat. "Mrs. Lee," Comstock said, "certainly knew how to make fritters. Man! I can taste them yet."[59]

Comstock left on the next morning, a Sunday, and the Lees went about their chores, not so heavy this day in observance of the Sabbath. Mrs. Emily Irwin visited the Lees that morning, but cut her visit short. There was a small footbridge over the

Clear Fork, but it did not look safe with the rising water. Mrs. Irwin left before noon and returned home. Shortly after noon, Able Lee, called "Professor" because of his part time work as a singing-school teacher, was relaxing in a rocking chair, reading the weekly newspaper and enjoying the breeze that blew through his south-facing covered hall connecting the two main rooms. Lee probably had no worry of Indians—after all, Fort Griffin was sixteen miles upriver and was a buffer between Indian Territory and the settlements farther downriver. Just then, White Horse's raiders burst from the bank of Kings Creek. A rifle bullet crashed into Abel Lee and his body slumped from the chair, dead on the floor, a great red stain covering his white Sunday shirt. Hearing the whooping Indians, the rest of the family tried to run out the back toward the river. The warriors caught Mrs. Lee before she could exit and shot an arrow in her back. Two pounced on her, one scalping her and cutting off both of her ears and the other chopping off her arms. The children got out first and stumbled through the vegetable garden and into the cornfield. Frances (14) was killed by a single arrow. Millie (9) stopped to help her sister and was captured. Susanna (17) and John (6) were hunted down in the corn, still too short to hide in, and were seized.

The Indians, as usual, plundered the house, ripped open the feather beds, took the ticking and stripped the place of any other articles that suited their fancy. Before they rode off with their prisoners, they killed a milk cow and the family dog. One warrior shot Abel Lee with two more arrows, just to make sure.[60]

Emily Irwin had been home only a few minutes when she heard shots coming from the direction of the Lee house. She alerted her husband, John, and he headed for his neighbor Johnnie Hazellett. The men got some help from a few cowpunchers of Murphy's cattle outfit, but by the time they got to the ford, the river was too high to cross and horses could not go on the rickety footbridge. They waited until the next day and forced their way across. The men prepared to bury the dead about fifteen steps from the back door. Just then, Lieutenant Erasmus C. Galbraith, 11th Infantry, with ten soldiers and a few Tonkawa scouts, rode to the river's edge. He did not want to try to cross the high water, but learned of the tragedy by shouting across to the grieving neighbors who were then wrapping the bodies in quilts. Galbraith reported the news back at Fort Griffin.

In a few more days, White Horse had his raiders and prisoners back in Indian Territory at their Rainy Mountain camp. The warriors were treated as conquering heroes and the villagers celebrated with an all-night dance. White Horse's mother forced the heart-broken, exhausted Susanna to carry buckets of water for the celebrants, and even to take part in the scalp dance. The next day the three children were parceled out to tribe members as slaves.[61]

At the Kiowa and Comanche Agency, Lawrie Tatum quickly learned about the raid and wrote to Major George W. Schofield, commander at Fort Sill, stating that the Indians were uncontrollable. He asked for the military to arrest the guilty parties, but Superintendent Enoch Hoag denied his request. As historian W. S. Nye said it, these "benevolent pollyannas" thought that kindness and conference could reform the Indians.[62] Tatum and Schofield knew better.

As usual, Chief Lone Wolf appeared at the Wichita-Caddo Agency and demanded that Agent Jonathan Richards pay him for the captives. He made the demand to Richards because he was afraid of the troops at Fort Sill. Richards informed Tatum of Lone Wolf's demand, but Tatum would not make any concessions. He would pay nothing and would not distribute rations until the captives were freed. While the Kiowas were considering his ultimatum, a conference was set to convene at old Fort Cobb on July 25, 1872, much to Tatum's disapproval, because he knew that while he had the Kiowa women and children clamoring for coffee and sugar and the chiefs weakening, at a council many presents would be distributed which would counteract his strategy. Nevertheless, the council met on the appointed day. It was to include the Five Nations, the Kiowas, Comanches, and Cheyennes. While waiting for the tardy Kiowas, Tatum received a message that his wife was ill and he returned to Fort Sill. The Kiowas did not arrive until August 3. White Horse swaggered up to Agent Horace Jones and asked, "Where is Bald-Head (Tatum)?"

"Gone to Sill," Jones answered.

"Well," White Horse threatened, "I was looking for him to kill him. And you too. But he is gone, and you are of little value, not worth bothering about."[63]

The impertinent warriors made it tough for their chiefs to bargain. The leaders of the Five Nations admonished the wild tribes to stop their raiding and settle down and the white agents and commissioners made their pleas, but little was accomplished. The Indians had heard the same words before, but were not inclined to change their life style until they had been soundly defeated in battle. Lone Wolf echoed the thoughts of many. When Cyrus Beede, representing Enoch Hoag, demanded that they return the captives, Lone Wolf said that they would do so when the government vacated Fort Sill and the Indian country and returned Chiefs Satanta and Big Tree from prison in Texas. The council broke up with little settled other than Beede's threat that unless the Kiowas complied, the military would be sent against them. The Kiowas had heard that before.

One Kiowa chief, Kicking Bird, was not sure that Lone Wolf was taking a wise course. He privately met with Beede and told him that in ten days he would deliver up the three Lee children to the Wichita Agency. Beede was skeptical, but Kicking Bird convinced the other chiefs that compliance was the right thing. On August 18, Lone Wolf, Kicking Bird, and Big Bow brought Susanna and Milly Lee to Agent Richards. Although they had been told they would get no reward, Richards issued them two-weeks' rations. He had the Caddo, George Washington, take the children in a wagon to Fort Sill, while Lone Wolf, Sun Boy, and seven other Kiowas rode alongside. When they delivered the two girls to Tatum, he asked about John Lee. They told him he was too sick to ride, but his sisters said, "that the boy was well and cried to go with them."

Tatum stood firm and said they would not receive rations until the boy was surrendered. The sullen Kiowas rode away. While hoping the Indians would deliver John Lee, Tatum placed the girls in the agency school. He wrote their relatives in Texas, and waited for word. It took until September 30, but finally the reluctant Indians brought in John Lee. He was greeted by his sisters and his elder brother, who had just arrived from Texas. Two days later they all climbed in a wagon and started back to their desolated home, trying to continue their lives that were shattered by the vengeful White Horse four months before. Tatum claimed that they "were the first captives ever recovered from the Kiowas without paying from $100 to $1,500 for each one."[64]

ARVILLA AND JOSEPHINE MEEKER
AND FLORA ELLEN PRICE
Colorado, September 29, 1879

Arvilla Delight Smith was born March 5, 1815, in Cheshire, Connecticut. Her family moved to the Western Reserve in northeast Ohio when she was a little girl. Arvilla had gray eyes, small hands, and was slender and shy. She met Nathan C. Meeker in 1843, while Meeker worked northeast Ohio as a traveling salesman. Meeker, born July 12, 1817, in Euclid, Ohio, was the

Author's photo

Near Meeker Agency site, Colorado.

proverbial jack-of-all-trades and master of none. He roved the country widely and held many jobs, as a newspaperman, teacher, shopkeeper, novelist, and salesman. Meeker was also a visionary, a devotee of utopian Fourierism with its communal ideals. When Arvilla first met Nathan, she was not sure if she trusted him, she being a Congregationalist, and he being an atheist espousing socialism. Nevertheless, Nathan was smitten, and he agreed to join Arvilla's church. She, in turn, agreed to move with him to a utopian community at Braceville, Ohio. While Nathan was idealistic and enthusiastic, Arvilla, he said, "is entirely passive." He was amazed that the only thing that seemed to concern her was that the community "had soft water!"[65]

Arvilla married Nathan in 1844. Ralph was born in 1845, and George in 1847. The financial Panic of 1857 ruined Meeker, and he fled his creditors to southern Illinois, where he opened a general store. During the Civil War, Meeker was a war correspondent for Horace Greeley's New York *Tribune*. In 1865, Meeker became Greeley's agricultural writer and the family moved to New York. They had three other children: Rozene (1848), Mary (1853), and Josephine (1856).

Things were looking up when Greeley envisioned an agricultural colony in the west, and sent Meeker to begin the work. Arvilla was hesitant about moving west. Her fears were real, for they had hardly arrived in 1870, when George died of tuberculosis, Rozene worried about never having a dowry, and Mary and Josephine

443

pouted over wearing second-hand clothes. The colony struggled, Nathan lost money, and by 1878, in debt and uncertain what his future would hold, he applied to become Indian agent for the Utes.[66]

With Senator Henry Teller's support, Meeker became the new Ute agent at White River, located near present-day Meeker, Colorado. Leaving Rozene and Mary in Greeley to take care of their home and business, Nathan, Arvilla, and Josephine moved to northwest Colorado.

Nathan was a creative agent, but his utopian ideals and lack of tact made enemies of many Utes. Building the agency, Meeker ruined what the Utes considered to be fine horse pasture and racing grounds. Meeker figured that horse-raising interfered with agricultural pursuits, and tried to halt it. The animosity between Meeker and his charges grew worse every day.

Meeker built a new agency, a boardinghouse and a school, but to the Utes, all they did was ruin valuable land. Josie Meeker (22) ran the school, but one by one, her pupils dropped out, and by the spring of 1879 she had only one left. Josie also ran the boarding house and Arvilla worried about her working herself to a frazzle. Josie did have a number of adult admirers, a young Ute named Persune, for one. The Utes, as well as a few other hired white employees, also liked Flora Ellen Price. Flora was the wife of Shadrach Price, a dull but quarrelsome Kansan, who boasted he had killed nine "redskins" while crossing the plains to Colorado. Price could be annoying, but he was a good farmer. Flora (16) had already given birth to two children: May (3) and Johnnie (1). She was a pretty, shapely, Illinois farm girl, but seemingly unaware of how she affected the men around the agency as she "threw her wide curves around the boardinghouse with the innocent abandon of a babe in its bath."[67]

In the summer of 1879, the Utes were accused of setting fires in the forests, leaving the reservation to hunt and steal, and refusing to give up horses and begin farming. In early September, as Meeker ordered another horse pasture ploughed, Chief Johnson came to his house, pulled him outside and threw him against a fence, injuring him badly. Meeker wrote for help, and troops were sent to restore order. Major Thomas T. Thornburgh responded by gathering a force of 153 men of the 3rd and 5th Cavalry, and heading out from Fort Fred Steele in Wyoming Territory. Thornburgh got as far as Milk Creek, about twenty miles northeast of the agency. The Utes, under Colorow and Ute Jack, saw it as an invasion of their reservation, and on September 29, about 300 of them

444

attacked. Thornburgh and thirteen soldiers were killed and forty-seven were wounded during a six-day siege. Three hours after the Milk Creek fight began, a Ute messenger rode to the agency and spread the alarm. Meeker was feeling better since things seemed to have calmed down. He had just penned a letter to Thornburgh. "Things are peaceful" he wrote, and said that Douglass, one of the Ute chiefs, "flies the U.S. flag." Meeker handed the letter to an employee to deliver to Thornburgh, but he never made it. The Utes killed him.

A short time later, Douglass and twenty Utes struck the agency. They killed Shadrach Price and Art Thompson first, then five other agency employees. Flora Price, her two children, Arvilla and Josie saw the opening shots from the boardinghouse. A young Greeley man, Frank Dresser, was shot in the leg and stumbled inside. He grabbed Shad Price's Winchester and began firing back, killing the Ute, Jata. The women and children ran into Josie's bedroom and crawled under the bed. The Utes set the place on fire and Dresser led them out and to the milk house. They held out until evening. Josie tried to calm everyone and believed the Utes would not harm them, but Flora was terrified, certain that she would die a torturous death. At twilight they tried to escape, but the Utes saw them and chased them down. Dresser got miles away before they caught and killed him. They shot Arvilla in the thigh and she fell. A Ute named Thompson helped her up and made her go back to the house and find all her money. The Ute, Persune, captured Josie and stood guard over his prize. A small Uncompahgre Ute named Ahutupuwit claimed Flora.

As the Indians gathered up their stolen goods and finished torching what remained, Arvilla saw a body about 100 yards south of her house. She went to it and saw that it was her husband. Nathan Meeker had been shot in the side of his head. Arvilla knelt beside him for a minute before she was told to leave. They all rode away: Flora Price with Johnnie on her lap, Josie carrying May, and Arvilla on a horse behind Douglass. That night Douglass began drinking whiskey and threatened the 64-year-old Arvilla with rape. She was beyond caring by now. Back at the agency, the last remaining Utes put a log chain around Nathan Meeker's neck and had a horse drag him around the grounds. When done with their sport, they drove a barrel stave through his open mouth and pinned his head to the ground.[68]

News of the massacre caused an uproar. How long would the Indians be coddled and fed on reservations while they killed whites and took hostages without punishment? As was the usual case, most westerners wanted the Indians killed or removed, while easterners sought to place blame on the army or greedy white settlers. The military closed in on Colorado and was poised to begin a campaign of destruction. Secretary Carl Schurz, however, demanded a halt in order to protect the lives of the captive women and children. General Sherman seethed while Schurz and President Rutherford Hayes sought to make peace.

In mid-October, Charles Adams, former Ute agent, took four other whites and thirteen Indians up onto Colorado's Grand Mesa, to find the Ute camp and negotiate for the prisoners. The Utes expected them. When Adams entered the village, Josie Meeker stepped out of a tipi, holding May Price's hand. She recognized him and said, "I'm so glad to see you, Mr. Adams!" Adams was anxious about their condition. He asked if the others were all right, and Josie answered, "Quite well, considering." Only Arvilla was still hampered by her wound.

Adams had several more questions about who had killed the employees at the agency and if the Indians had committed "any indignity" to them. "Nothing of that kind," Josie answered. Adams was relieved, although he noted that Josie seemed to have prepared all her answers and glanced furtively from side to side to see who might be listening.

When Adams met the chiefs he told them that they must deliver up the hostages and that he would call off the army. The chiefs, Ute Jack, Johnson, Sowerwick, and Douglass, argued that the army must first leave, or they would kill the women. Adams would not budge, and finally, after five hours of debate, the chiefs agreed to Adams's demand. When the women and children were turned over to Adams, he saw how badly Arvilla looked. He tried to console her, but she didn't seem to care. She was glad to be freed for Josie's sake, but "Mr. Meeker is gone," she said. "I have nothing to live for."[69]

There was no full-scale war, but the Utes were removed to smaller reservations in southern Colorado and in eastern Utah. The authorities demanded that the Utes turn over the guilty parties who killed the whites at the agency, but they never did. Secretary Schurz was happy, believing that "the Utes should be given credit for their good treatment of the captives." But how good was their treatment?

After a three-day journey down to the Los Pinos Agency, Ralph Meeker met them and escorted them by wagon to Denver, and then up to Greeley. While they waited at Los Pinos, the women gave Indian Bureau Inspector William J. Pollock a different story.

He sent his report to Commissioner Edward A. Hayt, with a note on the back page, that stated: "I have also a statement given to me personally and in confidence of a character too delicate to mention here as to the personal treatment they severally received from the Indians during captivity."

The note troubled Adams. Now he would have to investigate further. On November 4, he met Flora Price in Greeley, wondering how he might broach the subject, knowing full well the Victorian belief that heroines would always prefer to kill themselves before or soon after an "outrage." Flora was getting over her ordeal and the loss of her husband, and told Adams that she was sick of the notoriety and happy that a Greeley man had just proposed marriage to her. It would not be easy for Adams to drag any unpleasant details from her, but they would be necessary if they could get the guilty Utes in for a trial. Adams tried several ways to ask the question, and Flora answered that no Indians struck her. He persisted. What else did they do?

"I do not like to say," she answered. "You know them, of course, and can judge."

Adams said this was an official investigation and he could not guess.

"It will not be made public in the papers, will it?" she asked. Adams said it would not come out through the Ute Commission and Flora added, "I would not want—my fiancé to know. Men are funny about those things." Adams said her privacy was his first consideration. Finally, Flora said, "Well, this Uncompahgre Ute and Johnson outraged me."

"Was it by force?" Adams asked.

"Of course!" Flora snapped.

Finally Adams heard the details. Johnson threatened to kill her unless she yielded. His wife didn't know what he had done or she would have killed Flora. She was even raped the very day that Adams had rescued her. Flora became angrier. "I want to have the privilege of killing Johnson and that Uncompahgre Ute myself!"

Adams next visited Josie Meeker. He asked her if Persune kept her the whole time and she said he did. He asked if he had a wife. Yes, Josie said, two wives and two children. Adams asked if he treated her well and Josie looked around the parlor and pursed her lips. "I do not know, Mr. Adams. Of course we were insulted." What did that consist of, Adams asked. "Of outrageous treatment at night," she answered, and went on to say that she was raped several times a night and against her will. Once she asked Persune if he wanted to kill her. He said he did, and Josie, sick of her situation, told him to "Get up then and shoot me and let me alone." She said the Indians raped all the women the first night they were captured. "Of course, they were drunk," she said. "We dared not refuse them to any great extent."

Adams asked if she had told anyone this story, and Josie said she had told Pollock and Doctor. Alida Avery in Denver. She did not want anyone to know, she said, but she was afraid that the papers would get the news. She said the Indians bragged throughout the village about raping the women. Adams asked if they thought it was wrong. "No sir," Josie said. "They thought it was a pretty good thing to have a white squaw." Adams was struck by how matter-of-fact and un-Victorian Josie was, in contrast to Flora.

Lastly, Adams talked to Arvilla. She was almost apathetic in manner and described the outrage in toneless ease. Douglass had raped her, and only because his wife was not there. "It was made known to me that if I did not submit I would be killed," Arvilla said. "And after I gave up nothing was said about it."

Adams knew that if word of these events got around to the public, that nothing would stop the angry Coloradans from making war on their own, with or without the army. He wrote to Schurz and Colorado Governor Frederick W. Pitkin that it must be kept quiet, "for the wish of the women themselves" as well as for "the furious excitement this would raise in this State...."[70]

Regardless of their efforts, word leaked out, and there was a public outcry, but time had cooled many tempers and nothing seemed to be getting done about finding the guilty Utes. Surprisingly, it was Rozene Meeker who tried to keep the pot stirred up, realizing that the family might get some reparation money. While Josie and Arvilla tried to keep things quiet, Rozene went on a lecture circuit and told everyone what dastardly things the Indians had done to her mother and sister. Finally, Arvilla moved to Rozene's side, realizing she could get nothing for her or her children without exposing Schurz's suppression of the truth. In late December 1879, papers published a letter from Arvilla that admitted to the horrors the three women faced. She thought she had done all that was necessary, she said, "by telling these officers the sickening and most humiliating misfortune that can befall a woman, and if they and the Interior Department have not done their duty by the people of Colorado, it is they who are to blame, and not me."

The letter, with its admission of outrages and hint of government cover-up, electrified the nation. The Utes would definitely be removed from much of Colorado. In January 1880, a

Ute delegation went to Washington to ask for fair treatment, and Douglass surrendered in Kansas City, hoping that it would stop the investigation.[71] In the end, nothing was done to the twelve Utes deemed most responsible for the massacre at White River. Douglass was released from Fort Leavenworth prison after one year. Secretary Schurz said it was no use in trying to prosecute them, for he believed they were either all dead or had fled to Canada. Senator Teller succeeded in arguing for compensation of $3,500 for the Meekers, Price, and other families of the murdered agency employees, to be debited out of Ute funds. The White River Utes, who had caused most of the trouble, were forced out of Colorado and to the Uintah Reservation in Utah. The Utah agent reported them as indolent and flippant, with no desire to learn farming as the Uintah Utes were doing. They laughed at the Uintahs for farming and told them, "they ought to fight, and then Washington would furnish them with plenty to eat."[72] It was the same lesson that the Plains Indians learned.

Flora Ellen Price apparently never married the Greeley man who proposed to her. In September 1880, she and her two children were living with her parents in Ellensburg, Washington. She wrote to Arvilla to tell her how nice it was to have a father and mother to talk to, that the children were fine, and asked if Arvilla knew if they were going to get any money from the government, for she hadn't heard anything.

As for the Meekers, once again they were in financial difficulty. Mary died in 1883. Rozene, in order to save money, fed Arvilla little else but skim milk and bread, and her health deteriorated. Ralph made her move to White Plains, New York, to live with him. When Chester Arthur became president, he made Henry Teller his new Secretary of the Interior. In 1881, he hired Josie Meeker as his "copyist," and later as his assistant private secretary in Washington, at $17 per week. She sent five dollars a week to Arvilla. In December 1882, after a spell of cold, rainy weather, Josie caught pneumonia. Ralph came to visit her. On the morning of December 29, Josie clutched Ralph's hand and said she felt she was going blind. Then her voice failed and she fell unconscious. In an hour, she was dead. Josie was only 26 years old. Ralph escorted her body back to Greeley, Colorado, for burial at the Linn Grove Cemetery, next to her father. Arvilla lived quietly, infirm, and senile, dying in 1905, at age 90.[73]

CHARLES W. MCCOMAS
New Mexico, March 28, 1883

Hamilton C. McComas was born in Parkersburg, Virginia, in 1831. He studied law and was admitted to the bar at age 21. He moved to Illinois, and in 1859, married his first wife, Louisa K. Pratt. They had two children, but divorced during the Civil War. Hamilton joined the Union Army and became lieutenant colonel of the 107th Illinois. In 1868, McComas moved to Fort Scott, Kansas, and practiced law. In 1869, Hamilton married Juniata M. Ware.[74]

Juniata had two daughters, and in November 1876, a son, Charles Ware McComas. His father always called him Charley. Hamilton went to New Mexico Territory in 1880, practicing law and engaging in various mining and business operations. In March 1882, his family finally followed him out to the wild southwest. In December of that year, Hamilton purchased a substantial brick home for them in Silver City. On March 7, 1883, Juniata turned 37 years old.

On March 26, Hamilton received a telegram from Lordsburg, New Mexico Territory, saying that the Pyramid Mining and Milling Company needed his services. Juniata had been in Silver City for one year and had never been to Lordsburg. Her husband figured it would be fine for her and Charley to accompany him. They rented a buckboard and loaded it. The journey should have been safe, but Hamilton took along his Winchester and a Colt pistol, just in case. They stayed that evening at a hostelry called Mountain Home, about seventeen miles southwest of Silver City. The next morning they crossed the Continental Divide and rode down Thompson Canyon, a sandy, twisting trail through the Burro Mountains. If there was any chance of an ambush it would be in the narrowest part of the canyon, just as the road exited out the western edge. The McComas's passed safely out of the mountains. Perhaps breathing a little more easily, they continued one mile into the flat Animas Valley and saw a large walnut tree. It was about noon, and they decided to stop and have a picnic lunch.[75]

The timing of the McComas's journey was extremely unfortunate. On March 21, a twenty-six-person Apache raiding party swept out of Mexico's Sierra Madre and into Arizona Territory, seeking guns and ammunition. Chato led the raiders, who included Naiche, Mangus, Bonito, Dutchy, Tzoe, Beneactiney, and Kautli. They first hit a charcoal camp in the Canelo Hills southwest of Fort Huachuca. They killed four white men, but Beneactiney was killed in the attack. The furious Apaches continued north and east, stealing, cutting telegraph lines, and killing and mutilating twenty-two more whites. Apache atrocities were commonplace. Whenever an Apache was harmed, be it by Mexican or American, it was Apache custom that all members of that group were held responsible and could be indiscriminately killed. As white eyewitnesses such as Colonel Richard I. Dodge and General Nelson Miles saw for themselves, the Apaches liked to torture and kill. And they were proud of it. Asa Daklugie, the son of the Nednhi Apache Juh, boasted, "We had the Sioux beat [for cruelty], especially the Nednhi and Chiricahua."[76]

In this frame of mind and in the mood for revenge, Chato's raiders entered New Mexico in the area of present-day Virden, and rode to the southern end of the Burro Mountains. Near the mouth of Thompson Canyon they ran right into a few white people having a picnic. The McComas's saw the Apaches coming and ran for the buckboard. The judge tried to turn the horses around and run up canyon, but he was shot. He leaped from the seat with his Winchester while Juniata tried to take the reins and continue. Hamilton ran to the walnut tree to try and hold off the Indians. He got off three shots while running and four more at the tree before about five more bullets hit him. Other Apaches chased the buckboard about 300 yards when the right horse was hit and fell. Juniata jumped out, ran around the back and tried to pull Charley out. A warrior rode up and smashed her head with his rifle butt, and then dismounted and hit her two more times with his pistol to make sure she was dead. Generally raiders would murder children with no second thoughts, but this time they decided to keep the blond six-year-old.

Two Indians quarreled over who had a right to the prisoner, but Bonito rode up and said he would settle the dispute by claiming Charley for himself. He tied Charley with a rope to his own waist and put him on his horse. The Indians plundered the buckboard and stripped the two bodies, but did not mutilate them. There was no time. The most prized findings were Hamilton's Winchester, Colt, and ammunition. The Apaches headed back to Mexico. Within the hour, two whites, John Moore and Julius C. Brock, discovered the bodies and sped away to spread the alarm.[77]

Lieutenant Colonel George A. Forsyth was leading companies of his 4th Cavalry from Fort Cummings toward Arizona in the hope of catching Chato's raiders. When he received word of the McComas killings, instead of heading south toward the border to cut off the Indians, he insisted on first going to the attack site to personally find the trail. While he did, Chato headed east of Lordsburg and south across the line.

The raid sent shockwaves throughout the nation. General George Crook sent his men to scour the ground, but no one even spotted a hostile Chiricahua. What the raid did, however, was to give Crook an excuse to chase them into Mexico.

While campaign preparations were made, Eugene Ware, Juniata's brother, went to Silver City to arrange sending the two bodies back to Kansas. He remained in New Mexico to try to find and ransom little Charley. The McComas's were buried in the Evergreen Cemetery in Fort Scott, Kansas, on April 8.

After checking with Mexican authorities, Crook got the go ahead. He would travel light and fast. The force included forty-two men of Company I, 6th Cavalry, under Major Adna R. Chaffee, and 193 Apache scouts under Captain Emmet Crawford and Lieutenant Charles B. Gatewood. They took rations for sixty days, 150 rounds of ammunition per man, and all 350 packhorses in the department. Among the scouts were Al Sieber and Archie McIntosh. The Apache, Tzoe, who had been on part of Chato's raid, but dropped out before the McComas killings, was one of the guides. Mickey Free, who had been an Apache captive as a youth, was an interpreter. They crossed the border into Mexico on May 1.[78]

The command went up the Bavispe River in Sonora, following the river into the mountains and just across the border into Chihuahua. There, on May 15, Crawford's Apache scouts found Bonito and Chato's village and attacked. Although Crook ordered that no women and children were to be killed, the scouts charged in and firing was indiscriminate. They killed nine and captured four children and one young woman. The mother of an Apache named Speedy was killed in the chaos. The enraged warrior saw the white boy being led away up into the canyon. He ran up to him, "and using rocks, brutally killed the small white captive." Ramona Chihuahua, the daughter of the chief and one of those captured, saw the incident and later told another young Apache, Jason Betzinez, what had happened. The Apaches later told the soldiers that the white boy was with them, but at first attack, he ran away and was never found. Chato and Bonito were going to keep the boy and use him as a bargaining chip whenever they might have to surrender, but now that possibility was gone.

The Army/Apache victory over the hostiles deep in territory once considered impregnable convinced many of them to surrender. Chiefs Nana, Loco, Ka-ya-ten-nae, Geronimo, and Naiche turned themselves in during the following months. Crook marched 123 warriors and 251 women and children back to reservations in the

United States, but Charley McComas was not among them. The Apaches kept up the fiction that a few people had escaped and took Charley with them, and over the years stories circulated of a wild white renegade who ran with the last Apache holdouts well into the 20th Century.[79]

Chapter nine notes

[1] McConnell, *West Texas Frontier*, in www.forttours.com/pages.tocbuddav; Winfrey and Day, *Texas Indian Papers 4*, 330, 376, 378, 426-27; Leckie, *Buffalo Soldiers*, 101-02; Ashton, *Indians and Intruders*, 88-89; Hunter, ed., "Harrowing Experience," 32-33; Heard, *White Into Red*, 108-09; Hudson, "Chief Geronimo's Captive," 354; Simmons, *Renegades*, 65-68. The Martha Terry capture was also said to have occurred in January 1871.

[2] Zesch, *Captured*, 5-6.

[3] Zesch, *Captured*, 3-4, 6-12, 17-18.

[4] Zesch, *Captured*, 18-19, 41, 64, 122, 128-29, 143-44; Battey, *Quaker Among the Indians*, 87-88; Ashton, *Indians and Intruders*, 84-85.

[5] Lehmann, *Nine Years*, 43; Zesch, "Adolph Korn," 522-23, 526; Michno, *Encyclopedia of Indian Wars*, 258-59.

[6] Tatum, *Red Brothers*, 139-40; Zesch, "Adolph Korn," 528-29.

[7] Zesch, "Adolph Korn," 531-33; Zesch, *The Captured*, 183-84, 191-92.

[8] Zesch, *The Captured*, 289-92; Zesch, "Adolph Korn," 534-36; Smith, *Boy Captives*, 121. Scott Zesch, a great-great-nephew of Adolph Korn, recently completed a moving tribute to Adolph and several other captives in his 2004 book, *The Captured*.

[9] Lehmann, *Nine Years*, 1; Neal Jr., *Valor*, 359n6. In Lehmann's book, his father's name is given as Maurice, his death year 1864, and his mother's remarriage in 1866. J. Marvin Hunter transcribed while Lehmann dictated and possibly got the information wrong.

[10] Lehmann, *Nine Years*, 1-3; Zesch, *The Captured*, 90-91, 314-15n7; Ashton, *Indians and Intruders*, 95.

[11] Lehmann, *Nine Years*, 5-6; Zesch, *The Captured*, 92.

[12] Neal Jr., *Valor*, 53-56; Lehmann, *Nine Years*, 10-12; Zesch, *The Captured*, 95-97.

[13] Lehmann, *Nine Years*, 13-15, 17-19.

[14] Zesch, *The Captured*, 99-101; Lehmann, *Nine Years*, 23-24, 32.

[15] Lehmann, *Nine Years*, 40-41. It is possible that this attack was against the Whitlock Family, which occurred in Llano County in December 1870. The mother, father, and two or three children were killed, but reportedly only William Whitlock (4) was captured. Winfrey and Day, *Texas Indian Papers 4*, 330; McConnell, *West Texas Frontier*, in www.forttours. com/pages/tocwhitlock.

[16] Zesch, *The Captured*, 140-41, 193; Athearn, *Sherman*, 289-91. Sherman quickly learned that the Texans were telling the truth when he almost lost his own life two weeks later when he narrowly missed being attacked by a large war party that massacred a wagon train just after Sherman passed by.

[17] Zesch, *The Captured*, 133, 135-36, 208-212; Lehmann, *Nine Years*, 98-102; Gillett, *Six Years with the Rangers*, 42-44. Gillett makes no mention about shooting and missing Herman's head. Whether he purposely left it out of his book, or Herman made it up in his, is debatable. Gillett and Lehmann met again forty-nine years later at an Old Trail Drivers' Association reunion in San Antonio.

[18] Lehmann, *Nine Years*, 124-28, 141-44.

[19] Zesch, *The Captured*, 219-22, 227-32.

[20] Lehmann, *Nine Years*, xxiii, 212, 235; Zesch, *The Captured*, 232, 240-42, 256-58, 260-62, 277-78.

[21] Nye, *Carbine & Lance*, 99.

[22] Nye, *Carbine & Lance*, 102-03, 107, 111; Leckie *Grierson*, 177-78.

[23] Nye, *Bad Medicine*, 143; Gottlieb Koozier Depredation Claim #10263. Victoria Peak, now known as Queen's Peak, is 1,189 feet in elevation and is located four miles north of Bowie, Texas. It was a good spot for both Indian and whites to view the surrounding countryside.

24 Potter, *Montague County*, 97-98; Koozier Depredation Claim #10263.

25 Potter, *Montague County*, 96-97; Koozier Depredation Claim #10263; McConnell, *West Texas Frontier*, in http://forttours.com/pages/tocvictor. Jett Davis also said that one of the Slaughter brothers was killed.

26 The name is spelled as Goodlip, Godleib, Kooser, Koozer, and other variations.

27 Koozier Depredation Claim #10263; McConnell, *West Texas Frontier*, in http://forttours.com/pages/tockoozer.

28 Many authors have said that Mrs. Koozier was taken with her five or six children. Three of the captives were her children, two were her step-children, and one (Kilgore) was a neighbor's child.

29 Koozier Depredation Claim #10263; Methvin, *Andele*, 97. The letter to Elizabeth came from Tatum.

30 Koozier Depredation Claim #10263; Tatum, *Our Red Brothers*, 38-40.

31 Koozier Depredation Claim #10263; Tatum, *Our Red Brothers*, 41-43.

32 Koozier Depredation Claim #10263; Methvin, *Andele*, 98; Tatum, *Our Red Brothers*, 43-47. Some of Tatum's reasoning is suspect. He didn't "pay" for the captives, but he "gave" the Indians presents for returning them. Nevertheless, his interpreter, H. P. Jones, never believed he could get them so cheaply. A few years earlier, Jones said it would have cost several hundred dollars for each captive. The previous year, Lieutenant Colonel Custer had the same thoughts about not paying for captives (see Anna Morgan).

33 Koozier Depredation Claim #10263.

34 Koozier Depredation Claim #10263.

35 Potter, *Montague County*, 93-94; Jesse Maxey Depredation Claim #962; McConnell, *West Texas Frontier*, in http://www.forttours.com/pages/tocbeale.

36 Most references indicate the day of the raid was September 5, however, in Jesse Maxey's depredation claim signed on September 23, 1871, he states that the raid occurred on October 5, as do several other witnesses. Tatum, *Our Red Brothers*, 49, however, reported that Jesse Maxey came to the agency on September 25, 1870, to report a September 5 raid. Nye, *Carbine & Lance*, 118, says the raiders were Kwahadi Comanches, but all eyewitnesses of the raid describe them as Kiowas.

37 Potter, *Montague County*, 94; Maxey Depredation Claim #9673; McConnell, *West Texas Frontier*, in http://www.forttours.com/pages/tocbeale; Battey, *Quaker Among the Indians*, 85.

38 Potter, *Montague County*, 95; Maxey Depredation Claim #9673; McConnell, *West Texas Frontier*, in http://www.forttours.com/pages/tocbeale; Tatum, *Our Red Brothers*, 49-51; Nye, *Carbine & Lance*, 118;

39 Tatum, *Our Red Brothers*, 134.

40 Michno, *Encyclopedia of Indian Wars*, 258-59; Zesch, *The Captured*, 163; Tatum, *Our Red Brothers*, 138; Battey, *Quaker Among the Indians*, 82.

41 Potter, *Montague County*, 95-96; Tatum, *Our Red Brothers*, 138-39, 142; Battey, *Quaker Among the Indians*, 82, 85-86.

42 Maxey Depredation Claim #962, #9673.

43 Rister, *Fort Griffin*, 38-40; Webb and Carroll, *Handbook of Texas 2*, 595.

44 Clayton and Farmer, *Clear Fork*, 217; Rister, *Fort Griffin*, 41; McConnell, *West Texas Frontier*, in http://www.forttours.com/pages/tocledbet.

45 Clayton and Farmer, *Clear Fork*, 218-22.

46 Clayton and Farmer, *Clear Fork*, 223-24; Rister, *Fort Griffin*, 41; McConnell, *West Texas Frontier*, in http://www.forttours.com/pages/tocledbet.

47 Smith, *Boy Captives*, 10-13, 21-22. The exact place the Smiths lived is in question. Their various correspondence indicates Comal County, Drippings Springs, and Boerne, in Kendall County.

48 Smith, *Boy Captives*, 29-30; Zesch, *The Captured*, 103-04; Ashton, *Indians and Intruders*, 89.

49 Smith, *Boy Captives*, 31; Zesch, *The Captured*, 104-05.

50 Zesch, *The Captured*, 108-09; Smith, *Boy Captives*, 36-37, 43-47.

51 Smith, *Boy Captives*, 56-59, 64-65; Zesch, *The Captured*, 109-10, 138.

52 Smith, *Boy Captives*, 71-73, 90-91, 100, 116-18, 130-32; Zesch, *The Captured*, 119-20.

53 Ashton, *Indians and Intruders*, 88-93; Zesch, *The Captured*, 146.

[54] Zesch, *The Captured*, 168, 183, 187-88; Smith, *Boy Captives*, 140, 169-72, 175-80; Tatum, *Red Brothers*, 137-38; Battey, *Quaker Among the Indians*, 82-84.

[55] Smith, *Boy Captives*, 184-85, 193, 197, 203-04.

[56] Zesch, *The Captured*, 194-96; Smith, *Boy Captives*, 208-09, 211-12. In Jeff Smith's version of his recovery, his Apache band was in a battle with Mexican soldiers and he was captured by the victorious troops. They took him to town where they held him until they could contact his father and claim a $1,000 reward.

[57] Smith, *Boy Captives*, 213-17, 222, 224, 226-29; Zesch, *The Captured*, 200, 243, 252-53, 265, 272-75, 278, 281-82.

[58] Williams, *Last Frontier*, 154-57; Michno, *Encyclopedia of Indian Wars*, 254-55; Nye, *Carbine & Lance*, 152-53.

[59] Rister, *Ft. Griffin*, 93-94; Nye, *Carbine & Lance*, 153.

[60] Rister, *Ft. Griffin*, 94-95; Nye, *Carbine & Lance*, 153-54; Ledbetter, *Ft. Belknap*, 202; McConnell, *West Texas Frontier*, in www.forttours.com/pages/toclee.

[61] Rister, *Ft. Griffin*, 95; Nye, *Carbine & Lance*, 154.

[62] Nye, *Carbine & Lance*, 154-55.

[63] Nye, *Carbine & Lance*, 155-56; Tatum, *Red Brothers*, 125; Rister, *Border Captives*, 177.

[64] Tatum, *Red Brothers*, 125-27; Rister, *Border Captives*, 177; Hoig, *Kicking Bird*, 172-73; Nye, *Carbine & Lance*, 156-57.

[65] Sprague, *Massacre*, 7-8; Thrapp, *Frontier Biography* 2, 968.

[66] Sprague, *Massacre*, 9-12, 20, 24; Decker, *Utes Must Go*, 81, 85, 89, 92.

[67] Decker, *Utes Must Go*, 97, 99, 106-07; Sprague, *Massacre*, 147, 149, 165-66.

[68] Sprague, *Massacre*, 228, 234-38; Decker, *Utes Must Go*, 138-39, 141.

[69] Sprague, *Massacre*, 253, 255-58; Decker, *Utes Must Go*, 150-51.

[70] Sprague, *Massacre*, 264, 276-86; Decker, *Utes Must Go*, 153-55; Emmitt, *Last War Trail*, 263-64, 266, 268.

[71] Sprague, *Massacre*, 300-05, 308; Decker, *Utes Must Go*, 157-61. Sprague says Douglass turned himself in; Decker says it was Johnson.

[72] Decker, *Utes Must Go*, 170-71, 175, 190; Sprague, *Massacre*, 324.

[73] Decker, *Utes Must Go*, 198; Sprague, *Massacre*, 319-21.

[74] Simmons, *Lordsburg Road*, 5, 6, 9, 10, 14, 17. Juniata was a sister of Eugene F. Ware, who fought in the 4th and 7th Iowa Cavalry in the west during the Civl War, and wrote of his experiences in his book, *The Indian War of 1864*.

[75] Simmons, *Lordsburg Road*, 22, 73, 75, 100-01, 106-09.

[76] Kraft, *Gatewood & Geronimo*, 24; Betzinez, *Geronimo*, 102; Michno, *Encyclopedia of Indian Wars*, 345; Simmons, *Lordsburg Road*, 25-26, 35; Ball, *Indeh*, 78. Some sources incorrectly place Chihuahua as the leader of the raid.

[77] Simmons, *Lordsburg Road*, 109-16. A deputy marshal, S. L. Sanders, later disputed the story of non-mutilation. He said Juniata was tortured and the Apaches "broke off branches of the elder bushes and thrust them deep into her body, as many as they could."

[78] Simmons, *Lordsburg Road*, 123-24, 130, 144, 149; Crook, *Autobiography*, 247; Bourke, *Border*, 453; Betzinez, *Geronimo*, 118.

[79] Thrapp, *Apacheria*, 285-87; Betzinez, *Geronimo*, 118, 120; Simmons, *Lordsburg Road*, 160, 163, 167, 181, 186.

Conclusion

T here were many more captives taken by Indians across the breadth of the old West than can be detailed in one volume. Of about 300 hostages taken in 1862 in Minnesota alone, only a representative sample is provided here. Unlike Minnesota, which had nearly all of its prisoners taken during one month, Texas lost hundreds of captives in constant raids during a period of fifty years. Kansas and Nebraska were hit less. Indians captured many Spaniards and Mexicans in Arizona and New Mexico, but fewer white Americans of northern European background.

The thousands of Spanish and Mexican captives would deserve a volume larger than this. Most lived out their lives as prisoners of the Navajos, Apaches, Comanches, or Kiowas, but some were ransomed back to their kin in Mexico or the territories. One, Tomassa Chandler, was captured as a young girl in Mexico about 1850, was kept by the Comanches for years, and ransomed back to Mexico. There, a wealthy family took her as a peon, and after a short time, she returned to the Comanches. Eventually, she married Joseph Chandler, and then George Conover, and lived in Indian Territory.

American authorities rescued some Mexicans. Agent Lawrie Tatum recovered a number of them. Kiowas captured Jose Andres Martinez (10) near Las Vegas, New Mexico Territory, on October 10, 1866. He was one of the last Mexicans redeemed by Agent Tatum before his resignation in March 1873. Before that, Tatum was instrumental in recovering a dozen or more Mexican prisoners, including Martina Diaz (Martha Day), Seferino Trevino, Juan Buenavides, Jesus Maria Buenavides, Levando Gonzales, Manuel Valla, Vidal Roderique, Manuel Dhieriia, Esteban Dhieriia, and Prescilliaro Gonzales, who Tatum called Presleanno.[1]

One Mexican boy whose capture had far-reaching consequences was Felix Martinez, the son of Jesusa Martinez and Santiago Tellez. When the father died, Jesusa moved to Sonoita, Arizona, where she lived with John Ward, who adopted the boy. Apaches captured him in January 1861, which precipitated the confrontation in Apache Pass between Lieutenant George Bascom and Cochise, and led to the first war between the Apaches and the Americans. The boy, adopted into the White Mountain Apache tribe, later served as a scout for the U.S. Army and became known as Mickey Free. Another Mexican, Merejildo Grijalva, was captured by Chiricahuas in 1849, and remained with them ten years. He reported that the treatment of captives was harsh. Even after a decade of assimilation, when Grijalva had the chance to get away from Cochise in January 1859, he took it. He became one of the Army's most effective scouts in the 1860s and 1870s.[2]

While researching western Indian captivities, one must sort through historians' prejudices to get at the truth. A number of authors of the late twentieth and early twenty-first century have obvious biases in favor of the Indians and against the white settlers and U.S. Army. The historical trend is to tread softly on events that might offend ethnic groups, but truth cannot be suppressed or history altered for the gratification of any group.[3]

Today's trends extend beyond indictment of the military; in the current politically correct way of reporting Indian behavior in the nineteenth century, even acts of hostage taking are sugarcoated, distorted, or denied. A recent example is seen in *Halfbreed*, David F. Halaas and Andrew E. Masich's biography of George Bent, in which the anti-settler, anti-military prejudice is evident. The authors whitewash the experiences of the seven captives taken in August 1864 (see Nancy Morton and Laura Roper). The women wrote or told of their ordeals, which entailed beatings, rapes, and tortures. Cheyenne apologists Halaas and Masich blame the Lakotas for many Cheyenne misdeeds, but the women were clear that Cheyennes captured and mistreated them.

Laura Roper wrote of her experiences in 1927, sixty-three years after her capture, and told the Marysville *Advocate Democrat* of one pleasant memory when a "squaw" dressed her and combed her hair. The authors used that one statement as representative of the women's experience. On the same page cited by Halaas and Masich of Roper's "good" treatment, she also stated, "the squaws jumped on me and pulled my hair and beat me until I began to think my time had come." In fact, Laura Roper was so "happy" with her time spent with the Indians, that she wrote to Ann Marble, the mother of captive Danny Marble, that she hoped Ann's "wish will come true that every one of the Indians will be extinguished."[4] The authors' portrayal is deceitful.

Halaas and Masich have similar comments about Nancy Morton, stating that she had suffered hardships, "but had not suffered sexual abuse." It is a preposterous claim. Morton stated that, "I was subject to their passions and lusts, and the most brutal treatment that mortal being could be subjected to." She also said "she suffered from all the abuse and indignity that could be practiced toward her not only by one Indian, but by many. . . ." The Indians treated Lucinda Eubank even more harshly, if that was possible, with multiple rapes, beatings, and starvation.[5]

Halaas, Masich, and Jean Afton in their *Cheyenne Dog Soldiers* ledgerbook, list a chronology of Cheyenne depredations, but it amounts to only a brief summary. Nothing is mentioned about the August 1864 captures of Nancy Morton, Danny Marble, Laura Roper, Lucinda, Isabelle, and Willie Eubank, or Ambrose Asher. When Sarah and Joseph Morris were captured in January 1865, the entry only says "wife and child missing." The July 1867 captures of the Ulbrich and Campbell children are omitted. The October 1868 abductions of Clara and Willie Blinn and Anna Morgan are not mentioned.[6] It is deception by omission.

Another Cheyenne apologist, Peter J. Powell, badly distorts the captivity experience of Anna Brewster Morgan and Sarah White. One might get the idea from reading Powell that being an Indian captive was akin to enjoying a picnic in the park. On the contrary, Morgan was beaten and raped by her captors, and later gave birth to a half-Indian child. She told her rescuers about her horrible treatment, things that the soldiers were reluctant to repeat. When she returned to the white world, her husband made her life intolerable by never letting her forget the misery she had experienced. Anna told a female friend that she would rather be poor than have the "dreadful facts" of her captivity be known. She said her capture placed a blight upon her life that would follow her to her grave.

In 1907, five years after Anna died in an insane asylum, her friend, Emily Harrison, printed a story of Anna's captivity in which she said that one of the Indians Anna "married" treated her kindly, and that "after I came back, the road seemed rough, and I often wished they had never found me."[7] Even if Harrison's rendition of Anna's words are correct, it is less of a praise for Indian life than it is an indictment of an intolerant white society that could make life hell for an ex-captive. Powell, *Sacred Mountain*, 717, cites none of the abundant sources to the contrary, but takes Harrison's rendition and uses it to show captives had it relatively good living with the Cheyennes. Jeff Broome, in *Dog Soldier Justice*, 144, takes Powell to task and states that his account comes "from the frontier of the imagination and not the frontier of the West." Powell also claims that Anna's reported statement "was not the first time a captive had expressed longings to return to the People (Cheyenne), after being taken from them," but offers no other example. His biases are even more glaring when he writes of the Cheyenne treatment of the German children in 1874 (see Catherine German).

Some of Powell's claims of benign treatment come from Joanna Stratton's, *Pioneer Women*. She says that fear played a large role in the settlers' dealings with the Indians, which was true, but she also claims that "few families personally experienced intimidation or violence by the Indians," which is nonsense. Settlers filed more than 10,000 depredation claims against the Indians, and they are likely a small percentage of those who could have filed, but did not because of lack of knowledge, means, or ability. Stratton mentions some of the atrocities committed by the Cheyenne and Lakota in Kansas in 1868, but falls back on Anna Morgan's reported words that she wished she had never been found, as if that was a valid summation of "the personal truth" of what captivity was really like. The picture Stratton leaves us with is more in tune with her own biases than with reality.[8]

Sandra Myres in her book *Westering Women*, tells us it was men who said women feared Indians, but the women rarely were in fear, and the view of victimized white women is a view fostered by twentieth century writers. She claims women on the frontier had only benign thoughts about Indians, and she uses 1830s Arkansas, Missouri, Iowa, and Minnesota, as examples. Obviously, she did not include Texas, for that would have destroyed her contention. Myres says that Indian attacks on isolated frontier cabins occurred "with far less frequency than one might think," and claims that the frightened pioneer woman was more a creation of "penny dreadfuls" than of fact. She admits attacks occurred, but her survey of a tiny sample of captivities is not representative of the true picture. Myres mentions the Indian attack on the Whitmans, but throws quotation marks around the word "massacre" as if questioning its legitimacy. She mentions Helen Tarble (Carrothers), Minnie Carrigan (Busse), and Josephine Meeker. Her depiction of the attack on Matilda Friend and its accompanying horrors is glossed over, and no mention is made of the captives who were taken.[9] If Myres believes this is a representative sample of the frequency of attacks on homesteads, then her scholarship is suspect.

Myres makes several questionable generalizations, one of them being, "Most of the captivity accounts included at least one comment on friendly or kind treatment from one or more of their captors."[10] One needs only to reference the accounts in this book to realize that the statement is a distortion. There were many more "bad" experiences than "good" ones, and the "good" ones are very qualified, many being psychological and emotional mind games practiced by the Indians to break the resistance and will of the hostages. If a captive received "good" treatment one day, he or she was likely subjected to abuse the next day. Punishment, hard labor, starvation, and beatings were alternated with isolated acts of kindness. Many of the captives became emotional wrecks.

Glenda Riley would also have us believe that captivities were not so bad, and white women and Indians were kindred spirits. In her book, *Women and Indians on the Frontier*, Riley disparages captivity narratives, saying they were only written to make money. But women's diaries and letters tell us what they really felt, which is a rather strange argument, because in private letters we sometimes find more of the horrible details about captivity that the women did not want made public. Riley claims that newspapers exaggerated the dangers of western travel, but such was not always the case. There were occasions when just the opposite was true, with newspapers underplaying the danger so as not to stifle emigrant travel and hurt business.[11]

Riley says that Oklahoma women dealt better with Indians than Texas women. Of course! There were no white female homesteaders in Oklahoma during the years of heaviest raiding, and they did not suffer as the Texas women did. Riley says that "rape, pillage, and burn" was not the key phrase in understanding white women-Indian experiences, and that women and Indians were not adversaries. Again, the claims are hollow. Certainly not all women experienced capture, rape, and torture, but we cannot dismiss the thousands of them who did. For Riley, white men were the most to blame for Indian problems. She says scholars today read men's reports, not women's, which is an unfathomable argument, for if scholars looked closely at captive women's reports they would find the true magnitude of the situation.[12] It appears that Riley is subject to the selective amnesia posited by Michael Kammen, in *Mystic Chords of Memory*. He says that Americans have an inclination to depoliticize the past to minimize memories and causes of conflict. We try to remember only the aspects of history that will render it acceptable to as many people as possible.[13] If this is true, it contributes to paving the road for the march of political correctness that currently distorts our past.

Glenda Riley wrote another volume that included similar arguments. In *The Female Frontier*, she disparaged women's captivity narratives, and said they only claimed to be factual, but injected much fiction and maudlin sentimentality. Riley apparently doesn't believe some of the first-hand accounts of white captives are accurate, calling Abigail Gardner's experiences in Iowa, "the so-called Spirit Lake Massacre," and implying that Emeline Fuller (see Reuben Van Ornum) only "claimed to have witnessed" Indians torturing women on the way to Oregon.[14] It is remarkable how modern writers can claim to know more about what happened in the nineteenth century than those who experienced it, or how they tend to conceptualize the characteristics of an historical person or group in terms of their own sensibilities and experiences.[15]

Riley affirms that not all captives' experiences were negative, that some formed bonds of affection and often wanted to stay with their captors. Indeed. Much of this can be written off to a common survival mode that many captives entered, which has been called the "Stockholm Syndrome," and can be found in many hostage experiences, particularly in the ordeal of Patty Hearst. The younger and more passive the hostages, the more easily they can be coerced into empathizing with their captors and participating in their lives. But the hostages are not making life changes on their own free will. They are forced to adapt to survive, and even after release they will parrot much of what they learned during their "brainwashing."[16]

Using statistics of captives taken in New England between 1675 and 1763, Riley finds that about 62 percent of the captives were male and 52 percent were adults. She posits that data collected for the trans-Mississippi West would show a similar pattern. It does not. In the West, only 35 percent of the captives were male and only 25 percent were adults. If the Eastern statistics are correct, it may reflect a random pattern, or a slight Indian preference for capturing older males. In the West, a strikingly different capture pattern occurs that does not appear to be caused by luck-of-the-draw. There is a significant preference for young females.

Riley does not believe that Indians routinely sexually abused female captives, forced them into unwanted marriages, or assaulted them. She says numerous women's accounts do not "even hint at sexuality."[17] She is quite mistaken.

To support her contention that captives were sometimes treated well and frequently wanted to return to their Indian families, Riley cites the cases of Olive Oatman, Elizabeth Fletcher, Minnie Carrigan, Bianca Babb, and a few secondhand tales by unnamed captives whose stories cannot be substantiated. Oatman, Riley says, spent much of the rest of her life wishing to return to her Indian husband and children. Fletcher supposedly became an

Arapaho and wanted to remain with them. Carrigan and Babb had some kind words to say about the Indian women who acted as their "mothers." One only has to read the above stories of these captives to see that Oatman, at 14 years of age, was raped and treated horribly. The only reason the others were not raped is that they were 10, 7, and 3 years old! Still, their overall captivities were not at all pleasant. Only Babb had a more or less benign experience. Gelo and Zesch, in their article, "Every Day Seemed to be a Holiday," also play up this supposed "good time" that Bianca had. Regardless, when her rescuers came for her, she had no hesitation in telling her Indian "mother" that "I wanted to go back."[18] Even if they all had a wonderful time, it does not excuse the Indians from abducting them in the first place. Riley's attempt to use them to support her thesis falls flat.

Scott Zesch, who wrote an excellent study of nine white prisoners in *The Captured*, weakens his arguments by using his small sample to make generalizations. He claims that "many" captured children preferred the Indian life and resisted attempts to rescue them, and "nearly all" preferred Indian society once they had lived with them more than one year. He also claims that Indians "received the child captives warmly and without prejudice," rarely purposely hurt their boy captives, and didn't treat them any harder than they did their own sons. Zesch's statement that most of the captives preferred the Indian life is true—but only among the nine subjects of his study. When the captive base is expanded to include all captive children, then the true statement would be that very few of them preferred the Indian way of life. In some respects, Zesch has studied only the exceptions and generalized that they were the rule.[19]

Ty Cashion, in *A Texas Frontier*, accuses "Anglos" of distorting fact and hiding behind myths, apparently not realizing that some of the "New Western" historians he idolizes are the very ones doing the distorting. Cashion makes statements typical of his chosen school of thought: few frontier families experienced death or captivity; Indian fights in frontier Texas were infrequent during the Civil War; and frontier violence was not as common as traditional Turnerian historians, who "pandered" to popular appetites, would have us believe. Cashion also makes the unsubstantiated claim that "only women and children suffered the horrors of prolonged captivity."[20] This study shows that males were the prisoners in seven out of ten of the longest captivities.

Among the most biased histories, is Gary C. Anderson's, *Conquest of Texas*. Whereas a century ago, white pioneers and soldiers may have been nearly always depicted as "good," and the Indians as "bad," Anderson has distorted the picture in the opposite direction. Almost all white Texans, and especially the Rangers, appear in Anderson's eyes as reprehensible thieves, rapists, and murderers. Anderson disparages Robert Utley's study of the Rangers, *Lone Star Justice*, which was fair and balanced, but not nearly harsh enough for Anderson, who sees Texans as martial, violent, profit-lusting racists. He believes captivity narratives were only creations "of some supposed Indian attack." Anderson either has not studied the narratives, or does not wish to admit their true nature. He states "the women were safe then from sexual assault—and the captivity narratives demonstrate this . . ." Anderson also states that most Indian depredations were fabrications, and it was the Indians who were the victims, not the Texans. His research is thorough, but his anti-Texan, pro-Indian biases dramatically skew his arguments and make them nearly worthless. Anderson laments that the Anglo Texans distorted their history. Unfortunately, Anglos are still distorting it; Anderson is a prime example.[21]

June Namias blames white men for nearly all frontier troubles, including exaggerating white captives' ordeals for their own libidinous gratification or as nation-building propaganda. She claims there were three kinds of female captive archetypes: the "Survivors" of the colonial era; the "Amazons" of the Revolution and early Republican era; and the "Frail Flowers" of the expansion era from 1820 to 1870. It is the latter which most concerns us. Namias characterizes the "Flowers" as the fainting, "poor me" type, who would not resist capture, denied sexual attraction, and saw only brutality and lust in Indian men.[22] This categorization is only marginally true. The women of this model did deny sexual attraction and saw only brutality and lust in Indian men—they loathed the experience. But the primary characteristic of her model, that they were "Frail Flowers" and did not resist, is completely false. The paucity of captivity narratives in her study leads her to this incorrect conclusion. In the "Flower" archetype, Namias lists twenty-two captives, however, examination reveals that one of these is a fictional account (Mrs. Edwin Eastman), one is likely fictional, three were not captured in the time frame she constructed, and three cannot be located in her index. This leaves fourteen legitimate female captives with which to generalize. Namias claims that a prime characteristic of the "Flower" type is a penchant to wilt when faced with adversity.[23]

This study shows that the females of 1830 to 1870 resisted more than fainted, and even fought back more than the males did. There were more females who resisted capture than there were subjects in Namias's entire archetype. Dolly Webster fought back, was going to kill a chief, and threatened the Indian women who tormented her. Ann Harvey fought until Indians broke her arm. Sarah Horn fought her female master and fared better afterwards. Rachel Plummer fought her female tormentors, beat one with a bone, and found she was better off. Jane Crawford knocked a warrior in the head with a stick when he threatened her daughter. Jane Simpson fought back so hard she was killed. Jane Wilson escaped rather than submit to abuse. Lydia Noble always resisted her captors, and was finally killed because of it. Larcena Page tried to grab a pistol to shoot an Indian, and then wrestled with him. Eliza Van Ornum killed an Indian while trying to escape and was killed for her effort. Mary Schwandt resisted her captors. Mildred Durkin was killed while defending her family. Hannah Akers fought back. Sarah Kemp fought back and escaped being captured. Arrena Savage fought back, was lanced, but was not taken. Mary and Margaret Box fought back. Nancy Morton tried to run, was shot, and refused to go with the Indians. Matilda Friend fought back and was wounded. Elizabeth Bell resisted and was killed. Sarah White resisted and was raped, and Martha Russell resisted and was raped and killed. Emma Metzger resisted and was killed. There were more.

On the contrary, the males taken in the same period were the real "Frail Flowers." John Parker, Thomas Coleman, William Gilleland, William Simpson, and George and Meredith Wilson did not resist capture. Nelson Lee, a full-grown man, was captured without a fight. Tobe Jackson, William Wilson, James Taylor, Lon White, Herbert Weinand, and James Savage gave up without a struggle. Frank Buckelew didn't resist capture, but only thought about stabbing sleeping Indians. Fremont Blackwell and Thomas Sullivan ran and then gave up. Ole Nystel, Danny Marble, Ambrose Asher, John Kuykendall, and Thomas Bailey submitted to the Indians. Lee Temple Friend, Nat McElroy, Washington Wolfe, George Cullen, Adolph Korn, and Charles and Daniel Koozier didn't resist.

Namias does not know the subjects of her study. She could only guess that unlike the New England captives of the colonial era, she believed, "at least some white women experienced humiliating sexual treatment on the plains," but how common the experience was, she concluded, "is unclear." As a citation for this summation,

Namias cites only the contradictory accounts of Stanley B. Kimball and Lonnie J. White.[24] With such a superficial investigation, it is no wonder that she is unaware of the sexual abuses heaped upon her "Frail Flowers," and how much they resisted as compared with their male counterparts.

Not only do some historians whitewash the horrors of the individual captive experience, some would gloss over entire chapters. Roy Meyer, in his *History of the Santee Sioux*, likens the captives' stories in the Minnesota Uprising to a type of Falstaffian farce that crumbles upon close examination. He never tells the story of one captive, claims there were only occasional instances of torture and mutilation, and apparently believes that the hundreds of people who were captured, wounded, or escaped from the rampaging Santees were exaggerating or hallucinating. Meyers cites one doctor who accompanied a burial party and did not see any mutilated bodies, and therefore, fallaciously generalizes that bodies weren't mutilated. He calls the atrocities "isolated instances" and says they "were multiplied in the imagination of refugees . . . ." The number of white casualties during the Uprising was estimated at about 700 killed, 300 captured, an uncounted number wounded, plus an untold number of dead that were never found. Settlers filed 2,940 damage claims with the Sioux Commission, for property destruction of more than two and a half million dollars. The unlucky victims told of numerous horrors and atrocities. Meyer, however, pretentiously asserts that their accounts are exaggerated and cannot be accepted by "sober scholarship."[25]

In a *Journal of the Indian Wars* article, Ellen Farrell takes a similar line. The Dakotas, she said, "were not engaged in a wholly indiscriminate rampage." Whites provoked them, based on fear, racial prejudice, and land hunger, and much of the supposed Indian barbarism was the result of self-serving white imagination.[26] If only these authors could have been in Minnesota in 1862, to explain this to the settlers.

Although most captives were abducted from their frontier homes, the overland trails were not safe from marauding Indians. Just as there has been a whitewashing of Indian culpability in hostage taking, so too there exists a trendy attempt to show that there was no great danger from Indians along the western trails. One of the early attempts to downplay the hazards comes from Robert Munkres, in a 1968 article in the *Annals of Wyoming*. Munkres claims that Indian attacks on wagon trains were more numerous in movie plots than in reality. This may be true, but only because there were so many movies, and not because there were so few Indian attacks. Munkres studied sixty-six diaries of overland travelers between 1834 and 1858. He stopped his study in 1860 in time, and at Fort Bridger in space. Why? Because there were more emigrants before 1860, because there was less fighting east of Fort Bridger during those years, and more fighting everywhere after 1860. Munkres wanted to show there was little danger in traveling west, so he set narrow space and time parameters to a test area that he already knew would prove his thesis, and *voila*, he "proved" it. It made about as much sense as if one were to count casualties in the European Theater in WWII, but stop counting in 1943, and leave out the Eastern Front. Even so, Munkres's study may not have proved what he wanted. He said that only thirteen diaries contained reports of Indian attacks, which meant an "overwhelming majority" of diarists encountered no Indian attack. Thirteen attacks out of sixty-six, however, means that about 20 percent of all emigrant parties were attacked. That makes a tremendously dangerous travel proposition.[27]

Like a bad record that keeps repeating, historians built on Munkres's invalid study to promote the idea that western trails were relatively safe from Indian attack. John Unruh in *The Plains Across*, cites Munkres's article and takes a similar viewpoint that the overlanders exaggerated Indian danger and that most travelers before 1860 were killed west of South Pass (as if being murdered in Idaho as opposed to Nebraska made a difference).

John Faragher in *Women and Men on the Overland Trail*, cites Munkres and Unruh for more of the same; the early trail years east of South Pass were relatively safe from Indian attack. Glenda Riley repeats the chant. Sandra Myres too, in *Westering Women*, cites Unruh and makes the absurd affirmation that Indian attacks on wagon trains "simply did not take place," but paradoxically adds that most of the killings occurred west of South Pass.

In Stuart Udall's crusade to make our future a better place by denying past frontier violence, he cites Unruh, repeats many of Munkres's specious arguments, and adds that most of the supposed attacks on wagon trains were mythical.[28] Kent Steckmesser in *The Western Hero*, says that once a story gets embedded in successive accounts, by simple repetition it is accepted as truth. People, he affirms, believe that reliability of a story lies in the number of times it gets repeated, without considering its original source.[29] The tale of minimal danger from Indians while traveling west, like Harriet Beecher Stowe's Topsy, was generated from suspect origins and just "grow'd."

Despite all of the efforts made by the above writers to deny frontier violence on the Oregon-California Trail, their arguments are greatly weakened by other major flaws. First, they looked only at emigrants, neglecting many other travelers, freighters, mail riders, drovers, stages, and assorted business operations that were attacked. Second, they concentrated on only one trail and its branches. Had they also examined the other western trails, such as the Central Overland, the Santa Fe, the Butterfield, the Gila, the Spanish, the Southern Upper and Lower Roads, or Beale's Road for instance, examples of trail dangers would have increased dramatically. But then, it would have ruined their argument. This study has included a number of women and children who were captured while traveling the trail of choice for Munkres, *et. al.,* including Fanny Kelly, the Van Ornums, and Fletchers, but it also includes the Blinns, Oatmans, Germans, Wilsons, Horns, Harrises, Websters, Whites, and others who were on different roads and not counted in their statistics. In addition, there were more attacks and captures discussed above, on Munkres's "peaceful" half of the trail and in the "peaceful" years of his study, that he did not mention.

Not all contemporary historians, however, are attempting to whitewash Indian atrocities. Louise Barnett, who has extensively studied captives, explains in *Touched by Fire,* that hundreds of white women were taken prisoner in Minnesota, and hundreds more, perhaps thousands, were taken across the west. Statistically speaking, several thousand captives were a small minority compared to millions of people along the frontier from the Canadian to the Mexican border, nevertheless, almost all the women lived in fear of Indian captivity. And, Barnett concludes, there were certainly more women "whose lives were permanently damaged or shortened by the experience as opposed to women who recovered fully."[30]

Lest critics believe that this study takes into consideration only white settlers' viewpoints in its judgment of Indian behavior, one might want to examine Quintard Taylor's assessment, in his book *In Search of the Racial Frontier.* Taylor also belies the ideas of any women-Indian affinity. Indians were the common enemy of blacks and whites on the frontier. Particularly in Texas, the blacks hated and feared the Comanches and Kiowas as much as did the whites, for they killed and captured women and children of all races. Blacks even had to be wary of tribes other than the wild nomadic ones. Slaves in Texas could not easily escape to freedom by running north, for Indian Territory was the second largest slaveholding region in the west. The "civilized" tribes of Cherokee, Choctaw, Chickasaw, and Creek kept slaves. The Cherokees had laws against black and Indian intermarriage, and after the Civil War, Choctaws and Chickasaws drove freedmen out of their territory or enacted black codes to regulate the labor and behavior of those who remained. At one time the civilized tribes held 5,000 black slaves, about 6 percent of their population.[31]

The institution of slavery among Indian tribes is not as well known as its white counterpart, but it perhaps partially explains the Indian affinity for captive taking. According to Russell Magnaghi, in "The Indian Slave Trade," Indian slaveholding was a pre-Columbian practice that was given fresh impetus when they learned they could raid other tribes and sell captives to Europeans. In the West, the early Spanish and French traders gave the tribes an outlet for their captives, and the number of captives incorporated into the tribes lessened as Europeans stimulated the profit motive. About 1694, Navajos captured some Pawnees and brought them to Santa Fe, demanding money for their lives. When the Spanish did not pay, the Navajos killed their hostages, causing the Spanish to issue a decree authorizing the use of royal funds to ransom captives. It had long-range repercussions. Indians fully realized that captives could be used as bargaining chips or sold for a profit. It started a vicious cycle.[32]

In the southwest, the Comanches were the primary slave traders; preying first on the Apaches, then the Spanish, and then on the Americans. It was a Comanche custom that before they offered captive girls for sale, they would deflower them, and say, "Now you can take her—now she is good."[33]

James Brooks, in *Captives & Cousins*, says Spanish, Mexicans, and Comanches seemed to accept the established captive process, a situation that white Americans moving into the southwest could not tolerate. Patrimony and kinship bonds were challenged by the American penchant for property and profit motives. As the American presence became dominant, the age-old customs of raid and capture, intermarriage and sale, became less viable. Indian raiders needed guns and ammunition, and horses, cattle, white women and children were the necessary commodities. The Americans threw the proverbial wrench in the gearbox. One of the reasons Americans tried to get Indians onto reservations was to break the captive exchange economy and begin free labor capitalism. Brooks states that the view of native peoples on the fringes of civilization as subsistence economies with little inter-group conflict is false. Indians could be violently competitive, and buying captives only fueled the system. When it ended, it brought the Indians dependency and wage labor. Brooks believes that the Indians were once capitalists in a slave economy.[34]

One can see such trends in captive-taking using only the years of this study (Table 1). Prior to 1860, Comanches and Kiowas held their captives longer, perhaps seeing them as possible future kin and as tribal replacements. After 1860, they generally held captives for a shorter time, likely realizing that their immediate needs for food, clothing, or weapons outweighed the long-term goal of tribal population increase. Captives were turned over quicker, the goods changed hands, and the Indians proved to be budding entrepreneurs. Among the captives taken after 1870, a few, like Korn, Lehmann, Maxey, and the Smiths, were kept longer than usual, possibly because the Indians finally realized that they could no longer cash them in.

The possibility of becoming an Indian captive on the frontier was very real, and although a western overland trip could be hazardous, the stay-at-home frontier settlers faced dangers many times worse. There are no comprehensive statistics available to accurately total up the number of captives taken during the American western movement. Below, however, are some various estimations that give a hint of the problem's enormity. Prior to the period of our study, from 1540 to 1820, estimates range from 5,000 to 10,000 people captured by Indians along the Texas-Sonora border. Durango alone lost 1,446 women and children as prisoners to the Indians between 1822-1855. The Kiowas estimated that from 5 to 7 percent of their population were captives. In 1821, the Comanches held 900 prisoners, but by 1855, they held 2,000. Probably about 1,000 Americans were taken captive between 1860 and 1875.[35]

The official count of casualties in the 1862 Minnesota Uprising was established at 644 dead, plus about 300 captives. In Kansas and Nebraska there were about 400 citizens murdered in 1866 and 1867. In Nebraska, fifty-two were killed, wounded, or captured in just ten days in August 1864. In Kansas in 1867-68, the State Legislature visited five counties: Ellsworth, Saline, Ottawa, Cloud, and Mitchell, and took 120 depredation claims totaling almost $59,000. War Department statistics for Kansas in 1868-69 showed 158 people murdered, sixteen wounded, forty-eight scalped, fourteen women "outraged," one man, four women, and seven children captured. There were far more noncombatants killed in the Indian Wars than in the Civil War.[36]

Along the western ends of the California and Oregon Trails from 1862 to 1865, there were eighty-one whites killed in non-military actions. In 1850, in New Mexico Territory, Navajos held between 300 and 500 captives. In 1858, one attorney was trying to get reparations for the murder or capture of 100 New Mexicans and for the stolen property in excess of one half million dollars for 244 other civilians. In 1862, New Mexico Territorial Governor Henry Connelly complained that in the past several years, Indians murdered "hundreds of our people, and carried our women and children into captivity."

Superintendent Michael Steck reported in 1863, that in the past three years New Mexico Territory suffered 200 deaths and the loss of about one half million sheep. From his Arizona Superintendency the same year, Charles D. Poston reported 150 citizens killed. In 1867, New Mexico Territory Superintendent A. B. Norton complained to the commissioner that since the U.S. acquired the territory, there still remained almost two million dollars in unpaid Indian depredation claims.

Arizona Superintendent George L. Andrews, in his 1870 report, stated he could not begin to accurately count the number of lives lost and property destroyed in the past year, but provided an example from Pima County alone, where forty-seven citizens were murdered, six wounded, and one carried into captivity, plus 500 cattle stolen and $10,000 worth of property damaged or destroyed. Historian Dan Thrapp concluded that the civilian loss in the struggle for Arizona and New Mexico "was the most costly, in human lives, of any in the history of America."[37]

Texas was particularly hard hit. In the years 1865 through the first half of 1867, thirty-five counties reported a total of 162 killed, twenty-four wounded, and forty-three captured, plus 2,430 sheep and goats, 3,781 horses, and 30,838 cattle stolen. Wise County reported that between 1865 and 1870 it was raided twenty-one times and had twelve citizens murdered and five captured. One estimate is that about 400 people were captured within 100 miles of Parker County, Texas. Jack County reported 200 citizens killed and captured between 1859 and 1871. Montague County lost forty-three citizens killed or captured in 1866 alone. In other Texas counties between 1873 and 1875 there were forty-five killed, fifteen wounded, and two captured. A compilation showing depredations from 1865 to 1879 shows 407 Texans killed by Indians, seventy-six wounded, and eighty-one women and children carried off, plus 20,521 horses and mules, and 43,392 cattle stolen. The report also stated that seventy-seven Indians were killed, twenty-nine wounded, and three captured, along with the recovery of 6,871 horses and cattle.[38]

Ida Lasiter Huckabay, a long time resident of Jack County, remembered the pioneer days as all right for men and dogs, but "hell on women and horses." The old saying was fairly accurate, except that it might not have been all that good on men or dogs either. Perhaps one unnamed Comanche most succinctly summed up how women and children fit into the scheme of things. A female captive who had been raped all winter, learned some Comanche language. When she returned to Texas she reported to have heard one Indian say, "Didn't these damn fools, the Americanos, give us fine things for the few Texas rats we delivered to them?"[39]

No matter how much some authors would like to deny or whitewash the sexual abuse of the captives, it was a very common occurrence. Colonel Richard I. Dodge in his 1877 book, *The Plains of the Great West and Their Inhabitants*, wrote that "in the last twenty-five years no woman has been taken prisoner by any plains Indians who did not as soon as practicable become a victim to the lust of every one of her captors." In another book, *Our Wild Indians*, published in 1882, Dodge wrote, "Indians always prefer to capture rather than kill women, they being merchantable property. White women are unusually valuable, one moderately good-looking being worth as many ponies as would buy from their fathers three or four Indian girls." The Commissioner of Indian Affairs report for 1866, also stated that Indians "boastfully say that stealing white women is more of a lucrative business than stealing horses."

In 1940, Carl Rister wrote in *Border Captives*, that profits from the sale of white captives "far out-weighed Indian grievances—misdeeds of the whites, slaughter of the buffalo, and settler-occupation of favorite hunting grounds—as a motive for raids and outbreaks." In 1952, Wallace and Hoebel wrote that rape by the Comanches was rare, "except upon captives." In 1974, Fehrenbach wrote, "there was never to be known a case of white women captives who were not subjected to abuse and rape."[40] A contrary view comes from Michael Tate in his 1994 article, "Comanche Captives." He claims the charge that Comanches routinely raped female captives and thus the women were better off dead, was only based on the biased attitude of the nineteenth century. Tate says it "is not an accurate assessment of the situation," and adds that Texas captivity narratives are "virtually silent on this matter."[41]

In reality, reports of routine rape were legion, accurate, and the narratives are not silent on the matter. Texas captivity reports from Rachel Plummer in 1836, to Elizabeth Koozier in 1870, are replete with stories of sexual abuse. Indians routinely raped captive women—from the Comanches in Texas, to the Utes in Colorado, to the Cayuse in Washington, and from the Yavapais in Arizona to the Dakotas in Minnesota. The sweeping generalizations by Dodge and Fehrenbach are overstatements—but only slightly. Certainly they are more accurate than Tate's assessment, along with distortions being spread by other contemporary scholars. Apparently the Plains Indians did not read some of our New Western historians.

In this study we can see that of the eighty-three captured women who were 13 or older, forty-eight (58 percent) were certainly raped, twenty-nine (35 percent) were probably raped, and only six (7 percent) stated that they were not "compromised" or kept their "honor." In the twenty-nine probable cases there is not enough information given, or the victims simply did not admit it. If only half of them were actually raped, than the rape total increases to about 75 percent. In the white world it was a disgrace to have been so handled, especially by men who were considered to be of an inferior race. We can see what a hell some men made for their returning wives (see Anna Brewster Morgan). For the few who exaggerated their sexual abuse to perhaps make their stories more attractive to a potential publisher, there were likely many more who were raped, but denied it.

In the 1830s, Josiah Gregg noted the presence of Mexican captives with the Comanches along the Santa Fe Trail. He was surprised to learn that some of them preferred to remain with their captors "rather than encounter the horrible ordeal of ill-natured remarks on being restored to civilized life." Rosalie Tavaris of Monclova, when freed from captivity in the late 1840s, would not make public her sexual assault because of the stigma attached to cross-racial rape.[42] In the 1850s, Olive Oatman, who was captured at age 14, later told the soldiers that she was only 11, to make her appear to have been too young to be sexually abused. In one of her reminiscences, she claims never to have been touched by the Indians, but the evidence shows that she bore two half-Indian children.[43]

In 1867, Veronica Ulbrich was captured and raped, but years later in an Indian depredation claim her father pleaded with the authorities not to make her real age known; she had told her husband she was only seven at the time of capture, instead of 13, to make it appear that she was too young to have been raped. In

1879, Flora Price did not want her rape revealed to her potential suitor.[44]

The phrase, "a fate worse than death," is a common one, echoed by hundreds, perhaps thousands, of men and women who were captured or faced the possibility of capture. It was a nearly universal tenet in the West that white men and women would be better off to kill themselves than be captured alive. Corollary with this belief was the idea to "save the last bullet for yourself." George Custer's wife, Libbie, understood she was in double jeopardy—in peril of rape, torture, or death if captured, or to be killed by friends to prevent her capture. Other army wives, such as Ellen Biddle, Martha Summerhayes, Lydia Lane, and Sarah Canfield were well aware of their tenuous position. At the besieged Fort Phil Kearny, Colonel Henry B. Carrington made preparations to place the women and children in the powder magazine to blow them up if it appeared the Indians were about to capture the fort.[45]

All women "knew" that they should die rather than be captured, but only until they were actually faced with the choice did they realize that almost all of them desperately wanted to live. Fanny Kelly wrote, "it is only those who have looked over the dark abyss of death who know how the soul shrinks from meeting the unknown future. Experience is a grand teacher. . . ." she said, and quickly learned to "pause upon the fearful brink of eternity, and look back for rescue."[46] Anna Snyder, on the other hand, saw her husband murdered, tried to escape, failed, evidently believed that she could not exist as a captive, and hanged herself. Some women fought and died before letting themselves be captured. Other women took intermediate courses and survived the best they could. A portion of those who returned to the white world perhaps wished that they had died.

Several books attempt to summarize the white captive experience. Derounian-Stodola and Levernier in *The Indian Captivity Narrative*, said that there were tens of thousands of captives in America and the threat of captivity touched the minds of everyone. The authors claim that Indians took captives for revenge, ransom, replacement of tribal members, and for slaves. To that list they might have added, for fun and profit. They found that Eastern tribes sexually abused captives less than did Western tribes, but offer the unsubstantiated reason that the difference was because Western tribes "came to emulate white society's less civilized war practices." Frederick Drimmer in *Captured by the Indians*, notes this same phenomenon, but thankfully offers no such absurd reason. Wilcomb Washburn, editor of the *Narratives of North American Indian Captivities*, who should know better, states that rape was "never true generally." Apparently, he has only referenced the more numerous eastern narratives, for this study clearly shows such a case was not true in the West.[47]

Derounian-Stodola and Levernier make some minor errors with individual captives, such as in calling the Babb family the Dots, but one of their erroneous generalizations is more damaging. They claim that many captives grew to love their Indian families and would not leave them. Again, we assume the authors must only be speaking of captives east of the Mississippi, for their statement is definitely not correct in the West. Washburn estimated that in New England, 54 percent of captured girls between ages seven and 15 refused to return to their white families. Glenda Riley makes similar comparisons with Colonial New England and the trans-Mississippi West. In the former, she claims that nearly 33 percent of female captives stayed or returned to the Indians, but less than 10 percent of the males stayed. Riley, without studying the matter, believes that a similar situation may have existed in the West.[48] It did not.

This study shows a remarkable difference for Western captives: only one girl (2.5 percent) of the forty in the 7 to 15 age group stayed or returned to the Indians, *or tried to*, when given the choice. Four of the forty, Alice Todd, Virginia White, Mary Hamleton, and Elizabeth Fletcher, were either killed, never found, or never received a viable option of returning, so no preference could be determined. The one girl who wanted to remain with the Indians, but was not allowed to, was Cynthia Parker, who was captured when ten years old, spent twenty-four years with the Indians, and had a husband and three children. Yet, Cynthia is universally cited as proof that white girls preferred to remain with the Indians. As for the boys in the West, two out of fifty captives (4 percent) returned to live with the Indians (Thomas Coleman and Rudolph Fischer). Several others had yearnings, but never made a complete break with white society and returned to Indian life.

J. Norman Heard in *White Into Red*, analyzed many captivities to learn why some prisoners preferred death to capture, while others were more easily assimilated. Heard found that family background, religious training, race, national origin, and length of time held were not significant in determining how easily a captive would assimilate, although length of captivity did increase the likelihood of assimilation. He determined that age was the critical factor; with few exceptions children captured under the age of 12 were more easily "Indianized," with 12 being the limit for girls and

14 the limit for boys. Heard, who studied a sampling of Eastern and Western captives, says that teen-aged female captives had a greater desire to return to the white world, an analysis that differs markedly from Washburn's, who claims that more than half of the captured girls, even as young as age seven, wanted to stay with the Indians.[49] This study shows that only a tiny percentage of white girls wanted to remain with the Indians.

In the West there were hundreds, perhaps thousands of white captives. Almost all of them had bad experiences; most of the captured women were raped, most of them never assimilated, and most of them never returned to the Indians. Contemporary writers who deny or whitewash these facts have not studied the subject thoroughly, or are purposely distorting the truth.

One might want to compare the countless Indian atrocities perpetrated on the white captives with similar atrocities perpetrated on the Indians. Although scalpings and mutilations were sometimes practiced by both sides during and immediately following battles, white soldiers and civilians followed no accepted systematic practice of torture and rape, notwithstanding the fingers that will immediately be pointed to the Sand Creek incident. In November 1864, about 700 Colorado troops attacked a village of about 500 Cheyennes and Arapahoes on the Big Sandy in Colorado Territory. The attack has been depicted as a great massacre, and there were atrocities committed after the fight that were disgraceful.[50] The reader may decide whether the white soldiers' conduct at Sand Creek and in several lesser incidents during the Indian wars was much different from the treatment many white captives received at Indian hands on numerous occasions. The Colorado soldiers were rightfully condemned for mutilating some of the Indian dead, and particularly heinous is the oft-repeated example of "scalping" female genitals. One must remember that Cheyennes also mutilated and scalped the "private parts" of some females in the massacred Eubank Family (see Lucinda Eubank), an atrocity perpetrated three months before Sand Creek.

Indian Agent Samuel Colley made a statement regarding atrocities that apologists seem so prone to make, inadvertently exposing the reality of the situation. The Cheyennes "were butchered in a brutal manner," he said, "and scalped and mutilated as bad as an Indian ever did to a white man."[51] What Colley was saying is that an Indian fought in that manner, but a white man should not. In this age of egalitarianism it would be hard to argue that two races should be held to different standards of behavior.

There are some today who would argue, albeit incorrectly, that white atrocities at Sand Creek began the Indian Wars and caused the Indians to commit atrocities in retaliation. The contention is nonsense.[52] In the West, the Indians were heaping atrocities upon innocent settlers for three decades before Sand Creek.

For years Indian groups have pushed the U.S. government to make reparation payments for deaths and losses they suffered at Sand Creek and in other confrontations. The reparations issue can be seen as the proverbial can of worms, for, if the Indians are eligible for reparations, then certainly the whites are eligible. It can be argued that white settlers suffered more killed, and lost much more property than did the Indians, and we can see in a sampling of depredation claims in this study that they were seldom allowed payment. For example, of all the depredation claims filed for losses as a result of the August 1864 raids along the Platte and Little Blue in Nebraska, no one received money except Nancy Morton; the government did not pay a penny to the rest.[53] The government protected its Indian wards from thousands of claims filed against them.

In 1796, the U.S. Congress passed a law to provide compensation to both Indians and whites for depredations committed upon each other. Claims were filed and adjudicated as late as 1920. Poor record keeping and lost files make it impossible to determine exactly how many claims whites filed because of losses due to Indian depredations. They numbered in the thousands up to 1891, when all remaining cases were sent from Congress to the Court to settle. From 1891 to 1920, the Court tried 10,841 cases, and paid less than 13 percent of the damages claimed. From 1796 to 1890, only three percent of the claims were paid. Untold thousands of white settlers lost lives and property due to Indian raids. Life and limb were not remunerated—only property—but even so, pitiably few were compensated.[54]

Gary Ebersole summarized much of the above discussion in a cogent observation in his book, *Captured by Texts*. He explained that captivity narratives have been used by scholars of the late twentieth century for their own agendas, such as in trying to prove the existence of unconscious archetypes, as cultural myths of redemptive violence, as vehicles for feminist issues, and as the results of ideological repression. They seldom used the narratives for what most of them were—personal accounts of the horrors of captivity—but rather as metamorphosed hybrids to further their own designs.[55] Rather than accepting the narratives as factual glimpses of how harsh the pioneers' existence could be, they are often twisted and agendized until nearly unrecognizable.

The controversy about how to treat the white-Indian conflicts of the past is still unresolved. Michael Tate in *The Frontier Army and the Settlement of the West*, argued that New Western historians have turned the old stereotype upside down and sponsored a flawed view of the past that is more in line with fictional films like *Soldier Blue*, *Little Big Man*, and *Dances With Wolves*. Neither image is wholly correct. A more schizophrenic assessment is seen in Patricia Limerick's *Legacy of Conquest*. On one hand, she acknowledges that modern society has interchanged the usual terms: white Americans are now the barbarians, savage and greedy, while Indians lived with ecological wisdom and saintliness. These role reversals, said Limerick, do little to illuminate history. On the other hand, she seems little inclined to better balance the equation, for she also states that past historians wrote too often from the viewpoint of righteous bearers of civilization, and hopes that these "ethnocentric predecessors can be credibly and rapidly disowned." Modern Indians, Limerick says, want history that belongs to them and makes them feel better about themselves— which, according to Arthur Schlesinger, Jr., is actually heritage, not history.

Even the courts get into the argument. In the 1980 case to determine if the whites needed to once again pay the Lakotas for the Black Hills, Justice William Rehnquist said that Congress had no right to reopen a case that had been decided long ago, and that the Court and Congress could not "rewrite history by putting all the guilt for Indian-white conflict on the whites." He said it was "unfair to judge by the light of 'revisionist' historians or the mores of another era actions that were taken under pressure of time more than a century ago." Rehnquist's plea did not persuade his colleagues.[56]

Trying to restore truth in history is an uphill battle. For so many decades white Americans have been told that they are evil, that it appears many of them have come to believe it. This great guilt that they bear not only manifests itself in contemporary self-flagellation, but it is transferred into the past. If we are so wicked today, the bad seeds had to have come from heinous ancestors. It is a fallacious and destructive mind-set. Our great-grandparents were good people, but we project our self-hatred onto them and rewrite their history with our images. Much of it stems from the several-decade bombardment by revisionist historians who, seemingly from the simple reason that they believed traditional

Turnerian frontier history was bankrupt, felt they needed to substitute it with something different. Interpreting the West through the eyes of women, Indians, Hispanics, Orientals, or any number of diverse groups is a good thing, but the stage can be shared instead of usurped. One group need not be torn down for another to rise. Giving all the groups their necessary place in the spotlight does not have to be at the expense of the American pioneers who built the country, for without them there would be no stage for the others to stand upon.

All the above discourse aside, we are left with an evident conclusion: an Indian captive in the American West was almost assured of a horrible ordeal, and for many women it was truly a fate worse than death.

Conclusion notes

[1] Tatum, *Our Red Brothers*, 145-48, 153-54; Corwin, *Comanche & Kiowa Captives*, 105-07; Methvin, *Andele*, 29-30, 93; Winfrey and Day, *Texas Indian Papers 4*, 426-28.

[2] Thrapp, *Frontier Biography 1*, 518; Sweeney, *Grijalva*, 1, 8, 11-12.

[3] Marshall, *A Cry Unheard*, 13.

[4] Halaas and Masich, *Halfbreed*, 129; Ellenbecker, *Tragedy at the Little Blue*, 23; Ann Marble Depredation Claim #892, as cited in Becher, *Massacre Along the Medicine Road*, 438.

[5] Halaas and Masich, *Halfbreed*, 378n53; Czaplewski, *Captive of the Cheyenne*, Sec. 1, 72; Nancy Morton Depredation Claim #332; Carroll, *Sand Creek Documentary History*, iii.

[6] Afton, Halaas, and Masich, *Cheyenne Dog Soldiers*, 290-91, 294, 307, 316.

[7] Stratton, *Pioneer Women*, 124-25.

[8] Stratton, *Pioneer Women*, 111, 121, 126.

[9] Myres, *Westering Women*, 38, 53-54, 59-60, 64.

[10] Myres, *Westering Women*, 61.

[11] Riley, *Women and Indians*, xiv, 94; Broome, *Dog Soldier Justice*, 141. Myres, *Westering Women*, xviii, says we can't trust pioneer captivity narratives, reminicenses, diaries, or letters! Apparently we must only trust what she says.

[12] Riley, *Women and Indians*, 157, 159, 164-65, 208-9, 215, 247, 251-52.

[13] Kammen, *Mystic Chords of Memory*, 701.

[14] Riley, *The Female Frontier*, 9-10, 44-45, 78.

[15] The latter is a historical fallacy of ethnomorphism, discussed in Fischer, *Historians' Fallacies*, 224-25.

[16] Riley, *Women and Indians*, 208-09; Castiglia, *Bound and Determined*, 90-100.

[17] Riley, *Women and Indians*, 209.

[18] Riley, *Women and Indians*, 210-14; Gelo and Zesch, "Holiday," 65.

[19] Zesch, *The Captured*, xviii, 63-64, 102, 114-15. Zesch also claims (p. 142) that settlers chasing after raiders were "virtually never successful," but pursuits by settlers or soldiers did result in a significant number of rescues, including John McSherry Jr., Juliet Watts, Rebecca and William Gilleland, Rhoda and Margaret Riggs, Hannah Akers, William Wilson, Paula Carrolton, the Bell children, Washington Wolfe, and Willie Lehmann.

[20] Cashion, *A Texas Frontier*, 12, 22, 64, 79, 281, 286-87.

[21] Anderson, *Conquest of Texas*, 5, 7-8, 12, 15, 37-38, 41, 135, 223, 361, 380n11, 420n16, 421n18, 428n8.

[22] Namias, *White Captives*, 24, 40, 81-82, 97, 99, 140, 271.

[23] Namias, *White Captives*, 24, 295n5.

[24] Namias, *White Captives*, 102, 315n39.

[25] Meyer, *History of the Santee Sioux*, 120; Oehler, *Great Sioux Uprising*, 234-36; Folwell, *History of Minnesota 2*, 392; Bryant and Murch, *Indian Massacre*, 421.

[26] Farrell, "Dakota Conflict in White Imagination," 30-34.

[27] Munkres, "Plains Indian Threat," 242-43, 263, 273.

[28] Unruh, *The Plains Across*, 184-86; Faragher, *Women and Men on the Overland*, 31-32; Riley, *Women and Indians*, 97-98; Myres, *Westering Women*, 56-57; Udall, "The 'Wild' Old West," 67.

[29] Steckmesser, *The Western Hero*, 247.

[30] Barnett, *Touched by Fire*, 182.

[31] Taylor, *Search of the Racial Frontier*, 58-62, 116; Brooks, *Captives & Cousins*, 307.

[32] Magnaghi, "The Indian Slave Trade," 1-2, 51, 68-70, 112. The situation has similarities to terrorist hostage taking in the 21st Century.

[33] Magnaghi, "The Indian Slave trade," 111, 114, 140.

[34] Brooks, *Captives & Cousins*, 6, 24-26, 37, 67, 258, 291-92, 331, 365-68.

[35] Brooks, *Captives & Cousins*, 180, 191, 249, 326, 354; Tate, "Comanche Captives," 244.

[36] Garfield, "Defense of the Kansas Frontier 1866-67," 344; Garfield, "Defense of the Kansas Frontier 1868-69," 471-72; Wooster, *U. S. Indian Policy*, 213. Garfield's count of captured women is low.

[37] *Commissioner of Indian Affairs 1865*, 472-74; *Commissioner of Indian Affairs 1862*, 397; Watts, *Depredations in New Mexico*, 65; *Commissioner of Indian Affairs 1862*, 110, 383; *Commissioner of Indian Affairs 1867*, 196; *Commissioner of Indian Affairs 1870*, 115; Bender, *March of Empire*, 263n15; Thrapp, *Conquest of Apacheria*, 366.

[38] Winfrey and Day, *Texas Indian Papers 4*, 235-36, 314, 330, 390, 438; Marshall, *A Cry Unheard*, 18; Brooks, *Captives & Cousins*, 354.

[39] Huckabay, *Jack County*, 217; Fehrenbach, *Lone Star*, 533.

[40] Dodge, *The Plains of the Great West and Their Inhabitants*, 305-08; Dodge, *Our Wild Indians*, 530; *Commissioner of Indian Affairs 1866*, 281; Rister, *Border Captives*, viii; Wallace and Hoebel, *Lords of the South Plains*, 240; Fehrenbach, *Comanches*, 287.

[41] Tate, "Comanche Captives," 237. Tate also states that Comanches condemned rape, and "pledged abstinence while on the raiding trail." His contention is not based on reality. Perplexingly, he cites Wallace and Hoebel, who affirmed that Comanches did rape captives.

[42] Brooks, *Captives & Cousins*, 190, 289-90.

[43] Stratton, *Oatman*, xii, 231, 286; Hunter, "Southwestern Captivity Narratives," 196.

[44] The fact that many returning ex-captives were treated as pariahs and may have been better off dead than "red," has been a recurrent western movie theme in films such as *The Unforgiven* (1960), *Comanche Station* (1960), *Two Rode Together* (1961), and epitomized in John Ford's *The Searchers* (1956). See Slotkin, *Gunfighter Nation*, 462-72.

[45] Barnett, *Touched by Fire*, 169-71.

[46] Kelly, *My Captivity*, 42-43.

[47] Derounian-Stodola and Levernier, *Indian Captivity Narrative*, 2-6; Drimmer, *Captured by Indians*, 12-13; Stratton, *Oatman*, xii.

[48] Derounian-Stodola and Levernier, *Indian Captivity Narrative*, 5-6; Riley, *Women and Indians*, 210.

[49] Heard, *White Into Red*, 1, 24, 48, 116, 135.

[50] The standard treatment of the episode is in Stan Hoig's, *The Sand Creek Massacre*, while a different viewpoint is found in Greg Michno's, *Battle at Sand Creek*.

[51] "The Chivington Massacre," 29.

[52] Michno, *Encyclopedia of Indian Wars*, 355.

[53] Becher, *Massacre Along the Medicine Road*, 419.

[54] Skogen, *Depredation Claims*, 32, 120, 151-52, 195, 212

[55] Ebersole, *Captured by Texts*, 264, 270.

[56] Tate, *Frontier Army*, viv-xv; Limerick, *Legacy of Conquest*, 215, 219-20; Worster, *Under Western Skies*, 132.

APPENDIX

TABLE 1. Captivity Lengths 1830-1889

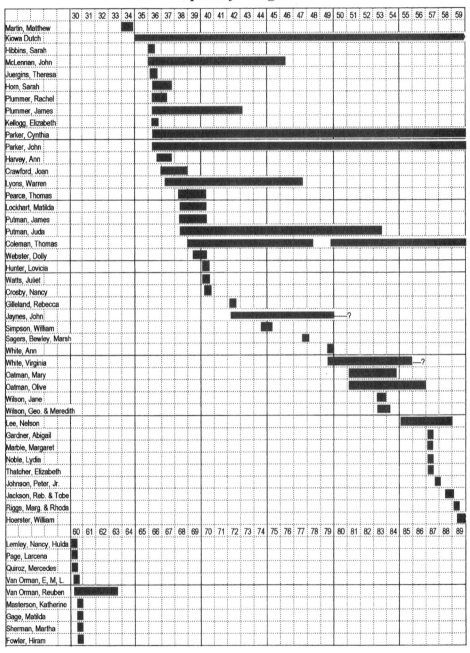

Captivity Lengths 1830-1889

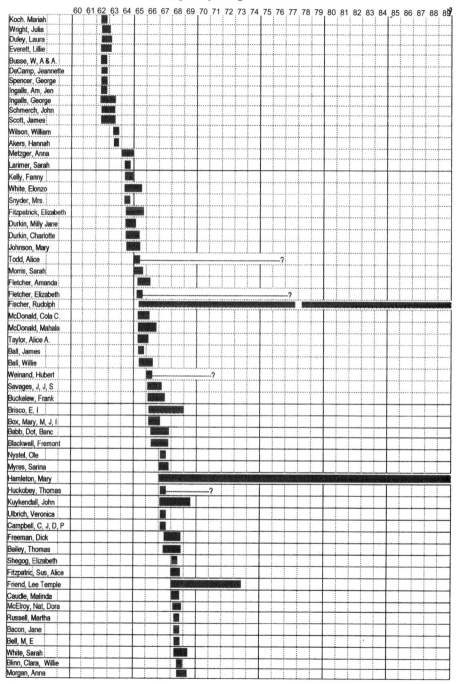

Captivity Lengths 1830-1889

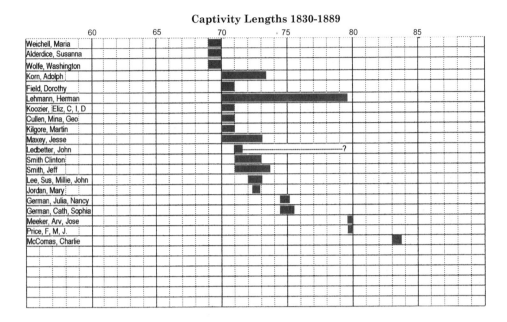

APPENDIX 1

(People not listed in a title in *Italics*)

Alderdice, Susanna 5-30-69
Alderdice, Alice 5-30-69
Akers, Hannah 7-25-63
Anderson, Mary 8-18-62
Asher, Ambrose 8-7-64
Babb, Bianca 9-14-66
Babb, Theodore A. 9-14-66
Bacon, Jane 8-12-68
Bailey, Thomas 9-67
Ball, James 9-20-65
Ball, William 9-20-65
Bell, Esther 8-12-68
Bell, Margaret 8-12-68
Benson, James 1865
Bewley, Crockett 11-29-47
Bewley, Esther 11-29-47
Blackwell, Fremont 10-66
Blair, James 2-28-64
Blinn, Clara 10-9-68
Blinn, Willie 10-9-68
Boyeau, Mary 8-62
Box, Mary 8-15-66
Box, Margaret 8-15-66
Box, Ida 8-15-66
Box, Laura 8-15-66
Box, Josephine 8-15-66
Bridger, Mary Ann 11-29-47
Brisco, Eliza 6-66
Brisco, Isaac 6-66
Brown, Elizabeth J. 8-63
Brown, Matilda 1836
Buckelew, Francis M. 3-11-66
Buenavides, Juan
Buenavides, Jesus Maria
Busse, Wilhelmina 8-18-62
Busse, Amelia 8-18-62
Busse, August 8-18-62
Campbell, Christiana 7-24-67
Campbell, Daniel 7-24-67
Campbell, Jessie 7-24-67
Campbell, Peter 7-24-67
Canfield, Sally Ann 11-29-47
Carrolton, Paula 1-5-68
Carrothers, Elizabeth 8-18-62

Carrothers, Helen Mar Paddock 8-18-62
Carrothers, Tommy 8-18-62
Carrothers, daughter
Carter, Elijah 10-13-64
Caudle, Malinda 2-5-68
Chandler, Tomassa 1850
Coleman, Thomas 2-18-39
Cortez, David M. 11-29-47
Cox, Tommy 7-41
Crawford, Jane Goacher. 2-37
Crawford, daughter
Crawford, boy (Jane brother)
Crawford, boy (Jane brother)
Crosby, Nancy 8-7-40
Crosby, child
Cullen, George 7-10-70
Cullen, Mina 7-10-70
Davis, Bud 1870
De Camp, Jannette 8-18-62
De Camp, Willie 8-18-62
De Camp, son
De Camp, son
Dhieriia, Estaban
Dhieriia, Manuel
Diaz, Martina
Duley, Laura 8-20-62
Duley, Emma 8-20-62
Duley, child 8-20-62
Durkin, Charlotte 10-13-64
Durkin, Milly Jane 10-13-64
Earle, Amanda Macomber 8-18-62
Earle, Julia 8-18-62
Earle, daughter
Eastlick, Lavina 8-20-62
Eastlick, John 8-20-62
Eastlick, Merton 8-20-62
Eubank, Lucinda 8-7-64
Eubank, Isabelle 8-7-64
Eubank, Willie Jr. 8-7-64
Everett, Lillie 8-20-62
Ewbanks, Thomas 6-66
Field, Dorothy 2-27-70
Fischer, Rudolph 7-29-65
Fitzpatrick, Elizabeth Ann Carter 10-13-64
Fitzpatrick, Mrs. 1-6-68
Fitzpatrick, Alice 1-6-68

Fitzpatrick, Susan 1-6-68
Fitzpatrick, son
Fletcher, Amanda 7-31-65
Fletcher, Elizabeth 7-31-65
Foster, Miss 8-12-68
Fowler, Hiram 11-26-60
Free, Mickey 1-61
Freeman, Richard 9-67
Friend, Lee Temple 2-5-68
Gage, Matilda 11-26-60
Gardner, Abigail 3-8-57
Gebhard, Frank 9-67
German, Catherine 9-11-74
German, Julia 9-11-74
German, Nancy 9-11-74
German, Sophia 9-11-74
Gilleland, Rebecca 4-42
Gilleland, William 4-42
Gluth, August 8-18-62
Gonzales, Levando
Gonzales, Prescilliaro
Hall, Rachel E. 11-29-47
Hamleton, Gus 4-67
Hamleton, Mary 4-67
Hardy, Jack 2-73
Harris, Mrs. 4-4-36
Harris, daughter
Harris, Caroline 8-35
Hart, son of Timothy 3-50
Harvey, Ann 11-36
Hays, Rebecca 11-29-47
Hibbins, Sarah Creath 2-36,
Hibbins, son
Hobbs, Jim 1836
Hoerster, William 7-19-59
Holt, Alexander 9-67
Horn, Sarah 4-4-36
Horn, John
Horn, Joseph
Houston, John Charles Fremont
Huckobey, Thomas 7-3-67
Hunter, Marion Robertson 8-18-62
Hunter, Lovicia 4-40
Ingalls, Amanda 8-19-62
Ingalls, George 8-19-62
Ingalls, Jennie 8-19-62
Ireland, Ellen 8-20-62
Ireland, Rosa 8-20-62
Jackson, Rebecca 10-21-58
Jackson, Tobe 10-21-58
Jaynes, John 7-10-42
Johnson, Mary 10-13-64
Johnson, son
Johnson, daughter

Johnson, Peter 12-31-57
Jordan, Mary Smith 8-19-72
Juergens, Mary Theresa 4-1-36
Juergens, son
Juergens, son
Kellogg, Elizabeth D. 5-19-36
Kelly, Fanny 7-12-64
Kelly, Mary 7-12-64
Kilgore, Martin B. 7-9-70
Killough, Miss 10-38
Kimball, Harriet 11-29-47
Kimball, Susan S. 11-29-47
Kiowa Dutch 7-35
Kitzmann, Ludwig 8-18-62
Koch, Mariah Christina 8-20-62
Koozier, Elizabeth 7-1-70
Koozier, Charles 7-10-70
Koozier, Daniel 7-10-70
Koozier, Ida 7-10-70
Korn, Adolph 1-1-70
Krause, Dorothea 8-18-62
Krieger, Henrietta 8-18-62
Krieger, Justina 8-18-62
Kuykendall, John 7-11-67
Landin, Bernave 9-67
Larimer, Sarah 7-12-64
Larimer, Frank 7-12-64
Ledbetter, John 1-71
Lee, Nelson 4-3-55
Lee, John 6-9-72
Lee, Millie 6-9-72
Lee, Susanna 6-9-72
Lehmann, Herman 5-16-70
Lemley, Hulda 2-7-60
Lemley, Liddie 2-7-60
Lemley, Nancy 2-7-60
Lockhart, Matilda 10-38
Luster, Sarah 9-14-66
Lyons, Warren 7-37
McKinn, James 10-85
McComas, Charles 3-28-83
McDonald, Cola Caroline Taylor 8-8-65
McDonald, Mahala 8-8-65
McDonald, Rebecca J. 8-8-65
McElroy, Dora 5-68
McElroy, Ellen 5-68
McElroy, Nathaniel 5-68
McLennan, John 3-36
McSherry, John, Jr. 2-36
Manson, John 11-29-47
Manson, Stephen 11-29-47
Marble, Daniel 8-8-64
Marble, Margaret 3-13-57
Marsh, Mary E. 11-29-47

Martin, Matthew W. 5-15-34
Martinez, Jose Andres 10-6-66
Masterson, Jane 11-26-60
Masterson, Katherine 11-26-60
Maxey, John 9-5-70
Maxey, Rhoda 9-5-70
Meek, Helen Mar 11-29-47
Meeker, Arvilla 9-29-79
Meeker, Josephine 9-29-79
Menasco, Lizzie 1-5-68
Menasco, May 1-5-68
Metzger, Anna 2-64
Morgan, Anna Brewster 10-13-68
Morris, Sarah 1-14-65
Morris, Joseph 1-14-65
Morris, Charlie 1-14-65
Morton, Nancy 8-8-64
Myres, Sarina 4-67
Noble, Lydia 3-9-57
Nystel, Ole 3-20-67
Oatman, Mary Ann 3-19-51
Oatman, Olive 3-19-51
Page, Larcena Pennington 3-16-60
Parker, Cynthia 5-19-36
Parker, John R. 5-19-36
Pearce, Thomas 5-38
Powers, boy 1840
Plummer, Clarissa 8-35
Plummer, Rachel Pratt 5-19-36
Plummer, James Pratt 5-19-36
Price, Flora Ellen 9-29-79
Price, Johnny 9-29-79
Price, May 9-29-79
Putman, Elizabeth 10-38
Putman, James 10-38
Putman, Juda 10-38
Putman, Rhoda 10-38
Quiroz, Mercedes 3-16-60
Riggs, Margaret 3-16-59
Riggs, Rhoda 3-16-59
Robertson, Mrs. Andrew 8-18-62
Robertson, Frank 8-18-62
Roderique, Videl
Roper, Laura 8-7-64
Ross, Lizzie 1855
Russell, Martha 8-68
Sager, Catherine 11-29-47
" Elizabeth
" Hannah Louise
" Henrietta Naomi
" Matilda Jane
Sales, Amos 11-29-47
Saunders, Mary 11-29-47
Savage, James 3-2-66

Savage, Jennie B. 3-2-66
Savage, Samuel 3-2-66
Schman, Fred 4-16-79
Schmerch, John 8-21-62
Schmidt, sons of Henry M. 2-71
Schneider, son of Johanes 12-51
Schwandner, Albert 11-64
Schwandt, Mary 8-18-62
Scott, Henry 1861
Scott, James 8-21-62
Sera, Marcela 4-20-72
Shaw, Mrs. 8-12-68
Shegog, Elizabeth 1-5-68
Shegog, child
Sherman, Martha 11-27-60
Simpson, Jane 11-3-44
Simpson, William 11-3-44
Smith, Joseph 11-29-47
Smith, Hannah 11-29-47
" Mary
Smith, Clinton 2-26-71
Smith, Jefferson 2-26-71
Smith, son of James 1-41
Snyder, Mrs. 8-14-64
Spalding, Eliza 11-29-47
Spencer, George 8-18-62
Stringfield, Adolphus 3-16-71
Stringfield, Thomas 3-16-71
Sullivan, Thomas 10-66
Tavares, Rosalie
Taylor, Alice Almeda 8-8-65
Taylor, Dorcas A. 8-8-65
Taylor, James 8-8-65
Terry, Martha 2-73
Thatcher, Elizabeth 3-9-57
Thomas, Eve 1865
Thomas, Sarah 1865
Todd, Alice 1-7-65
Trevino, Seferino
Ulbrich, Peter 7-24-67
Ulbrich, Veronica 7-24-67
Urban, Mrs. 8-18-62
Valla, Manuel
Van Ornum, Eliza 10-9-60
Van Ornum, Lucinda 10-9-60
Van Ornum, Minerva 10-9-60
Van Ornum, Reuben 10-9-60
Wakefield, Sarah 8-18-62
Wakefield, James O. 8-18-62
Wakefield, Lucy E. 8-18-62
Watts, Juliet 8-9-40
Webster, Dolly 10-1-39
Webster, Booker 10-1-39
Webster, Patsy 10-1-39

Weichel, Maria 5-30-69
Weinand, Herbert 1-27-66
White, Ann 10-24-49
White, Virginia 10-24-49
White, Elonzo 7-25-64
White, Sarah 8-13-68
White, Urania Frazer 8-18-62
White, Julia
White, Frank
Whitlock, William 12-70
Williams, Elizabeth 10-38
Williams, Mattie 8-18-62
Williams, daughter of Mr. 11-54
Wilson, Jane 9-25-53
Wilson, George 9-25-53
Wilson, Meredith 9-25-53
Wilson, William 7-25-63
Wolfe, Washington 6-22-69
Wood, Lucinda 2-7-60
Worman, Mrs. 9-59
Wright, Julia 8-20-62
Wright, Dora 8-20-62
Wright, John 8-20-62
Wright, Mary 2-22-71

Texas Captives Listed on Map B.

TEXAS CAPTIVES

1. Matthew Wright Martin 5-15-34
2. Kiowa Dutch 7-35
3. Sarah Creath Hibbins, John McSherry Jr. 2-36
4. John McLennan 3-36
5. Mary Hennecke Juergens 4-1-36
6. Sarah Horn, Mrs. Harris 4-4-36
7. Rachel Plummer, James Plummer, Elizabeth Kellogg, Cynthia Parker, John Parker 5-19-36
8. Ann Harvey 11-36
9. Jane Goacher Crawford 2-37
10. Warren Lyons 7-37
11. Thomas Pearce 5-38
12. Matilda Lockhart, James Putman, Rhoda Putman, Elizabeth Putman, Juda Putman 10-38
13. Thomas Coleman 2-18-39
14. Dolly Webster, Booker Webster, Patsy Webster 10-1-39
15. Lovicia Hunter 4-40
16. Nancy Crosby 8-7-40
17. Juliet Watts 8-9-40
18. Rebecca Gilleland, William Gilleland 4-42
19. John Jaynes 7-10-42

20. Jane Simpson, William Simpson 11-3-44
21. Jane Wilson, George Wilson, Meredith Wilson 9-25-53
22. Nelson Lee 4-3-55
23. Peter Johnson 12-31-57
24. Rebecca Jackson, Tobe Jackson 10-21-58
25. Rhoda Riggs, Margaret Riggs 3-16-59
26. William Hoerster 7-19-59
27. Hulda Lemley, Nancy Lemley 2-7-60
28. Katherine Masterson, Matilda Gage, Hiram Fowler 11-26-60
29. Martha Sherman 11-27-60
30. William Wilson, Hannah Akers 7-25-63
31. Anna Metzger 2-64
32. Elonzo White 7-25-64
33. Elizabeth Fitzpatrick, Charlotte Durkin, Milly Jane Durkin, Mary Johnson 10-13-64
34. Alice Todd 1-7-65
35. Rudolph Fischer 7-29-65
36. Cola Caroline McDonald, Mahala McDonald, Rebecca McDonald, Alice Taylor, James Taylor, Dorcas Taylor 8-8-65
37. James Ball, William Ball 9-20-65
38. Herbert Weinand 1-27-66
39. James Savage, Samuel Savage, Jennie Savage 3-2-66
40. Frank Buckelew 3-11-66
41. Eliza Brisco, Isaac Brisco 6-66
42. Mary Box, Margaret Box, Josephine Box, Ida Box, Laura Box 8-15-66
43. Theodore Babb, Bianca Babb, Sarah Luster 9-14-66
44. Fremont Blackwell, Thomas Sullivan 10-66
45. Ole Nystel 3-20-67
46. Mary Hamleton, Sarina Myres, Gus Myres 4-67
47. Thomas Huckobey 7-3-67
48. John Kuykendall 7-11-67
49. Richard Freeman, Thomas Bailey 9-67
50. Elizabeth Shegog, Paula Carrolton, Lizzie Menasco, May Menasco, Mrs. Fitzpatrick, Susan Fitzpatrick, Alice Fitzpatrick 1-5 and 1-6-68

51. Lee Temple Friend, Malinda
    Caudle 2-5-68
52. Nathaniel McElroy, Dora McElroy,
    Ellen McElroy 5-68
53. Martha Russell 8-68
54. Washington Wolfe 6-22-69
55. Adolph Korn 1-1-70
56. Dorothy Field 2-27-70
57. Herman Lehmann, Willie
    Lehmann 5-16-70
58. Martin Kilgore, Elizabeth Koozier,
    Charles Koozier, Ida Koozier,
    Daniel Koozier, Mina Cullen,
    George Cullen 7-9 and
    7-10-70
59. John Maxey, Rhoda Maxey 9-5-70
60. John Ledbetter 1-71
61. Clinton Smith, Jefferson Smith
    2-26-71
62. Susanna Lee, Millie Lee, John Lee
    6-9-72

APPENDIX 2

CAPTIVES HELD AT WHITMAN MISSION.

Bewley, Crockett (killed a few days after capture)
Bewley, Esther Lorinda
Bridger, Mary Ann (Jim Bridger's daughter)
Canfield, Sally Ann
" Albert (3)
" Clarissa (7)
" Ellen (16)
" Oscar (9)
" Sylvia (5)
Cortez, David M. (released)
Hall, Rachel Eliza
" Ann E. (6)
" Gertrude J. (10)
" Mary C. (8)
" Rebecca (1)
Hays, Rebecca
" Henry C. (4)
" child
Kimball, Harriet
" Byron E. (8)
" Mina A. (1)
" Nathan M. (13)
" Sarah S. (6)
" Susan M. (16)
Manson, John (16) (released)
Manson, Stephen (17) (released)
Marsh, Mary E. (11)
Meek, Helen Mar (10) (daughter of Joe Meek, died of measles)
Sager, Catherine (13)
" Elizabeth (10)
" Hannah Louise (6) (died of measles)
" Henrietta Naomi (4)
" Matilda Jane (8)
Sales, Amos
Saunders, Mary
" Alfred W. (6)
" Helen M. (14)
" Mary A. (2)
" Nancy J. (4)
" Phebe (10)
Smith, Joseph
Smith, Hannah
" Charles (11)
" Edwin (13)
" Mary (15)
" Mortimer (4)
" Nelson (6)

Spalding, Eliza (Henry Spalding's daughter)
Young, Elam
Young, Irene
Young, Daniel (21)
Young, John Quincy Adams (19)

APPENDIX 3
ANNOTATED COMPILATION OF MARION P. SATTERLEE'S LIST OF WHITE CAPTIVES FREED AT CAMP RELEASE, MINNESOTA, SEPTEMBER 26, 1862.

1. Adams, Mrs. Hattie (John), captured near Hutchinson.
2. Brown, Mrs. Angus, captured with the Joseph R. Brown family.
3. Busse, Wilhelmina (7), captured at Middle Creek.
4. Busse, August (14).
5. Busse, Amelia (4).
6. Burns, Mrs. Sarah, captured at Lower Agency.
7. Burns, child of Sarah.
8. "
9. "
10. Butler, M. A.
11. Buhrman, Tobet (18), captured at Lower Agency.
12. Carrothers, Mrs. Elizabeth (David).
13. Carrothers, infant of Mrs. David Carrothers.
14. Clausen (Classen), Mrs. Martha (Frederick), captured near Beaver Creek.
15. Clausen, infant daughter of Martha.
16. "
17. Cardenelle (Cardinal), Mrs. Margaret, captured near Beaver Creek.
18. Cardenelle, child of Margaret.
19. Consalle, Nancy (8), captured at Lower Agency.
20. Consalle, Philomena (4), sister of Nancy.
21. Earle, Amanda M. (Jonathan), captured at Beaver Creek.
22. Earle, Julia (14), daughter of Amanda.
23. Earle, Elmira (7), daughter of Amanda.
24. Eisenreich (Isenridge), Mrs. Balthasar, captured at Beaver creek.
25. Eisenreich, Peter.
26. Eisenreich, Sophie.
27. Eisenreich, Mary.
28. Eisenreich, Joseph.
29. Frass (Frace), Mrs. Justina (August), captured at Sacred Heart Creek.
30. Frass, child of Justina.
31. "
32. Gluth, August (14).
33. Huggins, Mrs. Sophia J. (Amos W.), captured at Lac qui Parle.
34. Huggins, Charles.
35. Huggins, Lettie.
36. Inefeldt (Eindenfield), Mrs. Wilhelmina (William), captured in Beaver Township.
37. Inefeldt, infant of Wilhelmina.
38. Ingalls, Amanda (14), daughter of Jedidiah Ingalls, captured with the Brown family.
39. Ingalls, Jennie (12), sister of Amanda.
40. Juni (Eune), Benedict, Jr. (14), captured near Lower Agency.
41. Kitzmann, Ludwig (14), son of Paul Kitzmann, captured at Sacred Heart

Creek.
42. Krieger, Henrietta (5), daughter of Justina Krieger.
43. Koch, Mrs. Mariah C. (Andreas), captured at Lake Shetek.
44. Krause, Mrs. Dorothea, captured at Sacred Heart Creek.
45. Krause, child of Dorothea.
46.   "
47. Krause, Pauline, sister of Dorothea.
48. Laramie, Mrs. Mary, captured at Sacred Heart Creek.
49. Laramie, Louisa (18).
50. Laramie, Edward (15).
51. Lammers, Mrs. Sophia (William), captured at Sacred Heart Creek.
52. Lammers, Fred (7), child of Sophia.
53. Lammers, Charles, infant of Sophia.
54. Lenz, Augusta, daughter of Ernest Lenz, captured at Middle Creek.
55. Launt, Mrs. Susan, captured at Lower Agency.
56. Launt, child of Susan.
57. La Blaugh, Mrs. Antoine, captured at Lower Agency.
58. La Blaugh, child of above.
59.   "
60. Lange, Mrs. Amelia.
61. Lange, child of Amelia.
62.   "
63. La Belle, Louis, captured near Upper Agency.
64. McLane, Mrs. Rosalie, captured at Upper agency.
65. McLane, child of Rosalie.
66.   "
67. Nicholls, Henrietta (12).
68. Patterson, Mrs. Mary, captured near Madelia.
69. Patterson, Antoine, child of Mary.
70. Patterson, Peter, child of Mary.
71. Piquar, Elizabeth, daughter of Eusebius Piquar, captured at Birch Coulee.
72. Record, Elizabeth (3), niece of Mrs. Cardenelle.
73. Rosyuse, Mrs., captured at Upper Agency.
74. Renville, Mrs. John, wife of mixed blood.
75. Rousseau, Peter, trader, captured near Upper Agency.
76. Rouillard, Peter, trader, captured near Upper Agency.
77. Schmidt, Minnie (4), captured at Middle Creek.
78. Schwandt, Mary (14), captured near Ft. Ridgely.
79. Spencer, George (30), captured at Lower Agency.
80. Thompson, George (18), captured at Lower Agency.
81. Urban, Mrs. John, captured at Sacred Heart Creek.
82. Urban, Ernestine.
83. Urban, Rose.
84. Urban, Louise.
85. Urban, Albert.
86. Valiant, Mrs. Harriet, captured at Lower Agency.
87. Valiant, child of Harriet.
88.   "
89. Vanasse, Mrs. Matilda, captured near Ft. Ridgely.
90. Vanasse, child of Matilda.
91.   "
92. Williams, Mattie, captured near Ft. Ridgely with Mary Schwandt.
93. Woodbury, Mrs. Mary, captured at Lower Agency.
94. Woodbury, child of Mary.

492

95.   "
96.   "
97.   "
98. Wright, John (3), son of Julia Wright, captured at Lake Shetek.
99. Wakefield, Mrs. Sarah (John), captured near Redwood River.
100. Wakefield, James (4), child of Sarah.
101. Wakefield, Lucy (Nellie) (2), child of Sarah.
102. White, Urania, S. (Nathan), captured at Beaver Creek.
103. White, Julia (14), child of Urania.
104. White, Frank, infant son of Urania.
105. Wohler, Mrs. Frances (Leopold), captured at the Samuel Brown home.
106. Wilson, Eunice (18), captured at Lower Agency.
107. Yess, Henrietta (3), daughter of Michael Yess, captured at Sacred Heart Creek.

APPENDIX 4

SOME AMERICAN CAPTIVES RESCUED THROUGH THE EFFORTS OF INDIAN AGENTS.

Jesse Leavenworth (15): Cola Caroline Taylor McDonald, Rebecca Jane McDonald, Mahala Louisa McDonald, Alice Almeda Taylor, James Taylor, James Ball, William Ball, James Benson, Elizabeth Carter Sprague Fitzpatrick, Fremont Blackwell, Ole Nystel, John Kuykendall, Alexander Holt, Susan Fitzpatrick, Alice Fitzpatrick.

Lawrie Tatum (12): Lee Temple Friend, Elizabeth Koozier, Charles Koozier, Ida Koozier, Daniel Koozier, Mina Cullen, George Cullen, Martin Kilgore, John Lee, Clinton Smith, Jefferson Smith, John Maxey, Adolph Korn.

Edward Wynkoop (5): Laura Roper, Danny Marble, Isabelle Eubank, Ambrose Asher, Malinda Caudle.

S. T. Walkley (5): Richard Freeman, Thomas Bailey, Nathaniel McElroy, Dora McElroy, Ellen McElroy.

APPENDIX 5

Texans often mentioned the full moon or "Comanche Moon" as a dangerous time when Indian raids on settlements seemed to occur more frequently. Below are names of captives taken on a full moon or within three days before or after the full moon. "0" is full moon, and - 1, 2, 3, or + 1, 2, 3, are the number of days before or after the full moon. In the below list, the 17 captures that occurred within that seven-day full moon span represent 27% of the 62 captivities referenced on the Texas Capture Location Map. The seven-day window of capture opportunity surrounding the full moon is not significantly different from any other random week in any given month, where chance of capture would be about 25%. At least in terms of Indian raiding where captives were taken, "Comanche Moon" week was no more dangerous than any other week of the month.

0   Mary Juergens
+1 Peter Johnson
-1 Rebecca and Tobe Jackson
-2 Rhoda and Margaret Riggs
0   Hulda and Nancy Lemley
-2 Katherine Masterson, Martha Gage, Hiram Fowler
-1 Martha Sherman
-2 Elizabeth Fitzpatrick, Durkins, Johnsons
+1 McDonalds, Taylors
-3 Herbert Weinand
+1 Savages
0   Ole Nystel
-3 Susan and Alice Fitzpatrick
-3 Lee Temple Friend and Malinda Caudle
-2 Washington Wolfe
+1 Herman and Willie Lehmann
-3 Kilgore, Kooziers, and Cullens

BIBLIOGRAPHY

Abney, A. H. *Life and Adventures of L. D. Lafferty*. New York: H. S. Goodspeed & Co., nd. Reprint.

Wilcomb E. Washburn, ed. *The Garland Library of Narratives of North American Indian Captivities* Vol. 89. Washington, D.C.: Smithsonian Institution, 1976.

Adjutant General's Office. *Chronological List of Actions &c., with the Indians from January 15, 1837 to January, 1891*. Washington: GPO, 1891.

Anderson, Gary Clayton. *The Conquest of Texas Ethnic Cleansing in the Promised Land, 1820-1875*. Norman, Oklahoma: University of Oklahoma Press, 2005.

_____. *Little Crow Spokesman for the Sioux*. St. Paul, Minnesota: Minnesota Historical Society Press, 1986.

Anderson, Gary C. and Alan R. Woolworth, eds. *Through Dakota Eyes: Narrative Accounts of the Minnesota Indian War of 1862*. St. Paul, Minnesota: Minnesota Historical Society Press, 1988.

Ashton, Sharron Standifer. *Indians and Intruders Vol 3*. Norman, Oklahoma: Ashton Books, 1998.

Athearn, Robert G. *William Tecumseh Sherman and the Settlement of the West*. Foreword by William M. Ferraro and Thomas J. Murphy. Norman, Oklahoma: University of Oklahoma Press, 1995.

Austerman, Wayne R. *Sharps Rifles and Spanish Mules: The San Antonio-El Paso Mail, 1851-1881*. College Station, Texas: Texas A&M University Press, 1985.

Babb, Bianca (Mrs. J. D. Bell). "A True Story of My Captivity and Life With the Indians." TMs. Decatur, Texas: Wise County Heritage Museum, nd.

Babb, Bianca. Untitled Manuscript. Decatur, Texas: Wise County Heritage Museum, nd.

Babb, T. A. *In the Bosom of the Comanches*. Amarillo, Tezas: T. A. Babb, 1912. Reprint, Azle, Texas: Bois d'Arc Press, 1990.

Ball, Eve, with Nora Henn and Lynda A. Sanchez. *Indeh An Apache Odyssey*. Foreword by Dan L. Thrapp. Norman, Oklahoma: University of Oklahoma Press, 1988.

Bancroft, Hubert Howe. *The Works of Hubert Howe Bancroft Volume XXX History of Oregon Vol. II 1848-1883*. San Francisco, California: The History Company, 1883.

Banta, S. E. *Buckelew the Indian Captive*. Mason, Texas: Mason Herald, 1911. Reprint, Washburn, Wilcomb E., ed. *Garland Library of Narratives of North American Indian Captivities* Vol. 107. 1977.

Barnett, Louise. *Touched by Fire The Life, Death, and Mythic afterlife of George Armstrong Custer*. New York: Henry Holt & Company, 1996.

Barnitz, Albert and Jennie. Robery M. Utley, ed. *Life in Custer's Cavalry: The Letters of Albert and Jennie Barnitz*. Lincoln, Nebraska: University of Nebraska Press, 1977.

Barry, Louise. *The Beginning of the West: Annals of the Kansas Gateway to the American West 1540-1854*. Topeka, Kansas: Kansas State Historical Society, 1972.

Battey, Thomas C. *The Life and Adventures of a Quaker Among the Indians.* 1875. Reprint, Williamstown, Mississippi: Corner House, 1972.

Becher, Ronald. *Massacre Along the Medicine Road: A Social History of the Indian War of 1864 in Nebraska Territory.* Caldwell, Idaho: Caxton Press, 1999.

Bender, Averam B. *The March of Empire Frontier Defense in the Southwest 1848-1860.* New York: Greenwood Press, 1968.

Bennett, James A. Brooks, Clinton E. and Frank D. Reeve, eds. *Forts & Forays A Dragoon in New Mexico, 1850-1856.* Foreword by Jerry Thompson. Albuquerque, New Mexico: University of New Mexico Press, 1996.

Bernhardt, C. *Indian Raids in Lincoln County, Kansas, 1864 and 1869.* Lincoln, Kansas: The Lincoln Sentinel Print, 1909.

Berthrong, Donald J. *The Southern Cheyennes.* Norman, Oklahoma: University of Oklahoma Press, 1963.

Bettelyoun, Susan Bordeaux. *With My Own Eyes: A Lakota Woman Tells Her People's History.* Lincoln, Nebraska; University of Nebraska Press, 1999.

Betzinez, Jason, with Wilbur Sturtevant Nye. *I Fought With Geronimo.* Harrisburg, Pennsylvania: Stackpole, 1959, Reprint, Lincoln, Nebraska: University of Nebraska Press, 1987.

Bourke, John G. *On the Border With Crook.* Lincoln, Nebraska: University of Nebraska Press, 1971.

Bradley, Lieutenant James H. *The March of the Montana Column A Prelude to the Custer Disaster.* Edited by Edgar I. Stewart. Foreword by Paul L. Hedren. Norman, Oklahoma: University of Oklahoma Press, 1991.

Brill, Charles J. *Custer, Black Kettle, and the Fight on the Washita.* Foreword by Mark L. Gardner. Norman, Oklahoma: University of Oklahoma Press, 2002.

Brooks, James F. *Captives & Cousins: Slavery, Kinship, and Community in the Southwest Borderlands.* Chapel Hill, North Carolina: University of North Carolina Press, 2002.

Broome, Jeff. *Dog Soldier Justice: The Ordeal of Susanna Alderdice in the Kansas Indian War.* Lincoln, Kansas: Lincoln County Historical Society, 2003.

Broome, Jeff. "Libbie Custer's Encounter with Tom Alderdice. . .the Rest of the Story." In *Custer and His Times, Book Four*, ed. John Hart, 63-93. LaGrange Park, Illinois: Little Bighorn Associates, 2002.

Brown, John Henry. *Indian Wars and Pioneers of Texas.* Austin, Texas: L. E. Daniell, 1880. Reprint, Greenville, South Carolina: Southern Historical Press, 1978.

Bryant, Charles S., and Abel B. Murch. *A History of the Great Massacre by the Sioux Indians in Minnesota.* Cincinnati, Ohio: Rickey & Carroll, Publishers, 1864. Reprint. Scituate, Massachusetts: Digital Scanning, Inc., 2001.

"The Burr Oak Tragedy." *Field & Farm.* Denver, Colorado: June 17, 1911.

Campbell, John R. "An Indian Raid of 1867." In *Collections of the Nebraska State Historical Society* Vol. XVII, ed. Albert Watkins, 259-62. Lincoln, Nebraska: Nebraska State Historical Society, 1913.

Carley, Kenneth. *The Dakota War of 1862: Minnesota's Other Civil War.* St. Paul, Minnesota: Minnesota Historical Society, 1976.

Cashion, Ty. *A Texas Frontier The Clear Fork Country and Fort Griffin, 1849-1887.* Norman, Oklahoma: University of Oklahoma Press, 1996.

Castiglia, Christopher. *Bound and Determined.* Chicago, Illinois: University of Chicago Press, 1996.

Cates, Cliff D. *Pioneer History of Wise County From Red Men to Railroads—Twenty Years of Intrepid History*. Decatur, Texas: Wise County Old Settlers' Association, 1907. Reprint, Decatur, Texas: Wise County Historical Commission, 1975.

Clodfelter, Michael. *The Dakota War: The United States Army Versus the Sioux, 1862-1865*. Jefferson, North Carolina: McFarland & Company, Inc., 1998.

Colton, Ray C. *The Civil War in the Western Territories: Arizona, Colorado, New Mexico, and Utah*. Norman, Oklahoma: University of Oklahoma Press, 1959.

Corwin, Hugh D. *Comanche & Kiowa Captives in Oklahoma & Texas*. Lawton, Oklahoma: By the Author, 1959.

Cox, J. C. "The Capture and Rescue of Lon White." *Frontier Times* 6, no.2 (November 1928): 59-61.

Crawford, Samuel J. *Kansas in the Sixties*. Ottawa, Kansas: Kansas Heritage Press, 1994.

Crook, George, Martin F. Schmidt, ed. *General George Crook His Autobiography*. Norman, Oklahoma: University of Oklahoma Press, 1986.

Custer, Elizabeth B. *Following the Guidon*. New York: Harper & Brothers, 1890. Reprint. Introduction by Shirley A. Leckie. Lincoln, Nebraska: University of Nebraska Press, 1994.

Custer, George Armstrong. *My Life on the Plains*. Introduction by Edgar I. Stewart. Norman, Oklahoma: University of Oklahoma Press, 1962.

Czaplewski, Russ. *Captive of the Cheyenne: The Story of Nancy Jane Morton and the Plum Creek Massacre*. Lexington, Nebraska: Dawson County Historical Society, 1993.

Dary, David. *The Santa Fe Trail: Its History, Legends, and Lore*. New York: Alfred A. Knoph, 2000.

Decker, Peter R. *"The Utes Must Go!" American Expansion and the Removal of a People*. Foreword by Ben Nighthorse Campbell. Golden, Colorado: Fulcrum Publishing, 2004.

Derounian-Stodola, Kathryn Zabelle, and James Arthur Levernier. *The Indian Captivity Narrative, 1550-1900*. New York: Twayne Publishers, 1993.

DeShields, James T. *Border Wars of Texas*. 1912. Reprint, Austin, Texas: State House Press, 1993.

Dodge, Richard I. *Our Wild Indians: Thirty-Three Years' Personal Experience Among the Red Men of the Great West*. Hartford, Connecticut: A. D. Worthington and Co., 1882.

_____. *The Plains of the Great West and Their Inhabitants*. New York: Archer House, Inc., 1877.

Dolbeare, Dr. Benjamin. *A Narrative of the Captivity and Suffering of Dolly Webster Among the Camanche Indians in Texas*. Clarksburg, Virginia: M'Granaghan & M'Carty, 1843. Reprint, New Haven, Connecticut: Yale University Library, 1986.

Drimmer, Frederick, ed. *Captured by the Indians: 15 Firsthand Accounts, 1750-1870*. Mineola, New York: Dover Publications, Inc., 1985.

Dunn, J. P., Jr. *Massacres of the Mountains: A History of the Indian Wars of the Far West 1815-1875* New York: Harper and Brothers, 1886.

Ebersole, Gary L. *Captured by Texts: Puritan to Postmodern Images of Indian Captivity*. Charlottesville, Virginia: University Press of Virginia, 1995.

Ellenbecker, John G. *Tragedy at the Little Blue*. Introduction by Lyn Ryder. Niwot, Colorado: Prairie Lark Publications, 1993.

Ellis, Mrs. Charles. "Robert Foote." *Annals of Wyoming* 15 (January 1943): 51-62.

Ellis, Richard N. *General Pope and U.S. Indian Policy*. Albuquerque, New Mexico: University of New Mexico Press, 1970.

Emmitt, Robert. *The Last War Trail The Utes & the Settlement of Colorado*. Boulder, Colorado: University Press of Colorado, 2000

Erb, Louise Bruning, Ann B. Brown, and Gilberta B. Hughes. *The Bridger Pass Overland Trail 1862-1869 Through Colorado and Wyoming*. Littleton, Colorado: Erbgem Publishing Co, 1989.

Exley, Jo Ella Powell. *Frontier Blood: The Saga of the Parker Family*. College Station, Texas: Texas A&M University Press, 2001.

Faery, Rebecca Blevins. *Cartographies of Desire Captivity, Race, & Sex in the Shaping of the American Nation*. Norman, Oklahoma: University of Oklahoma Press, 1999.

Faragher, John Mack. *Women and Men on the Overland Trail*. New Haven, Connecticut: Yale University Press, 1979.

Farley, Alan W. "An Indian Captivity and its Legal Aftermath." *Kansas Historical Quarterly* 2, no, 4 (Winter 1954): 247-56.

Fehrenbach, T. R. *Comanches: The Destruction of a People*. New York: Da Capo Press, 1994.

_____. *Lone Star A History of Texas and the Texans*. New York: Collier Books, 1968.

Fischer, David Hackett. *Historians' Fallacies: Toward a Logic of Historical Thought*. New York: Harper & Row, 1970.

Folwell, William Watts. *A History of Minnesota* 2. St. Paul, MN: Minnesota Historical Society, 1961.

Foreman, Carolyn Thomas. "Colonel Jesse Henry Leavenworth." *Chronicles of Oklahoma* 13, no. 1 (March 1935): 14-29.

Frazer, Robert W. *Forts of the West*. Norman, Oklahoma: University of Oklahoma Press, 1965.

Frazier, Donald S. *Blood & Treasure: Confederate Empire in the Southwest*. College Station, Texas: Texas A&M Press, 1995.

Frederick, J.V. *Ben Holladay the Stagecoach King*. Glendale, California: Arthur H. Clark Co., 1940. Reprint, Lincoln, Nebraska: University of Nebraska Press, 1989.

Fuller, Emeline L. *Left by the Indians and Massacre on the Oregon Trail in the Year 1860*. Fairfield, Washington: Ye Galleon Press, 1992.

Gard, Wayne. *Frontier Justice*. Norman, OK: Univeristy of Oklahoma Press, 1949.

Gardner Sharp, Abigail. *History of the Spirit Lake Massacre and Captivity of Miss Abbie Gardner*. Des Moines, Iowa: Mills and Company, 1885. Reprint. Des Moines, Iowa: Wallace-Homestead Book, Co., 1971.

Garfield, Marvin H. "Defense of the Kansas Frontier 1864-65." *Kansas Historical Quarterly*, 1, no. 2 (February 1932): 140-52.

_____. "Defense of the Kansas Frontier 1866-67." *Kansas Historical Quarterly*, 1, no. 4 (August 1932): 326-44.

_____. "Defense of the Kansas Frontier 1868-69." *Kansas Historical Quarterly*, 1, no. 5 (November 1932): 451-73.

Gelo, Daniel J., and Scott Zesch, eds. "'Every Day Seemed to be a Holiday:' The Captivity of Bianca Babb." *Southwestern Historical Quarterly* CVII, No. 1 (July 2003): 35-67.

Gerboth, Christopher B., ed. *The Tall Chief: The Autobiography of Edward*

W. Wynkoop. Denver, Colorado: Colorado Historical Society, 1994.

Gillett, James B. *Six Years with the Texas Rangers 1875 to 1881*. Edited and Introduction by M. M. Quaife. Lincoln, Nebraska: University of Nebraska Press, 1976.

Grace, John S., and R. B. Jones. *A New History of Parker County*. Weatherford, Texas: Weatherford Democrat, 1906. Reprint, Weatherford, Texas: Parker County Historical Association, 1987.

Gray, John, "The Santee Sioux and the Settlers at Lake Shetek." *Montana The Magazine of Western History*, XXV, no. 1 (Winter, 1975): 42-54.

Green, Rena Maverick, ed. *Memoirs of Mary A. Maverick*. San Antonio, Texas: Alamo Printing Co., 1921. Reprint, Introduction by Sandra L. Myres, Lincoln, Nebraska: University of Nebraska Press, 1989.

Grinnell, George Bird. *The Fighting Cheyennes*. New York: Charles Scribner's Sons, 1915. Norman, Oklahoma: University of Oklahoma Press, 1981.

_____. *Two Great Scouts and Their Pawnee Battalion*. Cleveland, OH: Arthur H. Clark Co., 1928. Reprint. Foreword by James T. King. Norman, Oklahoma: University of Oklahoma Press, 1973.

Groneman, Bill. *Battlefields of Texas*. Plano, Texas: Republic of Texas Press, 1998.

Guild, Thelma S. and Harvey L. Carter. *Kit Carson A Pattern for Heroes*. Lincoln, Nebraska: University of Nebraska Press, 1984.

Hafen, Leroy, and Francis Marion Young. *Fort Laramie and the Pageant of the West, 1834-1890*. Lincoln, Nebraska: University of Nebraska Press, 1984.

Hafen, Leroy R. and Ann W. Hafen. *Relations with the Indians of the Plains, 1857-1861*. Glendale, California: Arthur H. Clark Company, 1959.

Haines, Joe D., Jr. "'For our sake do all you can': The Indians Captivity and Death of Clara and Willie Blinn." *The Chronicles of Oklahoma* 2, Vol. LXXVII (Summer 1999): 170-183.

Halaas, David F. and Andrew E. Masich. *Halfbreed The Remarkable True Story of George Bent*. Cambridge, Massachusetts: Da Capo Press, 2004.

Haley, J. Evetts. *Charles Goodnight Cowman and Plainsman*. Norman, Oklahoma: University of Oklahoma Press, 1949.

Hamilton, Byrde Pearce. "Albert Schwandner, a Captive of the Lipans." *Frontier Times* 14, no. 9 (June 1937): 403-05.

Heard, J. Norman. *White Into Red: A Study of the Assimilation of White Persons Captured by Indians*. Metuchen, NJ: The Scarecrow Press, Inc., 1973.

Harris, Caroline. *History of the Captivity and Providential Release therefrom of Mrs. Caroline Harris*, New York: Perry and Cooke, 1838.

Herron, Lee. "Story of the Box Rescue." St. Paul, Nebraska: n.d. Denver Public Library, M 349.

Hoig, Stan. *The Battle of the Washita*. Lincoln, Nebraska: University of Nebraska Press, 1979.

_____. *Jesse Chisholm Ambassador of the Plains*. Norman, Oklahoma: University of Oklahoma Press, 2005.

_____. *Kicking Bird and the Legend of the Kiowas*. Niwot, Colorado: University Press of Colorado, 2000.

_____. *The Peace Chiefs of the Cheyennes*. Foreword by Boyce D. Timmons. Norman, Oklahoma: University of Oklahoma Press, 1980.

_____. *Tribal Wars of the Southern Plains*. Norman, Oklahoma: University of Oklahoma Press, 1993.

Huckabay, Ida Lasater. *Ninety-Four Years in Jack County 1854-1948*. Waco, Texas: By the author, 1949.

Hudson, G. B. "Chief Geronimo's Captive." *Frontier Times* 5, no. 9 (June 1928): 354-55.

Hughes, Michael A. "Nations Asunder: Western American Indians During the American Civil War, 1861-1865." *Journal of the Indian Wars* 1, no. 3: 69-114.

Hunter, Carolyn Berry. "Ten Southwestern Captivity Narratives." Ph.D. diss., Northern Arizona University, 1992.

Hunter, J. Marvin. "Horrors of Indian Captivity to be Retold." *Frontier Times* 14, no. 5 (February 1937): 193-94.

Hunter, J. Marvin, ed. "Once a Prisoner of the Comanches," *Frontier Times* 1, no. 11 (August 1924): 7.

_____. "The Capture of Mrs. Wilson." *Frontier Times* 1, no. 9 (June 1924): 22-23.

_____. "Harrowing Experience of Mrs. Kirby." *Frontier Times* 4, no. 10 (July 1927): 32-33.

_____. "Memoirs of Mrs. Maverick." *Frontier Times* 2, no. 5 (February 1925): 1-7.

_____. "Mrs. Rebecca J. Fisher." *Frontier Times* 3, no. 8 (May 1926): 6.

Hunter, John Warren. "The Battle at Ball's Ranch." *Frontier Times* 4, no. 12 (September 1927): 22-34.

_____. "The Tragedy of Legion Valley." *Frontier Times* 1, no. 4 (January 1924): 20-22.

_____. "The Trail of Blood Along the Texas Border." *Frontier Times* 1, no. 4 (January 1924): 14-15.

Hyde, George E. *Life of George Bent Written From His Letters*. Edited by Savoie Lottinville. Norman, Oklahoma: University of Oklahoma Press, 1968.

_____. *Red Cloud's Folk: A History of the Oglala Sioux Indians*. Foreword by Royal B. Hassrick. Norman, Oklahoma: University of Oklahoma Press, 1975.

_____. *Spotted Tail's Folk: A History of the Brule Sioux*. Norman, Oklahoma: University of Oklahoma Press, 1961.

Jauken, Arlene Feldmann. *The Moccasin Speaks: Living as Captives of the Dog Soldier Warriors*. Lincoln, Nebraska: Dageford Publishing, Inc., 1998.

Jenkins, John Holmes III. *Recollections of Early Texas: The Memoirs of John Holland Jenkins*. Foreword by J. Frank Dobie. Austin, Texas: University of Texas Press, 1958.

Johnson, Dave. "'Wild Bill' Hoerster." *Mason County Historical Book Supplement II*. Mason, Texas: Mason County Historical Commission, 1994.

Jones, Douglas C. *The Treaty of Medicine Lodge*. Norman, Oklahoma: University of Oklahoma Press, 1966.

Josephy, Alvin M. *The Civil War in the American West*. New York: Alfred A. Knopf, 1991.

Justus, Judith P. "The Saga of Clara H. Blinn at the Battle of the Washita." *Research Review* 14, no. 1 (Winter 2000): 11-20, 31.

Kappler, Charles J., ed. *Indian Treaties 1778-1883*. Mattituck, New York: Amereon House, 1972.

Kavanagh, Thomas W. *The Comanches A History 1706-1875*. Lincoln, Nebraska: University of Nebraska Press, 1996.

Kelly, Fanny. *My Captivity Among the Sioux Indians*. New York: Carol Publishing Group, 1993.

Kenner, Charles L. *The Comanchero Frontier: A History of New Mexican-*

Plains Indian Relations. Norman, Oklahoma: University of Oklahoma Press, 1994.

Kingman, Samuel A. "Diary of Samuel A. Kingman at Indian Treaty in 1865." *Kansas Historical Quarterly* 1, no. 5 (November 1932): 442-450.

Kraft, Louis. "Between the Army and the Cheyennes." *MHQ* (Winter 2002): 48-55

_____. *Gatewood & Geronimo*. Albuquerque, NM: University of New Mexico Press, 2000.

Kroeker, Marvin E. *Great Plains Command William B. Hazen in the Frontier West*. Norman, Oklahoma: University of Oklahoma Press, 1976.

Lamar, Howard Roberts. *The Far Southwest 1846-1912: A Territorial History*. Albuquerque, New Mexico: University of New Mexico Press, 2000.

Lavender, David. *Bent's Fort*. Lincoln, Nebraska: University of Nebraska Press, 1972.

_____. *Land of Giants The Drive to the Pacific Northwest 1750-1950*. Lincoln, Nebraska: University of Nebraska Press, 1979.

Leckie, William H. and Shirley A. Leckie. *Unlikely Warriors General Benjamin Grierson and his Family*. Norman, Oklahoma: University of Oklahoma Press, 1984.

Lecompte, Janet. "The Manco Burro Pass Massacre." *New Mexico Historical Society Review*. (October 1996): 305-18.

Ledbetter, Barbara A. Neal. *Fort Belknap Frontier Saga: Indians, Negroes and Anglo-Americans on the Texas Frontier*. NL Ranch Headquarters, Texas: Lavender Books, 1982.

Lee, Lorenzo P. *History of the Spirit Lake Massacre*. New Britain, Connecticut: By the Author, 1857. Reprint. Fairfield, Washington: Ye Galleon Press, 1996.

Lee, Nelson. *Three Years Among the Comanches: The Narrative of Nelson Lee, The Texas Ranger*. Santa Barbara, California: The Narrative Press, 2001.

Lee, Wayne C. and Howard C. Raynesford. *Trails of the Smoky Hill*. Caldwell, Idaho: Caxton Printers, 1980.

Liberty, Margot and John Stands in Timber. *Cheyenne Memories*. Lincoln, Nebraska: Univeristy of Nebraska Press, 1972.

Limerick, Patricia Nelson. *The Legacy of Conquest*. New York: W. W. Norton & Company, 1987.

Lockley, Fred. *Conversations With Pioneer Men: The Lockley Files*. One Horse Press, 1996.

McConkey, Harriet E. Bishop. *Dakota War Whoop: Or, Indian Massacres and War in Minnesota, of 1862-'3*. St. Paul, Minnesota: Wm. J. Moses Press, 1864. Reprint. Chicago, IL: R. R. Donnelley & Sons Company, 1965.

McConnell, Joseph Carroll. *The West Texas Frontier, or a Descriptive History of Early Times in Western Texas*. 2 Vols. Palo Pinto, Texas: Texas Legal Bank and Book Co., 1939.

Madsen, Brigham D. *The Shoshoni Frontier and the Bear River Massacre*. Foreword by Charles S. Peterson. Salt Lake City, Utah: University of Utah Press, 1985.

Marshall, Doyle. *A Cry Unheard: The Story of Indian Attacks in and Around Parker County, Texas 1858-1872*. Annetta Valley Farm Press, 1990.

Mattes, Merrill J. *The Great Platte River Road*. Lincoln, Nebraska: Nebraska State Historical Society, 1969.

Mayhall, Mildred P. *The Kiowas*. Norman, Oklahoma: University of

Oklahoma Press, 1971.

Methvin, J. J. *Andele The Mexican-Kiowa Captive A Story of Real Life Among Indians*. Introduction by James F. Brooks. Albuquerque, New Mexico: University of New Mexico Press, 1996.

Meyer, Roy W. *History of the Santee Sioux*. Lincoln, Nebraska: University of Nebraska Press, 1993.

Michno, Gregory F. *Battle at Sand Creek: The Military Perspective*. El Segundo, California: Upton & Sons, 2004.

———. *Encyclopedia of Indian Wars Western Battles and Skirmishes, 1850-1890*. Missoula, Montana: Mountain Press, 2003.

Millbrook, Minnie Dubbs. "The Jordan Massacre." *Kansas History* 2, no. 4, (Winter 1979): 219-230.

Miner, Craig. *West of Wichita: Settling the High Plains of Kansas, 1865-1890*. Lawrence, Kansas: University Press of Kansas, 1986.

Minnesota Historical Society. *Collections of the Minnesota Historical Society* VI. St. Paul, Minnesota: Minnesota Historical Society, 1894.

Minnesota Historical Society. *Collections of the Minnesota Historical Society* IX. St. Paul, Minnesota: Minnesota Historical Society, 1901.

Monahan, Doris. *Destination: Denver City The South Platte Trail*. Athens, Ohio: Ohio University Press, 1985.

Moneyhon, Carl H. *Texas After the Civil War The Struggle for Reconstruction*. College Station, Texas: Texcas A & M University, 2004.

Montgomery, F. C. "United States Surveyors Massacred by Indians Lone Tree, Meade County, 1874." *Kansas Historical Quarterly* 1, no. 3 (May 1932): 266-272.

Mooney, James. *Calendar History of the Kiowa Indians*. Washington, D.C.: Smithsonian Institution Press, 1979.

Moore, Stephen L. *Savage Frontier Indians, Riflemen, and Indian Wars in Texas Volume 1, 1835-1837*. Plano, Texas: Republic of Texas Press, 2002.

Morrell, Z. N. *Flowers and Fruits in the Wilderness; or Forty-Six Years in Texas and Two in Honduras*. St. Louis, Missouri: Commercial Printing Company, 1872. Reprint, Irving, Texas: Griffin Graphic Arts, 1966.

Munkres, Robert L. *Saleratus & Sagebrush: People and Places on the Road West*. Zanesville, Ohio: New Concord Press, 2003.

Myres, Sandra L. *Westering Women and the Frontier Experience 1800-1915*. Albuquerque, New Mexico: University of New Mexico Press, 1982.

Namias, June. *White Captives: Gender and Ethnicity on the American Frontier*. Chapel Hill, North Carolina: University of North Carolina Press, 1993.

Nye, Wilbur Sturtevant. *Bad Medicine & Good Tales of the Kiowas*. Norman, Oklahoma: University of Oklahoma Press, 1962.

Nye, Wilbur S. *Carbine & Lance: The Story of Old Fort Sill*. Norman, Oklahoma: University of Oklahoma Press, 1969.

Nystel, Ole T. *Lost and Found or Three Months with the Wild Indians*. Dallas, Texas: Wilmans Brothers, 1888. Reprint, Clifton, Texas: Bosque Memorial Museum, 1967.

Oehler, C. M. *The Great Sioux Uprising*. New York: Oxford University Press, 1959.

Oliva, Leo E. *Fort Union and the Frontier Army in the Southwest*. Southwest Cultural Resources Center Professional Papers No. 41. Santa Fe, New Mexico: NPS, 1993.

Olson, Greg. "Tragedy, Tourism, and the Log Cabin: How Abbie Gardner Sharp and Charlotte Kirchner Butler Preserved and Promoted the Past." *Iowa Heritage* 82, no. 2 (Summer 2001): 56-77.

BIBLIOGRAPHY

Pace, Robert F. and Donald S. Frazier. *Frontier Texas History of a Borderland to 1880*. Abilene, Texas: State House Press, 1004.

Passmore, Leonard. "The Captivity of Mrs. Charles Wattenbach." *Frontier Times* 1, no. 11 (August 1924): 20-25.

Peery, Dan W. "The White Kiowa Captive." *Chronicles of Oklahoma* 8, no. 3 (September 1930): 257-71.

Plummer, Clarissa Plummer. *Narrative of the Captivity and Extreme Sufferings of Mrs. Clarissa Plummer*. New York: Perry and Cooke, 1838.

Potter, Mrs. W. R. *History of Montague County, Texas*. Reprint. Salem, Mississippi: Higginson Book Company, 1957.

Powell, Father Peter John. *People of the Sacred Mountain*. San Francisco, CA: Harper & Row, 1981.

Propst, Nell Brown. *The South Platte Trail: Story of Colorado's Forgotten People*. Boulder, Colorado: Pruett Publishing Co., 1989.

Prucha, Francis Paul, ed. *Documents of United States Indian Policy*. Lincoln, Nebraska: University of Nebraska Press, 1990.

Quaife, Milo Milton, ed. *Kit Carson's Autobiography*. Lincoln, Nebraska: University of Nebraska Press, 1966.

Ramsay, Jack C. Jr. *The Story of Cynthia Ann Parker Sunshine on the Prairie*. Austin, Texas: Eakin Press, 1990.

Reeves, George. "The Scalping of Matilda Friend." *Frontier Times* 5, no. 2 (November 1927): 49-52.

Report of the Commissioner of Indian Affairs 1862-1870. Washington: GPO, 1863-1870.

Richardson, Rupert N. *The Comanche Barrier to South Plains Settlement*. Austin, Texas: Eakin Press, 1996.

Riley, Glenda. *The Female Frontier*. Lawrence, Kansas: University Press of Kansas, 1988.

_____. *Women and Indians on the Frontier 1825-1915*. Albuquerque, New Mexico: University of New Mexico Press, 1984.

Rister, Carl Coke. *Border Captives: The Traffic in Prisoners by Southern Plains Indians, 1835-1875*. Norman, Oklahoma: University of Oklahoma Press, 1940.

_____. *Comanche Bondage: Beales's Settlement and Sarah Ann Horn's Narrative*. Glendale, CA: Arthur H. Clark Company, 1955. Reprint, Introduction by Don Worcester. Lincoln, Nebraska: University of Nebraska Press, 1989.

Roberts, Captain D. W. "Restoration of Warren Lyons." *Frontier Times* 4, no. 4. (January 1927): 24.

Roberts, Virginia Culin. *With Their Own Blood: A Saga of Southwestern Pioneers*. Ft. Worth, Texas: Texas Christian University Press, 1992.

Robinson, Charles M. III. *Satanta: The Life and Death of a War Chief*. Foreword by William H.Leckie. Austin, Texas: State House Press, 1997.

Roenigk, Adolph. *Pioneer History of Kansas*. Lincoln, Kansas: Privately published, 1933. Reprint, Lincoln, Kansas: Lincoln County Historical Society, 1973.

Sabin, Edwin L. *Kit Carson Days 1809-1868. "Adventures in the Path of Empire."* Lincoln, Nebraska: University of Nebraska Press, 1995.

Sager, Catherine. *The Whitman Massacre of 1847*. Fairfield, Washington: Ye Galleon Press, 2004.

Sanford, Mollie D. *Mollie: The Journal of Mollie Dorsey Sanford in Nebraska and Colorado Territories 1857-1866*. Introduction by Donald F. Danker. Lincoln, Nebraska: University of Nebraska Press, 1976.

Satterlee, Marion P. *Authentic List of Victims of the Indian Massacre and*

War 1862 to 1865. Minneapolis, Minnesota: By the Author, 1914.

————. *A Detailed Account of the Massacre by the Dakota Indians of Minnesota in 1862*. Minneapolis, Minnesota; By the Author, 1925.

Schellie, Don. *Vast Domain of Blood: The Story of the Camp Grant Massacre*. Tucson, Arizona: Westernlore Press, 1992.

Schlicke, Carl. *Left by the Indians and Massacre on the Oregon Trail in the Year 1860*. Fairfield, Washington: Ye Galleon Press, 1992.

Schultz, Duane. *Over the Earth I Come: The Great Sioux Uprising of 1862*. New York: St. Martin's Press, 1992.

Schwandt, Mary. *The Captivity of Mary Schwandt*. Fairfield, Washington: Ye Galleon Press, 1999.

Shannon, Donald H. *The Utter Disaster on the Oregon Trail: The Utter and Van Ornum Massacres of 1860*. Caldwell, Idaho: Snake Country Publishing, 1993.

Sheridan, P. H. *The Personal Memoirs of P. H. Sheridan*. New York: C. L. Webster, 1888. Reprint. Introduction by Jeffery D. Wert. New York: Da Capo Press, 1992.

Simmons, Marc. *Massacre on the Lordsburg Road A Tragedy of the Apache Wars*. College Station, Texas: Texas A&M Press, 1997.

————. *Ranchers Ramblers & Renegades True Tales of Territorial New Mexico*. Santa Fe, New Mexico: Ancient City Press, 1984.

Settle, Raymond W., and Mary Lund Settle. *War Drums and Wagon Wheels: The Story of Russell, Majors and Waddell*. Lincoln, Nebraska: University of Nebraska Press, 1966.

Smith, Clinton L., and Jefferson D. Smith. *The Boy Captives*. Bandera, Texas: Frontier Times, 1927.

Smith, David Paul. *Frontier Defense in the Civil War Texas' Rangers and Rebels*. College Station, Texas: Texas A&M University Press, 1992.

Smith, Maurice E. "The Oregon Trail's Utter Tragedy." *Wild West* (April 2000): 42-48, 80.

Sonnichsen, C.L. *The Mescalero Apaches*. Norman Oklahoma: University of Oklahoma Press, 1958.

Sowell, A. J. *Early Settlers and Indian Fighters of Southwest Texas*. Austin, Texas: Benjamin C. Jones & Co., 1900. Reprint, Austin, Texas: State House Press, 1986.

————. *Rangers and Pioneers of Texas*. 1884. Reprint, Austin, Texas: State House Press, 1991.

Sprague, Marshall. *Massacre The Tragedy at White River*. Boston, Massachusetts: Little, Brown, 1957. Reprint.

Lincoln, Nebraska: University of Nebraska Press, 1980.

Stratton, Joanna L. *Pioneer Women Voices from the Kansas Frontier*. Introduction by Arthur M. Schlesinger, Jr. New York: Simon & Schuster, 1982.

Stratton, R.B. *Captivity of the Oatman Girls*. Foreword by Wilcomb E. Washburn. Lincoln, Nebraska: University of Nebraska Press, 1983.

Sweeney, Edwin R. *Merejildo Grijalva Apache Captive Army Scout*. El Paso, Texas: Texas Western Press, 1992.

Tate, Michael L. "Comanche Captives People Between Two Worlds." *Chronicles of Oklahoma* LXXII, No. 3 (Fall 1994): 228-263.

————. *The Frontier Army in the Settlement of the West*. Norman, Oklahoma: University of Oklahoma Press, 1999.

Thompson, Jerry. *Confederate General of the West Henry Hopkins Sibley*. Foreword by Frank E. Vandiver. College Station, Texas: Texas A&M University Press, 1996.

BIBLIOGRAPHY

Thrapp, Dan L. *The Conquest of Apacheria*. Norman, Oklahoma: University of Oklahoma Press, 1967.

———. *Encyclopedia of Frontier Biography* 3 Vols. Lincoln, Nebraska: University of Nebraska Press 1991.

Tolzmann, Don Heinrich, ed. *German Pioneer Accounts of the Great Sioux Uprising of 1862*. Milford, Ohio: Little Miami Publishing Co., 2002.

Unrau, William E., ed. *Tending the Talking Wire: A Buck Soldier's View of Indian Country, 1863-1866*. Salt Lake City, Utah: University of Utah Press, 1979.

Unrau, William E. "The Role of the Indian Agent in the Settlement of the South-Central Plains, 1861-1868." Ph.D. diss, University of Colorado, 1963.

Unruh, John D., Jr. *The Plains Across: The Overland Emigrants and the Trans-Mississippi West, 1840-60*. Urbana, Illinois: University of Illinois Press, 1993.

Urwin, Gregory J. W. and Roberta E Fagan. *Custer and His Times Vol. 3*. University of Central Arkansas Press: Little Bighorn Associates, Inc., 1987.

U. S. Congress, House of Representatives. "Difficulties With Indian Tribes." 41st Congress, 2nd Session. Executive Document 240.

U. S. Congress, House of Representatives. *Report of the Secretary of War*. 40th Congress, 3rd Session. Executive Document No. 1. Washington, GPO, 1868.

U. S. Congress, House of Representatives. *Report of the Secretary of War*. 41st Congress, 2nd Session. Executive Document No. 1, part 2. Washington, GPO, 1869.

U.S. Congress, Senate. "Massacre of Cheyenne Indians." *Report of the Joint Committee on the Conduct of the War*. 38th Congress, 2nd Session. Washington: GPO, 1865.

U.S. Congress, Senate. "Sand Creek Massacre." *Report of the Secretary of War*. Senate Exec. Doc. 26. 39th Congress, 2nd Session. Washington: GPO, 1867.

U.S. Congress, Senate. "The Chivington Massacre." *Report of the Joint Special Committee on the Condition of the Indian Tribes*. Senate Report 156. 39th Congress. 2nd Session. 1867.

U.S. Department of the Interior. Bureau of Indian Affairs. *Reports of the Commissioner of Indian Affairs. 1861-1870*. Washington: GPO.

U.S. War Department. *The War of the Rebellion: A Compilation of the Official Records of the Union and Confederate Armies*. Washington: GPO, 1880-1901.

Utley, Robert. *Frontiersmen in Blue: The United States Army and the Indian 1848-1865*. New York: Macmillan Company, 1967.

Utley, Robert M. *Lone Star Justice The First Century of the Texas Rangers*. New York: Oxford University Press, 2002.

VanDerBeets, Richard, ed. *Held Captive by Indians: Selected Narratives, 1642-1836*. Knoxville, Tennessee: University of Tennessee Press, 1994.

Wakefield, Sarah F. *Six Weeks in the Sioux Teepees: A Narrative of Indian Captivity*. Shakopee, Minnesota: Argus Books and Job Printing Office, 1864. Reprint. Introduction by June Namias. Norman, Oklahoma: University of Oklahoma Press, 1997.

Ware, Eugene F. *The Indian War of 1864*. Introduction by John D. McDermott. Lincoln, Nebraska: University of Nebraska Press, 1994.

Watts, John S. *Indian Depredations in New Mexico*. Washington, D. C.: Gideon, 1859. Reprint. Tucson, Arizona: Territorial Press, 1964.

Webb, Walter Prescott. *The Texas Rangers: A Century of Frontier Defense.* Austin, Texas: University of Texas Press, 1991.

Webb, Walter Prescott, and H. Bailey Carroll, eds. *The Handbook of Texas.* Two Volumes. Austin, Texas: Texas State Historical Association, 1952.

Webber, Bert. *Oregon Trail Emigrant Massacre of 1862 and Port-Neuf Muzzle-Loaders Rendezvous Massacre Rocks, Idaho.* Medford, Oregon: Webb Research Group, 1987.

White, Lonnie J. *Hostiles and Horse Soldiers: Indian Battles and Campaigns in the West.* Foreword by Merrill J. Mattes. Boulder, Colorado: Pruett Publishing Company, 1972.

White, Lonnie J. "White Woman Captives of Southern Plains Indians, 1866-1875." *Journal of the West* VIII, no. 8 (July 1969): 327-354.

Wilbarger, J. W. *Indian Depredations in Texas.* Austin, Texas: Hutchings Printing House, 1889. Reprint, Austin, Texas: Eakin Press, 1985.

Wilson, Jane Adeline. *A Thrilling Narrative of the Sufferings of Mrs. Jane Adeline Wilson During Her Captivity Among the Comanche Indians.* Rochester, New York: Dellon M. Dewey, 1854. Reprint, Fairfield, Washington: Ye Galleon Press, 1971.

Winfrey, Dornum H., and James M. Day, eds. *The Indian Papers of Texas and the Southwest 1825-1916.* 5 Vols. Austin, Texas: Pemberton Press, 1966. Reprint, Introduction by Michael L. Tate. Austin, Texas: Texas State Historical Association, 1995.

Wooster, Robert. *The Military & United States Indian Policy 1865-1903.* Lincoln, Nebraska: University of Nebraska Press, 1995.

Worster, Donald. *Under Western Skies: Nature and History in the American West.* New York: Oxford University Press, 1992.

Zesch, Scott. *The Captured A True Story of Abduction by Indians on the Texas Frontier.* New York: St. Martin's Press, 2004.

_____. "The Two Captivities of Adolph Korn." *Southwestern Historical Quarterly.* CIV, No. 4 (April 2001): 515-540.

_____. "The Search for Alice Todd." TMs (photocopy).

Zwink, Timothy A. "E. W. Wynkoop and the Bluff Creek Council, 1866." *Kansas Historical Quarterly* 43, no. 2 (Summer 1977): 217-239.

NATIONAL ARCHIVES

National Archives and Records Administration, Washington, D.C. Records Group 75 and 123, U.S. Court of Claims, Indian Depredation Files.

Babb, Hernando C. RG 123 #4606
Bainter, James #1020
Ball, James S. RG 123 #10172
Bell, Mary RG 75 #3532
Bissonette, Joseph RG 75 #2208
Davenport, James RG 123 #5732
Ecoffey, Jules RG 75 #2208
Emery, Charles RG 123 # 1019, #1620,
Eubank, Joseph RG 123 # 1117
Field, Patrick RG 123 # 8448
Fletcher, Amanda RG 123 # 5072
Friend, John S. #3379
Huckobey, William R. RG 123 # 3474
Jordan, Mary Ann #9469
Kalus, Margaretha #454
Koozier, Gottlieb RG 123 #10263

BIBLIOGRAPHY

Maxey, Jesse RG 123 # 962, # 9673
Menasco, Daniel #4211
Morgan, James RG 75 #3644
Morton, Nancy RG 75 #332
Shaw, Simeon #3705, #6441
Shegog, Louis C. #4360
Snow, Hester RG 75 #3718, #10349, #10350
Springs, Martha RG 75 #3704
Ulbrich, Peter #6220
Wolfe, George RG 123 #10315

INTERNET SOURCES

American West-History-Women of the West-Narcissa Whitman. http://www.
  tu-chemnitz.de/phil/amerikanistik/projekte/west/narissa.htm.
Cason, Mary Marsh. "The Whitman Massacre As Recalled by Mary Marsh
  Cason." http://gesshoto.com/whitman.html.
Crosby, David F. "The Battle of Brushy Creek." http://americanhistory.
  about.com/library/prm/blbattleofbrushycreek.htm.
Gaston, Joseph. "The Centennial History of Oregon 1811-1911." The
  Whitman Massacre. http://gesswhoto.com/centennial-whitman-massacre.
  html.
Handbook of Texas Online. www.tsha.utexas.edu/handbook/online
Heard, Isaac. "Dakota Conflict Trials." http://www.law.umkc.edu/faculty/
  projects/ftrials/dakota/trialrec3
"The Everett Family." Waseca County Historical Society. http://www.
  historical.waseca.mn.us/family.htm
"Killough Massacre." www.tsha.utexas.edu/handbook/online/articles/print/
  KK/btk1
Kingman, Samuel A. "Diary of Samuel Kingman." http://www.kshs.org/publicat/
  khq/1932/32_5_kingman.htm
"Koch Cabin Lake Shetek." http://www.rrcnet.org/~historic/kcabin.html.
La Foy, R. Aubrey. "Margaret Ann Marble." www.iowagreatlakes.com/_his/_
  memlane/margannmarble
McConnell, Joseph Carroll. The West Texas Frontier, 1939. http://www.forttours.
  com.
Nowak, Kate. "Painted Post Crossroads." www.forttours.com/pages/ewhite.asp.
NPS Historical Handbook Number Thirty-Seven, 1962. "The Massacre." http://
  www.cr.nps.gov/history/online-books/hh/37p.htm.
Oregon Pioneer Association – Twenty-First Annual Reunion. http://www.1st-
  hand-history.org/opa/21/095.jpg.
PBS-The West. "Letters and Journals of Narcissa Whitman." http://www.pbs.
  org/weta/thewest/resources/archives/two/whitman2.htm.
"Selected Families and Individuals." http://www.pehoushek.com/GENEALOGY/
  pafg283.htm
"Shetek Massacre." http://www.rrcnet.org/~historic/shetekll.htm.
Whitman Massacre. "Preliminary Events." "Whitman Massacre." "The
  Aftermath." "Whitman
Massacre Roster." http://www.oregonpioneers.com/whitman1.htm.
Zwink, Timothy. "Bluff Creek Council." http://www.kancoll.org.khq/1977_2_
  zwink.htm

THE AUTHORS

Gregory and Susan Michno are Michigan natives. Greg attended Michigan State University and did post-graduate work at the University of Northern Colorado. An award-winning author, he has written two dozen articles and several books, dealing with World War II and the American West. His books are *The Mystery of E Troop, Lakota Noon, USS Pampanito: Killer-Angel, Death on the Hellships, The Encyclopedia of Indian Wars,* and *Battle at Sand Creek.* He also participated in editing and appearing in the dvd history, *The Great Indian Wars 1540-1890.*

Susan Michno also graduated from Michigan State University and has researched Western History with Greg for many years. She recently published articles on Abbie Gardner and the Spirit Lake Massacre and the captivity of the Box Family of Texas. *A Fate Worse Than Death* is their first joint venture.

Greg and Sue currently live in Longmont, Colorado, where they completed or are working on other books, including *Fountain of My Tears, The Snake War,* and *Circle the Wagons.*

INDEX

517

Sherman, Ezra, 185
Sherman, Joe, 185
Sherman, Martha, 7, 36, 183, 185, 186
Sherman, William T., 153, 269, 308, 333, 350, 355, 361, 415, 446
Shibell, Charles A., 122
Shira, Mr., 289
Shropshire, Ben, 372
Shuman, Jacob S., 131
Sibley, Henry H., 113, 201, 204, 211, 216, 217, 223, 223-26, 230, 236, 237
Sieber, Al, 452
Silbaugh, Mr., 196
Simmons, Seneca G., 113
Simpson, George, 100
Simpson, Jane, 79-81, 465
Simpson, Nancy, 79-81
Simpson, William, 79-81, 465
Sitting Bull (Lakota), 134
Skaggs, M. S., 183
Slater, Stephen T., 80
Slaughter, John B., 419, 422
Slaughter, M. C., 372
Slayton, John P., 425
Slaughter Slough, 236, 240
Sloat, Benjamin, 15, 80, 81
Smith, A. A., 139
Smith, Angeline, 331
Smith, Ben, 312
Smith, Caroline, 436
Smith, Clinton, 392, 410-12, 429, 432-38
Smith, Dixie Alamo Dyche, 437, 438
Smith, Edward A. P., 334
Smith, Edward P., 393
Smith, Ellen, 109
Smith, Fannie Short, 432
Smith, George H., 429
Smith, Harriet, 432
Smith, Henry M., 432, 433, 435-37
Smith, Henry Watson, 232, 233, 240
Smith, James, 45
Smith, James, 136
Smith, James H., 272
Smith, Jane Cox, 109
Smith, Jefferson D., 432-34, 436-38
Smith, Jennie, 331, 332
Smith, John, 333
Smith, John W., 70
Smith, Joseph, 95, 96
Smith, Josephine, 331
Smith, Laura, 331
Smith, Martha A., 331, 332, 334
Smith, Mary, 95, 96, 97
Smith, Mr., 23
Smith, Mrs., 136, 137
Smith, Persifor, 171
Smith, Sophia, 233, 234
Smith, Thomas I., 15
Smith, Washington, 330
Smith, William, 109
Smith, William F., 139
Smith, Zona Mae, 438

Smithwick, Noah, 9, 10
Snana (Sioux), 201
Snyder, Anna, 88, 143-44, 474
Snyder, Bertel A., 191, 192
Snyder, Henry, 123, 124, 126, 128
Snyder, John, 143
Soper, Elijah, 301, 302
Sowerwick (Ute), 446
Spalding, Eliza, 91, 95, 97
Spalding, Henry, 91, 92, 97
Spangler, J. W., 37, 186
Spaulding, Charles, 47, 48
Speedy (Apache), 452
Spencer, Charles, 100
Spencer, George, 189, 223-26
Spillman Creek raid, 326, 327, 328
Spotted Horse (Lakota), 140
Spotted Leopard (Comanche), 116
Spotted Tail (Lakota), 308
Spotted Wolf (Cheyenne) 308
Spotts, David L., 324, 325
Sprague, Owen A., 267
Spring Creek battle, 56, 63
Stance, Emanuel, 413
Standing Buffalo (Sioux) 227
Standley Family, 376
Stanfield, Joe, 94, 96
Stanley, Henry M., 308
Stanley, John M., 97
Stanton, James M., 75
Starkey, Capt., 240
Steck, Michael, 471
Steckmesser, Kent, 467
Stephens, John, 343
Stephens, William, 343
Stevens, George, 142
Stewart, John, 115
Stewart, Milton, 319, 324
Stewart, Mrs., 194
Stickus (Cayuse), 92
Stillwell Family, 66
Stillwell, Mr., 67
Stinnet, Claiborne, 11
Stockholm Syndrome, 462
Stoeffens, Louis, 260
Stone Calf (Cheyenne), 160, 161, 162
Stone Forehead (see Medicine Arrow)
Stowe, Harriet Beecher, 468
Strange, John, 328
Stratton, Joanna, 460
Stratton, Royal B., 108
Stricklin, Frank, 181
Stringfield, Adolphus, 407
Stringfield, Thomas, 407
Strong, Mrs., 193
Stroud, Jack, 178
Stroud, Jonathan, 427, 428, 430
Stumbling Bear (Kiowa), 265
Sturm, Jacob, 281, 361
Styles, Richard, 3, 4
Sullivan, Fremont, 363
Sullivan, Margaret, 363, 365

OTHER TITLES ABOUT
THE WEST
FROM
CAXTON PRESS

Massacre Along the Medicine Road
The Indian War of 1864 in Nebraska
by Ronald Becher
ISBN 0-87004-289-7, 500 pages, cloth, $32.95
ISBN 0-87004-387-0, 500 pages, paper, $22.95

A Dirty, Wicked Town
Tales of 19th Century Omaha
by David Bristow
ISBN 0-87004-398-6, 320 pages, paper, $16.95

Our Ladies of the Tenderloin
Colorado's Legend in Lace
by Linda Wommack
ISBN 0-87004-444-3, 250 pages, paper, $16.95

Necktie Parties
Legal Executions in Oregon, 1851 - 1905
by Diane Goeres-Gardner
ISBN 0-87004-446-x, 375 pages, paper, $16.95

Colorado Treasure Tales
by W. C. Jameson
ISBN 0-87004-402-8, 200 pages, paper, $13.95

For a free catalog of Caxton titles write to:

CAXTON PRESS
312 Main Street
Caldwell, Idaho 83605-3299

or

Visit our Internet web site:

www.caxtonpress.com

Caxton Press is a division of THE CAXTON PRINTERS, Ltd.